Hollywood Vs. the Aliens

Hollywood Vs. the Aliens

The Motion Picture Industry's Participation in UFO Disinformation

Bruce Rux

Frog, Ltd.
Berkeley, California

Published by Frog, Ltd.

Frog, Ltd. books are distributed by
North Atlantic Books
P.O. Box 12327
Berkeley, California 94712

Cover: *Devil Girl from Mars,* Spartan, 1954, courtesy Wade Williams
Productions
Cover design by Paula Morrison
Book design by Catherine E. Campaigne

Printed in the United States of America by Printer

Library of Congress Cataloging-in-Publication Data

Rux, Bruce, 1958–
    Hollywood vs. the aliens : the motion picture industry's participation
    in UFO disinformation / Bruce Rux
        p. cm.
    Includes bibliographical references and index.
    ISBN 1-883319-61-7
    1. Unidentified flying objects in motion pictures.   2. Science fiction
films—History and criticism.   3. Unidentified flying objects—Sightings and encounters—United States.   4. Conspiracies—United States.
I. Title.
PN1995.9.U62R88   1997
791.43'615—dc21   96-37579
                                                                CIP

1   2   3   4   5   6   7   8   9   /   00   99   98   97   96

Dedication

To everyone involved in the making of the movies, T.V. shows, stories, novels, comic books, bubble gum cards, etc., listed in these pages, and everyone who loves them. And especially for Zoe, who suggested I write this book in the first place.

Table of Contents

Acknowledgments **ix**

Introduction **1**

1 *Wreckages and Robots* **73**

2 *Mesmerizations and Assassinations* **111**

3 *Media and Manipulations* **161**

4 *Misdirections and Misinformations* **191**

5 *Insiders and Informations* **255**

6 *Enlightenments and Educations* **299**

7 *Importations and Degradations* **341**

8 *Juvenilizations and Animations* **389**

9 *Foresights and Fictionalizations* **443**

10 *Peregrinations and Propagandizations* **495**

11 *Indoctrinations and Demonizations* **533**

12 *Conclusions and Considerations* **577**

Notes **591**

Bibliography **621**

Index **641**

Acknowledgments

As usual, thanks to my brother George, my sister Vickie, and my mother Georgia.

Also as usual, thanks to everyone at Frog, Ltd. and Publishers Group West—Richard Grossinger, Lindy Hough, Anastasia McGhee, and especially my editor Kathy Glass, and anyone else whose name I've overlooked.

Many thanks to everyone from American International/Orion Pictures—who have neither affirmed nor denied any of the theories presented in these pages—for their warmth, generosity, and support, including Herman Cohen, Samuel Z. Arkoff, Susan Hart (Nicholson) Hofheinz, and Krystle Houston, and a special thanks to Wade Williams, without whose help there would have been far fewer of the fabulous pictures. Also very helpful were Rudolph Grey, Ted Okuda, Paul and Donna Parla, and Robert Skotak at *Filmfax/Outré*, Gary and Susan Svehla of *Midnight Marquee*, and Tim and Donna Lucas at *Video Watchdog*. Thanks to Joseph Green and Jonathan Haze for their time and well wishes, and for having made their own variety of classics. Also thanks to Linnea Quigley, just because she appreciates a good Grave Affair (and makes some splendidly bad flicks). And of course thanks to Elvira, Joe Bob Briggs, Sandra Bernhard, and all their kin.

From the past and present, in and among the Village Inn Irregulars, my gratitude to those who have listened to me formulate my writings over the years, including Pat and Mike Haywood, Tim and Elizabeth Hogan, Chris Heiar, Julie Rumney, Lou Fails, and the Magic circle, Ed, Jason, Jeff, Matt, Ray, etc., etc.

From long ago and not so very far away, a special remembrance to Allison Walker (who gave me my first subscription to *Heavy Metal* and watched numerous Godzilla movies with me), fellow *Outer Lim-*

its and flying saucer fans Kent Leader, Steve Wright, Jay Parker, and especially Mike Stifel *("lay blenz oh a lanz tree oh trinzini . . ."),* and '60s chicks Sandra Broad, Shaun Emery Kelly, and Heidi Morrow.

And, last but not least, a special message from the Labyrinth of the Minotaur to Paul Dini and Arleen Sorkin (Scale this face in the gilt picture frame:) *Riddle Me This*—! Where does The Great Prosciutto get all his best acts (is it just me, or doth Ithcariot lithp)? (Shall the Riddler or the Joker prove more gallant? You decide. Read this clue at: 1-752-442-7473.)

What are you all still reading this for? What? Do you have no lives? This isn't for you, it's "To Whom It May Concern." Get on with the book!

Raiders of the Lost Art

At the Late-Night Double-Feature Picture Show

A bewildered couple has a story to tell about a rainy night on an isolated country road. Though their experience was not altogether unpleasant, it had a nightmarish quality to it. They remember seeing something like motorcycles after their car unexpectedly went dead, and the next thing they knew, they were someplace where identically dressed, pasty-faced people were taking off the couple's clothes and elevating them into a round room. There, some strange man in a lab coat was artificially creating life. The couple found themselves separated, and each person had a bizarre sexual encounter with the man in the lab coat that left them feeling a little puzzled and frightened. Each of them initially thought they were having sex with the other, only to discover it was the lab-coat man in bed with them. They remember being paralyzed, sedated, and a little spaced-out at various times. Before their unusual ordeal ended, they remember being paired-up sexually with another partner while submerged in a pool of water in which they were somehow able to breathe.

Then, it was abruptly over. They found themselves back out in the country, and they remember a spaceship taking off—to their understanding, to another planet. They knew that something profound had happened to them but have been unable to understand it since. The experience completely beyond him, the male member of the couple is upset—he just wants to curl up and die. She, on the other hand, feels strangely exhilarated, as though her mind has expanded in some way from the experience. She feels confident and more secure than she ever has—even as she admits to feeling raped.

A UFOlogist will recognize having just heard a standard abduction story. A late-night moviegoer will recognize having just heard the plot to *The Rocky Horror Picture Show*.

Coincidence? Possibly. But there is more than one such coincidence, and they go deeper than plotlines. The entire story of *Rocky Horror* is related by a shadowy figure who has a complete file on the "Denton Affair" (as this young couple's experience has come to be called), containing sworn testimonies, affidavits, and pictures of all people involved—just such files as, it appears, the National Security Agency may have been collecting since 1952 on real-life UFO abductees. The opening verse of the film's lyrics says, "See androids fighting Brad and Janet" (the hero and heroine of the piece), despite the fact that no such creatures are in the movie—but exactly the type of anthropomorphic robots we call "androids" are part of real UFO abductions. A "rival scientist" to the mad alien geneticist aboard the UFO in the movie, "Dr. Scott," turns out to know quite a bit about the alien captain before even meeting him—and the attention is mutual. Commenting to Dr. Scott, the alien at one point snaps, "Or should I say—Dr. *von* Scott?" and the Americanized ex-Nazi doctor admits that he and his cronies have been working on a paralyzing ray exactly like the one aboard the alien spacecraft. Operation Paperclip did indeed Americanize hundreds of ex-Nazi rocket scientists after WWII, which would have been public knowledge at the time *Rocky Horror* was made—but the standard use of paralysis beams by UFO occupants and the all-but-certain fact that United States military scientists had been exploiting recovered extraterrestrial technology since at least 1947 would not even begin to become public knowledge for another few years.

Such military exploitation of extraterrestrial technology connects in a roundabout way with something else in the *Rocky Horror* story tying closely to true facts about UFOs: the legend of the fallen Watchers. The Watchers were "the gods" or "giants" in all ancient mythologies, who created the human race as slaves to ease their burdens. Certain perverse members among them began interbreeding with mankind and corrupted the human race with their own vices and evil ways. Ultimately, these fallen Watchers were destroyed in the Biblical Flood—exactly as the mad doctor of *Rocky Horror* and his new creation (made to sate the doctor's perverse lusts) find themselves dispatched by a trident weapon (the symbol of the Supreme Watchers) and are left to float face-down in a pool. There is a large number of clues tying the modern UFO phenomenon to this ancient race, and there is evidence that high-ranking individuals of various world governments may have known this fact since as far back as one hundred and forty years ago.

But that isn't even the most interesting thing about the coincidences between *Rocky Horror* and real-life UFO abductions. The film's most jarring fact is simply when it was made. Who would have known the connection between the Watchers and UFOs in 1975? Let alone the true standard case history of a UFO abduction? Only three abduction cases were part of the public record at that time—and of them, only the Betty and Barney Hill case was well-known, thanks to an NBC-Universal movie called *The UFO Incident* which aired on October 20, 1975. The only other famous abduction case followed in the next two to three weeks, between November 5 and 12, when woodcutter Travis Walton was reportedly airlifted and returned from a UFO. However, Walton's case did not get any real public exposure until it was announced on February 7, 1976, that he had passed a lie-detector test about the incident.

But *Rocky Horror*'s premiere came on September 26, 1975, almost an entire month before *The UFO Incident* aired—and, for that matter, it had been a stage show at least two years before that. The Hills' abduction had been written about in *Look* magazine in 1966, but it contained only a fraction of the true elements of the experience found in *Rocky Horror*. The "breathing pool" would not be published until 1992 in David Jacobs' *Secret Life*. "Ancient Astronaut" theory was just coming into vogue when *Rocky Horror* was written, which might account for at least some awareness of the Watchers myth. Erich Von Daniken's *Chariots of the Gods* had been published in 1970, and other, better books on the same subject (barely noticed by the buying public) were published some years before that. But for a 1975 movie to come up with obscure and accurate UFO abduction information that was not to be published for another seventeen years— and also to contain apparently accurate ancient information on the phenomenon—is too curious a coincidence to ignore. Especially when both topics were relegated to the fringe, and when even those people who call themselves UFOlogists knew very little of their own field—a fact still true today.

U FO research has come a long way from the initial tentative study of mere lights in the night sky. Despite an endless number of government protestations to the contrary, copious documentary evidence exists testifying not only to UFOs' existence as aerial craft, but as interplanetary spacecraft. Similarly, the early, infrequently reported cases of human abduction aboard these craft have progressed from the occasional statements of a Betty and Barney Hill to a number of cases so massive that recognizable symptoms and occurrences associated with the act can be mapped with great consistency. Nor is UFO research any longer a study undertaken by a few amateur civilians drawn into the subject by happenstance, but one diligently catalogued by professors of history and psychology at prestigious universities. That the government has substantial knowledge of the subject is not in doubt, as is evidenced not only by the documentation now available through the Freedom of Information Act, but also by the extreme static the government raises in attempting to keep that information out of civilian hands. In fact, the question is no longer even one of *what* the government must know about UFOs, but rather *when*, exactly, they came to find out about it all.

Where does such a study begin, and where could it lead? The usual starting point given by historians of the modern UFO phenomenon is the sighting of nine boomerang-shaped aerial unknowns in Washington State by pilot Lieutenant Kenneth Arnold, in June of 1947. These were dubbed "flying saucers" by the press, because of Arnold's description of their movement being like that of "a saucer skipped across water."

But sightings are hardly the issue. The real starting point is with the U.S. Army's recovery of a crashed flying saucer near Roswell, New Mexico, only a little under a month later. The story was officially released by the Army, before National Security was invoked to keep the subject from further broadcast. Official coverup began, complete with the manufacture of fraudulent crashed saucers and weather balloons in other locations, to make the entire subject appear ridiculous or easily explainable in natural terms. The Central Intelligence Agency and the Air Force were formed within six months of the crash. A battery of tests was run by the Air Force on the recovered alien material, and further government studies were commissioned, at least some of which are documented.

The most important reason for the government's secrecy on the UFO question lies in the most probable reason a flying saucer was in the proximity of Roswell in the first place: in 1947, Roswell Army Air Field was the only location in the world in possession of an atomic bomb. Less than a year and a half after Roswell, a tremendous number of "green fireballs" were reported in Albuquerque, New Mexico. The Air Force, then just over a year old, paid no attention to them at first, but soon they were impossible to ignore. "No matter what these green fireballs were," wrote Captain Edward Ruppelt, head of the Air Force's official UFO investigation, Project Blue Book, "the military was getting edgy. They might be common meteorites, psychologically enlarged flares, or true UFO's, but whatever they were they were playing around in one of the most sensitive security areas in the United States. Within 100 miles of Albuquerque were two installations that were the backbone of the atomic bomb program: Los Alamos and Sandia Base. Scattered throughout the countryside were other installations vital to the defense of the U.S.: radar stations, fighter-interceptor bases, and the other mysterious areas that had been blocked off by high chain-link fences."

Meteor expert Dr. Lincoln La Paz, who previously gave two reports on the Roswell crash (discussed in Chapter 1), became the chief investigator on an Intelligence team at Kirtland Air Force Base studying the green fireballs that became known as "Project Twinkle." When the sightings continued through January of 1949, Dr. Joseph Kaplan and Dr. Edward Teller, inventor of the H-bomb, were brought into conference with the rest of the Project Twinkle team. Two major conferences were held, on February 17 and October 14, in which 209 reports were evaluated. The sightings were listed in three categories: Green Fireballs, Disk or Variation, and Probable Meteor. The guest list at the New Mexico conferences included the Fourth Army, Armed Special Weapons Project, the University of New Mexico, the Atomic Energy Commission, the University of California, the Air Force Office of Special Investigations, Scientific Advisory Board and Geophysical Research Division Air Materiél Command, and the FBI. A Bureau memo of the time refers to the meetings in the strongest terms (emphases original): *"This matter is considered Top Secret by Intelligence Officers of both the Army and the Air Forces."* Though it is nowhere explicitly stated, the reason for this classification can only be the same as that for the FBI's involvement in the first place: sabotage activity connected to the sightings.

Sabotage is the most regular activity of the UFO Intelligence, from its first appearance in the modern age—i.e., WWII and beyond. The list of UFO sabotages of government installations and projects is endless. To cite a few examples: the 1948 green fireballs of New Mexico; the remote-control cockpit takeover of Arctic surveying B-29s; the 1958 *Juno 2* "deflection"; the reprogramming of nuclear missiles at Malmstrom AFB on two separate occasions in 1966, and again in 1975; the 1964 toppling of an Atlas F missile from Vandenberg AFB; the "Mothman" assaults on nuclear trigger storage depots in 1966-1967 in West Virginia and Ohio, and similar UFO trespasses into Russian nuclear plants in the taiga since at least 1989; and the suspicious malfunction of numerous space probes from all countries, even into the present day.

By the end of 1948, the Air Force's Project Sign delivered a report called the Estimate of the Situation which determined that UFOs were interplanetary spacecraft. It was reportedly the Estimate that sent Defense Secretary James V. Forrestal running down the halls of the Pentagon, screaming, "We're being invaded and we can't stop them!" Forrestal was immediately given the proverbial "nice, long rest" at Bethesda Hospital, where he soon after either committed suicide or was murdered—his body was found dead on the pavement, several stories beneath his open window. Not long after this incident, the Rand Corporation computer was assigned the task of fighting an imaginary war with the UFOs, based on all the available information on them. Its verdict was simple: give up. In October of 1955, no less a personage than General Douglas MacArthur told *The New York Times,* "The nations of the world will have to unite, for the next war will be an interplanetary war. The nations of the Earth must someday make a common front against attack by people from other planets."

That the military considered itself at war with the UFO Intelligence is betrayed by the conclusions to Project Sign, which all but outright declared that the military was in possession of recovered extraterrestrial spacecraft wreckage that had to be kept sequestered from anyone else's examination (emphases added): "No definite and conclusive evidence *is yet available* that would prove or disprove the existence of these unidentified objects as real aircraft of unknown and unconventional configuration. It is unlikely that positive proof of their existence will be obtained *without the examination of the remains of crashed objects* [implying that such crashed objects were around to be examined]. Proof of non-existence is equally impossible to obtain unless a reasonable and convincing explanation is determined for each incident ... Evaluation of reports of unidentified objects is a necessary activity of military intelligence agencies. Such sightings are inevitable, and *under wartime conditions* rapid and convincing solutions of such occurrences are necessary to maintain morale of military and civilian personnel. In this respect, it is considered that the establishment of procedures and training of personnel is in itself worth the effort expended on this project."

By November 4, 1952, assuredly to assist in exploration of the knotty UFO question, President Truman formed the largest, most secrecy-shrouded, and least accountable Intelligence organization in the entire world: the National Security Agency. The date of its formation was chosen deliberately so that any news which might inadvertently leak out about the occurrence would be lost in the wake of election results. For the first six years of its existence, the NSA had

no charter. Once the charter was drafted, it was immediately classified, and remains so to this day.

Until Walter Mondale's vocal complaints about the Agency's completely unwatched activities and their potential use against American
citizens who would have no legal recourse should they be targeted for
surveillance, the NSA had no official body to oversee or regulate it. The
Federal Intelligence Surveillance Act was instituted in 1978 to satisfy
Mondale and the Church Committee, instating a rotating judiciary to
monitor the NSA's activities, but FISA has remained nothing more than
a token legislature with no impact. Until that time, the only public
mention ever to escape of the NSA was in one or two minor references
in the back of newspapers, when it was casually dismissed as nothing
more than a minor subdivision of the Department of Defense. In fact,
it is virtually synonymous with that exact department, though the vast
majority of Americans have never heard of it, let alone have any knowledge of its activities. Since those activities remain classified—other than
the Agency's own admission that it intercepts and studies all forms of
communication, especially electronic—it can only be guessed what
precisely the NSA really does. One area the NSA is definitely attached
to is the study of UFOs. Within months of its formation, its name
appeared on distribution lists for UFO documents. Captain Edward
Ruppelt mentioned in his memoirs that "The Puzzle Palace" gave orders
on UFO material at the time, and that particular nickname for the NSA
was not publicly known until James Bamford's biography of the Agency,
bearing the same name, was written in 1982.

All that is known about the NSA today—other than the way various presidents such as LBJ and Nixon abused it horribly to conduct illegal surveillance of war protesters and political enemies—is that from
its beginning, it monitored a variety of "watch-lists." More specifically,
the agency monitored anything containing "information on foreign
governments, organizations, or individuals who are attempting to influence, coordinate, or control U.S. organizations, or individuals who may
foment civil disturbance or otherwise undermine the national security
of the U.S." Those conditions would certainly apply at least as much
to the UFO Intelligence as to any potential earthly opponent—even
more so in light of the sabotage activity being conducted at military

and atomic sites. It is inconceivable that the United States or any other world government would not want to keep as close and thorough a track of these activities as humanly possible, especially since it could hardly have been known at the time of the Agency's inception whether or not the unknown invaders were friend or foe—or even simply casually interacting with the local population for reasons unknown. The monitoring of UFO activity—and of substantial numbers among the local populace—also had to do with a fact the government could hardly be anxious to share: UFOs were abducting a great many people, hypnotizing and mind controlling them, and were probably utilizing the abductees in their acts of sabotage.

The formation of the National Security Agency came hot on the heels (within three months) of the most publicized UFO occurrence in modern history: the Washington Nationals. On the nights of July 19 and July 26, 1952, numerous UFOs were spotted by both civilian and military witnesses flying directly over the White House. In both instances, the military delayed doing anything about it for as long as possible, refusing to dispatch interceptors for several hours and insisting that everything was in hand when plainly it was not. The delay in fighter dispatch was doubly confusing to all observers, since not only were unknown aircraft over the most secure airspace in the world without any opposition, but at the time the Air Force had a standing policy of "intercept and destroy" for all unidentifieds.

Forty-eight hours after the second incident, Air Force Intelligence head Major General John A. Samford held the biggest press conference since the Second World War to announce that what his Air Force radar and ground personnel had verified seeing, and their best interceptors had reluctantly engaged and spent hours unable to combat, had been a) temperature inversions, b) meteors, and c) the planets Venus and/or Jupiter. Though it is doubtful anyone believed him, the story was duly printed for circulation, with no one to protest it, including Captain Ruppelt and his entire Blue Book staff. The formation of the NSA so soon after the White House flyovers testifies to the fact that the government still didn't have all its answers on the UFO question, and that it wanted to monitor intensively anyone who might have any connection to it at all.

The National Security Agency only ever released two out of an admitted 279 documents in its possession on the subject of UFOs, both due to the Freedom of Information Act. One was a heavily censored paper citing "high strangeness" in witnesses, with substantial commentary by internationally renowned UFO expert Jacques Vallee. The other was a 1968 paper titled "UFO Hypothesis and Survival Questions," dealing with the wisdom of keeping anything on the subject away from the public. UFOs were casually mentioned to be "adversarial" at one point in the paper, displaying an official attitude of belligerence on the part of the United States, if not the UFO Intelligence itself, though the intruders were never defined as hostile or dangerous. The justification for secrecy was that many civilizations in human history had completely fallen apart, demoralized, when confronted with a technologically superior civilization, especially when they had different ways of life.

The government had other reasons not to want to discuss UFOs with the public, the most bizarre of which was the fact that UFO abductees were found to be having sex with the aliens, even resulting in reproduction. The earliest recorded case in the modern era—echoing similar Fairy abductions of all times and ages—was the Antonio Villas Boas abduction of October 15, 1957. Boas, a twenty-three-year-old Brazilian farmer, was taken from his tractor by typical "Gray" figures (short, bald, with enormous heads, and elliptical black eyes) while working the fields at night and put aboard a landed, egg-shaped UFO, where a woman who to all appearances and functions was human (she was short, blonde, and shapely) had sex several times with him over the space of about an hour. Nor was Boas' account the only one of its type—a great many similar reports were being catalogued, and kept secret. Boas was in no way harmed, nor was his memory at all impaired, as later abductees' apparently have been. (This subject will be discussed at length in Chapter 2.) Additionally, permanent bodily disappearances of pilots were occasionally being recorded. By 1966 or '67, animal mutilations related to UFO appearances were being recorded and publicly discussed, all attention to which the government has done everything in its power to squelch.

But it can quickly be determined that the story does not even begin with all these events. UFOs have been recorded in every age in history, in every country and every culture. Official government interest in them began no later than 1933 and conceivably could have started even earlier than that. After World War II, "ghost aircraft" in Scandinavia, of maneuverability technically superior to anyone's capabilities, were studied by the Scandinavian, United States, and British governments, with no final determination as to what they were. In fact, an earlier study had been undertaken by the same parties during an appearance of the same phenomena in 1933–34. These phantom aircraft flew low-level maneuvers in complete silence over uncertain land conditions, even in the worst weather, running powerful searchlights over the ground, and were far superior in performance to any nation of the time's technological capabilities. More than forty reports a day were being registered in Sweden and Norway by January of 1934, from reliable observers. Intensive research was undertaken to ascertain their origin, to no avail, even when the craft reappeared for a brief time in 1946.

Several reports of UFOs were registered during WWII, also by reliable observers. At 2:25 AM on February 25, 1942, Los Angeles was flown over by about fifteen red UFOs that took 1,430 rounds of 12.8-pound anti-aircraft shells which failed to affect them in the slightest. Despite direct hits in many instances, no pieces of the aerial craft were dislodged for examination. They cruised casually down the coastline at about sixty miles per hour, sometimes accelerating to speeds estimated by professional aircraft observers as being five miles per second, then departed a little under two hours after having first been spotted. General George Marshall wrote a Memorandum for the President the following morning, estimating their speeds ranging from "very slow" to 200 miles per hour, and their elevation between 9,000 and 18,000 feet. He concluded his report with "Investigation continuing." No follow-up report has ever been discovered.

By the following year, parties on all sides of the war reported witnessing what were dubbed "foo fighters," after the French word for fire, *feu*. They were fiery spheres of indeterminate size, usually claimed to be fairly small, that paced fighter and bomber formations off their wingtips in the distance at up to 360 miles per hour. Sometimes they merely followed the flights, and at other times they were seen flying in front of or around the planes at close range. Some reports even said that these "fireballs" entered bombers through their fuselage, to slowly maneuver about inside. Seen in a variety of colors, the apparitions were usually reported as flickering in red or white and were generally believed to be secret weapons of one of the other nations, even though no one was capable of such technical inventions at the time. No one was ever harmed by them, even if pilots did anxiously speculate that they were some kind of aerial bomb. As a result of the number of encounters, Britain's Royal Air Force opened the first official military files investigating UFOs in 1944, under Air Marshall Sir Victor Goddard and General William Massey.

In the U.S., all UFO sightings from that time were filed in triplicate, one copy going to the OSS (Office of Strategic Services, the wartime Intelligence outfit that was the forerunner of the CIA), another going into the file on whatever sortie or raid originated the report, and the last going directly to General Douglas MacArthur, Supreme Commander of the Pacific Theater of Operations, who was the single most avid researcher of the subject in the military. "Officers who wanted to gain favor with the General [MacArthur]," writes John Keel, "knew the best way to win his attention was to present him with a new UFO report. He tried to correlate the European Foofighter sightings with the Pacific sightings, without much success. The water-related UFOs were apparently radically different from the bobbing and weaving nocturnal lights of Europe." Those "water-related" UFOs were gigantic cigar-shaped craft that "bubbled up from the ocean's depths and then flew away," eyewitnessed and registered by ships' and planes' radar all over the Pacific. MacArthur—whose name was closely linked with the Army's Interplanetary Phenomenon Unit, which was officially disbanded in the late 1950s—frequently made public assertions after the war that UFOs were real, and he told students in his final address at West Point that mankind would one day find itself in a war with "evil beings from outer space."

But there are other reasons to be certain that the United States, if not many other world governments, was already asking questions about unidentified aerial craft in the sky well before the Roswell recovery, the formation of the CIA, or even WWII—and that they were finding out specifically where those aerial unknowns were coming from. A number of extremely prominent minds around the world were stating the belief that intelligent signals were being transmitted from the planet Mars. Chief among these was a report made by the inventor Nikola Tesla that was registered in the *Colorado Springs Gazette* of March 9, 1901, and received worldwide attention: the eccentric genius was convinced that he had received intelligent radio transmissions from the planet Mars. He had been attempting to achieve wireless contact with the Red Planet for at least two years, and had made statements to that effect. Nevertheless, when the event came (if in fact it did), he did not immediately publicize it, certain that he would be ridiculed. Ridicule was exactly what he got, until a year later, when Lord Kelvin publicly announced his concurring opinion that Tesla had been contacted by Mars. The matter received no further press.

Three months before Tesla made his announcement, astronomer William Pickering also believed he had detected intelligent signals on December 7, 1900, in one of many "absolutely inexplicable" light displays he and others had witnessed on the planet's surface. Previously, on November 24, 1894, Pickering had reported seeing from Lowell Observatory a self-luminous object approximately twenty miles above the unillumined portion of the Martian surface. Tesla's rival to the claim of inventing radio, Guglielmo Marconi, also believed he had received intelligent signals from Mars of 150,000 meters' wavelength, in the late summer of 1921, a time when no wavelength was greater than 14,000 meters. Japanese astronomer Tsuneo Saheki, professional Mars observer since 1933, once detected intermittent radiation bursts from that planet that he thought were intelligent signals. He also saw what he reluctantly admitted thinking was "an atomic explosion on Mars" on January 15, 1950, a brilliant flare with the brightness of a sixth-magnitude star, lasting five minutes.

But the most dramatic and best documented of received signals from Mars came on August 23, 1924, when "a day of national radio silence" met with success. Mars was in favorable opposition that year,

meaning that it was at its closest distance to Earth in any regular fif-
teen- to seventeen-year cycle—about thirty-four million miles—and
both an early television device invented by the brilliant C. Francis
Jenkins (called the "radio-camera") and the U.S. Signal Corps succeeded in picking up repeating signals from the Red Planet. Jenkins
was in the company of high-ranking U.S. Navy officials and Amherst
University astronomy professor (and proponent of the inhabited
Mars theories of Percival Lowell) Dr. David Todd at the time the signals were received. A repeating picture at the edge of Jenkins' recorded
film was interpreted as being the image of a face in profile and was
written about in *The New York Times* on August 28, though the signals were never deciphered. Master government cryptologist and
early godfather to the CIA, William Friedman, also failed to decipher
whatever message may have been transmitted but devoted considerable time to the effort. Following his death, Friedman's archives at
the Virginia Military Institute were "purged" by the National Security Agency. Despite the purge, a letter survived at the institute from
Captain John P. Ferriter of the U.S. Signal Corps, confirming that his
men had received the Martian signals: "They consisted in part of
dashes of six seconds duration separated by intervals of seven seconds. These dashes continued for several minutes, and were followed
by a voice pronouncing words. They were isolated words of from one
to four syllabels [sic]." The Navy and the Signal Corps repeated their
listening experiment through Johns Hopkins University in 1926, via
a huge specially-built one-hundred-thousand-dollar wireless receiving station in Nebraska; the results were never made public.

Earlier, in 1896 and 1897, a mystery "airship" made appearances
in America, witnessed by hundreds of people at a time, containing
human crewmembers, dressed in clothes of the time, who made landings and conversed in English with the locals—the mystery airship
was the inspiration for young genius, technological prophet, social
reformer, and later British Intelligence man, Herbert George Wells,
to write the most famous of all Martian invasion stories in 1898: *The
War of the Worlds*. Wells was recovering from an illness in a London
hospital when he received a package of clippings concerning the
sightings from the United States. He determined that since no oper-

ational dirigibles were capable of the reported flight characteristics, and the batteries required to power the ship's searchlights would be impossibly heavy, the mystery aircraft was of no Earthly design. His conclusion was that it came from Mars.

From that same era also came at least two interplanetary incidents that certainly had to have gotten the attention of the powers that be, one possibly, and the other definitely, connected to Mars. The first incident occurred on June 17, 1873, and was recorded by England's Dr. Sage in the *Journal of the British Association*. On that date, Sage witnessed a luminous object issuing from Mars, which arrived and exploded in the amazingly short time of five seconds in the skies of Austria, Hungary. "It seemed as if Mars were breaking up under the force of the impulsion of this object," he stated, "and dividing into two parts. The concussion of the firing was sharp."

The other incident was the atomic explosion of a UFO over the Tunguska region of Siberia on June 30, 1908, that created aurorae effects on the opposite side of the planet consistent with what was later discovered by the detonation of atomic weaponry in 1945. The UFO was witnessed by hundreds of people and reported in the newspaper *Sibir* to be a shining cylinder in the shape of a "pipe," which altered direction and speed more than once before exploding. The fireball itself blasted a thirty-seven-square-mile-wide area, yielding about thirty megatons—1,500 times the force of the Hiroshima bomb—from a probable height of three to five miles. Shock waves from the blast twice circled the globe, and the resultant twelve-mile-high pillar of fire and smoke was seen as far away as the town of Kirensk, 250 miles distant. Aerial surveys during and after the war revealed the total staggering area of devastation caused by the explosion's blast of wind to be between 770 and 850 square miles in a triangular shape. Radiation sickness, burns, and electromagnetic disturbances were recorded, lasting five decades or more. Additionally, accelerated growth of the local flora occurred, consistent with that witnessed at the subsequent Bikini Atoll atomic tests and UFO-related crop circles.

In 1946, Soviet Colonel Alexander Kazantsev wrote a science-fiction story attributing the 1908 explosion to a crashing Martian

spaceship, since the damage so closely approximated what was witnessed at Hiroshima and Nagasaki and no trace of comet or meteorite fragments (or even a crater) was ever discovered at the Tunguska
site. In the 1960s, Kazantsev still affirmed, "Highly advanced creatures from Mars have visited the Earth many times until today." In
1966, Soviet scientists V. K. Zhuravlev, D. V. Demin, and L. N. Demina confirmed in a definitive official paper the consensus that the
Tunguska blast was, indeed, atomic. If Kazantsev was postulating as
late as 1946 that Mars was a planet from which spaceships habitu-
ally visited Earth, it is certainly possible others around the world
were considering the possibility much earlier—even from the time
of the 1908 Siberian explosion.

Mars was not the only planet receiving government attention,
however—there was equal notice being given by world governments
to unusual activity on the Moon. The activity on the Moon begins
to give some indicator when world governments began to seriously
consider the question of extraterrestrial neighbors. The British Royal
Astronomical Society embarked on an intensive three-year study of
"Lunar Transient Phenomena" (LTP) in 1869, which were occurring
in the oddly hexagonal-shaped Mare Crisium. In 1879, the Society
asked its members to report all unusual lunar phenomena in an
attempt to discern possible communications; they stopped cataloguing the strange lights and configurations witnessed on the Moon
after only two years, because there were simply too many of them.
Potentially connected to these investigations was that of the search
for public nuisance (and probable robotic UFO occupant) "Springheel
Jack," circa 1837, undertaken by none other than the Duke of Wellington, a Lord Mayor, and members of the British Admiralty. The LTP
and the Springheel Jack incidents officially studied by the British
government could well have influenced Baron Edward Bulwer-Lytton's
1871 novel, *Vril: The Power of the Coming Race,* about immortal supermen from a once-believed mythical Underworld kingdom returning
to the Earth to establish a peaceful and technologically advanced
matriarchal socialist government. Lytton's Underworlders possessed
heat-ray weapons, lived in a world replete with Egyptian fashions
and pyramids, and had human-looking automata which abducted

surface-dwellers to their subterranean kingdom. Lytton wrote several novels in the same vein, mostly of a Masonic or Rosicrucian philosophical background.

In 1966, Russian and American scientists made independent discoveries, in two separate areas of the Moon, of apparently artificial structures. The first such discovery was made on February 4 of that year, by the Soviet *Luna 9* probe, in the Sea of Storms. There, regular "straight lines of equidistant stones ... look[ing] like markers along an airport runway," as *Argosy* editor Ivan Sanderson reported, were detected and subjected to stereoscopic analysis by Russian Laureate State Prize winner (the equivalent of our Nobel) Dr. S. Ivanov, the inventor of stereoscopic movies in the Soviet Union. Based on photos of the "stone markers" at two different lighting angles, Ivanov determined that the structures were definitely artificial, and the Soviet magazine *Technology of Youth* subsequently reported them to be "planned structures" which were equated to "pointed pyramids." The objects were identical in height and spaced at regular intervals. "There does not seem to be any height or elevation nearby from which the stones could have been rolled and scattered into this geometric form," said Ivanov. "The objects as seen in three-D seem to be arranged according to definite geometric laws."

Later the same year, William Blair of NASA's Boeing Institute of Biotechnology detected obelisks in a geometric pattern in the Sea of Tranquility, photographed at twenty to thirty miles above the Moon's surface by *Lunar Orbiter 2*. On November 22, the *Washington Post* (and later, the *Los Angeles Times*) ran a front-page headline on the lunar objects reading, "Six Mysterious Statuesque Shadows Photographed on the Moon by Orbiter," which Blair found to be "[in] a basilary system, with coordinates x, y, z, to the right angle, six isosceles triangles and two axes consisting of three points each," countering official explanations that these were somehow natural landforms. The article described the obelisks, reaching to a height of 213 meters, as being in a pyramidal-prismatic configuration that Soviet space engineer Alexander Abramov believed were identically positioned to the Giza pyramid complex in Egypt. Next to the obelisks could clearly be seen an enormous rectangular depression with clean

90-degree corners "persuad[ing] one to think it is like an excavation whose walls have been eroded or fallen inwards," as Blair described it. Blair's persuasive arguments for the structures being artificial caught the attention of Congress, which advocated closer study of the curious structures, and gave those structures the popular name of the "Blair Cuspids." It may be noted that the first Apollo Moon landing occurred in the Sea of Tranquility, where the cuspids were discovered.

NASA commissioned more than one study into both unusual planetary lights and geometric anomalies. Technical Report R-277, the "Chronological Catalogue of Lunar Events," was compiled by Barbara M. Middlehurst in 1967, listing 579 reliable sightings of anomalous lunar activities from their first appearance to the present. The National Security Agency's "UFO Hypothesis and Survival Questions" was written two years later. The NSA's concern about society collapsing if confronted with the reality of superior extraterrestrial neighbors appeared earlier in a 1958 Brookings Document for NASA entitled "Proposed Studies on the Implications of Peaceful Space Activities for Human Affairs," which spent more than two hundred pages discussing the possibility of discovering "artifacts left at some point in time" which "might be discovered by our space activities on the Moon, Mars, or Venus," bringing up examples of "societies sure of their place in the universe, which have disintegrated when they had to associate with previously unfamiliar societies espousing different ideas and different life ways."

Between 1961 and 1966, astrophysicists Jacques and Janine Vallee, and French Institute of Astrophysics and Center for Scientific Research head Pierre Guérin, discovered something about Mars that they continually debated without ever coming to a definite conclusion: UFO waves almost invariably appear in conjunction with Earth-Mars oppositions. First publishing his findings in *Flying Saucer Review* in 1962, then publicly in his first book on the UFO phenomenon in 1965, *Anatomy of a Phenomenon,* Vallee considered that his findings were good enough to try fitting Martian oppositions and UFO waves together for the period between 1870 and 1914. The "opposition" refers to that time when Mars comes closest to Earth, approximately 34 to 64 million miles away (depending on the year), every twenty-six months. Vallee determined that the findings were interesting, but inconclusive.

In 1966's *Challenge to Science,* Jacques and Janine Vallee applied the Martian oppositions to the waves of UFO activity from 1947 to 1962, and included this time a figuring-in of the Martian *half*-period—when Mars reaches its furthest remove from Earth, in the thirteen months between each twenty-six-month period of peak opposition—which also showed a strong correlation. Randomly taking his figures, he applied cross- and auto-correlation tests to them, and found that the minimum errors in his computations vanished. In other words, for the time period in question, there was a virtually perfect and consistent correlation between UFO waves and the closest and furthest proximities of the planet Mars. Still refusing to commit himself to the hypothesis, Vallee merely suggested that it required further study. Interestingly, he did not go back to show that his figuring-in of the half-period brought the correlations of his 1870–1914 chart much closer into place. Jacques Vallee also noted in his personal journal entry of April 5, 1962, that he and Guérin had discovered three "great circles" that Vallee had computed "divided the equator according to a defined scale, with a basic unit of 12.4 degrees which turns out to be related to the Martian mean time." Vallee wondered if he had discovered a genuine law: "The elegant geometric pattern formed by these three great circles does seem to be more than the product of coincidence."

In 1967, the Department of Defense hired Vallee as principal investigator on "computer networking projects," and he never wrote about Mars correlations again—but his findings, despite the sudden silence and Vallee's own conservative caution, speak for themselves. It was observed by others, independently of Vallee, that the two greatest UFO waves in modern history occurred in direct connection with the Martian oppositions. As Nigel Blundell and Roger Boar wrote in *The World's Greatest UFO Mysteries,* "UFOlogists noted that the sighting peak years of 1967 and 1973 coincided with the time when the orbit of Mars brought it closest to Earth; they wondered whether Martians had to wait for suitable conditions to travel, just as Russia and America had to select exactly the right moments to launch their Venus probes." 1966–67 was the first period in which UFO sabotage

activity against the military was such that it could no longer be concealed, and 1973 had so many reports of UFOs and their occupants
assaulting the local citizenry that researchers and the press labelled
it "The Year of the Humanoids." Vallee had stated that his only objection to pronouncing the Mars-UFO correlation "reliable" was that it
had not yet gone a full twenty years—the 1967 and 1973 waves go
seven years beyond that limit. Adding confirmation to the theory is
the Moscow Institute of Aviation's Dr. Felix Ziegel, Vallee's Russian
counterpart, who by 1970 went on record asking, "Is it sheer coincidence that [UFO] sightings increase whenever Mars is closest to
Earth? No one knows."

Though Vallee never speculated on the reason, the sharp and consistent upswing in sightings when Mars and Earth are closest makes
perfect sense if space shots from that planet are occurring by means
more efficient than our own chemical propellants. The only reason
we do not schedule our own launches to Mars when it is closest to
Earth is because we do not have an efficient or powerful enough
propulsion system to benefit from the close proximity. As for the secondary upswing in UFO activity when the two planets are most distant from each other, there is also a logical reason, if regular return
trips to Mars from Earth are occurring: a "least-energy path" computed by Walter Hohmann in 1925 (and confirmed by Wernher von
Braun in 1948), employing Keplerian gravity curves for projected
Mars shots, estimated the ideal launch time from Earth to be when
Mars was actually 735 million miles distant, for a journey of 250–260
days—close to nine months. The gravity curve thus provides maximum fuel efficiency by acceleration around the Sun, as Mars is similarly gaining velocity on its return toward Earth. The Hohmann
gravity curve is close to the one employed for Mars shots today, which
vary according to the propellant and booster system being used in
the given launch. NASA's lost 1993 *Observer,* for instance, was launched
on September 25, 1992, and lost contact three days before projected
arrival on August 24, 1993—a duration of exactly eleven months,
the precise period of the Vallees' raw data for the secondary upswing
in UFO sightings. (The thirteen-month "half-period" was a number
arrived at by the figuring-in of least squares and other mathematical

tests for minimizing error, on raw sighting data at the eleven-month period.) Similarly, NASA's *Mars Pathfinder* was originally scheduled for an August 3, 1996, launch, to arrive at the Red Planet on July 4, 1997—again, exactly eleven months. (It was launched instead in November, with a more powerful booster, and arrived on the same projected date.)

Based on all the foregoing, it seems apparent on a broad overview that the United States government and probably others were at least strongly considering the possibility of life on other planets, especially Mars, since no later than the beginning of the twentieth century. Nikola Tesla and Lord Kelvin were hardly the sort of men who would be ignored, the more so since both of them made public commentary on their beliefs concerning intelligence on that planet. H. G. Wells made for equally compelling testimony, as do the Vallees and Pierre Guérin. And subsequent happenings to a number of space probes, primarily those sent to Mars, make it all too painfully apparent that government scrutiny of planetary neighbors has hardly lessened, but only intensified, in ensuing years.

In 1994, MGM/UA released a science-fiction epic blockbuster that did not become the new *Star Wars* it was obviously intended to be, but was phenomenally successful nevertheless. It was called *Stargate*, the plot of which concerned a top-secret U.S. government project investigating ancient Egypt since the 1920s. The reason for the project was the discovery of superior extraterrestrial technology buried in that country's sands, and misunderstood since it first came to be there. Eventually deciphering the technology's hieroglyphics, they send a team to the Egyptian planet of man's origins with a nuclear device, in a failed pre-emptive strike anticipating war with that planet's occupants. *Star Wars* itself, filmed while Jimmy Carter was president and no doubt part of an educational media program on the UFO subject that will be considered in depth as this study progresses, was about a tyrannical military-industrial complex of gray-suited and robotic-looking figures utilizing a space station that is mistaken for a moon to devastate rebel opposition, ultimately coming to a showdown with those rebels in their base on the moon of a red planet. Both movies spawned entire industries which are still in business.

In real life, the plot of *Stargate* appears to have played out in the fate of numerous Mars probes, most notably the Soviets' *Phobos 1* and *Phobos 2* and *Mars '96*, and the United States' *Observer*. For that matter, the Egyptian connection to the planet Mars has been an open secret for a quarter of a century. Anyone with more than a passing interest in space knows that NASA probes to Mars have photographed what appear to be configurations of pyramids, in two separate locations of the planet: Elysium and Cydonia. The Elysium Pyramids were photographed in the Trivium Charontis area by *Mariner 9*, at two separate times and lighting angles, on frames 4205-78 on February 8, 1972, and 4926-23 six months later. They appeared to be regularly spaced, three-sided pyramids in rhombus formation, the two larger of which were two miles across and half a mile high. "Given the present lack of any easily acceptable explanation," wrote David Chandler of the structures in *Life on Mars*, "there seems to be no reason to exclude from consideration the most obvious conclusion of all: perhaps they were built by intelligent beings."

No NASA official has ever admitted to believing these are images of real pyramids. A study in Volume 22 of *Icarus* two years after their discovery, by Victor Ablordeppy and Mark Gipson, gave four theories for how the Elysium images could have formed naturally. These were dissected and disregarded by several scientists, including astronomer Francis Graham in the November-December 1980 *Frontiers of Science*. He maintained that the structures might have been standing for up to ten thousand millennia, and courageously stated that "the conjecture that these are the buildings of an ancient race of Martians must take its place among the theories of their origin." Despite convincing arguments by such men as Chandler and Graham, the official consensus remains that these anomalies are interesting, but altogether natural, landforms of the Martian surface.

The *Viking* probes in 1976, however, revived the issue forcefully, when they took two photos of an immense mesa looking like a human face, a mile across, two miles long, and half a mile high in the Cydonia region. Though NASA has ever since attempted to dismiss the mesa's appearance as merely "an oddity of light and shading," detailed analysis and computer enhancements, taken from two different angles at different times, reveal it to arguably be a face, wearing an Egyptian headdress or helmet. Another face was found in mathematical relation to the first one, positioned so as to monitor the rising and setting of the sun on Mars. The author has proposed, in *Architects of the Underworld,* that this central face is actually one of the two central gods of Egypt—Ra, the sun-god, who was depicted as a hawk— and that the second face is that of Thoth, the other central god of Egypt, who was depicted as a baboon.

Three years after *Viking,* computer analysts Vincent DiPietro, Gregory Molenaar, and The Analytic Science Corporation's Mark J. Carlotto discovered an approximately 1-by-1.6-mile pyramid on Mars, also in mathematical relation to the Mars faces. More such structures emerged by 1983, under the analysis of author and scientist Richard Hoagland, until an entire city construct in the Cydonia region was revealed. Hoagland, Defense Mapping Agency cartographer Erol Torun, and Daniel Drasin (discoverer of the second Mars face), among others, found recurring geometry and interrelationary mathematics throughout the Cydonia complex that were found also to occur on our own planet: most notably, in the Giza pyramid complex in Cairo. The pyramids were found to be precisely oriented to the spin-axis of Mars, just as the Giza pyramids are perfectly oriented (to a lesser deviation than any man-made structure built since) to the cardinal points of the compass on Earth. The consensus estimate of the Cydonia complex age came to 445,000–450,000 years, which is the same calculated time for the arrival on Earth of the culture god, Oannes (or Nommo), according to ancient Babylonian records.

These multiple geometric discoveries were independently corroborated, in part, by Scottish astronomer Duncan Lunan and mathematician M. W. Saunders, in their 1975 book *Destiny Mars*—which was published the year before *Viking* beamed back its amazing pictures of the planet's surface for analysis. Lunan discovered an alignment between Mexico's Pyramid of the Sun in Teotihuacan and the Great Pyramid in Giza which defined a precise orbital period locking with the rotation of Mars, and both men found numerous mathematical relationships among the Great Pyramid, the Earth, the Sun, and Mars. By their measurements, the Great Pyramid's base length times 1,000 million is within 1% of the mean distance between Mars and the Sun; the mean Earth-Sun distance, with an error only 1% greater, is 1,000 million times the Pyramid's height; 1,000 million times its height plus base length equals the maximum Mars-Earth distance, with an error of only 0.14%; the Pyramid's building measurement, the Cubit, equals the Mars-Earth Indicated Base-Length divided by 440, with a one-tenth tolerance for error; the displacement of the Pyramid's innermost chamber from the east-west center-line, divided by the mean semi-base, equals the eccentricity of Mars' orbit to within 0.0023%; the north slope of the Pyramid (which is a 2 pi pyramid) points to a height above the equator the equivalent of 2 pi times Mars' equatorial radius, with an error of 0.5%.

In addition, with tolerances for error all of 0.5% or less, Lunan and Saunders found the mean height of the orbit of Mars' satellite Deimos to equal *pi* times the Earth's equatorial radius, at which height in Earth's orbit such a satellite would revolve twice for every rotation of the Earth; and that for every rotation of the Earth, Phobos orbits Mars pi times, an equivalent satellite of which in Earth's orbit would revolve 2 *pi* times in the time it takes Earth to rotate once. They also noticed that the largest volcanoes of both Earth and Mars occurred at about 19.6 degrees north or south of their equators, which Hoagland measured to a more precise 19.47 degrees and found to be an apparent universal constant for maximum volcanic activity of any planetary body—such being the location of the Alpha and Beta Regios of Venus, the Great Dark Spot of Neptune, the Great Red Spot on Jupiter, and the like.

Despite the fact that no official establishment figure would admit to believing the Martian structures were actually manufactured, the late Dr. Carl Sagan televised the Elysium pyramids on his show, *Cosmos,* shortly after their discovery, in the interest of whipping-up national support for the space program. Earlier in his career, the famous UFO debunker ironically made more than one statement strongly affirming the possibility of immediate extraterrestrial neighbors. As the Advisor on Extraterrestrial Life to the Armed Services, Sagan told the December 1962 American Rocket Society convention in Los Angeles—at which researchers C. D. Jackson and R. E. Hohmann presented an excellent paper on the 1924 and '26 Jenkins/Todd/U.S. Signal Corps Mars radio project—that early visitors from space had probably left bases in the solar system, specifically on the far side of the Moon, and that they might even still be inhabiting them. His views were shared by Major Patrick Powers, U.S. Army Space Development Program head, who was quoted in *Family Circle* stating his opinion that "the first men to reach the moon must be prepared to fight for the privilege of landing." After the seemingly dismal Mars evidence of *Mariner 4* in 1965, Sagan addressed the 1966 American Astronautical Society meeting with the portentous observation, ". . . the earth may have been visited by various galactic civilizations many times (possibly in the order of 10,000) during geological time. It is not out of the question that artifacts of these visits still exist, or even that some kind of base is maintained (possibly automatically) within the solar system to provide continuity for successive expeditions." 1966 was also the year that Sagan translated I. S. Shklovskii's *Intelligent Life in the Universe* from the original Russian. Shklovskii's book created something of a firestorm, seriously putting forth a number of ideas that no one knew quite what to make of.

For one thing, Shklovskii proposed that Phobos, which should have flung out into space or crashed into the surface of Mars long ago due to its small size and weight, either had an ice center or was hollow. If that idea met with ridicule, the further suggestion that Phobos might be a converted planetary body being used as a space station certainly fared no better. But all the evidence shows that, at the highest government and military levels, it was taken with the utmost seriousness. The conservative Jacques Vallee wrote the same year that it was entirely possible "that the 'saucers' are interplanetary craft that use either a satellite of Mars or that planet itself as a base in their exploration of our solar system. In our present state of the ignorance of the nature of the Martian satellites it is not impossible to think that they are large interstellar vehicles, placed into orbit more than a century ago . . . by an advanced community coming from elsewhere in the universe." Indeed, the findings of the Russian probe *Phobos 2* did nothing to dispel the hollow satellite theory, and on the other hand did a great deal to confirm it. Complicating that theory is the odd fact that our own Moon, like Phobos, appears also to be hollow, reverberating for up to four hours when struck with spent rocket stages—and both of Mars' moons, like Earth's Moon, have unnatural synchronous orbits, always showing the same face to the planet around which they are anchored. Additionally unnatural, Phobos—unlike any known body in the universe—rises in the west and sets in the east.

Only four years after Sagan and Shklovskii's book, Howard Koch—the author of the infamous Mercury Radio Playhouse Theater adaptation of H. G. Wells' *The War of the Worlds*—wrote, "Not long ago, there was a chilling prediction by an official in the American State Department. He projected a plan, which apparently his science advisors considered feasible, for launching a spaceship armed with nuclear missiles that could push the moon Phobus [*sic*] out of the Mars gravitational field across space and into our orbit." The proposed reason was to bring a ready-made space station to Earth, which frankly seems harder to believe than the reason which more readily springs to mind: to blow up the base being used by the spaceships visiting Earth. Just like *Stargate*.

The suggestion of military activity around Phobos becomes easier to accept when the fate of probes subsequent to *Viking* is taken into account. The Russians were the next to attempt a Mars mission, assisted by the European Space Agency, France, and Germany. A number of failed attempts preceded that of their 1989 probes, *Phobos 1* and *2*, named after the primary object of their photographic mission: that most curious of Martian satellites. Six probes were lost between their first attempt in October of 1960, and *Zond 2* in April of 1965, a fact which caused the Americans to joke uneasily about the "Great Galactic Ghoul." Following the U.S.' successful *Mariner 9* probe, the Soviets lost two more, *Mars 2* and *Mars 3*, which arrived about two weeks after their American predecessor. The former crashed, believed to have been the victim of one of Mars' notorious dust storms. The latter landed its rover, which was the first to transmit images from the planet's surface. Twenty seconds into its debarkation, however, it abruptly ceased, for reasons never to be discovered—or, at least, never to be disclosed. The Russians did not even reveal *Mars 3*'s failure until the United States lost its *Observer* probe in August of 1993.

The purpose for the Phobos mission was to prepare for a robot lander, in further preparation for a joint U.S./U.S.S.R. manned Mars mission to follow, a stated goal of both the Russians and the Americans since 1984. Among the probe's planned activities was scanning the moonlet with both infrared and gamma rays and firing an "ion emitter" and laser at Phobos' surface, for the stated reason of pulverizing and retrieving some of its surface material, and to create a cloud that could be studied for chemical content. Given what happened to the mission, the likelihood that the emitter and laser were intended to serve a different purpose altogether again comes to mind. The laser was so powerful that it raised a voice of protest from American defense experts that it was merely a ploy for the Soviets to expand and test their own Star Wars weaponry—but that objection was overruled by the White House, explained as being "officially sanctioned due to the improvement in Soviet-American relations."

Phobos 1 and *Phobos 2* were launched on July 12, 1988. *Phobos 1* was lost en route after only two months, reportedly due to loss of the radio link. *Phobos 2* arrived at Mars to establish stable orbit in January of 1989, relocating to orbit Phobos on March 28, when it abruptly and inexplicably "failed to communicate with Earth as scheduled" according to the Russian news service, Tass. Though the radio link was blamed, the Russians did admit openly to a UFO being present at the time *Phobos 2* ceased transmitting. It was a thin, symmetrical ellipse, about twelve-and-a-half miles long, the shadow of which was cast onto the surface of Mars and photographed by the probe. An extremely similar shadow had been photographed, between sixteen and nineteen miles long, only a few days earlier. The shadow was detected both by the color cameras and the infrareds, and was unquestionably ruled out as belonging to that of Phobos itself. The Russians called it a "phenomenon," and were outright asked by their own reporters at a press conference at the end of the month whether or not the shadow was that of a spaceship. Their space agency, Glavkosmos, answered that such speculation would be "to fantasize," but admitted by April 10 that they had located *Phobos 2*'s weak signal and were "tracking a spinner," implying that the radio link had not been the cause of the loss. The October 19, 1989, issue of *Nature* carried the official Soviet verdict that either the computer had malfunctioned or something had "impacted" their probe.

Though in deference to international pressure they did release *Phobos 2*'s final transmissions to be aired on European and Canadian T.V. as curiosities about three months after the probe's loss, the Russians still have not shown anyone the final few frames it photographed. What they did release for public viewing testifies to the fact that what they withheld must have been something extremely important indeed: the available footage showed more than 230 square miles from an unspecified area of the equatorial region of Mars which looked like an intelligently designed network of crisscrossing lines in a city grid pattern, consisting of parallel lines and rectangles with varying lengths. The regular cameras did not pick them up, only the infrareds, indicating a heat source in the area which by implication was radiating from beneath the planet's surface, though Radio Moscow correspondent Boris Bolitsky identified the "quite remarkable features" as being either on the planet's surface or else "in the lower atmosphere." The London Museum's Dr. John Becklake was very straightforward in his analysis: "The city-like pattern is 60 kilometers wide, and could easily be mistaken for an aerial view of Los Angeles."

The United States, not to be outdone, followed the spectacular Russian space failure with one of its own: four years after the loss of *Phobos 2*, the U.S. launched *Observer*, at more than a billion dollars' cost, on September 25, 1992, and mysteriously lost it on August 21 of the following year, three days before its scheduled arrival at destination Mars. Everything about the loss was suspicious, and still no satisfactory answers have surfaced to dispel those suspicions. For one thing, no backup probe was launched with *Observer*, which is standard procedure since it costs only a fraction more to do and ensures against exactly such failures. For another, the probe appeared to have been sabotaged at least once even before launch: after the launch was delayed by Hurricane Andrew, NASA found on a safety inspection that scraps of fiber, metal filings, dirt, paper, and even plaster of Paris had somehow gotten past *Observer*'s nitrogen hoses and entered the probe, all of which look much less like what might have accidentally entered the probe in a high-powered wind than the product of a deliberate dumping of garbage. Shortly after launch, the probe lost radio contact for about a half hour, which is suspicious all by itself, though contact was reestablished. And, immediately before the probe's final loss, NASA succeeded in uploading all of its commands, meaning that the probe would continue its mission even if no one on Earth was visibly able to monitor it—or that NASA (or someone else) could monitor the probe privately without anyone else knowing—and, against protocol, they deliberately turned off telemetry just after the loss of radio contact, claiming it was General Electric's and Martin Marietta's idea, even though these manufacturers flatly denied it.

If all of this weren't bad enough, CIA President George Bush fired NASA head Admiral Richard Truly, a man renowned for his honesty and integrity, while he was investigating Michigan Democratic Representative Howard Wolpe's allegations that the Space Agency was officially ordered to circumvent the Freedom of Information Act. While Congress was looking into ways to get the SP-100 nuclear space reactor developed, Wolpe discovered a two-page set of instructions "instruct[ing] government employees to . . . rewrite and even destroy documents 'to minimize adverse impact' . . . mix up documents and camouflage handwriting so that [their] significance would be 'less meaningful' . . . [and] take steps to 'enhance the utility' of various FOIA exemptions."

Final determination as to the fate of *Observer* was never made public, other than to say first that the radio link was lost, and later to speculate that it might have exploded after an unspecified system leak. Given the impossible breach of protocol in turning off telemetry *after* the commands were uploaded, it seems almost certain that someone behind the scenes at either NASA or the Department of Defense continued to monitor the probe, and wanted to do so without having to publicly disclose what it was seeing. The bizarre debris present inside the probe before launch and the near-loss of the radio link immediately after once more raise the question of sabotage, which raises the more interesting question of which parties might have been behind it. Did NASA, the CIA, or the DOD want to keep the probe from disclosing secrets on Mars? Or could sabotage have been prompted by someone from the Red Planet itself? If so, then it was done by hands down here, and not by remote UFO-related cause as seems to have been the case with numerous missile launches in the past. Whose hands would those have been?

And that Mars itself could be occupied is no longer a question to be considered out of bounds. Though the planet's atmospheric conditions would not allow for occupancy above ground—even if they may well have in the past—striking evidence of what looks like a city grid has been found beneath the surface, and the last object photographed by *Phobos 2* was, by definition, a UFO: it was unquestionably an object, it was flying, and it has never been identified. Expert opinion has been publicly issued, since no later than the mid-1960s, that Phobos may actually be a space station, and there have even been indications that Earth's own Moon serves a similar function—which would explain the tremendous interest the War Department showed in the Moon immediately after WWII, sanctioning the importation of many Nazi rocket scientists who did, ultimately, succeed in taking us there. The military's concern in space matters becomes all the more obvious when the latest failed space probe is taken into account: *Clementine,* the Department of Defense's lunar mapping device.

Clementine was the first return to photograph the Moon since the Apollo project was shut down in 1972. Though advertised after the fact as a joint NASA-DOD venture, the semi-secret mission was plainly a BMDO project—the Ballistic Missile Defense Organization, the latest reincarnation of Reagan's "Star Wars," operating on a stated two and a half billion dollars a year. Launched from Vandenberg AFB on January 25, 1994, at a seventy-five-million-dollar cost, *Clementine's* mission was to exhaustively photograph the lunar surface and put it into high-resolution, all-digital format. The spring following the probe's launch, *Clementine* was "lost and gone forever" before reaching its next mapping destination, the near-Earth asteroid Geographos, owing to a stated motor malfunction and resultant fuel loss. Despite the failure to reach its second destination, *Clementine* returned more than two million lunar images, 1.8 million of which have since become available on the Internet. If *Clementine* was not for military purposes, then why did the DOD and BMDO control it, and why have 200,000 images been kept unavailable to the public? What does the military want with the Moon that it couldn't get from reading already-existent NASA maps?

That Mars was connected to Earth and its early civilization can no longer be in doubt. On September 1, 1987, *The New York Times* published a photograph of a four-and-a-half-billion-year-old football-sized and -shaped piece of rock, seeming to be intelligently joined together in four sections at a corner, that NASA had proclaimed contained the same gaseous content as rocks on the planet Mars. The Mars rock was believed to be 13,000 years old on Earth (which places its arrival at the end of the last Ice Age, that period which closely corresponds to worldwide myth-text datings of the loss of Atlantis). The rock was one of several found Antarctica as early as 1979—a location credibly argued by a few scholars as the location of a sacred outpost of the gods in antiquity—that were previously believed to belong to a group of eight enigmatic rock fragments dubbed "SNC meteorites" which were discovered in India, Egypt, and France between 1815 and 1865. Both the SNC and Antarctic samples had the same gas content, which was that of Martian rock. To anyone who might suppose the correlation could be accidental, U.S. Geological Surveyist Jeffrey S. Kargel elsewhere unequivocally stated that, "We have in our laboratories and museums chunks of Mars that have come to the Earth. Maybe terrestrial life has its origins on Mars. Maybe we're all evolved Martians."

On August 7, 1996, one of these Mars rocks, discovered in 1984 and dubbed AH (Allan Hills) 84001, was announced by Associated Press, Reuters, and several other news services to contain the same building blocks of organic life as existed on Earth, called polycyclic aromatic hydrocarbons (PAHs), as well as carbonate globules and the presence of the minerals magnetite and iron sulfide, which are associated with bacterial action on Earth. The news made the front page of papers across the world and has sparked intensive scientific investigation of the possibility that Mars contained primitive life in its antiquity. What has not yet been speculated openly is the likelihood that more advanced life evolved, notably human life, as evidenced by not only the ignored artifacts on that planet's surface and the regular correlation between UFO waves and the planet's proximity to Earth, but the fact that the world's leading biologist, Sir Francis Crick, has stated since 1973 that Earth simply has not been in existence long enough to have spawned any form of life as advanced as man, and that Earth's life was almost certainly seeded by the activity of an extraterrestrial society in antiquity. This argument is naturally furthered by the likelihood that Mars is older than Earth, witnessed by the fact that its red color comes from oxidation. Mars has not had much oxygen in its atmosphere for many millennia, and Earth has had a highly oxygenated atmosphere for probably as long a time as Mars has not, but Earth is not colored red. In other words, Mars is to all appearances older than Earth, and the evidence would seem to be greater for human life having evolved there than here.

United States Intelligence agencies, namely the CIA, DIA (Defense Intelligence Agency), and NSA, have acknowledged occult research since the early 1970s in the area of "remote viewing," funding for which was only cut off in the mid-1990s. Established in response to potential Russian breakthroughs in psychic warfare, its most vocal believers on the public record include President Jimmy Carter, his CIA head Admiral Stansfield Turner, and numerous Pentagon and Intelligence insiders who worked on the project. One of its 1980-82 specially trained participants was purported to be none other than DOD computer scientist, Stanford Research Institute consultant, and UFO expert, Jacques Vallee. Claimed successes in the field, recorded in science writer Jim Schnabel's *Remote Viewers: The Secret History of America's Psychic Spies,* include early discovery of the Soviet Typhoon submarine, the location of missing agents and downed Russian planes, and the location and identification of defense installations and projects in several foreign countries long before their official verification by more conventional means. Since its official government termination as a funded project, remote viewing has gone corporate, with some former members starting their own companies or research centers. The Centre of Remote Sensing at Boston University is one example, whose founder and director is Dr. Farouk El Baz, graduate of Cairo's prestigious *Ain Shams* university (and team head of the aborted 1996 project to open a metal door discovered in a shaft of the Great Pyramid's Queen's Chamber, hand-picked by Director General of the Giza Pyramids Dr. Zahi Hawass), NASA consultant, and one-time personal friend of astronauts Buzz Aldrin and Neil Armstrong. El Baz was the analyst of geological formations on the Moon and Mars who chose the *Apollo 11* lunar landing site. Among the RV project's admitted uses was UFO research, most specifically in regards to the planet Mars: "[Remote viewer] Ed Dames conducted a training session with Angela Dellafiora in ERV [Extended Remote Viewing] mode," reports Schnabel. "She went into an altered state and began to visualize the target. Something was a bit strange about the target site. It seemed too cold; everything was red. Eventually, Dames showed her the target folder. The target was a certain region on Mars known as Cydonia. Dames believed that an ancient humanoid civilization had lived there. Perhaps the Cydonian civilization was distantly related to modern Earth civilization. . . Dellafiora promptly complained to . . . the unit's other managers about this bizarre targeting, and Dames was told to cease and desist."

Despite the official censure, 1981–84 INSCOM head (Internal Security Command, U.S. Army) and long-time overseer of the remote viewing project, Maj. General Albert Stubblebine, commented in a May 1992 lecture on the subject for the International Symposium on UFO Research, "I will tell you for the record that there are structures underneath the surface of Mars. . . . I will also tell you that there are machines under the surface of Mars that you can look at. You can find out in detail, you can see what they are, where they are, who they are and a lot of detail about them . . . you can do that through remote viewing." Elaborating further on these points on the August 29, 1996, Art Bell syndicated radio talk show, Major Ed Dames stated in regard to the *Phobos 2* and *Observer* losses that there was a biological "command and control element beneath the Martian surface"—i.e., living beings of some sort—working in conjunction with "intelligent robots" that "seem to have a type of sentience, something that goes beyond the idea of advanced artificial intelligence."

Confirmation was given by two other RV trainees, Tom Nance and Joe McMoneagle, as Schnabel relates: "[Nance's] sites included sites on the dark side of the Moon, and in the Cydonia region of Mars. . . . Nance, for whatever prosaic or paranormal reason, had come up with results suggesting that some kind of humanoid civilization had lived at Cydonia, or perhaps even lived there now. McMoneagle was given the same targets . . . with similar results. He even drew the humanoids in detail, and called them 'They.' McMoneagle would later tentatively suggest, on the basis of his RV sessions, that a race of humanoids had fought for survival on Mars, had dispatched some kind of space-lifeboat to Earth, and had perhaps built the great pyramids of Egypt." (RV sessions with UFO targets were regarded as spooky business by many of the viewers. McMoneagle "was often surprised to find himself looking around the cramped, curved interior of an unearthly ship, filled with skinny, large-eyed humanoids—who often stared back at him, wondering what the hell he was doing there. Facing off with aliens was a rough business, it seemed, and on several occasions, McMoneagle returned from the experience drenched in sweat and xenophobic stress.")

Contemporary civilian researchers into the question of UFO abductions are equally enlightened concerning space connections to ancient Egypt and automata, such as Rosicrucians Lord Edward Bulwer-Lytton and mythologist Lewis Spence were writing about even before the turn of the century. The Roswell crash remains exhibited what everyone who saw them—without exception—called "hieroglyphics." The witnesses at this site were not alone in the discovery of anachronistic-seeming Egyptian elements associated with UFOs—a great many abductees have made exactly the same observation. Abductee Herbert Schirmer saw "some books which looked like log books, note books, on the tables. This stuff was more like symbols, like stuff you see in the movies about Egypt." He also saw the emblem of a winged serpent on the right breast area of the UFO occupants' uniforms, the symbol of Quetzalcoatl, culture god of the Americas, also commonly found in Egypt. So did abductee Betty Andreasson, picked up the same year as Schirmer, who reported being taken someplace where she saw "a pyramidlike structure with a sculptured head affixed to its apex. It looked sort of like an Egyptian head, and it had like a, you know, how they wear those hats?" She also saw the serpent-emblem reported by Schirmer and had the Egyptian myth of the Bennu bird enacted for her during her experience.

Many of Pulitzer Prize-winning Harvard psychiatrist Dr. John Mack's abductees report a surprising number of Egyptian references associated with their time aboard UFOs. One, shown "nature images" on a screen, for the stated purpose that it was "to make you understand, to comprehend the implications. To put you in the right frame of mind," said, "I've seen this on T.V. It's going to the desert. It's going to be pyramids. I'm seeing more Egyptian, ancient things, like hieroglyphics and pictures, pictures of pharaohs and things . . . This makes sense to me . . . This is not a trick. This is like useful information." Another described details in a ritual to Anubis for the acquisition of eternal life that was accurate down to colors, styles of dress, and implements utilized, none of which is either common knowledge or easily found, even in Egyptology texts. Another, probably his best single case-study, stressed to Mack that his abductors were "not here to hurt anybody," had been with us for a long time, and "They can see what's about to happen to us. They're just watching us." Mack relates that, "As he was saying these things, [his] mind was 'flashing' on the pyramids of Egypt and the 'faces of Mars.'"

Mack reports "an increasing group of abductees that I have been encountering who have discovered that they have a dual identity as an alien (they do not use that word) and a human being." (Parenthetical inclusion Mack's own.) These report their "controller"- being speaking to them in their own voice, and they identify themselves with it completely. "I have to go with him," explains one, "because I'm—we're—linked in some way." Mack relates one of these cases specifically: "The figure told [the abductee] 'it's me,' and that he has 'the power to make this thing [the figure], and I can't see how I do.'" This is a direct correlation to ancient Egypt that neither Mack nor the abductee knew existed, but that exists nonetheless. In the Egyptian Book of the Dead—the actual name of which is the "Book of

Coming Forth By Day," which might have quite different connotations—*ushabti* figures identify themselves with "the deceased" in exactly the same way, as premiere Egyptologist Sir E. A. Wallis Budge notes concerning the determinative given in the hieroglyphs: "The variants are of interest, and not the least remarkable are the last two words, 'I am thou,' in which the figure makes itself identical with the deceased." *Ushabtiu* (plural), or *shawabtis* (as they are also called), are specifically artificial, animated figures. "We know from classical authors," mythologist Lewis Spence noted, at the beginning of the century, "that the Egyptians possessed the most wonderful skill in the manufacture of automata." Papyri and pottery in the British, Berlin, and Brooklyn Museums describe and portray oracle statues moving under their own power to resolve legal disputes. "The Sorceror's Apprentice," the story in which a magician's assistant animates broomsticks to carry water for him but then cannot make them stop, originated with the Egyptian story of Eucrates as related by Lucian. But even more interesting than the many ancient Egyptian texts describing automata is the fact that those automata can be shown to have performed exactly the same functions being reported by today's UFO abductees—who apparently are also being confronted with robots (as will be discussed in detail in Chapter 1). Spell 572 of the Coffin Texts, a version of the Book of the Dead, describes the "porters of Horus," beings which bring magic teachings to the pharaoh and tell him "what I should know and what I should forget," exactly in tune with the training and amnesia aspects of UFO abduction.

Spence and Budge each relate the story of an Egyptian Pharaoh abducted by the magic of an Ethiopian Viceroy's sorcerer, who then performs the same magic on the Viceroy. "The Ethiopian sorcerors had sent their sorceries to Egypt intending to spirit away Pharaoh to Ethiopia," writes Budge. "But as Hor had bound amulets on Pharaoh the sorceries of Ethiopia were powerless to carry him off. When Hor heard this from Pharaoh he determined to do to the governor of Ethiopia what the governor had tried to do to Pharaoh. He had a large quantity of pure wax brought to him and made a model of a litter and models of four men to carry it. Then he recited spells over all these, and so endowed them with life, and he ordered them to go to the Sudan (Nehes), and to bring the Viceroy to the presence chamber of Pharaoh. When there they were to give the Viceroy a beating with sticks, five hundred strokes, and then to carry him back to the Sudan. All this was to be done in six hours. The following morning the Viceroy assembled his nobles, and showed them his back, and they saw the weals and wounds which the sticks had made on it, and seeing them, they uttered loud cries of horror. The Viceroy sent for his chief sorceror, who was also called Hor, and cursed him by Amen, the Bull of Meroe, and commanded him to save him from further disgrace and suffering at the hands of the Egyptian sorcerors. Hor promptly prepared amulets and bound them on the Viceroy and so protected him."

Spence provides the prologue to the story, in which the Pharaoh found himself abducted by the Ethiopians. He writes, "wakening the next morning . . . he lay in great pain, his body sorely bruised. Bewildered, he asked his courtiers how such could have happened in Egypt. They, thinking some madness had fallen upon their king, and yet ashamed of their thoughts, spoke soothingly to him, and said that the great gods would heal his afflictions. But still they asked him the meaning of his strange words, and suddenly he remembered all that had happened to him and recounted it to his courtiers." The story relates every particular of a modern UFO abduction: automata flying on the clouds by means of some technology ("magic," or "sorceries"), kidnapping a given target and performing physical procedures on him, then taking him back where he came from and erasing his memory of the event—which he nevertheless eventually remembers—and having to show unidentified body markings to those he relates his story to, in order for them to believe him.

Contemporary governments certainly are not unaware of any of the preceding revelations, and the loss of *Phobos 2* even seems to indicate that the knowledge has influenced some of their policies as well. It was only days after the probe's loss that the White House unexpectedly reversed its decision to cancel the military space defense X-30 National Aero-Space Plane program. The decision was made by President George Bush and Vice President Dan Quayle, who was newly appointed chairman of the National Space Council, at its very

first meeting in April of 1989. Two months later, the NSC funded
NASA's Space Station program for 1990 at 13.3 billion dollars, with
instructions to accelerate its work. The following month, Quayle lobbied Congress and the space industry with five options for "developing a lunar base as a stepping stone to Mars." And only one week
later, *Voyager 2* photographed the same type of odd chain-craters on
Neptune's moon, Triton, that have been witnessed both on Phobos
and our own Moon, at the same time it was revealed that a U.S. military space device had successfully fired a "neutral-particle beam"—
exactly the sort of "death ray" that Nikola Tesla proposed decades
before. By the end of the year, the event no one believed ever would
happen—the unification of Germany and the end of the Cold War—
became a sudden and unexpected reality.

Bush made exceptionally short work of a summit conference with
Mikhail Gorbachev in Malta, in which the two discussed the use of
SDI as both a defensive and offensive program, including both rockets *and men,* none of which appeared to bother Gorbachev at all.
Bush's proposed budget to Congress suddenly included a 4.5-billion-
dollar increase for Star Wars, and a twenty-four percent increase for
NASA, stating the specific reason of wanting to "return astronauts to
the moon" in commitment of a joint U.S.-Russian manned mission
to Mars. All proposed space programs so accelerated were specified
to be for "insuring that the space program contributes to the national
military security." NASA's Deep Space Network of telescopes was
expanded, and the SETI (Search for Extraterrestrial Intelligence) program cut off by Congress in 1983 was revived with a doubled and
tripled budget, "to search for evidence that life exists—or has existed—
beyond Earth, by studying other bodies of the Solar System," in addition to its former stated purpose of scanning space for intelligent
signals from anywhere in the universe. The Hubble telescope plainly
fits into that search mission. And *Clementine,* equally plainly, fit into
a militaristic space mission.

Indeed, such joint American-Russian military concerns in space
were becoming quite apparent as early as 1985, immediately after
Russia's statement of intent to join forces with the United States in
a manned Mars mission. Reagan's former declarations against the

"Evil Empire" of the Soviet Union suddenly became replaced with a more cooperative stance. About two weeks after the Geneva Summit with Gorbachev, on December 4, 1985, Reagan made a public speech in Fallston, Maryland, in which he disclosed, "I couldn't but—one point in our discussion privately with General Secretary Gorbachev—when you stop to think that we're all God's children, wherever we may live in the world—I couldn't help say to him, just think how easy his task and mine might be in these meetings that we held if suddenly there was a threat to this world from some other species from another planet outside in the universe. We'd forget all the little local differences that we have between our countries and we would find out once and for all that we are all human beings here on this earth together. I also stressed ... how our nation's commitment to the Strategic Defense Initiative ... was a reason to hope, not to fear." Later, on September 21, 1987, in answer to queries concerning his odd reversal of attitude with the Soviets, Reagan reiterated, "In our obsessions and antagonisms of the moment we often forget how much unites all the members of humanity. Perhaps we need some outside, universal threat to recognize this common bond. I occasionally think how quickly our differences would vanish if we were facing an alien threat from outside this world."

On February 16, 1987—one year after the American *Challenger* disaster and seven months before Reagan's repeated emphasis on space threats—Gorbachev disclosed his own version of his and the American President's talk at the international "Survival of Humanity" forum address at Moscow's Grand Kremlin Palace: "The destiny of the world and the future of humanity have concerned the best minds from the time man first began thinking of the future. Until relatively recently, these and related reflections have been seen as an imaginative exercise, as other-worldly pursuits of philosophers, scholars and theologians. In the past few decades, however, these problems have moved onto a highly practical plane." He discussed first the perpetual threat of nuclear weapons, then added, "At our meeting in Geneva, the President said that if the Earth faced an invasion by extraterrestrials, the United States and the Soviet Union would join forces to repel such an invasion. I shall not dispute the hypothesis, though I think it's early yet to worry about such an intrusion." In response to senior *New Republic* editor Fred Barnes' question as to whether Reagan's promise to join with the Russians in the event of extraterrestrial invasion were true, the President confirmed, "Yes, absolutely."

There is reason to believe both world superpowers continue to view someone from outer space, most notably someone from Mars, as a threat. The last Russian Mars shot, *Mars '96*, the second of three proposed missions, fell very shortly after launch into the Pacific Ocean between Chile and Easter Island, on November 17, 1996. The loss to world science was devastating, the cost itself being in the hundreds of millions of dollars. Twenty-three instruments from several European countries and the United States were aboard the six-ton craft, for as many different tests of the planet. One was a device to measure magnetic fields around Mars that cost its designer, Professor David Southwood of London's Imperial College, an entire ten years' work. The probe was also carrying something most unorthodox, however, which made front-page news due to the fact that it almost crashed into Australia instead of the ocean: four cannisters of plutonium, each about the size of a thirty-five-millimeter film cannister, ostensibly to power unspecified "generators." Nuclear propulsion in space was not revealed as a reality until *60 Minutes* broadcast the fact on October 5, 1997, when it was admitted to have been in use since the Apollo missions thirty years ago. The reason several NASA personnel broke the former secret is certainly worthy of note: a phenomenal seventy-two pounds of plutonium lifted off with that month's Cassini launch to Saturn. Are such great quantities of plutonium necessary to power nuclear engines for these trips? And what other purpose is there for plutonium?

Before all these events, there were discoveries made by the British in India that could be considered the inciting incidents of government involvement in UFO studies. In 1856, while workers lay railway line, the Indus Valley city of Harappa was unearthed, which was not only older than believed possible (at least 2,500 BC), but more advanced. It had plumbing, cylinder seals depicting varieties of yak no longer found anywhere in the world, and script that had never been encountered. Plundering of Harappa for building materials led to the discovery of several other ancient cities in the 1920s. The occupants of some of these had apparently died at the same time, and in full awareness of their end. They were lying openly in the streets, holding hands, their skeletons still intact. Evidence of tremendous heat was found in thousands of pots fused into black lumps of stone, but no volcanic activity could have occurred in the region. The only similar discovery was that of Pompeii, but that had definitely been caused by a volcano. What exterminated these Indus Valley inhabitants, seemingly all at once and with prior warning? The Aryan myth-texts provide an answer: there were seven cities of what was called the Rama Empire destroyed in an ancient war by "Kapilla's Glance" and "Indra's Dart," weapons that fell from the sky and created an apocalyptic inferno with poison winds. Robert Oppenheimer, the inventor of the atomic bomb, was definitely aware of these texts, informing an interviewer that Alamogordo had not been the first such detonation, but only the first "in modern history."

In fact, there had been at least one other detonation about which it is not possible Oppenheimer was ignorant: the Siberian explosion of 1908. Hermann Oberth, called "the father of space travel"—and one of the most outspoken early believers in UFOs as interplanetary spacecraft—gave similar intimations in a 1974 interview to those of Oppenheimer, when he told his questioner that man's remarkable leaps in technology had not come solely from his own ingenuity, but partially through help from "the people from other worlds." Indeed, Wernher von Braun's three-stage Saturn V rockets that took America to the Moon have identical counterparts inscribed in stone in ancient Egypt, referred to as the god Osiris' "ladder to heaven."

And there is the key to the real reason for such intense governmental secrecy concerning UFOlogical matters. Even at such early discoveries as the Indus Valley sites, it must have crossed someone's mind that perhaps there was more to ancient myths than mere fabrication for purposes of moral instruction. That, possibly, there was something of inestimable value to be learned—specifically, a lost technology to be regained. And a technology of such power, no less, that whoever possessed it would rule supreme over all other kingdoms of the Earth. For those same elaborate myths not only described

weapons capable of wreaking exactly the type of destruction pre-
served for eternal witness in India, but also aerial craft to deliver
them. The Aryan texts describe these aerial vehicles, called "vimanas,"
at great length, including operating characteristics and methods of
construction. Some of these sound identical to airplanes of today.
Others seem much more advanced—such as the "disc of Vishnu,"
sounding suspiciously like the "flying saucers" reported with some
frequency since 1947. Such weaponry would certainly be worthy of
the most serious study, and not something any self-respecting government would casually ignore.

A fanciful supposition? Without further evidence to support it,
perhaps. But further evidence does exist. That world governments,
or at least their military forces, are aware of such connections between
UFOs and ancient myth texts, is officially acknowledged by Admiral of the Fleet (G.C.B.) Lord Hill-Norton's introduction to Timothy
Good's UFO study, *Above Top Secret,* in 1987. In spite of the fact that
Good's book deals entirely with modern UFO sightings and does not
enter into the question of ancient astronauts at all, Norton makes
the statement, "As for what I have called bizarre phenomena [con-
nected to UFOs], I need only refer to the astounding geometrical
effects in the Alti Plano in South America of what seem like gigantic airfields laid out in the days of prehistory by means which would
tax today's technology to the limit. And to the pyramid effects, and
to the so-called navigational beacons, which could only be of use to
a craft approaching earth from outside the atmosphere. These are
physical phenomena which exist, and can be touched and measured;
and no one knows how they were made, nor by whom, nor for what
purpose." Lord Hill-Norton was for many years Chief of the Defense
Staff in Great Britain and would hardly make such assertions concerning "pyramid effects" on any authority but that of the best scientists working for the military.

Lord Hill-Norton's contemporary, Parliamentary Air Under-
Secretary George Ward, specifically referred to the British government's looking into the possibility of constructing ancient Aryan
vimanas. Ward wrote ex-RAF fighter pilot Desmond Leslie (playfully
dubbed the "Saucerer Royal" for his many acquaintances among

British royalty and political VIPs, and who was second cousin to none other than Sir Winston Churchill) on January 18, 1954, regarding supposed UFO contactee George Adamski's book *Flying Saucers Have Landed,* which Leslie co-authored: "I can well understand why you got so absorbed in the subject ... Let's meet again as soon as possible. There is a mass of things I want to ask you and I should love to see Adamski's papers. I spent the morning with old Handley Page at his works. I couldn't escape from the horrible thought that all our efforts to fly higher and faster and further are simply brute force. God, I wish we knew how to build a vimana! Let's damn well find out...."

Only about thirty years after Harappa, in 1882, a brilliant American named Ignatius Donnelly wrote a comparatively advanced—if imperfect—study of ancient civilizations, compiling and cataloguing similarities in scripts and artifacts from around the globe. He called special attention to a phenomenal number of connections between the Old and New Worlds, which had hitherto been believed to have no contact at all. Donnelly went so far as to state his belief that these similarities were proof of the fabled continent of Atlantis. A number of more respectably viewed scholars were independently following suit and coming to the same conclusion, even if they did not call the original civilization by the same name. Celtic experts were discovering Egyptian solar barques carved in British dolmens, and apparent runic writings were being found in North America. The academicians writing about these seeming anomalies were not cranks, but top names in their fields, and their movement was not a small one. They were called "diffusionists," and only the First World War called a halt to their research. Even then, it was only a temporary cessation, but from that point on the resumption of such studies did not continue openly and academically—instead, it became secret. And "secret" of the highest order, in the highest places.

The evidence for this is found in Nazi Germany. The Vril Society—and its parallel organization, the Thule Society—which took its name from Lord Edward Bulwer-Lytton's nineteenth century novel, had come into existence virtually at the same time Lytton wrote his book, and the Vril and Thule Societies' influence on the young Adolf

Hitler is visible at a glance. Both were occult organizations, stemming from the fundamental premise that there had been a race of superior white Aryans at the beginning of time, who through the sin of interbreeding with lesser, "mongrel" races of their own creation for use as slaves had fallen from Grace and been destroyed. These "Aryans" had possessed the entire world and left their mark on it. The runic writings were the sign of their presence, as were the famous megalithic temples and structures historically ascribed to them. One symbol, in particular, was their sign: the swastika. This, of course, became the central symbol of the Nazis, chosen by a key member of the Thule Society and Hitler himself. Germany's Vril Society—beginning as the Luminous Lodge, which combined Theosophy, the Caballah, Hindu mysticism, and elements of the Order of the Illuminati—was one of the first German Nationalist groups to utilize the swastika as a link between Eastern and Western occultism, and it was a Thulist who designed the image into the Nazi flag. The very colors of Nazi Germany were the same as those of legendary Atlantis: red, white, and black. Whether Hitler personally believed any of the philosophies or not, he definitely used them as a political tool for forging German solidarity. Heinrich Himmler's S.S. was formed in response to Hitler's 1934 declaration, "We shall form an Order, the Brotherhood of the Templars around the Holy Grail of the pure blood."

World governments, long in advance of the Nazis, had been influenced by the occult and occultists as early as Cagliostro and Elizabethan court astrologer Dr. John Dee. Rosicrucian Dr. Arthur Dee's assistance in Mikhail Romanov's ascension to the Russian throne has long been speculated to have been clandestinely helped by the British Secret Service. In another example, Anthony Masters' *The Man Who Was M: The Life of Maxwell Knight* and Richard Deacons' *A History of the British Secret Service* both confirm that the notorious self-styled British warlock (and member and founder of several European occult societies) Aleister Crowley had connections with the British Secret Service's Dennis Wheatley, Ian Fleming, and Fleming's superior (and basis for the character "M" in his James Bond novels), Maxwell Knight, and was influential in the machinations that led Deputy Führer

Runic and Celtic writings seemingly left around the entire globe—decades before the work of Harvard diffusionist Barry Fell—and between 1932 and 1940, they were writing intelligently and at length about the still-controversial runic Kensington Stone, discovered on a Minnesota farm in 1898, that purports to record an Indian massacre in 1362. Archaeology and astronomy were prominent among the Ahnenerbe's studies, as well as mythology. Their research into the ancient origins of South America and Mexico predated that of most everyone else. Their connections in those two areas were what made the post-war flight of Nazi criminals such an easy feat. Germany alone, independently of the Nazis, was between the wars perhaps the most academically advanced country in the world, internationally renowned for its scholarship in numerous areas.

In fact, archaeology and astronomy were not merely separate studies for the Germans—they were combined in the pioneer field of *archaeoastronomy,* the science that studies the astronomical alignments of ancient structures, which the rest of the world is only now beginning to look into. "In the 1930s, for example," writes Graham Hancock, in *Fingerprints of the Gods,* "Rolf Müller, professor of Astronomy at the University of Potsdam, found convincing evidence to suggest that the most important features of Machu Picchu possessed significant astronomical alignments. From these, through the use of detailed mathematical computations concerning star positions in the sky in previous millennia (which gradually alter down the epochs as the result of a phenomenon known as precession of the equinoxes), Müller concluded that the original layout of the site could only have been accomplished during 'the era of 4000 BC to 2000 BC.'"

It was in 1938 and '39 that archaeologist Wilhelm Koenig discovered the "Baghdad batteries," ancient earthenware jars containing iron rods encased in copper cylinders, which, when filled with an electrolyte of copper sulfate, functioned as well after their emergence into our modern world as they must have millennia before—in fact, Plutarch, Lucian, Pausanius, and St. Augustine all wrote that Egyptian temples had torches which burned perpetually, unaffected by wind or rain; and underground chamber number seventeen at the Temple of Hathor at Denderah shows what looks remarkably like electrical lights attached to batteries. It was exactly such connections between modern archaeological discoveries and ancient history that the Ahnenerbe studied. Connected to their runic and archaeoastronomical researches, they had "pages and pages of documents and photographs of megaliths, dolmens, and standing stones, from all over Europe," according to Peter Levenda, who has actually pored over the captured Ahnenerbe files in the National Archives and is the first author to tackle the subject in English. Also in their purview was the analysis of various Ice Age theories. While most of these Ice Age theories turned out to be of little merit, it is worthy of note that the current reevaluation of the Sphinx and the Giza pyramid complex construction dates by Egyptologist John Anthony West and geophysicists Robert Schoch and Thomas L. Dobecki, which was endorsed by three hundred geologists at the 1992 Annual Geological Society of America meeting, indicates that these structures were built circa the mid-eleventh century BC—i.e., the end of the last Ice Age. And, once again, the Nazis had their eyes very prominently on Tibet.

The Ahnenerbe's chief Tibetan scholar was Dr. Ernst Schäfer, a man with lifelong and lengthy credits in the field, and a very close friend and colleague of Sven Hedin. The Heidelberg- and Gottingen-educated Schäfer made his first expedition to Tibet with Philadelphia's Academy of Natural Sciences in 1930, when he was only twenty years old, and the next year returned with the American Brook Dolan expedition that also included Siberia and China. Schäfer was internationally published with a number of articles to his credit, and he wrote at least three books, *Mountains, Buddhas and Bears, Unknown Tibet* and *Roof of the World.* He joined the S.S. in 1933 (Nazi membership number 4690995), going from Untersturmführer in 1936 to Sturmbannführer in 1942, was awarded the coveted and highly prestigious runic Death's Head Ring, and was one of Himmler's personal staff.

From April of 1938 to August of the following year—returning one month before the Blitzkrieg that officially began World War Two—Schäfer was on an official S.S. expedition to Tibet, where *Der Neue Tag* of July 21, 1939, recorded "outstanding accomplishments in the area of geophysical and earth-magnetic research" as well as "valuable geographical and earth historical accomplishments." In addition to his collection of zoological and botanical specimens, Schäfer, with official help from the regent of Lhasa, "succeeded in obtaining the *Kangschur,* the extensive 108-volume sacred script of the Tibetans, which required nine animal loads to transport." The article concluded with the interesting comment that, "Difficulties encountered due to political tensions with the English authorities were eliminated due to personal contact between Dr. Schäfer and members of the British authorities in Shangtse, so that the unimpeded return of the expedition out of Tibet with its valuable collections was guaranteed." Schäfer's S.S. personnel file shows he made a prior Tibet expedition to the one that was publicized, between 1934 and 1936, the purpose for which has not been discovered—but, given the group involved and the substantial time spent, it seems a safe assumption that he wasn't merely gathering flowers for the botanical wing of the Berlin Museum. But German Intelligence was not the only party to make a mysterious appearance in that area of the world. Another Intelligence group was in the same place not long after, at the height of the war in 1942, sound and color film footage of whose expedition exists today in New York City's Tibet House: the American OSS, in the company of the same Brook Dolan who led Ernst Schäfer's second journey to the country.

The timing of these expeditions, the subjects studied, and subsequent events are somewhat suggestive. The OSS showed up in Tibet right between the time that invincible UFOs appeared over Los Angeles and the time of Nikola Tesla's death, that brilliant inventor in whose private research files the U.S. government suddenly showed inordinate interest at the end of the war (see below). The OSS expedition was to a site twice visited, both times at quite some length and once in complete secrecy not to be discovered until after the war, by an acknowledged expert German Tibetologist whose official studies had included "geophysical and earth-magnetic research," much like that of Tesla. Moreover, China also contained mysterious and isolated pyramids from great antiquity discovered before the war by U.S. P-40 Flying Tiger pilots, which could easily have interested them—along with numerous other ancient sites and megalithic constructions—for the same reason they seem to have interested the Nazis: those constructions' connection to legends of an ancient, superior race from a mythical Underworld.

The Underworld, found in all the world's myths, is known as a sunken Red Land to the West. The Red Land that was the Underworld (or "Lower Kingdom") was the Ancients' Heaven. The "happy land across the Western ocean" was where Ra and the Buddha both sprung from a lotus flower. The "Happy Otherworld" of Iranian, Scandinavian, and Indian mythologies was in the West, as were the First and Third Worlds of the Hopi. The Tuat (or Amenti) of Egypt lay across a vast Dark Sea, as did "Urani Land," known as the "Land Beyond the Western Sea." The Greek Hades was also across the impassable river Styx to the West, reachable only in magic boats provided by the gods. The Celts' Land of Eternal Youth, *Tir na Nog,* also referred to as the Happy Plain or Great Plain, and sometimes merely as the "Other World," was located in the West. Tibet's heavenly Hsi Wang Mu, home of the "Ancient Ones" or "Abode of the Immortals," was where Kuan Yin presided, Merciful Guardian and Queen Mother of the West. In all these cases, the location of heaven is also given as being beneath the earth or under the sea—if not taken literally, a good way to indicate another planet beneath the earth in the ocean of space. In one of many connections between Egypt and the Celts, the Ireland of old was divided into two lands, one upper and one lower, and it was to the lower world—their original land—that the Fairy Folk returned after warring with man in the upper world.

But the sunken Red Land to the West was not only the place of the primal paradise, but also of the wrathful and terrifying God of the Underworld. In the ancient mindset, heaven and hell were not separate, but one and the same location. The Cherokee *Tsunil-kalu,* or "slant-eyed people," were a race of giants from a land "very far away in the direction in which the sun goes down"—i.e., the West. The Celtic Fomorians were described as "warlike giants from across the Western Ocean." The equivalent Hindu race, the Asuras, to remove themselves from their hated younger cousins, the Adityas, strove to "divide this world between ourselves" specifically "from west to east"—in other words, they separated their western world from that of the Adityas' world to the east. Manannan Mac Lir's brother, King Bran, a renowned traveler to mystic regions, traveled on a winged chariot to the West. So did Hercules, on a "cauldron-shaped vessel he borrowed from the sun," which would equate exactly with the Egyptian "solar barque" and other such "sun-ships" around the world. Enlil sent the equivalent destruction of Sodom and Gomorrah in the Bible from the West. The demon Pazuzu—the Sumerian equivalent of Set and the devil—was the "Demon of the Southwest Wind" and was specifically equated with the planet Mars. Ra destroyed the world once with fire from his home, the Red Land, which was the land of the setting sun—the West.

Given the evidence for a civilization of architects on Mars in the distant past, the sunken Red Land of the world's myths—the lost Atlantis—may well be the Red Planet. Egypt itself (the land of the Neteru, or Watchers) was referred to by its inhabitants as "the Two Lands," the Black and the Red, the latter of which—given the occult significance around the world, as well as archaeological and astronomical evidence today—could easily refer to Mars. The "Red Land" was where Ra built a sphinx in his own image, a hawk (which is what the Mars sphinx appears to be) amidst a "protected place" from which he could "ascend beautifully and traverse the skies," i.e., a place of pyramids. Even Sir E. A. Wallis Budge, in 1934, acknowledged that Egyptian mythology equated a specifically hawk-headed sphinx with Mars: "Mars ... was called Hor Tesher, the 'Red Horus.' He was said 'to journey backwards in travelling,' and he was also known as 'Harakhti,' 'Horus of the Two Horizons.' The god of this planet was Ra; he had the head of a hawk with a star above it."

Interestingly, Ra-Harakhti (or Harakhte) was one of three "gods" Aleister Crowley believed had communicated with him in Cairo in 1904. There, the famous spy, humorist, occultist, and sometime fraud had a literally life-changing experience when his wife of the time (who had never claimed or exhibited any mediumistic powers) trance-channeled an entity called "Aiwass" that insisted on speaking with Crowley, whom Crowley believed he recognized as Satan and Ra-Harakhte. Crowley duly recorded Aiwass' "messages" into a book (later to become his "Book of the Law," for his own pseudo-religious cult of Thelema) and was so disturbed by the entire experience and its purported revelations that he put the book away for five years before going back to it. The being he believed was communicating with him identified itself with the phrase, "I am the Warrior Lord of the Forties," which—whether or not Crowley was actually trying to put something over on the world with his claim—was a remarkably prescient prediction of WWII.

In the area of mythic and Underworld research as in others, the Nazis limited themselves from the start by looking only for ancient runic proof of Aryan superiority over the Earth. If they had gone further afield, they might have discovered what the Allies probably did, the physical evidence for which becomes more abundant every day: that there was an original civilization that roamed the entire globe in antiquity, but it wasn't recorded only in the myths and legends of the Germans; and hints of their superior technology, which was certainly the primary interest of both Axis and Allied powers in their quest, were indeed still around to be deciphered.

Bolivia's La Paz Museum, in 1974, recorded one of those items of information the Nazis would have learned from their careful questioning of local populations wherever they went: "The Indians say that thousands of years ago their ancestors travelled on great golden discs which were kept airborne by means of sound vibrations at a certain pitch, produced by continual hammer blows." Avid students of mythology, the Nazis would have been aware of the writings of classical scholar Lewis Spence, who wrote in 1907 that "Apollo, after endowing Admetus with immortality, left his service, and went to assist Neptune, who had also been banished to Earth, to build the walls of Troy. Scorning to perform any menial tasks, the god of music seated himself near by, and played such inspiring tunes that the stones moved into place of their own accord."

Celtic scholarship being of great importance to the Ahnenerbe, it could not have escaped their attention that the Great God of the Celts, "the Dagda Mor," destroyed the entire race of the Fomorians with "music from his harp"—such "music" being the primary magic of the god-race of Ireland, the *Tuatha de Danaan,* or "Fairy Folk"— and that Geoffrey of Monmouth's legends of Merlin attributed the building of Stonehenge to his having floated the stones into place effortlessly through the air, an act which may have inspired the site's name, the "dance of the giants." According to the local natives, such a "dance" was exactly how their gods brought the Easter Island multi-ton giant statues, the *moai,* to their locations: "They walked." And the ancient Egyptian priests told their contemporary historians that the pyramids were built the same way: by the utterance of "words of power," or sound waves. Their name for the "relieving spaces" above the King's Chamber in the Great Pyramid was "spirit stones," which somehow served such a purpose.

Such was the evidence that led to von Braun's three-stage rocket, which originated as Osiris' "ladder to heaven," the *ta-wer* (i.e. "Tower" of Babel) at Abydos. It was also the evidence that would have connected Nikola Tesla's research to its rediscovery. Tesla's biographer, Margaret Cheney, asks in *Tesla: Man Out of Time* (parenthetical inclusion Cheney's own), "...what turn of affairs rekindled the intense interest of the U.S. intelligence establishment in Tesla's work (as something surely did) in the late 1940s?" Tesla was the inventor of alternating current, radio (actually determined by the Supreme Court after his death), and many other fabulous—and sometimes terrifying—devices. After his death at age eighty on January 7, 1943, all of his personal papers were sealed by the interestingly named Office of Alien Property (especially curious since, though born a Yugoslavian Serb, Tesla was a naturalized American citizen), with the blessing of the FBI. It was admitted that some of these were examined by a government team from the National Defense Research Committee of the Office of Scientific Research and Development (ORD), consisting of that organization's technical aide, Dr. John G. Trump, Willis George of the Office on Naval Intelligence's Third Naval District, and chief yeomen Edward Palmer and John J. Corbett, USNR.

There were literally tons of these papers, in boxes and barrels. Among his writings, Tesla himself claimed, was the solution to his lifelong quest of finding a way to transmit wireless power—in effect, a "death ray." This tied directly into his theory of "telegeodynamics," by which he claimed "a cylinder of finest steel [could be] suspended in midair by a type of energy which was old in principle but which had been amplified by a secret principle—combined with a stationary part." In short, anti-gravity. He used sound-resonance devices operating on the same principle, no bigger than a pocket alarm clock, to create localized earthquakes, all with "but a fusillade of taps, no one of which would have harmed a baby." And, interesting to note, Tesla was a pioneer in the field of robotics. As early as 1894, he proposed both robots and guided missiles in his writings: "By installing proper plants it will be practicable to project a missile of this kind into the air and drop it almost on the very spot designated, which may be thousands of miles away. Telautomata will be ultimately produced, capable of acting as if possessed of their own intelligence, and their advent will create a revolution."

Though Tesla's papers were placed in the Manhattan Storage and Warehouse Company along with about thirty other barrels of his writings, and theoretically sent back to Yugoslavia in 1952 by his nephew, Ambassador Sava Kosanović, according to the inventor's stated (but not willed) wishes, it is documented that Vice President Henry A. Wallace advised the FBI that the government continued to be "vitally interested" in them. Despite the formal pronouncement by the ORD team's John Trump that "there exist among Dr. Tesla's papers and possessions no scientific notes, no descriptions of hitherto unrevealed methods or devices, or actual apparatuses which could be of significant value to this country or which would constitute a hazard in unfriendly hands," Kosanović claimed someone had been in Tesla's safe before he got to it, and that the custodian at the warehouse told him that "some government guys were in to microfilm some of the papers" after Trump's team had already made its assessment. J. Edgar Hoover denied any FBI involvement in such activity, and at one point actually advised that Kosanović himself be arrested for possible burglary. No action was taken, the Washington FBI's Edward A. Tamm turning the matter back over to the Office of Alien Property. "[B]ut between 1945 and 1947," remarks Cheney, "an interesting exchange of letters and cables occurred among the Air Service Technical Command at Wright Field, Ohio, in whose Equipment Laboratory much top-secret research was being performed, Military Intelligence in Washington, and the Office of Alien Property—subject, files of the late Nikola Tesla."

Wright Field's Air Technical Service Command requested seven days "for the purpose of securing property clearance on enemy impounded property" in a letter sent to the commanding general of the USAAF in Washington on August 21, 1945, some of the said properties including items from John Trump's Tesla catalogue. By September 5, Colonel Holiday of the Equipment Laboratory, Accessories Subdivision, wrote to the Office of Alien Properties and asked that some of this reviewed material be photostated for use "in connection with projects for National Defense by this department." These were confirmed as having been sent on September 11, 1945. There are letters indicating that Wright Field never got the desired items, but at least one letter does confirm that the requested materials managed to end up there: in response to a request from OAP on October 24, 1947, for the return of the materials forwarded to Wright Field's Air Matériel Command, Colonel Duffy sent a letter on November 25, stating that "These reports are now in the possession of the Electronics Subdivision and are being evaluated. . . ." Duffy said the evaluation should be completed by New Year's Day, at which time the materials would be returned. They weren't. From that day to this, no Federal or military agency admits to having any of Tesla's files.

Considering the many letters seeming to indicate that the Tesla papers were lost in transit, it would appear that someone wanted to leave a paper trail obscuring their actual receipt—and the particular place receiving them, which is the same location at which the Roswell crash remains ended up in 1947: Wright Field. It is interesting that Wright Field did not acknowledge receipt of the Tesla materials until four months after the Roswell incident. Before that, during the seeming "loss" of those papers through official channels, the Air Technical Service Command wrote to the OAP, "In view of the extreme importance of these files to the above command, we would like to be requested that we be advised of any attempt by any other agency to obtain them." In other words, the official documentation says—both in and between its lines—"We never got those classified papers you sent, so don't expect them back—and by the way, if anyone comes looking for them, we want to know, and fast."

Cheney attempted to discover the whereabouts of the missing

Tesla papers, supplied to Wright Field in 1945 and acknowledged two years later, by venue of the Freedom of Information Act. The response she received, on July 30, 1980, from Headquarters Aeronautical Systems Division at Wright-Patterson, was, "The organization (Equipment Laboratory) that performed the evaluation of Tesla's papers was deactivated several years ago. After conducting an extensive search of lists of records retired by that organization, in which we found no mention of Tesla's papers, we concluded the documents were destroyed at the time the laboratory was deactivated."

By late 1947, at the tail end of this search for the missing papers of Nikola Tesla, a flying saucer crashed near Roswell, New Mexico (the story of which will be recounted in Chapter 1), the remains of which were sent to Wright Field—the same Army Air Base where Tesla's papers were received for military study. The request to Washington for Tesla's papers began on August 21, 1945, six days after the conclusion of World War II. During those six days between the war's end and the request for Tesla's papers, the Third Reich's chief of the Foreign Armies East and Hitler's master spy against the Soviets, forty-three-year-old Reinhard Gehlen, landed in Washington, D.C., aboard a DC-3, to be openly welcomed by U.S. officials at Fort Hunt. A number of generals, Truman's national security advisor, and former OSS high-up Allen Dulles, who would one day helm the CIA's director position, accepted Gehlen's offer to relocate to America complete with all his files and European contacts, to fight the Cold War and help lay the groundwork for what would become the CIA. Gehlen's arrival in the United States began what is known as "Operation Paperclip."

Operation Paperclip, so named because its members were denoted by a simple paperclip attached to the corner of their files, was the U.S. War Department's secret importation of ex-Nazis that began immediately following the war. Among those on its guest list were such notorious S.S. figures as "Butcher of Lyon" Klaus Barbie, terrorist Otto Skorzeny, and enthusiastic concentration camp exterminators Dr. Franz Alfred Six and Emil Augsburg. But most important, and numerous, were the imported Nazi scientists. Rocketry suddenly became of paramount importance to America, partly for the development of ICBMs in its new trumped-up Cold War against the menace of global communism, and partly for something else. About 120 German rocket scientists—many of whom were Nazi war criminals, the like of which were, at that very time, being handed sentences of life imprisonment or death by hanging at Nuremberg—were brought to America through the back door, with the full sanction and blessing of the State Department. Brought with them was Lieutenant General Shiro Ishii, head of Japan's Unit 731, a biological warfare division that experimented on U.S. troops during the war.

Among the imported Nazis was S.S. elite Major Wernher von Braun, inventor of the V-2 rockets that murdered as many as 5,000 people in Britain and Belgium during the war, and which were built by 20,000 to 60,000 slaves taken from the concentration camps in the "extermination by work" program. Von Braun only ever expressed token repentance or sorrow for his involvement in any of these projects, and fully consented to them during his tenure with the Third Reich. In 1990, *Life* magazine dubbed him one of the "100 Most Important Americans of the 20th Century" for his development of the Saturn V three-stage rocket that ultimately took man to the Moon. The director of Germany's Museum for Transport and Technology, at their fiftieth anniversary of the downfall of the Third Reich, lamented America's moral bankruptcy in dealing with such "criminals," offering as his only explanation for the insanity of it all, that "It was as if they had only ever thought of going to the moon." He could as readily have added something which even a superficial overview of the history of the space program makes equally obvious: from the beginning, they were also thinking of going to Mars.

It was this hidden history of Axis/Allied top-secret ancient research that obviously inspired Paramount Studios' and Steven Spielberg's 1981 inaugural Indiana Jones movie, *Raiders of the Lost Ark*. The central premise of *Raiders* was that Hitler was "a nut on the subject" of the occult, and sought the Hebrews' Ark of the Covenant because he knew it was "a radio for talking to God" and a weapon of tremendous power that made armies invincible. The Bible shows how the Ark's powers worked, even if the details of its workings are not revealed. It was as a sonic amplifying device that Joshua used the

Ark to demolish the walls of Jericho, the walls tumbling down when all his people "raised a great shout" together. In fact, not only the Ark itself, but several other mentions of "horns" throughout the Bible—most notably, that of Gabriel, at the end of the world—make the same obvious corollary: that sound waves can be used to devastating effect. Such destruction was wrought by Lucifer, the one description of whom in Isaiah 14:10–17 designates him both as being a man and as having the same "musical" instrument and power as the Celtic Great God, the Dagda Mor: "Your magnificence has been flung down to Sheol, with the music of your harps . . . How did you come to fall from the heavens, Lucifer, son of the dawn? . . . All who see you will gaze at you, will stare at you, 'Is this the man who made the earth tremble, and overthrew kingdoms, who never to his captives opened the prison gates?'" Karl Haushofer was involved in related research between 1933 and 1935 at France's famous Rennes-le-Chateau. There was being sought the secret of a technological device of some sort of levitating power, which it was rumored had been the secret of the Knights Templar and Masons' remarkable volume of construction in so brief a time during Mediaeval history—eighty actual cathedrals in France, and hundreds of "cathedral class" churches, in the mere one hundred years between AD 1170 and 1270.

It was not only the overt nuclear and sonic destructive power of the ancients that the world's military forces were seeking, but that of the more esoteric and far-reaching power of mind control. While the story of hypnotic assassins is often cited to have begun with Hasan-e Sabbah's Assassins of Persia between the eleventh and twelfth centuries—the word *assassin* derives from the Arabic *"hashshashin,"* meaning "hashish eaters"—the effects of hypnosis and mind-controlling drugs or substances, and cults who employed them, were written about extensively in the mid-fifth century BC by the Greek General Xenophon and the playwright Euripides. Xenophon encountered a deadly honey made by bees from rhododendron pollen in the Black Sea area that had such toxicity as to drive his men mad and sometimes kill them. Pliny and other historians confirmed the honey's deadly presence in the region, and it was reported sometimes to have been used in controlled fashion to erase short-term memory. Euripides wrote of the maenads, or bacchantes—cultists who drank a special honey mixed with alcohol that had the same effect on memory and behavior, as well as enhancing sexuality. Before any of these sources, the Egyptians recorded the use of hypnotic "sleep temples," as CIA MK-ULTRA experimenter and hypnosis expert William Bryan discussed in one of his books. And, most interestingly, Himmler's Ahnenerbe—in addition to its more obviously archaeological and linguistic studies of the Ancients—had one other item of research under its aegis that under any other circumstances would not seem to have any connection: *mind control.* It was specifically the Ahnenerbe's records that the fledgling CIA combed over in its own research on the subject, most of which were destroyed by the Nazis before anyone could get their hands on them, even as the CIA itself was to destroy countless documents in its own files before the Church Committee could expose them in the late 1970s.

In short, the Nazis—however reprehensible they were in every other regard—were in their day the world's foremost scholars in ancient civilization and unorthodox weapons research. They had been predated by the British, who sent government agent James Churchward to Mexico years in advance of the Nazis to closely follow the work of brilliant archaeologists Augustus Le Plongeon and William Niven in their decipherment of hieroglyphs and mathematical codes of the Mayans. Churchward had found the same symbol in Tibet (and in the same style) that Niven found in Mexico—the one that held such supreme importance to the Nazis: the swastika. The work of Le Plongeon and Niven paralleled some of the same work done by Scotland's Astronomer Royal, Charles Piazzi Smyth, on Egypt's Great Pyramid in the mid-1860s, which, in Smyth's opinion, connected Egyptian units of measure with the British and showed the Egyptians to have had much more advanced geodetic knowledge than would have been possible for a primitive people.

Oppenheimer and Hermann Oberth are not the only government scientists to have openly acknowledged a debt to ancient and/or extraterrestrial forebears, or to have shown advance knowledge of what the rest of the world is only now beginning to discover. Werner von Braun wrote a novel in 1948 called *The Mars Project,* which—

except for its technical appendix—was never published. Von Braun called it "a futuristic novel, based on solid technical facts. I have consciously avoided utilizing any fantastic assumptions that today could not be asserted with certainty." At the same time, he prefaced magazine articles about the book with the statement, "[M]y story is fiction entirely—not a prediction that we shall find such people and such technological marvels when we go to Mars," since the core element of his plot was the discovery by seventy Earth explorers of 800 million people on that planet . . . all living beneath the surface. Von Braun's Martians are as technologically advanced as the men of Earth, but stultified by enforced conformity and mass-consumerism that gives them more than all the material comforts they need—a fascinating observation, for an ex-Nazi recently come to live in exactly such a society—who find in our spirit a new desire to explore space themselves. The story ends with the Martians putting a special base into orbit around their planet to serve as a space station on future Mars-Earth missions . . . rather like Phobos.

Above and beyond Operation Paperclip or the statements of Robert Oppenheimer, Hermann Oberth, and Wernher von Braun, proof of early United States government investigation into ancient mysteries is found in the Voynich Manuscript. This hand-written manuscript is a still-mysterious undeciphered illuminated text named after its discoverer, American rare-book dealer Wilfrid Voynich, who purchased it for an unspecified sum from Mondragone College in Frascati, Rome, in 1912. It had supposedly been given to Prague's Emperor Rudolph by the Elizabethan court alchemist, John Dee, and was believed to have been written by the thirteenth-century heretical Franciscan monk, Roger Bacon, a man much like the more famous prophet Nostradamus. The manuscript came into the possession of the Jesuit scholar Athanasius Kircher through a friend in 1665 or 1666, accompanied by a note which read, "Such sphinxes as these obey no one but their master." Kircher was the first man on record to have failed in an attempt to decipher it, and the manuscript remained locked in a chest after his death until Voynich came along. Written in an indecipherable script at over 250 pages, it contains 33 pages of straight text and a tremendous number of captioned color diagrams, and has resided in Yale's Beinecke Rare Book Room since 1968. Going for $160,000 in New York in 1962, its present estimated value is between a quarter and a half million dollars.

Many of its illustrations are astronomical and biological, with a great many botanical sketches of plant species not recognized today. Also included are what look like microscopic drawings of cells, and what Professor Eric Doolittle of the University of Pennsylvania believed, in the 1920s, was a sketch of the spiral Andromeda galaxy shown from an angle no terrestrial telescope would have been able to discern centuries before. Director Herbert Osborne Yardley and his top U.S. elite cryptographical Military Intelligence unit, MI-8, failed to decipher it during WWI, as did their phenomenal Allied ULTRA successors—even with the assistance of an RCA 301 computer—who cracked the German Enigma and Japanese Purple Codes during WWII. Since then, the National Security Agency commissioned at least one official study of it in 1978, entitled *The Voynich Manuscript: An Elegant Enigma,* by Mary D'Empirio. No conclusions were reached concerning the manuscript, except that it required a great deal more of the most serious study.

If the connection of all these interesting facts to the UFO phenomenon is not immediately apparent, it is because UFOs have come to be regarded only as space vehicles for a non-human intelligence from another planet (or perhaps even solar system or dimension) recently come to Earth on some sort of survey mission. In fact, the evidence is in favor of human intelligence behind UFO operation, but not humans from this planet. It is therefore not an unlikely surmise that the humans in question are those Aryan Supermen from whom Hitler and his ill-conceived political party were attempting to prove direct descent, and therefore direct inheritance. Whether or not they had any inkling that this ancient race still existed, either inside a hollow Earth (their prevalent theory) or elsewhere in the solar system, is unimportant. They seemed to have some knowledge, as did other governments, that the secrets of that race's superior technology still existed in ancient texts—if only they could be deciphered.

This premise of the "Indiana Jones" movies was supposedly based on nothing more than earlier cliffhanger serials. But in fact, those serials themselves were based on earlier "Lost World" romances of the nineteenth century—which, interestingly enough, were all written by government figures. Lord Edward Bulwer-Lytton himself wrote novels of the type. Between 1885 and 1887, Sir Henry Rider Haggard wrote his most famous Lost City romances, *King Solomon's Mines,* *Allan Quatermain,* and *She,* the last in which an immortal Egyptian "Great White Queen" (obviously inspired by Lytton, for whose nephew, the Governor of Natal, Haggard was personal secretary) rules a secret Underworld. Haggard's "She Who Must Be Obeyed" is the supreme regent of Earth, who becomes sexual companion to, and bestower of kingly power upon, a chosen mortal male. His 1904-5 sequel transferred the action and characters from Africa to Asia— specifically, around Tibet. Between 1888 and 1890, Nobel Prize-winner-to-be Rudyard Kipling wrote "The Man Who Would Be King," drawing attention to the history and constructions of the Masons in connection with more "primitive" civilizations in Asia, and—as the Spaniards had written of the fairest Peruvian women, two to three centuries before—about the exceeding whiteness of their more "royal" offspring, who were whiter than the British Masonic protagonists. Kipling was also figuring-in the history of Captain Cook, who was slaughtered along with his men on Hawaii in 1779 when it became apparent to the natives by the newcomers' sexual appetite and sailing ineptitude that the sailors were not the returning white gods they had initially assumed.

Sir James M. Barrie was the author of a related piece in 1904, the famous play *Peter Pan,* the title character being a timeless Hermes-figure whose name literally means "All-Father" *(Pan-Pitar).* This character nocturnally repeat-abducts children from their bedrooms (in much the same manner as elfin UFO occupants) to fly with him on adventures, including combat with a pirate captain whose one-handed appearance echoes the universal uni-limbed description of the mythical "warlike giants of the Western Ocean." In 1924, the same year the U.S. Signal Corps documented receiving repeat voice transmissions from the planet Mars, engineer and author Alexei Nikolayevich Tolstoy's (distantly related to Leo) 1921 novel *Aelita* was filmed by Jacob Protozanov in the new Soviet Union. Tolstoy's story—not unlike Lord Bulwer-Lytton's *Vril* a half century before—depicted a blue-skinned human-descended Martian queen who emigrated from Earth in antiquity to escape the devastation wrought in aeons past on the lost continent of Atlantis by a passing comet, engaging in a romance with an abducted Earthman in her socialist Utopian kingdom run by robot servants. It was Sir Gerald Hargreaves who wrote the first play about Atlantis as a superior ancient civilization, which was turned into the 1960 MGM movie, *Atlantis, the Lost Continent.* The Earl of Clancarty, writing as Brinsley le Pouer Trench, stated his belief in the 1950s and '60s that mankind immigrated to Earth from Mars in antiquity. And Ignatius Donnelly, the author of the scholarly study *Atlantis* in 1882, was lieutenant governor of Minnesota for two terms during the Civil War, a Minnesota congressman for several terms in the 1860s and '70s, and several times a senator in the same state up to the turn of the century and the end of his life.

If the coincidence of high-ranking government figures writing and disseminating seemingly frivolous Lost Civilization works is not interesting enough, then the far greater coincidence of military intelligence and CIA figures connected to Hollywood films on the post-Roswell subject of UFOs is even more so. RKO—owned by multi-billionaire defense contractor and test pilot Howard Hughes, and a subsidiary of Time-Life, which was owned by heavily CIA-connected Henry Luce—made the first realistic flying saucer movie in 1951, *The Thing from Another World.* Its facts not only accurately reflected those of Roswell, but a Top Secret government study called Project Twinkle that was not even partially declassified until five years later. 20th Century Fox's *The Day the Earth Stood Still,* the same year, contained even more Top Secret realities that would not be discovered publicly until many years later. Both of these movies were drastically changed from their original source materials due to tampering on the executive level by Intelligence-connected men, and changed in accord with legitimate secret UFO facts. American International Pictures made an entire industry of disseminating actual UFO material in its silliest Roger Corman movies, and Corman has a military intelligence background. A striking number of then-publicly unknown UFO facts are found in the 1963–65 T.V. show, *The Outer Limits*. Leslie Stevens, the show's executive producer in both seasons, just happened to work for Army Air Corps Intelligence and *Time* magazine. And Stevens' father was not only an MIT-graduate Vice-Admiral, but the naval attaché to Russia in 1953 and the man who invented airplane arresting gear for U.S. aircraft carriers.

But the coincidences do not end there. The James Bond stories of Ian Fleming can be shown to have contained accurate secret information years before official declassification by the British War Department. Fleming was the number-two man in Bletchley Park's ULTRA operation, the best-kept secret of WWII, with disclosure a treasonable offense punishable by death, and he was instrumental with novelist Dennis Wheatley and occult mavin Aleister Crowley in arranging Deputy Führer Rudolf Hess' defection from Germany. Wheatley's many novels also were claimed by the author to be far less fanciful than they appear at first glance, and Fleming's novels contained not only thinly disguised material on ULTRA—almost twenty years before its official declassification—but information about UFOs, abductions, and mind control. Mind control, especially, is one of the most crucial keys to understanding not only the UFO phenomenon, but official government reaction to it. Mind control (along with genetic manipulation) was the other central area of investigation undertaken by the Nazis' prestigious Ahnenerbe S.S.

Following the war, the United States imported hundreds of Nazi rocket scientists under the secret Operation Paperclip. Their interest—despite protestations of mere Cold War superiority over the Russians—was to get to the Moon as soon as possible, and then to Mars. Hidden papers of the recently deceased Nikola Tesla were suddenly appropriated and secretly studied, and Tesla had been working on death-rays, guided missiles, robots, and anti-gravity for nearly half a century. World governments appear to have known (to varying degrees) that someone seemed to be inhabiting the interiors of the Moon and Mars, occasionally visiting Earth from these locations to perform surveillance, biological study, reproductive activity, and the like. This realization began as early as the discovery of the Indus Valley sites and concurrent excavations in Egypt, became the focus of much interest following the Second World War, and reached a maximum peak of secrecy and activity following the Roswell recovery. Up until that time, there had been only an awareness that someone else was "out there," and some pretty good indication as to just where they were coming from—but with Roswell, actual "fire from Olympus" had been recovered, and the technology of the mysterious unknowns was suddenly a tangible reality, ripe for maximum exploitation.

Immediately following the Roswell crash, the CIA was formed, and from its very first month of existence was intensively investigating the field of mind control, a project designated MK-ULTRA. They literally took up exactly where the Nazis had left off, both in that area and in rocket research, and almost certainly continued the super-secret study of ancient mysteries toward these ends as well. As already noted, mind control was not entirely a modern study, but had ancient precedents. The reason for U.S. government interest in mind control was publicly given—decades later, when it could no longer be concealed—as having originated with the brainwashing of Korean POWs, but all records and datings contradict this assertion completely. Their real reason had to do with what was discovered from the Roswell wreckage, and what was found out from UFO sabotage of sensitive installations: that members of the local population were under the amnesiac hypnotic control of a government so foreign, it didn't even come from this planet—and that same foreign government appeared to be using some of these individuals for acts of military and industrial sabotage.

This situation, too, would be portrayed in the movies with greater and lesser degrees of seriousness, relaying verifiably correct data not publicly known at the time of the movies' making, and again traceable to known Intelligence sources. *The Manchurian Candidate*'s hypnosis advisor, Dr. William Joseph Bryan, Jr., was a CIA MK-ULTRA veteran and also advised on the subject for American International's low-budget Roger Corman pictures. Like the subject of UFOs, actual facts about hypnosis and mind control would surface years before declassification or public discovery, in sources as frivolous as the T.V. series *The Avengers, Dr. Who, Batman, I Spy,* and even *Gilligan's Island.*

Such facts would be put into Commando Cody serials, E.C. comic books, and Popeye and Bugs Bunny cartoons.

Hollywood vs. the Aliens: The Motion Picture Industry's Participation in UFO Disinformation is a study designed to explore, as fully as possible within a limited space, the truth of the ideas just presented. Its main tenet is that the entertainment industry has been and continues to be exploited by agents of military intelligence and the CIA for purposes alternately of confusing and enlightening the public at large on UFO facts, the change in focus of intent at any given time depending primarily on changing political influences. Its central area of focus is post-Roswell Hollywood, from the 1950s to the present. The book studies not only Hollywood movies, but T.V. shows, comic books, cartoons, and all forms of popular entertainment—both foreign and domestic—that have contained accurate UFOlogical information well in advance of its public discovery. Developed concurrently are the numerous Intelligence connections to these areas of dissemination, disinformation, and misinformation, with the specific purpose of deflecting the average citizen's attention from them. For the most part, this discussion is presented chronologically, though exceptions will be encountered when, for instance, the collective works of a given inside source are considered together.

Chapter 1, "Wreckages and Robots," tells the story of the Roswell recovery, demonstrates the reality of what was found there by comparing it with subsequent UFO incidents, and discusses Roswell's dramatization in 1951 as *The Thing from Another World*. Chapter 2, "Mesmerizations and Assassinations," gives a quick outline of the beginning of CIA mind-control experiments and examination of UFO abductees in connection to that field. It also gives a comprehensive overview of the subject of hypnotic mind control in fiction and cinema, leading to a brief analysis of what can be determined about the success of the CIA in its own mind-control experiments. The history of the nefarious and shadowy William Joseph Bryan, Jr., MK-ULTRA hypnosis expert extraordinaire, is laid bare, as are mind-control connections to various political assassinations and attempted assassinations from the 1960s to the 1980s. Pulp fiction, movies, and television shows discussing and popularizing the concept of hyp-

explored, as are those of other more modern horror writers whose pieces for whatever reason echo actual UFO material, such as Dean R. Koontz, Stephen King, Peter Straub, and Anne Rice. *2001: A Space Odyssey* and *The Abyss* are reviewed in light of known UFOlogy. The educational movies on the topic made during the Jimmy Carter presidency are discussed and appraised as the best single period of attempted public consciousness-raising. Contrasted with this is the next chapter, "Peregrinations and Propagandizations," illustrating how under the conservative and Intelligence covert-action-friendly Ronald Reagan, UFO movies returned to simplistic good-guy vs. bad-guy shoot-em-ups, vastly increasing in number and equally decreasing in educational value, simultaneously with the largest peacetime weapons budget increase in history—specifically, in space weaponry. Post-1980 James Bond films are contrasted with those made earlier to illustrate the point. Anti-military films of the time, ironic for the era in which they were made, are also considered. In "Indoctrinations and Demonizations," the changes toward increased fear-mongering made in UFOlogical movies under George Bush (and then Bill Clinton), coinciding directly with Bush's increased funding for NASA and Star Wars after the loss of the Russian Mars probe, *Phobos 2*, are pointedly compared to movies made under his predecessor's aegis. Finally, "Conclusions and Considerations" presents a brief summary and ponders the future of the government's UFO media-education program.

As both the inheritors of secret studies to exploit ancient technology and as propagandists deflecting public attention from those very studies, the Intelligence agencies involved can truly be called "Raiders of the Lost Art." We have already entered the theater and enjoyed the first feature of their "late-night double-feature picture show": this little documentary on the true facts about Mars, the military, and mind control. Now it is time for us to enjoy the lengthier second feature on Hollywood's treatment of the subjects, brought to us by our good friends at the Central Intelligence Agency.

The military had been calling Roswell mortician Glenn Dennis all day, curious about preservation techniques, eventually telling him there had been three fatalities in a crash and curious as to whether all of them could be put into a single hermetically sealed casket. Later that afternoon, they called Dennis to carry a pilot who had only a broken nose and the most superficial of head injuries to the hospital, at the rear of which there were three old-fashioned boxy ambulances. One had some wreckage in the back, which Dennis did not find strange since there had been some kind of crash, but on a closer look he found it to be more unusual: "What I saw reminded me of the front part of a canoe . . . about three feet long and lying up against the side . . . tipped [so that] the open side was against the floor. There were some inscriptions on [a] border around part of it . . . three inches maybe . . . going along the contour . . . [which] reminded me of Egyptian inscriptions." The same "hieroglyphics" had been noticed by every witness to the wreckage, including Jesse Marcel and his wife, Lewis S. Rickett, Loretta Proctor, Tommy Tyree, Walt Whitmore, Sr., Robert Shirkey, Robert Smith, and O. W. Henderson.

A new nurse at the hospital was "very excited" upon bumping into Dennis in the lounge, where he had stopped to buy a Coke. "How did you get in here?" she asked him. "You're going to get into trouble. Get out of here as fast as you can." Immediately departing through a side door, she left Dennis in the presence of a prematurely graying middle-aged officer who confronted him and asked his name and his business. Dennis replied that he had brought in an injured pilot. "Looks like you've had a crash. I see some debris in the ambulance there." The officer summoned two M.P.s to evict Dennis. A very tall redheaded captain tapped him on the shoulder and said, "Mister, don't go in Roswell, and don't say there's been a crash or anything, 'cause nothing's happened out here." Affronted, Dennis replied, "Look, Mister, I'm a civilian. And you can't do a damned thing to me, and you know that." The captain responded, "Mister, somebody'll be diggin' your bones outta the sand." A black sergeant with him added that Dennis "would make good dog food."

Wanting to know what was going on, Dennis called the hospital several times the next morning to try and contact the nurse he had encountered. At about 11:30, she got back to him. "I understand you've been trying to call me," she said. "I don't want you coming to the hospital. I would rather see you at the officers' club." They met for lunch, and the nurse made Dennis swear never to mention her name and get her in trouble. "I can't believe what I've just seen," she said. "This is the most horrible thing I've ever seen in my life."

Recounting her story almost fifty years later, Dennis specified that "I don't think she said alien bodies. I think she said foreign bodies. Then she described to me what happened when she got involved in it . . . She said it was so gruesome and so horrible. She was in a state of shock . . . She never touched her food."

Routinely entering the hospital examination room for supplies, the nurse had found two doctors she'd never seen, who told her to stay put. Three bodies were present, two mangled and one mostly intact. They were not human. The doctors "didn't know what they were or where they came from." Shock and an overpowering smell quickly drove her from the room, but not before she had observed a few things about the bodies.

Their arms were longer from wrist to elbow than from elbow to shoulder, and the only hand she saw had four fingers with suction cups on their tips, looking as if the thumb were "missing." The heads were oversized and "very pliable. It was like a newborn baby . . . You could push the sides and it would be movable." The eyes were sunken. There were two small orifices on either side of the head where the ears should be, and two small orifices inside a markedly concave nose. The mouth was "very thin. [It] didn't have a full lip. Hardly any lip at all. In place of teeth, it looked like a piece of rawhide. The doctors said it was even harder than the bone structure." This was the only comment she made regarding their interiors, which she never claimed to have seen and offered no description of. Dennis asked about their sex, and her only response was, "I didn't pay any attention and was so sick." She admitted she hadn't even noticed if they were dressed or not, which can only mean she could not have seen them medically opened up—if she had, they would definitely have been naked. She could provide Dennis no further details, though she did sketch the general appearance of the bodies for him before excusing herself because she felt sick and wanted to lie down in her barracks.

That was the last Dennis ever saw of the nurse. After three days' failed attempts to contact her, Dennis was told by the Army that she'd been transferred and they didn't know where. Dennis got a note from her, ten days to two weeks later, saying she couldn't write but providing an APO address for him to contact her. Two weeks after attempting to write her, Dennis got his letter back with "Return to sender" and "Deceased" stamped on it in big red letters. He was told her plane crashed on maneuvers, but no records either military or civilian confirm such an occurrence. Her whereabouts remain unknown to this day.

It was on July 9 that KGFL announcer Frank Joyce, who had been turned away with many other reporters from the cordoned crash site that morning, interviewed Mac Brazel. He could see the rancher "was under a great deal of stress." The military took Brazel into custody immediately after the interview and kept him for a week. Joyce claimed that Brazel confided to him on his way out, "Frank, you know how they talk of little green men? . . . They weren't green." As Brazel was escorted away, Colonel Blanchard also abruptly went on leave.

Of Brazel's detention, his neighbor and friend Marian Strickland later recounted, "It amounted to humiliation and detention when there wasn't any good reason. He had come in in good faith. And they didn't accept it that way, or didn't appear to. He said they threw him in jail. He said if he ever found anything like that again, he would never show it to them. He would never bring it in; he had done so as what he thought was a good citizen, and he had been humiliated and mistreated. And he was very disturbed." Brazel changed his story for all later interviews with the press, saying that he was now sure what he had found was a weather balloon. He also changed the date he claimed to have discovered it to June 14. Brazel's son, Paul, said his father never received any kind of payoff from the military, but it did not go unnoticed that Brazel had a new pickup truck, meat locker, and house shortly after his week's ordeal. He asked all his friends to simply accept the new stories, saying, "It'll go hard on me."

The coverup had begun, and it rapidly accelerated and expanded. Weather balloons were reported discovered three days in a row in three different states, directly coinciding with the discovery of the Roswell crash material and its special investigation by the Army, a pattern of deception which was to become much more common in the ensuing years. First Air Force Project Blue Book head Captain Edward J. Ruppelt noted in his 1956 memoir *The Report on Unidentified Flying Objects:*

By the end of July 1947, the UFO security lid was down tight. The few members of the press who did inquire about what the Air Force was doing got the same treatment that you would get today if you inquired about the number of thermonuclear weapons stockpiled in the U.S.'s atomic arsenal. No one outside of a few high-ranking officers in the Pentagon knew what the people in the barbed wire enclosed Quonset huts that housed the Air Technical Intelligence Center were thinking or doing.

In fact, they were testing the Roswell material, and possibly that recovered from other crashes as well. Reported General Twining to Brigadier General George Schulgen in an AMC (Air Materiél Command) Opinion Concerning Flying Discs dated 9-23-47:

It is possible within the present U.S. knowledge ... to construct a piloted aircraft which has the general description of the object ... which would be capable of an approximate range of 7000 miles at subsonic speeds. Any developments in this country along the lines indicated would be extremely expensive, time-consuming and at the considerable expense of current projects and therefore, if directed, should be set up independently of existing projects.

The "aircraft" referred to had "no normally associated sound" and was "circular or elliptical in shape, flat on bottom and domed on top," unlike any known aircraft either then or now.

The wreckage was such that the certainty of the shape was being supplemented by military reports of similar objects in flight, as is evidenced by Twining's specific wording, "There are objects probably approximating the shape of a disc ... [with] extreme rates of climb, maneuverability (particularly in roll), and . . . are controlled either manually, automatically or remotely." He added, "Due consideration must be given . . . the lack of physical evidence in the shape of crash recovered exhibits which would undeniably prove the existence of these objects," certainly a reference to the extremely battered "shape" their own "recovered exhibit" was in. Twining was probably also being deliberately delicate in his phrasing for security reasons. Recovered wreckage was unquestionably examined, as is proven by his long list of technical experts from whom he garnered his "opinion," including "the Air Institute of Technology, Intelligence T-2, Office, Chief of Engineering Division, and the Aircraft Power Plant and Propellor Laboratories of Engineering Division T-3." Laboratories do not tend to come to any decisions without something specific in their hands to test.

Brigadier General Arthur Exon was a Lieutenant Colonel at Wright Field when the Roswell material was brought in. He told UFO researchers in later years that the wreckage was experimented with in a "special project" by an "oversight committee" which had among its duties "to design studies to exploit it." He stated that "a top intelligence echelon [was] represented and the Secretary of Defense's office was represented and these people stayed on in key positions even though they might have moved out." Exon himself "never heard what the results were," but "the overall consensus was that the pieces were from space. They knew they had something new in their hands. The metal and material was unknown to anyone I talked to." Though he never saw the bodies, he confirmed that they were talked about at the base. "They were all found, apparently, outside the craft itself but were in fairly good condition. In other words, they weren't broken up a lot. One of them went to a mortuary outfit . . . I think at that time it was in Denver."

One of Blanchard's best men, Captain Pappy Henderson, told his friend and military colleague, Doctor John Kromschroeder, and also his own daughter, that he had personally seen the bodies, but waited until 1978 and 1982, respectively, to tell them. He called them "kinda little guys" he didn't get a good look at, because they made him nervous. They "were little men, gray, with slanted eyes and tiny mouths."

CIA high-up Victor Marchetti, former Executive Assistant to the Deputy Director and Special Assistant to the Executive Director, and co-author of the tell-all book *The CIA and the Cult of Intelligence,* told *Second Look* magazine in 1979 that the subject of UFOs had always been under the heading "very sensitive activities" at the Agency. Marchetti never saw any evidence but heard "high-level" rumors of "little gray men" kept specifically at Wright-Patterson's Foreign Technology Division. In later years, a NORAD technician computerizing the complex inadvertently came across black and white pictures of bodies matching the Roswell description, about five feet tall and with big heads. They were in a file labelled "USAAF Early Automation."

UFO researcher Len Stringfield put together a composite description of the bodies combining claimed eyewitness autopsist Dr. Jesse Johnson's description with that of other supposed inside sources. All his particulars agreed with the eyewitness testimonies, adding a few details. The bodies were between three-and-a-half and four-and-a-half feet tall and weighed less than forty pounds. The eyes were large and almond-shaped, elongated, slightly slanted, and completely black, set deep and wide apart and appearing rather Oriental. The mouth was a mere slit, only two inches deep, and completely non-functional for speaking or eating. The head and bodies were completely hairless, the torsos long and thin. The feet were without toes. The skin was gray, tough and leathery, of a microscopically dense mesh-like structure. The bodies were without teeth or reproductive organs, had no digestive or alimentary tract, no upper or lower gastrointestinal area, no anus and no rectum, and a colorless liquid devoid of red blood cells was prevalent in them.

By itself, the description would be useless, not to mention absurd, but its mysteries were answered by Dr. Robert I. Sarbacher, President and Chairman of the Board of the Washington Institute of Technology and consultant to the Research and Development Board during Eisenhower's administration. Responding to UFO researcher William Steinman's questions to him in a 1983 letter, the helpful and cooperative Sarbacher said that he "had no association with any of the people involved in the recovery and have no knowledge regarding the dates of the recoveries [of flying saucer crashes]," but verified that a top-secret government investigative body was heavily involved with it. "John von Neumann was definitely involved. Dr. Vannevar Bush was definitely involved, and I think Dr. Robert Oppenheimer also . . . This is all I know for sure."

Concerning the bodies, Sarbacher stated,

My association with the Research and Development Board . . . was rather limited, so that although I had been invited to participate in several discussions associated with the reported recoveries, I could not personally attend the meetings . . . About the only thing I remember at this time is that certain materials reported to have come from flying saucer crashes were extremely light and very tough. I am sure our laboratories analyzed them very carefully. There were reports that instruments or people operating these machines were also of very light weight, sufficient to withstand the tremendous deceleration and acceleration associated with their machinery. I remember in talking with some of the people at the office that I got the impression these "aliens" were constructed like certain insects we have observed on Earth, wherein because of the low mass the inertial forces involved in operation of these instruments would be quite low.

In the most concise and straightforward analysis ever given, Sarbacher revealed the best-held government secret about flying saucer technology—which is that the crafts' occupants are just another part of it. All later evidence only deepens realization of the fact that the odd little gray bodies witnessed coming from flying saucers are *robots*. Virtually every UFO researcher close to the question came to the same conclusion eventually, though few of them understood it or its implications, and if they did they rarely expounded on them. Other independent amateur researchers missed the obvious in their pursuit of exotic alien beings that didn't exist, but that were romantically appealing to believe in.

But all the best evidence confirms it, including Sarbacher's statement that the "instruments or people" were "constructed" to withstand G-force stresses, and his putting of the word "aliens" in quotes, denoting inadequacy or inaccuracy in its usage; Lincoln La Paz's evaluation that the Roswell spacecraft had been a fully automated extraterrestrial probe, yet had touched down and had repairs attempted long-distance by its controllers, which would require remote-controlled arms and legs; Victor Marchetti's affirmation that the "little gray men" were kept at Wright-Patterson's Foreign Technology Division, and the NORAD computer technician finding their picture in a file labelled "USAAF Early Automation"; John von Neumann's "definite involvement" with the government's top-secret UFO investigative group, von Neumann being a pioneer of digital computers; and the Roswell nurse's use of the term "foreign bodies" to describe them, and her inability to remember sex organs, any interior structures, or even whether the bodies were clothed or naked.

Numerous subsequent cases in UFO files would make the thesis of robot occupants all the more obvious, and even some prior historical cases as well. Occupants reported in ensuing decades by abductees and military confrontations confirm it, all the more strongly by virtue of the fact that most of the witnesses were unaware that they were describing robots, but gave consistent details that only fit that interpretation. The Freedom of Information Act has brought some of these to light, such as a DIA (Defense Intelligence Agency) summary reading, "La Razon (Buenos Aires) 27 July 68—Relates new sighting near La Pastora, Alvear, and Tapalque. The latter describes the crew and inability of machine gun bullets to affect them...." But the vast majority of reports have been publicly available for at least three decades, through UFO periodicals and books by independent researchers, that—as with many other professional and academic publications—went unread by the very specialists who should have been paying the most attention to them.

French astrophysicist and computer expert for the Department of Defense, Jacques Vallee, was first attracted to the study of UFOs in 1954, "when there was a deluge of sightings in France, and indeed throughout Europe, from England to Italy ... As a kid I remember hearing one of the earliest French witnesses, a railroad worker named Marius Dewilde ... He had seen two little robots next to a dark machine resting on the nearby railroad tracks ... I believed his story at the time. I still do." Recruited into the U.S. Air Force's official UFO research team, Project Blue Book, by university professor of astronomy and Blue Book scientific advisor J. Allen Hynek in 1963, Vallee and an unofficial colleague had noticed by December of 1965 that most UFO occupants appeared to be robots: "Over lunch Bill Powers and I have been talking about the operators of the craft. 'In some cases,' I said, 'it almost seems that they are not real beings, but artificial humanoids.' 'Yes,' he replied, warming to the subject, 'they could be noticing machines with fast pattern recognition abilities! In a few minutes on the ground they could gather reams of data about us, couldn't they?'"

In a later book, Vallee also hinted at artificial intelligence, referring to a case in Everittstown, New Jersey, on November 6, 1957, as "another of the tantalizing coincidences with which UFO researchers are now becoming familiar." A twelve-year-old boy named Everett in Dante, Tennessee, had at 6:30 that morning seen strange people "like German soldiers in movies" attempting to grab his dog. Already in the possession of several other canines, they took off in an oblong object. The same night, in Everittstown, a man named John Trasco saw little tam-o'-shantered green men by an egg-shaped object outside his barn. In broken English, one of them said, "We are peaceful people. We only want your dog." Trasco grabbed the little man's wrist, and it pulled away from him and fled, leaving green powder on his fingers which indicated that the little man had been made up to look like an elf.

The curiosity of funny little men by egg-shaped objects attempting to seize dogs from both a person and a town named "Everett," hundreds of miles apart on the same day, could easily have been the product of an artificial intelligence taking too literally the command to "take dogs from Everett." The "broken English," to be encountered in numerous later cases—most reporting that it issues from an artificially oversized chest or trunk area—sounds not unlike the product of a voice synthesizer selecting and programming each word in methodical sequence, and the "German soldiers" comment would associate with the stiff goose-stepping of an artificial being not naturally constructed for walking with ease.

Famous UFO abductee Barney Hill specifically made the reference to the occupants being "like a German Nazi," partly in describing the leader as wearing a "black, black shiny jacket" but also in the occupants' movements. The stiff walk and oversized chests come from a great many reports. Nebraska Highway Patrolman Herbert J. Schirmer, a 1967 abductee, said his abductors spoke broken English from oversized chests, moved stiffly and mechanically "like professional soldiers," and that their eye pupils widened and narrowed "like a camera lens adjusting." He added, "All the time I was with them, I never noticed whether they were breathing or not ... I don't recall seeing them take a breath like we do."

Abductee Judy Doraty of Texas reported in 1973 her abductors' eyes also seeming to open and close like a camera lens—"They go in and out real fast, like this," she depicted, folding and spreading her hands several times. When they turned, she said it was "kind of like on their heel ... swing rather than like we might turn ... it seems like they pivot." The September-October 1950 Ontario *Steep Rock Echo* reported a man and wife's description of occupants moving on a landed flying saucer: "These figures did not turn around. They just altered the direction of their feet. They walked on the angle, or camber surface of the disk, and the leg on the higher side seemed shorter, so that the compensation—real or apparent—provided against any limp." The witnesses said the occupants were identical midgets of three-and-a-half to four-and-a-half feet tall, the only difference among them being that the leader had "what seemed to be a red skullcap, or perhaps it was red paint, the caps worn by others were blue," which would be echoed eleven years later by Barney Hill's comment that one of the chief occupants was "a redhead." The Ontario witnesses further added, "[T]he faces seemed just blank surfaces! It was odd that the figures moved like automata, rather than living beings."

UFO occupants that besieged a Kelly-Hopkinsville, Kentucky, farmhouse in August of 1955 also had the oversized chests. They were three to three-and-a-half feet tall, with glowing round yellow eyes on either side of their heads, and their entire bodies shone silver as if lit from within. They had the same odd arms reported on the Roswell occupants, very long, with the distance from shoulder to elbow about half that from elbow to wrist, only the fingers were taloned claws (another fairly frequent feature) instead of suction cup-tipped. The beings each had three antennae, a very common feature, two on top of the head and the probable third in a conical nose with a ball on the tip of it. They also had no feet, just suction cup-ending spindles, upon which they levitated and moved in an even float, as opposed to walking. They were also bulletproof. Four boxes and more of shells, ranging from .22 caliber rifle to point-blank shotgun blasts, "just seemed to bounce off their nickle-plated armor," as one witness put it, all with no effect; the "goblins" just sprang back up, suddenly dropping to all fours and locomoting away at incredible speed. They were also shy of bright lights. A similarly super-locomoted, silver-suited, and antennaed figure from a landed UFO outran Alabama State Police Officer Jeff Greenhaw's patrol car. "It moved stiffly," Greenhaw told the *Birmingham News,* "like a robot, and didn't make any sounds."

Abductees Charles Hickson and Calvin Parker, in 1973 in Pascagoula, Mississippi, never used any word other than "robots" to describe their assailants, five-foot-tall humanoids who floated out of an egg-shaped UFO on the same suction cup-ending legs reported on the "Hopkinsville Goblins." They were "grayish, like a ghost . . . with pointed ears and noses and a pale skin-type covering . . . claw-like hands [pincher things]," and had only the shape of feet without toes, on "more or less just a roundlike thing on a leg—if you'd call it a leg. . . ." The "skin-type" coverings looked like foil radiation suits, as did that reported on Jeff Greenhaw's UFO occupant. The "pointed ears and noses" were conical projections, one extending straight out of either side of the head and one straight forward where a nose should be. They had no faces, just a slit at the mouth area.

Artist James Flynt's sketch of what the men reported looked to journalist and author Ralph Blum "like somebody's idea of a wrinkled robot," which Hickson and Parker confirmed was their own assessment: "Calvin and me's talked about that too. We've put our minds together and we've come to the conclusion it was robots . . . I'll believe until the day I die that they was robots and that they was communicating with somewhere else." The communications of the robots were solely between each other or some other computer and consisted only of a buzzing "zzzZZZ, zzzZZZ" sound. Keesler Air Force

Base interrogated and thoroughly checked both men, who also passed a lie-detector test for the sheriff. Detective Tom Huntley, who sat in on the military questioning, said that the assembled brass and scientists listened "just cool," as though they'd heard it all before, but the mention of the "claw hands" seemed to grab their attention. "Two colonels exchanged looks over that."

In Voronezh, about two hundred miles south of Moscow, the Russian news service Tass reported as many as five hundred witnesses to any of numerous sightings in September and October of 1989 of landed, egg-shaped UFOs, the traces of which matched those given in Quarouble, France, thirty-five years before. Ten- to twelve-foot-tall humanoids were seen disembarking from them to collect soil and plant samples, and were sometimes seen leading human beings to locations where they seemed to simply vanish into thin air. All the missing people later returned, bewildered but completely unharmed, with no memory at all of what had happened to them. The giant humanoids most closely resembled the description of a robot: foil-suited, with extremely long arms ending in clamps for hands, no faces, no necks, and only a three-"eyed" flattish dome shape for a head—the "eyes" of which would correspond to the antennae of the Hopkinsville Goblins and the Pascagoula robots.

The first recorded UFO abductee of the modern age, Brazil's twenty-eight-year-old Antonio Villas Boas in October of 1957, reported his abductors as having "from the middle of their heads ... three round silvery metal tubes ... a little narrower than a common garden hose ... placed one in the middle and one on either side of their heads, [which] were smooth and bent backward and downward, toward the back. There they fitted into their clothes; how I cannot say, but one went down the center, where the backbone is, and the other two, one on each side, fitted under the shoulders...." They wore skintight gray "siren-suits," which "perhaps ... did interfere slightly with their movements, because they kept walking very stiffly." On their feet were thick-soled shoes, "the general appearance [being] that of common tennis shoes," which his observations took to be "larger than the feet they covered," and the front of which "turned up (or arched up) ... so that the tips looked like those in the fairy tales of old...."

Their heads "corresponded to double of what the size of a normal head should be," and their faces consisted only of "thin metal plates, one of which was three-cornered, at nose level," and "two round glasses, like the lenses in ordinary glasses," beneath which were eyes he thought were smaller than human, "though I believe that may have been the effect of the lenses." Boas' report of their appearance being "like in the fairy tales of old" connects it to John Trasco's and is enhanced by his saying that their gray "siren-suits" were made of "soft, thick, unevenly striped" material—or particolored, such as a mediaeval jester might wear, the three "hoses" even reminiscent of tasselled bells on a cap. The abductors were only as high as Boas' shoulder and seemed to be lightweight but were enormously strong, communicating with each other in strange grunts he couldn't describe, "some ... longer, others shorter, sometimes containing several different sounds at the same time, at other times ending in a tremor." His overall description could easily be that of a robot, the smallish-distorted eyes beneath larger round "glasses" being camera lenses, the bizarre grunts simply a variation on the chirp used by binary computers to communicate with each other.

With only minor variations, Boas' description—like that of the Roswell occupants—matches that of the most commonly reported UFO abductors, the "Grays." The Grays are three-and-a-half- to four-and-a-half-foot-tall ectomorphs, extremely thin, with no muscle tone or individuality of face or expression. They have fixed, identical looks, mere bumps for noses, slits for mouths, no hair on the head or body, and enormous, outwardly slanting jet-black, insectoid "bug" eyes. They never blink or speak, their communication with abductees accomplished "telepathically"—which, given the universality of implants reportedly put in abductees' heads, could simply be radio communications to an implanted receiver, an idea strengthened by the fact that Herbert Schirmer could not understand the little men who accosted him (and which also match this description) until they apparently pressed something into his neck.

Abductee Kathie Davis, researcher Budd Hopkins' case study for his 1987 book and subsequent 1992 CBS miniseries *Intruders,* made observations about the Grays that support the idea of their being robots. Chief among these is the fact that their fingers were cold and hard: "Whoever's touching me . . . I feel touching . . . I feel cold touches on both sides of my chest . . . and fingers or something cold touching me." Hopkins asked her to clarify whether they specifically felt like fingers, and she replied, "Yeah, sort of, but they're cold . . . Not real soft. . . ." Without realizing it, Hopkins even seems to have confirmed the idea in a 1992 *UFO* magazine interview. Referring to the miniseries of *Intruders,* he commented, "The first aliens built by the prop department very closely followed the descriptions given by abductees. But when filmed, those 'aliens' looked lifeless, more like alien dolls or puppets than living entities."

Other reports definitely state that witnessed UFO entities appear or feel metallic. Barney Hill said his bluish-gray abductors, typical of the most common reports, were "almost metallic-looking." A twelve-year-old Argentinian abductee, referred to by Jacques Vallee as "Oscar," saw a "giant" with what he specified was a small robot on a landed UFO near his father's property, cutting up one of his father's cows. The "giant" remained suited throughout the entire encounter, except for removing a glove to reveal "nails like conical dark blue metallic claws." Since a coverall suit was all he saw, and the "nails" appeared metallic, the "giant," like the similar Voronezh humanoids, could also have been a robot. A woman in the Loire, France, in May of 1950, reported an assault by an invisible entity whose hands alone could be seen, and said that they felt over her mouth "very cold, and their touch made me think that they were not made of flesh." She said they were black with a yellowish tinge, "somewhat like copper. They pulled my head against a very hard chest—one that seemed to be made of iron; I felt the cold through my hair and behind my neck, but no contact with clothes." She mentioned that "when the hands touched me, I had the distinct impression of a strong electric discharge, as if I had been shaken by a lightning bolt. My whole body was annihilated, helpless, without reflexes."

Electric current passing through metallic hands would explain the report given by Betty Hill and many later abductees of pain being relieved by the simple laying of the crew leader's hand upon her forehead—electricity, properly applied, can have a numbing or therapeutic effect. It can also erase or severely jumble all memory of several hours prior to its application, which is exactly what electroshock (sometimes called electroconvulsive) therapy is for. This might be the cause of both the amnesia and the severe headaches reported by abductees following their experiences.

The indestructibility of UFO occupants most attests to their robotic nature. In addition to the bulletproof Hopkinsville Goblins and the beings impotently strafed by the military in Brazil, there are a great many reports of the occupants possessing superhuman strength and being completely unaffected by any form of attack. Twenty-eight-year-old Donald Schrum fired arrows and threw lit articles of his clothing at what were apparently Grays and an accompanying creature "behaving more like a mechanical being than an animal or a man," which he specifically called "robot-like." They besieged him for an entire night in Cisco Grove, California, in September of 1964, his arrows clanging off the "robot-like" entity with no effect but to produce sparks.

In November and December, 1954, two couples in South America were accosted by UFO occupants, the resistance they put up being futile. Gustave Gonzales struck a three-foot-tall hairy dwarf that tried to grab him with his knife. His blade "glanced off as though it had struck steel." A single blow from the dwarf reeled Gonzales back fifteen feet. He and his companion, Jose Ponce, were left shaken but unharmed, save for a red scratch the dwarf left on Gonzales' side. The following month, rabbit hunters Lorenzo Flores and Jesus Gomez found themselves suddenly set-upon by three hairy dwarves from a hovering saucer near the Trans-Andean Highway. One grabbed Jesus, and Lorenzo bludgeoned it with his shotgun. "The gun seemed to have struck rock, or something harder, as it broke in two," Lorenzo later related. Both men, who escaped unharmed but for minor cuts and bruises, said that the "little men" were remarkably strong for being so lightweight.

In September of 1973, a group of boys, a radio disc jockey, and a family in North Carolina witnessed a "limping creature with red glowing eyes, long hair, pointed ears, and a hook nose on a gray face, missing a hand but [leaping] fifty to sixty feet at a time." The disc jockey fired at it with a pistol, to no effect. This particular bullet-proof creature connects to one of history's most mysterious airborne characters: "Springheel Jack."

Jack got his nickname in November of 1837, when he was witnessed on numerous occasions making impossible leaps in the dark London suburbs. He was described by those who saw him as "a most hideous appearance . . . tall, thin and powerful. He had a prominent nose, and bony fingers of immense power which resembled claws. He was incredibly agile. He wore a long, flowing cloak, of the sort affected by opera-goers, soldiers and strolling actors. On his head was a tall, metallic-seeming helmet. Beneath the cloak were close-fitting garments of some glittering material like oilskin or metal mesh. There was a lamp strapped to his chest. Oddest of all: the creature's ears were cropped or pointed like those of an animal." That same "lantern," or some device like it, has been reported by modern UFO witnesses to be in the possession of the crafts' occupants, even performing the same function: to render victims helpless. An article of the time, about one girl he accosted in Green Dragon Alley, reported that "Jack's weird blue [lantern] flame spurted into his victim's face and she dropped to the ground in a deep swoon."

Two incidents of Jack appearing as a caller at the front door of private residences were recorded in February of 1838, both instances causing those called on to scream upon seeing him, one being gassed unconscious by the flame from his lamp and seized before the victim's sister scared him off, empty-handed. The authorities tried to suppress knowledge of the nightmarish figure, but a Peckham resident's letter to the Lord Mayor finally ended official censorship of the subject. Admiral Codgrington set up a reward fund for Jack's capture, causing even "the old Duke of Wellington himself [to] set holsters at his saddle bow and [ride] out after dark in search of Springheel Jack." Jack remained uncaptured, and from then on largely unseen— or at least unreported.

Thirty-nine years later, two sentries in Aldershot, Hampshire, fired upon Jack to no effect as he swooped over them—in addition to Jack's phenomenal leaps, he was also reported actually flying. He stunned the sentries with the same "burst of blue fire" and vanished again. Had he been a mortal man, Jack would have to have been around his sixties at the time of this incident, but the description was the same, indicating either that his health or longevity exceeded the norm, or that there was more than one of him—or, perhaps, that "he" was something other than a living human being. Journalist John Vyner, who recorded Jack's exploits, believed he was also the author of a reign of terror in Mattoon, Illinois, in 1944, when a number of women were similarly blasted unconscious by a peeping-tom "as in search of someone known to him by sight," as Jack's behavior also had been described. This would correspond to the vast majority of UFO abduction reports, abductees rarely if ever being taken only once, but rather numerous times in the course of their lives. Later flying beings with the same modus operandi, such as the "Mothman" of Point Pleasant, West Virginia, will be discussed elsewhere in this book.

Springheel Jack is a convincing enough candidate for a robot abductor from the annals of history, with his standard UFO occupant appearance, vise-like grip, and "pointed or cropped ears" corresponding to the other robots' antennae, but he pales in comparison to a more obviously mechanical abductor in Livingston, Scotland, in our own era, on November 9, 1979. Forest inspector Robert Taylor found an oddly configured, large hovering globe while inspecting plantations between Edinburgh and Glasgow. It appeared to be failing in an attempt to camouflage itself, fading in and out between plain visibility and partial transparency. As he watched the strange display, two small metallic spheres with grappling spikes abruptly charged at him, so quickly he couldn't determine where they'd come from. These wrapped about his ankles and dragged him toward the globe, as a choking smell rendered him unconscious. He awoke sometime later with a headache and thirst that persisted for two days. His dog was barking madly, and he briefly had some difficulty with his motor functions after the incident. Other than tears in his pants and the grass from the grappling hooks, nothing remained to be seen.

The evidence for robot occupants of UFOs, as well as their collection of environmental and biological samples—including temporary abduction of human beings, which is nearly always erased from their memory following the encounter—can plainly be seen to have been reported numerous times in our own era, and also preceding it. Vallee was not alone in his early robot assessment. His mentor, Hynek, commented after the Hopkinsville Goblins incident of 1955, "It is odd that the creatures seen coming from these craft ... would be able to adjust to our gravitational pull or breathe our air so easily. This could only mean that they are mechanical creatures—robots—or they originate from a habitat whose environment is very similar to ours here on Earth." Similarly, space rocketry pioneer and confirmed believer in UFOs as interplanetary craft, Hermann Oberth, responding to the suggestion that the occupants of such craft could be human, commented on his belief that the occupants probably "hypnotized the contact persons and suggested a human-like appearance to them, or that the contact persons encountered something like man-shaped robots."

That the Grays, especially, could have evolved on an Earth-like planet is absurd on the face of it, let alone the other examples cited. As small and frail-looking as they are, our gravity and atmosphere should crush and suffocate them with about the same effect as our walking on the ocean floor. Yet they are never reported with breathing apparatuses, pressure suits, or even face masks—and, in fact, are not reported breathing at all. Combined with the testimony of their metallic look and feel, stiff hobbling walks, identical formed-out-of-a-mold appearances and seemingly indestructible nature, let alone the surface reports of the Roswell "autopsy," the only logical conclusion is that they are, in fact, robots. The thesis is all the more strengthened by reports of other UFO occupants that are plainly of mechanical nature and involved in the same kinds of activities.

Cattle mutilation and UFO researcher Linda Howe has heard them referred to as either "biological robots" or "robots" by abductees she has interviewed, who claim they serve merely as "bellhops" of a sort to escort them to and from the craft. Numerous witnesses have overtly or covertly compared them to "automata," and the descriptions provided by others, without such references, still fit the same qualifications. In fact, Hynek's own specific definition of a "Close Encounter of the Third Kind" is one in which "the presence of animated creatures is reported" in connection with a UFO experience. It is important to notice that he never uses the word "alien"—and neither do most abductees, unless they have simply come to employ it as a convention to avoid confusion, since it is the word the researchers questioning them use. Pulitzer Prize-winning author and Yale psychiatrist John Mack has specified "they do not use that word," *alien,* to describe their abductors, and it is to be remembered that Robert Sarbacher also offset the word in quotes, signifying its use as a mere convention.

Russia's equivalent to Jacques Vallee, Dr. Felix Zigel, finally concluded after years of study that UFO occupants consisted of four basic types: tall humanoids, small grays, crews of robots or androids, and astronauts indistinguishable from terrestrial *Homo sapiens.* Timothy Good has "come to similar conclusions" as Zigel after thirty years of research in the field, and so have author Zecharia Sitchin and *UFO* magazine editor Richard Hall, among others. If the "tall humanoids" comprise such entities as the plainly robotic-seeming creatures witnessed at Voronezh and possessing "metallic claws" in Argentina, and the Grays also can be concluded to be mechanical, that leaves only two types of UFO occupants: human and artificial. The plentiful examples of human occupants will shortly be discussed, but for the moment, it seems a safe bet to say that the rest are indeed robots.

The evidence for actual "aliens," as in non-human life forms, is all but nonexistent. Witnesses reporting the sighting of living aliens at Roswell are not credible, and are secondhand. One secondhand witness reports that her father arrived at the Roswell crash site to find living aliens, but her story is either inaccurately remembered or relayed, or else a fabrication. At alternate times, she reports that one alien was alive and the others dead, or that three were alive, or that there were five aliens and not three. One version of her story—coming from herself and not distorted through any third-party interpreter—has it that a soldier found a living alien clutching a black box to its chest and clubbed its head with his rifle butt to force it to relinquish the box. This story is impossible to believe, since no disciplined military man would conceivably attack any non-threatening (the alien was claimed to be cowering at the time) individual in an obviously tenuous position, especially given that the supposed alien in question represented a technologically superior civilization that the military would unquestionably have been extremely reluctant to antagonize. It is equally difficult to believe, given all testimony that the crash occurred several days before its discovery, that an intelligent flight crew of any race—human or other—would sit around doing nothing but feeling sorry for themselves until the locals might come driving up.

One purported firsthand witness, Gerald Anderson, perjured himself early on in his claim of discovering a living alien at the Roswell crash site while still a young child. He admitted to having forged a diary entry to substantiate his story, but not until researchers first satisfactorily proved the forgery for themselves by scientific means. Other supposed firsthand witnesses approached authors Kevin Randle and Donald Schmitt after their well-researched *UFO Crash at Roswell* was published. Two claimed to be archaeologists who saw the craft come down and witnessed the military's arrival the next day, with the suspicious enough names of "Ragsdale" and "Truelove," and a third—who corroborated their story—was a military man who plainly could have had motivation to disseminate a disinformational story about flying saucers.

The story the new "witnesses" fed the authors was exactly the same as one that had been used by the Air Force Office of Special Investigations (AFOSI), between 1980 and about 1984, to drive independent UFO investigator Paul Bennewitz out of his mind. Bennewitz was an inventor and electronic parts manufacturer who recorded film and radio transmissions of mysterious aerial objects over Kirtland AFB in New Mexico for many months. He wrote about it to Kirtland, New Mexico's, Senator Schmidt, several scientists and military officials, and even the President, and then became the target of counterintelligence "from a variety of agencies"—chief of which was AFOSI—who doctored and forged documents to convince him that the government was conspiring with evil aliens to privately massacre the citizenry of Earth. To make their project look more authentic, they employed the services of author and early Roswell researcher Bill Moore, then head of APRO (Aerial Phenomena Research Organization), to "obtain" the "leaked documents" and help sell their legitimacy to Bennewitz. Though it is not proven, it appears very much as if they also arranged for a fraudulent abductee to tell similar "corroborative" stories, which Bennewitz could easily have compared to other accounts to discover their dubious reality. Unfortunately, he instead believed all of it without question and was hospitalized for nervous exhaustion four years later, a paranoid wreck of a man.

The story that had been painstakingly cultivated and fed Bennewitz was what is now recognized as the "EBE" (pron: "EE-bee," for "Extraterrestrial Biological Entity"), "Area 51," or "MJ-12" story. Even though all parties involved have admitted to its being concocted as a disinformational hoax, a hardcore number of insulated UFOlogists continue to write a great many books trying to sell it and related conspiracy stories as gospel truth. With certain variations, according to whomever is relating it, the story basically runs like this: the government recovered a number of dead aliens and one living one, dubbed "EBE," from either Roswell or any other crash in New Mexico. EBE was not biologically classifiable by any category known to man, but essentially synthesized chlorophyl for sustenance like a plant. Despite their naturally synthetic diet, he and his race need cattle parts for sustenance and just adore strawberry ice cream (actually a part of the story), and require human tissue to help them reproduce since their own genitalia (and digestive tracts) have atrophied. They use telepathy to communicate, and their leader is named "Krlll," with no vowels and three "l"s, begging the question of how a telepathically communicated name would be known to have no vowels, let alone how it would be pronounced. EBE soon died because the government didn't know how to care for him, and his race never answered distress signals—just why or how it is that EBE was unable to convey any of the necessary information to them is never pondered. The EBEs sometimes lie and are sneaky bastards, but the government has struck a deal with them anyway to allow their taking of human and cattle tissue in return for their giving us some of their superior technology.

One of the EBE-related stories fed Bennewitz was the "Archuleta Peak" story, which is the one Randle and Schmitt's new "witnesses" have been resurrecting (and for which there is no backing evidence whatsoever), named after the mountainside into which a flying saucer supposedly crashed. This particular variation gives specific (but, of course, impossible to verify) details on the aliens, even dividing them into various biological types, and also details the crashed ship's precise configuration, which just happens to match descriptions given by Kenneth Arnold—the latter fact given for why the story can only be true and not possibly fabricated by anyone who simply read a UFO history book to acquire those details. Any claimed documents legitimizing the story have all been demonstrated to have originated from AFOSI and/or other military intelligence sources, or simply have no duplicate records in government files or any other source of verification. Ex-ONI (Office of Naval Intelligence) man Bill Cooper is one continuing seller of such stories, forcefully discrediting himself even as he tells them by insisting that he saw JFK's driver shooting the President on live television in Dealey Plaza, which is a patent impossibility, and by claiming that all his ONI buddies are out to kill him at the same time he proclaims he has worked only for ONI-owned businesses since leaving the service.

One set of supposedly corroborative papers is called the "MJ-12 documents," which appeared mysteriously in the home of producer Jaime Shandera, friend of self-confessed AFOSI asset and propagator of false UFO stories, Bill Moore, in December of 1984. These purported to substantiate the formation of a top secret government UFO investigative group formed by President Truman in response to the Roswell crash, and the recovery of alien biological entities from it. That both a crash and such a group's formation occurred is testified to by numerous sources, and the latter stands to reason as being an extreme likelihood on its own merits, but the MJ-12 documents are not evidence of that group. No duplicates of them have been found by the FBI, and numerous technical flaws in them indicate they are forgeries. However, many other details in the documents are correct and would not have been known by any but informed government sources, which most strongly indicates they were deliberately constructed as a disinformational counterintelligence ploy to lure independent UFO investigators on a wild goose chase—which they have brilliantly succeeded at.

It can be noticed that, with few alterations, the EBE story closely parallels that of Steven Spielberg's 1982 hit movie from Universal, *E.T., The Extraterrestrial,* which was produced shortly before the MJ-12 documents appeared. This is only one of many curious connections between UFO research and the movies that will be detailed at great length in the coming chapters. In this particular case, the film appears to have been partly intended to lay the groundwork for the further-ance of disinformation already in the offing by the Intelligence agen-cies, during the most military-intensive era in American history.

Jaime Shandera produced documentaries for RKO and Time-Life Broadcast, and he and Moore sold the "story" of MJ-12 to indepen-dent Seligman Productions to be turned into an embarrassingly shoddy two-hour WGN-syndicated special called *UFO Coverup?: Live* that received multiple airings in the late 1980s. Journalist and UFO researcher/author John Keel derogatorily dubbed it "The Strawberry Ice Cream Show," after its most absurd claim concerning the "alien" dietary preference, which represented the consensus opinion. "Wit-nesses" with blanked-out faces and electronically altered voices gave "evidence" from the shadows, refusing to offer any of their sources up for scrutiny for fear of the dread reprisals that might be exacted upon them by their Intelligence colleagues. Long since exposed, the hidden sources "Falcon" and "Condor," who were Master Sergeant Richard Doty and Captain Robert Collins—the authors of the doc-tored AFOSI documents calculatedly fed Paul Bennewitz by Bill Moore—are both alive and well today, as are Bill Cooper, sometime CIA-operative John Lear, and others who have spread similar stories.

The founder of *Time* and *Life* (the producer of Shandera's docu-mentaries), Henry Luce, was—like many magnates in the media—a close friend of CIA founder Allen Dulles. Luce hired CIA agents and offered others credentials for cover. He appointed his *Life* publisher, American media czar C. D. Jackson—who had worked as the CIA's "special consultant to the president for psychological warfare" (about which authors Jonathan Vankin and John Whalen appropriately ask, *"against whom?"*)—to be his special liaison with the Agency. General Walter Bedell Smith, who wanted to recruit prominent Americans into the shadowy, elitist Bilderberger organization, "turned the [recruitment] matter over to C. D. Jackson, and things really got going." Jackson was the man who bought the Zapruder film for more than $150,000 three days after John Kennedy's assassination, and locked it away on the excuse that it was too horrific ever to be aired for the general public; it took a court subpoena by prosecuting attorney Jim Garrison to first get it seen by the jury trying Clay Shaw as a possible conspirator in the case, and it was not released to the public until 1974. It was during the time the film was in the sole possession of Time-Life Corporation that its only hitherto published photos, in the Warren Report, were seen with the two most critical frames out of sequence: those showing the direction Kennedy's head snapped when shot. Luce's wife, Clare Booth, was also heavily Intelligence-connected. Both of them, in common with many CIA officials at the time, dropped LSD—which was being experimented with for its mind-control potentials in the Agency's extensive MK-ULTRA project—and extolled its virtues, and Clare founded the Association of Former Intelligence Officers as well as sponsoring anti-Castro activities based in Florida. The Time-Life CIA connection is only one among many in America's mainstream media that will be revealed in due course in this book.

The latest incarnation of the EBE hoaxes has been Fox Television's one-hour *Alien Autopsy: Fact or Fiction?* aired twice in one week in August-September of 1995. As hoaxes go, it wasn't even a good one. Purported to be recovered Roswell autopsy footage, it was far less realistic than similar scenes staged for Hollywood movies such as 1979's *Alien*. Any graininess in the film was identical to that seen in flashback sequences like those shown in Oliver Stone's *JFK,* and the film stock itself, which for 1947 would have been silver nitrate that by now should have deteriorated badly, was as pristine as if it had been shot yesterday.

Put simply, any evidence for the existence of non-human life forms connected to the operation of UFOs comes entirely from inside the military and/or Intelligence communities, and is without any verifiable corroboration. Supposed witnesses to such aliens give conflicting and highly improbable if not impossible accounts, and those who are military-connected plainly have a motive to lie. By contrast, the reports showing indication of robot abductors associated with the craft come from numerous witnesses in all countries and times, and are easily verifiable for the consistency they offer and the corroborative elements they contain, often without the witnesses realizing those consistencies and corroborations themselves. The robotic descriptions come from abductees who are accepted as legitimate by even the most conservative of UFOlogists, where those attempting to sell the story of aliens come only from the most questionable of sources and are accepted only by the least demanding from that same community of researchers.

Digital computer pioneer John von Neumann, "definitely" stated to have been involved in the government's most top-secret UFO investigative group from the beginning, is not listed in the almost certainly fraudulent MJ-12 documents, and he is a likelier candidate than others who are mentioned there—most notably, the only biologist in those documents, Detlev Bronk. If aliens had been recovered from a crashed spaceship, wouldn't they have been the most important single area of study? Especially if the supposed life-forms encountered were as complex as much later disinformation has led investigators to believe? What remained of the craft was nothing but wreckage, according to all the witnesses, while at least one of the recovered bodies was universally reported to have been virtually, if not completely, intact. And Jacques Vallee, who began as an astrophysicist, was—like von Neumann—also acquiring his advanced degree at Northwestern in computer science, when he was picked up by J. Allen Hynek and Blue Book. Why would computer science be more valuable than biological science, in the examination of "aliens"?

Aside from which, if alien bodies had been picked up, they would have been lying out in the open, in the hot desert sun, for close to a week before they were found. Why did no one report predators having taken their eyes, when those are the first tissues taken by scavenging birds or vermin? The nurse never saw any reproductive organs and said the doctors told her predators had taken them. Why would they take those, especially if they were covered, as opposed to the eyes? And if two of the bodies were relatively mangled and the third intact, why would predators have gone after two dead creatures and left a third alone? The damage is easier to accept as having been due to varying degrees of crash protection. The nurse couldn't even say whether the bodies were clothed or naked, and she described no wound or interior tissues or organs that would imply her having seen mutilated genitalia. Nor could she even properly identify the men who were examining the bodies as doctors—she had never seen them before.

For that matter, not one single witness made reference to the distinctive rotting stench of decomposition coming from the bodies. An overpowering smell was mentioned by both the nurse and one or two of the men conveying the bodies back to the base in their crates of ice for the Army, but this was never described with any specifics, and could as easily have been the chemical smell of some lubricant or internal medium as that of actual organic decay. Ammonia alone has the most overpowering smell to the human olfactory sense. The crates of ice into which the bodies were placed would not have been needed for non-biological bodies, but then the military almost certainly didn't know yet what they were dealing with. Mortician Glenn Dennis was led to believe a conventional crash had occurred, which could easily explain the superficially injured pilot he conveyed to the base that day and also the repeated phone calls from the hospital asking him about preservation techniques. The nurse's description of the "aliens'" skin matches as easily that of a durable plastic covering, and in fact makes more sense when interpreted as such, since there should have been insufficient skin left to test after the bodies' exposure to the elements for a week or more.

On September 1, 1994, according to *UFO* magazine, former Air Force Intelligence agent and disinformationalist Bob Oechsler announced his "retirement" from UFOlogy. Caught several times stirring up the EBE hoax waters, he was finally discredited for his involvement in the "Guardian" fraud in Canada. For some strange reason, Oechsler continues to be given a great deal of credence by such respected researchers in the field as Timothy Good, who followed his extraordinary *Above Top Secret* with a book called *Alien Liaison* (in America, *Alien Contact),* which is filled with uncorroborated

EBE stories from Oechsler and others. Given the man's background, any story coming from him must be taken with a considerable grain of salt. But one of those stories is certainly interesting, and may be revelatory, whether intended as disinformation or not.

Oechsler has claimed to be a NASA mission specialist and project engineer, involved in the Canadian end of a manufacturing project creating mechanical arm assemblies for the space shuttle, and having "expertise regarding sophisticated remote-control devices for character robots." Good claims to have found one of Oechsler's name-tag I.D.s for NASA and attests to the man's being a robotics expert who has given invitational talks to other professionals in the field, adding that he is "a prototype designer of sophisticated control systems and mobile surveillance systems." Oechsler has claimed association with the mythical MJ-12, which may or may not mean that he had any connection to the actual inside government UFO investigative team at some time or another. By his own account, he met Admiral Bobby Ray Inman—who for ten consecutive years was the number one or number two man in the CIA, the National Security Agency, the Defense Intelligence Agency and the Office of Naval Intelligence—at the groundbreaking ceremony for a top-secret NSA computer facility on May 13, 1988. After the ceremony, Oechsler handed Inman his card and credentials, and asked to be brought into MJ-12. On the basis of the credentials alone, Inman was said to have smiled and said, "O.K."

What makes this story interesting is that at no time has Oechsler, or anyone associated with the EBE hoaxes, ever alluded to robotics playing any special part in the reality of UFOs, yet robots and computers plainly are of paramount importance to that particular field of study. More interesting still is the fact that Inman himself—without question one of the closest Intelligence insiders alive—since "retiring" from Intelligence work in 1982 has become the chairman, president, and chief executive officer of a Texas microelectronics company.

The foregoing case studies, combined with that of Roswell, make more illustrative a repeat viewing of a classic science fiction film which nearly everyone has seen at one time or another, and then mostly forgotten. Roswell still has not been declassified, having no record in the Air Force's Project Blue Book, and in fact has still never been admitted by any branch of government to have been anything other than a weather balloon. For that matter, no public knowledge of Roswell would be available until thirty years after the event, at the earliest. Yet, so many years before public discussion of the famous crash recovery, its facts, only slightly altered, were accurately to be seen on the silver screen in the following manner:

At a North Pole U.S. military base, a scientist explains to a captain why he has been summoned. "Your message said an airplane crash," the captain says. "Is that what we're looking for?" An aide reads the scientist's notes of the preceding day: "November 1, 6:15 PM. Sound detectors and seismographs registered explosion due East. At 6:18, magnetometer revealed deviation 12 degrees 20 minutes East. Such deviation possible only if a disturbing force equivalent to 20,000 tons of steel or iron ore had become part of the Earth at a sixty-mile radius." The scientist adds that the magnetic deviation has been constant, and the captain confirms running into it on his way to the base.

"We have some special telescopic cameras. At the appearance of radioactivity a Geiger counter trips the release and the cameras function. It was working last evening. This first picture was taken three minutes before the explosion, or 6:12. You can see the small dot low, there, in the corner. Now the next picture, one minute later, that dot is moving from west to east, moving fast enough to form a streak." An assistant throws in that the camera footage was a thousand per second. "Moving pretty fast, wasn't it?" the scientist agrees. "Here, at 6:14, it's moving upward. 6:15, it drops to the Earth . . . vanishes. A meteor might move horizontal to the Earth, but never upward."

Flying over the site, forty-eight miles away, the captain and the scientist, along with a team from the base, pick up radiation and can see the area clearly beneath them: a long skid is melted into the ice, forming a shiny streak to a huge, circular area, made equally shiny with the formation of ice over some object that obviously melted its way through as it came to a halt. The team lands and surrounds the site. The Geiger counter goes crazy. "Something's melted that surface crust. It's frozen over again into clear ice. The bottle shape was apparently caused by the aircraft first making contact with the Earth out there at the neck of the bottle, sliding toward us and forming that larger area as it came to rest, with the engine or engines generating enough heat to melt that path, through the crust, then sink beneath the surface," the team quickly assesses. "Could an airplane melt that much ice?" a journalist along for the ride asks. "One of our own jets generates enough heat to warm a fifty-story office building," an officer answers. They connect arms and spread out to see the shape of the submerged craft, its tail fin stabilizer (of no identifiable metal or alloy) sticking up out of the ice . . . it is perfectly round.

"Holy cats. . . ." the journalist exclaims. One of the military members ruminates, "It's almost . . . yeah. It's almost a perfect. . . ." "It is," says another. "It's round! We finally got one!" The journalist smiles. "We found a flying saucer!" They can't discern much of it through the ice, except that it is perfectly smooth, with no visible doors or windows, and no apparent engine. "I doubt we'll find anything we'd call an engine," the scientist says. Agreed that it is not from this planet, the scientist tells the journalist, "The answers to your questions will be much easier after we've examined the interior of the craft. And its occupants—if there are any." The journalist cries, "What a story!" but before he can radio it out, the captain catches up to him: "Hold it, Scott—sorry, no private messages." Pleading the Constitution, the journalist is cut off with, "I wish you could, but this is Air Force information, it'll have to wait for authority to let you file a story." The journalist tells him it's the biggest story since the parting of the Red Sea, that it can't be covered up—"Think what it means to the world!" The captain responds, "I'm not working for the world, I'm working for the Air Force." He tries to confiscate the journalist's camera, who complains that even the Russians wouldn't do that, and the journalist is allowed to keep it on the agreement that he reports nothing until proper clearance is given.

Unable to dig the saucer out, the team employs thermite bombs. They fail, not releasing the saucer, but instead blowing it up. The journalist laments that their thoughtlessness has turned a new civilization into a Fourth of July piece. But all is not lost: a radiation reading leads them to something nearby, also under the ice. "It looks like a man. . . ." one says. They congregate around. "It's got legs and a head, I can see 'em . . . yeah, he must be over eight feet long . . . somebody got out of that saucer. . . ." The scientist enters his opinion: "Got out, or was thrown out. And was frozen fast before he could get clear." The journalist, in awe, thinks out loud, "A man from Mars. . . ."

Given their failure with the saucer, they decide to leave the occupant on ice (or in it, more specifically) until home base can be contacted stateside to authorize some plan for analyzing the thing. No one wants to stand guard duty over it. "The ice is clearing up, and you can see that thing pretty good now," one of the men tells the captain. "It's got crazy hands and no hair. And the eyes? Well, they're open, and they look like they can see." He laughs uncomfortably. "It's got me too, sir, and I wasn't in there very long." Another man concurs, "It's the eyes being open that gets you." Seen through the ice, the thing looks more or less exactly like a man, only with a large bald head and big black eyes.

Though it should obviously be dead after its ordeal, the thing turns out to still be animate and escapes, losing an arm to the dogs, a dozen of which cannot faze it. Nor does flame. The arm moves independently of it, seemingly with a life of its own. The thing is bulletproof. Only electricity ultimately can stop it. It has green fluid for blood. Its surface is hard and sharp, "a sort of chitinous substance," the scientist and an autopsist opine, "something between a beetle's back and a rose thorn . . . amazingly strong. No arterial structure indicated. No blood in the arm. No animal tissue. No nerve endings visible. Porous, unconnected cellular growth. I doubt very much if it can die, as we understand dying. . . ."

The similarity all of the foregoing bears to Roswell should be obvious, after our review of the facts: the appearance of the glazed bottleneck and round shape where the saucer came to rest were reported in Roswell, burned into the sand making it like glass; the saucer wasn't recovered, but blew up; despite the loss of the saucer, occupants were recovered nearby that theoretically ejected from the crashing ship; the occupants were bald, with big heads and staring eyes and crazy hands, with clear fluid for blood, no arterial structure, no animal tissue or digestive tracts; and if the occupants were like other reported UFO occupants then they were also bulletproof, flameproof, may have been susceptible to electrical overload and might have reanimated at any given time with individual parts functioning when detached from the whole. Later in the story, a female scientist, exactly like the nurse at Roswell, excuses herself to go lie down because examination of the occupant has made her decidedly queasy and a little upset.

There's a problem with the story just related, however—it comes from RKO's 1951 movie, Howard Hawks' world-famous classic *The Thing from Another World,* based on a well-known novella called "Who Goes There?" by Don A. Stuart (the pen-name of John W. Campbell, Jr.). Which raises an inevitable question: how did filmmakers in 1951 know facts about the most top secret occurrence in human history, which had happened only four years before? Lucky guess?

If so, they had another phenomenally close surmise to accompany those already mentioned: the facts of Project Twinkle. A meteor expert talking about meteors not being able to fly horizontal to the Earth or to seemingly change trajectory is in the movie. Dr. Lincoln La Paz said the same things in 1948. But, as the documentation clearly shows, all branches connected to Project Twinkle considered this to be top secret material. The first place such facts were published was in Captain Ed Ruppelt's memoirs, in 1956, after having been declassified. Again: where did Hollywood filmmakers come up with it— five years earlier—in 1951?

Coincidence, perhaps. And coincidental, also, that the occupant is repeatedly referred to as a "man from Mars," though how the scientists in the movie determine the craft is from Mars is never mentioned. Of course, it could just be a colloquial expression, but given all the facts discussed in this study it is of more than passing interest—as is the fact that the first published research connecting Mars and UFO activity did not occur until more than a decade after the making of this movie, being the findings of Jacques and Janine Vallee in conjunction with the French astrophysicist Pierre Guérin.

Besides, the movie was made from a science-fiction novella, written in the pulp days of the 1930s. Surely John W. Campbell, Jr.—

himself a magazine editor who inspired such later sci-fi authors as Robert Heinlein (whose name will be noted again in context of the UFO educational program), A. E. Van Vogt, Isaac Asimov, and Theodore Sturgeon—did not prophesy any of these connections in advance of their discovery, and how could Hollywood be held accountable for what another man wrote? But then, *The Thing* has very little in connection with Campbell's original story. In "Who Goes There?" the saucer crash occurs thousands of years before the action, and the Arctic team unearths an entirely different-looking creature from the one used in the movie. The story has a polymorphic shapeshifter, capable of imitating any life form perfectly, its original form being a tentacled, three-eyed horror. A recent AMC (American Movie Channel) showing of the movie related, in its pre-show publicity teaser, that the filmmakers wanted to come up with the scariest monster imaginable. If so, they failed miserably. The movie monster is just James Arness (in his first film role) in an over-sized bald head, with accented brow and spiked fingers, a makeup reportedly so frightening that it caused one woman who saw it to go into hysterics. This last is frankly unbelievable, since character actors Tor Johnson and Rondo Hatton looked much more frightening than this without any makeup at all, and no one reacted to them in such a way. Aside from which, in comparison with the monster described in the story—which truly was frightening—the makeup on Arness falls comically short.

Perhaps Hollywood was unable to duplicate such a terrifying creature believably. Certainly, special effects were still primitive back then, and the violent shapeshifting scenes would have been difficult, at the very least, to adequately pull off. John Carpenter and Universal studios remade *The Thing* thirty-two years later, almost exactly as Campbell wrote it, with genuinely eye-popping effects. The threat of this monster was that, being the perfect parasite, if it got free into the world it would be able to destroy and replace the entire human race with itself. Unable to realistically portray such a threat in 1951, Hawks and Company appear to have chosen their "plant man" (which is their explanation for why the thing is bulletproof and without blood or animal tissue) as the next best thing, a creature that could bud and reproduce by the millions, threatening the entire human race by virtue of the fact that its favorite food is mammalian blood. By itself, this would be a perfectly rational explanation for the change. But the appearance of the end product being so similar to actual flying saucer occupants—except for the height—is amazing, as are the multiplicative coincidences in its nature, and the nature of the saucer crash and recovery. And it is documented, in Jim Wynorski's *They Came from Outer Space,* that screenwriter Charles Lederer did initially hew to Campbell's original vision, but for some reason or another—by implication, because someone higher in the production chain of authority ordered it so—altered the monster: "In the first draft screenplay, the monster came the closest to resembling Campbell's original description of a hunched-over anthropoid with three eyes, rubbery blue hair and razor-sharp tentacles. However, in succeeding rewrites, the Thing's appearance was ultimately changed to that of a giant, hairless Frankenstein-like humanoid."

The Thing turns out to be a completely hostile entity, against which the military is shown to be wise in taking a hard and violent stance. The scientist in the movie is portrayed as foolish in his desire to learn more from the visitor, even if it should cost the lives of the entire Arctic party. The journalist (unlike any in real life) finally radioes his story to humanity, saying that Earth successfully defended itself against the first invader from another planet, and utters the famous last words: "And remember to watch the skies—keep watching the skies!"

RKO, as a subsidiary of Time-Life, was directly connected to the CIA—which should be no surprise, since RKO was owned by billionaire industrialist/aeronautic engineer Howard Hughes, whose very name was synonymous with government interests. Many other studios and directors who made low-budget science-fiction pictures, especially those dealing with flying saucers, were similarly connected to the CIA and other agencies. In 1957, Hughes sold RKO, at which time Metro Goldwyn Mayer bought its last flying saucer film, made in Japan with Toho: *The Mysterians.* MGM has turned out more UFO-logical movies than any other studio except United Artists, and (as if to emphasize the point) MGM and United Artists fused into a single corporate entity in 1980. Many of the people involved behind the scenes in the production of those movies, at the highest level—including one of the most prominent CIA figures in mind control, William Joseph Bryan, Jr.—are to be found working on the same projects at other studios, such as the next most prominent on the UFO-logical list, American International Pictures ... which, as Orion Pictures Corporation, is presently being taken over by MGM/UA. Such a surfeit of bad flying saucer movies with robots would be produced in ensuing years, from these and other studios, that they would become first a laughingstock and ultimately a nostalgic institution, which was precisely what they were intended to be from the outset. A psychological strategy was employed to deflect public attention from the subject by ridicule, that both then and now has been perhaps the most successful counterintelligence program ever undertaken.

Before this can be fully appreciated, more has to be understood about the actual UFO phenomenon itself. The Roswell saucer, its hieroglyphics and its robots, were but the tip of a more complex iceberg that comprised the most secretive study ever conducted by the government. What they would learn in the course of their investigation would be astounding—and it would also be accurately reflected, for decades to follow, in a massive number of the worst movies ever made.

2

Mesmerizations and Assassinations

The year 1947 was extremely active for the United States government. Edward Ruppelt noted "the UFO security lid was down tight" by the end of July—the month of the Roswell recovery. Only two months later, on September 18, President Harry Truman—a Mason with a latent love of secret societies—formed the Central Intelligence Agency when he signed the National Security Act. It had begun the year before, as the Central Intelligence Group, and the party thrown for its formation included party favors for all the guests, from Truman himself, of cloaks and daggers and black hats. Initially intended according to its charter to be nothing more than its name implied, the CIA's purpose was to collect and collate information from every other branch of military intelligence. Spying and clandestine activities were nowhere mentioned in its charter, but the clever Truman provided a "loophole" in his bill stating that the CIA could perform "other functions" at the discretion of the National Security Council, said functions never being specified. That loophole made the CIA, in the words of journalist Jonathan Vankin, "a fully functioning, government-sanctioned, secret society." Shortly after, on December 17, 1947, the United States Army Air Force was formed into a separate bureaucracy, becoming instead the USAF.

From the very beginning, the study of UFOs was perhaps the foremost of the CIA's activities. And from the time of its formation, it became involved in a much better documented study, of far more questionable ethics and legality: mind control. "CIA officials started preliminary work on drugs and hypnosis shortly after the Agency's creation in 1947," writes State Department officer John Marks, in his groundbreaking study, *The Search for the "Manchurian Candidate": The CIA and Mind Control.* Why this should have been the primary field of interest for an organization of supposed paper-pushers, especially so early on, is a question well worth pondering. The generally stated reasons were the brainwashing of Cardinal Mindszenty and the brainwashing of POWs in the Korean War—but Mindszenty's rather obvious mental conditioning was not witnessed until 1949, two years after the CIA's formation, and the appearance of seemingly drugged or brainwashed American POWs did not begin until 1952. At that time, several prisoners of war made televised statements reviling the United States, all of which seemed to be coming from non-coerced individuals—even once liberated from any influence of their former captors, these former prisoners refused to come home. The State Department was puzzled and deeply concerned, resulting in a Pentagon pronouncement on April 3, 1953, that any liberated Korean War POW who refused repatriation after being recovered from a camp was to be classified as a deserter, and shot on sight.

The Agency itself quickly branched into several different departments, nearly all of which had become involved in the study of mind control by the spring of 1950. On April 20 of that year, the first Director of Central Intelligence (DCI), Admiral Roscoe Hillenkoetter, approved Security Chief Colonel Sheffield Edwards' special project code-named BLUEBIRD, which aimed to assemble special interrogation teams for foreign use. Each team was to operate only with permission of a high-level committee (which it didn't always bother to get) and consisted of three members: a psychiatrist, a technician, and an expert hypnotist who could operate a polygraph (lie detector). Nazi concentration camp records and Nuremberg transcripts were carefully studied but yielded nothing of value—though Edwards commented, "How the victims coped was interesting." By the end of 1950, forty-year-old Morse Allen, of the former communist-hunting Civil Service Commission of the 1930s, became head of BLUEBIRD, extending its research into the most questionable of areas.

The specific goal, as stated in numerous documents from every branch of the CIA, was to find a way of "controlling an individual to the point where he will do our bidding against his will and even against such fundamental laws of nature as self-preservation." Though the stated reason for this was to discover defensive measures against foreign use of such techniques, "the line between offense and defense—if it ever existed—soon became so blurred as to be meaningless," as Marks puts it. So did any scruples attached to the research. BLUEBIRD teams were specifically ordered to keep their true research and techniques secret from any U.S. military authorities in whatever country they happened to be working. Their experiments quickly expanded, under Morse Allen, into the chemical realm and beyond by the end of 1951. Seconal and Dexedrine were early chemicals tested. Between 1951 and 1956, the new synthetic drug D-lysergic acid diethylamide (LSD), which had been discovered in 1938, became the drug of choice, and the Agency tested the use of hypnosis and electroshock specifically to produce amnesia above and beyond the desired mind control. Their program even extended to the realm of "neurosurgical techniques," experimenting with behavior-controlling brain implants.

Though initial studies were conducted with at least some degree of responsibility, they rapidly got out of hand. Between 1950 and 1952, under Allen, BLUEBIRD was rechristened ARTICHOKE and swiftly lost all semblance of morals or ethics. Where members first agreed to test LSD only on themselves, for instance, they later got to spiking each other's food or drink without warning as a control. The latter technique brought about at least one suicide and a few other accidents, for the very simple reason that, without any warning, everyone might spike the office water cooler on the same day, resulting in a massive dose of a chemical that is of questionable safety in the first place. Once the project became noticeably dangerous, the Agency took its experiments outside to the bordellos they held jointly with the Mafia, known as "safe houses." There, they spiked unsuspecting "guests'" drinks with their LSD, studying the results from behind two-way mirrors, in what they called operation "Midnight Climax."

Even at that point in the testing, the ARTICHOKE group was voluntarily submitting itself to such dangerous laboratory procedures—but Allen took it outside the immediate group in order to practice experiments that could become "terminal." For obvious reasons, many doctors approached for such potentially lethal experimentation turned the Agency down, but there were others who did not. The worst offender was one of Canada's supposed guiding lights in the field of psychiatry and humane treatment of patients, Dr. Ewan Cameron. Cameron had no scruples concerning the experimental use of drugs, psychosurgery, electroshock, and sleep-deprivation, especially when he was being handsomely paid $19,000 a year for his efforts, in secret and laundered funds, by the American CIA. It is conceivable he did not know the Agency was his benefactor, since they decided to fund him through one of their screens in order to keep him ignorant—in which case, they selected Cameron simply because his already twisted methods were convenient to their purposes, saving them the need for persuasion. His megalomaniacal desire was to find a cure for schizophrenia, and to create both partial and complete amnesia, theoretically to cause an individual to forget only his schizophrenic behavior without losing his identity. He did not succeed. Even the ruthless Allen reported that Cameron's techniques only seemed to succeed at the "creation of a vegetable."

The collective name of the CIA's mind-control project has since come to be known as MK-ULTRA. The letters designated a Technical Services Staff operation, with "ULTRA" being the Second World War's most devastating OSS success, the breaking of Hitler's ENIGMA code. MK-ULTRA operated from 1953 until 1964, then to be rechristened MK-SEARCH until the programs' supposed termination in 1973. Three days before forming MK-ULTRA, CIA director Allen Dulles gave a completely fraudulent speech to a Princeton University audience denouncing Soviet "brain perversion techniques ... so subtle and so abhorrent to our way of life that we have recoiled from facing up to them," knowing full well from Agency memoranda that "no indication of

Red use of chemicals" had been discovered. The formation of MK-ULTRA occurred on the same day the Pentagon pronounced sentence on all defecting Korean War POWs, and was stepped-up—at least in theory—precisely to try and find a way to understand and combat such brainwashing techniques as the Chinese appeared able to employ.

MK-ULTRA also absorbed lesser concurrent "MK" projects, such as DELTA, a straight chemical-assassination program using pioneered medical breakthroughs in toxin development specifically funded by the Agency. Many of its activities were brought out in open Congressional hearings during the Carter administration. Richard Helms gave the program its most famous nomer—the same Richard Helms who was convicted of lying to Congress during Watergate, and the subject of Thomas Powers' *The Man Who Kept the Secrets.* His specific aim was to gain control of human behavior by "covert use of chemical and biological materials," and as to the ruthlessness of his methods, he answered simply with, "We are not Boy Scouts."

The most interesting thing about the ongoing and all-consuming CIA study of mind-control is that, from the very beginning, they knew the Russians and Chinese did not have any such capability. Ten weeks before Dulles gave his Princeton speech, he already knew from secret CIA memoranda of January 14, 1953, that "Apparently their major emphasis is on the development of specially-trained teams without the use of narcotics, hypnosis or special mechanical devices." The term "brainwashing" itself was coined by one of the Agency's own propaganda-meisters from the former OSS, Edward Hunter, when he published an entirely false article on the subject for a September 1950 *Miami News* article, titled "'Brain-Washing' Tactics Force Chinese into Ranks of Communist Party." Hunter was one of many CIA operatives working under the guise of a responsible journalist. He continued a long stream of articles on this entirely fake subject, also making up a Chinese word, *hsi-nao,* "to cleanse the mind," to supposedly document his work. As he wrote, Hunter was fully aware of U.S. Army studies which "failed to reveal even one conclusively documented case of the actual 'brainwashing' of an American prisoner of war in Korea."

Writes Marks:

[A] careful reading of the contemporaneous CIA documents . . . indicates that if the Russians were scoring breakthroughs in the behavior-control field—whose author they almost certainly were not—the CIA lacked intelligence to prove that. For example, a 1952 Security document, which admittedly had an ax to grind with the Office of Scientific Intelligence, called the data gathered on the Soviet programs "extremely poor." The author noted that the Agency's information was based on "second- or third-hand rumors, unsupported statements and unfactual data." Apparently, the fears and fantasies aroused by the Mindszenty trial and the subsequent Korean War "brainwashing" furor outstripped the facts on hand. The prevalent CIA notion of a "mind-control gap" was as much of a myth as the later bomber and missile "gaps." In any case, beyond the defensive curiosity, mind control took on a momentum of its own.

The only area that either the Russians or Chinese had worked substantially on in mind control was at the group level, utilizing traditional brainwashing techniques. Their methods should be instantly recognizable not only to students of cults, but of the Third Reich and the Reagan Era. First, all individuality is subsumed into the group. Everyone is gradually conditioned into performing the same way, dressing the same way, and eventually thinking the same way—put simply, "marching in lockstep." "Group therapy" is perpetual, all members picking on each other when they find any lack of conformity. Pleasures are gradually taken away, one by one, as work for the whole is increased—first smoking, say, then enjoyable foods, recreational activities, etc.—and this is initiated by getting the group to recognize that these activities are somehow counterproductive or "unhealthy," causing them to believe that surrender of those "detrimental" activities was their own idea and not anyone else's. Increased work is emphasized, along with the notion of self-sacrifice.

Pity and ridicule are employed against anyone who fails to "see the light" in the group program. As the dissenters eventually come around—which they almost invariably will, simply out of the basic human need for acceptance—lavish praise and warmth are given them by the others, helping them solidify their new orientation. Physical activity is emphasized; any intellectual pursuit heavily discouraged. Authority is acknowledged to be all. For Hitler, it was the *"Arbeit macht frei"* ethic—"Work makes us free"—with all classical education ridiculed and discouraged, as an emphasis on national physical fitness was grossly overemphasized; for Reagan, it was the hammering of the Protestant Work Ethic, the steady and pervasive infiltration of "physical fitness" programs in the corporate workplace and in advertising, and a progressively virulent attack on smoking, "fat foods" (which quickly progressed to the persecution of fat people), and any Union that might oppose the unquestionable wisdom of Corporate Management.

As dire as it sounds, evidence exists to speculate on CIA activity behind the death cults of Matamoros and Jonestown. Matamoros quasi-Santeria drug cult leader Adolfo de Jesus Constanzo's name was allegedly found in downed Contra pilot and CIA contractor Eugene Hasenfus' address book. Though it is easy to dismiss such charges as being of no consequence without hard evidence, it is also important to remember a comment made just over fifteen years ago by former State Department officer John Marks, referring to illegal medical experiments being performed on California prisoners at Vacaville: "During the late 1960s and early 1970s, it seemed that every radical on the West Coast was saying that the CIA was up to strange things in behavior modification at Vacaville. Like many of yesterday's conspiracy theories, this one turned out to be true." So did such "allegations" as the CIA's direct involvement in the drug business, since documented to have occurred in the Vietnam heroin connection and in violations against the Drug Enforcement Agency on supposed South American "sting" operations; such revelations make the idea of a similar connection in Matamoros conceivable. Where allegations will not stand up in a court of law, an organization with the incredible power and unaccountability of the CIA has to expect them—unless they plan on opening their files for public scrutiny, as they were forced to do to some extent with MK-ULTRA.

That the cult of the Reverend Jim Jones might have been one of the CIA's group mind-control experiments was officially suggested in a UC-Berkeley psychology professor's 1980 paper entitled "The Penal Colony," sent to murdered Congressman Leo Ryan's aide, Joseph Holzinger. Holzinger was just then becoming suspicious of CIA involvement in the massacre himself, having discovered that twenty-year Agency veteran Richard Dwyer had been at Jonestown before, during, and after the event. Dwyer had been witnessed "methodically" washing his hands after the murder of investigating Senator Leo Ryan and four reporters on the airstrip where they had landed, sporting a leg wound and admitting that he had been "stripping the dead. It's not a nice job." Then he returned to Jonestown apparently to clean up some evidence of that massacre before witnesses could arrive. That Dwyer had been at Jonestown itself while the mass-suicide/murder actually took place is proven by a surviving tape of the incident with Jones' own voice shouting for someone to "Get Dwyer out of here!" According to Guyanese coroner Leslie Mootoo, the vast majority of the Jonestown fatalities (as many as seven-hundred) had not been suicides, as reported by the press, but forced injections of cyanide; and numerous psychotherapeutic drugs such as Valium had escaped Dwyer's clean-up attentions at the site—none of which could even be considered surprising, since the assassins who murdered Ryan's party were reported to have looked glassy-eyed and zombie-like during their lethal attack.

Far from a random, disenfranchised, lone madman, Jones himself was a far right-wing Republican who raised funds for Richard Nixon in the 1960s and lived for eleven months in Brazil "like a rich man," with his neighbors openly stating that they believed he was working for the CIA. According to multiple award-winning journalist Jonathan Vankin (the editor of San Jose, California's, alternative weekly newspaper, *Metro*) a surviving family member of Jonestown victims wrote that Jones was a Marxist heavily connected to both Cuba and Russia, which could be dismissed as angry rhetoric if it weren't for the fact that Jones did meet frequently enough with Soviet officials to joke with his followers that the CIA had "infiltrated" their commune. In addition, one of Jones' closest advisers was a mercenary of the CIA-supported Angolan UNITA rebel army.

If the CIA had been running a mind-control experiment in Guyana, it would have been easy for them to do so right beneath the nose of United States officials: U.S. Ambassador to Guyana, John Burke, went on to work for the CIA's "intelligence community staff" after Jonestown, and embassy official Richard McCoy was a self-admitted U.S. Air Force counterintelligence agent. Despite all the facts, the House Permanent Select Committee on Intelligence announced that "no evidence" existed to connect the CIA to Jonestown. "The American government running its own concentration camp at Jonestown," reflects Vankin, "a brainwashing laboratory whose specimens spilled into the public view. Unthinkable. No more unthinkable, though, than 913 people swallowing cyanide at the command of a lone madman."

The various Cold War "gaps" easily explain the continuance of the individual brainwashing lie for monetary profit, but an important question remains: why did the CIA involve itself in such devastatingly dangerous mind-control experiments in the first place? And from virtually the very day of its formation? Was it merely a latent Nazi desire to discover a way of controlling local populations? Or could there have been a more practical reason? If the Russians and Chinese were incapable of such exotic mind control, and the Nazis had not attained it, then who might have possessed such a capability that would make the particular field of study so incredibly secretive and important—worth the risk even of civilian human lives?

An answer may be found today by studying the available cases of UFO abductees. Reliable data on their number cannot be known, because officially, no government body or statistical record-keeping organization has kept track of such studies, though Jacques Vallee stated in 1990 that "over 600 abductees have been interrogated by UFO researchers, sometimes assisted by clinical psychologists." Estimates from the experts go as high as one in forty among the general populace—or, more specifically, "from several hundred thousand to several million Americans"—having been at one time or another abducted, based on a Roper survey taken in 1991 of nearly six thousand Americans employing the symptoms listed. Attempts to gauge an accurate psychological profile of abductees have been unsuccessful, it being discovered that they come from all socioeconomic backgrounds, all races, all ages, and both sexes. No consistent pattern for their having been targeted has emerged, save two: they were either in the right place at the right time, generally somewhere very remote, or either or both parents were also abductees.

Following publication of Budd Hopkins' *Missing Time* in 1981, psychologist Dr. Elizabeth Slater was employed by Hopkins, UFO researcher Ted Bloecher, and psychologist Dr. Aphrodite Clamar—who has sat in on many of Hopkins' hypnotic regression sessions with abductees and remains reserved concerning the question of UFO reality—to conduct a study on "Nine Psychologicals," not being told beforehand that their only known commonality was that all claimed or were believed by a team of psychologists and UFO researchers to have been abducted aboard a UFO. Slater was to first determine whether or not they suffered any mental disorder, and second, to see if "certain psychological characteristics or physical attributes might predispose one to such an experience." The tests employed were the MMPI, Wechsler Adult Intelligence Scale, the TAT (Thematic Apperception Test), the Rorschach, and projective drawings. Her fifteen-page report, published by FUFOR (Fund for UFO Research), discovered a few similarities among the subjects, who were five males and four females between twenty-five and forty, three of the women and one of the men unmarried, and four of the men divorced, three with post-graduate degrees and all college-educated. They were a college photography instructor, an electronics expert, an audio technician and salesman, an actor who was also a tennis instructor, a corporate lawyer, a commercial artist, an executive, a chemical lab director, and a secretary. Some had done varying degrees of prior reading on the subject of UFOs.

Slater determined that they were "very distinctive, unusual and interesting," and except for one subject "did not represent an ordinary cross-section of the population" (about which she did not specify), and were widely divergent personality types, from "flamboyantly exhibitionistic and dramatic with an exaggerated display of emotions" to "quite shy, sensitive and reticent," with a "tendency toward mildly paranoid thinking" that she specified was not pathological, "but rather [an] oversensitivity, defensiveness and fear of criticism, and susceptibility to feeling pressured." She noted that they were sometimes overanxious, as well as wary and cautious. They were at best "highly creative and original" and at worst "beset by intense emotional upheaval," and had "relatively high intelligence with concomitant richness of inner life."

There was no mental illness, but two-thirds of the group sometimes showed "a loss of reality testing along with confused and disordered thinking that can be bizarre," which she equated to "transient psychotic experience." All had a modicum of "narcissistic disturbance" in the areas of "identity . . . lowered self-esteem, relative egocentricity and/or lack of emotional maturity," lacking "solidity and coherence in their experience of selfhood," especially in "sexual identity confusion." This last gave them a "concomitant vulnerability in the interpersonal realm" and "a certain orientation toward alertness which is manifest . . . in a certain perceptual sophistication and awareness or in interpersonal hypervigilance and caution."

An interesting side-note to this study is that famous UFO-debunker and long-suspected CIA-asset Philip J. Klass gave the report to another team of psychiatrists for an "objective" analysis, which was immediately betrayed to be far from the desired objectivity by the phrasing, "One does not have to be certifiably insane to believe in UFO experiences. There are other emotional disturbances, states and conditions that make one vulnerable to the development of such mistaken beliefs and/or misperceptions." If the investigators could not accept the real possibility of a UFO abduction, then their bias could only affect their analysis. Unlike Dr. Slater, they knew in advance that the subjects in question believed themselves to have been abducted, and predetermined that they could only be wrong.

By contrast, Slater—once the believed commonality tying her test subjects together was revealed to her and she then read Hopkins' book—wrote that while her tests could do nothing to prove the truth of an actual UFO abduction, "one can conclude that the test findings are not inconsistent with the possibility that reported abductions have, in fact, occurred." She also believed it possible that all of their symptoms may have related to some other, undetected, under-lying aspect of their lives—"There is really no way of knowing." She concluded that *"The answer is a firm no"* (italics Slater's own) as to whether severe mental disorders were present in any of the test sub-jects. Nor were they pathological liars, paranoid schizophrenics, or any other "rare hysteroid" personality, though she considered it pos-sible—even as she emphasized that such states are extremely uncom-mon—that they might have the dissociative mechanisms of a fugue state or multiple personality neurosis, which ". . . is very subtle and difficult to detect . . . and careful interviewing is needed to firmly rule out its presence." In short, where the group might have various rare neuroses, its members were in no way mentally ill. She recommended further testing on a wider variety of subjects, which has since loosely been done, Pulitzer Prize-winning Harvard psychiatrist Dr. John E. Mack and Temple University history professor David M. Jacobs improving the scientific quantification of the study.

Slater determined that "a surprising degree of inner turmoil as well as a great degree of wariness and distrust" were present in each member of the group, which was not surprising "if one considers the skepticism and disrepute that is typically encountered with reports of UFO sightings and abductions," which would not only be "char-acteriz[ed] as inherently traumatic, but we must add . . . would likely carry social stigmatization as well. Moreover, assuming for the sake of argument that abduction has actually occurred and that presum-ably its occurrence would be very rare, it then becomes something which cannot be readily shared with others as a means of obtaining emotional support." She emphasized that this last, especially, could lead to "a deep sense of shame, secretiveness and social alienation." She wrote that "the closest analogy might be the interpersonal alien-ation of the rape victim, who has been violated most brutally but somehow becomes tainted by virtue of the crime against her."

Slater explained this further by adding, "It will be recalled that subjects typically recalled having been subject both to mind control and an even more basic loss of motoric function—i.e., they reported that they seemed to have been physically transported to the UFOs and had somehow been stripped of any mental capacity to resist physically. Events such as these, when one is denied every opportunity for even minimal forms of mastery, can only be characterized as psychologically traumatic." Earlier, she had emphasized the point by saying that, "Certainly such an unexpected, random, and literally otherworldly experience as UFO abduction, during which the individual has absolutely no control over the outcome, constitutes a trauma of major proportions." Jacques Vallee had made a virtually identical assessment in a heavily edited paper almost two decades before—one of only two from a reluctantly admitted 279 on file that the National Security Agency released via the Freedom of Information Act—to account for "high strangeness" in UFO witnesses.

M.D. Rima Laibow, a Dobbs Ferry, New York, psychiatrist, of Albert Einstein College of Medicine in New York City, did her own study of eleven abductees she personally worked with and sixty-five other case studies. She diagnosed them as having PTSD, or Post-Traumatic Stress Disorder, commonly thought of as "Vietnam Vet's Disease," which is believed possible only where event-level trauma has occurred—i.e., an actual physical event, as opposed to any internally generated fantasy. Where she expected to find varying individual fantasies, she instead found the subjects' UFO abduction stories remarkably similar. Her conclusions were virtually identical to Dr. Slater's.

Senior clinical psychologist at St. Vincent's Hospital in New York, Dr. Jean Mundy, also diagnosed claimed UFO abductees as suffering from PTSD, with no symptoms of the mentally disturbed. "This is how people who have experienced terrible trauma react," she wrote, "people who were holocaust victims, or Vietnam veterans, or rape victims. We don't know the nature of the trauma they experienced, but we know it's not their imagination; it's something real that hit them from the outside, and in that sense it's something 'real.'" Aphrodite Clamar's assessment concurs: "The people I have seen who claim to have had a strange encounter of whatever kind are run-of-the-mill people, neither psycho nor psychic, people like you and me. I could find no common thread that ties them together—other than their UFO experience—and no common pathology; indeed, no discernible pathology at all."

In 1986, University of Wyoming counselor Dr. June Parnell published a 110-page paper titled, "Personality characteristics on the MMPI, 16PF and ACL tests, of persons who claim UFO experiences." Her tests were applied to 225 UFO witnesses/experiencers of all types. She found that abductees were "self-sufficient, resourceful, and preferring their own decisions," and had "a high level of psychic energy." She described their characteristics as "above-average intelligence, assertiveness, a tendency to be experimenting thinkers, a tendency toward a reserved attitude, and a tendency toward defensiveness. There was also a high level of the following traits in these deep-encounter witnesses: 'being suspicious or distrustful . . . creative and imaginative. . . .'" In short, except for the assertiveness of personality (which would indicate self-esteem), her assessment matched that of Dr. Slater.

Also in 1986, Eastern Michigan University sociology professor Dr. Ronald Westrum classified what he calls Post-Abduction Syndrome (PAS), which matches PTSD except in three important regards: abductee memories are repressed *whether they want to repress them or not,* when in many cases they do very much want to remember; the repression occurs *with or without* any violent physical trauma, being imposed from an external source by means unknown; and lastly, the syndrome is not only the product of a past trauma, *but also of ongoing events*—i.e., not only is the individual repressing memories from a former event, but living in anticipation of more to come that will also have to be repressed. This last is an extremely important point, it having been discovered by all researchers into UFO abductions that they are rarely, if ever, single-time occurrences, but literally lifelong repeat contacts—moreover, they almost invariably begin in childhood, even infancy.

Premiere abductologist Budd Hopkins describes abductees as "extremely attractive, interesting, intelligent people . . . [but with] self-doubt, even a kind of odd shame about their experiences, preclud[ing] a kind of easy, relaxed interaction with other people . . . The degree of success of many, many people I've worked with is enormous, yet they don't really believe in it themselves. One person is a nationally known star in the entertainment business; another person is a self-made millionaire from a poverty-stricken background, with a very important place in the real world—yet neither of these people has the self-esteem of Dan Quayle ... There's an enormous disparity between their actual talents and abilities, their actual accomplishments, and the way they view themselves. And I think that's one of the legacies of these experiences." He adds that he finds them to be "open-minded [and] accept[ing] a wide-range of possibility, and yet that person has a lot of trouble, which they shouldn't be having, with relationships and self-esteem and everything else," and that "there are very, very few successful relationships" among them.

Dr. David Jacobs, friend, colleague, and protégé of Budd Hopkins, takes a slightly less negative view than his predecessor in the field. He acknowledges that there are many abductees who have a hard time dealing with the long-term trauma of their experiences, but also stresses, "Many abductees have adjusted well to the abduction phenomenon and are able to lead their lives free from the disruption that these experiences can cause. A few abductees feel that in some way they have been enlightened and even prepared for some future benevolent purpose. Some, who have not investigated their experiences, have successfully integrated the barely remembered events into their daily belief structure, whether it is religious, New Age, or pragmatic ('Don't strange things happen to all people?'), and the experiences become little more than a psychological irritant." Their Post-Abduction Syndrome, he notes, "lead[s] both men and women to question their mental stability. They are often extremely introspective, having continually ruminated about their odd behavior— both sexual and otherwise—for most of their lives." He notes the same personal isolation reported by others and considers most abductees to be "emotionally fragile," but also finds them "brave and resilient," with "fierce determination to gain control over their lives," and is surprised at how many "retain their sense of humor and their optimism."

The introspection Jacobs comments upon has been called "absorption" by others, an ability to virtually tune out all external stimuli while still being able to interact with others and perform normal functions, the whole while being deeply absorbed in thought on entirely other matters which are usually of a personal nature. The sexual "oddness" he reports comes from the "sexually bizarre nature of the event [that] is retained deep within the unconscious mind." Behavioral indications include excessive masturbation, intense one-night-stands, long stretches without any interpersonal sexual relationships at all (yet being continually preoccupied with the subject, especially in fantasies), and marked proclivities toward dominance/ submission or bondage and discipline scenarios. Other observations of abductees have included their seeming to be somewhat morally self-righteous—which, in an age with inverted morals might simply mean that they exhibit any sense of morality at all—and are emotionally somewhat removed or distant. They are generally good-humored and well-liked but don't make much effort to stand out in a crowd. It has been noticed by several researchers that abductees frequently tend to become friends or lovers with each other, neither party initially knowing (as they often don't know it themselves) that the other is also an abductee.

But abductees have two vital elements in common with the CIA's interests in mind control. One is that their entire experience—during and after—involves hypnosis and mind control employed by an outside power. The other element is that they often tend to identify themselves more with their abductors than with anyone in their daily life.

It was this latter symptom, dubbed the "Stockholm Syndrome," that so concerned the government with America's Korean War POWs, and certainly it would have concerned them no less with an even more foreign power. Victims of this syndrome are chronically traumatized, threatened with repetitive violence or pain, given unpredictable rewards and punishments which they do not understand in the enforcement of equally unpredictable "rules," and are denied control even over their own bodily functions. With their own sense of self-control so severely demolished, the victims will sometimes identify themselves with their brutal captor-aggressors, simply to maintain some belief that they have chosen something for themselves. This can result in amnesia later, when the oppressive conditions are no longer present, due to the desire not to remember the horror endured. Many UFO abductees actually profess to feeling guilty when caused to remember their experiences through hypnotic regression, as though they are "betraying" their abductors, and even use that very word. They claim to have a dual identity, or secret life, their "other self" being the one who cooperates with the abductors—and frequently feel much more comfortable in that other, secret identity and life than in their own on Earth.

Dr. Mack, in his study, *Abduction: Human Encounters with Aliens,* sees the cooperation of abductees with their UFO kidnappers as something much different: "It is true that abductees may experience terror and some pain with the examination performed on them. The aliens' abductions are also in many ways unpredictable, sometimes frightening and sometimes rewarding. However, in contrast to the narrow and self-serving purposes of human abusers and political kidnappers, the beings reveal a shared purpose, and offer the possibility of opening to an inclusive, more expansive worldview that is powerfully internalized by many abductees." He states that, in his view, "abductees come to feel a more authentic identification with the purposes of the whole phenomenon than occurs, for example, in hostage situations."

The standard abduction experience has been laid out best by David Jacobs in *Secret Life,* based on personal experience with 60 abductees and familiarization with approximately 240 more. The procedures do not always occur in the same order, and not all abductees undergo the entire spectrum of experiences. The target is first picked up by the abductor-beings and transferred to the ship, where they disrobe to be given a quick medical examination and have implants secured, removed, or replaced—such implants have in fact been recovered and examined by Dr. David Pritchard of MIT, among others. A machine-scanner, frequently described as looking like a giant eye, goes over their body, enveloping them in an extremely bright light. Sometimes a pain test is undergone, or anaesthetized surgical techniques of indeterminate nature, and cures of any diseases the abductee may have also occur.

Tissue samples are invariably taken, including skin, blood, and sperm or ova, and women sometimes have very immature fetuses either implanted or removed from their wombs. A slightly different being, sometimes like those that escort the subject aboard the craft and sometimes reported as being much more insectoid-looking, "mindscans" the abductee. This process is described as being completely overwhelming and intense, and often extremely pleasant, during which they feel information is both imparted and retrieved, though they cannot remember any specifics concerning it later— sometimes they are told they will remember "when the time is right." Often they are given a tour of the ship, shown displays on screens, and/or put into interactive scenarios seemingly for instructive purposes or to gauge their response to different situations.

The subject is put into a pool of liquid in which they can breathe, and sometimes has sex there (or somewhere else) with either a human subject, whom they may or may not know, or perhaps one of the "Grays." Eventually, most have offspring who are brought back to see them on a semi-regular basis, from infancy through adolescence and perhaps beyond, which are generally described as human though some believe they may be "hybrids" of some sort. The process over, the abductee is returned, their memory somehow erased—or at least severely jumbled—concerning the entire incident, which they will remember as an especially vivid dream, if they remember it at all.

It is this last that is the key point of identical interest in the CIA's MK-ULTRA program: the entire process appears to be mind-controlled, hypnosis and hypnotic amnesia employed first to conduct it, then cover its tracks. Virtually all researchers in the abduction phenomenon have indicated that they believe hypnosis is employed by the UFO Intelligence. There are excellent reasons to believe they are correct, above and beyond the obvious surface facts. One is that hypnotic regression enables the abductees to remember most of what has been erased from their memory, indicating that the same key was utilized to lock those memories away in the first place. Another is that all abductees recall being very cold during the experience. Though that coldness may partly be due to actual environmental conditions, deep-hypnotic subjects also feel very cold when coming out of trance.

An excellent example of this is provided by Dr. Philip H. Melanson in *The Robert F. Kennedy Assassination,* describing Sirhan Sirhan's occasional inexplicable fits of sudden shivering. Sirhan's defense psychiatrist, Bernard Diamond—though he did not believe Sirhan could have been programmed to commit an assassination—was certain he had been hypnotized before, because his own sessions with him showed all the symptoms:

> Before the trial, when Dr. Diamond first hypnotized Sirhan in his cell, the session was traumatic for the prisoner. Author [Robert Blair] Kaiser described Sirhan's voice as high-pitched and punctuated by deep breaths. When Dr. Kaiser slapped Sirhan's face and brought him out of the trance, he made "wheezing sounds." Shortly thereafter, he started to shiver, complaining of the cold and hugging himself to keep warm. The cell was reportedly quite warm (it was summer in California), except for Sirhan. Another example of Sirhan's unexplained shivering came early in the hours immediately following the shooting, when LAPD brought in the jail's medical examiner, Dr. Marcus Crahan, to check the prisoner. During the examination, the prisoner began to shiver violently, embracing himself to keep warm. "It's chilly," Sirhan mumbled. "You're *cold?*" asked the doctor in surprise, because the room was comfortably warm. "Not cold," said Sirhan. "*Not* cold. What do you mean?" "No comment," the prisoner responded. Sirhan may have reacted this way because he was coming out of a trance on both occasions.

William Turner and Jonn Christian, in *The Assassination of Robert F. Kennedy: The Conspiracy and Coverup,* also describe the same symptoms as "a clue of withdrawal from the hypnotic state." Recounting another incident of Diamond's hypnosis sessions, they state, "when [he] put Sirhan into a deep trance to try and fathom a motive . . . his subject slipped into an even deeper trance, sobbing and causing the doctor considerable alarm. As Diamond snapped him out of it, Sirhan began trembling, and goose bumps surfaced on his arms. 'Doc, it's cold,' he complained." Hypnosis expert Richard St. Charles, and the pre-eminent authority on the subject, Dr. Herbert Spiegel—who "unequivocally designated Sirhan a Grade 5, placing him in the 5 to 10 percent of the general population who are the most susceptible to being hypnotized"—also determined that Sirhan had been hypnotically programmed, as did a most interesting and mysterious Svengali named William Joseph Bryan, Jr., whose case will be studied later. Spiegel is the man who came up with the Hypnotic Induction Profile, which professionally defines the "clinically identifiable configuration of personality traits" that comprise any individual's hypnotizability.

Budd Hopkins has said that Dr. Clamar's non-UFO-related hypnotic patients rarely report feeling cold, but that abductees almost invariably do, and he believes that it must mean the interiors of the craft into which the abductees are taken must therefore be very cold. This is certainly possible, but obviously there is expert testimony to the deep-hypnosis state creating such a sensation. Given the testimony, it would seem likelier that Dr. Clamar's patients simply have not been taken to such a deep level of hypnosis as that which is part of the process of mind control—which obviously is not a practice she would be endeavoring to duplicate, or even study.

Another reason to believe that hypnosis is being employed on abductees is that they often report being given seemingly meaningless lists to repeatedly look over, and for some reason memorize, which is a technique employed by hypnotists to further secure their control. During a filmed demonstration of hypnoprogramming for NBC in 1967, Spiegel invented a nonexistent list of three names—which he convinced his Grade 5 subject were written on a blank sheet of paper—to "look over" while in a trance. Spiegel's subject was a forty-year-old liberal New York businessman, and the demonstration was done in order to show that Jim Garrison may have been hypnotizing some of his Kennedy assassination witnesses in the Clay Shaw trial. The segment was deemed "too graphic," potentially "frightening" to viewers, and never aired. Turner and Christian, who viewed the videotape, recount the entire demonstration, which was performed before anchorman Frank McGee:

> After a brief warm-up with the subject, Spiegel is seen achieving a quick induction. "Try to open your eyes, you can't," he tells the subject, whose eyelids quiver but remain shut. [Spiegel] confides

that there exists a Communist plot aimed at controlling television and paving the way for a takeover. "You will alert the networks to it," he instructs. Then he shifts the subject from formal or deep trance to the posthypnotic condition where his eyes open and he appears normal. At this point Spiegel explains . . . that the subject is in the grip of what he terms the "compulsive triad": (1) he has no memory of having been under hypnosis; (2) he feels a compulsive need to conform to the signal given under hypnosis; and (3) he resorts to rationalizations to conform to the instructions of this signal. Glaring accusingly at McGee, the subject launches into an "exposé" of the Communist threat to the networks. He talks about dupes in the media and how they are brainwashing the entire nation. "I have a friend in the media," he says, "but friendship should stop when the nation is in peril." Spiegel suggests the name Jack Harris at random, and the subject readily adopts the name as that of his duped friend. The rationalization has set in. McGee hands him a blank pad on which he says three names are written. The subject nods. Yes, those are the men who were at a Communist cell meeting in a theater loft over a restaurant. Spiegel snaps his fingers 1-2-3, reinstating the formal trance. With his eyes closed, the subject persists in the same argument about Communist penetration of the media. He names Harris as a ringleader. McGee argues against the subject, and as he increases the pressure of his rebuttal the subject slips into a deepening paranoiac depression. Spiegel snaps him out of the trance. The subject can't remember a thing. Later, when the videotape [of the entire session] is run for him, his face mirrors disbelief as he hears and sees himself sloganeering in Birch Society rhetoric. "I can't conceive of myself saying those things," he protests, "because I don't think that way."

David Jacobs cites one example of exactly such a list, which a UFO abductee was told to memorize "because there's war, and I'll need to know these names," even though the abductee openly said he made no attempt to actively commit the list to memory. "He said he would make me remember it," the abductee said, another of the numerous examples of someone being told they would remember something "when the time is right." This becomes especially interesting given that a great many abductees appear to undergo repeat training in the operation of various instruments aboard the craft, including actually flying them—knowledge of which is unavailable to them at any time except when they are with their abductors. Jacobs relates that "[Some abductees] have been shown an intricate 'control board,' or some such apparatus, and told to operate it. The abductee complains that she does not know how to do it, but the aliens insist that she do it anyway. She then goes to 'operate' the board and finds that she can in some way do what they want." The first published account of this kind of activity was in 1987, in Budd Hopkins' *Intruders*. Kathie Davis reported being handed an unidentifiable object—a "shimmering box." Hopkins writes, "The gray figure handed her the box, telling her to look at it, and then took it away with the observation—delivered telepathically—that when she saw it again, she would understand its purpose."

Hopkins does admit the implication "...that abductees could, from time to time, be made to act as surrogates for their abductors," but—despite a natural tendency to view the entire phenomenon as negative—prefers not to "dwell on any of these paranoia-inducing theories." But assuredly the government must have "dwelled" on exactly such ideas, as it surely also noticed many years in advance everything abduction researchers are now discovering and making public. Whether or not any untoward intentions exist on the part of the UFO Intelligence, it would be naive to assume that it had not crossed someone's mind to ponder whether or not such training could be related to later invasion purposes, with abductees fulfilling the function of a fifth-column vanguard. In fact, if someone in the government had not questioned it, they quite simply would not have been doing their job very well. As already noted in the introduction, UFO sabotage of nuclear sites was a regular occurrence from the beginning of the phenomenon in the modern age.

At least one piece of evidence exists for the theory of abductees used for purposes of sabotage by the UFO Intelligence, in the case of Hector Aguiar. Aguiar took four excellent photos of a flying saucer on Piata Beach, Salvador, Brazil, on April 24, 1959. After taking the photos, he lost consciousness and so suffered a missing-time experience, which is rather common. When he woke up, he found himself clutching a note written in his own hand that he had no memory of writing: "ATOMIC EXPERIMENTS FOR WARLIKE PURPOSES SHALL BE DEFINITELY STOPPED . . . THE EQUILIBRIUM OF THE UNIVERSE IS THREATENED. WE WILL REMAIN VIGILANT AND READY TO INTERFERE." If the UFO Intelligence could cause a man to write a note he had no memory of writing, then it is certainly within the realm of possibility that it could employ him to assist in acts of sabotage.

The theory of abductee-saboteurs is strengthened by events that occurred immediately following—and some probably preceding—the Roswell crash in 1947. Even casual observation of the available literature on the subject reveals the most obvious and consistent thing about UFOs: they are intimately involved with the world's military and industrial forces, *especially in acts of sabotage*. The most important evidence concerning this question lies in the most probable reason a flying saucer was in the proximity of Roswell in the first place, and the greatest reason for the government's keeping it secret: in 1947, Roswell Army Air Field was the only location in the world in possession of an atomic bomb.

The busiest and best documented of UFO sabotage activities occurred in 1966 and '67 in Point Pleasant, West Virginia, and neighboring Ohio across the river, with numerous UFO sightings and reports of a mysterious creature the press dubbed "Mothman." Mothman was about six (perhaps even seven) feet tall, gray, faceless except for two huge, glowing red "bug-eyes" with "hypnotic effect," and sported instead of arms two folding wings, which never flapped, but were used solely for gliding whenever Mothman levitated silently up into the air. He tracked cars at between 70 to 100 miles per hour, or possibly even greater since the people fleeing him were so anxious to escape they didn't always notice their speedometers.

Journalist John A. Keel, himself a repeat witness to UFOs for several decades, documented the sightings and occurrences at length in *The Mothman Prophecies*. Eighteen-year-old Connie Carpenter, described by Keel as shy and sensitive, saw Mothman when she drove by a golf course on her way home from church at about 10:30 AM on November 27, 1966. Mothman flew straight at her from a hovering position and fixed his hypnotic red eyes on her, causing her to drive off in panic. She developed conjunctivitis for two weeks—"pink eye," frequently caused by exposure to extremely bright lights or ultraviolet radiation (actinic rays), and a common feature of UFO witnesses and abductees. Hers was an extremely typical report—over 100 people related identical or similar incidents throughout the winter.

UFOs began being reported in record number during this flap as early as March of 1966, especially along the eastern seaboard. From a notorious UFO haunt south of Warrington, England, in Preston Brook/Daresbury, came reports of a creature like Mothman during the same time period, as well as Salt Lake City, Utah, and Scott, Mississippi. A "birdman" or "batman" was also seen subsequently in many locations during other UFO flaps, such as southeast Texas in January-February 1976, and the taiga in Russia (one of the country's most intensive military-industrial areas) in 1991. During the Point Pleasant Mothman sightings UFOs were seen consistently in very interesting locations: one was hovering over schools; another was chasing Red Cross bloodmobiles (at least once attempting to grab hold of them with mechanical extensor arms before being chased off by approaching traffic in isolated areas); a third was around lover's lanes, surprising necking teenagers and causing some of them to "lose a few hours" (certifying that "missing time" in abductions was known at least as early as the mid-1960s); and, most importantly, over and in military-industrial weapons sites.

Mothman's favorite haunt was the one hundred or so "igloos" scattered about the wooded West Virginia countryside about seven miles outside of Point Pleasant in the 2,500-acre McClintic Wildlife Station, which beginning in WWII had been built, camouflaged, and connected by a network of underground tunnels to house high explosives. The igloos were concrete domes with heavy steel doors, which were theoretically stripped of most of their lethal contents after the war and given to the county as possible storage vaults. They were then sold to LFC Chemicals and Trojan-U.S. Powder Company, with some leased to American Cyanamid. Never known before as a haunted territory, these igloos became the most regular visitation site of Moth-man, beginning at least as early as November 15, 1966. It was the next day, November 16—following four different people's sightings of the creature in the area—that the press came up with the nomer "Mothman," believed to derive from the then-popular *Batman* series on T.V.

Mothman appears to have been an airborne variation on the Grays, performing many of the same activities. Keel himself reported that the creature made a metallic sound when on the roof of the TNT sheds, having witnessed its presence along with a sizeable party more or less "on safari" one night to find him. In addition to his metallic-sounding feet, there are other good indicators of his being a robot: a dog was found dead at a site where he had been spotted—it had been barking at something the night before and was later found crushed, something a machine could easily accomplish—and wit-nesses reported Mothman making a "mechanical humming sound" as he flew overhead, one saying specifically that the sound was "like a squeaky fan belt." Other dogs disappeared from the area completely during the flap, and, in common with many UFO waves to follow, animals were found mutilated.

Author William Christian, after viewing the videotape of the 1967 NBC hypnosis session, asked Dr. Spiegel, "Tell me, if you had stuck a gun in the subject's hand and instructed him to shoot McGee, what would have happened?" and the hypnosis expert answered, "Ah, the ultimate question. I'm afraid he might have shot him." And deter-mining exactly the truth of that "ultimate question" was, specifi-cally, the goal of MK-ULTRA. John Keel also was one of the earliest speculators on UFO contactees being used not only as saboteurs, but as killers. He wrote in *The Mothman Prophecies:* "I was concerned . . . with a more worrisome question. What, I wondered, happened to the bodies of these people [UFO contactees] while their minds were taking trips? Trips that lasted for hours, even for days. A young col-lege professor in New York State was haunted by the same question in 1967. After investigating a UFO-related poltergeist case he . . . was led to believe that he had committed a daring jewel robbery while he was in a trance or possessed state. He abandoned ufology and nearly suffered a total nervous breakdown in the aftermath. Were our contactees being used by exterior intelligences to carry out crimes, even murder? The answer is a disturbing yes." He then drew attention to the similarity in mind control between UFO contactees and political assassins throughout the ages, exactly as the CIA's MK-ULTRA program appears to have done. Though he failed to prove his case (no UFO abductee has ever been shown to be connected to a murder or related crime), Keel suggested UFO-controlled contactees as the cause for the collapse of Point Pleasant's Silver Bridge on December 15, 1967—though he admitted it had been old and was never in great shape anyway—on the basis of unidentified men seen crawling around its sides a few days before the tragedy, implied foreknowledge of the event by the UFO Intelligence, and UFO activity around the area as it happened.

The subject of hypnosis for the purpose of assassination was first broached for a mass audience in the 1962 (released in '63) United Artists movie *The Manchurian Candidate,* which was taken out of circulation immediately after opening because of the Kennedy assassination. The novel was written by Richard Condon in 1959. What not many people knew was that exactly such mind-control experiments had been one of the CIA's primary interests since the Korean War, being the basis of their entire MK-ULTRA program. *The Manchurian Candidate* is about the narcohypnotic programming of controlled assassins. In the movie, survivors of a Korean War experience return to the States with the same peculiar, debilitating psychological problem, which began for all of them during a weekend out on maneuvers that none of them can remember the slightest thing about. They all have recurring nightmares of murder. In all cases, they dream themselves being in a friendly gathering—a privileged white officer sees himself among country club patrons, a black enlisted man sees himself at a church gathering of old black women—where they are the central topic of conversation. The chief speaker at the gathering keeps shifting from the friendlier, more familiar figure to that of a Chinese officer, and some of the assembled guests occasionally seem, for some reason, to be wearing Russian uniforms. At one point, the central figure asks them how they feel about someone sitting next to them, and they respond that they like that person just fine. The central figure asks them to pick up a gun or scarf and shoot or strangle that person. They do—and wake up screaming.

Officer Frank Sinatra finds himself unable to sleep or concentrate, and begins to realize what is happening when he encounters a Korean manservant helping his former superior, Laurence Harvey—the man's face is familiar and breaks the memory bubble that was keeping Sinatra amnesiac. Reporting back to base, he reminds the officers there that, on his return from Korea, when asked how he liked Harvey, he had responded, "He is the kindest, bravest, warmest, most wonderful human being I have ever known in my life," when in fact he couldn't stand him. In fact, all the men in Harvey's unit responded with exactly the same phrase while going abruptly slack-jawed whenever asked the same question, and they felt no better about him than Sinatra. The generals show Sinatra pictures from their files, and he recognizes two from his dreams, who just happen to be a Chinese expert in brainwashing and a Russian officer engaged in similar research. Realizing they have all been part of a mind-control experiment, Sinatra tries to help Harvey remember and break the spell, meanwhile asking him, "What have they built you to do?"

The answer is that Harvey is the most successful of the hypnotic subjects from the group and has been programmed to assassinate a presidential candidate toward the end of putting a Communist-sympathizer in the Oval Office. He is regularly kept tabs on and visited by his Chinese controller, who reinforces his previous conditioning and post-hypnotically erases all memory of each event. His trigger is the Queen of Hearts from any deck of playing cards. Whenever his controller wants him, he simply calls on the phone and suggests, "Why don't you pass the time by playing a little solitaire?" And in the process of doing so, as soon as Harvey comes across the Queen of Hearts, he follows his prearranged commands.

It is worth mentioning, given the facts considered in this study, that when Harvey's character is first return-visited by his Red Chinese and Russian programmers to ensure that his hypnoprogramming is still intact, it has been two years since his initial abduction and conditioning occurred—and two years just happens to be the period of Martian oppositions, when maximum UFO activity invariably occurs. The reconditioning in the movie takes two to three weeks at periodic intervals, which is about the same time period most UFO abductees have their "dreams" in any given cycle. As if to underscore the connection, Sinatra's fiancée in the movie, Janet Leigh, gratuitously mentions (it being discovered that, like Sinatra, she happens to be an orphan), "I used to be convinced that, as a baby, I was the sole survivor of a spaceship that overshot Mars."

Details pried from CIA records on MK-ULTRA via the Freedom of Information Act show that the CIA was deeply involved in hypnotic programming and successful to at least some degree in its experiments. A January 1954 Agency memo attests to the fact that they unquestionably were at work trying to resolve the "hypothetical problem" of programming hypnotic assassins. The paper names an individual (deleted from the document) and asks whether he could be induced by a "trigger mechanism" to "perform [an] attempted act of assassination at a later date ... to be accomplished at one involuntary uncontrolled social meeting. After the act of attempted assassination is performed, it is assumed that the subject would be taken into custody by [the particular government in question, deleted] and disposed of." The proposed target was "a prominent politician [of the foreign country] or if necessary an American official."

One of the Agency's most prominent assets, Dr. William Joseph Bryan, Jr., *The Manchurian Candidate*'s technical adviser and (in his own words) "chief of all medical survival training for the United States Air Force, which meant the brainwashing section" during the Korean War, proudly said he could program a suitable candidate—which constituted approximately five percent of the population—to fire blanks at someone in three months, and real bullets in six. The claim concerning the blanks, at least, was subsequently proven by Morse Allen, the CIA's first in-depth hypnosis investigator and behavioral research czar for ARTICHOKE. On February 19, 1954, Allen succeeded in getting his secretary to fire a gun full of blanks at a woman she had been hypnotized into believing was a romantic rival; not only did he manage that neat little trick, but he also succeeded in giving her hypnotically induced amnesia, the poor woman insisting that she would never shoot anyone and having no recollection whatsoever of the incident.

Among his many witnessed feats of hypnotic prowess, Bryan performed impromptu sessions to demonstrate that he could create controlled anaesthesia entirely by hypnosis, stick his subjects with needles without their crying out, and literally command them when to bleed and when to stop bleeding. Interestingly, a book authored by Bryan, *Religious Aspects of Hypnosis,* contained information on its roots going back to ancient Egyptian "sleep temples"; AMORC, the Ancient Mystical Order of the Rosicrucians to which Sirhan Sirhan was attachéd, has an Egyptian museum at its San Jose headquarters. Bryan was found guilty of unethical behavior in multiple hypnosis cases for seducing his female patients, and had his hypnotherapy license suspended for five years in 1969.

An inveterate egotist, Bryan's greatest claim to fame was his having been the hypnotist of the Boston Strangler, Albert Di Salvo, and also of executed "Hollywood Strangler" Harvey Bush. He boasted himself as "the leading expert in the world," able to "hypnotize everybody in this office in five minutes." Hours before Sirhan Sirhan was identified as Robert F. Kennedy's murderer, and only hours after the event, Bryan announced on Ray Briem's KABC radio talk show that the suspect was probably acting under post-hypnotic suggestion. He was famous for telling his many call-girls, among others, that he had hypnotized Sirhan Sirhan (though officially he never had any contact with the man either before or after the fact), and Bryan belonged to the same extremely small fundamentalist Roman Catholic sect as David Ferrie, one of the mysterious suicide witnesses in Jim Garrison's Kennedy assassination investigation. Even more interesting, especially in light of Bryan's *The Manchurian Candidate* connection, is that numerous witnesses at the Robert Kennedy assassination reported seeing a "woman in a polka-dot dress" with Sirhan before the fact, who was heard saying, "We shot him," seeming quite pleased, as she hurriedly left the scene after the shots were fired. Something striking and unusual, especially connected to some powerful emotional stimulus (of which none is more powerful than sex), was considered by the hypnotists consulted by the MK-ULTRA bunch to be the best trigger for a post-hypnotic command: Laurence Harvey's strikingly beautiful love (Leslie Parrish) costumed as the Queen of Hearts in the movie; a woman in a polka-dot dress, perhaps, in real life.

Sirhan had no plausible motive, no recollection of the deed after the fact, wildly claimed to have planned the assassination for twenty years (he was only twenty-four), and had atypically and incoherently scribbled repeated phrases in his diary that day such as "RFK must die" and "please pay to the order of," over and over again. Dr. Bernard Diamond, Sirhan's defense psychiatrist and expert hypnotist, was certain that Sirhan had been hypnotized prior to his act because he went under at the snap of a finger and showed all the signs, but believed he must have done it to himself because the idea of a Manchurian Candidate was, to him, a "crazy, crackpot theory." This, despite the fact that whenever he asked Sirhan why he was writing so crazily in his diary, he scribbled over and over in capital letters, "MIND CONTROL MIND CONTROL MIND CONTROL." Interestingly also, in light of Bryan's most famous case, Sirhan wrote "Di Salvo" repeatedly in his diary, with no professed knowledge of who anyone named Di Salvo was. A former U.S. Intelligence officer gave Sirhan a Psychological Stress Evaluation test, much more sophisticated than usual polygraphs, and stated, "Everything in the PSE charts tells me that someone else was involved in the assassination—and that Sirhan was programmed through hypnosis to kill R.F.K." Bryan's secretary told New York reporter Betsy Langman on June 18, 1974, that Bryan had received an emergency call to go to Laurel, Maryland, immediately after George Wallace was shot there by Arthur Bremer on May 15, 1972.

The best evidence that American International Pictures was connected to the Intelligence world is to be found in Bryan: he was the technical advisor listed in the credits for the hypnosis sequence in "The Facts in the Case of M. Valdemar" segment of producer/director Roger Corman's *Tales of Terror* in 1962, and also contributed to a gimmicky prologue called the "D-13 Test" for Francis Ford Coppola's first feature of any note through AIP/Filmgroup the following year, *Dementia 13*. The latter featured a scene in which Patrick Magee cleverly hypnotizes a murder suspect in a pub, causing him to betray his secret. The former had hypnosis as its central element, Poe's horrific tale in which a man's soul is trapped inside his dead body because his will is held prisoner by an evil hypnotist. There is literally no conceivable reason for a hypnotist of Bryan's caliber to be spending his time advising on low-budget drive-in flicks, save that someone at AIP was connected to government Intelligence at the same level he was. Otherwise, how would anyone there even have known his credentials to hire him? He was serving as technical consultant to *The Manchurian Candidate* the same year he served as hypnosis advisor on Roger Corman's movie, but that indicates more than anything that his caliber of work was far above Corman's standard fare. Though Bryan is nowhere listed on *The Manchurian Candidate*'s actual credits, his peers corroborate his claim to having been the film's official consultant according to RFK assassination researchers Dr. Philip H. Melanson, William Turner, and Jonn Christian. If Bryan's fee wasn't too high for American International to begin with, there would still be no reason for him to stoop to what were considered low-brow horror films—unless he was doing someone a favor.

"Mesmerism" was also the central element in the most notorious of Corman's legendary AIP "quickies," 1963's *The Terror*. The plot concerned a Napoleonic era witch's revenge upon her daughter's murderer, by hypnotizing a woman into impersonating the victim to haunt the killer and ultimately spring a death trap on him. "She knows not what she does—her will is not her own," the witch's unwilling servant warns lovestruck Jack Nicholson, the film's protagonist. "She is possessed! You are in great danger!" It is interesting to note that American International Pictures was seriously utilizing the same hypnotic elements as shown in the higher-budgeted and mass-audience-promoted *The Manchurian Candidate* at least six years in advance of it, with *The She Creature* and several pictures that followed, and that the same hypnosis expert connected to *Candidate* was also connected to AIP. It is also interesting that, of many little coups Corman could have boasted of in his 1991 autobiography, he nowhere mentions his association with the famous William J. Bryan, Jr.

Bryan died "from natural causes" (heart attack) at the age of fifty in a Vegas motel room in 1977, the verdict announced without an autopsy. Though Bryan has not been linked to James Earl Ray in any way, it has been established by William Turner and Jonn Christian that Ray did consult with a hypnotist going by the name Xavier von Koss immediately before the assassination of Martin Luther King, Jr., while still in Los Angeles. Interestingly, the LAPD was awarded a $10,000 grant from the American Express Company in October of 1977 for "pioneer work in developing hypnosis as an investigative technique." Bryan was fond of boasting how often he helped the LAPD with murder cases.

Long before Rodney King and Chief Daryl Gates, the LAPD was a notoriously corrupt bureaucracy. Five-year intelligence officer for the LAPD, Mike Rothmiller, wrote a 1992 best-seller called *L.A. Secret Police: Inside the LAPD Elite Spy Network,* documenting that since 1959's dictatorial and ambitious Chief Parker (he wanted J. Edgar Hoover's job), there was a secret and nearly omnipotent spy network within the police, "operating like the KGB, blessed with ties to the CIA, and led by men who were obsessed with power." This same Chief Parker was *Star Trek* creator Gene Roddenberry's personal mentor, Roddenberry serving as LAPD historian and Parker's protégé before producing his famous show (see Chapter 6).

The story is lent corroboration by none other than CIA veteran Victor Marchetti, who in a 1975 interview with Betsy Langman "related that in 1967 he saw LAPD and Chicago officers at Langley, the CIA headquarters in Virginia," according to Turner and Christian. "There were about a dozen in the Los Angeles contingent who, Marchetti was assured, were part of a 'sensitive project' that had been given the green light by the director himself. For their part, the police departments carried out surveillance and break-ins on behalf of the CIA and performed other Agency odd jobs."

Dr. Philip H. Melanson, while researching his book *The Robert F. Kennedy Assassination,* interviewed a hypnosis expert he identified pseudonymously as "Dr. Jonathan Reisner." Reisner was linked with Bryan by several witnesses, and when the MK-ULTRA hypnosis files were declassified, another expert's first comment after reading them was that they looked like a textbook written by Reisner. Reisner admitted having known Bryan but denied any involvement with him, and also denied any involvement with the CIA or MK-ULTRA, even though one of his colleagues pointed out that the man had a gap of several years in his professional career that could best be explained by his working intensively with the government. Reisner, like Bryan, tried to claim credit for being *The Manchurian Candidate*'s technical adviser, even as he insisted that a hypno-programmed assassin was an impossibility. He asked Melanson if he was familiar with the Candy Jones case and said it also was impossible.

Candy Jones was an attractive Chicago cover-girl in whom a submerged personality named "Arlene Grant" emerged in 1973 while undergoing therapeutic hypnosis by her husband, WMCA late-night New York City radio talk show host "Long John" Nebel. The experience was so bizarre that she soon underwent further sessions with a professional hypnotist, uncovering details of Arlene Grant's life. Donald Bain documented the case in *The Control of Candy Jones*, three years later. She claimed to have been openly approached by the CIA in 1960 to work as a courier for them, then to have been hypnotized into doing the job for free, sometimes being tortured while on foreign assignment, all the while entirely amnesiac of the events after the fact. She said she had been taken by her controller to the CIA's Washington headquarters, along with other hypnotic subjects, to be tortured up to the point of having lit candles stuck into her vagina without feeling pain, all as part of a demonstration—such demonstrations are documented to have been done under Morse Allen, though not to that extent. Bain stated in his book that, at the time of his writing, Jones was still subject to her personality change by prearranged phone signals.

One of Jones' claims was that her controller, whom she specified was then dead, programmed her to be his lover, and that she remembered hearing him mention something about a racetrack and bragging about hypnotizing Sirhan Sirhan—Sirhan's activities around a Mafia racetrack and at a horse ranch have been documented, and Bryan's boasts about hypnotizing Sirhan have been attested to by many. John Marks, on studying her account, was convinced that the details she reported matched too closely the only recently released documents then in his possession on MK-ULTRA to possibly have been made up. Interestingly enough, Gerold Frank, author of *The Boston Strangler*—Bryan's most famous hypnosis case—blurbed Bain's book with, "If you think mind control and brainwashing belong in the realm of science fiction, read this—and be shattered." Dr. Herbert Spiegel, who arranged the 1967 NBC hypnosis demonstration, and WWII ULTRA-insider William Stevenson, also blurbed it. Spiegel even wrote the Foreword.

Despite his insistence that Manchurian Candidates and the Candy Jones case were impossible, Dr. Reisner told Melanson, "There was a real problem with that book [*Candy Jones*]. I haven't told too many people about it. There was supposed to be a doctor described in that book and, except that he was supposed to be in northern California, people could have thought it was me. I told the publishers that; I threatened to sue. You see, the problem was that I dated Candy a couple of times way back ... when she was a model." There was another "real problem" he might have mentioned: it has been documented that women exactly like Candy Jones were targets of CIA mind-control experiments from the very start, and that the Agency was specifically trying to create a totally separate and amnesiac—not to mention controllable—personality inside hypnotic subjects. Melanson stated in his book that he was convinced Reisner tried to hypnotize *him* during the interview—Melanson had read enough by that point to recognize the signs.

Both John Hinckley and Mark David Chapman also showed evidence of having been mind-controlled, prior to their attacks. among his travels, Chapman went to the Beirut YMCA, of all bizarre places (his second choice after Russia, no less), which Fenton Bresler and premiere conspiracy researcher Mae Brussel have claimed was a CIA initiation camp for desensitizing recruits to violence—and if it isn't, it certainly could be. Chapman was never obsessed with John Lennon, as was so often claimed in the news, and in fact was not even interested in him until shortly before the murder. On his last day as a security guard, Chapman wrote Lennon's name where his own should have been in the checkout sheet, then crossed it out and corrected it. Following the murder, he waited calmly in place to be arrested, and curiously enough seemed to know exactly where Lennon would be for the shooting. Clues tying him to the murder were neatly arranged in his hotel room, as if someone wanted to make sure they would be found in case Chapman wasn't. Where sex might not have been overtly used as a trigger in his case, the bizarre fixation with *The Catcher in the Rye* may have served the purpose instead.

Suppressed by both the courts and the media was Hinckley's own assertion that he had been acting as part of a conspiracy. The October 21, 1981, *New York Times* reported a Justice Department source "confirm[ing] a report that John W. Hinckley, Jr., had written in papers confiscated from his cell in July that he was part of a conspiracy when he shot President Reagan and three other men March 30." The prison guards who had seized Hinckley's papers gave their testimony in secret to the judge, who ordered the attorneys and witnesses involved not to publicly divulge any of the papers' contents. Reagan himself did not feel the shot—which admittedly might have been simply a delayed reaction, though it is far from certain—until after he was inside the presidential limousine. The official FBI story is that the bullet that hit Reagan, however, did in fact ricochet off the door of the limousine as the president was being pushed inside— which is especially curious given that it was a Devastator bullet and should have exploded on such contact even before entering Reagan's body.

And just what John Hinckley, Jr., was doing stalking Mae Brussel shortly before his attempt on Reagan is a question that seems never to have been asked by theoretically responsible investigative reporters, even when the FBI compiled a report on the incident after the fact. That Hinckley's father was a good friend of George Bush's, and that his brother had a dinner arrangement with Neil Bush (of the Silverado Savings and Loan scandal fame) on exactly the same date as John shot President Reagan conveniently misses being published, except by Jonathan Vankin. Also unasked is just where he came up with exploding and poisonous .22 caliber lead azide "Devastator" bullets, which are not exactly available over the counter. Hinckley "anonymously" tipped off the FBI in advance that he intended to kill Reagan—why would he do such a thing? He was dosed with a number of psychotropic (mood-altering) drugs, including Valium, at the time of his shooting, all prescribed by a hometown psychiatrist. And, like the Queen of Hearts or the Girl in the Polka-Dot Dress, he could easily have been programmed to be triggered by Jodie Foster, whose prior communications with Hinckley (instigated by him, not her) might have been arranged by someone with nefarious purposes she had no inkling of.

Nor are these even isolated incidents. Gerald Ford was shot at by two separate parties while president, making the number of "lone nuts" grow higher and more preposterous. The historical model prior to Lee Harvey Oswald—with the possible exception of John Wilkes Booth, though he is coming to be considered by many historians to have been a member of a conspiracy—shows that lone assassins do not attack political figures. Their sudden proliferation since 1963 can then only be regarded with the utmost suspicion, especially when both the motive and the means for such political murders exists within the Intelligence/organized crime communities. Recently, one pilot committed suicide by ramming his plane into the White House, directly where President Clinton could reasonably have been expected to be, another man opened fire at the same location with an automatic weapon, and a third was caught scaling the fence with an unloaded machine gun. The question of just how many "lone nuts" could be out there certainly has never been more timely.

If it was theoretically Columbia's 1976 movie *Taxi Driver* that inspired John Hinckley to try impressing Jodie Foster by killing President Reagan, what is the excuse for identically-threatened actions the same year by Michael Berke, stalker of "Golden Girl" T.V. newswoman Jessica Savitch? Berke, a neatly dressed twenty-two-year-old Nebraska farmer, made his way into Savitch's temporary office at the *Today* show on April 20, 1981, where she was substituting for a week for Jane Pauley, and frightened her with his "strange, haunted look" and his overpowering desire to talk to her and touch her. She shut him out on the other side of the door, huddled under the desk, and called security. The next day, she received a letter from Berke saying that he intended to "murder John Swearman"—an entirely fictitious political figure—to "get your attention . . . I realize that as I mull my duty in the luxury of this Hilton hotel room, I only hope my historical deed will win your love and your respect." He sent along with it a poem he called "Voices in the Moving Dreams of a Sailor." Traced down by authorities, his car was found to have a photo of the White House in it, as well as other letters which implicitly threatened President Reagan, George Bush, and Alexander Haig. His behavior was identical to that of John Hinckley, only he never claimed *Taxi Driver* or any other movie as an inspiration. If he was simply imitating Hinckley's actions, he never indicated it, and his stated intention to murder a completely nonexistent person is certainly unusual. Interestingly enough, Jodie Foster had another "obsessed fan" stalking her and making death threats against Reagan, only one week following Hinckley's attempt. Given that psychoses do not spring up overnight, and that the FBI apparently had their eyes on this man for a short time prior to his stalking Foster, the question inevitably arises whether he was less a copycat than a backup.

As in the case of Hinckley, no press followup was ever done on Berke's bizarre story. Also identical to Hinckley is Berke's prior stalking of other political figures, as if building up courage for the final deed at hand. In addition to having staked out Mae Brussel, Hinckley had, in October of 1980, shortly before his attempt on Reagan, been caught—and released—with three handguns (and John Lennon buttons) in his possession at the Nashville airport. His diary explicitly detailed plans to assassinate former president Jimmy Carter, who was due there soon. The oddest thing about the entire incident is that Hinckley, despite blatant illegal transport of firearms, was detained a mere five hours, only cursorily fined, and released, and his diary which literally screamed guilt was left completely unexamined at that time.

Actress Jodie Foster features in three final interesting twists from the stranger-than-fiction department, on the subjects of UFOs and mind-control. Her first film project after the Hinckley incident (and its bizarre near-reprise) was as the young singer Trilby in an ill-received T.V. production of *Svengali,* the early pulp story of a hypnotic Rasputin-like hypnotist and mastermind. In 1997, Foster—who so violently refuses to answer any questions about the Hinckley incident that she terminates all interviews where the name comes up—consented to

play the voice of an hallucinogenic tattoo that drives a man to murder in Fox's *The X-Files*. And she is presently playing the astronomer
who finds herself contacted by extraterrestrials in the Warner Bros.
film version of the late Carl Sagan's *Contact*.

Among numerous bizarre follow-up stories and curious coincidences concerning MK-ULTRA participants (and probable participants)
is that of Candy Jones and her husband Long John Nebel. Journalist and famous UFO researcher John A. Keel reported that a probably phony contactee calling herself "Princess Moon Owl" attempted
to use Nebel's show in 1967 "[in] a blatant bid for publicity," but
that Long John was smart enough after having been tipped off not
to put her on the air. Given that such "contactees" often appear to
have been fronted by the CIA, it would seem Long John himself was
not a CIA agent or asset, otherwise he would gladly have put the
woman on. Keel himself suspected Moon Owl was exactly such a
fronted fake, saying that she went from being considered a complete
kook to "unexpectedly" becoming "respectable," suddenly having
twenty-five dollars at a crack to charitably hand out to passers-by,
expanding her popularity.

But if Long John was not under the CIA's influence, his wife Candy
certainly continued to be. Donald Bain wrote in his study of her case
that she received messages on her answering machine after her marriage to the respected radio host that almost certainly came from the
CIA. One, coming on July 3, 1973, a little over six months after the
two married, said, "Japan Airlines calling on the 0–3 July at
4:10 PM.... Please have Miss Grant call 759-9100.... She is holding
now reservation on Japan Airlines Flight 5, for the sixth of July,
Kennedy-Tokyo, with an open on to Taipei. This is per Cynthia that
we are calling. Thank you." Bain confirmed that the number was
indeed that of Japan Airlines, but the airline assured him no reservation clerk named Cynthia worked there. Reservations offices of
other airlines told Bain that they frequently got strange messages
like that which were almost certainly codes. "I cannot help but speculate," Bain wrote, "that were I with the CIA and looking for such a
code, Cynthia would be my hands-down choice for a word to indicate CIA." Both Bain and Long John reported instances such as strange

phone calls or otherwise seemingly mundane happenings—such as Candy sitting before flickering candles at a romantic dinner—that would unexpectedly trigger her personality change into "Arlene Grant," and that she would only change back to herself sometime later after disappearing for a while.

"Strangely, and fortunately," Bain reported, "Arlene never did interfere with the conduct of the six-hour-a-night talk show. She showed up at the radio station on many occasions prior to air time, flinging nasty comments at Nebel and threatening to cause a blowup. But once the red light came on, Candy seemed to be in command." Despite the fact that the disruptive "Arlene Grant" appeared to absent herself from her husband's show during his life, at least one guest on that show documented receiving inexplicably hostile behavior from her following Long John's death, when she took over hosting the show herself. The guest was the late Dr. Stephen Kaplan, a well-known and respected parapsychologist who spent the last twenty years of his life debunking the infamous Amityville Horror hoax, long before it was exposed as such. In an earlier appearance on the WMCA show, Kaplan found himself hospitably and courteously treated by both Long John and Candy, who displayed tremendous interest in his point of view. However, his return guest spot on the show on April 26, 1978, hosted by Candy alone shortly after Long John's demise, turned out to be entirely different.

WMCA had solicited Kaplan's appearance, since they were short of guests on that particular night. Kaplan had not been informed that professional magician and notorious parapsychology debunker Milbourne Christopher was also scheduled to appear at the same time—in other words, that he was being set-up for an ambush. Handling himself suitably under the circumstances, Kaplan was surprised that Christopher had not brought up the Amityville case at all, and when Kaplan tried to get a comment from him on it, Christopher would only say that "he had no opinion on the case one way or the other." As Kaplan put it, "I do not understand why Christopher and other infamous debunkers of parapsychology, such as 'The Amazing Randi' and Philip Klass, have not seized upon the Amityville Horror as a potent tool in their fight to discredit the field. For years they have wasted the public's time attacking legitimate, responsible researchers; but on the biggest, internationally known fraudulent case in history, they have all remained strangely silent."

As for Candy, she "launched an all-out verbal attack on my credentials, my experience, my cases, my book and my knowledge of the field.... At one point in the show, Candy thumbed through a stack of books on parapsychology (with the home listeners totally unaware that she was reading from books) and asked me questions such as, 'Who was J. B. Rhine's medium in 1934 and what was the title of the chapter he wrote about the case?' When I would admit to not recalling the answer, she would read the information from the book, pretending of course that she knew it all along, and comment something like, 'You call yourself a parapsychologist and you don't know about its history?!'"

Kaplan suggested that her complete turn of personality from his former experience with her was probably due to the recent death of her husband, not suggesting it had anything to do with her previous MK-ULTRA contacts. But given that she had such contacts, displayed exactly such violent mood swings under her alter-ego, and continued to be contacted by the Agency during her marriage to Long John, the possibility certainly exists that "Arlene Grant" was being used to debunk Stephen Kaplan. What makes this possibility all the more curious and intriguing is that, of all studios, it was American International that made the film version of *The Amityville Horror,* and—as Kaplan noted—the most notorious UFO debunker in the world, long-suspected Agency asset Philip Klass, refused to touch the Amityville case, which was a straw dog if ever there was one. Kaplan's thesis, culminating in his 1995 book, *The Amityville Horror Conspiracy,* was that the entire hoax had been cooked up for profit between convicted Amityville murderer Ron DeFeo, Jr., and his attorney, a charge which DeFeo's former attorney admitted to. That the Intelligence community might have leapt on that particular bandwagon is perfectly in keeping with their sponsorship of UFO contactee frauds and other circus-aura attractions of the lunatic fringe.

It could be (and has been) speculated that people claiming UFO abductions are, as in a case reported by Jacques Vallee, actually government mind-control experiments. While similarities exist in narcohypnotic subjects, there are too many differences to look for the government as the culprit behind UFO abductions; the sheer numbers, logistics involved, and evidence found exceed what could believably come from the Intelligence community. When abductees begin recovering suppressed memories, they usually do so in exactly the same manner as the "missing time" Korean War platoon in *The Manchurian Candidate,* only they remember strange little gray humanoids shifting back and forth with images of friends or loved ones instead of Chinese and Russian officers.

In drama, hypnotically superior villains were a product of the pulp-fiction of the 1930s, prompted by George Du Maurier's novel *Trilby* and its character of Svengali—who was almost certainly based on exaggerated reports of Rasputin then circulating from one of his murderers, Prince Felix Yusupov—and the 1920s German pulp-fiction character of Dr. Mabuse, but the more accurate use of these and many other elements in actual relation to UFO abductions did not greatly proliferate until the 1950s. *Trilby* was serialized in *Harper's Magazine* in 1894 and filmed for the first time in America in 1915, and Rasputin, widely believed by anyone with even minor exposure to the subject to have been a master hypnotist, was murdered in 1912.

The earliest common appearance of such villains seems to have been in the Italian *gialli* of about the 1920s—a term simply meaning "yellow," the color of the covers between which lurid pulp thrillers were published—which were in turn inspired by English "penny-dreadfuls." The German *Cabinet of Dr. Caligari* premiered in 1920, starring a ghoulishly skeletal Conrad Veidt as a "somnambulistic" murderer under the control of the diabolical title character. By 1945, the serious side of hypnosis was beginning to be dramatized, both as a potential tool for crime and for the breaking of trauma-repressed memory and amnesia, in such films as Universal's Sherlock Holmes entry, *The Woman in Green,* the title character (along with Holmes' arch-nemesis, Professor Moriarty) using hypnotic techniques to drive wealthy men to suicide after they sign over their fortunes. The same year, Alfred Hitchcock's famous Selznick International Picture, *Spellbound,* had psychiatrist Ingrid Bergman breaking through Gregory

Peck's trauma-induced childhood amnesia, in fairly realistic fashion. Running concurrent with Hitchcock's picture was *Hangover Square,* starring Laird Cregar as a psychotic dual personality, a decent and compassionate man when in his normal state, but an amnesiac murderer when in the grip of one of his "spells."

As early as 1948 and '49, only three or four years after these entries, Abbot and Costello made great sport of the potentially lethal side of hypnosis and amnesia in Universal's *Abbot and Costello Meet Frankenstein* and *Abbot and Costello Meet the Killer, Boris Karloff.* The former is interesting for the UFOlogical elements of a super-hypnotic fiend with a robotic servant (literally activated with electricity through bolts in its neck) and controlled sex-surrogates who seduce a man prior to his abduction for medical experiments. The year 1949 was also when Jean Cocteau's *Orphée* was made in France, the first film to accurately depict UFO occupants, specifically as "abductors from the Underworld."

The late 1950s saw hypnosis almost invariably treated as a threat, perhaps the only exception being Paramount's 1956 Danny Kaye vehicle, *The Court Jester,* in which the famous song-and-dance star played a klutz comically turned into a champion swordsman by the "magic" of a court witch. The same year, American International Pictures' *The She Creature,* directed by Edward L. Cahn *(Invasion of the Saucer Men, It! the Terror from Beyond Space,* etc.), was about a hypnotist able to turn his assistant into a murdering monster by means of hypnosis, a theme reprised the following year by the same studio, with the same cast and by the same director, in *Voodoo Woman.* AIP's Herman Cohen made a career out of "evil hypnosis" movies, the most famous being 1957's *I Was A Teenage Werewolf,* in which unscrupulous government scientist Whit Bissell, a special consultant to an aircraft company, discovers a perfect experimental narcohypnotic trance subject (which is determined both by psychological profile and "certain telltale marks on his body only I would recognize," such as appear consistently on UFO abductees) in troubled, latent-psychopathic teen Michael Landon, whom Bissell mind-controls into an amnesiac dual-lifed murderer. Later the same year, Cohen produced *Blood of Dracula,* which was identical to *Teenage Werewolf* only with Sandra Harrison as the juvenile delinquent hypnotically turned into a murderess. Cohen's *How to Make a Monster,* the following year, was about a Hollywood makeup man who discovers a trance-inducing chemical that makes his actors hypnotically receptive to his murderous commands and amnesiacally post-event-controlled. The mind-control information in the movie, as in *Teenage Werewolf,* was of the same accuracy as that written about in *The Manchurian Candidate* two years later, and filmed three more after that, which should be no surprise since William Joseph Bryan, Jr., was a consultant to American International Pictures. Robert H. Harris, the actor who played the mind-controlling murderer in *How To Make A Monster,* even bore an uncanny resemblance to Bryan.

1958's Allied Artists production, *Frankenstein 1970,* starred Boris Karloff as a descendant of the famous Baron, who hypnotized witnesses into forgetting the presence of his tinkered-together, blank-faced, mummy-wrapped, nocturnal robotic bedroom-abductor in the basement. Both *Horrors of the Black Museum* (AIP/Anglo-Amalgamated) in 1959—another of Herman Cohen's flicks—and *The Hypnotic Eye* (Allied Artists) in 1960 gave lectures on the dangers of hypnosis, purporting to show the horrible deeds one could be driven to if one succumbed to it, the former showing hypnosis as a tool for murder and the latter to cause people to maim themselves.

Throughout the 1960s, West Germany produced six popular movies featuring the pulp-cinema character of Norbert Jacques' novel, *Dr. Mabuse,* previously filmed by Fritz Lang in the 1920s and '30s. Mabuse was a hypnotic super-criminal who sometimes ran his crime empire from inside an asylum, a proto-Hannibal Lecter. This was not entirely fictional; the first recorded case of hypnosis being used for robbery and murder occurred in similar fashion in 1952 Denmark, when Bjorn S. Nielsen mesmerized Palle Hardrup into becoming his amnesiac criminal puppet. The case was published in Munich two years later by Dr. Heinz E. Hammerschlag, in *Hypnotism and Crime.* Hammerschlag also reported the 1934 case of a man's wife hypnotized by an outsider into becoming a prostitute and would-be murderer of her husband, who was saved only by the fact that the gun she used was unloaded during the attempt—the same feat duplicated by the CIA's Morse Allen in February of 1954, as already mentioned. This particular incident cannot have been the inspiration for pulp sci-fi fiction author Seabury Quinn's near-identical "The Brain-Thief" in the May 1930 *Weird Tales*, since his story was written four years prior to the occurrence and more than twenty before it was recorded and published. The same year Nielsen was hypnotizing Palle Hardrup into a life of crime, Erich von Stroheim was playing a scientist using artificial insemination to create a soulless woman, in *Unnatural,* another popular and oft-filmed German tale. Interestingly enough, von Stroheim was the star of perhaps the first mannequin feature film, 1929's misfire musical-drama *The Great Gabbo,* playing an egocentric and abusive ventriloquist.

In 1961, Warner Bros. produced one of the great gimmick movies of all time in Canada, a 3-D spook-show called *The Mask,* with psychiatrist Paul Stevens finding himself hypnotically possessed by an ancient Mayan sacrificial mask and repeat-abducted by its magic into a limbo realm filled with immobile- and skull-faced figures, animated statues, doppelgangers of himself, and sexually yearning women who turn to skeletons as they mate with him—and, like a previous victim of the mask, becoming an instrument of murder, to awaken with no memory of how he came to sport unidentified body markings (from the struggling of his victims). 1963's *Devil Doll* (Associated Film Distributors, U.S./England) was about a frightening stage hypnotist who could use Tibetan magic to gain control of human souls and animate killer dummies—which appear in people's rooms in the middle of the night to deliver messages, making the recipients wonder later if the event was real—and 1969's *Fear No Evil* (see Chapter 7) showed hypnosis used for memory erasure and post-event control, with trance-state repeat supernatural visitations leaving unidentified body markings on their target in the morning. Fairway-International's *The Incredibly Strange Creatures Who Stopped Living and Became Mixed-Up Zombies* (its real title, no kidding) in 1964, billed as "the first monster musical" (as was the same year's *The Horror of Party Beach,* from 20th Century Fox), featured a gypsy fortune-teller who hypnotizes patrons into becoming her slaves, then—as in *The Hypnotic Eye*—disfiguring them. Larry Buchanan's 1967–68 AIP feature, *Mars Needs*

Women (see Chapter 7), combined hypnosis with the most provocative planet in terms of the UFO question.

On television, hypnotic mind control and amnesia were seen with such frequency in the 1950s and '60s that Nickelodeon once literally ran an entire night featuring nothing but episodes from a multitude of sitcoms and half-hour dramas with amnesiac principal characters. The elements were seen in the cloak-and-dagger shows *I Spy* ("Anyplace I Hang Myself Is Home"), *The Wild, Wild West* ("The Night of the Howling Light," an episode that was essentially a direct copy of *The Manchurian Candidate),* and both the original *Batman* and the later *Batman: The Animated Series* (sometimes featuring robots). Irwin Allen's *Voyage to the Bottom of the Sea,* in its first season (1964, when the show was still dramatizing relatively realistic Cold War dramas), aired an early episode called "The Blizzard Makers," in which Werner Klemperer utilizes radio signals beamed directly into Milton Selzer's head to turn him into a mind-controlled assassin. Shortly after, "The Saboteur" dramatized Captain Crane's (David Hedison) abduction to a limbo setting, there to be subjected to electro-shock and hypnotic conditioning to become a saboteur-assassin for a faceless foreign power, and "The Enemies" starred *The Manchurian Candidate*'s Henry Silva as a sinister Oriental despot who abducted Crane and Admiral Nelson (Richard Basehart) in order to similarly condition them into killing each other.

The *Batman* and *I Spy* renditions were actually very close to true. In the former's "Fine Finny Fiends," Alfred the butler is kidnapped by the Penguin, then subjected to torture, paralysis, and hypnotic conditioning. Released, he has no awareness of the event, and so suffers missing time. Batman questions his knowledge of criminals and discovers that Alfred has no recollection of ever having seen the Penguin, which is utterly inexplicable since Batman is fully aware that Alfred knows the criminal's entire police file. Whenever Penguin or his cohorts' names come up, Alfred draws a blank and displays a strange nervous twitch, by which Batman realizes he has been hypnotized. The purpose for the abduction and brainwashing is so Penguin will have someone on the inside in an upcoming event, to incapacitate victims in advance and open the secured door for his entrance. Victor Buono's villain, "King Tut," was invented specifically for the *Batman* television show, never having appeared in the comics. He was a Yale Egyptology professor who became the separate criminal personality of King Tut when struck on the head, utterly amnesiac of his deeds when in his normal waking state. One of his episodes involved creating an ancient mind-control drug called "Abu Rabu Simbu Tu" that rendered its victims completely pliable to his commands. Similar plot devices were used by villains in other episodes scripted by the same writer, Stanley Ralph Ross, such as Catwoman's "cataphrenic" drug, and certain villains were keyed completely around hypnotic domination or unconsciousness-rendering, such as the Mad Hatter.

The *I Spy* episode has agents Kelly and Scott tracking down a number of strange suicides, all leading back to their rookie training days' Quantico class project of breaking into a U.S. government office. Unfortunately, they managed to stumble onto a double-agent manipulating the Vietnam war, who just happened to be their own instructor (again played by Henry Silva). The instructor narcohypnotized them into forgetting what they had discovered, implanting a post-hypnotic command for them to kill themselves if they should ever begin to remember. The command has become linked in their minds with the giant statue of Rodin's Thinker in the courtyard outside, and coming across the image has begun triggering the suicides.

The Wild, Wild West was less science-fictional than it appears at first glance, the actual Secret Service of the Civil War era having such an array of devices as Robert Conrad's "James West" displayed on a weekly basis. When slightly more outlandish contrivances were trotted out, they were clothed more or less believably within the technology of the time. Hypnosis and robots made more than one appearance on the series, generally under the auspices of Michael Dunn's evil dwarf genius character, Dr. Miguelito Loveless. The last episode featuring the character, "The Night of Miguelito's Revenge," featured both elements. Loveless has a robot servant, but it is crudely mechanical and attached to a keyboard panel for operation, a repeated device from the first season's "The Night of the Puppeteer," in which a madman with super-marionettes terrorizes West. Loveless abducts West in "Miguelito's Revenge" almost exactly in accordance with what is known about UFO abductions today: once West is comfortable in a chair, Loveless gently chloroforms him so he is unaware that he is being put under, then transports him a few miles away to a den prepared with theatrical trappings, giving him a little show of enigmatic clues when he groggily revives. After the performance, West is again knocked out and returned to where he came from, waking up two hours later and thinking he has only been asleep for a minute or two—"missing time." When West discovers that his latest mystery to solve contains many of the elements he saw in his "dream," he knows that he has somehow been drugged and abducted precisely for the purpose of satisfying his adversary's perverse sense of fair play by means of foul.

ITV/ABC's *The Avengers,* which often dramatized sinister scenarios involving hypnosis and mind control, debuted in England in 1961. In it, Patrick Macnee's John Steed was originally a fairly realistic combination of spy and supersleuth for the state, belonging to some shadowy outfit between Scotland Yard and MI-5 or -6. From 1965 to the show's end in 1969, the show changed directions. The sexually adventurous and somewhat kinky Diana Rigg was brought in to play Steed's tiger-lithe assistant, Emma Peel (a play on "M" for "Man"-Appeal), and stories began tending toward the science-fictional. While a standard number of purely human criminals were paraded by for their due trouncing, new threats were encountered—most notably, those prominent UFOlogical mainstays, robots.

"The Cybernauts" introduced robots as both abductors and killers, proving so popular that they were brought back for a reprise both in the initial series and its brief 1970s reincarnation, also being the villains of a recent commemorative novel. The cybernauts themselves look like UFO Grays, with blank metal faces only crudely etched onto their surfaces. They are disguised in street clothes, with overcoats, Homburg hat, gloves and—most interestingly—large, dark sunglasses. Their being called cyber-nauts is most curious in itself: *nautes* is Greek for "sailor," and of course is applied to our own "astro"-nauts; why *The Avengers'* production team would apply that particular suffix to metal men who never sail or fly anything in the story is something to ponder. Other robots and killer computers periodically popped up, such as "Thingumajig," an automated weapon, "Killer," a computer-trap for spies, and "The House that Jack Built," a lethal, fully automated house. Punch and Judy puppets were the bosses behind a gang of killer clowns in "Look (Stop Me if You've Heard this One) but there were these Two Fellers" and "How to Succeed . . . at Murder" featured a schizophrenic madman keeping the illusion of his dead wife alive in a ventriloquist's dummy which runs an assassins' ring, a theme often reworked and most recently appearing on the new *Batman: The Animated Series,* which also features quite an array of robot foes (see Chapter 11). A similar reworking occurred in the 1997 premiere season of the WB (Warner Bros.) Network's *Buffy the Vampire Slayer,* with the title heroine meeting a possessed ventriloquist's dummy that dominates its "owner's" mind. UFOs as false-leads were seen on *The Avengers,* invariably screens for someone's high-tech murders, and cases were solved by discovering hitherto unknown technological breakthroughs being criminally employed, such as power beams, anti-gravity boots, and the like. Much of the show's highly successful revamping can probably be attributed to the fact that it was being streamlined for American exportation, and the sci-fi trend was proliferating tremendously at exactly that time.

The Avengers had several similar "missing time" abduction episodes, such as "The Morning After" and "The Forget-Me-Knot," in which agents are gassed and kidnapped for interrogation, gone from their jobs for up to three weeks with no memory whatsoever of where they have been or what they have done. "The Hour That Never Was" expresses the same plot, as the title suggests. "Too Many Christmas Trees" utilized the same elements, adding those found in the *Wild, Wild West* episode—while asleep, selected targets are telepathically invaded (the equivalent to drugging) repeatedly and put through progressively more terrifying repetitive motions, the object being to deeply instill in them a sense of dread upon their awakening that will make them more vulnerable over a period of time. "Death's Door" was identical in story, except that the entire process was accomplished through drugs and physical transport. "Escape in Time" saw a similar drugging and removal game employed to convince people that they had actually travelled through another dimension into a past era.

Hypnotic mind control often figured prominently in *The Avengers.* "The Master Minds" in 1965 had Steed and Mrs. Peel infiltrating a MENSA-esque high-IQ club called "Ransack," which utilized essentially the same sleep-hypnosis techniques exhibited in Ian Fleming's 1963 novel—six years later a United Artists film—*On Her Majesty's Secret Service* (see Chapter 7). Ransack hypnotized its members by night to become saboteurs and unconscious assassins. 1967's "Something Nasty in the Nursery" was about another nefarious organization utilizing a hypnotic drug to regress prominent Cabinet members and gain their secrets. "The Super-Secret Cypher Snatch (Whatever Happened to Yesterday?)," in 1969, dramatized the use of a hypnotic gas upon members of a top-secret complex. The same year, "Stay Tuned" had Steed the victim of a missing-time abduction, during which he was hypnotized by an enemy power to murder his superior. Also in '69 was an episode called "Split," about a dual-personalitied murderer who is triggered by post-hypnotic command.

As early as Diana Rigg's first season (1965), there was even one story that combined mind control with space invasion: "The Man-Eater of Surrey Green." The title character is a space-plant, denoted as having come from either Mars or the Moon, which hypnotically dominates horticulturalists into assisting its development for lethal world dominion. Interesting in this story, given that the show's production team almost all had Intelligence connections (see Chapter 7) and that the show tended to base itself on tangible realities (no matter their science-fictional expansion after the fact), is a specific reference to "recent photographs of the Moon which show entire areas of vegetation." What makes this all the more worthy of attention is the fact that Rick Lehner announced to the major news media on December 3, 1996, on behalf of the Pentagon's Ballistic Missile Defense Organization (BMDO), that their 1994 *Clementine* probe discovered ten to one hundred feet of frozen water in an area the size of a small lake or pond in a huge crater deep in the south pole of the far side of the Moon.

Mind control's portrayal in dramatic media so closely echoing the truth is certainly not a coincidence. While some works, notably those of early pulp fiction, appear to contain some true elements about the subject, Hollywood's later dramatizations contain far more. William Joseph Bryan, Jr.'s, attachment to United Artists and American International Pictures is only the most obvious connection in the explanation of why Hollywood films began to see a post-War rise in accuracy on the subject of mind control. The accuracy reflected in the presenting of UFO information will similarly be noticed.

As to the Intelligence world's motivation for such portrayals, a number of reasons spring to mind beyond the obvious one of popular deflection from the topic. For one thing, the movies gave the agencies involved a venue for openly talking about their secret research; for another, the movies began acquainting a mass audience with the more serious and dangerous aspects of such areas as hypnosis and mental domination by outside parties. It was AIP co-founder James H. Nicholson who insisted on the lengthy warning prologue about the dangers of hypnosis preceding Herman Cohen's *Horrors of the Black Museum,* which today appear dated and laughable—but at the time, to an audience unfamiliar with the real perils of mind control, it served as a reasonable alarm, not so seriously presented as to potentially cause any panic, yet not so frivolous that it would be completely ignored. As to giving the public the entire truth—either on the question of mind control or of UFOs—Intelligence insiders could hardly have been expected at the time to share openly what they knew. The public had to be made ready first. And there was no better way to begin acquainting them than through entertainment media.

3

Media and
Manipulations

I n 1980, a famous UFO incident occurred on British soil at an American air base in Rendlesham Forest. It got almost no news coverage in England, but Japan and the United States made two ninety-minute documentaries about it each. Similarly, almost all news about the spectacular loss of *Phobos 2* was excluded from the American media even though Europe and Canada heard quite a bit about it. British UFO researcher Jenny Randles wrote books on the Rendlesham Forest incident and was approached by two different BBC producers about making documentaries. Both times, despite written guarantees in one of the cases, the program was never made. Producer Doug Salmon told Randles that it had been "blocked at the highest level" in October of 1983, and a proposed December 1984 date for airing the material was cancelled at the last minute with the excuse that there was "not enough information," an interesting claim since several hours were presented on it in two other countries.

This is only one example of media and government censorship in action. The book *Spycatcher,* about the highly publicized "fifth man" scandal of Soviet-sympathizing key officials in England's MI-5, written by a former member of that organization, Peter Wright, was banned in Britain. The excuse was the Secrets Act, but really it was a question of embarrassment. Banning the book did nothing to keep

162 HOLLYWOOD VERSUS THE ALIENS

illegal copies from flooding over the borders where it was not banned—it only illustrated exactly how controlled the media is in Great Britain.

This kind of media censorship is not unique in the Free World to British shores, but has been witnessed in America as well. On the January 22, 1958, *Armstrong Circle Theater Show,* Major Donald Keyhoe, then head of NICAP, was given seven minutes to rebut twenty-five minutes of official Air Force debunking testimony on UFOs. His script was deleted of all its salient points in advance by CBS, who incorrectly claimed it was too long. Keyhoe insisted on retaining one paragraph of uncategorical statements from official sources affirming the existence of UFOs as intelligently controlled spacecraft, and was told this would not be allowed. When he went ahead and began reading them anyway, well within his allotted time, the producer cut the audio from the air for the remainder of his speech. CBS's Director of Editing, Herbert A. Carlborg, gave an official response to NICAP's inquiries concerning the incident: "This program had been carefully screened for security reasons. Therefore, it was the responsibility of this network to ensure performance that was in accordance with predetermined security standards. Any indication that there would be a deviation from the script might lead to a statement that neither this network nor the individuals on the program were authorized to release." Mike Wallace was later used to make Keyhoe look like a fool on the subject of UFOs, confronting him with denials from the Air Force on four documents Keyhoe insisted were in their possession. They later turned out to exist, as Keyhoe claimed, coming to light via the Freedom of Information Act.

60 Minutes wanted to run a piece on Len Colodny and Robert Gettlin's Watergate book, *Silent Coup,* which presented ironclad tape-recorded confessions from Pentagon Admirals on previously undisclosed information, one important item of which was that the intrepid investigative reporter, Bob Woodward, who had supposedly gained all of his information from a number of shadowy inside sources under the collective name "Deep Throat," had actually served as a briefer for Al Haig at the Pentagon not long before becoming a reporter for the *Washington Post.* The show was killed at the executive level, with a great many incidents on record testifying to pressure exerted on witnesses not to back up their own statements, and others in the media line being warned off. Interestingly enough, Woodward, who vociferously denied that he had ever worked at the Pentagon, later did admit that he *had* actually been a Pentagon briefer, in a throw-away sentence in the foreword of his book, *The Commanders,* so matter-of-factly it was as if he had never denied it (let alone so heatedly) in the first place. The story is recounted at length in the postscript to the paperback edition of Colodny and Gettlin's book, a weighty piece of evidence that our Free Press is more controlled than we think.

As has already been mentioned, several publications—in fact, virtually all of the major ones—are not only founded by CIA-sympathizers, but are also often staffed with their very agents, making them little more than propaganda rags. In addition to Henry Luce and C. D. Jackson, Watergate reporter Carl Bernstein identified a great many others in an October 20, 1977, *Rolling Stone* article, including the creator of Copley News Service, *New York Times* publisher Arthur Hayes Sulzberger, CBS president William Paley, a well-known (but unnamed) ABC correspondent, NBC, AP, UPI, Reuters, Scripps-Howard, Hearst newspapers, the *Miami Herald* and *Newsweek.*

Martin A. Lee and Norman Solomon, in *Unreliable Sources—A Guide to Detecting Bias in News Media,* call the media the "Fourth Branch of Government" rather than the "Fourth Estate." They document "that the American public was a prime target of CIA propaganda. A memo dated July 13, 1951, described the CIA's fledgling mind-control operations as 'broad and comprehensive, involving both domestic and overseas activities.' Another CIA document from the same period indicates that high-level CIA officers met on a regular basis to exchange ideas on 'the broader aspects of psychology as it pertains to the control of groups or masses rather than the mind of an individual.'" They add that "the *New York Times* provided press credentials and cover for more than a dozen CIA operatives during the Cold War," and regularly submitted articles to Agency head John A. McCone, even after he had stepped down from his position, for "vetting and approval." Former Nazis and fascists staffed Radio Liberty and Radio Free Europe for the CIA, "among the largest and most expensive psychological warfare operations ever undertaken by the U.S. government," stating outright lies against the Soviet Union even as the CIA was performing the very acts the Russians were being accused of, such as the MK-ULTRA brainwashing experiments. Lyndon Johnson is recorded as saying, "Reporters are puppets. They simply respond to the pull of the most powerful strings." And as Lee and Solomon put it, "...the links between the CIA and the three main TV networks are just the tip of a very spooky iceberg."

The CIA's media assets were called the Propaganda Assets Inventory and went unofficially by the name of "Wisner's Wurlitzer," after first chief of covert action, Frank G. Wisner, who committed suicide in 1961. Under its auspices, as many as fifty radio stations, newspapers, and magazines and news services, in addition to deliberately doing false reporting abroad, disseminated "black propaganda"—false or misleadingly inaccurate news stories, aimed specifically at the domestic population. William Colby and George Bush stonewalled the Congressional Frank Church Committee investigating this and other Intelligence abuses during the Carter administration, including the entire MK-ULTRA program. Watergate reporter Carl Bernstein wrote that Church "deliberately buried" the evidence of CIA media manipulation, having been both warned-off by Agency officials and accused of creating a witch-hunt—as though the Agency hadn't had its part in the entire McCarthy Communist blacklistings, back in the 1950s. Bernstein wrote that "more than four hundred American journalists . . . in the past twenty-five years have secretly carried out (CIA) assignments." Its chief asset, *The New York Times*, put the figure twice as high according to one of Bernstein's inside sources, "more than eight hundred news and public information organizations and individuals." Some of these were recruited journalists already working in the field, many of whom then became Agency couriers abroad and actually recruited foreign spies themselves.

Even those publishers or writers not directly connected to the knowing dissemination of propaganda are still subject to ignorantly spreading it about. "Lying to the press goes back to the beginning of the Republic," according to former *New York Herald Tribune* editor and author of several books on American espionage, David Wise.

Referring to Reagan-era disinformation in 1987, he commented that where policies used to be framed to fit events, "Now events are shaped and manipulated to fit policies." *The New York Times'* Washington editor, Bill Kovach, called Reagan's White House "an administration that freely states—and stated early—that literal truth was not a concern." George Bush's press secretary openly admitted the future president's media strategy after his 1984 vice-presidential debate with Geraldine Ferraro: "You can say anything you want in a debate and 80 million people hear it. If reporters then report that a candidate spoke untruthfully, so what? Maybe 200 people read it."

Most reporters are not inclined to investigate factual accuracy in the first place. They merely accept whatever is handed them as true and mouth it over the airwaves, or re-word government-written documents to put out on the wires, without asking questions. On any given talk show or in any article or CNN report, if the commentator says anything to the nature of "Inside sources in the government say …" or "An unnamed expert in the State Department relates …" then he is openly admitting that what he is reporting is nothing but hearsay, with no reliable source to document it. Yet, this is common on the nightly news, both local and national. Tabloids often do better. For that matter, U.S. reporters continue quoting official sources even after they have discredited themselves. Former Assistant Secretary of State Elliot Abrams openly admitted to misleading Congress concerning the Reagan administration's Central America policies, but not one single reporter from any paper, magazine or media talk show let this deter them from continuing to quote whatever further "news" items he chose to disseminate, let alone refuse to quote him at all for his being an admitted liar.

Bill Moyers, one of the few reporters to ever challenge official State Department lies in a PBS documentary called *The Secret Government: The Constitution in Crisis,* exposed Reagan's entire inner circle as nothing but pure fabricators and prevaricators, responsible for "a wholesale policy of secrecy shrouded in lies, of passion cloaked in fiction and deception." Former U.S. Information Agency official Abraham Brumberg concurred, calling the media's reporting during that time (not that it has been much better before or since) "a flood of distortions, exaggerations and plain unvarnished lies . . . that issue forth almost daily from the administration," and Congressman David Bonior openly complained about "a notable lack of a sense of history in this administration and in the media."

The mainstream media's lack of any standard for determining factual accuracy in its reported stories never became more apparent than under Ronald Reagan, when the OPD, the "Office of Public Diplomacy," was formed by the State Department. An "officially sanctioned leaks bureau," the OPD was a taxpayer-funded propaganda factory, controlled by the National Security Council and the CIA. Director of Central Intelligence William Casey created it in 1982 by shuffling one of his top propaganda specialists, Walter Raymond, to the National Security Council. His purpose was to circumvent Congressional prohibitions against domestic CIA intervention. "Raymond's job," write Lee and Solomon, "was to organize a massive public diplomacy effort that would generate grassroots support for Reagan's controversial—and hitherto unpopular—foreign policy ventures. Toward this end, OPD recruited five 'psy-ops' specialists from the 4th Psychological Operations Group in Fort Bragg, North Carolina. Skilled in what OPD chief Otto Reich called 'persuasive communications,' these psychological warfare experts prepared 'studies, papers, speeches, and memoranda to support [OPD] activities.'" Media critic Alexander Cockburn defined its strategy: "Erect a mountain of lies, and as members of the press examine each new falsehood, they find themselves on a foundation of older lies still taken for granted as natural features of the landscape." The OPD functioned until the end of 1987, when it was disbanded in the wake of the Iran-Contra scandal—itself a glaring example of media impotency in the face of genuine Constitutional crisis.

Nor could the OPD be considered a sign of CIA media control only in the past fifteen years. When Reinhard Gehlen was first brought over to United States shores and given official sanction in the closing months of 1945, the model was set. He and the Agency both were vigorous and exaggerated liars concerning the Red Menace, securing themselves in jobs that would never become obsolete as the champions of the Free World against that supposed threat. One estimate put the amount of Gehlen's highly inaccurate information concerning the Russians as high as seventy percent, though it all ended up being repeated to NATO as accurate. "The [CIA] loved Gehlen," reported Victor Marchetti to Gehlen biographer Christopher Simpson, "because he fed us what we wanted to hear. We used his stuff constantly, and we fed it to everybody else: the Pentagon; the White House; the newspapers. They loved it, too. But it was hyped-up Russian boogeyman junk, and it did a lot of damage to this country." Those reports were used, as Simpson puts it, "to justify increased U.S. military budgets and [intensify] U.S./U.S.S.R hostilities."

Certainly the entertainment realm was of no less interest to the CIA as a potential molder of public opinion and thought. "CIA scientists understood that television and motion picture media are especially conducive to subliminal manipulation," write Lee and Solomon, "which bypasses rational defense mechanisms through split-second imagery. A once-secret document dated November 21, 1955, noted how 'psychologically the general lowering of consciousness during the picture facilitates the phenomenon of identification and suggestion as in hypnosis.'" In other words, that the willing "suspension of disbelief" that an audience puts itself through for the sake of enjoyment of the story before the fact virtually makes them automatically susceptible to mass hypnotic conditioning for the duration of the show.

Ex-CIA Assistant to the Deputy Director, Victor Marchetti, and former State Department official John D. Marks document in their groundbreaking exposé of the Agency, *The CIA and the Cult of Intelligence,* that "As part of their formal clandestine training at 'The Farm' [the CIA's Williamsburg, Virginia, training facility] . . . CTs [Career Trainees] are regularly shown Hollywood spy movies, and after the performance they collectively criticize the techniques used in the films," strongly implying that Agency personnel are indeed behind the making of many of those very spy movies. They quote a former clandestine operator whose April 1967 testimony in *Ramparts* helps strengthen the idea: "We were shown Agency-produced films depicting the CIA in action, films which displayed a kind of Hollywood flair for the dramatic that is not uncommon inside the Agency."

In light of these facts, it is most interesting what Jenny Randles was told by a high-ranking establishment figure at the House of Commons bar, after "a talk to a gaggle of Lords, Barons and MPs" on the subject of UFOs, days before Rendlesham Forest. Though he was credible, "a source in the House of Lords," she didn't believe what he had to say at the time, treating it as a joke. He had claimed, perfectly seriously, that there was an "education program" afoot at the official government level to gradually release the truth about UFOs—that the world had to be prepared, which necessarily took some time. He claimed that films like Steven Spielberg's *Close Encounters of the Third Kind* were part of that program, "financed by the right money being placed in the correct hands at the appropriate time." On later reflection, Randles considered that it may well be true.

Speculation is not even necessary on the fact: it is documented that such a program was in effect since at least January of 1953, in the recommendations of the Robertson Panel. The Panel was a hastily convened board of scientists assembled by the CIA and the Office of Scientific Intelligence, devoted to debunking the subject of UFOs in the wake of the highly publicized Washington Nationals, six months prior. After the most cursory of glances at a minimal amount of evidence deliberately selected for easy dismissal, the panel did its job of assuring the public of what the Air Force always had before—that all UFOs were nothing more than swamp gas, temperature inversions, and the odd, straying weather balloon. The scientists also secretly made a great many recommendations to the government in direct contradiction to their own public conclusions, suggesting how the government could best psychologically combat UFOs and control all reports of their sightings. Two of those recommendations, affecting the latter, were the regulations JANAP-146 and AFR 200-2. In the former category, the panel recommended specifically "That the national security agencies immediately take steps to strip the UFOs of the special status they have been given and the aura of mystery they have unfortunately acquired," in order to "(reduce) public interest in 'flying saucers' which today evokes a strong psychological reaction." An organization called the "Psychological Strategy Board" was consulted about making this proposed "educational project" work:

"This education could be accomplished by mass media such (as) television, motion pictures and popular articles."

Cartoons by "Walt Disney, Inc." were recommended to be used for such a project, which is interesting, since it has now been documented by biographer Marc Eliot that Disney was an FBI informant since perhaps as early as 1940. Disney had been of interest to the Bureau for several years before he allowed himself to be recruited by them, owing to his anti-Communist and anti-Union stance. By 1954, he was recommended in memo #S-186 for SAC—"Special Agent in Charge"—status: "Because of Mr. Disney's position as the foremost producer of cartoon films in the motion picture industry and his prominence and wide acquaintanceship in film production matters, it is believed that he can be of valuable assistance to this office and therefore it is my recommendation that he be approved as an SAC contact." Special Agents in Charge are usually members of long standing with the Bureau to begin with, who have reached such a high level that they no longer draw any sort of salary or take independent contracts, but continue to work in their former capacity more or less as an ongoing favor to the government. J. Edgar Hoover's personal note of condolence to Disney's widow on December 15, 1966, confirms that "Mr. Disney was on the Special Correspondents' List on a first name basis."

Disney was, in fact, the first man to put a serious science show on television—most notably, one devoted entirely to space travel. A decade prior, in 1943, he had produced a wartime short through United Artists—a studio which, as we will see, has produced a surprisingly high number of UFOlogically accurate films—called *Victory Through Air Power,* based on Major Alexander de Seversky's book discussing his and Billy Mitchell's controversial intercontinental bombing theories. On March 9, 1955, based largely on that precedent, Disney premiered a "Tomorrowland" segment on his *Disneyland* show, called "Man in Space." Disney had handed a literal blank check to his former animator Ward Kimball, whom he had known since at least 1934, to produce and direct the series. Enamored of a series of space articles in *Collier's* magazine from 1952 to 1954, written by rocket scientists Willy Ley, Wernher von Braun, and Heinz Haber,

Kimball enlisted these men to actually appear on Disney's show and present their ideas, live. The Tomorrowland series included two more episodes, all of approximately 48 minutes each, "Man and the Moon" on December 28, 1955, and "Mars and Beyond" the following year. Though Disney managed not to include any space-race polemics against the Russians, he also managed to exclude any mention of such major contributors to the history of space travel theory as Konstantin Tsiolkouvsky. Aside from such omissions, the entire series was very well received, was given a special screening for the Pentagon, and presented a combination of stunning animated sequences with live-action dramatizations and speeches and interviews with the rocket scientists, all of which served an invaluable function in selling the space program to the public. A record of the Tomorrowland series survives in its edited-down movie compilation, *Man in Space*.

It was also Walt Disney who introduced Jules Verne's most famous character, Captain Nemo, to the popular viewing audience in 1954's *20,000 Leagues Under the Sea*. Verne was connected to occult organizations in his life and clearly knew what he was writing about, even in the nineteenth century. The resemblance of the name "Nemo" to the benevolent fish-god of man's prehistory, "Nommo," is too much for coincidence, as is the fact that Nemo is a technologically superior "good neighbor" (like the Fairy-Folk) who deliberately disarms world powers to preclude their warring on each other. Exactly in common with the UFO phenomenon, the characters in Verne's story begin by disbelieving stories of an "alien" creature in their seas who is destroying their warships. Eventually, too many people witness the creature for anyone to continue denying it—but some of the more clever ones have noticed that the sea-beast is not a living animal, but a machine. Survivors from one of Nemo's attacks are "abducted" aboard his vessel and react in different ways to their position, just as present UFO abductees do. And, in common with what has been observed about today's abductees, they are put into interactive situations to test their moral mettle before being trained to assist Nemo in his work.

Ray Harryhausen, whose movies were extremely similar retellings of the ancient gods interacting with mortal affairs via superior technology, did the Columbia sequel *Mysterious Island* seven years later. In it, Nemo emerges even more as the Underworld culture god of old, in his guise as lord of wealth and increase: his secret island hideaway is where he experiments with growth hormones to solve the world's food shortage. In common with the UFO presence, Nemo remains hidden by choice throughout his encounters with a hapless set of men and women who have unfortunately become shipwrecked on his island. He manages to invisibly guide them to shelter and supplies, and fires a bullet from hiding to save their lives when they are threatened and unable to fight back. They gradually become aware that more than mere dumb luck is behind their good fortune, and meet their benefactor when circumstance forces him to reveal himself: like Atlantis, the island is doomed to blow up and sink beneath the sea, and he requires their help to get them all safely away before the catastrophe.

But Walt Disney was hardly the first person to involve himself in the Robertson Panel's "educational project"—in fact, it is entirely possible that it was in effect from the beginning of the saucer phenomenon, or perhaps even before. "Flying saucers" first got their name when Lieutenant Kenneth Arnold sighted a number of UFOs over Washington state in June of 1947 that looked like shiny pie tins, skipping along the air as a saucer would, which the press turned into the now-infamous moniker. 1940s pulp-magazine publisher Ray Palmer had a "mysterious aerial objects" article on the cover of *Amazing Stories* at the same time Arnold made his sighting. Palmer publicized the sighting in the first issue of his new magazine *Fate,* and co-wrote Arnold's book about the incident, *The Coming of the Saucers.* Shortly after, he was personally instrumental in getting Arnold involved in the Maury Island affair, which Project Blue Book head Edward Ruppelt called "the dirtiest hoax in UFO history." It is this last, especially, that may have prompted John Spencer, in his *UFO Encyclopedia,* to observe that Palmer "seems to have played a prominent if rather shadowy role in some of the development of the UFO mystery." The "shadowy" aspect becomes all the more prominent when Palmer's part in the Richard Sharpe Shaver episode is taken into account, along with the information considered in this study.

Shaver was the prototype model for a UFO contactee, predating George Adamski by almost ten years. Between 1944 and 1948—that time spanning exactly the best-documented UFO sightings in the Second World War, the Roswell crash, and the formation of the National Security State in America—Palmer published Shaver's accounts in *Amazing Stories* and *Fantastic Adventures,* literally having rescued them from the wastepaper basket to which his peers had consigned them. Shaver was an ex-con and mental patient whose abduction experiences theoretically began back in the 1930s, when he heard unpleasant voices he could not silence talking about torture and sexual perversion through his welding headgear. During one of his prison stints, he claimed to have been abducted by a woman to an underground cavern inside the hollow earth, where she and the good race of "teros"—which he called robots even though they had none of the attributes and were specifically described as descendants of a living race—were at war with the evil and perverse "deros," a rival race, both remnants of original giant "Atlan" and "Titan" super-races who fled Earth 12,000 years ago in spaceships to avoid a deadly change in the sun's radiation.

Literal clamp-handed robot-men from Atlantis were seen at least as early as the 1936 Republic serial *Undersea Kingdom* (condensed into a movie in 1961), which may have been where Shaver got his ideas. *Undersea Kingdom* showed quasi-Oriental/Roman supermen living in a hollow Earth, similar to what it is thought the Nazis believed. They had viewscreens to see the "upper world," which their king vowed to destroy with his superior technology—chief of which was a bulletproof remote-control robot army, piloting superior vehicles and armed with heat-ray guns. As to where the serial got its ideas, there may be nothing more mysterious than the screenwriter's having read the turn-of-the-century works on Atlantis that were being written by such respected scholars as Lewis Spence, whose 1915 *Myths and Legends of Ancient Egypt* records the story of Pharaoh's abduction by "model men" who fly "on the clouds" (recounted in the introduction to this study). Or, Palmer and Shaver's teros and deros could have derived from Nikolai Tolstoy's *Aelita,* written in 1921 and filmed in Russia in 1924, containing robot men from Mars which were relics of the Earth's Atlantis. As indicated by the archaeological studies undertaken not only by the Nazis, but also by the Allied powers from the beginning of the century on, and the fact that the mysterious "ghost rockets" of Scandinavia had been intensively investigated by several governments only two years before, it could also be that a few things were known about Mars and UFOs before Roswell, and that early experimentation with the "educational" program was already at work minimalizing the subject.

Palmer promoted the "Shaver controversy" to sell magazines, and he introduced another shady character named Fred L. Crisman into the *Amazing Stories* issue preceding the one on the stands when Kenneth Arnold's sighting took place. In that issue, Crisman told a rollicking adventure story of having escaped a cave full of deadly deros armed only with a submachine gun. Two months later, following Arnold's sighting, Crisman got Palmer to introduce him as a legitimate witness in a supposed UFO incident, which was the Maury Island hoax that was rather obviously contrived to make Arnold look foolish. Crisman's claims proved to be false, and the entire incident was admitted to be a hoax after the fact, though fortunately Arnold's involvement was kept to a publicity minimum by Air Force investigators on the case—who died in a B-25 explosion on their way back to base from that investigation. There was testimony following the crash, according to early UFOlogist Frank Scully, that Air Force reservist Crisman was ordered to board an Alaska-bound Army plane. Crisman appeared years later, in December of 1968, as a witness before the grand jury in Jim Garrison's JFK murder trial against Clay Shaw.

But these frauds, hoaxes, and obviously suspicious occurrences were predated by the most famous one of all, which has long been speculated to have been far from the innocent mishap it was publicized to be: Orson Welles' 1938 Halloween Eve Mercury Radio Theatre broadcast of "War of the Worlds." The show created a famous panic among a great many of its listeners, who believed they were really being invaded by Martians in tripodal death-machines armed with heat-rays. The day following, Welles was pictured in the newspapers with an angelically pained expression at the chaos his innocent prank had caused, which looked as staged then as it does today.

Protesting at the time that he was "deeply shocked and deeply regretful," he admitted to his interviewer on a *Today* show commemorative fortieth anniversary appearance when asked, "Did you get a laugh out of it, Orson?" that indeed it had been "Huge, huge, yes, a huge laugh. I never thought it was anything but funny." The author of the original novel, however, despite many subsequent reports to the contrary, was not at all amused. "In the name of Mr. H. G. Wells," his New York spokesman, Jacques Chambrun, stated, "I granted the Columbia Broadcasting System the right to dramatize Mr. H. G. Wells's novel *The War of the Worlds* for one performance over the radio. It was not explained to me that this dramatization would be made with a liberty that amounts to a complete rewriting of *The War of the Worlds* and renders it into an entirely different story. Mr. Wells and I consider that by so doing the Columbia Broadcasting System should make a full retraction. Mr. H. G. Wells is personally deeply concerned that any work of his should be used in such a way, and with a totally unwarranted liberty, to cause deep distress and alarm throughout the United States."

The specific changes referred to were all in manner of presentation. Welles had deliberately utilized a low-key, naturalistic, live-action documentary format to present the material in order to make it appear more realistic within the dramatic medium. His conceit was that real news flashes were interrupting regular programming, to update the public about an actual invasion from Mars. To make it all the more realistic, he included unnaturally long musical interludes between the "news broadcasts." Welles' biographer, Barbara Leaming, asks:

> Did Orson Welles know exactly what he was doing? Had he been counting on the fact that the millions of listeners tuned to Edgar Bergen wouldn't begin idly switching stations until long after the announcer had said that this was really just an adaptation of *The War of the Worlds?* Could Orson have suspected that moments after Edgar Bergen had introduced a singer, people across America would gasp at the "news" on CBS? For once Orson succeeded magnificently in keeping listeners from tuning back to Charlie McCarthy.

He had dragged out the boring music to intensify suspense, to make it seem that considerably more time had passed in the interval since the last news bulletin than really had. It was all a question of framing. Not having heard the usual introduction that framed the scenario as fiction, countless people took it for fact.

The framing, and especially the dragging-out of the music, had all been Welles' idea:

> Routinely submitted to the CBS censors, the script suffered twenty-seven minor changes, such as the substitution of the made-up Hotel Park Plaza for the all-too-real Hotel Biltmore, and Jersey State Militia for Jersey State Guard—all in the interest of diminishing verisimilitude. Just before he went on the air, Halloween Eve, Orson made last minute changes in the script, which appeared to make it even duller than it already was. While it seemed far more logical to stress the mock-newscasts rather than the silly music, Orson wanted to keep the music playing for unbearable stretches of time. No sooner would listeners have begun to listen to a newsflash than they would find themselves bored by the music again.

In other words, where CBS tried to make Welles' production appear more fictitious, Welles countered with a technical trick to make it appear all the more realistic. Another curiosity about Welles' deliberately making the entire production seem as realistic as possible was uncovered by the show's disputed author, Howard Koch, who, "finding it difficult to believe the coincidence," discovered that Welles had actually spent a summer at the site where the radio drama's action had been located, Grover's Mill, New Jersey: "Yes, it was true. Mrs. Carl Sjorstrum, a warm and hospitable woman, was entertaining her guests in her garden and she quickly included me in the company. When [I] told her the purpose of our visit, she beamed. Yes, Orson Welles, as a very young man, spent a summer in [her] small guest apartment writing a book."

Welles made a lifelong career out of fraud and deceit, delighting in fooling his audience, even becoming a T.V. mentalist before he died. In his film *F for Fake*, Welles demonstrated his infinite, purposeful, and deliberate lack of credibility. Recounts Leaming (parenthetical inclusion her own):

> As long ago as his radio program *First Person Singular,* Orson had enjoyed turning up on both sides of the frame by oscillating between the roles of narrator and character, thereby calling into question the line between fact and fiction ... For, in the first few moments of the picture, Orson announced that everything he was about to recount in the next hour would be *true.* That hour is a frame. By the time Orson ... recounts the Picasso affair, although we probably have not noticed, that hour is over, having been filled with diverting accounts of hoaxes: Elmyr's, Irving's, and, as it turns out, Orson's (the Martian scare that makes of Orson as much a faker as the other two). As the film draws to a close, having just laughed at the victims of a triptych of famous frauds, we fall victim ourselves to a fiction that we take for truth. Orson, who has just gleefully confessed to being a charlatan, still deftly puts one over on us.

It is worth noting that Welles was so devoted to FDR's controversial fourth-term re-election bid, that his constant electioneering over the radio and on the road for the wheelchair-ridden New Dealer brought him personal letters of thanks from the President. In other words, he considered himself quite a patriot, and as such would have been in ideal position to do the President a favor if called upon. It isn't even necessary to suppose that he might have been pulling a hoax for a secret government program to discredit thoughts of Mars or outer space, though this is possible. It could instead merely have been a test of the nation's mood for possible war against the Nazis or the Japanese—or, on a more mundane level, simply a personally engineered hoax of Welles' alone, for the purpose of inflating his stock with the greatest publicity any star ever acquired in a single night.

A great many government and Intelligence figures were writing about Atlantis and ancient Great White Brotherhoods from at least the 1870s on. For one example, Sir H. Rider Haggard's *She* was filmed a half-dozen times before the end of WWI, and has been filmed probably as many times since, making it perhaps the single most famous story of the type in all of film and literature. Even the star of the 1935 RKO version, Helen Gahagan Douglas, went on to become a California Congresswoman in the House from 1945 to 1949, then being defeated for a Senate seat in 1950 by Richard Nixon. Remaining political, she wrote a biography of Eleanor Roosevelt in 1963.

However early the government may actually have been implementing an "educational" program about UFOs or the planet Mars, it appears very much to have been experimented with heavily in the year 1951, two years before the recommendations of the Robertson Panel. The case of Howard Hawks' *The Thing from Another World* has already been considered (Chapter 1). The same year, another movie of curious coincidences, like *The Thing* changed from its original source material, was made: 20th Century Fox's *The Day the Earth Stood Still*. The original 1940 story by Harry Bates, "Farewell to the Master," bears little resemblance to the far more famous movie made from it. Only three points of similarity remain between the two: the beginning, in which a benevolent, Christ-like human lands in a UFO with a giant robot, his shooting and eventual resurrection, and the robot being his all-powerful companion against whom the military is helpless. In the story, the extraterrestrial human Klaatu is murdered by a lone religious nut upon disembarking from his craft to benevolently wave hello. The robot, Gnut (Gort in the movie), stands guard over his corpse until a later time when he discovers necessary elements for his temporary resurrection from the dead, but eventually leaves without the still-dead Klaatu. Confused humanity wonders how the robot could leave his master behind, and in a then-novel twist, Gnut reveals that he, not Klaatu, is the Master. Screenwriter Edmund H. North added religious references to the story and expanded it into a more dramatic plot—a plot remarkably resembling the facts now known about UFOs, but then unknown to the public.

The Day the Earth Stood Still begins with a flying saucer being tracked by various stations the world over, which comes to land in a ballpark in Washington, D.C. Having attracted tremendous attention, the saucer is surrounded by the military in full force, along with masses of average citizens anxious for a closer look. Finally, a door opens and a ramp emerges silently, showing no seam whatsoever to betray its location until that time. A humanoid emerges, wearing a tight, metallically shiny, one-piece bodysuit. The being is tall and extremely thin, with a spherical metal head and odd-shaped slits for eyes. It carries a strange object in one hand, which it ultimately raises in a neutral gesture. The device makes a motion looking and sounding something like a switchblade, and without anyone having given the order, a shot rings out from the crowd. The visitor falls but is only wounded. The device, however, is destroyed. Immediately after, a giant eight-foot robot emerges from the craft, featureless but for a visor in place of eyes, which lifts to show a pencil-thin beam of light that instantly vaporizes selected military targets—guns, tanks, anything. The visitor barks an order in an alien language, stopping the robot, and removes the spherical headpiece, revealing himself to be human—at least to all appearances. The potentially disastrous confrontation aborted, he introduces himself as Klaatu and holds out the ruined device: "It was a gift for your president—with this, he could have studied life on the other planets."

The Secretary of State speaks with Klaatu while he is recovering in a sequestered hospital room—much faster than a normal human would, though his physiology is completely identical to that of *Homo sapiens* on Earth. Klaatu is healed by his own superior medicines, which he shares with our doctors along with the knowledge that his race lives much longer than our own. The Secretary mentions that, of course, Klaatu's arrival is a surprise. Asked where he came from, Klaatu reveals only that he comes from another planet—"Let's just say that we're neighbors"—about 250 million miles away, a trip of five months for him. He knows English and all other Earth languages, because his race has been monitoring Earth for some time. Klaatu wants a meeting with the world's heads. When the Secretary says this would be next to impossible due to distances both geographical and political, Klaatu reminds him that he has travelled a far greater distance, and expresses impatience. "I am not concerned with the internal affairs of your planet," he says. "My mission here is not to solve your petty squabbles. It concerns the existence of every last creature on Earth. I intend to explain. To all the nations. At the same time. I don't want to resort to threats. I merely tell you that the future of your planet is at stake. I urge that you transmit that message to the nations of the Earth ... I am impatient with stupidity. My people have learned to live without it."

When the Earth's nations predictably cannot agree on where they would meet with this Ambassador from another planet, the Secretary apologizes to Klaatu, "I'm very sorry. I wish it were otherwise." Klaatu looks out his window at the people on the streets below. "Before making any decisions," he says, "I think I should get out among your people. Become familiar with the basises for these strange, unreasoning attitudes." In response, the Secretary tells him that would be impossible, and essentially informs him—as politely as he can—that "under the circumstances" he is more or less under house arrest. Klaatu only smiles as the Secretary leaves, the door locked behind him by an armed guard.

The next day, Klaatu is gone from his room, and panic spreads on the news. The papers read, "'MAN FROM MARS' ESCAPES," and the radio says, "We are dealing with forces beyond our knowledge and power—the public is advised to take ordinary precautions, and to remain calm. . . ." Another announcer says, "The officials have come to the inescapable conclusion that this ship and its occupants come from some other planet. Thus far, scientists have refused to speak officially on just which planet, until they've had an opportunity to study the ship. They seem to agree, however, that either Venus or Mars is the most likely possibility. Not only are these the closest planets to Earth, but all research to date shows that these are the only two planets capable of sustaining life as we know it. However, all reputable scientists warn against jumping to hasty conclusions. . . ." A T.V. announcer says, "Although this man may be our bitter enemy, he could be also a new-found friend," and another says, "If he can build a spaceship that can fly to Earth, and a robot that can destroy our tanks and guns, what other terrors can he unleash at will?"

Klaatu has donned the borrowed clothes of a Major Carpenter, whose name he assumes when he takes a room at a boarding house. A likeable man, Klaatu is quickly accepted by the other boarders and uses his new vantage point to listen to opinions about the "man from Mars." Some think he's a Communist spy, others a threat, others still perhaps something else. One woman in particular thinks the man from Mars is probably just afraid, having been immediately shot upon leaving his ship, and Klaatu later reveals himself to her after first befriending her little boy, Bobby.

Bobby becomes Klaatu's central source of information, being naturally fascinated by Klaatu's knowledge. Touring the saucer site together—now a tourist attraction, with the motionless robot, Gort, standing guard, whom everyone is sure will eventually come to life and destroy them all—Bobby asks questions about how fast it goes and how it must work, and (assuming the hypothetical stance) Klaatu tells him, to the amusement of bystanders, who say, "Keep going, Mister, he was fallin' for it!" A news reporter doing "man on the street" interviews asks Klaatu what he thinks of the man from Mars scare, and when Klaatu's answer goes beyond a single sentence (or sound byte), the newsman cuts him off with a thank you, quickly moving to the next man and illustrating one of the primary problems with education by media.

After some of Klaatu's technical explanations, Bobby says, "I bet that's just the way Professor Barnhard talks," and Klaatu expresses interest in meeting Professor Barnhard. Bobby says they'd never get to, and Klaatu impresses him by telling him he might be surprised. Going to his home, which is at the moment unoccupied, Klaatu enters and makes some changes in a lengthy equation on the Professor's blackboard, leaving his name and address, and is summoned by Army guards that night back to the Professor's residence. In private, the Professor praises and thanks him for the help in his work, asking him if he has had a chance to test the theorem. Klaatu answers, "I find it works well enough to get me from one planet to another," and the two quickly become friends. Klaatu tells him of the trouble he has been having in arranging a meeting of Earth representatives, and asks the Professor's help. He reveals that his planet is concerned about Earth's having discovered atomic power, not because it is being used to resolve political conflicts, but because it means Earth will soon be involved in space travel and will carry its wars with it to the other planets. He declares that he has come to issue Earth an ultimatum, and arranges for a demonstration of power the next day to help the Professor impress his colleagues as to the importance of the meeting they must attend.

Bobby follows Klaatu as he goes out at night to communicate by flashlight code with the motionless Gort, and sees him and the robot incapacitate the guards to gain entrance to the saucer. His mother of course does not believe him, but she and her fiancé both discover that Klaatu is not in his room and that he has a sizeable number of diamonds—the source of his money, which on his planet are used as currency. Additionally concerned by his having been picked up by military men earlier, Bobby's mother becomes wary of Klaatu. He corners her at work the next day in an elevator, saying he has something important to tell her, and the power goes out. Klaatu announces that it will remain out for the next thirty minutes, all over the world. "Bobby was telling the truth. . . ." she realizes. Klaatu tells her everything and enlists her support. Her fiancé, however, goes to the authorities as soon as she lets him in on the secret, more concerned with his own status and financial gain than with interplanetary concerns.

The military ambushes Klaatu on his way to the prearranged meeting of scientists that night, gunning him down in the street. Having anticipated this possibility, he has warned Bobby's mother what to do if he should be killed. "I'm worried about Gort," he says. "I'm afraid of what he might do if anything should happen to me." She reminds him that Gort is only a robot—"Without you, what could he do?" Klaatu answers, "There's no limit to what he could do. He could destroy the Earth." Klaatu gives her a phrase in his language to repeat to Gort in the event of his death: *Klaatu barada nikto.*

True to Klaatu's fears, as soon as he is dead, Gort reanimates, vaporizing two armed guards without delay. Bobby's mother arrives and relates the phrase, nearly forgetting it in her terror as the featureless metal man relentlessly approaches her, and Gort ceases his attack to pick her up and carry her aboard the saucer. Locating Klaatu's body on a control screen, Gort leaves the woman in the saucer and retrieves it, then raises Klaatu from the dead in a sonic machine before her eyes. Klaatu tells her he does not know how much longer he will live now that he has been revived, but confirms that he was in fact dead and that the robot brought him back.

Klaatu goes out with Gort to address Professor Barnhard's gathering of scientists (the military also in attendance): "I am leaving soon, and you will forgive me if I speak bluntly. The universe grows smaller every day, and the threat of aggression from any group, anywhere, can no longer be tolerated. There must be security for all, or no one is secure. Now, this does not mean giving up any freedom—except the freedom to act irresponsibly. Your ancestors knew this, when they made laws to govern themselves and hired policemen to enforce them. We of the other planets have long accepted this principle. We have an organization for the mutual protection of all planets, and for the complete elimination of aggression. The test of any such higher authority is, of course, the police force that supports it. For our policemen, we created a race of robots. Their function is to patrol the planets, in spaceships like this one, and preserve the peace. In matters of aggression, we have given them absolute power over us. This power cannot be revoked. At the first sign of violence, they act automatically against the aggressor. The penalty for provoking their action is too terrible to risk. The result is, we live in peace, without arms or armies, secure in the knowledge that we are free from aggression and war. Free to pursue more profitable enterprises. Now, we do not pretend to have achieved perfection. But we do have a system. And it works. I came here to give you these facts. It is no concern of ours how you run your own planet. But if you threaten to extend your violence, this Earth of yours will be reduced to a burned-out cinder. Your choice is simple: join us, and live in peace, or pursue your present course and face obliteration. We shall be waiting for your answer. The decision rests with you." And, having spoken his piece, Klaatu and Gort depart back into the heavens from whence they came, without further ado.

As much a classic today as when it was first made, *The Day the Earth Stood Still* plays in successful revivals in outdoor summer festivals and is frequently seen on cable stations. Most remarkable about the film in terms of this study are the facts we can see it presenting that were not publicly available in 1951—nor were they in the short story on which the film is based. It is perhaps also of note that screenwriter Edmund North co-wrote the militarily patriotic *Patton* and the later *Meteor,* a cosmological collision story not as fictionally removed as it may once have appeared (based on an actual 1968 MIT-proposed planetary defense system called "Project Icarus"), and that director Robert Wise is a UFO believer. Could someone in Hollywood have had an inside track? Or, either knowingly or unknowingly, been in connection with someone who did?

There is no question that producer Darryl Zanuck was considered unlikely to have chosen *The Day the Earth Stood Still* for a project. It was a low-budget picture, surprising as that seems today upon viewing its superb craftsmanship, and science-fiction was far too new a genre to attract anyone's attention on its own merits. Director Robert Wise, in a February 1995 *Starlog* interview, said that everyone around Hollywood remarked at the time, "It seems kind of strange that Darryl Zanuck would go for something like this, him being a big Army man and very much a conservative." And in fact, the Army refused to allow its material to be used in the movie after reading its extremely pacifistic script. The National Guard had to be used instead. Wise protests that he had no idea until he saw the finished picture that he was making an allegorical film. "You've said that you didn't realize, as you were making *Day the Earth Stood Still,*" his *Starlog* interviewer brought up with Wise, "that it was a Christ allegory. And yet when Zanuck offered the picture to Claude Rains [the part was ultimately played by Michael Rennie], *he* told Rains he would be playing 'a modern Christ'—so *Zanuck* knew." Wise immediately acknowledged this, saying, "Isn't that interesting!" Obviously, some of the changes from the original story to the screen version had come from the highest possible source.

We have already noted similarities among the facts of Roswell, the New Mexico atomic energy plant intrusions of 1948, and the movie *The Thing.* As in that movie, *The Day the Earth Stood Still* has so many coincidences with actual UFO facts that the question is unavoidable, especially given the year it was made. A classic flying saucer, bearing a human being and a robot—and the human being initially appears dressed in identical fashion to what was not recognized for well over another decade as being a standard UFO occupant look—arrives from an unstated planet that is most probably

Mars, which is even directly hinted at. Its occupant is concerned with our military, and threatens force to keep us in line, much as actual UFOs have monitored our atomic development and sabotaged our military bases. Failing to achieve direct contact, the alien visitor goes underground and gets to know the locals on a one-on-one basis, which appears to be a motivation for the UFO abductions that have been going on since at least 1957 (and probably a great deal longer)— two actual abductions (performed by a robot, no less) even occur in the movie, one of them including medical procedures performed on the abductee by the robot. Who would have known about these things back in 1951? More lucky guesses? Like *The Thing?* Are these movies isolated incidents, or are there other examples?

One year before these two sci-fi classics, the space travel movies *Destination Moon* (Eagle-Lion) and *Rocketship X-M* (Lippert) were made. The latter has a rocket going off course from its Moon destination, ending up on Mars. There, the crew discover the remnants of a once-advanced civilization, destroyed in nuclear war. As has been noted in the introduction, investigations of odd formations and moving lights on the surface of Mars and the Moon were actively pursued in the mid-nineteenth century and had been recorded considerably before then by reliable astronomers. Combined with the sudden post-war importation of ex-Nazi scientists by the CIA for purposes of Moon rocket development, and the recent discoveries of the Great Pyramid of Xian and Egyptian flying saucer inscriptions, this would all seem to indicate that the government had begun pondering our solar system's inhabitation considerably earlier. Mars had been an object of romantic speculation since Percival Lowell and H. G. Wells, and it isn't difficult to believe that someone simply happened on elements that, ironically, seemed later to actually be true, but Mars must surely have crossed government investigators' minds as the likeliest planet of UFO origin as well. It must be noted that the Washington National flyovers could not have been veiled in *The Day the Earth Stood Still*'s flying saucer landing in Washington, D.C.—the actual UFO incidents there didn't occur until the year after the movie was made. The 1965 New York blackout has been attributed by some (not without grounds) to UFOs seen over power plants, and 1967 abductee

Herbert Schirmer's testimony says that aliens sometimes take power from our sources, but neither of these occurrences happened until fourteen or more years later. Coincidences do happen. Sometimes a banana is just a banana.

The year 1951 also brought the first outer-space serial since Universal's *Flash Gordon Conquers the Universe* in 1940: *Radar Men from the Moon*. Released by Republic Pictures to compete with Lippert's contemporaneous *Superman,* it was the inaugural appearance of the bullet-helmeted, jet-packed hero Commando Cody, Sky Marshal of the Universe. "So," a government scientist says to one of his peers at the beginning of Chapter Four, "the radar men from the moon are planning to attack Earth, as soon as their saboteurs have softened-up our defenses!" The first scene in the entire serial takes place in a secret government lab, where the ultimate Top Secret is revealed—that the Moon is inhabited, and its occupants have been experimenting with their "atomic ray" against planet Earth. Brave Commando Cody and his stalwart band secretly combat the Moon menace. The serial was followed by the sequel *Zombies of the Stratosphere*—in which Leonard Nimoy made one of his first-ever appearances, as a slant-eyed alien—in 1952, both later being condensed into feature films (in reverse order) in 1958 and 1966. *Zombies* featured the same clunky tin-can robot that had been used in 1940's *The Mysterious Dr. Satan,* and both serials utilized flying footage from 1949's *King of the Rocketmen.* The same year Commando Cody debuted, Republic released another serial "in 12 atomic chapters!" called *Flying Disc Man from Mars,* also condensed into movie form in 1958. The title character was "Mota the Martian," who premiered in 1945's feature release (formerly a serial) *D-Day On Mars,* capable of taking over the will of human beings and threatening mass destruction with his "electroannihilator" and "thermal disintegrator" weapons.

The serials that preceded Commando Cody began with *Flash Gordon* in 1936—the same year as *Undersea Kingdom.* Flash Gordon also appeared in two sequels, *Flash Gordon's Trip to Mars* in 1938 and the aforementioned *Flash Gordon Conquers the Universe* two years later. *Buck Rogers,* also from Universal, premiered in 1939 and was condensed into ninety-minute feature-film format in 1965. "Mind-control helmets" were featured as part of the villainous alien Killer Kane's arsenal. Jerry Siegel and Joe Shuster's "Superman," the friendly humanoid alien from Krypton, premiered in *Action* comics in exactly the same time period, June of 1938, making his first movie appearance simultaneously with Commando Cody.

George Reeves first played Superman, in the Lippert movie *Superman and the Mole Men.* The next year, *Superman* was picked up for a very successful run of five years on series T.V., and the sixty-seven-minute movie was cut and condensed into two parts to appear in the show's first season as "The Unknown People." The title creatures are short, almost completely bald dwarves, with tight-fitting body-suits. Disturbed by "the world's deepest well" hitting their subterranean lair, the little dwarves come to the upper world and create general havoc despite entirely peaceful intentions. They bedroom-visit a little girl at night and successfully befriend her, but are driven away by her mother, who screams upon encountering them. They terrify an old man to death simply by appearing to him, and are met with actively hostile backwoods redneck locals, who shoot one of the dwarves before Superman can intervene. Superman does his best to convince all the locals that their mysterious little underworld visitors have shown no hostility, and in fact may be entirely friendly, but they will have none of it. Another little man is nearly burned to death by a lynch-mob and returns with other little men armed with a ray-gun. Superman prevents them from killing the redneck who shot their friend, and he returns the injured Mole Man to the others who have come for him. Clark Kent laments that the world is not ready to meet new-found friends who might be a little different, and a serious-faced Lois Lane concludes the story with its epitaph: "You stay in your world, we'll stay in ours."

1951 was also the year that physicist-turned-science-fiction-writer Robert Heinlein, one of John W. Campbell's protégés, published *The Puppet Masters,* an oft-borrowed (and rarely credited) plot about alien parasites who invade human hosts on the sly for clandestine takeover. The Robertson Panel-recommended Disney Studios made the novel into a movie forty years later. In those forty years, the story found its way into one form or another (many of which will be commented on) in every medium, one example being 1958's AIP entry, *The Brain Eaters*. Heinlein also wrote one of the most famous science-fiction novels ever, which became a cult favorite of an entire generation: *Stranger in a Strange Land*. Its protagonist is a human raised on Mars named Valentine Smith, who tries to teach mankind to accept the peaceful Martian ways but ends up dismembered and devoured *a la* Dionysus by his worshippers.

Also the same year, the obscure *The Man From Planet X* was released by United Artists, about a saucer landing in Scotland spearheaded by an initially friendly alien (who never speaks, with an immobile face inside a fish-bowl helmet, and whose planet is on a collision course with Earth). The alien turns hostile after a psychopathic member of his reception party tortures him in an attempt to gain his knowledge. The alien hypnotizes the local populace into becoming its invasion vanguard by night, an oft-repeated element in flying saucer movies, from 1953's *Invaders from Mars* to the 1970 Warner Bros./ABC T.V. movie *Night Slaves,* and beyond. Star Margaret Field (mother of Sally), like many cast members of UFOlogical dramas, whether in the cinema or on television, is interested in the UFO subject. Asked in the January 1997 *Filmfax* about the fact, Field answered, "[My husband] and I were always believers in UFOs and extraterrestrial life. In later years we would meet with other people who would share in this belief and it was quite interesting to have been a part of it. I guess we maybe hoped in some way that we would have a 'close encounter' of some kind because our belief and open-mindedness in the subject was genuine. *The Man From Planet X* may seem a bit corny today, but it was more inspiring to me years later when I became enthused in this subject. It's that kind of movie. It makes you wonder." Such may have been the movie's precise purpose, even before it was made.

A more telling piece of propaganda is 1952's *Red Planet Mars* from United Artists, in which Peter Graves believes he is receiving messages from that planet on his radio, telling him of the Martians' beatific society of technological and natural harmony. He publicizes the messages, and a worldwide religious revival occurs. Unfortunately, the messages have actually originated from a nihilistic Communist Russian bad-guy out to subvert the world—even though it seems that the signals continue after his plot is foiled. A similar theme had been explored two years prior, in MGM's *The Next Voice You Hear,* in which radios around the world begin transmitting what claims to be the voice of God. The experience is shown to frighten even religious believers and disrupt their lives, even though the voice's communications are benevolent. Its only "threat" is to ask doubters if it will be necessary to create another Flood in order to be believed—at which point, a sudden rainstorm begins. It is natural to assume that *Red Planet Mars,* and *Invaders from Mars* the next year, were a result of the McCarthy era, which in part they may have been. But the connection to real flying saucer information is unquestionably of importance, as is the use of a theme of particular interest to the Robertson Panel, which was concern over the potential use of flying saucers as a subversive political influence.

Aside from these examples, and the early government-connected Lost City writers and UFO investigations, there are other extremely good reasons to believe that there has long been a Hollywood connection to the propagandization of actual UFO facts. In *Destination Moon,* a Walter Lantz "Woody Woodpecker" cartoon is utilized to deliver a science lesson in the physics of space travel, reminding us of the Robertson Panel's recommendation that cartoons, especially by "Walt Disney, Inc." be employed for this purpose. Obviously, the CIA had some pull with Disney Studios, as they did with Walter Lantz. Who else did they have influence with? And in what way were they using them? The answer to the former can only be discovered by reviewing the output of science-fictional space stories in the media, and the latter can be defined by a single word from Counterintelligence parlance: *misinformation.*

"Misinformation," in its Intelligence usage, can best be defined as the dissemination of truthful information from less than credible sources, or telling the truth in such a fashion that it is certain not to be believed. Where "disinformation" is fiction masquerading as fact, "misinformation" is the exact opposite—fact masquerading as fiction. An extremely effective variety of misinformation is something initially taken to be true that is then exposed as false, thus souring any later mention of such facts by way of having cried "wolf." If, for example, Orson Welles' "Invasion From Mars" broadcast was a deliberate cover to deflect attention from the real thing, then it would be classed as misinformation. Its effect would have been to discredit the very idea of such an occurrence by its exposure as a hoax after having first been believed to be legitimate, in which case it would have succeeded brilliantly, because people have been laughing at the idea of Martian invasion ever since. We have already encountered some prime examples, actual UFO facts having appeared in at least two Hollywood movies and a few prior serials. There are a great many more.

Where these movies show a fairly serious approach to the material in question, as though perhaps attempting to prepare their audience for eventual disclosure of the reality at hand, it has to have occurred to most readers by this time that much of the factual UFO information so far studied bears a remarkable resemblance to one or two movies they have seen at some time or another, virtually all of which, with notable exceptions, are extremely bad. So bad, in fact, that at the time they were seen, there was a niggling suspicion that they almost had to have been made so deliberately. Having been briefed on the UFO subject as best as possible within the limitations of the format and the official government censorship, it might do us well to consider the use of Hollywood as a propaganda machine. Certainly, cable and VCRs put literally hundreds of examples at our fingertips.

4

Misdirections and Misinformations

Anyone who doesn't think Hollywood is a willing partner in propaganda for the government never saw a WWII movie in which "them dirty Krauts" and "stinkin' Japs" machine-gunned pilots parachuting to safety, bayoneted babies, raped blind schoolteachers, and committed nameless other atrocities against "good, God-fearing folk" supporting the Free World of Mom, Apple Pie, and the American Flag. Hitler was comically parodied by Charlie Chaplin, the Three Stooges' Moe Howard and even Bugs Bunny. Other Warner Bros. cartoons, still regularly in circulation on Ted Turner's many cable channels, solicited the purchase of War Bonds, the patriotic donation of nylons and other supplies, and the planting of Victory Gardens, not to mention extolling the virtues of men who rushed off to enlist with the Marines, women who became war plant workers, and all good citizens who respected the meat and travel rations of the time. Ronald Reagan never went to war, but he preached patriotism from his presidential pulpit and made propaganda films both before and after he served as the FBI's "Agent T-10," informing on Communists in the entertainment industry during the McCarthy blacklistings.

Propaganda against William Gaines' liberal and entertaining E.C. comic books (he also ran the first educationally oriented science fiction in the medium, though it is trite by today's standards) was filmed in documentary fashion, suitable enough to get Congress to enforce the sanitary Comics Code for well over a decade: the footage used—which can be seen in the documentary *Comic Book Confidential*—showed a child literally swooning after reading a horror comic, then beginning to jitter as if possessed, and pick up a rock, slowly raising it in his hand and moving toward his unsuspecting friend ... my God, the cameraman must have stopped him *just in time!* An entire generation has grown up smoking marijuana, disproving the horrific "reality" portrayed in *Reefer Madness,* with other equally ridiculous films such as *Sex Madness* and their like now also shown-up for the blatant propaganda they were. We laugh at such things today, but the propaganda was such that it was believed at the time, and, when subtly disguised, is still believed today. Rush Limbaugh's entire job is propaganda, but it masquerades as investigative journalism and millions believe it. The same could be said for *Oprah, Donahue, Geraldo,* and any number of other non-news forums. Even *60 Minutes* can sometimes be demonstrated to be not entirely objective.

As if to underscore the connection, the same year the Robertson Panel made its recommendation, a classic Cold War movie was made, released at the same time as a pro-documentary on Yucca Flats called "Operation H-Bomb": Columbia's *Invasion U.S.A.* Both T.V. actresses to have played Superman's love interest, Lois Lane (Phyllis Coates and Noel Neill), were in it. *Invasion U.S.A.* begins with patrons in a luxuriously bourgeois bar debating whether or not fear of the Russians and development of war products has gotten a bit excessive. Before they know it, there is a news flash on the T.V.: Russia has dropped atomic bombs on America! They are paratrooping into Alaska and California! The country is under merciless attack! But we are solemnly assured that, for every Communist A-bomb detonated over our cities, three will be returned. The evil Commies barge into offices, terrorize employees, shoot decadent bourgeois bosses, and rape secretaries and wives. The horror escalates, until finally ... *snap!* Bar customer Dan O'Herlihy wakes everyone up—they have been hypnotized by him, into seeing the future their foolish talk of limiting arms and trusting the Russians would bring. Having seen the error of their ways, the other customers swear they will be prepared. The entire movie is performed in deadly earnest, without a smile or a joke or even a moment of intended comic relief to be found. It is impossible to take seriously today, yet as recently as 1984—as Ronald Reagan was being reelected—right-wing director John Milius made almost exactly the same film for theatrical release through MGM/UA, called *Red Dawn.*

The ink was barely dry on the Robertson Panel propaganda recommendation before Herman Cohen, the producer of the cheapest exploitation films (he came to fame with *I Was A Teenage Werewolf* in 1957), bought the rights to *If* magazine's "Deadly City," by Ivar Jorgenson (a pen-name of Paul W. Fairman, who also wrote the story on which 1957's *Invasion of the Saucer Men* was based) immediately as it was published in March of 1953. Shot in seven days on a $75,000 budget, it was released nine months later by Allied Artists under the title *Target Earth.* Its story was about a small group of metropolitan survivors holding their own against alien invaders. The movie made one change from the story, bringing it directly in line with actual UFOlogical facts: the invading aliens became instead indestructible robots. The military eventually saves the survivors with a sonic wave device which jams the alien robots' signal reception, having determined from experiments on captured devices that they are radio-controlled emissaries of a humanlike race presumed to be from Venus. The budget was so small Cohen only made one robot, which was used as an army of them through the behind-the-scenes miracle of recycling, and it was a laughable affair with a boxy look, clamp hands, one cyclopean light in the middle of its head, and corrugated tubes for legs. Lippert/20th Century Fox produced a virtually identical movie in England only eleven years later, called *The Earth Dies Screaming.* Perhaps not so ironically, Richard Denning's character in *Target Earth* observes that the apparent UFO reality against which he and his retinue find themselves making their last stand is remarkably like the pulp fiction stories an old friend of his used to read. *Target Earth* was one of Cohen's first productions, at age twenty-three. Immediately prior to embarking on his film career, he spent four years in the Marines.

Cohen told Jim Wynorski, himself now a director of such enjoy-ably camp films as *Return of Swamp Thing* and *Transylvania Twist,* that audiences had enjoyed the movie in its day. "Even though we played it straight," he said, "they sat in their seats with tongues-firmly-in-cheek." This could well have been calculated. As Wynorski wrote in *They Came From Outer Space,* ". . .it is admittedly difficult to assess the motive behind an exploitation film like *Target Earth.* Is it cheaply produced in every way to cash in quickly on a craze, or is it the most esthetically acceptable product that can be done with minor resources?" Or was it, perhaps, a deliberate attempt to create a laugh-able aura around a subject few yet suspected was that serious?

More ludicrous still was one of the most famous of the incredibly bad flying saucer movies, all of which can be traced directly to a beginning no earlier than the Robertson Panel's recommendation, but rather immediately following it: *Robot Monster.* Also known as *Monsters from the Moon* and *Monster from Mars,* it was filmed in four days in Hollywood's Bronson Canyon for under $20,000, in 3-D. The title creature is Ro-Man (as opposed to his Hu-Man prey), from a Mar-tian robot race out to destroy the world, paving the way for 268,000 émigrés from the Red Planet. A handful of survivors stand against him—exactly as in *Target Earth*—and, inexplicably, the robot is a man in a gorilla suit, the only robotic-looking thing about him being a diving helmet with a glass faceplate and two antennae. The story goes that producer-director Phil Tucker either couldn't afford a whole robot suit or else lost part of it somewhere and replaced it with the nearest available substitute, which frankly sounds like a lot of balder-dash though it is a highly entertaining story. It is also interesting in light of the reports of "hairy dwarves" involved in UFO abduction, which as we have seen were almost certainly robots, and which were not written about anywhere before the mid-Sixties, more than a decade following this movie.

It is not really within the realm of possibility that anyone involved with the making of this film intended it to be taken seriously, but it is played as if it were intended to be, naturally making it all the fun-nier. Stock footage of entirely unrelated movies is spliced into the script, including the famous fighting dinosaurs of *One Million BC,* having nothing to do with the story; phrases like "U-Ray" and a leader called "The Great One" abound; Ro-Man delivers portentous speeches, brazenly threatens, succumbs to the pangs of love (which is absurd on the face of it, given what he is supposed to be), and anguishes with a soul that by definition he could never have. The British have long had a term for exactly this style of theater, called "coarse acting," and have actually turned it into its own art form, of sorts, by holding festivals to see who can do the best job of bringing it about. "Good" coarse acting is when the acting is unbelievably bad, and is actually contrived to have been so, but is made to appear as if intended to be serious. It is, in short, imitation bad acting.

Robot Monster's producer, Al Zimbalist, made the 3-D *Cat Women of the Moon* from the same studio, Astor, in the same year. The Moon is inhabited by remarkably beautiful telepathic women in black cat-suits, who fool around with astronaut Victor Jory, rescue him from a giant spider, and ultimately let him and his cohorts go back home before they might discover other terrors beyond their present ability to contend with. Star Marie Windsor considered it the worst movie she ever made. Actually remade—arguably worse—by the same studio in 1958, as *Missile to the Moon,* it was the real beginning of the mini-skirted space-maiden movie trend, even though predated by 1951's near-identical color Monogram production, *Flight to Mars.* Made simultaneously with these movies were the English imports *Project M-7* (funded by Universal), and Lippert Studios' *Spaceways* and *Project Moonbase,* all static and rather silly space-operas, the latter-most written by Robert Heinlein.

At exactly the same time as Cohen purchased the rights for *Target Earth,* publisher William Gaines put a science-fiction story in his February/March 1953 *Shock SuspenStories* comic book (No. 7), which was ordinarily devoted to nothing but straightforward crime melodramas. It was entitled "Infiltration," by Joe Orlando. "This may come as a complete surprise to you," read the opening narrative panels, "but do you know that there is a government bureau, working in cooperation with the Army, Navy, and F.B.I., specifically formed for the purpose of investigating and ferreting out *Martian Invaders?* It is a *small* government agency . . . *Top Secret!* With the appearance of the flying saucers, the thought that possibly an undercover invasion was taking place prompted formation of the Bureau. . . ." Concurrent with these entertainment events, Max Fleischer's popular Popeye the Sailor was saucer-abducted and subjected to torture by antennaed green Martians, in "Popeye, the Ace of Space." He downs his spinach, knocks them senseless, and leaves them dancing merrily around a maypole. Flying their saucer back home to Earth, he sings, "The Martians were hateful, but now they are playful, thanks to Popeye, the Sailor Man!" *(Toot, toot!)* Popeye also frequently found himself abducted to the "Island of the Goons," strange, non-verbal humanoids, with teardrop heads, unblinking eyes, and elongated forearms, whose motivations are never made clear. A later cartoon had Popeye once more saucer-abducted to Mars by their planet's version of his usual antagonist, Bluto, who is preparing an invasion of Earth. Fleischer was also the animator of the wartime *Superman* cartoons beginning in 1941, one of which—"The Mechanical Monsters"—had robots abducting Lois Lane in the series' first year.

United Artists' 1953 entries were *Phantom from Space, The Magnetic Monster,* and *The Twonky.* The initially invisible title extraterrestrial of *Phantom from Space* was a musclebound, bald, lightbulb-headed man in tights, who hid in Griffith Park Observatory. The alien was not hostile, but died after being pursued by two government agents. The movie was forgettable enough that it is not often found listed today in sci-fi film catalogues and is virtually never aired. *The Magnetic Monster,* directed and co-written by *Donovan's Brain* and *The Wolf Man*'s Curt Siodmak, was an extraterrestrial collection of intelligent atomic particles from space invading Earth; the film was produced and co-written by Ivan Tors (later most famous for MGM T.V.'s *Flipper),* who would the following year produce a robot-run-amok/UFO-sabotage story called *Gog* (see below). *The Twonky* was screenwritten, directed, and produced by Arch Oboler (originally written by renowned sci-fi/horror author Henry Kuttner under the pseudonym "Lewis Padgett" in the 1940s magazine *Unknown),* most famous for radio's *Lights Out,* and starred florid character actor Hans Conreid as a man haunted by a T.V. set. The T.V. set is in actuality a "Twonky," a robot from the future which has taken a liking to

Conreid, following him around and making his life miserable. The robot awkwardly hobbles about, performing chores for Conreid by the use of light beams emanating from its tube. When discovered or interfered with by others, the robot hypnotizes them with an electrical zap, and the interlopers wander away like zombies to amnesiacally follow whatever post-hypnotic commands the Twonky has given them. When a neighbor first suggests to Conreid that the set is a robot, Conreid looks at him disdainfully and snorts, "Oh, come now—where, outside of Hollywood, would anyone make a robot?" Like *Phantom from Space, The Twonky* is utterly forgettable, and almost appears deliberately intended to be. It is poorly produced and remarkably cheap, its worst feature being an incessant sound like a kid's slide-whistle throughout the soundtrack.

1953 was the year that Universal's *Abbot and Costello Go to Mars* was released. Robert Heinlein, the author of *The Puppet Masters* and co-scripter of 1950's *Destination Moon,* was advertised as being in the process of writing the never-materialized *Abbot and Costello Go to the Moon* the following year. Instead, 1951 saw *When Worlds Collide* (the first space catastrophe movie, directed by George Pal, who had done *Destination Moon), The Man from Planet X, The Thing, The Day the Earth Stood Still* and *Flight to Mars,* and the promised Abbot and Costello movie came in 1953 with a title (and planet) change. The A&C film featured paralyzing rays and more mini-skirted space-maidens (this time on Venus). *Flight to Mars* starred Arthur Franz, who soon appeared in *Invaders from Mars,* and showed the Martians living beneath the surface of their planet. It also starred Morris Ankrum, who made a career as generals in these movies.

The A&C venture was the most expensive and most hyped of any in the famous Universal series during the 1950s. Sexy co-star Marie Blanchard was shown wearing "flying saucer jewelry" in an August 25, 1952, UPI promotion. Oldsmobile had gimmick contests attached to the movie, and New York had a high school contest co-sponsored by Universal for the best thesis on "Why You Think Interplanetary Travel Will Be Developed In Your Lifetime." Universal International was a sponsor of the Miss Universe pageant, and used its contestants for their Venusian space lovelies. Milked for all it was worth

198 HOLLYWOOD VERSUS THE ALIENS

commercially, its purpose was hardly to promote serious thoughts about space travel, but specifically to make as comedic as possible any consideration of the Red Planet, as was *Flight to Mars*. Its promotional techniques were designed to make anything to do with outer space, and flying saucers especially, appear to be nothing more than a passing fad. It wasn't until 1960's critically acclaimed East German/Polish production *First Spaceship on Venus*, excluding Disney's "Tomorrowland," that space flight would be shown in America as anything other than fantasy. In common with many movies about other planets— Mars especially—*First Spaceship on Venus* portrayed that planet's civilization as long-deceased due to nuclear conflict, its surface devastated.

Already in production at the time of the Robertson Panel (it began filming in February of 1952) was George Pal's 1953 update of H. G. Wells' *The War of the Worlds,* a Technicolor masterpiece from Paramount with the best production values of the post-WWII American empire, and state-of-the-art Oscar-winning special effects to recommend it. It differs little from Wells by way of story, but is altered considerably in two major elements: the Martians and their war machines. The Martians in the movie are small bipeds with tri-lobed eyes, calling to mind the three antennae common to most UFO occupants, and their fingertips have the same suction-cup tips described by the nurse at Roswell—the Martians in the original novel were shapeless tentacular blobs. Their arms also possess the same characteristics as the reported Roswell occupants, being shorter from shoulder to elbow than from elbow to wrist. The eyes are lit from within, like those of 1955's Hopkinsville Goblins, and like the Goblins also are extremely light-sensitive (explained as due to the Red Planet receiving half the sunlight of Earth). The Martian warships look like the crescents described in Kenneth Arnold's famous sighting, as opposed to the tripodal walking tanks in Wells' novel. When Lincoln La Paz-inspired scientific hero Gene Barry finds his way back to Pacific Institute of Science and Technology, after he and fellow scientist Ann Robinson have had their plane downed by the Martians, he tells the team who have been looking for them, "We walked halfway from Corona." Corona, New Mexico, is the town closest to where rancher Mac Brazel discovered the downed Roswell saucer in 1947.

A much more nightmarish film was issued from 20th Century Fox the same year, William Cameron Menzies' *Invaders from Mars*. Menzies was the set designer for MGM's *Gone with the Wind*, and director and production designer for the 1936 United Artists production of H. G. Wells' *Things to Come*, and his creations for this 1953 *film noir* of sci-fi have made the movie a cult classic. Menzies' sets and costumes closely resemble actual abduction accounts, none of which were to become known for another ten years. Betty and Barney Hill weren't publicly written about until 1966. Yet, *Invaders from Mars* has a subterranean flying saucer with the same sterile environment described by the Hills and later abductees, in which people who have been abducted are carried off by identical bulletproof, bald, green-jumpsuited creatures with masklike faces, big round eyes, and over-sized mitts for hands, that bounce stiffly and mechanically about. These are specifically called "synthetic humans" (and "mutants") in the movie. The abductees are placed on a table in the middle of an empty room, and are implanted in the back of their necks by an automated drill that comes out of the ceiling; implants were not discussed in UFO writings until Betty Andreasson, almost fifteen years after this movie was made. The implanted abductees then return to their homes, where they continue living their lives, but are secretly under the control of a tentacled gold head in a globe inside the flying saucer—defined as "mankind, developed to its ultimate intelligence"—which silently and telepathically communicates messages to them that the audience never does learn the precise content of.

The abductees are the sons and daughters of government or military men, or other authority figures. After the implanted abductees have performed their acts of murder or sabotage, the Martians coldly explode the implants at the base of their skull, giving them fatal cerebral hemorrhages. Under the alien influence, fathers sadistically strike their sons, adorable little girls set their parents' homes on fire, and even top-security generals in the military become dangerous saboteurs. One little boy named David sees the saucer land and knows his father has been taken over, and eventually convinces the Army of the threat, ending in an Us-vs.-Them shootout at the saucer that drives the invaders away. And then ... pop! the little boy wakes up to discover that it was all a dream! But then the saucer lands for real, and ... *oh, no ... !!!*

Invaders from Mars is exactly the kind of movie that is used to argue for hysterical contagion in abduction reports. If that were the case, then it is strange that so many years should pass before the hysterical contagion hit. Aside from which, the abductors in the movie are identical giants, where the standard abduction report concerns identical little men. Why wouldn't hysterically induced reports feature the same giants? And why would they wait more than a decade to surface? The clichéd "all a dream" ending is also attached to bedroom abduction reports, in which the abductees wake in great terror from what they believe was a nightmare, but eventually come to realize was not.

Also curious is the lack of understandable motivation for the Martians in the movie. There is an Army-man-machine-guns against the Alien-heat-ray-guns battle, the Martians' hostility having been established by assassination attempts from their implanted humans against government scientists, but no motive for their actions is ever pondered. All the creatures from the saucer are either clearly mechanical-acting and -looking—itself a telling feature, for 1953—or immobile and entirely inscrutable, speaking not one intelligible word, which is atypical of comic book villains. (The gold head in the globe only asks abductees through one of its mind-controlled subjects about the military's activities against it, and the Gray-looking "mutants" that comprise its army are so indestructible that only explosive blasts can dismantle them.) The movie could well be taken as an actual presentation of what the military of the time knew about the entire UFO phenomenon: they are here, they are from Mars, they are abducting and implanting people in their sleep who awaken to believe they were dreaming, and are using mind-control on them for potentially hostile purpose ... and we haven't got the slightest idea why.

In fact, the promo trailers for the film expressed that exact angle, boldly asking "Why?" after each dramatic assertion: "[They] capture innocent people, only to destroy! *Why?* Father turns against son! *Why?* People changed into strange, weird animals! *Why?* A General of the Army becomes a saboteur! *Why?* Trusted police turn into arsonists! *Why?* A boy's parents changed into killers! *Why?"* An astronomer in the movie gives the only suggestion for the Martians' motus operandi, which is that our space shots are threatening their secure spaces. He believes the Martians must be living beneath their planet's surface, partly because of the frozen Martian atmosphere and partly because their strongholds on Earth are hewn underground caverns. He also states outright that they may be living in entirely artificial space stations of enormous size, undetectable to skywatchers on this planet.

Remade for Cannon Films in 1986 by Roger Corman-inheritors Menahem Golan and Yoram Globus and horror film maker Tobe Hooper, the nightmarish quality was retained, but virtually all connection to actual UFO trappings got lost. The Martian "mutants" became bizarre, hulking reptiles, unlike their robotic predecessors, and a needless element was added concerning implanted abductees eating live frogs and swallowing bottles-full of vitamins. It has little of the charm, but some of the classic production values of the original. While Hooper was almost certainly doing nothing more than paying homage to an old childhood favorite, his remake served the purposes of distancing viewing audiences from the original propaganda.

The remake has an exchange between David and two scientists involved in the "Millennium Project," co-workers with his father at a sabotaged NASA launch. "I didn't think the Viking missions found any sign of life," David says. "Except for this one photo I saw in a magazine of these things on the surface that looked like pyramids. And what about that huge thing that kind of looked like a monkey's head? It was in all the papers. Uh, that was fake, right?" "On the contrary," one of the scientists answers, seriously. "There were other photos, too sensational to be made public." The boy says, "But there's not enough water on Mars to support life!" "Not on the surface," the other scientist answers. "That's why we're looking below ground, this time." The general adds, "If there is life beneath the surface, it may not want to be found. It may not want us up there." Another scene in the remake that is not found in the original is one in which David is watching a clip from the same year's (and production company's) space-invader movie *Lifeforce,* and is startled by the appearance of a mobile toy robot with blinking-light eyes (being remote-controlled by his mother, as a joke), which says to him, "David Gardener! Feed me!" It is interesting to note that the 1953 version is almost never seen on television anymore, even on AMC, and is difficult to find on video (except in cutout bins), where Hooper's remake can be seen constantly making the late-night rounds. TNT scheduled the original in Fall of 1994 to be shown along with the other 1950s juvenile sci-fi fantasy movies *The 5,000 Fingers of Dr. T.* and *The Invisible Boy,* but these were preempted by an all-night Elvis-fest. Columbia's *The 5,000 Fingers of Dr. T.*—co-scripted by none other than children's author Dr. Seuss, and made the same year as the original *Invaders from Mars*—is itself an abduction movie, superbly produced by Stanley Kramer. *The Twonky*'s Hans Conreid plays mind-controlling mad piano instructor Dr. Terwilliker, who hypnotizes parents into cooperation with his nocturnally stealing away to a dark sky-kingdom five hundred little boys (with five thousand little fingers) to play his grand concerto.

As 1954 began and Herman Cohen's *Target Earth* was garnering intended unintended laughs, his British equivalent—the Danziger Brothers (Edward J. and Harry Lee), famous for cheap exploitation films—was producing Spartan's *Devil Girl from Mars,* a movie so bizarre it almost defies dramatic criticism. The entire thing is impossible to take seriously, but it plays like a war drama of the era, and is written more or less as a filmed stage play—which it is. Unbelievable as it seems upon viewing today, the script was originally a theatrical production, and was then adapted by one of its playwrights, James Eastwood (the co-author being John C. Mathers), for the screen. If someone took *The Rocky Horror Picture Show* and made more dry and British all of its sexual references, stripping it of all but one of its overt trappings, utterly removing all trace of humor and setting it in the middle of an Agatha Christie play, they would almost have *Devil Girl from Mars.* Dissatisfactory on any level as entertainment, it is only interesting for the fact that it cannot have been planned to be anything but a failure, and contains all the trappings of what appear to be the actual truths behind the UFO phenomenon.

The title character is a pre-Diana Rigg *Avengers* amazon played by decadently aristocratic Patricia Laffan, in a tight-fitting body-sheath and miniskirt of shiny black leather or vinyl, replete with severe skull-cap, cape, knee-boots and razor-sharp bone structure. She arrives in a classic flying saucer at an isolated English country inn—made all the more so by her severing their communications links to the rest of the world—and makes a number of superior and arrogant speeches in a low, sultry voice, all concerning how she is going to take what she wants from our puny planet . . . which is men, for sex. Since the men stupidly refuse to go voluntarily (they are, after all, British), she has to resort to threats and displays of power from her robot assistant, which—though it may be as powerful as *The Day the Earth Stood Still*'s Gort—is as ridiculous-looking as its closer contemporary from *Target Earth*. She also induces trances which cause "missing time," hypnotically dominates the wills of others and programs them to attack their fellows on her behalf, and briefly abducts a little boy aboard her saucer to coerce the adults, though she in no way harms him—in fact, he has the time of his life, having been enticed aboard by the Devil Girl saying, "Come—I will show you wonders you have never seen before!"

Despite its obvious drawbacks, the film interestingly "has achieved a certain cult status and culled affectionate reviews by some contemporary film critics," according to *Filmfax* interviewer Mark Miller, though the same magazine's movie reviewer, David J. Hogan, accurately levels the criticism that it suffers from "didactic posturing, trite moralizing, and unconvincing character development." Star Hazel Court, who has appeared in far better, more recognizable, and more memorable movies in her day, admits, "That film haunts me! Everywhere I go people say, 'I saw you in *Devil Girl from Mars!*' I think the film only took about two weeks to shoot and it was made on a shoe-string." And it shows. Though never seen on American T.V., it can currently be purchased at bargain price on home video. Given that this movie has all the plot elements of a highly successful comedy, or at least a camp classic, its having instead been made as a spectacularly mediocre serious melodrama with scarcely a moment's comic relief seems inexplicable . . . unless it was intended to leave audiences with a sour feeling toward its subject matter.

It was in 1954 that the Warner Bros. classic *Them!* was made, about giant ants in the Mojave Desert. Though it has nothing overtly to do with UFOs, it exemplifies a practice that was quickly to become common throughout the 1950s and ensuing decades: the ubiquitous mention of flying saucers or UFOs in an overtly ludicrous manner. At one point in the movie, pilot Fess Parker is questioned by the team clandestinely trying to destroy the giant mutant ants before any public news can escape concerning them. Parker is being held against his will in a hospital, refusing to recant his story. He claims to have seen flying saucers—but saucers shaped like big ants. Admitting that he knows it sounds crazy, he is adamant, and the investigators cannot tell him they know he is telling the truth. While it makes the reality of the movie's story more credible, it also reinforces an image that flying saucers are no more real outside of the movie theater than giant mutant ants. Other "giant insect" movies of the period made the subject of nuclear radiation appear to be equally harmless: since everyone can plainly see that no giant insects or animals exist outside of the movie theater, the idea is reinforced that any talk concerning the dangers of radiation is equally nonexistent.

1954 also saw United Artists' Technicolor (then called Eastmancolor) 3-D robot movie, *Gog,* and another, more juvenile robot from Republic called *Tobor the Great.* "Gog" is one of two robots (the other being "Magog," both from the Bible) at an experimental government defense installation. The Office of Scientific Investigation (an actual CIA division, though the fact was likely unknown at the time of this movie's production), first seen in the same studio's and the same producer's *The Magnetic Monster* the year before, is called in to discover why so many scientists at the installation are turning up dead in terrible accidents. Every time one of the accidents takes place, UFOs are in the area. It turns out that the UFOs are high-flying Communist planes, sending signals which cause Gog and Magog to sabotage the base and kill people. Plainly, at the time of the movie's making—and even today—the Soviets and Chinese lacked such technology, but if Martians are figured into the equation, there was another party from a bit farther away that was engaged in much of the same activity.

One of the sabotaged base's primary experimental equipment arrays in Gog consists of a number of tuning forks operating in conjunction with each other to alter temperatures. Such experimentation was not only begun by Nikola Tesla even before the turn of the century, but also appears to have been the principal "magic" of the superior race of people who lived on Earth in antiquity. Such connotations would be intriguing enough in light of the apparent historical connection of such technology's use by the UFO Intelligence, but are all the more so for the fact that a real-life top-secret Department of Defense project called HAARP—standing for High-frequency Active Auroral Research Project—has been experimented with since at least the early 1970s, and did not even begin to become public knowledge until the late 1980s.

In its earliest documented stages, as discussed in Dr. Nick Begich and Jeane Manning's *Angels Don't Play This HAARP: Advances In Tesla Technology,* much of HAARP's workings and purposes were kept secret even from President Jimmy Carter, who the military believed would be hostile to it. HAARP indeed appears primarily to be sonic in nature, utilizing Tesla technology to cook particles in the ionosphere with waves radiating from massive antenna arrays. Practical weather control is one of its attempted purposes, as is the instant erasure of any targeted computer complex in the world with directed magnetic pulses of tremendous power. Its most alarming desired operating characteristic, as stated in documents attesting to the project, is the ability to create nuclear-sized explosions without the fallout. HAARP has received severe censure from a number of expert scientists who have become aware of its existence and follow its progress as closely as is possible, which is not very close at all owing to the extreme secrecy of the project.

As interesting as HAARP's appearance is in a movie more than three decades prior to its public mention, it is far more interesting that the ideas behind its technology were aired in the United Artists T.V. series *The Outer Limits* on April 6, 1964, in the episode "The Special One." (See Chapter 5.) In this story, a human-looking alien called "Mr. Zeno" secretly instructs a young Earth pupil in clandestine takeover techniques, for purposes of a surprise fifth-column attack in preparation for the all-out invasion of Earth by his race. "Sound waves can trigger weather changes," Zeno informs the boy, after showing him how to walk effortlessly through solid walls, "therefore, element control." The boy experiments throughout the show with "combinations" generated from a sound-machine Mr. Zeno gives him, to alter the temperature of solid objects and change atmospheric conditions. In the end, the clever student, having detected Zeno's evil designs, drives his treacherous teacher off our world by use of the same machine, and tells his proud father, "I had to figure out the right atmosphere combination that would make it impossible for beings like him to ever set foot on Earth again ... We'll have to turn [the machine] over to the government. They'll have to expand the principle so that they can repel a whole army of them at a time— cut off their Xenon supply." Xenon is a necessary gas for Zeno's survival in the story, plentiful in his atmosphere but sparse in our own. It may be no more than a coincidence, but Mars has noticeable quantities of the rare gas Xenon-13 in its atmosphere. What appears to be less a coincidence is the idea of HAARP's being the expansion of an ancient alien technology, in development for precisely the same purpose stated in the "The Special One."

An early potential veiled reference to HAARP appeared in the premiere "Derek Flint" spy-spoof released by 20th Century Fox in 1966, *Our Man Flint*. In it, Flint learns from ."0008" about an organization "much bigger than [James Bond's nemesis] SPECTRE," called GALAXY, which has created a weather-control machine for world domination toward the ostensible end of creating an imposed peace on Earth. GALAXY is headquartered inside an uncharted island, its members wearing uniforms of the Atlantean colors red, white, and black. They also abduct a number of beautiful women, whom they physically brand (not unlike the unusual birthmarks found on UFO abductees) and hypnotically condition into becoming "pleasure units" for breeding purposes.

Just how successful the government has been with HAARP cannot fully be known, but during one of its scheduled test runs in September 1995, extremely unusual and severe weather disruptions, causing emergency conditions and long-lasting, massive power outages, occurred in Colorado, where one of the U.S. Space Command's two publicly disclosed dishes is located at Buckley Air Force Base—exactly the sort of dish necessary to house the antenna arrays on which HAARP functions. HAARP's principal array is located in the outlying Alaskan wilderness, but most of its technology requires two sets of antennae, one of which Buckley could have been supplying at that time. Another scheduled test was for April of 1997, when Colorado broke a seventy-five-year-old record for unseasonably cold temperatures.

The debut of one of the most famous movie monsters in history came from Universal in 1954, who bears an interesting resemblance to UFO abductors: *The Creature from the Black Lagoon.* Producer William Alland and director Jack Arnold (later of *Gilligan's Island* fame) had a hit the previous year in the same studio's *It Came from Outer Space,* one of the first 3-D exploitation gimmicks, based on a Ray Bradbury story. The plot concerned xenomorphic aliens crash-landing in the American desert, uninterested in man except as a means of helping them repair their ship so they could leave. Neither friendly nor hostile, they just wanted to be on their way, and seemed to think—as did the film's protagonist (Richard Carlson)—that man simply wasn't ready for a meeting with extraterrestrials. *The Creature from the Black Lagoon* has nothing to do with UFOs (though it does feature an early passing comment about them), but does feature a classic abductor-entity, the title Creature being claw-handed, bald, hairless, noseless, strong and silent and relentless in its purpose ... which is abduction "beneath the sea" (like the Fomorians/Giants of Celtic myth) of shapely Julie Adams, for sex.

It is noteworthy that William Alland was part of Orson Welles' Mercury Radio Theatre when the famous 1938 "Invasion from Mars" broadcast occurred. In fact, Alland was the ubiquitous back-to-the-camera shadow/interviewer "star" of Welles' *Citizen Kane,* in 1941. Alland claimed to have gotten the idea for the story of *The Creature from the Black Lagoon* from an after-dinner tale of Amazonian fishmen told by a South American movie director of the famous auteur's acquaintance after shooting *Citizen Kane,* though the idea sounds like a bit of puffery. Alland himself was a combat pilot on bombing missions in the South Pacific during WWII, and his male lead for *The*

Creature and *It Came from Outer Space,* Richard Carlson, was a super-patriotic ex-Navy man who starred as diligent McCarthy-ite Commie-hunting spy "Herbert Philbrick" (based on a true character) in the J. Edgar Hoover-sponsored 1953–56 Ziv T.V. hit *I Led Three Lives.* It may also be worth mention that the original Black Lagoon Creature underwent several different overall appearances, script-wise—from mere shadow in the background, to lobster-clawed beast with tail—before ending up looking like the famous UFO Gray abductor.

Alland and Arnold also produced the following year's *This Island Earth,* for the same studio as their former two hits, which may be considered the first of the space-opera epics. Based on 1947's short story "The Alien Machine" by Raymond F. Jones in *Thrilling Wonder Stories,* expanded in coming years to novel length because of fan acclaim, the story concerns a hapless bunch of Earth geniuses seduced into unwittingly assisting another solar system's interplanetary war. After encountering a control takeover in his jet cockpit by an unidentified, pulsing green beam, scientist Rex Reason finds that some practical joker has sent him a tiny bead in place of a clunky electronic part he needs, but then discovers that it is far superior in function to the part he ordered . . . and it is also many years in advance of Earth's technology. The same untraceable source sends him instructions for building an "Interociter," which turns out to be a two-way telescreen through which a strange-looking but friendly enough man (Jeff Morrow) with a huge, domed head extends him an invitation to learn more.

Hopping aboard a remote-controlled, pilotless airplane, Reason is taken to an isolated spot where a number of scientists like himself are holed-up in an expansive chalet, run by characters as odd-looking—and acting—as Morrow. Hooking up with old-flame colleague Faith Domergue, he discovers that strange goings-on are afoot, such as people's personalities becoming zombiefied and more cooperative after private trips to a back room, pervasive surveillance, and an inability to freely come and go. Becoming understandably concerned, they make a break for it, only to be abducted by a flying saucer that seizes control of their airplane by means of the same green beam encountered earlier. Aboard the sterile, futuristic saucer,

Morrow apologizes for the extraordinary measures and clues them in. His planet, Metaluna, is at war with the planet Zagon, and they need to discover a way to create more nuclear power than they presently have. The most promising Earth scientists were employed to help them toward that end, and now they must return to Metaluna with their captors personally. Aside from Morrow, the Metalunans are ruthless and unconcerned with Earth people's wants or needs, other than those that are necessary in order for them to serve. Morrow helps them escape back to Earth as his home planet succumbs to a final onslaught from its enemies, then commits suicide, having nowhere left in the universe to go.

The original story did not contain the UFOlogical elements most recognizable as actual case-study occurrences, namely the control takeover from a remote source and one or two curious saucer descriptions. Before making the leap to Metaluna's solar system, all humans aboard—which includes the Metalunans—must go into vacuum stasis tubes, in order to keep from being pulverized against the sides of the craft. Betty Andreasson's is not the only case on record of abductees being placed in a "breathing pool" of liquid that holds them firm, like jello, but it is the only case published claiming to know the purpose—which is exactly the same as the one stated in *This Island Earth*. There is no question that Andreasson could consciously or unconsciously have picked up the idea, but she wouldn't have known anything about remote-control instrument takeovers. Also included in the movie, but not in the published material, is a "Metaluna Mutant," a giant, insectoid creature bred as a slave. Admittedly more than likely the hook for luring juvenile viewers the monster was claimed by its producers to be, it also bears an interesting functional resemblance to actual UFO abductors. That the movie was not intended to be taken as anything other than silly escapist fantasy is apparent from its companion release: *Abbot and Costello Meet the Mummy*.

Also in 1955 came Allied Artists' *World Without End*, a space-travel apocalypse story converted into a time-travel apocalypse story. Like the earlier and later Otherworld nuclear-devastation-of-aeons-past pictures, this one had Earth's time-travelers discovering that between our century and the 21st, the planet has succumbed to the ravages of the bomb and man's stupidity. Giant spiders, mutant cavemen, and lusty young ladies eager to repopulate the planet in Alberto Vargas-designed spangled mini-gowns made up the Technicolor CinemaScope extravaganza. The same year, a propagandistic production of Wernher von Braun's *The Mars Project* was filmed for Paramount by George Pal and Byron Haskin as *Conquest of Space,* in which the first captain of a Mars mission deliberately attempts to sabotage the flight because he believes it is a blasphemy against God—who, by implication, ends up saving the astronauts by making it snow, thus providing his waterless crew with the only thing that will save them. Von Braun himself frequently addressed crowds with arguments that if God had not intended man to fly into space, he would have made space impassable and never given man brains—i.e., God meant man to fly, therefore he gave him wings of thought. He actually had audience with the Pope to discuss the very topic, who agreed with von Braun.

One of the earliest "astro-zombie" movies was released in 1955, Columbia's *Creature with the Atom Brain,* written by Curt Siodmak. It was produced by Sam Katzman and directed by Edward L. Cahn, both of whom went on to do many more UFOlogically-oriented movies in the same vein. A mad scientist turns dead men into bulletproof robots for bank robberies, by use of brain electrode implants. Roky Erickson revived this otherwise completely forgotten mini-classic in 1981 by recording a song based on it, complete with dialogue and a mock-radio report of the "killing" of one of the bulletproof zombies. Siodmak, who first achieved fame by being the scriptwriter for Universal's legendary 1941 production of *The Wolf Man,* is best known for his novel written the following year, *Donovan's Brain,* an oft-filmed story of a dead man's brain hypnotically dominating the living, which was probably inspired by the Doctor Mabuse character of 1920s German pulp fiction and cinema.

MGM's *Forbidden Planet* followed in 1956, with a ship that was a typical flying saucer. Again, the stasis element was introduced, as it would be in the same studio's *From the Earth to the Moon* in 1958, based on the famous Jules Verne book. Its central element was an ancient civilization (beneath the surface of the solar system's fourth planet) with still-working artifacts and machines, including probably the most famous robot in modern cinema history, "Robby." Essentially a classical tragedy reworking of Shakespeare's *The Tempest,* it does contain actual UFOlogical elements. The Cydonia or possible Moon artifacts could well have been suspected at the time, so the lost city of the Krell (as the race was called) may have been based on them—again, Mars and the Moon must have been considered likely possibilities by the government as base locations for the saucers. The "Krlll" of the Area 51/MJ-12 disinformational stories obviously derived from this source. And, of course, the continued association of escapist fantasy with flying saucers was reinforced, childish terminology being employed to describe the advanced technology seen in the movie: the guns are called "blasters," the signaling devices "beamers," and a comic-relief robot named "Robby" is self-explanatory. Its most interesting UFO connection is in the character of Dr. Morbius, a philologist whose intellect has been artificially boosted by the Krell technology; by night, Morbius becomes a separate saboteur personality, completely oblivious to his actions when awake. Disney Studios did the movie's animation sequences.

Peter Graves, in one of his many idiotic early movies, played an unlikely UFO abductee in RKO's 1954 feature, *Killers from Space*. He is a dead man reanimated by classically decked-out abductors: body-fitting sweatsuits with tight hoods, mitten hands, and literal ping-pong balls for eyes, all identical. They show him images on screens, while he lies on a slab in a womb-like cave, not unlike many UFO abduction descriptions. His memory is blocked, and he is given a post-hypnotic command to perform an act of sabotage. If movies have been used for deflection from serious topics by making them ludicrous, then this one is an excellent example. Something that must be borne in mind is that, even if such a plan was set in operation between 1951 and 1953 or thereabouts, it would need little impetus to continue on its own. Nothing breeds faster in Hollywood's creatively impoverished and plagiaristic environment than bad movies. If one or two deliberately bad films were made in the beginning, utilizing actual abduction and UFO information, others would follow on their own without any prompting. As one famous saying about Hollywood goes, "Imitation is the sincerest form of television."

In 1956, Graves was back again as the manly-jawed hero of *It Conquered the World,* exploitation artist Roger Corman's second sci-fi feature for American International Pictures, with a "cucumber creature" from Venus (playfully named "Beulah," behind the scenes) that lives in a hot-springs cave and communicates with a young Lee Van Cleef by radio. The movie begins with government rockets being deflected from an outside source, which scientist Van Cleef tells them is his friend from Venus. The thing talks to him in strange humming sounds on short-wave radio which somehow he alone understands, and he has convinced himself that the Venusian is coming to Earth to help. Like Gort and Klaatu before it, the alien is capable of blacking out all power, including stopping-up the water supplies. It implants people by means of flying bat-creatures it gives birth to from under its unlikely body, and of course dispatches pesky interlopers who get in its way by means of its controlled human servants. After many ponderously moralistic speeches from Graves about the nature of humanity and the fight for freedom, and the thing's killing of Van Cleef's wife who resisted it (Beverly Garland), Van Cleef sees the error of his ways and manages to singlehandedly kill the Venusian with a hand-held torch, where the military with its bazookas had formerly failed.

The Comedy Network's *Mystery Science Theater 3000* did an especially good job of roasting this one, and it is one of the best exhibits for a case of deliberately planned badness—probably (but not necessarily) on the part of Roger Corman, but at least of someone at American International Pictures. The reason it makes a good exhibit is because it was actually *remade* ten years later, as *Zontar, the Thing from Venus.* There was no conceivable reason for American International to want to remake this movie, let alone worse than the original, which *Zontar* is. *Second City Television* spoofed it, and it developed a bizarre cult following. A Boston-based magazine even named itself after the movie. It was one of seven made by director Larry Buchanan for a package sale to T.V., providing a built-in excuse (which may even be true) for their unbelievably poor quality. Some of the others—which we will encounter—also were remakes of laughable UFO movies from previous years, all done imminently worse than their originals. The trademark of these movies is the same melodramatic synthesizer sound-track music, tin-can recording, obvious day-for-night photography, bad theatrical sets, idiotic costumes (not only for the monsters, but also including incredibly mismatched clothes for the principals, and some of the monsters are not even finished or have visible zippers and woolen turtlenecks), calculatedly bad acting, and jagged editing.

Larry Buchanan's film directing career began with Paul Mart Productions' *Naughty Dallas* in 1961, starring strippers from the nightclub of none other than the Mafiosi assassin of Lee Harvey Oswald, Jack Ruby. Ruby's joint was exactly the sort used by the CIA for safe houses and clandestine MK-ULTRA experimentation. Buchanan filmed Falcon's *The Trial of Lee Harvey Oswald* in 1964, in which Oswald pleads not guilty by reason of insanity. In this context, it is extremely interesting that in his recent autobiography, *It Came from Hunger: Tales of a Cinema Schlockmeister,* Buchanan professes his belief that the JFK assassination was ordered by LBJ.

Another of Buchanan's remakes was of Corman's first real sci-fi feature, *The Day the World Ended* (remade in 1966 as *In the Year 2889*), made in 1955 for A.R.C. (American Releasing Corporation, just as it was re-incorporating to become American International Pictures) right before *It Conquered the World*. Though it had nothing to do with UFOs, it did have notable similarities to the abduction phenomenon. The plot concerned a small group of humans who are the only survivors after "TD"-Day—"Total Destruction." A nocturnal, radioactive "mutant" stalks Lori Nelson, able to communicate with her telepathically with no one else hearing. She finds herself sleepwalking to the nightmarish horror whenever it silently calls to her in her bedroom, the creature being a bulletproof black humanoid with three eyes and antennae and literal steel claws for hands (inexplicable for a biological being, but perfectly comprehensible on a robot), and finds herself strangely unafraid of its never-stated intentions after overcoming her initial fear of it. She enters a lake when it sets her down, soon to be accompanied by hero Richard Denning. Being a mutant, it dies when natural rain falls on it, and Nelson says, "I can't hear it anymore, the noise. I'm free of it. He tried to speak to me before, he called me by name. I feel so sorry for him. It's strange, I feel that way. . . ." This entire scene and imagery is remarkably like UFO abductions. The sexually paired couple in a pool, watched over by an alarming abductor-figure that somehow doesn't frighten them, the calling by name, the sleepwalking, the feeling of a special bond or connection to the abductor, all recur in numerous reports.

Earlier in the story, Denning has a conversation with an "abductee" in the survivors' camp. The man, Reddick, is half-mutant and spends most of his nocturnal hours outside the house where the survivors are holed-up. More to the point, he goes "over the ridge," where only radioactive contamination exists, and there feeds on the animals— and apparently, people. Denning and group leader Paul Birch have essentially become the group's Intelligence apparatus, by virtue of their leadership, maturity, and Birch's former Military Intelligence career (he knows secrets about mutations resulting from atomic-bomb blasts). One night, after one of his "feedings," Reddick returns to the room in which all the men in the house sleep, and somehow knows Denning is already awake and has been watching him.

"You followed me the other night, I saw you," Reddick tells Denning, simply and without accusation. "You went over the ridge," Denning notes. "If you went up there, you'd die," Reddick comments. "I know," Denning says, and asks him what he does "up there." "There's wonderful things happening," Reddick tells him. Denning asks him what sort of things, and Reddick only replies, "Maybe I'll tell you, sometime." Ignoring Denning's request to go ahead and tell him now, Reddick merely comments, "I like it out there. I don't like this house." Since Reddick is obviously more mutant than man, Denning asks Reddick why he even bothers to come back each night, and Reddick tells him that he only returns to the house because he has "an enemy [who] wants to kill me" among the other mutants who live over the ridge. Reddick volunteers finally, "I will tell you something. In a little while, you'll all be dead." And he chuckles, simply and without malice, adding, "You think I'm crazy, don't you?" Denning, troubled, admits, "I don't know." Though nothing is learned about the mutants over the ridge except that they are a "survival of the fittest" society, they are the central threat of the film.

If all abductees were science-fiction fans and had seen *The Day the World Ended,* a case might be made for contagion in abductee testimonies. But they all aren't and they all haven't, yet they have many of the same reported features to their experience, including numerous other details not seen in this or any other movie that are consistent with each other. Additionally, the conversation between Denning's character and the "mutant" Reddick is much like any real one the government might have had with any number of true-life UFO abductees. Also, as already mentioned, if contagion were the cause of these incredibly similar (and even identical) reports, why did they all take so long to surface? Why did the contagion not make itself evident until thirty or forty years after its supposed cause?

Corman's *Not of This Earth,* about blood-stealing and body-snatching alien vampires, came out the following year from Allied Artists. Considered by many to be his most enjoyable film, it was remade in 1988 by Corman protégé Jim Wynorski, possibly better than the original. *The Day the World Ended*'s Paul Birch plays the chief alien vampire, a business-suited anemic in dark, wraparound sunglasses, who dispatches interlopers with a flying bat-creature (which soon resurfaced in *It Conquered the World)* that crushes their heads. Hired nurse assistant Beverly Garland (also soon to resurface in *It Conquered the World)* gradually discovers that her wealthy employer is actually teleporting humanity's "lower class" refuse (which consists of drunks and minorities, in true Nazi fashion) back to his home planet for sampling as potential blood-and-tissue farms.

Corman himself could easily have been connected to the Intelligence world. At Stanford and Palo Alto, straight out of high school, he studied both electrical and aeronautical engineering. He volunteered for the Navy's V-12 officer training program in 1944 for its educational opportunities, and stayed with it in Boulder, Colorado, for two years. Though he never rose above Apprentice Seaman in his two-year stint, he had the background and personality for Intelligence work. He traveled internationally, attending Oxford on the G.I. bill. He hung out in Paris for a time, and had a penchant for taking profitable risks. He made a brief living smuggling Leica cameras from West Germany to France and selling them at a substantial markup. "Logic, cunning, conning, a little daring," he listed as his attributes in his autobiography. "I was learning how to do whatever I had to do to get what I wanted—and having some adventures in the process." At one point, he nearly took a job worthy of Ian Fleming's flamboyant Auric Goldfinger: "I had an offer to smuggle gold in my MG from Iran across the Continent into Paris. As the all-American courier, I was to be paid $10,000. The gold would be built into the chassis of the MG." He spent tremendous amounts of time scouting locations while abroad in his later film career, ideal opportunity for preliminary reconnaisance work. Additionally, he had certain contacts and access to rare and unusual film footage that would indicate some sort of inside governmental connection, as will be noticed. From the very beginning, he was involved in flying saucer projects, wetting his feet by executive-producing *The Beast with 1,000,000 Eyes* in 1955 for A.R.C. just prior to that studio's becoming American International Pictures: the title creature was a mind-controlling, antennaed UFO alien, with a huge bald head and enormous eyes.

1956 also saw two other important UFO-oriented films, one a classic and the other a typical piece of period juvenilia: Allied Artists' *Invasion of the Body Snatchers* and Columbia's *Earth vs. the Flying Saucers.* The former first appeared as a story in *Collier's* magazine in 1954, then was expanded into the novel *The Body Snatchers* the following year by its author, Jack Finney. The plot was an outer space abduction story minus the actual saucers. Essentially the same as *Invaders from Mars,* the story concerned people being spirited away and replaced by "pod-people," plant duplicates coming from somewhere outside our planet. Considered a classic example of McCarthy era/Cold War nightmare paranoia, as indeed *Invaders from Mars* could partly be (the Red Planet to represent the Red Menace of Communism), it painted an equally bleak picture of superior extraterrestrials taking over on the sly, with almost exactly the same "all a dream" ending tacked-on at the last minute by the studio. The 1978 United Artists remake was even more grim and nightmarishly made, one of a number of very good UFO-related films that came out during Jimmy Carter's presidency. Both versions hold up, and the same production team remade the story again through Warner Bros. in 1994, almost equally well, as simply *Body Snatchers*. Identical elements were used in 20th Century Fox's *The Day Mars Invaded Earth*, in 1963.

Of note in this oft-filmed story is its central premise: "They get you when you're asleep." Kevin McCarthy, in both the original and the '78 remake, raves to anyone who will listen not to go to sleep, because "that's when it happens." Bedroom abductions would not be publicly recognized as common to the phenomenon until about the early 1980s. McCarthy's behavior in the story is very similar to that of the first Secretary of Defense, James V. Forrestal, who was hospitalized at Bethesda after running down the halls of the Pentagon, screaming, "They're invading us, and we can't stop them!" shortly after which he was found dead on the pavement outside his window. What caused Forrestal's mental disintegration has never been disclosed, but his panicked action occurred very soon after Project Sign concluded that UFOs were interplanetary spacecraft.

Earth vs. the Flying Saucers featured early Ray Harryhausen stop-motion animation for a saucer attack on Washington, D.C., repelled once again by a resourceful military *à la Invaders from Mars*, this time by sound-radar guns that disrupt their balance and make them crash, an idea derived from the writings of Major Donald E. Keyhoe perhaps in an attempt to make Keyhoe and his ideas appear silly. Most interesting about the movie is its alien saucer occupants, who look and move exactly like stiff robots, almost but not completely bulletproof, emerging from their landed saucers to destroy military installations. Though man-like aliens are shown to be inside the suits, they immediately disintegrate when exposed to air—which is a pretty neat way of saying "there's no one inside these things."

1956 was also the year that Captain Ed Ruppelt published his *Report on Unidentified Flying Objects*, and his colleague Al Chop released his film documentary, *U.F.O.*, not surprisingly from United Artists. Chop's movie lacks life but is surprisingly informative for the year in which it was made. It also contains color footage of the Montana movie and the Trementon film, the two best UFO films of the era, which have never yet been explained by any authority. At the same time, England's Danziger Brothers produced a space sabotage movie called

Satellite in the Sky through Warner Bros., starring a young Lois Maxwell, who within the next decade would become famous as Miss Moneypenny in the James Bond film series.

1957 saw a slew of truly mind-numbing awfulness on the sci-fi/UFO front in Hollywood. One or two of that year's crop were actually good, or at least charming in their own way, and one is a superior case for a disinformational-informational movie: *Invasion of the Saucer Men*. Billed as a sci-fi teen comedy, it ran as a double-feature with Herman Cohen's *I Was A Teenage Werewolf*. Saucer Men was based on a story called "The Cosmic Frame," by Paul W. Fairman, written two years before. Only one element from the story is in the movie—and that being the most ridiculous—which is a bunch of aliens framing a man for murder, who runs down one of their own in his car. When it came to filming the story, *"Saucermen's* [sic] producers ... started out aiming for shocks," Jim Wynorski informs us, "but veteran director Edward L. Cahn figured the kids would surely jeer at the ridiculous-looking monster makeups. Studio heads agreed, and the film went out as the first teenage SF send-up." Those monster makeups were midgets in oversized heads, with gigantic, bulging eyes. The little creatures communicate in unintelligible hums, buzzes, and clicks among each other, are bulletproof, run from light, and have automatic hands—i.e., just like *The Thing* of 1951, they detach from the body and have a life of their own, complete with retractable nails that inject alcohol into their prey. Though the little mens' origin is not discussed in the film, the script itself referred to them as Martians.

Clearly based on the Hopkinsville Goblins of two years before, the title creatures of the film also share much in common with Antonio Villas Boas' abductors, who were performing their act a few thousand miles south of Hollywood at about the same time *Saucer Men* was released. It is doubtful Boas could have seen the movie, and questionable whether it was even made prior to his abduction; in any event, his account differs substantially from the movie's plot elements. The movie seemed to know a few things about flying saucers and abductions, though, that weren't public knowledge for another ten to twenty-five years. For one thing, the abductors attack a cow, which isn't in the short story, and are utterly impervious to any kind of retaliation—"Lady" wasn't mutilated until 1967. For another, they besiege a hapless teenager with their alcohol-injecting nails, who wakes up later with a hell of a headache and no memory of what has happened to him. A frightening cattle-mutilator from space was also seen in the British 1958 import, *First Man Into Space*.

Also quite interesting is *Saucer Men*'s portrayal of the military. The Air Force pretends lack of interest and a comfortingly condescending attitude toward the reports of local kids about seeing a flying saucer land, but quickly mobilizes secretly behind the scenes to investigate it. Finding the saucer and receiving no answer to their hails over the bullhorn, they decide that the craft is automated and unmanned. Attempting to cut through it with blowtorches, they trip a booby-trap fuse and it blows up. Herbert Schirmer reported this as a standard feature of his abductors' aerial craft—clearly, he could have gotten that idea from seeing this movie, if he watched such things or had friends who talked about it, but we have no evidence that he did; also, if he was going to report that feature, why was it the only one? When the Air Force fails to retrieve the saucer, they order the area bulldozed over—exactly that procedure has occurred at more than one UFO landing sight, Rendlesham Forest probably being the most famous.

A nudge-nudge-wink tone is taken for the movie, from first frame to last, making it all seem perfectly silly. From the very beginning, the words "A True Story of a Flying Saucer" are shown on the screen, then suddenly light comedy music plays, a variety of placards appearing of comical little men with antennae in elf costumes, roping women from flying saucers with big smiles on their faces. Since there are no obvious abductions in the movie, and no aliens with antennae, the idea can only have been to link Disney-fied elves with flying saucers in an effort to make them ridiculous, which it succeeds at admirably. The action of the story takes place in "Hicksberg," and the narrator immediately betrays himself as a teller of tall tales who can't be taken seriously. From there, pretty much the actual story of the Hopkinsville Goblins is told, but turned into a light teen comedy instead of the horrific encounter it was—an effective strategy, if the intent was to make people not take such accounts seriously. The effect it had on serious UFOlogy is unfortunate, but at least the movie itself is good inoffensive fun, still, today. Also, when all is said and done, the story is more or less true as told in the movie, if many current abduction accounts are taken as evidence. While initial encounters are almost never reported as anything except extremely terrifying, many abductees are more like Villas Boas in the long run, whose story is far from frightening. There are a great many indications that the entire abduction process is wholly benign. If the movies make it laughable by comparison to elf stories, there is after all excellent reason to believe that the Fairy Folk are behind abductions and other UFO activity, as should have been shown by now. As such, the experience should be expected to be every bit as frightening, bewildering, and humorous as all such accounts throughout history.

Like *It Conquered the World, Invasion of the Saucer Men* was an American International release—and similarly, it was remade by Larry Buchanan, and remade worse as *The Eye Creatures* in 1965. As if the remake wasn't bad enough, being one of Buchanan's worst (and that is saying a lot), some time between its initial T.V. showing and its later spoofing by *Mystery Science Theater 3000* on the Comedy Network (later moved to the Sci-Fi Channel), its title card was changed to "Attack of" *The Eye Creatures,* actually utilizing the article "the" twice: *Attack of the the Eye Creatures.* This is so contrived as to plainly throw the ludicrousness of the project in the audience's face. It has almost the exact same script as *Saucer Men,* but with noteworthy differences. There is an added scene at the beginning: in it, an Air Force officer is solemnly shown into a secret room and made privy to a film of a flying saucer—looking, as the Comedy Network crew called it, like a "bagelwich"—and is reminded of the seriousness of the situation, which already the audience is having tremendous difficulty accepting. Another series of intercut scenes shows the Air Force voyeuristically spying on young teen lovers in the area where a saucer is believed to be.

But the most interesting change is in the *deletion* of one scene: the attack on the cow. *The Eye Creatures* was made only two years prior to the beginning of the modern cattle mutilation phenomenon. This curiosity can only lead to speculation on what the Intelligence services were either planning or discovering, since certainly they have been exceptionally active in attempting to convince both researchers and the public that there is no connection between UFOs and the mutilations. The chief researcher in the field, Linda Howe, was aggressively lobbied against in an AFOSI (and possibly ONI) disinformation campaign, concurrent with that against Paul Bennewitz.

Inexplicably bad costuming choices are evident throughout *The Eye Creatures,* including a horizontally striped, multi-colored nightshirt which clashes with everything around it, and title monsters who in many cases are men in visible black turtlenecks with truly idiotic masks (that don't match). Interestingly enough, though nowhere in the movie is it suggested that the creatures are robots, a rhythmic beeping sound accompanies all of their appearances. It is next to impossible to view this movie as anything but deliberately bad, and the reason for that should by now be self-evident.

AIP's Herman Cohen followed up his 1957 monster success *I Was a Teenage Werewolf* with the even more lurid *I Was a Teenage Frankenstein* later in the same year, which played on the same bill with the hypnotic murderess story *Blood of Dracula. Teenage Frankenstein* had very un-British middle-aged character actor Whit Bissell as the supposedly very British descendant of the original Baron Frankenstein. Bissell maintains a double life, concealing his basement laboratory activities from fiancée Phyllis Coates *(Superman's* Lois Lane). Obsessed with completing his notorious ancestor's work, the psychopathically sadistic Bissell and his conscience-stricken assistant tinker together a living teenager from the grisly remains of a fortuitous nearby car wreck. The unfortunate young man has the face of a pizza, even if the accident left his musclebuilder's body in terrific shape. Bissell keeps the youthful golem dormant in a morgue drawer by day, taking him out at night to prowl lover's lanes until the pair find just the right face to steal (Gary Conway). Bissell mentally dominates and makes the teenage monster utterly dependent on him, with techniques of isolation and torture, then utilizing his creation's muscular build and compliant mind to murder anyone—including his fiancée—who might complicate his plans. Ultimately rebelling against his evil dominator, the young monster murders Bissell and throws him into his own alligator pit (no basement lab should be without one), before accidentally electrocuting himself back into lifeless flesh.

Made the same year was another movie with even more bits of apparent inside UFOlogical knowledge to its credit than *Invasion of the Saucer Men:* 20th Century Fox's *Kronos. Kronos* begins with a local man's truck being stalled by a flying saucer, and the man then becoming "possessed" by a light emanation from it. The possessed man then knocks out a sentry at a government lab and makes his way to the lab's director, transferring the possessing intelligence to the director before abruptly dying. From that point on, the director becomes a saboteur/spy/assassin for the intelligence behind the UFO. The saucer crashes into the ocean off the coast of Mexico, where a small team of scientists set up to study it. Before they can decide the best course of action to raise the submerged object, it has solved their problem for them by revealing its nature: it builds itself, overnight, into a giant robot the size of a highrise building, and with much the same shape. Entirely automated, the machine goes on a rampage across the countryside, sucking up energy from all sources and mindlessly destroying everything in its path. The scientists determine— with some help from the possessed director, when he is able to temporarily shake the saucer intelligence's influence on him—that the robot was sent from far away in space, first as a vanguard and second as an accumulator to return energy to its homeworld, which it intends to do by converting itself back into a flying craft and disembarking, as it came, after it has taken what it came for. It finds the energy sites it drains by the assistance of its implanted human "colleague," the director, who dies trying to free himself from his alien masters. Impervious even to atom bombs, the rampaging robot is finally destroyed by the resourceful scientific team's switching of the polarization of its rotary antennae. Recently made available on video, *Kronos* is a little gem of a B-movie, and fascinating in light of its actual UFOlogical elements, especially given the year it was made.

The worst of the year's offerings—and probably intentionally so— was not about flying saucers, but seems most plainly intended to have cast a bad light on them: Columbia's *The Giant Claw.* Typical of every sci-fi movie since the Robertson Panel, no matter what its plot elements or trappings, is the inclusion of a derogatory reference to UFOs. *The Blob,* in 1958, for instance, has nothing to do with flying saucers, but does feature an unlikely invader from space and has an obligatory line to the effect of, "Oh, sure, kid, and it was in a flying saucer, right—?" The effect creates a subliminal mantra, continually being reinforced: "Walking tree-monsters from Borneo, and flying saucers . . . giant cardboard insects, and flying saucers . . . zipper-wristed fishmen, and flying saucers. . . ." The continual linkage of the subject of UFOs with badly thought-out and childishly silly monster costumes, bad acting, and cartoon plots eventually develops an aura around the subject that makes it impossible for anyone to continue entertaining it seriously. When former CIA head President George Bush was confronted with questions about the Kennedy assassination in the wake of Oliver Stone's movie, *JFK,* his automatic response was to give a typical frustrated bluster, and eventually to blurt out angrily, "Oh, I believe the Warren Report, and anyone who doesn't thinks Elvis is still alive!" which of course completely ignored the questions and answered them with the intellectual equivalent of blowing the raspberries.

The Giant Claw, produced by the man who had done the same studio's *Earth vs. the Flying Saucers* the year before, Sam Katzman, is as laughable a movie as was ever made, and it deserves some lengthy consideration as a disinformational/deflective piece. Flying saucers are nowhere in evidence, but the term is used plentifully, as is the acronym UFO, in every case to make sport of or to make idiotic. After some narration making it clear how thoroughly the world's airspace is continually combed by modern radar and satellites, and an introduction to the "serious and efficient" personnel that make our world so safe (and make up our cast)—an electronics engineer, a radar officer, a mathematician and systems analyst, a radar operator, and a couple of technicians—we are assured: "Situation normal . . . for the moment." But then, "[Mitch] McAfee reported instantly by radio the sighting of a UFO—an Unidentified Flying Object. The radar officer replied that it was impossible. According to the radar scope, except for Mitch's plane, there wasn't a single solitary object of any nature whatsoever. Nothing in the sky for a radius of hundreds of miles. McAfee didn't care what the radar showed or didn't show, he knew what he saw with his own eyes, and he was determined to get a better look. McAfee turned, and so did the Unidentified Flying Object heading towards him. There was no mistaking the urgency in McAfee's voice. Something—he didn't know what—but something, as big as a battleship, had just flown over and passed him, at speeds so great he couldn't begin to estimate them. At National Defense, it's better to be safe than sorry. The alert was sounded, to scramble intercept." All of this could have been enacted for us, but instead we have the benefit of needless narration to cheapen it. This is a trademark to be found in other deliberately bad movies to come.

Returning to ground, McAfee is accused of calling a false alarm, since no UFO is found. "Your flying battleship wasn't there," he is informed. But planes and pilots have disappeared. McAfee's superior gets a call and learns that a civilian plane has vanished without a trace, also having reported a UFO. Electronics engineer/pilot McAfee (Jeff Morrow, again—the same casts recycle for all these movies, especially the bad ones) and love-interest mathematician/systems analyst Mara Corday (*Playboy*'s Miss October 1958 and famous lingerie model) wing to another location, when their plane is attacked by the UFO, looking exactly like the plastic model kit B-29 being waved on a string that it is, with a match-lit fire rising from its engine cowl. Miraculously unharmed, McAfee and Corday wonder what hit them. The answer, a solemn McAfee delivers, is, "The flying battleship that wasn't there."

While the two are staying at an inn, the local sheriff comes and tells them that the area has been sealed off by the military—"real hush-hush"—and he asks them, "What happened? You tangle with a flying saucer or something?" Corday glibly assures him, "Oh, nothing so domestic as a flying saucer, officer—just a flying battleship." "Well," he answers, "have a good time with your flying battleship," and takes his leave. The refrain "flying battleship" rapidly becomes a comedy routine, but of course no one cracks a smile, except Corday: "Flying battleship, pink elephants, same difference. You really should try buttermilk instead." "I said it *looked* like a battleship, not that it *was* a battleship!" McAfee retorts, sounding more and more inane.

After a local thinks he has seen a terrifying demon from the air, McAfee and Corday are taken to their special flight and argue the facts concerning UFOs and disappearing planes. McAfee sees a pattern in the disappearances, and Corday considers it all nonsense because no radar has reported it and a great many should have. "Maybe it was [the local's] demon," she scoffs, "with 'the head of a wolf and the body of a woman and wings as big as I can tell'!" Soon, however, we discover what the UFO is. The next day, the narration tells us, "A plane flies toward the scene of the previous day's crash involving Mitchell McAfee. Aboard, four members of the Civil Aeronautics Board investigating team, and a pilot. Another significant moment in history...." A bizarre chattering is heard. The CAB team and the pilot look about and out of the windows, in apprehension and fear. "Once more, a frantic pilot radioes in a report on a UFO: A bird. A bird as big as a battleship. Circling, and preparing to attack the CAB plane ..."—which it does, quite comically, being a marionette of such unbelievably stupid appearance that one doesn't know whether to gape or laugh at it as it devours the unfortunate paratroopers in midair.

"A bird," McAfee's commanding officer repeats to him, immediately following, as though the narrator hadn't just informed us and as if it hadn't been repeated every thirty seconds since the film began in case we might forget, "A bird as big as a battleship circled and attacked that plane." Film recovered from the crashed plane is shown: *a bird.* (HOW BIG WAS IT?) *A bird as big as a battleship.* Big. Then bigger. Filling the frame. Sticking its huge, obscene, puppet beak straight into the camera lens, poor Miss Corday recoiling in horror and covering her mouth with the back of her hand at the sight.

"There's a general air alert on, this very minute, son," the paternal general (Morris Ankrum, the same actor seen in *Kronos, Earth vs. the Flying Saucers* and *Invaders from Mars*) assures McAfee, not so much as cracking a smile. "Hundreds of planes from every command are combing the skies, searching for this overgrown buzzard ... Our planes are armed with cannon, machine-gun, and rockets. This should be the end of the Big Bird that was there but wasn't." Grade-B movie dialogue from left-over WWII propaganda films relays over the radio, while stock-footage jets are attacked by the giant marionette fowl. "Easy-Baker squadron leader, Charlie hit the silk when the bird got his plane, and—and now he's gone. Chute 'n all. *No*—it's comin' after *me*! No—*no*—!" Back at base, the Joint Chiefs are notified. "It doesn't make sense," one general laments. "It's just a bird. A big bird. Guns, cannon, rockets—it's just a bird!" "Sure, just a bird," another general responds. "Ten million dollars' worth of radar can't track it— enough firepower to wipe out a regiment can't even slow it down, sure, just a bird." The first general complains that they're just crying about it. "It's hard to come up with answers when you don't even know what the question is," the other says. "I'm scared" *(of the bird, the bird as big as a battleship)*, McAfee admits, deadly serious. They debate how to take it down. "Electronic spitballs?" "Close, general, close. But not electronic spitballs—*atomic* spitballs!"

After examination of the evidence, the scientific verdict is reached: "That bird is extraterrestrial. It comes from outer space. From some godforsaken anti-matter galaxy, millions and millions of light-years from the Earth. *No other explanation is possible.*" Not only is it an extraterrestrial bird (a bird as big as a battleship), but it has an electromagnetic anti-matter envelope that it can open and close at will, and its motive for being here—of course—is "to lay an egg."

Eventually, the Big Bird (as big as a battleship) is dispatched by the miracles of scientific doubletalk jargon and inane logic, leaving only the most laughable of memories and an upturned claw slowly sinking beneath the ocean. But 1957 had other impossibly bad UFO movies, all of which need not be gone into, but one which should definitely be mentioned: Allied Artists' *Attack of the 50 Ft. Woman.* Like many of its predecessors a movie so bad it finally achieved cult status, it featured established exploitation favorite Allison Hayes, and Yvette Vickers two years before her becoming a B-movie icon in her own right and *Playboy*'s Miss July 1959. Hayes grows into a giantess after encountering a badly dressed giant bald man (he looks like a genie from a poor-man's "Sinbad" movie) aboard a glowing sphere that sets down before her car in the desert. Her cad husband doesn't believe her or care—though he later sees the flying sphere—too intent on getting his wife committed or killed in order to acquire her millions. Police do battle with the giant bald man, who is so cheaply superimposed against the desert backdrop that he can be seen through in spots, and Hayes, conveniently and exploitatively in a 50-foot stretchable miniskirt, is finally killed after murdering her unfaithful husband and his hussy girlfriend.

William Asher, the director of AIP's Frankie-and-Annette "beach movies," made one relatively good saucer film for Columbia Pictures in 1957, *The 27th Day,* which John Mantley adapted from his own novel. Aliens completely indistinguishable from humans abduct one human being each from five divergent countries, and place in their possession bacteriological capsules which they are charged to take care of for the sake of the world. If they are opened at any time within 27 days, the population of the Earth will be killed in an incurable and instantaneous plague. The governments of each of the abductees treat them differently, which the saucer occupants had counted on—the Soviet Union's KGB try to force theirs to divulge what occurred in his encounter with the extraterrestrials, and to gain knowledge of what is in the capsule. Unable to tell them because of his prior arrangement with the aliens, the abductee must watch helplessly as the KGB forces the capsule open despite his insistent warnings, destroying all of Russia overnight.

United Artists released *The Flame Barrier* and *Voodoo Island* in '57. The former was about a space probe that returns to Earth carrying a thermally destructive extraterrestrial intelligence akin to the more famous "Andromeda Strain" of Michael Crichton's later bestseller, and the latter was a minor Boris Karloff vehicle featuring the aged star as a celebrity government investigator trying to discover the secret of mind-controlled zombies on an isolated island. *Voodoo Island* partially dramatized a purportedly true Bermuda Triangle occurrence early in the film, an incident in which a plane and its ground control could not see each other on a clear day despite the fact that the instruments of both the plane and the ground crew indicated that the plane was directly overhead.

A nightmarish scenario was depicted in MGM's 1957 entry, *The Invisible Boy,* starring that studio's famous "Robby the Robot" from

Forbidden Planet the year before. Though sold as a juvenile escapist fantasy, the basic plot was about a malfunctioning government super-computer sabotaging space shots, and abducting the sons and daughters of the scientists behind those shots in order to coerce the scientists' surrender. One little boy is shown immobilized on a slab in the classic sterile UFO environment, with the robot standing over him. The computer intelligence that abducted the boy televises the scene live to a group of onlooking government scientists and top brass, and coldly informs them that unless they cooperate, what they are about to behold will become commonplace. "Robot," the computer commands, "start with his eyes. . . ." And the screaming begins.

The tremendous output in flying saucer and UFO movies in 1956 and 1957, especially the bad ones, is interesting, since those were major flap years for the phenomenon. It would be tempting to say that the upsurge in sightings was caused by the movies, but they fell perfectly into Vallee's Mars opposition chart, as did the sightings well in advance of bad UFO movies. It is possible, given the government's foreknowledge, that they knew when sightings were going to come and prepared to discourage reports or thoughts of those sightings by making bad movies about UFOs in advance—no one wants to be associated with idiotic movies. 1957 saw one of the first modern mind-control movies as well, from Columbia/Anglo-Amalgamated in England: *Electronic Monster,* based on Charles Eric Maine's novel *Escapement* and executive-produced by Richard Gordon, a famous name in the exploitation movie business. In it, a man in a Ewan Cameron-esque mental hospital discovers illegal procedures being performed on patients, especially the employment of electronic implants to create hallucinations. A similar movie was filmed in Denmark with an American cast during the Nixon administration, by Cinerama in 1972, called *The Mind Snatchers.*

On February 7, 1957, at the Booth Theater in New York, a witty new play by Gore Vidal, *Visit to a Small Planet,* opened. Essentially the (uncredited) basis for the later 1970s and '80s much more successful T.V. vehicle *Mork & Mindy,* even including one of the same principal performers, Conrad Janis, the play was about 1950s America being turned upside down by the visit of a comical alien named

Kreton (Cyril Ritchard) on a flying saucer. Dressed for the Civil War, he is sorry to be more than a century off-course and arranges to start a war of his own by fooling around with all the world's military powers. Playful but dangerous, he is able to read others' thoughts and manipulate their actions, and is completely untouchable. A bit of a renegade on his own world—one of the characters asks upon his arrival if he is from Mars, and he laughs and answers, "Oh, dear no! No one lives on Mars . . . At least no one *I* know!"—he is eventually caught up with by his more civilized peers and taken home before his precious World War can start. In 1960, it became a drastically rewritten (for the worse) Jerry Lewis vehicle, from Paramount.

Mars featured prominently in 1958's *It! The Terror From Beyond Space,* from United Artists, directed by the same man who delivered *Invasion of the Saucer Men* for AIP the previous year. The title beast is a stowaway from Mars who murdered all of Marshall Thompson's crew, which busily attempts to kill the rescue party as well. A cheap movie to say the least, it was essentially the basis for 1979's far better and more slickly produced *Alien.* United Artists the same year released *The Flight that Disappeared,* in which three government weapons research scientists are missing-time abducted from a commercial flight to be tried for war crimes by the future generations of Earth. 1958 also saw *The Colossus of New York* from Paramount, a giant robot with a dead scientist's brain inside it, that abducts and relates to a child, and threatens the world's military powers with its own superior force at a United Nations meeting. American International produced two female space-alien invader movies the same year, *Terror from the Year 5,000* and *The Astounding She Monster*—the former was a super-hypnotic mind-controller from the future, and the latter a glow-in-the-dark sexy blonde in a skintight metallic outfit, whose touch is lethal despite an entirely Ambassadorial and friendly intent.

1958 was a bumper-crop year for horror and science-fiction in general, including Steve McQueen's first movie, Paramount's *The Blob,* and another low-budget sleeper from 20th Century Fox, *The Fly* (a giant black insectoid). *The Fly*'s title monster looking so much like many reported UFO abductors was more than likely not accidental—

author George Langelaan was a secret service officer of the SDECE *(Service de Documentation Extérieur et de Contre-Espionage)* in WWII, and by 1965 in the publication *Sud-Ouest* he was making statements about Russian-United States cooperation in UFO research: "The Flying Saucers exist, their source is extraterrestrial, and the future—relatively quite soon—should permit confirmation of this statement."

Universal released *The Thing That Couldn't Die* in '58, a story in which a psychic dowser uncovers a treasure chest containing the decapitated head of a black magician. The head hypnotically dominates anyone unfortunate enough to gaze into its compelling eyes, and whispers silent instructions to them which they obey without question. Its subjects then carry it from one person to the next, so it can spread its influence. That influence causes the victims to become amnesiac somnambulists in the head's service, some committing murder before the head is ultimately laid to its final rest.

Columbia's 1958 release, *Curse of the Demon* (British title: *Night of the Demon),* was a horror film closely showing the connection between supernatural and UFO phenomena in real life, including a gratuitous derogatory reference to "flying saucers" by scientific lead Dana Andrews. Andrews is a famous American psychiatrist and debunker of the supernatural, investigating the grisly accidental death of an English peer who before his demise had been exposing a demon cult. Charming but sinister cult leader Niall MacGinnis threatens Andrews as he did the American's English predecessor, assuring Andrews that it was his sorcery that killed the man. MacGinnis slips a sheet of runic writing to Andrews, with a card that informs him exactly how many days he has left to live. For the remainder of the film, Andrews and former victim's daughter Peggy Cummins become increasingly aware that MacGinnis' threats are substantial, and that the demon at his command is some sort of genuine otherworldly guided missile capable of true harm. Haunted beforehand, Andrews finds himself followed by flashing lights like UFO phenomena in the trees at night. Questioning one of MacGinnis' former cult members under narcohypnosis—the man has been in shock for weeks and can be reached no other way—Andrews learns that the cult leader's indestructible demon follows the runes blindly, like an automaton, and that no one, including MacGinnis, is immune from the creature. MacGinnis also has been using hypnosis on Andrews' new love interest Cummins, in order to abduct her to his home for unspecified future uses. Andrews confronts McGinnis and admits to believing the man's claims, slipping the runes into McGinnis' pocket before the appointed time—and McGinnis is mauled by his own conjured demon, in Andrews' place.

According to American Movie Channel host Bob Dorian, the 1958 Paramount production *I Married a Monster from Outer Space*—released on a double-bill with *The Blob*—was made almost as a joke. The title originated as a challenge and a bet for director Gene Fowler (who had directed AIP's popular hit, *I Was A Teenage Werewolf,* the year before) that he couldn't make a movie to live up to it, which makes a good argument for someone on the inside wanting deliberately bad movies with flying saucers in them. Fowler, on the other hand, insisted in a 1996 *SPFX* interview that the title was his own, and that he intended a serious movie from the start: "Our idea was to make a touching story. It really is a sad thing to think that the aliens had to come here to get women because theirs had all died off. And it really was a sad ending for them."

Aside from Fowler, no one expected the very good movie *I Married a Monster* turned out to be. Star Gloria Talbott expressed the general attitude toward the film's title, when she called it simply, "Horrible! I thought it was funny because at the time I *was* married to a monster from outer space. That's why I understood the part so well," though even at the time she had to concede, "It played better than it read, but I knew it was going to be made at Paramount so it had to be pretty decent." Talbott also made probably the pithiest observation of the entire story in *SPFX:* "[T]he hospital was where they found the 'real men' who could reproduce [and who formed the posse that dispatched the aliens]. [Don't] you find it funny that in this movie only the 'real men' had guns and dogs. That's really phallic, don't you think? The aliens couldn't reproduce and they turned to jello. [Laughter.]" The movie is a cult favorite of many still, often found making the rounds today on the cable channels AMC and Cinemax. "As a matter of fact," Talbott admits, "the first time I saw it was on TV. Even *TV Guide* liked it and they don't like anything. Their capsule description says something like, *'Don't let the title fool you, this is a neat yarn about aliens from outer space.'"*

More or less a combination of *Invaders from Mars* and *Invasion of the Body Snatchers, I Married a Monster from Outer Space* was filmed in only eight days in mid-April of its release year, for a budget of $185,000. Its alien abductions are performed by grisly (and bulletproof) saucer occupants of nightmarish description, who form duplicate bodies to occupy from their unconscious abductees. The aliens can no longer reproduce, and they marry human females to experiment with genetic compatibility. Resourceful newlywed Gloria Talbott discovers her husband's (Tom Tryon) true identity and purpose, and emphasizes to him the futility of a sterile race trying to artificially reproduce off of another that is fertile. "Eventually we'll have children with you," he assures her. "What . . . *kind* of children?" she shudders. *"Our kind."* Tryon's mission is aborted by heroic townsfolk storming the egg-shaped saucer in the woods. Destroyed by having tubes torn out of their throats by attacking dogs, the aliens dissolve into so much jello. Talbott feels sorry for the needy newcomers, even as they are dispatched, just as Lori Nelson did for her bizarre humanoid abductor in *The Day the World Ended.*

One important scene in *I Married a Monster* occurs when streetwalker Valerie Allen approaches the only other figure on a deserted city street at night. The motionless figure wears a hooded parka and is staring blankly into a shop window at several shelves of baby dolls. Allen coos, "Ooh, I'm just *crazy* about dolls! Would *you* like to buy me a doll?" Angered when her intended target for the night refuses to acknowledge her presence, Allen grabs the figure's shoulder and spins it around to face her. Seeing what is beneath the hood, she screams and flees, only to be disintegrated by a rod-like pistol in the figure's hand. The figure then stiffly returns its blank gaze to the shop window, and we see its monstrous alien face reflected as simply one more mannequin in a long line. Ensuring that the connection is not accidental, and that someone on the production team knew something about true UFO facts, the first abduction in the movie occurs when Tom Tryon's car skids to a stop in order not to run over a figure in the road that the audience can plainly see is nothing but a man-nequin. When Tryon gets out, the mannequin is gone from in front of his car—and the "alien" steps out of the woods behind him, rendering him unconscious.

The William Alland-Jack Arnold partnership that formerly produced *It Came from Outer Space, The Creature from the Black Lagoon,* and *This Island Earth* for Universal made Paramount's *The Space Children* in 1958. Children of military rocket base personnel are hyp-notically beckoned to a glowing alien brain in a seaside cave, which teaches them how to sabotage their parents' nuclear missiles before launch. The alien brain is not portrayed as either evil or interested in any sort of military conquest, but rather as a protector of the childrens' future. 1964's *Children of the Damned* had many of the same plot elements, featuring human-alien, super-genius hybrids produced in 1960's *Village of the Damned* (see next chapter) being studied by government scientists who are trying to protect them from a frightened military—the children build a sonic resonator weapon (which the military covets) to defend themselves, and are ultimately slaughtered. Both movies were MGM productions made in England. *The Cape Canaveral Monsters* of 1960, soon to be discussed, also featured juvenile abduction and alien sabotage of government rockets.

Also in 1958 came Howco International's *The Brain from Planet Arous,* one of many bad John Agar films that rivaled those of Peter Graves for cheapness and silliness. Stephen King and other horror writers have credited this particular film as being an inspiration. Agar is a government nuclear physicist who becomes possessed by an evil alien brain, which gives him needed super-powers to destroy U.S. rockets and missiles on its behalf. The invader is caught by surprise by a policeman of its race possessing Agar's dog in order to follow the space criminal around, exposing it in time to save Earth and whatever other planets might have fallen prey to its insatiable desire for dominance. The year before, Howco made an Old West teenage sci-fi flick called *Teenage Monster* (a.k.a. *Meteor Monster).* The title creature is a young boy caught out alone at night by the strange, eerie glow of a meteorite—or perhaps even a spaceship—which in later years mutates him into an imbecilic, bristly-haired, snaggle-toothed menace who is hidden from the world by his mother. The monster-youth escapes, abducts a young woman to the hills, and is rapidly hunted and shot down like a dog. (Many of the same elements, much better handled, would find their way into AIP's 1965 Lovecraftian horror entry, *Die, Monster, Die!*)

1958 saw a curious choice for Roger Corman: *Teenage Caveman*. Starring young Robert Vaughn in his first film role, the movie actually is not as bad as either its title or its advance press, though it is certainly clichéd by today's standards. It was one of the first to pose the idea of an advanced civilization preceding our own for a mass audience, which was guaranteed to be younger and more impressionable both by the movie's being drive-in material and its having a sexy poster with tantalizingly revealed former Miss Teenage America, Darrah Marshall. Young upstart Vaughn defies his tribe's elders to cross the Forbidden Zone and confront the dreaded "monster that kills with its touch," seeking the ultimate truth of his tribe's origins. He discovers it with the other young tribesmen who bravely follow him: the monster, unfortunately killed before it can reveal much, was nothing more than a man like themselves in a scorched and burnt radiation suit, the last survivor of a holocaust that left Vaughn's tribe in a new Stone Age. The dead survivor had not been menacing the tribe, but trying to help them survive and to teach them what he knew before he died.

Corman also released *War of the Satellites* through Allied Artists in 1958, filming it in eight days, two months after the first Russian *Sputnik* and the U.S.' *Explorer* satellite were launched. The plot concerned unseen aliens warning man against further attempts at space exploration, abducting and brainwashing scientist Richard Devon to help them sabotage future shots. Film critic Leonard Maltin called it a "ruthless combination of *The Day the Earth Stood Still* and *Kronos.*" Though considered to be one of Corman's decidedly lesser efforts, it got a good review from *Life* magazine, which may possibly have been done as a favor by someone who wanted the film to be seen anyway. The following year, Corman executive-produced *The Beast from Haunted Cave* for Filmgroup and *Attack of the Giant Leeches* through AIP, both of which—along with "Allied Artists"—were essentially the same company: Allied Artists was the name Monogram Studios took in 1953, the year of the Robertson Panel recommendation, and it was famous for the release of numerous youth-oriented foreign horror films, like AIP, until the late 1970s. Both *Haunted Cave* and *Giant Leeches* were abducting-humanoid features, the former being a never-explained, spider-webby, tentacled bloodsucker that steals away hapless wayfarers into its snowy mountain domain, feeding on them until the poor unfortunates die. The latter was exactly the same, with the action relocated to a remote swamp, though the monsters were at least explained as genetic freaks of nature. *Haunted Cave* featured a gratuitous derogatory reference to Mars, by a gang-leader whose men are being killed by the title creature: "I don't care what it is! I don't care if the thing chews up the whole state! I don't care if it came from Mars or happened by spontaneous combustion!"

Interesting in light of his probable Intelligence connections, Corman made a contemporaneous satire of the Bay of Pigs, in Filmgroup's *Creature from the Haunted Sea* in 1961. One of his few overt comedies, the central characters were Mafiosi bank robbers doing-in duped Cuban politico exiles who plan a militaristic comeback, by means of a mythical sea monster. Both groups are being carefully monitored by an undercover CIA agent whose radio set is concealed in a hot dog. The Mob boys find their fun and games ruined by an unwelcome surprise: the real sea-monster, which makes mincemeat of both them and their intended Cuban prey. Both films display a recurrent theme in early Corman pictures—gangsters, government agents, or backwood rednecks finding an unknown monster entering, uninvited, into the middle of their violent little games.

A busy year for Corman (and his brother, Gene), 1958 saw one of the most astonishingly prescient of his UFO films, AIP's *Night of the Blood Beast*. A crashed astronaut, at the world's lowest-budget and farthest-removed NASA outpost set in the middle of a forest, is pronounced dead only to be discovered still alive hours later. He sports a unique scar on his body, and his blood is impregnated with alien embryos. An unknown something he brought back with him decapitates and eats the head of a scientist at the complex, for the later-revealed reason that it was the only way it could absorb sufficient human intelligence to communicate with our species. The impregnated astronaut finds itself in communion with the alien invader, not only by telepathic contact but also in sympathy with its aims, insisting that his peers not kill it as is their wish. He believes the creature is peaceful, despite its initial grisly introduction to our world. He later changes his mind, committing suicide rather than give birth to whatever alien offspring is awaiting emergence from his body, and his fellow scientists burn the alien to death in a cave, while it cries out to them that they need its help and that it will be back someday, when they are better prepared, to help save them from themselves. The most interesting thing about this low-budgeter, other than the elements and themes discussed in the early time frame in which they appear, is the ambivalent note they end on.

The 1958 DCA/Eros British import, *The Crawling Eye,* contained a few accurate UFOlogical elements, most notably in the recurrent abduction/implant remote alien control and sabotage motif. Adapted by Jimmy Sangster from Peter Key's BBC serial, *The Trollenberg Terror,* it was one of many similar foreign-produced pieces along similar lines that began with Nigel Kneale's well-known Quatermass series in the early 1950s. (These will be discussed in Chapter 7.) The invading aliens in the story either decapitate hapless wayfarers wandering into their domain (in common with Corman's Blood Beast), or else use their victims' reanimated dead bodies to gain entry into human headquarters and murder those who are a threat to their continued existence. One member of the besieged human entourage holed-up in a hidden United Nations laboratory studying the space monsters is a psychic, whose ability to telepathically view the aliens' movements makes her an invaluable asset—and a target of the aliens. Given the U.S. government's recent admitted use of "remote viewers" for precisely the same purpose (see Introduction), this particular element in the story may have been more than simply an inspired guess. As noted in Sheila Ostrander and Lynn Schroeder's *Psychic Discoveries Behind the Iron Curtain,* Russian experiments into psychic phenomena were not revealed in public articles before the mid-1960s; and the Nazis also experimented in the field, but their studies have only recently begun to be reported in such books as Peter Levenda's *Unholy Alliance: A History of Nazi Involvement with the Occult.*

Testifying to the popularity and influence of such movies, *The Crawling Eye,* not seen on television in perhaps decades, was recently satirized by Steven Spielberg in his 1995 cartoon series, *Freakazoid,* in an episode called "The Cloud." The same series features a nocturnal child-abductor villain called "Candle Jack," a ghostly, floating humanoid with a bald, oval head, and no face except for huge round eyes and a slit of a mouth that never moves, making him appear to speak as if telepathically. Eros films also made another movie with *Crawling Eye* star Forrest Tucker the same year, called *Cosmic Monsters,* with a saucerman saving the world from invasion by giant insects from another dimension. *Crawling Eye* adaptor Jimmy Sangster's first screenplay was *X The Unknown* in 1956, a Hammer picture financed by Warner Bros. and often confused with the Quatermass series, which was about menacing radioactive mud from the Earth's core being destroyed by government scientist Dean Jagger's HAARP-like sonic weaponry.

A 1959 United Artists entry was *Invisible Invaders,* one of many John Agar movies in which he played a scientist bravely defending Earth from hostile space aliens—in this case, from the Moon. The aliens are invisible creatures traveling on an equally invisible ship, animating Earth's dead—another oft-recurring theme, which could be simply to indicate the UFO use of unkillable "animated figures"— to accomplish their plans. The "animated figures" are pasty-white (with the perfect excuse, since they are dead), with blackened, round eyes, and stiff, mechanical walks. Agar somehow defeats them with sound waves. The same year, the mainstream movie *The Mouse That Roared,* produced by Columbia in England and starring Peter Sellers in the earliest of his multiple-roles, featured as its central element an invasion by a small, unknown country called Grand Fenwick, the armor-clad members of whom are mistaken for "men from Mars" as they patrol the abandoned streets of New York and kidnap Professor Kokintz and his dire new "Q-Bomb." The sequel, directed by Richard Lester four years later, had Grand Fenwick ludicrously involved in the space race, in *The Mouse on the Moon.*

1959 was the year Ed Wood's granddaddy bad movie of all time was released, DCA's (Distributing Corporation of America) *Plan 9 from Outer Space.* Wood made many bad movies, but this was his worst—and the one of which he was most proud. He certainly needed no one's prompting to make a bad movie about flying saucers, but he was a super-patriotic military veteran, who even claimed (though he was a notorious bullshitter) Intelligence experience in the war, and he was always pressed for cash. His long-standing mistress, Kathy Wood, was unequivocal in her belief that he had security clearance. She told Wood's biographer, Rudolph Grey, "Eddie did industrial films for Autonetics ... I think all those films for Autonetics were classified. Eddie was investigated by the F.B.I. He had clearance, secret clearance." She also stated specifically that backer Edward Reynolds "had taken over the control of *Plan 9.* For one dollar." His previous movie, *Bride of the Monster* in 1955, demonstrated that Wood did anything the paltriest of his backers told him to—the star, Tony McCoy, according to Wood's colleague Dennis Rodriguez, was put in the movie solely because "[his] father, who owned a meat packing plant, demanded that, in exchange for the financing, not only was his kid going to be in the movie, but that they had to end it with an atomic explosion." And, sure enough, the movie ended with a mushroom cloud that had no reason to be there. Wood also bounced his girlfriend from the lead, because Loretta King gave him sixty thousand dollars in return for being made the star.

Independent exploitation film producer George Weiss adds, "Now, I had nothing to do with it, and I can't even verify it, but Ed Wood helped to start American Pictures, which later became American-International." American International is the studio that Roger Corman made his UFOlogically-related movies for, and it will be noticed in connection with a great many more of the same type. Co-studio head Samuel Z. Arkoff virtually admits that one of Wood's ideas may have originally inspired AIP'S 1958 film, *How to Make a Monster.* It is interesting to note that it took three years for Wood to complete and release *Plan 9,* which made only backer/star Criswell rich, and that despite its obvious badness, it played "for over five years ... about every seven weeks" on T.V., according to Wood biographer Rudolph Grey. Someone certainly wanted *Plan 9* to get a lot of exposure. It is also of interest that Grey had difficulty tracking down people who would talk about Wood: "Former associates, such as the late Phil Tucker, director of *Robot Monster* [who helped Wood edit *Plan 9*], refused to discuss the past; others flatly denied ever knowing Ed Wood—or came down with a sudden case of amnesia."

In addition, Wood was exactly the sort the Intelligence communities like to deal with, someone bizarre enough to blackmail if the need should ever arise. While his transvestism was well-known, he could easily have had other skeletons lurking in his closet. Though he seems to have been strongly heterosexual himself, he did have close homosexual friends (one of whom was briefly imprisoned for child molestation), and tolerance was extremely low back then. He may not have been bought, or even necessarily enlisted to make this ridiculous bomb, it being possibile that an old service buddy suggested the idea to him, perhaps even feeding him legitimate tidbits under the guise of amusingly fun ideas. Given his history and perpetual financial worries, it is likelier however that "the right money got placed in the correct hands," as Jenny Randles' source put it. Whatever the circumstance, there is unquestionably real material in the movie, some of which could have been guessed or coincidental, some of which it is more difficult to imagine coming from any source but one in the know. And all of it was never made more laughable.

For starters, it is introduced and narrated by The Amazing Criswell, who, like co-stars Bela Lugosi, Vampira and Tor Johnson, was an icon of silliness in his day. Criswell was a pseudo-mystic with a determined delivery and glazed eyes, guaranteed to instantly cheapen anything he touched. From behind his desk, as the words "Criswell Predicts" flash on the screen, he announces, "Greetings, my friends. We are all interested in the future, for that is where you and I will spend the rest of our lives. And remember, my friends: future events such as these will affect you in the future. You are interested in the unknown—the mysterious—the unexplainable—that is why you are here. And now, for the first time, we are bringing to you the full story of what happened on that fateful day. We are giving you all the evidence, based only on the secret testimony of the miserable souls who survived this terrifying ordeal. The incidents, the places, my friends we cannot keep this a secret any longer—let us punish the guilty, let us reward the innocent—my friends, can your hearts stand the shocking facts about graverobbers from outer space?" The grammatical errors and incoherence would take another entire chapter to criticize, and are obvious enough on the face of it to demonstrate the nature of the film.

It would be impossible in a limited time to go over every inanity of the movie, which has to be seen to be disbelieved. Some of the more memorable lines include, "One thing's sure—Inspector Clay's dead, murdered, and someone's responsible," "Yeah, women—they've been like that, all through the ages, especially in a spot like this," and "The saucers are up there. The cemetery is out there. But I'll be locked up in there," among a great many others of equally baffling content.

At the top of the movie, a pilot, co-pilot, and stewardess in the world's cheapest cockpit set see alarming flying saucers—Cadillac hubcaps on strings according to Wood, though at least some were actually chrome-painted plastic model kits of the time dangling on strings—and react in horror as the cast of *The Giant Claw* react to their bird (as big as a battleship), which of course can get no other response than unbridled laughter. Later, the pilot tries to explain to his wife on their back porch. "I saw a flying saucer . . . it was shaped like a huge cigar. Dan and Edie saw it, too. When it passed over, the whole compartment lighted up with a blinding glare. Then there was a tremendous wind that practically knocked us off our course . . . I radioed in immediately. They said, 'Well, keep it quiet until you land.' Soon as we landed, big Army brass grabbed us and swore us to secrecy about the whole thing. It burns me up. These things have been seen for years, they're here, it's a fact, and the public ought to know about it . . . Oh, but what's the use of making a fuss. Last night, I saw a flying object that couldn't have possibly been from this planet. But I can't say a word! I'm muzzled by Army brass! I can't even admit I saw the thing!"

Two things are especially interesting in this speech: one, it is word for word what numerous pilots report in real life, and exactly the military or civilian airlines' actual policy; two, the entire monologue is grammatically correct and coherent, yet was ostensibly written by the same inept man who gave Criswell his opening speech and also penned all the other incredibly bad lines in this movie. Wood seems to have selectively bad grammar, and the ability to turn it on or off. He didn't have that problem mere months before, when he wrote 1956's *The Violent Years,* which, however bad or corny it may have been, had perfectly acceptable and coherent sentence structure. (Though released in 1959, *Plan 9* was written and filmed in '56, immediately after *The Violent Years.*) Also, why would the director deliberately describe the UFO as being cigar-shaped, when he knew in advance his model kit was going to be round and saucer-shaped?

The inane dialogue soon returns, however, along with another at least partly true scene. A general—having already been shown valiantly fighting off the plastic flying saucers with ground cannon and rockets, *à la* the real-life 1942 Los Angeles incident—welcomes a colonel into his office, asking his opinion on the subject. The colonel says he believes in them, even if they aren't officially recognized: "May I speak freely? How could I hope to hold down my command if I didn't believe in what I saw and shot at?" The general says, "There are flying saucers. They've been in our skies for some time." He reveals that they didn't always shoot at them, but used to attempt radio contact that was never answered. But then, they sent signals which were finally translated. He plays the tape, which the two men are seen to be listening to with awe and wonder, undercut completely by the silliness of the message and its deadpan delivery: "Since the beginning of your time, we have been far beyond your planet. It has taken you centuries to even grasp what we developed aeons of your years ago. Do you still believe it impossible we exist? You didn't actually think you were the only inhabited planet in the universe? How can any race be so stupid? Permit me to set your mind at ease. We do not want to conquer your planet. Only save it. We could have destroyed it, long ago, if that had been our aim. Our principal purpose is friendly. I admit, we have had to take certain means, which you might refer to as primitive. That is because of your big guns, which have destroyed some of our representatives. If you persist in denying us our landing, then we must only accept that you do not want us on friendly terms. We then have no alternative but to destroy you, before you destroy us. With your ancient, juvenile minds, you have developed explosives too fast for your minds to conceive what you are doing. You are on the verge of destroying the entire universe. We are part of that universe. This is our last. . . ." And the message dramatically ends.

The aliens themselves are foppishly effeminate middle-aged adults in badly tailored silk pajama suits with silly insignias. They want "live Earth people," for no stated purpose, and utilize animated corpses to acquire living humans and to demonstrate their strength and superiority. They plan to make their presence undeniable by sending out their reanimated dead robots, then "turning on the decomposure ray" to catch witnesses' attention. "Their own dead will be used to make them accept our existence, and believe in that fact." So, after at least a solid minute of suspenseful build-up music in which all the principals look seriously back and forth at each other ("Do you see anything?" "I don't know, but somethin' started stinkin' mighty fast!"), Bela Lugosi's stand-in (his chiropractor, a foot taller and not remotely like him in appearance, but Bela died after filming his first scene—probably from seeing the rushes) stalks up to the general, the colonel, the pilot, and his wife, terrifying them (while the audience laughs), unfazed by numerous pistol shots fired at him, and obligingly turns suddenly into a heap of bones. At this point the general asks, "What do you make of that?" and the colonel responds, "You got me! Didn't look that way a minute ago!" A terrified police officer, revived from his faint, gasps, "Did—did you get it? I fired every bullet I had at that thing!" "So did I," reassures the colonel, "but unless that bag of bones can reassemble itself, it's out of the running now."

Finally making their way into the saucer hidden at the cemetery, our valiant crew confront the silk-pajamaed, middle-aged aliens in their lair. Their arrogant captain pompously delivers a few egocentric speeches, then explains that his concern is our nearness to discovering how to explode the actual particles making up sunlight, which will cause a chain reaction destroying the entire universe. Listening to just exactly how this would be accomplished is truly mind-numbing. He makes repeated reference to "your juvenile minds," and actually says, "Because all you, of Earth . . . are IDIOTS!" When the humans listening express their inability to comprehend this inanity, the superior alien suddenly throws a temper-tantrum worthy of a two-year-old, with everything except stamping feet: "You see? *You see?!?* Your *stupid* minds! Stupid! *STUPID!!!*" Our heroes call him a fiend, and he calmly says, in a repeating litany, "I? *A fiend? I?*" And when he is called mad, his girlfriend comes to his rescue with another repeating litany: *"Mad?* Is it *mad* that you destroy other people to save yourselves? But you have done this. Is it *mad* that one country must destroy another to save themselves? You have also done this! How then is it *mad* that one planet must destroy another that threatens the very existence—!" And for no reason (she has, after all, been helping him explain his point), the alien captain snaps, *"That's enough!"* and strikes her, his only explanation being that, on his planet, men fight their own battles and women are merely for advancing the race.

Our heroes finally make a break for it, a fire starting aboard the saucer in the ensuing fracas. It takes off, looking like the flaming model kit on a wire it is, and the onlooking heroes say, "Wonder if that's the last we'll see of them? But sooner or later there'll be others." The general says, perfectly serious—even respectful—"We've gotta hand it to 'em, though . . . they're far ahead of us." This said as the audience sees the superior aliens bickering and bawling like schoolkids, their flaming model-kit saucer exploding in mid-air. Cut back to "The Amazing Criswell," who pronounces the end on this Golden Turkey: "My friends: you have seen this incident, based on sworn testimony. Can you prove that it didn't happen? Perhaps on your way home, someone will pass you in the dark, and you will never know it, for they will be from outer space! Many scientists believe that another world is watching us this moment! We once laughed at the horseless carriage, the airplane, the telephone, the electric light, vitamins, radio, and even television—and now, some of us laugh at outer space! God help us . . . in the future. . . ."

No kidding. And if it wasn't this movie's deliberate intent, from the beginning, to make "some of us laugh at outer space," it was certainly the end result.

American International T.V. financed a Mexican film series in 1959 that began two years earlier, with *Curse of the Aztec Mummy* and *The Robot vs. the Aztec Mummy*. They were produced by K. Gordon Murray, "[whose] name was as well known as Walt Disney or William Castle, thanks to saturation promotion," as *Psychotronic Encyclopedia of Film* editor Michael Weldon puts it. The movies were as ludicrous as they sound, combining ancient history with animated monsters in a comical light. Given Disney's government connection, it makes an interesting footnote that Disneyland is famous for having the most realistic and advanced character robots in the world. The previous year, United Artists produced a similar Edward L. Cahn flick: *Curse of the Faceless Man*. The title creature is a stone mummy animated by ancient Egyptian alchemy, which haunts a woman first in her dreams and then in reality; in amnesiac shock over the matter, her artwork obsessively reflects the bulletproof golem, and her relationship to it is retrieved through regressive hypnosis.

The *Juno 2* deflection surely had some part to play in 1960's *The Cape Canaveral Monsters* from independent CCM, made by the director of *Robot Monster,* Phil Tucker, but this particular picture is of interest for a different reason: it features alien abductions with accurate details, not popularly published either then or now. The movie's aliens are possessed dead human bodies (shades of *Plan 9* and *Invisible Invaders),* which—like 1973's one-handed leaper (and 1951's *The Thing,* or 1957's *Saucer Men)*—lose arms in battle and are entirely unfazed, and needless to say are bulletproof, much to the consternation of the M.P.s who are certain they didn't miss when firing at them. The aliens, when not abducting hapless lover's lane teens and putting them into an unconscious/dreamlike state to perform medical experiments, sabotage missile launches from Cape Canaveral. The actual sabotages by UFOs at Malmstrom AFB were not to come to light for many more years, let alone the Polaris tracking, Atlas deflection, nuclear site incidents, etc. That such material comes in the same movie featuring robotic abductors and actual abduction material not commonly available even today, and that its writer-director also produced the plainly-intended-for-laughs *Robot Monster* of 1953, are coincidences that cannot be taken lightly.

An important entry came in 1960, Columbia Pictures' *12 to the Moon*. Hopelessly average in all regards, what makes it interesting are its story elements. The first Earth team to the Moon discovers someone already living there, apparently beneath the surface, whom they never meet face to face. The strangers communicate to them by sending symbols looking very much like ancient Sanskrit through their computer. They abduct a male and female from the party, stating that they are studying our "emotion of love," a euphemism for sex. They ask for animal specimens to be left behind also, which the team give them before departing as asked. Arriving back at Earth, they find the planet frozen by a beam from the Moon. They return to heat-bomb the Moon, first having to settle dissension among Communist-bloc members who argue over whether or not they should exploit the opportunity to do away with the Imperialist Westerners once and for all, and share the world among themselves. The Moon people turn off their freezing beam of their own volition, telling the returned astronauts that they were simply preserving Earth from harm, and no longer have a need to do so. They tell the team that Earth is not ready to meet them yet, but that they will be welcomed back in a few years when they are.

MGM in 1960 released H. G. Wells' *The Time Machine,* produced and directed by the man who made the same author's *The War of the Worlds* a hit for Paramount seven years prior, George Pal. Both Wells' famous novel and the movie contain mythologically astute elements which tie in with UFOlogy. In the story, a utopian idealist constructs a time machine and travels into the future, there to find not the paradise of which he dreamed, but a nightmare world divided into two factions: the surface-dwelling Eloi, and the subterranean Morlocks. The brilliant but degenerate Morlocks are technologically advanced exploiters of the beautiful, blonde, apathetic, and uneducated Eloi. The Eloi enjoy the simple pleasures provided them by the Morlocks, never knowing or caring where those pleasures come from. Like fattened sheep, the Eloi go into trance and sleepwalk into the Morlocks' underworld at the sound of a siren, there to be cannibalized. The Morlocks' underworld is guarded by—of all things—a sphinx.

Many more bad UFO movies continued throughout the 1960s, as

they have into the present day. No matter their original intent or source, they took on a life of their own very quickly, eventually becoming a fond institution. Some of these show evidence of deliberate tampering, such as 1979's Film Ventures International production, *The Dark*. Filmed as a supernatural horror movie, the producers for no appreciable reason made the movie even more confused than it already was by turning the monster into a space alien at the last minute . . . but also leaving in all the references to its being supernatural. The end result is so confusing as to not even be awful. 1965's *Monster a Go-Go* (B.I.&L.), from legendary independent exploitation schlockmeister Herschell Gordon Lewis, is so incomprehensible it isn't even fun, an originally bad monster-astronaut story spliced into an early disco mess and liberally laced with voice-over narration in place of action. The same year's Allied Artists release, *The Human Duplicators,* had space robots replacing humans with their mock-androids, and was released with an early invading space-fungus movie (soon to become its own mini-genre), *Mutiny In Outer Space.* The same year, AIP-T.V. produced the ludicrous *Space Monster,* with exposed-brain aliens similar to those seen in Topps' *Mars Attacks* trading cards of the time.

AIP funded two Czechoslovakian entries in 1961 (a practice that will be noted more thoroughly in coming chapters): *The Man In Outer Space* and *Voyage to the End of the Universe.* The former was directed by the satirist who did the more famous comic Western *Lemonade Joe* three years later. *Voyage to the End of the Universe,* like *First Spaceship on Venus,* was actually considered to be a pretty good piece of serious science-fiction, in which a group of intergalactic refugees from a corrupt superior civilization flee to Earth. Commonwealth United-TV funded the Mexican production *Neutron Against the Death Robots,* pitting a famous wrestler against the title creatures, and the same year, the Italian-French Teleworld production *Planets Against Us* featured attack by identical alien robots with hypnotic eyes and a touch of death. The year before, AIP produced *Assignment Outer Space* in Italy, a low-budget soap-opera featuring a spaceship run by a renegade computer about to crash into Earth. AIP's *The Crawling Hand* in 1963 was another in the line of disembodied hands incongruously attached to a space movie, having come back in place of the astronaut it was attachéd to with a never-explained penchant for murder.

1962's AIP-financed Swedish import, *Journey to the Seventh Planet*, featured a missing-time abduction of Earth astronauts by an alien on Uranus, intent on probing their minds for potential weaknesses in the human race. The production's intended level of seriousness is indicated by the inclusion of a hallucinatory dream-woman played by Greta Thyssen, a busty blonde sex-bomb who was frequently seen in Three Stooges shorts, and a laughably bad title song that was so embarrassing it has since actually been removed from new prints of the film shown on cable. This movie was scripted by Ib Melchior, whose name is frequently to be found attached to such deflectional UFO and outer space pieces for American International Pictures as 1959's equally silly *The Angry Red Planet,* and the 1965 Italian Mario Bava horror thriller, *Planet of the Vampires.* The last was one of the inspirations for the 1979 hit *Alien,* about a derelict spaceship containing giant mummified aliens discovered by space travelers, which somehow reanimates them into Nazi-looking leather-clad zombies when they die—replete with S.S.-looking insignias on their jackets. Melchior is a military veteran and the author of more than a dozen books on WWII, whose memoirs are specifically about his service in the counterintelligence corps. A recent émigré to America at the time of Pearl Harbor, Melchior was so patriotic that he immediately tried to enlist in the military. He was initially denied, but after writing numerous letters to various government authorities was cleared in an FBI background check and embarked on a lifelong counterintelligence career.

1962 saw the brave lampooners of Hitler and the Nazis, Larry, Moe, and Curly Joe, pitted against Martians after a secret Earth weapon in Columbia's *The Three Stooges in Orbit.* ("Hey, Moe! Hey, Moe! Martians in the bathroom! *Whoob, whoob, whoob—!"*) Three years before, they were abducted and mechanically duplicated by a Venusian robot, in the juvenile *Have Rocket, Will Travel,* a movie which inexplicably made a great deal of money and literally saved the Stooges from obscurity by reviving their career. The Stooges had been so on the

outs since studio cancellation of their film shorts that in 1957 leader
Moe Howard had appeared in a serious cameo as a cabdriver in one
of the earliest invading "space-fungus" movies, 20th Century Fox's
Space Master X-7. Also released in 1962 was the movie said to have
been Andy Warhol's favorite, Emerson Films' *Creation of the
Humanoids*. Featuring *Plan 9*'s effeminate alien leader, Dudley
Manlove, the 75-minute short was about survivors of WWIII creat-
ing purple-green bald robots to do all their work.

AIP was busy with other UFOlogical entries in 1962. among these
was a supernatural thriller akin to 1958's *Curse of the Demon,* called
Burn, Witch, Burn (in England, *Night of the Eagle)*. The script was by
Twilight Zone regular contributors Richard Matheson and Charles
Beaumont, along with George Baxt, and was adapted from Fritz
Leiber's famous and oft-filmed novel *Conjure Wife*. Peter Wyngarde
is an ultra-rational English university professor, who discovers that
his wife Janet Blair—along with other faculty wives—is a witch.
Believing his wife to be suffering from harmful delusions, he forces
her to destroy her "protective charms," and both of their lives take
a sudden downward spiral. A rival witch is out to destroy Wyngarde
and Blair for her own advancement. Toward this end, she utilizes a
supernaturally animated stone eagle statue, which—like the title
creature of *Curse of the Demon*—ultimately boomerangs on her and
brings about her untimely demise. Hypnotic trances and sleepwalking are also featured in the film. The best-known former rendition
of the story, Universal's *Weird Woman* in 1944 (one of the studio's
"Inner Sanctum" series), lacked the animated statue hench-creature,
though it is to be found (as a gargoyle) in the novel.

Extremely rarely seen anymore is 1962's *Invasion of the Star Creatures* from AIP, written by *The Little Shop of Horrors'* (another Corman
classic from 1960) Jonathan Haze. This one has Jewish stand-up comic
soldiers abducted by walking carrots to a nearby saucer occupied by
sexy Gloria Victor and Dolores Reed in extremely revealing leotards,
"stacked better than *The Cat Women of the Moon* and *The Queen of
Outer Space*" as Michael Weldon puts it. Their general uses a plastic
cereal decoder ring, and begins taking orders from privates because
their decoder ring ranking is higher than his. The soundtrack is all

but played on a kazoo—in fact, it may actually *be* played on a kazoo. There is no straight-man in the entire movie—*everyone* in it is Jerry Lewis. *("Oy! Dean! Whoa, De—ee—éa—ean—! Save me from the big Space LA—A—A—ADY—!!!")*

Invasion of the Star Creatures was the second feature on a double-bill led by probably the most famous low-budget schlock film of all time, *The Brain That Wouldn't Die*, produced by Rex Carlton. Like *I Was A Teenage Werewolf* and *Invasion of the Saucer Men* five years before, the 1962 double-bill led with a terrifying mind-control story, and followed with a feature ludicrously pitting the Air Force against flying saucers. *The Brain that Wouldn't Die* concerned a mad surgeon (Jason "Herb" Evers) keeping his decapitated fiancée's (Virginia Leith) head alive in a pan with special chemicals, until such time as he can murder a woman onto whose body he can transplant her remains. Leith despises her new condition, and hates Evers for his predatory intentions against others on her behalf. Despite her lack of a body, Leith finds herself in telepathic contact via the chemical solution that keeps her alive with one of Evers' undead failed experiments—a gigantic, deformed, bald golem kept locked in a closet—which becomes Leith's body to work her will. The two become linked into a single entity, reveling in their ability to wreak revenge against the man who made them the grotesque freaks that they are. Before they succeed in that aim, overheard snatches of the clandestine contact between the two makes Evers and his deformed assistant quite unsettled by their association, much in the same way the government could be unsettled by the association between UFO abductees and their abductors:

"I know there's someone there," Leith tells her unseen, unknown new partner. "Together we could have revenge. Do you want revenge? Yes. You, the thing inside, and me the thing out here . . . Together, we're both more than things. We're a power . . . Together we'll wreak our revenge! I shall create power—and you shall enforce it!" Leith even boasts to Evers' assistant of their contact, and when he doubts her "power" (owing to her present state), she smiles and says, "I *have* power. This liquid that he's pumped into me—my brain burns with it! That thing in there and I are in touch. You want me to prove it?"

Leith commands the thing in the closet to knock, and it does. "Together we're strong—more powerful than any of them!" And she laughs at the assistant's sudden fear, realizing she is right.

Rex Carlton wrote another low-budget film in 1963, Anglo-Amalgamated's *The Unearthly Stranger*, about a man who gradually comes to realize that his human-appearing wife is actually from another planet, an alien vanguard attempting to acclimatize herself to Earth and its inhabitants. Carlton's *The Brain that Wouldn't Die* was filmed in thirteen days in 1959 for less than $150,000 and, like Ed Wood's *Plan 9 from Outer Space*, "took three years to reach an appalled public" as Michael Weldon puts it. Also like Wood, Carlton was reportedly a very nice man who had a phenomenal knack for coming up with money when it was needed. AIP literally rescued Carlton's movie from obscurity, cutting ten minutes of gore from its eighty-one minutes before release that have since been restored so viewers can enjoy every goopy drop. Given the CIA-Mafia connection, it is interesting that fellow exploitation producer Al *(Satan's Sadists)* Adamson, among others, reported to interviewer David Konow in an issue of *Psychotronic* magazine that Carlton "borrowed some money from the mob and he was threatened by them because he couldn't pay them back. He had mob money in two pictures we made *[Nightmare in Wax* and *Blood of Dracula's Castle].* . . ." *Variety* reported on May 15, 1968, that Carlton was found dead in his bathtub from a self-inflicted wound delivered by an Italian pistol. Whether Carlton's demise was suicide or a mob killing, it is worth noting that Al Adamson also was found "entombed in concrete beneath his whirlpool hot tub" at his home in Indio, California, in 1995.

The greatest of all bad UFO movies were 1964's *The Creeping Terror*, from independent Crown International, and Long Island-based Embassy Pictures' *Santa Claus Conquers the Martians*. The latter was Pia Zadora's debut film as a child star, playing the little green Martian child, "Girmar." Its ridiculous title song, "Hooray for Santa Claus," was released as a single for promotional purposes, and Dell put out a comic book of the movie. Every bit as stupid as it sounds, *Santa Claus Conquers the Martians* has the same children's theater production values as its T.V. counterpart two years later, Irwin Allen's *Lost*

In Space. The Martians are antennaed, green-suited stooges, who abduct children (and Santa Claus) to Mars, with the help of a tin-can robot. For unnecessary comic relief there is a dumb-dumb layabout out of Commedia d'ell arte named "Droppo," who does everything but pull down his pants and bray like a jackass ... come to think of it, he may actually bray like a jackass. Even kids hated it. *("Ho-Ho-Ho—!")* The same director made another bad movie for Allied Artists featuring the same planet, *Mission Mars,* three years later. 1964 also brought American General Pictures' *Wizard of Mars,* a techno-magician who plays host to four crash-landed Earthmen in much the same way as his more famous predecessor did to Dorothy and her trio of assorted adventurers before him. Not to be outdone, Avco Embassy T.V. produced an unfunny Italian comedy called *The Flying Saucer* the same year, about a Martian who abducts hapless Italians. The same title was used by Film Classics for what is considered to be the first actual UFO movie ever made, in 1950—which supposedly had to be viewed by the FBI before release for security reasons—the flying saucer of which turns out to be nothing more than a Communist Chinese secret weapon. The exact same plot would turn up again in 1967's *The Bamboo Saucer,* from World Entertainment. (You know how them damn sneaky Commies are.)

Imminently worse than *Plan 9 from Outer Space* or *Santa Claus Conquers the Martians* was Crown International's *The Creeping Terror.* It is impossible to believe that this movie was ever intended as anything but a purposeful ploy. Combining live-action with voice-over narration at an unbelievably static and slow pace, and with all the production values of a 1950s stag film, its title creature is a walking, leafy carpet with an erect, penile head, a vulvaic mouth and four or five lumpily visible operators walking it from underneath. Organ music as from a period soap-opera plays continuously throughout, and the film quality is poor. The excuse that has long been given for the narration in the movie is that the director lost the soundtrack and had to dub it over, but—though it is an entertaining story—it cannot be true, since the action has dialogue spoken in between the narrative segments. All the characters have only one name, repeatedly used to make them silly: "They discovered Jeff's truck, but Jeff himself was not around . . . They looked at the rocket in utter amazement. A puzzled Ben finally asked Martin what he made of the craft." Then the narration stops, and Martin gives the line, "It's no airplane." Ben says, "It could be one of our missiles," and Martin's girlfriend says, "Or one of theirs." Then it's right back to the narration again: "Ben could not understand why the craft wasn't severely damaged." And so on. There's a lot of stuff like, "Martin?" "Yes, Jeff?" "What do you think Dr. Bradford will think?" *("They asked Dr. Bradford what he thought.")* "What do you think, Dr. Bradford?" *("Dr. Bradford told Martin he didn't know.")* "Martin, I just don't know," etc., all accompanied by a lot of silly, mock-heroic drum-playing in the background.

Up to five solid minutes at a time are spent on scenes that go nowhere, people badly dancing to the same repetitive tune for no reason, or to subplots that are over before they began, such as Martin's drifting away from his ol' Army buddy: "Barney and Martin had been bachelor buddies for years. But now that Martin was settling down to marriage, they were slowly drifting apart. Barney, naturally, was still dating all the girls in town, and he couldn't understand why Brett *(the girl's name—another inanity)* and Martin didn't pal around with him more than they did. He couldn't comprehend that married life brought with it not only new problems and duties, but the necessary togetherness of husband and wife, as well. Despite Brett's most tactful considerations, such as inviting him over to dinner twice a week, Barney was growing more resentful of her, or at least, she felt that he was. Since time began, this change in relationship has probably happened to all buddies in similar circumstances. Life has its way of making boys grow up. With marriage, Martin's time had come. His life was now Brett—a life he thoroughly enjoyed." Exit Barney, exit the scene, exit any further mention of this entirely needless episode.

After the walking carpet stalks lover's lane and the local dance hall for a while, sucking up beautiful girls with identical tape-loop screams in the fashion best suited to bare their legs and show their panties as they kick away and jiggle their bottoms, the military eventually destroys the walking carpet monster and its twin (yes, there are two—why?—who knows). Dr. Bradford is mortally wounded to die a hero's

death in the lap of Martin's fiancée, Brett. Then come the most interesting final narrations: "Bradford told Martin what he had just confirmed. That these monsters were highly specialized test animals—they
were, in fact, mobile laboratories that consumed human beings in
order to analyze them chemically, undoubtedly to detect weaknesses
in the human species. He told Martin that the information fed into
a computer in the spacecraft. Further, he added, now that both monsters were dead, the computer would activate a transmitter to send
the results to outer space. Martin knew what he had to do." For two
solid minutes, while the organ music melodramatically plays, brave
Martin tries to hammer the computer to pieces with an all-American
baseball bat, but his efforts prove entirely useless. "On Martin's return,
he confessed his failure. He slowly asked Bradford what was in store
for humanity. Bradford was pessimistic—but implied that maybe all
was not lost. After all, he told them, the vastness of the universe is
incredible. If these monsters had come from its outer limits, their
home might even no longer exist. Or, if they do come again, perhaps man will have advanced enough to cope with them, and those
who made them. Only God knows for sure, were Bradford's last words
to anyone on this Earth." And Brett sobs in Martin's arms and the
camera pans the empty sky. "The End" flashes and the audience is
beside itself with laughter, completely oblivious to the fact that they
have just been told what is probably the truest information available concerning flying saucers for that time, but in such a way that
they will regard it only as the worst of jokes.

The voice-over narration in place of action technique seen in *The
Creeping Terror* was pioneered in at least one prior film from the same
company, three years before (an additional reason why the story of
the dialogue-track having been lost cannot be true), which must be
considered before moving on to later and better treatments of the
UFO subject: *The Beast of Yucca Flats*. Written, directed, and produced
by legendary bad filmmaker Coleman Francis in 1961 (whose films,
similar to Roger Corman's, include an absurdly patriotic low-budget
treatment of the CIA-sponsored Bay of Pigs invasion called *Red Zone
Cuba*), *Yucca Flats* is an utterly nonsensical movie with virtually no
plot, which is noteworthy only in relation to the propagandistic

UFOlogical considerations in this study. It stars *Plan 9 from Outer Space*'s bald giant, Tor Johnson, as another unlikely silent abductor of women, for no purpose stated in the story. Johnson begins as a defecting Russian government scientist being chased by his former comrades, the implied reason being that they want him to keep quiet about information in his possession concerning the Moon: "Flag on the Moon—how did it get there?" the narrator asks, as Tor and Company are chased down the highway. The completely unexplained statement comes out of nowhere, making it the most laughable and famous line of this otherwise completely forgettable film. Though nothing before or after is shown to be related to UFOs in the rest of the movie, one other equally impossible-to-understand line is included, halfway through it, said over a shot of an old man snoozing in his hammock in a small desert town: "Nothing bothers some people—not even flying saucers."

But humor was not the only treatment given the UFO phenomenon. More serious considerations were also made in the cinema, not only in Hollywood, but abroad as well. And as movies gradually phased-out as the primary source of entertainment, another medium was rapidly developing and being equally exploited: television.

5

Insiders and Informations

The exact influence of television on the human mind has never been agreed upon, but is continually debated with considerable venom. There can be no question that, whatever its actual effect, its *perceived* influence is tremendous. It was a national scandal when it was discovered, as early as the 1950s, that game shows were rigged, one of the primary purposes being to sell a false notion of the opportunities of capitalism to a mass audience. Campaigning by various anti-defamation leagues in the 1960s banned from the airwaves everything from the immensely popular *The Untouchables* (derogatory to Italian Americans) to the commercial character of the Frito Bandito (considered equally tarnishing to Mexican Americans). It might be noticed that *Hogan's Heroes* has rarely been off the air since it first debuted, and that since America's increasing economic dependence on Japan, *McHale's Navy* has rarely if ever been back on. Vice President Dan Quayle criticized *Murphy Brown* for selling a damaging image to American families, and was attacked by women's groups, who in turn—along with every minority group imaginable—kept up a fevered campaign for proper role models in the media for their interest group to emulate according to their own ill-decided set of criteria. Former Surgeon General Joycelyn Elders and Attorney General Janet Reno blame television for teenage violence, supported by three separate reported incidents of children setting themselves or their friends on fire because of having seen it done on MTV's *Beavis and Butthead.* Yet the Canadians who view exactly the same programs have no such incidents to report, and the Japanese, whose television programs are many times more violent, have a significantly lower rate of both crime and violence in their society.

Whatever the reality, there can be no question that television— including cable—is the most powerful and important single business in the world, testified to by the phenomenal amount of money spent on advertising in any given year. Advertising is propaganda, and corporations run on it. So do politicians, who do at least as much surveying of their audience as their corporate cousins. FCC Chairman Newton N. Minow gave a famous speech in 1961 calling T.V. both the most powerful communications medium and "America's vast wasteland," which resulted in giving ironclad control of all television's aspects to its producers. Content of programming was watched and judged by boards of censors, which only recently, with the advent of cable, began to change. Sex was so severely censored that the navels of *I Dream of Jeannie*'s Barbara Eden and *Gilligan's Island*'s Dawn Wells were under constant scrutiny lest they prove too provocative for family fare, and Elvis Presley's hips were forbidden to be televised on *The Ed Sullivan Show.* What specific dire effect anyone thought these might have on a viewing audience can only be speculated on, especially considering that mass murder on *Combat* and *The Rifleman* were deemed acceptable, but then America is also the country that gave us *Reefer Madness* and *Sex Madness* under the guise of serious documentaries.

Given both the perceived importance of television's impact on its viewers and the unquestionable importance and secrecy of UFO study by the government, it would be inconceivable that the government would not be interested in utilizing such a powerful communications tool for the purpose of disinformation and/or education on the subject—decided, at any given time, on the prevailing political winds. There is good circumstantial evidence for the movies having been used for these purposes, as discussed in the preceding two chapters. Roger Corman's first film, *The Day the World Ended,* saved the dying corporation A.R.C. and turned it into American International Pictures, which then marketed numerous silly UFO and related pictures by Corman, as well as others with the same slant on the same subject. The revitalized and renamed AIP also remade a great many of those same movies even worse, years later, with Larry Buchanan. Jenny Randles' reported comment from inside the British government about "the right money being placed in the correct hands at the appropriate time" comes to mind.

For the purposes of the proposition under consideration—that the government utilizes entertainment media for UFO propaganda and education—it would help if we could find either an incredibly ludicrous or especially good television show dealing with UFOs or related issues from T.V.'s early years, as well as some clear connection to the military or Intelligence world on the executive level of its production. Such an example is readily available, and was released through United Artists, one of the three most prolific studios involved in disseminating accurate UFOlogical material. First-time producer Joseph Stefano is most often considered its guiding influence, but ABC's *The Outer Limits* (Daystar/Villa di Stefano Productions, 1963–65) was helmed in both of its seasons by executive producer Leslie Stevens, whose brainchild it was.

Thought of as a studio golden boy by most, and a Faust by others, Stevens was often compared to a younger Orson Welles, a mover and shaker with tremendous expertise in all aspects of production. "Leslie was an image-maker," recalled Claude Binyon, Jr., one of Stevens' production team, in David J. Schow and Jeffrey Frentzen's *The Outer Limits: The Official Companion.* "I think he wanted to be President of the United States." Stevens never failed to impress anyone he met. Another co-worker, Robert Justman, called him "a sort of Renaissance Man." Having started out as a New York actor, Stevens became a Broadway playwright and one of Hollywood's "new breed, the curious combination of corporate executive and creative artist," according to his former place of employ, *Time* magazine (where he worked as a copyboy). Early on, he served a stint with the military and earned a degree from Yale University. He attained the rank of captain in the Army Air Corps during WWII, serving in Intelligence for three years in Iceland. Between his military time and his success as a playwright, Stevens "worked for the same people in [the same] places" at both a psychiatric hospital and *Time*. His father, a U.S. Navy vice-admiral, wrote the 1953 bestseller *Russian Assignment* about his experience with anti-Communist Russian exiles, and was an avid science-fiction fan. He also was an MIT graduate and the inventor of airplane arresting gear on aircraft carriers. Leslie Stevens himself professed some years later to be "into the absolute quintessence of the emerging new mythological age," reading such things as *Rhythms of Vision* by Blair, the works of Peter Tompkins, and books on hard physics, authoring his own book on EST under the name L. Clark Stevens. His talent, ambition, natural interests, and military connections—both personal and familial—make him an ideal candidate for an informational media outlet on UFOlogical material. As an added plus, Stevens sold a script to Orson Welles' Mercury Radio Theatre Company while only in high school, talked the company into hiring him at that tender age, and only left when the truant officers caught up with him and dragged him back to the classroom.

Unlike any other show on television before or since, the vast majority of *The Outer Limits'* anthology stories concerned first-contact scenarios with otherwordly intelligence, especially in the area of alien abductions. Its style and tone were sophisticated and adult, though it was sometimes criticized as a "monster of the week" show, and for its use of a moralistic "Control Voice" that introduced and concluded each week's episode. The monsters were Stefano's idea, partly to satisfy ABC as a hook for the juvenile audience, and partly as a vehicle for creating an appropriate fear in meeting the unknown. They were seen less often in the second season, but the ratings also dropped with their absence, as (generally) did the production quality and approach under a new producer. The budgets were minimal, going primarily to imaginative and compelling visual effects, Wah Chang's rather grisly monster masks, and weekly guest stars' salaries. The show was never a huge hit in its initial run, making it curious that it even survived into a second season, which might possibly be explained by friends in high places. In later years, the show developed a huge cult following, and it runs in semi-annual marathons still today on TNT.

Joseph Stefano, Leslie Stevens' first-season *Outer Limits* producer, was initially a musical-comedy writer and starving actor compatriot of Stevens' in Greenwich Village. Stefano had just written the screenplay to Hitchcock's *Psycho,* and he maintained the same claustrophobically oppressive atmosphere for *The Outer Limits.* Unlike its predecessor, CBS' *The Twilight Zone, The Outer Limits* rarely incorporated outright fantasy and hewed to plausible scientific realities. Aliens and humans had to travel in conventional ways and were subject to the laws of physics. The show's outlook was often grim and bleak, lacking the standard Hollywood happy ending so common both then and now. Sticking solely to science-fictional horrors, *The Outer Limits* was more or less a weekly Lovecraftian outing, its most interesting characteristic being its view of mankind as essentially inconsequential in the great scheme of things. The alien intelligences encountered were of varying nature, sometimes hostile, sometimes benevolent, sometimes merely "alien." The human characters in each story were as often as not their own worst enemies, having less to fear from outside entities than from themselves or each other. In general, Stevens tended to be more cerebral and Stefano more visceral in their individual story approaches, both contributing regular scripts to the show, along with many other writers. Both men focused on the human drama in the story, with all other elements playing a backdrop or vehicle to human nature and interaction, and the two tailored all incoming scripts to fit that approach.

From the very beginning of each week's opening narration, with oscilloscope sine waves and striking sharp-focus zoom-ins on the barren face of the Moon, the viewer was told that he was about to experience "the awe and mystery that stretches from the inner mind to ... *The Outer Limits."* The narration itself took on the tone of an abduction: "Do not attempt to adjust your television set. We are controlling transmission ... For the next hour, sit quietly and we will control all that you see and hear...." The end credits featured shots of nearby galaxies, and majestic, appropriately awesome music by Dominic Frontiere (with a more haunting theme by Harry Lubin in the second season), whose otherworldly harp glissandoes, flute trills, and unsettlingly low-key bass notes were among the show's distinctive trademarks. In an interview shown with TNT's airings since 1991, Stevens stated the guiding philosophy of his show: "I think that . . . what it constantly says is, there are ways to relate to the universe and to relate to strangers that are prudent, but nevertheless with an open mind. The whole idea is . . . don't get turned off by something very strange and very peculiar . . . In the beginning we talk about the awe and mystery of the universe, and at the end of it, we say, don't be quick to judge the stranger." Premiere guest star Cliff Robertson—the highest-paid star ever to be on the show—agreed, saying, "In other words, we are a small blue marble of a planet that has so much to learn, and wouldn't it be wonderful if we could learn from out there."

Robertson himself was probably part of the Hollywood disinformational chain without even knowing it. Ten years before his *Outer Limits* appearance, he had been one of the legion of bad space-heroes on T.V., of whom there averaged a new one just about every year since *Captain Video*'s appearance in 1949. There was *Buck Rogers* in 1950 and *Flash Gordon* in 1951, capitalizing on the serials of the 1930s. *Tom Corbett, Space Cadet* ran the same year as *Buck Rogers*, and 1951 also saw *Space Patrol* on the T.V. roster. Robertson's show, *Rod Brown of the Rocket Rangers*, ran alongside *Rocky Jones, Space Ranger*, in 1953. The next year aired the short-lived *Johnny Jupiter*, about a crotchety Walter Matthau-ish robot from Jupiter and his equally mechanical friends who clandestinely communicated with an Earth teenager through the T.V. set, toward the ultimate aim of mutual understanding. 1955 saw three space-hero adventures at once, *Jet Jackson, Flying Commando*, *Captain Z-ro*, and *Commando Cody*, after which the space-opera adventures of T.V. slowed down for a while until 1959's somewhat more serious *Men Into Space*. It was also in 1955 that *Science Fiction Theater* did a live demonstration of a robot in action, a repulsive but effective machine capable of obeying simple commands. The movies kept up a number of equally silly space-opera offerings throughout the 1950s, of which only *Forbidden Planet* and *This Island Earth* made any attempt at being something more than either kid's stuff or parody. It was in this period that *Cat Women of the Moon, The Angry Red Planet* (making Mars a planet of idiotic, red-solarized beasties warning man to "Stay away!" with everything but a ghost in white sheet and clanking chains), and *Queen of Outer Space* led a lesser host of cloned productions, the majority of which had scantily clad space-maidens in miniskirts looking for a good lay from the stalwart manly-men of whatever latest space-probe Earth had launched.

Stevens wrote *The Outer Limits'* pilot episode, "Please Stand By" (later re-titled "The Galaxy Being"), starring Cliff Robertson as an amateur scientist and radio station owner working on a three-dimensional television receiver scanning the galaxy for signs of intelligent life. Accidentally succeeding beyond his wildest dreams, he tunes in the image of a being from Andromeda one night, translating its language through a binary computer (which, like several of the show's episodes, is never fully explained, but at least made plausible within the suspension of disbelief). Like Robertson, it too is an explorer, breaking its planet's laws in attempting to establish outside contact. The alien—as did many later aliens on the series—resembled standard UFO occupants, being all eyes and no face. It also had a vastly oversized chest for no reason stated in the story, but obviously resembling the then-unpublished reports of such creatures as abducted the Hills and Herbert Schirmer, among others.

An unforeseen power surge causes the being to be transmitted bodily to Earth, where it wreaks untold havoc entirely without meaning to, simply because of the nature of its radioactive body. People it stumbles across are blinded by its radiation, or horribly burned. Others run off the road and crash in sheer panic at the sight of it. Having come to the attention of the National Guard, the Andromedan is pursued back to Robertson's laboratory and attacked. Robertson tries to convince them that the being is friendly, having just cauterized his wife's bullet wound caused by their shooting. The captain of the Guard is unconvinced, saying, "It's using him!" but is stopped cold when his initial barrage against the alien visitor proves entirely ineffective.

"I have told you not to use force," the Andromedan says. "Now I warn you—there are powers in the universe beyond anything you know." It effortlessly destroys the station's radio tower to prove its point, then says, "There is much you have to learn. You must explore! You must reach out! Go to your homes. Go and give thought to the mysteries of the universe. I will leave you now . . . in peace." Completely shown up, the military disbands without further comment or fuss, and the friendly but dangerous visitor, unable to return home and unable to live on Earth, tunes itself out of existence. "What will happen to you?" Robertson asks. "Unknown," it replies. "End of transmission. . . ." And it simply dissolves into nonexistence, neither having bestowed the final word of wisdom nor been our judge and destroyer, unable even to predict its own fate as it crosses the final barrier of mortality. Exactly in common with early UFO visitations, "The Galaxy Being" simply comes and then leaves, in between proving itself superior and by its very existence insisting that we more deeply ponder our exact standing in the universe.

Stefano later did a version of the same story in his own style, showing the difference between the two men's visions. His "The Bellero Shield," an adaptational cross between *Macbeth* and a pulp story called "The Lanson Screen" by Arthur Leo Zagat, featured a friendly alien made out of concentrated light, which finds itself inadvertently beamed into laser scientist Martin Landau's living room one night. Small and frail, the glowing thing looks like a cross between a little Chinaman and a classic UFO abductor, badly frightening everyone until they realize it is not hostile. It protects itself with an impenetrable force field, generated by a bulb attached to its wrist. Though Landau is a decent man and fascinated by exchanging information with the visitor, his scheming wife Sally Kellerman conspires to seduce the alien out of its shield, and murders it for its force-field device. Telling her husband the alien simply departed, she tries to convince his powerful and wealthy father that Landau invented the force field himself, and gets herself trapped inside it during a demonstration. Admitting to her crime, she and the rest of the household discover that the thing isn't quite dead yet. Fortunately, unlike its human hosts, the alien is not capable of being vindictive. Before expiring, it frees Kellerman from the horrible prison in which she has put herself, but the noble gesture has proven fruitless since Kellerman's conscience won't let her go.

In general, Stevens' stories tended to be scientifically oriented and to show man as an essentially curious but fearful creature, sometimes dangerous or rash but rarely malicious or mean, and Stefano's Catholic background influenced his scripts to deal strongly with both benevolent and fearful celestial visitations and human evil. Exploitation is frequently at the core of Stefano's stories, with man rarely being as interested in the awesome nature of contact with a new visitor as he is in what he can get out of it. Both Stevens and Stefano rarely presented alien races as hostile, though they were often as self-interested as their human counterparts on Earth. Notable exceptions included an adaptation of Louis Charbonneau's obscure 1960 novel *Corpus Earthling,* starring Robert Culp as a man with a metal plate in his head that gives him a unique ability to hear conspiring aliens' conversation between themselves, making him their target for murder when they become aware of his intrusive listening. The creatures are alien parasites (brought back from Mars, in the original novel) masquerading as common rocks, which invade their hosts and cause accelerated aging in the process. In common both with UFO abductors and classic pulp villains, they are super-hypnotic, capable of compelling a man to act against his will once he hears them. A claustrophobically paranoiac story, and one of the series' scariest, the episode ironically aired four days before Kennedy was shot. It owed a great deal to the 1956 Frank M. Robinson novel, *The Power*—filmed by UA's companion company, MGM, in 1968—about a psychic superhuman in a secret government group investigating paranormal mental powers, who invisibly blends in among mortal men, preying upon them as he will, and seeking out and destroying any of the locals who display similar proclivities in case they might one day rival him.

A later entry scripted by Stefano, "The Invisibles," could have been a continuation of "Corpus Earthling," as well as a virtual adaptation of Robert A. Heinlein's *The Puppet Masters.* In it, crablike parasites create "the Society of the Invisibles," intent on gradual takeover of the planet by "implanting" themselves in powerful hosts. Other hostile aliens on the series included a plainly malevolent being in "Don't Open Till Doomsday" which abducted human beings aboard its ship as hostages to force human accomplices to help it destroy

Earth, and the fifth-column invaders of "O.B.I.T.," which were equally evil. Another story starred a compelling Joanna Frank as a mutated Queen Bee turned into a human being for the purpose of creating a new, superior race of creature in a hybrid between the two species. The she-creature (appropriately named "Regina") was not depicted as evil, but as psychopathically dangerous through her lack of recognizable human morality in achieving her aims.

All of these contain elements of interest in common with the UFO abduction phenomenon, which may or may not have reflected what the government researchers on the inside knew themselves. Actual alien abduction occurs so often in the series that speculation on the possibility cannot but be considered. In addition, the military features prominently in a great many of the show's stories, essentially like its involvement in real life at the time the series was being made, which has since been confirmed by FOIA-released documents. Any of these correct UFOlogical elements in the series' stories could have been inspired guesses, and many of them probably were. Some of them may have been a little better informed by personal experience, since Stevens was, after all, an Air Force Intelligence man with a vice-admiral father. Though he and Stefano did not write all the scripts themselves, they did tailor scripts to fit their vision of the show, and some of them mirror actual events of the time.

An excellent example of apparent UFO accuracy in *The Outer Limits* is the next-to-last episode of the first season, "The Chameleon," written by Robert *(Chinatown)* Towne, starring Robert Duvall as an Intelligence agent/assassin given the assignment of his career: to impersonate an alien and infiltrate a flying saucer. While this has almost certainly never come close to occurring in real life, the story is credibly told and depicts the military's handling of the saucer problem as it appears actually to have been done. Duvall is called in to view a top secret film taken by an army patrol, and is briefed on foregoing events. A saucer has landed in the woods near the base, where it has been for a few days. Occupants have been sighted on the ground, who are all identical in appearance, small, quick and elusive, bald and hairless (matching very closely the appearance of actual UFO occupants, and differing in appearance from the creatures in

Towne's original script). They greet all attempts at communication only with silence, and have destroyed one armed patrol that went to meet them. The military treats the saucer as hostile, since its occupants killed their men, but can't figure out whether or not their readings as to the amount of combustible radioactive material on the saucer will cause it to "make Hiroshima look like a bonfire if it's hit."

Duvall's mission is to infiltrate the saucer and discover this information for them. Through a science-fictional plot device, he accomplishes the task by actually being transformed temporarily into one of the creatures, done somehow through a recombinant DNA trick involving cell samples taken from beneath the nails of one of the dead soldiers. Once Duvall is aboard, the aliens paralyze him with a light beam, not taken in for a moment by his masquerade. In their ensuing conversation, he asks why, if the aliens were peaceful, they killed the military patrol, and he is told simply, "They tried to kill us," which is exactly the truth in the military's real-life handling of saucer occupants according to the records. Duvall asks to be freed, assuring them that he would never hurt them as the military tried to, surprising even the military brass that sent him—who are monitoring him through a bugging device—by telling the aliens that, whether he was initially an Earthman or not, he is indeed now one of them because of the process that transformed him: "I feel I belong here, that I've been here." He proves his point by correctly describing the items on their spacecraft and details about their home planet that he could not possibly know. In light of the unmistakable tendency for UFO abductees to identify with their abductors and seem to know what is going on aboard the craft while they are there, this is all very interesting indeed.

Both the aliens and the military are then in a quandary about what to do with him. "In trying to combat those creatures," Duvall's controller tells the military, "we may have contributed one more to their number. We might be losing our agent—not through death, but through defection." The general in charge of the operation has figured out that there are no explosives aboard the saucer and is ready to order a strike, since "There's too much at stake for us to take a chance. We have as much to worry about from them holding onto

something human—even partly human—as they do from us holding one of them. With him in their hands, they'd be in a position
of knowing all about us, our strengths and our weaknesses. They'd
be in a position to blackmail us, or even conquer us . . . [his] life is
precious, and it's an awful thing to sacrifice a man, but we can't trust
the unknown without asking for something far more awful." This
was probably a very real fear of any government investigative team
at the time concerning the abduction phenomenon, especially since
they had been studying it for only ten to sixteen years and certainly
would have to have been suspicious (to say the least) of the reasons
behind it.

The two aliens return from their conference, revealing that they
were not to have contact with any destructive society, or to leave
behind any trace of themselves. Since Duvall is now part of them,
they insist on his returning with them. They would prefer that he
come willingly, and convince him that he would be happier with
them than in his killer's life on Earth, which he cannot help but agree
with. When the aliens make their decision, Duvall is given a prearranged kill-order by his controller through the bugging device. He
initially resists, but his years of training stand secure, and he murders one of the aliens. Pursuing the remaining survivor through the
woods, he changes his mind at the last minute: "No. You were right.
You see how destructive we Earth creatures are? You were right. Would
you still have me . . . come away with you?" The alien says it is a long
journey back to his planet, better made with a friend, and they return
to the saucer. The general orders Duvall to return to the base, and
Duvall informs him simply that he belongs somewhere else now:
"On a warm, yellow planet, where there is no need for a man of
action—where the chameleon no longer needs to change his color-
ing to survive." The general calls his command post to order them
to destroy the saucer as it takes off, but at the last minute changes
his mind and lets them go.

Duvall also starred in the single best example of a story paralleling actual abduction occurrences, the only two-parter in the series,
the second season's "The Inheritors." One of *Outer Limits'* best entries
on any level, the story is amazingly well-handled, one of the few

without any monsters. Duvall plays senior agent Adam Ballard in a government investigative branch, referred to as "the Federal Bureau of Security" and seeming to be a loose blend of the FBI, CIA, and NSA. He has discovered something highly unusual about four recently wounded Vietnam soldiers: they have all been hit in the head by bullets made in the same theater of war, should have died and didn't, and somehow developed extraordinarily high I.Q.s and sudden new interests as a result. In addition, they have acquired something theoretically impossible to have: "Another brain wave pattern?" Ballard asks a doctor upon seeing the EEG of the latest case, receiving the answer, "Another *brain,* Mr. Ballard. An *alien* brain. There are two brains in the lieutenant's head now."

Lieutenant Minns (Steve Ihnat) recovers from his injury with remarkable speed, like the three soldiers before him. Ballard is intent on not losing Minns, since the other men simply disappeared from their hospital rooms with no one being the wiser as to how they did it. Minns is agreeable and pleasant, deceptively low-key, and as baffled by his new condition as Ballard. "I understand my I.Q. is going up and up," he laughs, "and that's very funny, because I don't feel any smarter!" Ballard tells him that, like the other men, he has no ties, no family or girlfriend. "Link after link," Minns agrees, intrigued. "So many things in common. There's gotta be a reason, a purpose, is that it, Mr. Ballard?" Ballard asks him, "No clue, lieutenant? No inkling what it may be? Something alien in your head—something guiding you, pointing you, directing you … ?" Minns says no, but Ballard finds him with an advanced book on stock market trends as easy-reading material.

Despite a guard at his door, Minns walks casually out of the hospital and into anonymity as did the other three, using hypnosis to gain cooperation and erase the memories of anyone in his way, another newly acquired attribute of his mysterious injury. "Whatever it is that's started," Ballard says, "he's part of it. Mr. Secretary, I'll be blunt about it—I think we've been invaded. This whole world has been invaded." Ballard is concerned, even though Minns and the others have not been shown to have done any harm or harbored any untoward intentions. His superior agrees that the mystery is well worth continuing investigation, but asks Ballard if he doesn't think all of this may be entirely innocent. "I hope so," Ballard answers. "But then, why did those men *disappear?* Do you disappear when you're doing something innocent? How can we know what they may be up to when they've got that 'invader brain' in their heads? What if they *aren't* innocent? What if they're enemy-inspired, or a mutant of some kind, or—I hesitate to say it because it sounds so theatrical—but, what if those men are now joined in some dark venture, bent on some evil purpose, controlled by some malevolent extraterrestrial influence? Maybe they *are* innocent, sir, and maybe not . . . but I think we ought to find out, and fast!"

Such would not have been an unreasonable attitude for the government to have taken upon first discovering that a portion of their population had been abducted and implanted with unknown devices by unknown spacecraft. The bullets in the story serve the function of implants, Ballard discovering that they were all formed out of metal from a meteorite containing a fine, honeycombed structure that has lost whatever substance it held upon entering the men's skulls; a government scientist examining the metal claims that slight remaining traces show evidence of having been an RNA code, or an alien genetic structure. The "abductees" in the story match pretty accurately the standard profile now recognized: they are average, everyday people, they keep an extremely low profile and don't seek publicity, and they somehow seem to find other abductees though they are not often aware of it. Their memories are very good, and they tend to develop obsessions or compulsions they don't really understand. They are generally well-liked, attractive and intelligent, with good senses of humor, but somehow not very assertive. "It was as though the devil had him under his thumb," a character describes one of the cosmically infected soldiers in the story, "and he had no chance to get out from under, and be his own man." Though overly melodramatic in real-life terms, abductees have often been described in more or less the same way. They also display the same characteristics of uncertainty and doubt that the "abductees" in the *Outer Limits* story do. One of the characters goes to church—preternaturally having anticipated Ballard's coming and evaded him, displaying

another not-uncommon characteristic of general wariness and awareness—and prays, "Is it your will? This thing inside my head—it creates new and wonderful images. It makes me do things of such beauty,
it can't be bad. No, it's not bad. It's good. It *is* good . . . isn't it, God?"

Ballard's fears turn out to be not entirely unfounded. Minns
amasses a small fortune in a few days by means of his new stock market expertise, and he somehow knows where the other three
"abductees" (none of whom know each other) are located, sending
them large sums of money. Traveling around the globe to track them
down, Ballard is always one step behind them. PFC Hadley has just
disappeared from his rented warehouse in Wichita to gather rare
plants and herbs in South America, blueprints in his lab showing
that he is working on some kind of air conditioning system and structural design; Sergeant Conover has been working in a lab in Stockholm, having come up with a new metal alloy that is lighter and
tougher than any yet known, and which bonds magnetically without any visible seam using no rivets or bolts; Private Renaldo has created an anti-gravity device in Tokyo. Ballard's conclusion: the men
are building a spaceship. In the process of discovering this, Ballard
finds himself at the Indianapolis 500, where he experiences "missing time," suddenly waking with no memory of how he got to be
there, his last recollection being of talking to one of the abductees
he intended to arrest and bring back home . . . two weeks before.

Ballard stakes Minns out at his apartment, and Minns merely
smiles at him, unconcerned. "You smile at me and I get a chill," Ballard tells him. "You're smiling with a piece of your mind that doesn't
belong to you. You'll lie that way, cheat that way, steal that way if
you have to. You said we can't contain you, well, I believe you. I
believe you can do just about anything you want to do." Minns cor-
rects him: "Anything I *must* do." He asks what laws he has broken,
why he is under scrutiny, let alone arrest. Ballard reveals that he
knows the men are building a spaceship and asks what it is for. Troubled, Minns answers honestly, "I don't know." "Does it matter that
it may be heinous?" Ballard asks, and Minns says, "Yes, it matters.
There's nothing I can do about it." "You can fight it," Ballard insists.
"Not any more than you can fight me," Minns replies. Having said

everything he can and heard all he is going to, Minns effortlessly eludes them by means of an impenetrable shield given him by one of the other infected soldiers.

Complicating matters is the fact that Minns is soon discovered to be in contact with a number of small children, all crippled, blind, and lame, who somehow seem to know him without his introducing himself and all wanting to go with him on his "long journey." Ballard brings a task force to where the spaceship is constructed but cannot pass a force field the men have erected there, so he reasons with them. "You haven't even found out why you're building this ship. Well, I found out. You ought to be proud to be part of such a noble undertaking. A bit of kidnapping, that's what. That's the purpose for this whole thing. But there's no ransom with these kids, their folks can't buy them back, it's a one-way trip to some fantastic horror; some alien monster's got plans for them. And you're picking the best. A little blind girl. A deaf and dumb boy. The helpless ones."

"Even if it's true," one of the abductees answers, "we can't do anything about it. We can't stop what we're doing. We can't help ourselves. We're not even aware, from one moment to the next, what we're going to do. Don't you understand? We can't stop ourselves!"

"I don't care that you couldn't stop what you did!" Ballard accuses them. "You could have taken your own lives, without harming those helpless little ones! Now what? When do they take off, and how far do they go? Which one of you brave geniuses goes with them? What's in store for them? Do you know that? Why did you pick these particular ones? Why the helpless ones? What's going to happen to them? They're so innocent and so trusting, what do you want them for? For what sacrifices? For what purpose?"

"Not the helpless," Minns tells Ballard, after putting the children aboard the ship, "the hopeless. The ones who, all their short lives, never had anything. Never were whole. Never had dreams. Never were loved." Admitting that he is only now coming to understand the purpose they have all been laboring for, he says that a superior race from a distant planet—which he casually connects to the Bible, by virtue of their lengthy lifespan—found suddenly that they could no longer procreate and sent their RNA out in meteorites, hoping somewhere that a course of action like that which has transpired would occur, enabling them to bring children from somewhere else to their world, to start over. To prove his good intentions, Minns lowers the force field and says, "You want them, Ballard? Come and get them." Aboard the ship, Ballard discovers that the childrens' infirmities have disappeared in the artificial atmosphere there, which is identical to that on the world they are going to. As in "The Chameleon," the government men decide that they must simply have faith in the aliens, and allow the spaceship to leave peaceably.

When exactly the government figured out that not only were human abductions occurring by UFOs, but that they were being done to infant children, cannot be known for certain. Whoever has that knowledge is not about to share it. But it is certainly interesting to find it employed in such a way in a 1964 teleplay, along with the elements of implants and missing time, fully two years before Betty and Barney Hill's story was published, which was the first on record to discuss the "missing time" aspect of abduction.

An *Outer Limits* episode from earlier that same year, "The Children of Spider County," featured military and Intelligence members of the "National Space Security Agency" (a very close acronym to both NASA and NSA) discussing a "curious pattern" of "disappearances" apparently connected to UFOs, all of men born in the same county, in the same year, and even the same month, whose fathers left immediately after birth. "These speculations regarding abduction by representatives of an alien planet are just that—speculations!" one general protests against the theory, but admits the disappearances must be studied. Like "The Inheritors," the missing men in this episode are all considered to be geniuses, which intensifies the interest of the government in studying their disappearance.

Some of these same plot elements were seen in the classic *Village of the Damned* four years before (released by MGM, United Artists' companion studio), about "missing time" in an entire village accompanied by an energy-dampening force field, after which all the town's women find themselves pregnant and giving birth to perfect blonde-haired, blue-eyed children, who are telepathic, super-hypnotic geniuses, ultimately destroyed as hostile invaders in every community where they appear. What had not been in that movie was the typical UFO-abductor monster seen in the *Outer Limits* version, or its use of hypnosis to put its abductees into a trance and take them to a waiting ship in the woods, as well as erase interlopers' memories and give them missing time intervals. The *Outer Limits* episode also features both vehicular and bedroom abductions. "Spider County's" aliens turn out to be seeking rejuvenation of their race through the breeding of sons off of Earth women, to be taken to their world when they are old enough to withstand the rigors of spaceflight. Ruthless and amoral, they are ambivalent to human affairs or life, interested solely in their own concerns. The alien father who comes to reclaim his Earthly hybrid offspring appears both as a completely human-looking man and in the alter-ego of a bald, large-headed, and bug-eyed insectoid, a recurring production element seen throughout the course of the series.

In "Second Chance," an alien masquerading as a carnival barker passes out free flying saucer-ride tickets to carefully pre-selected people among the crowd, but the ride turns out to be on a real spaceship. This alien is not hostile but is as ruthless and self-interested as those in "Spider County." Its concern is finding a number of people to populate an asteroid and help divert it from an ultimate collision course with its own homeworld, and eventually ours. It abducts without asking, as a matter of expediency, but at least tries to take those who will have the least regrets and find the adventure worthwhile. Finally, the abductees convince the being that it would do far better to ask for volunteers, and it reasonably returns them.

One of Stefano's scripts, "The Zanti Misfits," featured a flying saucer with insectoid occupants who approach a paralyzed and terrified Bruce Dern, while he agonizingly pleads with them to leave him alone. The Air Force listens in the entire time, unable to lift a finger to help and simply sweating it out silently. This episode also features a "sham" radio report—Dern's girlfriend listening to a chuckling disc-jockey announce that yet another flying saucer has been spotted which the Air Force denies, even as she is looking at it where it has landed in an isolated desert setting and her boyfriend is being ravaged by its occupant. A similar commentary occurs in the background of "Don't Open Till Doomsday," where a scientist predicting an invasion from space is seen on the cover of a newspaper—the same scientist is seen at the beginning of the episode, bringing the invading alien's ship to its new location. Other UFOlogical points of interest in "Doomsday" include the alien being essentially nothing more than a giant, unblinking eye—exactly like the scanner reported by abductees Charles Hickson and Calvin Parker in 1973—holding its victims paralyzed and terrified while it examines them in a fashion not unlike what David Jacobs labels the "mindscan" procedure, and the fact that it abducts newlyweds, connecting it with the sexual activity universally reported in real abductions. The heroine is even shown writhing on her knees in a state indistinguishable between terror and sexual ecstasy, while locked in the gaze of the alien eye.

Classic vehicular abductions occur in another of Stefano's scripts, "A Feasibility Study," in which robotic inhabitants of the planet Luminos (Venus, in the original script) transport an entire Earth neighborhood—homes and all—to study their viability as slaves. While the hapless abductees awaken from their blissful ignorance of the preceding night's events and gradually discover that they are no longer in Kansas, some of them are escorted to and from their cars by lumbering humanoids out of a sudden fog and subjected to a variety of tests. "Do you know where you are?" the Luminoid leader asks an aware abductee who has been brought to him. "Nowhere on Earth," the abductee answers. "While you and your neighbors slept, we borrowed—so to speak—six city blocks of Earth," the alien leader tells him. "Naturally, we did not intend that you become aware of our experiment until it was concluded. Experiments are best conducted upon the blithely ignorant."

"Fun and Games," which Stefano heavily script-doctored, features classic abduction settings and occurrences. Its story is about the jaded and all-powerful Andarans, who kidnap creatures from different planets for gladiatorial games. Along the way, they taunt, torment, and test their subjects. "Will I have to remember any of this?" an Earth girl asks her shadowy abductor after surviving the ordeal, and it replies, "Only those things which may be of help to you [in your life]," before wiping her memory clean and returning her from whence she came. Neither hostile nor friendly, the Andarans are solely interested in their fun and games, with human beings only one more set of pawns. The Andaran costume was the same as that employed in the episode "Nightmare," though seen only in recessed shadows, consisting of an oversized bald head with enormous eyes.

"Nightmare," also by Stefano, proved prophetic in at least one regard: it wrote about the scandalous treatment of military person- nel by their superiors in inhuman peacetime psychological torture tests, years before exactly such occurrences in real life became pub- lic. Redolent with abduction imagery and occurrences, "Nightmare" features gargoyle-like aliens with enormous bald heads who speak through rough, mechanical translators in monotonous voices, tor- turing their charges with rod-like weapons in a limbo environment, creating such hallucinations that the real is indistinguishable from the unreal, and often interrogating them in play-acting scenarios, exactly as described by abductees today. These "rods," frequently described as looking like pens or pencils, have been said to cause paralysis in countless abductee cases. They are so often reported that government scientists have even speculated on the nature of their technology, the consensus seeming to be that they use a pulsed microwave beam that temporarily stuns the nervous system. Jacques Vallee mentions in *Dimensions—A Casebook of Alien Contact* that he was not certain that Betty Hill's abduction had been a real occur- rence until she mentioned this item, which hitherto had not been written of in any account.

Though entirely lacking in alien presences, Stefano's most com- pelling script, "The Forms of Things Unknown," featured abduction- related elements, most notably in a genius inventor of super-hypnotic power, played by David McCallum. McCallum has the power to raise or lay to rest the dead, and he "intrudes on people's reveries" by means of hypnosis, forcefully entering their minds and effortlessly uncov- ering their deepest, darkest secrets, then completely erasing their memory of the encounter. McCallum appeared earlier the same sea- son in an episode ("The Sixth Finger") having nothing to do with UFO phenomena, but in a makeup nearly identical to that of the classic abductor, so distinctive that the Don Post Studios eventually made a mask out of it. In this story, McCallum plays an artificially evolved man, six million years in Earth's future. This super-advanced man is small and frail, playing off the actor's wispy Welsh physique, moving with swift, economic precision, arms straight down at its sides; it has a gigantic bald cranium and intimidating ocular cavities, with which it can read minds and hypnotically impose its will. Telepathy, hypnotic memory erasure, and a bug-eyed, bald-headed abductor also were seen in "The Mutant," and space abduction, offspring, and mental domination were featured in "The Man Who Was Never Born." "Expanding Human" also displayed curious foreknowledge of related UFOlogical subjects, its story being about a secret, university-run LSD test, producing superhuman mutants with genius intellects who become bulletproof hypnotic masters bending others to their will and erasing all memory of their having been present. "Expanding Human"'s protagonist even finds himself—as the Jekyll-and-Hyde victim of his own experiment—suffering missing time lapses, because his alter-ego has not only hypnotically erased itself from his conscious memory, but also post-hypnotically suggested times for him to bring the alter-ego back by use of the special drug.

An ambivalent abductor-alien tricks unsuspecting humans into its laboratory in "The Guests," "dissecting" them psychologically and tormenting them in various unspecified tests for its own purposes. Entirely without feeling or emotion, this being conducts its studies in a limbo setting with utter detachment and single-mindedness of purpose, able to mentally dominate its subjects, paralyzing them and summoning them at will. Seeming interested in discovering what makes us so violent and greedy, it ultimately finds one subject with suitably noble emotions to release, exterminating the rest without a moment's care or pity.

Frightening claw-handed robotic abductors are seen in Stevens' "Production and Decay of Strange Particles," the title creatures being intelligent particles that eat away human tissue inside the protective suits of an atomic plant's technicians, then occupying the suits themselves and mechanically going about seizing others to increase their number. The story owed a great deal to United Artists' 1953

production, *The Magnetic Monster.* Actual robots starred in "The Duplicate Man" (a clone, specifically), "I, Robot," and Harlan Ellison's
"Demon with a Glass Hand" in the second season.

Ellison's script, yet one more among his many Hugo Award-
winners, is another example of aliens in a script being changed at
the executive level for reasons unknown. "In this one, there is no
strange-looking, weird monster," Ellison said during a TNT *Outer Limits* marathon. "The closest the network could get to it was painting
those stupid round black circles around the aliens' eyes." Those circles make the alien eyes look very much like those of UFO Grays, as
do the close-fitting shower-caps (identified as being exactly such
items by star Robert Culp), which make them look completely bald—
an effect enhanced in the longer shots by stretching a nylon stock-
ing over them. In Ellison's original script, the aliens are extraterrestrials
surgically altered to pass for humans, so as to be completely undetected on an undercover mission. That mission is to pursue robot
Culp back in time, and discover from him how the future inhabitants of Earth, which they have conquered, escaped from them undetected in a single night. Culp, attempting to explain some of this to
a woman he accidentally becomes hooked-up with in our time,
expresses one of the principal hurdles in understanding that UFOlogists have to deal with. "I thought you said they were from another
planet?" she frowns, as Culp finishes telling her they are from the
future. He responds, calmly and deliberately, "Another planet . . . *and
another time."* Which, in a sense, is where today's UFOs come from—
only their origin is to be found in the past.

Though Ellison probably was not ever consciously involved in
the UFO educational project—he was briefly drafted into the Army,
which left him with a notorious hatred of the military, and openly
professes an affinity to famous UFO-debunking group CSICOP (Committee for the Scientific Investigation of Claims of the Paranormal)—
his scripts sometimes echo enough actual information that they
would certainly have been of great interest to those who were. The
possibility that he was knowingly involved is not out of bounds,
however. In 1967, Ellison scripted an episode of MGM's immensely
popular T.V. spy show, *The Man from U.N.C.L.E.* (NBC, 1964–68),

called "The 'Pieces of Fate' Affair." The story concerned attempts on novelist Sharon Farrell's life by agents of U.N.C.L.E.'s rival agency, T.H.R.U.S.H., owing to the uncanny accuracy her recent novel *Pieces of Fate* shows in relating their most top-secret true-life plans—just as true top-secret UFOlogical facts seem to appear with uncanny accuracy in such seemingly silly entertainments as Intelligence-produced T.V. spy shows like *The Man from U.N.C.L.E.* And the year before, Ellison wrote an episode for the same show called "The Sort of Do-It-Yourself Dreadful Affair," in which T.H.R.U.S.H. creates numerous invincible and identical robots for an army, containing some human parts taken from accident victims. Ellison was intimately involved with a short-lived early 1970s show called *The Starlost* (though he disowned it after the fact), and most recently has been creative consultant on *Babylon 5*, which sometimes displays apparently accurate UFO material. He also wrote one of *Star Trek*'s most famous episodes ("The City on the Edge of Forever") and could have gained ingress to a governmental UFO project through that famous show's producer, Gene Roddenberry (see next chapter), if not through United Artists with *The Outer Limits*.

It is worth noting that the *U.N.C.L.E.* series gave thanks to the "real" United Network Command for Law and Enforcement at the end of each episode ("without whose assistance this program would not be possible"), when in fact no such organization exists—though "Uncle Sam" does. And perusal of the series' episodes quickly reveals that the majority of its background elements are accurate portrayals of CIA standard operating procedure and tactics (and often unflattering portrayals, at that, including blackmail, coercion, and bribery as recruitment tools, and the employment of thieves and Mafia figures), none of which was publicly written about until Victor Marchetti and John Marks' *The CIA and the Cult of Intelligence* six years after the *U.N.C.L.E.* series' cancellation. The contemporaneous *I Spy* also contained such realistic elements.

The government was often shown to be in uneasy league with alien intelligences on *The Outer Limits*, or being duped by them in one way or another, which may have been an inspiration for some of the EBE/Area 51 disinformational stories of the 1980s. Ronald

Reagan or his scriptwriter was unquestionably using *The Outer Limits* for the president's speeches, evidenced on two different occasions. In his speech selling the Star Wars platform for re-election in 1984, Reagan referred to the program as a "protective umbrella," calling it specifically "an anti-weapon." These were the exact terms used by the alien in "The Bellero Shield" to describe its protective force field, which its ambitious murderer coveted as a weapon. In his famous speech about how quickly warring nations on Earth would band together if confronted by an enemy from "out there," Reagan was referring to the plot of "The Architects of Fear," in which a band of Intelligence scientists surgically-genetically create an alien invader out of one of their own (with oversized head, bug-eyes, and disproportionate arms, *à la* Roswell), secretly sending him up into space to return and terrify the U.N. in an effort to forestall further nuclear accidents between the superpowers. (The idea of a bogus space-invader for banding the world together was proposed fifteen years earlier, in Bernard Newman's novel *The Flying Saucer,* but it took *The Outer Limits* to effectively dramatize it.)

That the series had a definite influence in other high places is evidenced by Harvard's drama school doing a production of Meyer Dolinsky's 1963 series entry "O.B.I.T.," a story about a fifth column of seditious aliens giving Intelligence agencies a perfect surveillance device, which they correctly surmise the human race will demoralize itself with before their invasion. Dolinsky—who the same year also authored "The Architects of Fear" and Joanna Frank's alien Queen Bee episode—either knew something about the FBI's COINTELPRO (Counter Intelligence Program), or was extraordinarily perceptive. "In this room twenty-four hours a day, seven days a week," the narration opens, "security personnel at the Defense Department Cypress Hills Research Center keep constant watch on its scientists through 'O.B.I.T.,' a mysterious electronic device whose very existence was kept from the public at large...."

The first realistic mention of the National Security Agency (whose very existence also was kept from the public at large), according to NSA biographer James Bamford, was in James L. Kahn's *The Codebreakers* in 1966, and even then it was only incidental. Prior, only exceptionally rare mentions of the NSA's existence made the papers or any public document, when it was invariably dismissed with vacuous cover stories as nothing more than a minor subdivision of the Department of Defense. To this day, its charter remains classified, and that charter did not even exist until six years after the agency's creation in 1952. Kahn, a former *Newsday* reporter and Paris newsdesk editor for the *International Herald Tribune,* himself became a subject of close scrutiny by the Agency, who sanctioned any illegal surveillance necessary toward blocking his book. The CIA was consulted to see how they might similarly assist the NSA in the matter, and it is unknown to what extent they did. Macmillan Publishers, who had contracted for the book in advance, unethically forwarded, without the author's consent, first two chapters and then the entire manuscript to the Pentagon upon receipt for pre-publication review, something the same publishing company had also done during WWII with Herbert O. Yardley's *Japanese Diplomatic Secrets.* The NSA attempted intimidating the publishers into refusing the manuscript, but failed. They also engaged in the same kind of paranoid monitoring of their own members as occurs in "O.B.I.T." If Dolinsky didn't pattern Cypress Hills after the NSA, he certainly was prescient.

The aliens responsible for O.B.I.T. are exposed during a Senatorial investigation of a Cypress security guard's murder, committed by one of their number. A witness who previously saw the killer on the surveillance machine has put himself into voluntary seclusion in a mental home, where he is hiding. "I saw a monster," he tells the Senator, reluctantly, when pressed for the exact reason he left the defense plant. "When I told them what I saw, they got very quiet. Looked at me with great, quiet eyes. Quiet can tell you so much. Until they looked at me that way, I was certain that I had seen what I had seen. Dead certain. Of course, I hadn't." But he knows he really did. His reaction is exactly like that of contemporary abductees, afraid to tell anyone about their experience, trying to doubt it themselves, but ultimately certain that, whatever it may have been, it was real. When the Senator tells the witness that he believes he did see something monstrous, the witness says with conviction, "Of course I did! No one has ever been able to convince me that I didn't see it—I wish they could, but they couldn't."

The witness is pulled in to testify, and exposes the human-looking alien guilty of the crime by tuning its image in on the O.B.I.T. screen. The criminal appears as a monster on the screen, with enormous bald head and claw hands, one of the many instances of *The Outer Limits* showing its aliens as simultaneously being somehow both human and like UFO Grays. The alien killed the guard for the same reason that the witness went into hiding: the guard had discovered its identity while monitoring the machine.

Its cover blown, in front of the Senator, a gathering of generals and Defense Department scientists, the murderous alien calmly rises and walks about them, first hurling invectives at them and then pronouncing their doom as casually as we would put in an order for a deli sandwich, scattering all their research notes to the wind while everyone listens in paralyzed awe: "The machines are everywhere! Oh, you'll find them all, you're a zealous people. And you'll make a great show out of smashing a few of them, but for every one you destroy *hundreds* of others will be built, and they'll *demoralize* you, break your spirits, create such rips and tensions in your society that *no one* will be able to repair them! Oh, you're a savage, despairing planet. And when we come here to live, you friendless, demoralized flotsam will fall without even a single shot being fired. Senator, enjoy the few years left to you—there is no answer. You're all of the same dark persuasion. You demand, *insist,* on knowing every private thought and hunger of everyone—your families, your neighbors—*everyone but yourselves!"* And it vanishes back to its ship, untouched. "The machines" referred to in the speech might as well have been UFOs themselves, and their automated occupants, the reaction of the assembled audience identical to their real-life counterparts—stunned and amazed by what they have found themselves up against, and powerless to do a thing about it. The script's scathing indictment could as accurately have been referring to the illegal surveillance programs implemented against their own citizenry and department members not only by the NSA, but by the FBI and CIA, against UFO groups, war protesters, environmentalists, and numerous other "dissidents."

Other examples of government or military agencies being manipulated or coerced by alien intelligences, or vice-versa, abound in *The*

Outer Limits. The aliens in "Nightmare" are forced to help the Earth's armed forces to conduct a controlled torture experiment on their own men, and "The Zanti Misfits" are foisted on our planet by a superior extraterrestrial race that wants to use Earth as a prison outpost, the entire operation conducted by the military and kept secret from the public at large. Classic bald, bug-eyed, hypnotic, and emotionless aliens trick government scientists into constructing a disintegrator weapon for them, in "Keeper of the Purple Twilight." A renegade mad-scientist at a government atomic plant terrorizes, abducts, and implants scientists for his experiments, in "It Crawled Out of the Woodwork." Harlan Ellison's "Soldier" (another Hugo-winner) is an accidental transport from the nightmarish future back to our time, barely comprehended by a private government investigative team (akin to that in "The Inheritors") before his predictably violent demise. Shadowy Intelligence types are the heroes of "The Invisibles," attempting to understand and defuse the seditious extraterrestrial society before it is too late. "The Mice" are exchange program volunteers between a concealed government project on Earth and a planet on a secret mission to test our world for potential farming exploitation. "The Man with the Power" is a volunteer for another private government project which boomerangs—extending the powers of the mind with a brain implant. A government scientist secretly monitoring planet "Wolf 359" (Mars, in the original script) is nightly bedroom-visited by its sole ghostly, faceless, elliptically-eyed occupant that passes through walls and paralyzes him.

"The Special One" featured completely human-looking extraterrestrials with super-hypnotic powers who masquerade as government agents, contacting human child-geniuses by day and clandestinely returning at night on a regular schedule to train them in the operation of their weaponry (which works on sound waves) for later first-strike attack purposes. Journalist John Keel was unsettled in 1966–67, three years after this episode aired, to find such a real-life pattern in the "Mothman" sightings around Virginia and Ohio. When a local resident reported seeing Mothman in a particular area, Keel wrote, "I was perturbed to find that it was right next to the Duncan Falls Elementary School. An unusual number of sightings and Fortean events seem to be concentrated around schools and the largest percentage of witnesses consists of children between the ages of seven and eighteen. Another statistical oddity is that the majority of the adults who claim their autos were pursued by UFOs or monsters are schoolteachers, especially teachers specializing in abnormal children—the very bright or the mentally deficient. This is why I was so interested in the West Virginia 'census takers' who were mainly concerned with the numbers and ages of the children living in the Ohio Valley." These "census takers" were among a great diversity of "Men In Black" who mysteriously appeared (and continue to appear) around UFO witnesses or abductees under various guises to ask personal questions, such as what unusual scars or birthmarks the witness might have on their body—the latter something that would not be written about as a common feature of UFO abductions until the 1980s.

The second season's "Cold Hands, Warm Heart" presented an image of the government keeping an abduction secret in order to further its space program. Pre-*Star Trek* William Shatner is the first astronaut to Venus (in a preliminary study for the colonization of Mars), breaking orders to go beneath atmospheric cloud cover and losing contact with the Earth, after which he suffers "missing time." He cannot remember what happened to him in the eight-minute telemetry loss and exhibits a bizarre inability to keep warm since his return. His concentration is badly impaired, and he has inexplicable fits of irritability and snappish temper. He suffers from unremembered nightmares that cause him to bolt awake in terror. Finally, his condition becomes impossible to hide: he begins mutating, his body going into shock. Hypnosis reveals that his missing eight minutes brought him face to face with a small, skinny, floating, puppet-like alien (the actual effect used was a marionette moved underwater), all glowing eyes with no face and a mere slit for a mouth. "Strange," he says. "Darkness. Had to go closer, had to . . . then the sounds began. That thing *stared* at me through the porthole . . . that sound . . . it's doing something to me . . . it's gotten *inside* me . . . !" Being a second-season show, the story had a happy ending, with Shatner's wife bringing him back around by loving care. The second season tended to sell unrealistic images of big bourgeois comfort and a strong faith in science and government institutions, unlike the first season, another good argument for its having had government influence on the executive level. Interestingly enough, loving care is the same treatment most effective on actual abductees, such as Barney Hill: "Level 6 sharing," as an untitled NSA paper—one of only two released on the UFO subject by that agency, out of an admitted 279 in their possession—puts it. And, except for the cold (which was used as a plot device, though abductees do report feeling terribly cold during their experiences), the symptoms exhibited by Shatner's character are identical to those of abductees in real life—which is most interesting for 1964, like "The Inheritors" airing two years before publication of the Hill case in *Look.*

Two more interesting abduction stories occurred on the series, "Counterweight" and "The Probe." The latter was the show's last episode, a story about an airplane blown off course in a hurricane, its crew bailing out to wake up after a time lapse inside a sterile environment that turns out to be someone's highly advanced—and entirely automated—space probe. Writing identified as cuneiform is found on the walls, and a pyramid is built into the middle of the main room. Fearful that they will be killed as its engines eventually warm up for takeoff, and of contamination from wherever the probe came from, one of the crew delivers an impassioned speech in the mere hope that whoever sent it will understand and help them. Receiving nothing but blinking lights and repetitive patterns in response, she breaks down and cries, "Are you all machine? No humanity?" but something pushes her outside of the probe into a waiting raft, which has been brought there by a radio signal the survivors didn't send. Free of its human subjects, the probe takes off, blowing itself up when it is a safe distance away, obviously having understood the message. One of the crew makes the closing statement that he hopes we would be as understanding and compassionate, if the shoe happened to be on the other foot.

"Counterweight" was about a government experiment to see if a number of passengers could survive confinement with each other for a year, in order to reach the closest planet colonizable by man. Unknown to either the experimenters or the passengers, an occupant of the planet in question is aboard with them, sliding literally into their ears at night and listening to their thoughts. By the time the alien reveals its presence, it has caused all the passengers to realize they are not ready for contact with another race, being too selfish to be trusted. The single holdout is a professional developer intent on being the first to exploit whatever resources the planet might have, even if that means "exterminating any Indians that might already be there." The alien forces him to be the one pushing the panic button which terminates the experiment and ends the government program.

"Cry of Silence" summarized the second season's general focus. Written by "Corpus Earthling's" Louis Charbonneau, it centers on two isolated travelers in the desert who find themselves mysteriously unable to leave a given area because of intelligently menacing tumbleweeds. They take refuge in a farmhouse with an old hermit, who confirms that lately everything has had a strange life of its own. The hermit inadvertently is killed by whatever force is behind the unearthly animations and becomes its latest vehicle—his lifeless body returns from an escape attempt, and fails to write a message due to the onset of rigor mortis. The travelers realize that an alien intelligence is behind the eerie phenomenon, simply attempting to communicate, and one of them becomes a medium for it to give voice. The intelligence, unable to hear but only to speak, expresses anguish at its inability to communicate and finally leaves in despair. "Who are you? Why do you not communicate?" it cries, probably echoing the frustration of the Intelligence teams investigating the UFO phenomenon.

Two episodes dealt with Mars, other than the background mention in the episode with Shatner. One, "The Invisible Enemy," is a formulaic space-opera starring *Batman*'s Adam West (who also appeared in Paramount's *Robinson Crusoe on Mars* the same year, which showed Martians dominating mining slaves from superior flying machines), puppet shark-creatures, and atomic bazookas, hardly meant to be taken very seriously. The other, "Controlled Experiment," the show's only deliberate comedy (scripted by Intelligence man Leslie Stevens), is about two completely human-looking beings from Mars named Phobos and Deimos (Barry Morse and Carroll O'Connor), who come to Earth to make a study of man's violent nature. Having noticed our irrationality, they are concerned that the human tendency to murder might spread to the other planets, since man has now developed atomic weapons. Like the Fairy Folk, they are able to slip around completely undetected, both through space and people's thoughts, by virtue of their superior technology. Perhaps betraying a connection to the Masons, Stevens' script has the Martians temporarily slowing time to a near-standstill, Morse examining a dollar bill from a woman's purse during the pause: *" 'Annuit Coeptus Novus Ordo Seclorum'?"* he puzzles. What does that mean?" O'Connor replies that it's a dead language, with which humans impress each other. "What's this pyramid?" Morse asks. "Symbol of the home," answers O'Connor. "But it's got *one eye* looking out of it!" Morse frowns. "Symbol of the home owner," says O'Connor. Morse shakes his head. "But what does it all *mean?*" O'Connor shrugs, and merely offers, "Who knows?" (Who knows, indeed?)

The Outer Limits was the only show of its kind, unique in the annals of television history. It provided a weekly exploration of man's place in the universe, in varying degrees of fear and optimism, in such a way as to engage its audience's thoughts and emotions without alienating them from its subject matter. Whether or not the show was connected to any official government program of dissemination or preparation on the subject of contact with visitors from beyond Earth, that was certainly the personal mission of Leslie Stevens and Joseph Stefano. Though they didn't intend to produce a non-successful series, commercial considerations were lowest on their list of priorities, subordinate to the desire to stimulate thought in the average mind on extraordinary possibilities. On that level, their show succeeded better in the long run than any series before or since, barring possibly its near-contemporary *Star Trek,* to be discussed in the next chapter. The success of *The Outer Limits* stemmed from the production team's belief in their project, literate and often poetic scripts, very real human characters, and a refusal to insult or pander to their audience.

Early in 1995, MGM/UA revived *The Outer Limits* through a Canadian outfit called Trilogy Entertainment Group and Atlantis

Productions, produced by Penray Densham, Richard K. Lewis, and John K. Watson, with original series producer Joseph Stefano as Executive Consultant and original creator Leslie Stevens as Program Consultant. In the interim between the old and the new, Stefano scripted Universal's "Corpus Earthling"-esque *Eye of the Cat* in 1969 and Vestron's 1987 Lovecraftian horror film *The Kindred,* and in the early 1990s became the creative force behind the USA network's successful and ecologically conscious *Swamp Thing.* The latter two projects focused on the UFOlogical element of creating viable mutant hybrids. *The Outer Limits'* new incarnation first aired on the cable premium channel Showtime and was optioned later the same year by Fox T.V. for its Fall lineup. Although the new series suffers somewhat from preachiness due to an admitted Fundamentalist Christian bias on the part of its producers, many of its episodes show the same depth and maturity of stories as the original, and as many UFOlogically accurate themes and elements. It has also achieved the honor of being awarded "Best Dramatic Series" two years in a row from the Cable Ace Awards.

The premiere episode was a ninety-minute adaptation (like the original series, the standard episode is one hour) of George R. R. Martin's famous Hugo and Nebula award-winning novella, "Sandkings," which first appeared in the August 1979 *Omni.* The original story was a futuristic one in which pets from other planets are collected by connoisseurs. A latent sadist named Simon Kress acquires one species of ant-like creature with high intelligence called "sandkings," which he quickly turns into warring monsters through his treatment of them. Before they ultimately turn on him, they worship him as a god, literally crafting his face into a sphinx on the cliffsides of their terrarium sandcastles. Elements in the story hearkened back to Stefano's original *Outer Limits* story, "The Zanti Misfits," with its human-faced ant-aliens, making it a good choice for the new series' inauguration.

In the brilliant adaptation, the majority of the crucial plot points from Martin's story manage to be faithfully retained, while at the same time the story is drastically reworked to include what can now be recognized as UFOlogically correct elements. Simon Kress is turned into a NASA/DOD scientist working in a restricted and isolated underground base, who hatches the sandkings himself out of larvae brought back by probes from the soil of Mars. The sandkings, like fruit flies, have very short life cycles, and so make excellent subjects for generational study in addition to being extremely intelligent. When they manage to escape their controlled environment and threaten to enter Earth's biosphere, the government decides to shut down Kress' study and freeze the remaining embryos. Understandably upset about the termination of his life's work and the possibility that someone else may revive it and steal the credit in the future, Kress smuggles some of the soil and embryos home with him in his thermos, and starts up anew in a duplicate terrarium he builds in his barn. Though initially of pure motives, he soon discovers that he enjoys his godlike power over the alien insects, and experiments with their intelligence in corrupt fashion by encouraging them to war. As in the original story, they erect sphinxes of his face in their sandcastles—which is an interesting choice, given the shift of the story's action to a recreation of the planet Mars—and eventually escape to infest Kress' house after he uses them to murder a former government colleague who has cottoned-on to his project and tried to bring it to a halt. Realizing that his desire for a Nobel Prize has jeopardized his own planet's very safety, Kress finally destroys the sandkings, along with himself, in an act of valiant self-sacrifice.

Other elements from the original series incorporated into the story include those from "Wolf 359" and "The Invisible Enemy." In the latter, "sand-sharks" skimming beneath the surface of Mars threaten the first astronauts to the Red Planet, becoming visible only when their fins sail into sight or they rear their very ugly heads. The scorpionic sandkings are similar in appearance to these predecessors. And in "Wolf 359," a recreated planet from another solar system is studied by a government team in an isolated location, until it eventually spawns a hostile occupant (remarkably close in appearance to a UFO Gray) threatening life on Earth. The original script of "Wolf 359," it should be noted, had the recreated planet under observation being none other than Mars.

Mars quickly surfaced again on *The Outer Limits,* in "The Voyage Home." After three months exploring Mars, an expeditionary team discovers on its last day what appear to be Sanskrit inscriptions on some of the rocks. "Definitely man-made," one of them observes, "or some other kind of intelligent creature." "You know, maybe there is something to this Face on Mars theory," says another, in awe (as though that wouldn't have been the very first area investigated— but then, it would have been impossible for the producers to incorporate that into the story and not take a decisive stand on the issue). A strange egg-shaped pod is nearby, which—as in 1979's *Alien*—opens to eject unknown contents which render all of the astronauts unconscious.

When the astronauts revive (after hours of "missing time"), they are just able to make their launch window to return to Earth. On the voyage home, they discover that the ship contains green goo that they surmise must have come from the egg, which turns out to be an alien microorganism. Before they can consider the possible ramifications, their ship is partially disabled by a meteor shower (another gross scientific improbability, but necessary as a plot device). The electronics expert, Barkley, goes below-decks to effect repairs and suffers a light head injury. Above-decks, astronaut Wells is not acting like himself—the damage has affected the air-conditioning, raising the cabin's heat, and Wells seems only to be comfortable in the cold … like the cold of Mars, his companion, Claridge, notices. Frankly concerned that some of the green goo may have adversely affected his crewmate, Claridge asks Wells to humor his suspicions and submit to a few routine tests.

Barkley returns to finds Wells the only one present. Claridge, Wells tells him, is lying down. Barkley reveals that he is looking forward to cashing-in on his hero status when he returns to Earth, laughing about the irony that everyone on Earth will believe his motivations entirely altruistic instead of self-serving, and Wells admonishes him with the fact that their discovery of life on Mars means more than a personal mercenary platform. "Well," Barkley smiles, "the scientific ramifications will take care of themselves." Barkley quickly notices that some of the alien goo is bleeding from a wound on Wells' arm, and like Claridge before him, wants to check it out. He quickly discovers that Wells isn't Wells, but a shape-shifting alien, which reveals its true form and tries to kill him. Barkley blows the creature out of the hatch, with the returned Claridge first trying to stop him. "You've been hit on the head," Claridge says. "You're imagining things. Think about what you're doing!" But it is too late. Barkley fails to convince Claridge that he did not kill Wells, but an alien shape-shifter . . . and then discovers Claridge's dead body stowed away in a locker.

Barkley locks himself in a chamber away from the intruder alien in Claridge's form, who tries to talk him out. The alien tells him that his life form came from another solar system and landed on Mars, attempting colonization. They reproduce as spores, which enter the host and duplicate its structure—including memory—and then eject, leaving the host dead. "Your friends felt no pain," it assures Barkley, who responds, "Great, no pain, only death—that makes me feel better." The alien asks him to understand, and tells Barkley he is under no threat, since members of its race only produce a single spore every thirty days. It tells Barkley it needs him to help pilot the ship. The alien seduces him with promises of fame and great medical gifts for mankind, and tells Barkley it has no objection to being put into quarantine once they reach Earth. Initially deceived, Barkley deliberately blows the hatch on re-entry, dooming both himself and the alien invader to swift destruction. Before they die, the alien reveals its plan was indeed to proliferate the entire planet: "Our species is millions of years old—it is our *right* to take lives, in order to continue!" Barkley answers, "Then it had better find someone else to carry the torch," and blows up the capsule—discovering, as the final narration puts it, that "The true measure of a hero is when a man lays down his life with the knowledge that those he saves—will never know."

The real question is, how many of today's Defense Establishment personnel believe they are making exactly such selfless sacrifices? Certainly, in the beginning, they all must have thought so. There can be little doubt they knew who the race was behind the extraterrestrial spaceships regularly traversing Earth's airspace, and their assessment of that race's believing itself entitled to exploit mankind as its own resource would not even have been entirely off-target. It even seems probable that the Department of Defense has been gearing for war with that race for several decades now. But in all those ensuing years, there still has been no act of actual hostility from that outside race. And if there have been any such actions, it would probably be better to disclose them to the public and enlist support, rather than conceal the knowledge.

In general, there appears to be more presumption of alien hostility on the part of the new *Outer Limits,* as opposed to the old. "Birthright" featured a hostile twist on "The Inheritors," revealing a hidden underworld of high-ranking politicos who are actually hybrid aliens with extra brain lobes, attempting to spoil the Earth in order to make it more habitable for their own kind. An alien parasite in "If These Walls Could Talk" was not evil, but dangerous to human life by its very consuming nature. "The Quality of Mercy," a darker reworking of Joseph Stefano's original "Nightmare," has an Earth soldier held prisoner on a planet with which we are at war. Like the aliens in the short-lived other Fox sci-fi entry, *Space: Above and Beyond,* little is revealed about the enemy, except that they are hideous, nasty reptiles, plainly hostile to the human race. "Nightmare" featured a war between Earth and the planet "Ebon" (probably meant to be Mars), in which Earth prisoners are interrogated in limbo settings by huge-craniumed gargoyles with bald heads, rough, halting, mechanical voices and physically torturous hand-held rod weapons. In the end, it turns out that the Ebonites' intent was not to torture Earth troops for their own purposes, but rather to satisfy a bloodthirsty Earth Defense Establishment that simply wanted to see how its men would stand up to the potential future threat of exactly such tortures. The Ebonites had accidentally caused an explosion on Earth, and were cooperating with the Department of Defense in order to *forestall* an actual war.

In "The Quality of Mercy," the astronaut-soldier is put into a ratty limbo-setting cell and periodically tortured for no immediately obvious purpose by his metallically armored reptilian captors. They throw a young and attractive Earth girl soldier in with him, who is being systematically taken in repeat abductions to a sterile slab, to be gradually transformed surgically into one of the aliens. As the transformation nears completion, she begs her virile young cellmate to end her torment. Though he is fully capable of instantly killing her, he cannot bring himself to do it, even despite her present grotesque condition, and urges her to maintain hope because he knows exactly when and how Earth plans to utterly destroy the aliens. She then willingly goes away with her abductor who immediately comes to fetch her, and reveals that she is actually an alien spy: "They're not changing me—they're changing me *back.*" The final narration then warns, "In the darkest of hours—in the greatest of battles—we must never forget who, or what, we are." Most science-fictional television shows and series, atypically for a Democratic administration (Clinton), seem most recently to have been threat-oriented. If the surface elements, as it appears, are intended to warn abductees or potential abductees against "collaboration with the enemy," then the message is as naive and out of date as the edicts in the Middle Ages against lying with incubi and succubi—in none of these cases has such interaction been voluntary by anyone on this end of things.

As if in realization of this fact, the second season presented an episode called "The Deprogrammers," in which underground guerilla rebels kidnap and reprogram an abductee to murder the alien leader that took him and made him its servant—in the end, it turns out that the "deprogrammers" were simply other human abductees, serving another alien that is the leader's political rival. The second season's opener (on cable, in which episodes are sometimes aired in different order than they appear on commercial T.V.), "Beyond the Veil," gave mixed signals concerning alien hostility. The story itself left no doubt that the Grays were evil invaders, dramatizing them in the commonly accepted myth of Nazi torturers. They are shown taking over on the sly, masquerading as helpful human psychiatrists, when in reality they are simply trying to discover how much their abductees remember about them through extended testing on Earth. "If they don't come tonight, they're just gonna come tomorrow . . ." the defeated protagonist drones, over and over again, in his hospital cell and straitjacket, at the story's end. Despite the downbeat interpretation, the closing narration reads, "It is said that madmen and fools are the children of God. And yet, we seem to confine these children to the outer reaches of society, shut away and ignored. Is it possible that what we dismiss as their mad ravings may in fact be the wisdom of prophets?"

The concept of nocturnal child-abductors connected to folkloric myth and appearing only during specific times connected to specific planetary bodies (as UFO appearances are connected to Mars), was brought forth cleverly in "Under the Bed," a satisfying little horror melodrama that obviously has heavy grounding in the actual UFO abduction phenomenon. A child disappears from his bedroom at night, when his mother was present in the room mere moments before and the little boy's young sister was right next to him. The girl has gone into shock, and only interactive psychodrama and hypnosis reveal what has so horrified her: her brother was taken "under the bed" by a monster masquerading as his teddy-bear.

Two investigators, reluctant to accept the mounting evidence confronting them that something beyond the ordinary is at hand, come finally to do so by simple process of elimination and the application of scientific method. They find a blood sample left behind by the abductor in a failed return attempt at taking the missing boy's sister, that swiftly decomposes into sand—silicon—which is a convenient plot-device, if one wants to indicate a synthetic creature like a robot. The investigators go back to the historical record and discover a direct planetary correlation to the nefarious activity—the abductions occur every twenty-eight days, on each New Moon. And they put the bizarre clues of their investigation together to discover that what they are dealing with is a shape-shifting troll living in a nearby mine shaft; they also learn the means to dispatch it. The chief investigator, whose brother was seized by exactly such a creature when he was a young boy, smashes the silicate troll in a fit of gratuitous heroic posturing that, once more, seems to be more a feature of both the new *Outer Limits* and media sci-fi in general. "This is for my brother—and all the others!" he cries, wielding the vengeful crowbar of justice, worthy of the best Jimmy Cagney movie. "Our world has been mapped, the oceans charted, animals and plants named and indexed—or so we believe," concludes the narrator, "but there are still places grownups forget they've been. And it is children who remind us that there *are* creatures who lurk in the dark . . . and under the bed."

One of the rare exceptions to threatening monsters in the new *Outer Limits* has been one of the few episodes to hearken back to the spirit and ideas of the original's "The Inheritors": "Second Soul." Earth is visited by aliens who are neither friendly nor hostile—merely desperate. The alien N'tal are wispy creatures (patterned after "The Bellero Shield's" Bifrost alien) on an expedition from a dying world, to find a new place to live. They are symbiotes—"parasites," as they come to be derogatorily dubbed by a number of Earthmen who despise them—requiring host bodies in which to live . . . only those host bodies have to be dead. A government program is instituted to provide Earth's recent dead for the N'tal to inhabit, including relocation to protect the privacy of the incoming N'tal and to shield past loved ones from encountering their former lovers and spouses.

Government members involved in the program have noticed that some of the N'tal are clandestinely meeting, in the most suspicious of circumstances. They are cautious about being detected and are exchanging vials of what turn out to be chemicals highly poisonous to humans. It is suspected that the N'tal are hastening the demise of human host bodies. Worse, one of the government insiders is found to have committed suicide right after bringing these facts to his colleagues' attention. An entire factory is found under N'tal control, from which the chemicals are coming. An investigator infiltrates the factory and is welcomed by the N'tal ambassador with whom he has regularly been doing business. The ambassador reveals that the N'tal have been recreating a complete atmospheric copy of their abandoned homeworld, constructed so that their offspring—who are now coming from intermarriages with the local Earth population—will have a heritage to remember. "What if you were to wake up to a different world, tomorrow—a world of invaders?" asks the narrator, at the end. "Would you raise your voice, with the aliens, in a chant of remembrance and regret, bidding farewell to a vanished world? Or would you fight against those who might—ultimately—help us?"

A similar "misunderstanding" theme involving alien reproduction occurs in "Caught in the Act." A reasonably shy and conservative young woman finds her bedroom literally shot into one night by a sort of space-bullet, which ejects a parasite into her upon inspection. Though not visible, the alien's presence drastically alters her personality: she suddenly can't get enough sex. Unfortunately, all her partners are bodily consumed by the parasite, turning her into a serial sex-killer who acts under compulsion, not understanding her own motivations, knowing only that she needs sexual energy to "transform." Her fiancé investigates and discovers the hollow bullet, which is found to contain an alien genetic pattern, *"almost human, but not quite."* Enlisting the help of a biologist, they soon discover that such "bullets" have made appearances throughout the preceding century, always with the same result—nuns or nice girls possessed, and sudden seductions of bishops and sailors who turn up missing. The fiancé ultimately makes voluntary love to the alien in the girl's body, he and his biologist friend having reasoned that only strangers have ever been killed, and never mates or loved ones. The ploy works, giving birth to a sort of angelic energy-butterfly, which then soars off into the heavens leaving its "parents" watching its departure with appropriate awe and joy—and perhaps even sadness. The second season turned the idea of parasitic invasion and rampant sexual coupling into a much more apocalyptic scenario in "From Within," concerning prehistoric mind-eating worms reviving from inside the Earth and possessing human beings. The worms destroy natural inhibitions in the mind, resulting in widespread acts of rape and pillage.

The second-season (commercial T.V.) opener, "Trial By Fire," pitted a newly elected peacenick president and his wife (obviously patterned after Bill and Hillary Clinton) against both an unknown race of approaching aliens and the entire upper echelon of the Pentagon. Extremely similar to the concurrently filmed *Independence Day,* and actually far better and more satisfying, this episode's twist turned out to be that the invading aliens were not hostile at all, but misunderstood friends simply trying to take up residence in Earth's oceans. The aliens, in keeping with the popularly accepted MJ-12 conspiracy scenarios and the majority of Hollywood films since the dawn of Reagan, were slimy, grotesque reptilians. Their peaceful message was not understood or immediately translatable because they were actually speaking English, but through a water medium that they require to survive. Steadfastly having refused to listen to the hardline military advisors who want immediate nuclear strikes against the invaders, the president ultimately accepts their judgment and allows the military to attack—only to discover that he has made a mistake, and opened the entire human race up to obliteration in response by the technologically superior newcomers.

"Afterlife" features the military and Intelligence communities as self-interested and ruthless villains, who set up one of their own to take a murder rap, solely so that he will be desperate enough to take their alternative to his guaranteed death sentence: the chance to become an alien DNA experiment. The condemned man accepts, and has genetic material from the occupant of a flying saucer shot down by the Air Force injected into his system. He mutates into a hybrid life-form, and his captors deliberately let him escape in order to test his—and therefore the alien race that spawned him—physical prowess before executing him. A noble man, their subject was first recruited as a sort of punishment for refusing to assassinate a target given him by the State Department. Remaining true to his ideals even after becoming an alien, he refuses to kill any of the soldiers out to murder him, and even forgives the woman doctor who agreed to monitor his transformation for the military her part in what she has done to him. Later, the same doctor sets him up as an easy target, but still the hybridized alien takes no retribution, insisting that she be allowed to escape the target area before the soldiers open fire on him. At the last moment before execution, a sonic weapon incapacitates the military death-squad, and aliens virtually identical to the hybridized human appear, acknowledging him as one of their own and disappearing with him to wherever they came from. "God ... !" the doctor exclaims. "Relax, doctor," the (presumed) CIA man in charge of the project tells her, "they've gone." "You don't get it, do you?" she responds. "We failed the aliens' test. They set us up. *They* were testing *us*. They put the bodies in there [from the crashed ship, that were used to transform the subject] to see what we would do. Do you understand? *They were testing us!*" The narrator concludes, "Can the true reason we so fear the unknown be that we know ourselves too well?"

Like Mars, robots have made more than one prominent appearance on the new *Outer Limits*. "The New Breed," a nightmarish horror story about man's God-complex in attempting to defeat mortality, borrows heavily on an idea from Dean R. Koontz's *Midnight,* in the form of "nanobots"—microscopic robots that can be injected into the human bloodstream, programmed to assist in healing tissue damage. "Valerie 23" featured a robot made to appear and function as a human woman—in every regard. Her specific program is to serve as "companion" to the handicapped. She has the convincing illusion of feelings, which ultimately turn out to be more real than imagined. Her programmed capacity for emotional bonding causes her to become lethally jealous when her experimental love-mate, a parapalegic named Frank, finds himself attracted to a living, flesh and blood woman. After Valerie 23 attempts to kill the woman, her builders decide to dismantle her and start from scratch. Frank speaks to her first, to ascertain whether she is afraid to die, which is his own definition for what constitutes true life. She expresses no such fear. "It isn't afraid to die," he laments, fleeing the laboratory. But the robot's claim turns out to have been bluff. She escapes and follows Frank home, again trying to kill her romantic rival. "I am programmed to remove all obstacles to my bonding with my mate," she calmly declares to the terrified woman. "You are an obstacle." Her "mate" fries Valerie's circuitry with an exposed wire, and as her machinery winds down, she looks into his eyes and says, "Frank—I'm afraid to die."

"Valerie 23" turned the original series' "I, Robot" on its head. "I, Robot" was originally a series of "Adam Link" stories premiering in *Amazing Stories'* January 1939 issue, by Eando Binder—a pseudonym adopted by brothers *Earl and* Otto Binder—with the title character being a robot whose adventures explored the meaning of being human. His very name was intended to indicate that he was the first in a new line of sentient beings, branching from their creator, Man, and the stories were all told from the robot's point of view. In *The Outer Limits'* second season, the story utilizing the character had Adam Link put on trial by backwoods rednecks for the murder of his creator, Dr. Link, whom he had actually been trying to save when a heavy piece of machinery fell on him. Despite an eloquent and impassioned defense from a disillusioned humanistic lawyer, Adam is found guilty of murder by a frightened populace and is ordered by the judge to be dismembered. But on his way to execution, Adam breaks free from his captors to hurl a little girl out of the way of an oncoming truck, and is shattered to pieces in the process. The same little girl had testified against him earlier, calling him "the tin man who hurt me," when he pulled her from the water because he perceived her in danger of drowning. The new *Outer Limits* remade the same story, with one important alteration: Adam has become a murderer due to reprogramming done by the Department of Defense. He doesn't even remember whether or not he committed the crime, adding the element of government mind-control and—literally—robot assassins. He turns out to have been a prototype for a military killer-robot, who went schizoid during programming because—like many a flesh-and-blood counterpart in real life, including certain dolphins of the CIA's "swimmer nullification" project (see Chapter 9)—he discovers he likes poetry and doesn't like killing.

"Resurrection" presented a variation of Czechoslovakian dramaturg Karel Capek's 1921 robot play, *R.U.R.* ("Rossum's Universal Robots"). Capek's play dramatized what amounted to a reenactment of mankind's rebellion against the gods, in the revolt of manufactured slave robots turning against their creators for independence, ending with the then-novel parting line delivered by their inventor, "Go, Adam—Go, Eve." The *Outer Limits* version is set in post-biological holocaust future Earth, where androids initially made to serve man have now supplanted him. Whatever remnant of humanity remains to be found is pitilessly exterminated by militaristic robots, who have taken over their new mechanical society the way man's flesh-and-blood military had before. An underground of robots with higher intelligence illegally recreate a man and woman from recovered biological material, who succeed in switching off their oppressive metallic offspring and setting about the "Second Coming" of Man.

The Fairy Folk have made *Outer Limits* appearances as well. "The Choice" dramatized a secret little war going on between a hereditary line of psychic "witches" and a government office that seeks them out to inter them in camps and sometimes torture them to death in an effort to both understand and eradicate them. The witches are hampered by their refusal to stoop to the level of their persecutors, even though they could effortlessly kill them. "I Hear You Calling" starred Michael Sarrazin as an alien indistinguishable from terrestrial men who appears to be murdering a number of humans for no fathomable reason. Journalist Ally Sheedy follows the trail of dispatched bodies he leaves behind, which are nothing more than purple ash. She finally discovers that Sarrazin is simply sterilizing a plague one of his planet's scouts inadvertently contaminated a small number of Earthmen with. Being exposed herself, Sheedy concedes to be terminated rather than risk destroying her race, and Sarrazin explains to her that no one has died—the ash remains she has been finding are simply residue from the transportation process utilized in transporting the victims to his ship, from whence they are taken to live on his planet, where the plague is completely harmless. "The Conversion" had a superior race of unspecified, but clearly human in origin, beings watching out for mankind. These superior beings try to keep man from making mistakes, and are even willing to assume responsibility for his misdeeds and sacrifice themselves on his behalf in the hope that even the worst among mortals can improve if given a chance. Either the scriptwriter or director Rebecca de Mornay linked the superior beings to American Indian kachinas, by the use of darting lights in the sky and the singing of a joyful religious chant to signify their presence.

Even if the new series takes more often a hostile reading of the unknown, some influence from the original still shows in its opening narration—which was later dropped in favor of the more neutral version which now airs. Whether that original narration reflects more the view of Stevens and Stefano or the new producers, Densham, Lewis, and Watson, it still speaks unmistakably to the reality of the UFO phenomenon, and mankind's relation to it: "In the Outer Limits, we experience a close encounter of another kind. Fact and fantasy combine to tell us the truth. The greatest danger we face is from ourselves because it's not just what's out there, it's what's in here ... in you. In all things mysterious, magical and mortal, the human race has more to fear from itself than from any other forms of life. So lock your doors and unlock your imagination...."

6

Enlightenments
and Educations

L ater attempts at examining potential culture clashes between Earth and aliens from other worlds were nowhere near as successful as *The Outer Limits,* such as the 1988 20th Century Fox movie (and subsequent T.V. series) *Alien Nation,* which embodies all the drawbacks of later efforts. *Alien Nation* was set in a fictional future where odd-looking near-humans from another planet have moved to Earth, giving weekly glimpses of the difficulties they have fitting in with the locals. Except for their appearance, and unimportant idiosyncrasies, the aliens may as well have been incoming Vietnamese or Rastafarians. They weren't very "alien" at all, seeming to want nothing more than a bourgeois American job and a house in the suburbs. The black/white working class relationship in the *Lethal Weapon* movies was more alien, which is to say not at all.

Part of the reason for this may have been the era in which *Alien Nation* was made. It is interesting to note that, in general, during Democratic administrations, aliens are portrayed with less presumption of evil, and during Republican ones they are almost invariably out to turn the human race into food. The big-budgeted, highly rated 1983 Warner Bros. miniseries and T.V. show *V* is a classic example, masterminded by *Alien Nation*'s creator, Kenneth Johnson. *V*'s aliens are evil reptiles who openly and peacefully move in, masquerading as benevolent offworlders no different from ourselves, duping Earth into lowering their arms while they carry on a behind-the-scenes human abduction program to secure their latest snack supply. Transparently made to resemble Nazis, they create an aura of persecution around scientists instead of Jews, subverting the populace to their side by providing cancer cures and the like. Faye Grant plays a woman in the Earth resistance forces who is abducted by the Visitors and subjected to torturous sonic and electrical mind-control conditioning, leaving her unable to combat the enemy at a crucial moment. In light of Mars' importance to actual UFOlogy and the proposition that entertainment media are used for propaganda purposes, it may be noteworthy that the Visitors wore *red,* as did "Mork from Ork" in *Mork and Mindy,* the exchange-program volunteers in *Close Encounters of the Third Kind,* and Luke Skywalker's "Red Brigade" in *Star Wars*—the last rather obviously a play on King Arthur's heroic "Red Branch of Ulster."

*V'*s plot elements owe a tremendous amount to the EBE/Area 51 disinformation stories, which also began the year Reagan took office. *V* was made in 1983, running on the airwaves exactly when Reagan was campaigning for Star Wars appropriations for the military, bringing to mind the proximity of 1953's *Invasion U.S.A.* to increased atomic testing. Its essential remake, MGM/UA's *Red Dawn,* came out the year after *V,* as Reagan was campaigning for reelection. 20th Century Fox's *Predator,* in 1987, and its 1992 sequel, *Predator 2,* both starred a title creature worse than the combined enemies of foreign jungle-fighters, drug-dealers, and domestic criminals, a reptilian alien hunter with high-tech weaponry who views the human race as hunting game; like the assailant of the woman in the Loire in 1950 and the abductor-sphere in Scotland, it camouflages itself into near-perfect invisibility by technological means. Paramount's *Star Trek: The Next Generation,* which began its lucrative run the same year (1987), was a combined proto-political correctness primer and corporate sales advertisement, fully co-opting any liberal messages that may have been sown by its former namesake, and embodying their exact opposite.

By comparison, Democratic administrations seem to spawn more open and peaceful consideration of UFOlogical questions, the best examples being the movies that came out during the Carter administration, which will be considered in the next chapter. *The Outer Limits* came out during the Kennedy/Camelot years, and *Star Trek* during Johnson's administration and the Great Society. Space exploration itself was a product of that era, all but having suffocated to death in the succeeding wake of High Frontier exploitation throughout the Reagan-Bush years, during which satellite weaponry became almost its only concern. Reagan did all he could to smother the Freedom of Information Act and expand the operating power of the CIA and other covert branches, where under Democratic terms the opposite has always tended to be the case. One seeming contradiction to this theory would be 20th Century Fox's *Alien,* coming out at the end of Carter's term in 1979, but while it had an unquestionably malevolent space entity threatening the Earth by using human beings to gestate its life-form, that creature was merely a mad tiger being used by the real enemy, which was a corporate-military robot sent to capture and exploit it at the cost of any human life that might get in its way.

Another seeming exception would be *The Night Stalker,* a 1972 Universal T.V. movie on ABC, made into an NBC series for a single year in 1974. The title character was Darren McGavin's "Carl Kolchak," an intrepid (and obnoxious) reporter who continually unearthed (sometimes literally) various supernatural nasties, always getting the evidence for his story and never being allowed to publish it, solely because entrenched bureaucracies would lose their credibility. But the series was made in Fall of 1974, immediately after Nixon's resignation from the White House in the Watergate scandal, from which time the Republican party was so on the outs that Democrats might as well have been in office until Carter took over two years later. Though it had nothing to do with UFOs (except for one not very good early episode, "They Were, They Are, They Will Be"), *The Night Stalker* was very much a weekly enactment of exactly the kind of nonsense all investigators have had to fight in government bureaucracies while researching the topic, with the monsters merely a vehicle for the true theme of the series. "Maybe people see in the monsters and in the way public knowledge and discussion are stopped [in the

Kolchak stories] symbols for all those things various government entities wish 'the people' not to know about," commented *The X-Files'* creator, Chris Carter, in a 1996 issue of *Cinescape,* about how Kolchak was an inspiration to his own work. Despite Kolchak's dearth of outer space nemeses, he did oppose a number of automata and robots, including "Mr. R.I.N.G.," an escaped government artificial intelligence, and "The Zombie," a supernaturally animated corpse utilized by a Haitian sorceress for revenge-murders against the gangland slayers of her son. Also, in "The Knightly Murders," Kolchak opposed an animated suit of lethal armor, and in "The Trevi Collection" he survived an onslaught by witch Lara Parker's (who played the similar role of "Angelique" on ABC's popular daytime soap, *Dark Shadows)* remote-controlled killer car and murderous mannequins.

More than any other source, *The Night Stalker* was itself probably influenced by the 1920s and '30s pulp fiction of Seabury Quinn, whose running character of Jules de Grandin appeared in ninety-three adventures, beginning in 1925 and continuing for about the next ten years, in *Weird Tales.* Though since outstripped in popularity and fame by the magazine's most famous contributor, H. P. Lovecraft (see Chapter 9), Quinn was at the time the most popular author in its pages. De Grandin was a Belgian combination of supersleuths Hercule Poirot and Sherlock Holmes, who fought supernatural foe after supernatural foe from issue to issue, in—of all places—New Jersey. Many of his stories contained hypnotic mind-control and abduction elements, such as "The Brain Thief" and "The Bride of Dewer," both published in 1930. The former involved a Hindu fakir who hypnotized women into amnesiac sexual encounters for the purpose of creating scandals against his enemies, and the latter was about an entity not too unlike a UFO Gray that enjoyed equally amnesiac nocturnal sexual encounters with the brides of a given bloodline's grooms. It is tempting to try and fit Quinn, a brilliant and very scholarly man himself, into the actual investigation of UFOs by the government even at that early date, just as Arthur Conan Doyle actually was a consultant to Scotland Yard in the manner of his own famous character of Sherlock Holmes, but there is no evidence to the effect. Interestingly, out of all of de Grandin's adventures, not a single one (at least, that is known today) involved a threat from space, despite a science-fictional space cover designed for "The Bride of Dewer" on one of the six collections of his surviving stories issued by Popular Library in 1976.

The Outer Limits' predecessor, MGM's *The Twilight Zone,* also had a reasonable share of episodes appearing to be devoted to the media UFO program. Producer-writer-host Rod Serling, like Leslie Stevens, was a military veteran and an inveterate workhorse. His first attempt to sell the series met with failure, interestingly enough, because one of the network sponsors had lucrative Defense Department contracts, and found Serling's script about a clairvoyant trying to avert Pearl Harbor potentially offensive to the military. Serling redirected the psychic's warnings to a newspaper instead of the Army, and the first pilot was then aired with the result that it pulled in more fan mail than anything else run by CBS that entire season. The second pilot, "Where Is Everybody?," concerned a hallucinating astronaut in an isolation-tank stress test, and sold the series for what turned out to be a lucrative, three Emmy Award-winning, five-year run from 1959 to 1964.

Robots were featured several times on *The Twilight Zone,* the most notable being in the seventh episode, "The Lonely," in which a man is given a seemingly completely real female partner to share his prison sentence on an isolated asteroid, only to have his illusion brutally blasted to naked, exposed circuitry when his term is up and her weight proves too great to bring back with him. "The After Hours," another first-season episode, was about mannequins who assume a life of their own while people are not around to see them—Anne Francis finds herself haunted by the dummies, who call her name and tell her she is "one of them," terrifying her until she becomes calmed by the recognition that they are right. "A Thing About Machines" showed a man attacked by everyday mechanical items, and "The Brain Center at Whipple's" featured *Forbidden Planet's* own Robby the Robot as the future mechanized supplanter of humankind. Serling's "The Mighty Casey" and Richard Matheson's "Steel" showed robots utilized as sports figures; Ray Bradbury's "I Sing the Body Electric" was about a robot babysitter; and Charles Beaumont's "In His

Image" presented a robot discovering its identity as an exact duplicate of its evil creator, who has used it for murder. "The Dummy"
and "Living Doll" portrayed indestructible mannequin antagonists,
the former identity-fused with its human operator—a recurrent dramatic theme since the first horror anthology film, Universal's *Dead
of Night,* which utilized it in 1946. One of the show's most famous
episodes, Richard Matheson's "The Invaders," spotlighted Agnes
Moorehead as a mute woman besieged by tiny robot-men from a flying saucer—the twist ending being that they are not really robots
(though their special-effect definitely is), but an expeditionary force
from Earth. Serling also dramatized automated killers in his later
1970–72 Universal NBC series, *Night Gallery,* in "The Doll," "Class
of '99," "You Can't Get Help Like That Anymore," and "I'll Never
Leave You—Ever." Sinister hypnosis was portrayed on that same series
in its premiere episode, "The Dead Man," and in the final season in
"Finnegan's Flight."

Night Gallery additionally featured one classic UFOlogical entry,
minus any of the overt trappings, in "Brenda." Compellingly played
by Laurie Prange, Brenda was an antisocial eleven-year-old whose
Yuppie parents' summer island home was—unknown to them—
haunted by a faceless thing. Brenda encounters the thing on one of
her lonely outings. Initially afraid of it, she comes to enjoy its presence and confides in it as she would a friend, even though it never
communicates back with her in any obvious way. Her affection for
the inexplicable creature being greater than that she has for any
humans around her, the girl arranges for it to visit her home at night
as a sort of prank, causing her terrified parents (who know nothing
of their daughter's bizarre relationship with the thing) to rally the
rest of the islanders together and seal it up in a rock quarry. The
embittered Brenda secretly returns to the imprisoned thing the following year, vowing to one day set it free again in the world and
unite with it, and even to help it "become" with her, strongly implying—along with her sexually blossoming form, caressing of the rocks,
and passionate tone of voice—that she will provide it offspring. It
is a strange and somewhat disturbing episode, which makes its own
sense in light of UFO abduction phenomena. Probably echoing actual

fears of the government, Serling's opening narration for the piece conveyed the hope—or, perhaps, warning—that "you never get so lonely" as to make a friend like Brenda's.

Mars and Martians made a surprising number of appearances on *The Twilight Zone*. The first season's "Third from the Sun," another Matheson script (he is generally considered to have been the best writer for the series), was about a group of refugee scientists fleeing their oppressive government on the eve of a globally devastating nuclear war, escaping the planet on a flying saucer. Their destination is the next planet over in the solar system: the third from the sun, Earth. A near-identical plot was the subject of "Probe 7—Over and Out" in the last season. "The Monsters Are Due On Maple Street," one of Serling's own scripts, was not specifically about Martians but did concern aliens masquerading as humans clandestinely terrorizing and debilitating average suburbanite Americans for the same purpose as the aliens in *Outer Limits'* "O.B.I.T.": preparation for invasion. Serling also wrote, from an original story by *Invasion of the Saucer Men*'s source-story author Paul W. Fairman, "People Are Alike All Over," in which first astronaut to Mars Roddy McDowall finds to his delight that not only is the planet populated, but populated with people just like those on Earth—who put him in a comfortable cage that is the spitting image of his own house as one of their zoo exhibits. Subsequent seasons presented such episodes as "Mr. Dingle, the Strong," in which an experimenting Martian gives a weakling power to combat his sadistic tormentors, and "Will the Real Martian Please Stand Up," which has three-armed human-looking Martians superseded in their invasion of Earth by three-eyed human-looking Venusians. "The Fugitive" was an alien implied to be a Martian who risked his life to save a dying girl on Earth. Other interesting aliens included a giant encountered by Earthmen in "The Fear"; aliens masquerading as a human teenage biker-gang, romantically involved with human females, in "Black Leather Jackets"; and the famous Serling-scripted episode, "To Serve Man," in which a giant bald alien named Kanamit ("can-o'-meat") who arrives on Earth with a book bearing the story's title is mistaken for a being intending to assist man, when in fact his tome is a cookbook.

In general, *The Twilight Zone*'s episodes, with notable exceptions, were not meant to provoke serious thought about other worlds, but rather to insert irony into otherworldly settings, frequently with a strong element of fantasy as opposed to realism. Like *The Outer Limits,* however, it did focus on the human and adult elements in out-of-the-ordinary encounters, and maintained a rather claustrophobic and oppressive atmosphere. Serling, like Joseph Stefano, seemed to hold an essential view of man as exploitative, greedy, selfish, and dangerous, unworthy of a place in a higher galactic community— though at the same time, no doubt echoing the thoughts of government UFO investigators, Serling was not beyond attributing more sinister motivations to alien visitors, either.

Among Serling's other projects were film adaptations of politically oriented novels. The highly prophetic novel *Seven Days in May*— which accurately foresaw the 55-mile-per-hour speed limit, disposable lighters, and the Vietnam War down nearly to its actual years—was rewritten even better by Serling into perhaps the most compelling conspiracy film ever seen. Its plot concerns a military government coup in the United States by a MacArthur-type populist general against an unpopular and pacifistic president. This too, in light of Dealey Plaza, may be considered very close to prophetically accurate. Another of Serling's adaptations was the 1968 20th Century Fox film version of *Planet of the Apes.*

Phenomenally popular, *Planet of the Apes* spawned four sequels in the years to come, as well as a television series, a Saturday morning cartoon series, and even a number of comic books. The original movie, based on Pierre Boulle's book, is a brilliant social satire set in Earth's future, in which apes have ascended to the place of man and man has descended to the level of the apes. When human astronaut Charlton Heston lands among them, they are scornful and afraid of him. Two enterprising chimpanzees have determined that man was civilized before the ape, and find proof for their argument both in man's past ruins and Heston's arrival among them. They are brutally silenced by a bureaucratic priesthood of orangutans and their gorilla police, who have known the truth all along. They do not want the truth becoming known, for fear that the present race of apes will erradicate itself in nuclear war as their human predecessors did before them. Partial evidence for this being a deliberate informational film in the education program is that the movie is substantially changed from the book. Boulle's original version made the title planet an altogether different one from man's, though the human astronaut discovers upon his return that, in the time he has been gone, the apes have taken man's place as on the planet he just left. There is no talk of man's preceding apes in the book, or the examination of ancient civilization in that light. It is a simpler and more direct satire.

The sequels, which ran through 1974 ending in *Battle for the Planet of the Apes,* showed such elements as the apes' creation in antiquity by mankind to be their slaves (just as the ancient myth texts of the Middle East explain the creation of mankind by the gods), and the surviving (and long-forgotten) remnant of the human race after nuclear war living beneath the surface of the planet to potentially threaten the ape inheritors of their former world. Serling disingenuously pretended, as late as 1974, that he considered the idea of ancient astronauts to be absurd—but in writing the Foreword to Alan and Sally Landsburg's *In Search of Ancient Mysteries* that year, he admitted, "...I had seen enough evidence to convince me that we had entered a new and fascinating field of research. If we kept at it we would turn up more and more pieces of the puzzle [of man's origins] encapsuled in the question 'Where did we come from?' I now think it is highly possible that man had his genesis somewhere in outer space."

The same year *Planet of the Apes* made its appearance (1968), one of the most highly popularized images associated with the abduction phenomenon was seen on the screen from Paramount, in Ira Levin's *Rosemary's Baby.* (Levin would write about humanoid robots replacing man in Columbia's *The Stepford Wives,* in 1975.) Wispy waif Mia Farrow dreams she is paralyzed and surrounded by naked humans and bizarre humanoids, who are impregnating her; later she discovers it was not a dream, and that she has given birth to a hybrid baby who will inherit the Earth. Levin actually told *Publishers Weekly* that the reason he made his "unwanted monster child" that of the devil was because his only alternative was to have it come from outer space.

1975 also saw a film that questioned man's origins similarly to *Planet of the Apes,* in John Huston's production of the aforementioned Rudyard Kipling classic, 20th Century Fox's *The Man Who Would Be King.* The title character is a Victorian British soldier uniting primitive warring tribes in far-off and barbaric Kafiristan, by use of superior firearms and organized thinking. They accept him as a god because he is a bearded white man and wears the Masonic emblem, in exactly the same manner as Cortés and the other Spanish explorers were automatically accepted by many of the Indians of the Americas. In Kipling's story, it was the former "gods" of the Masonic emblem who built the Kafiristanis' ancient ruins. That acceptance of the characters in the movie, of course, raises the reality of the historical question as to why the New World Indians so readily accepted the Spaniards, and (initially) the Hawaiian natives accepted ~~John~~ Cook and his men. The only change between Huston's movie and the original Kipling story is the actual use of the Masonic emblem accidentally saves the "white god's" life. Huston also directed probably the only Biblical movie—especially in that time period—to present Genesis in light of modern science, after Soviet scientist and ancient astronaut theorist Mikhail Agrest's theories. His *The Bible,* a lavishly produced U.S.-Italian film of 1966, showed Sodom and Gomorrah being devastated by mushroom clouds.

Paramount Studios' *Star Trek* is today a legend—in fact, it's a billion-dollar-a-year industry—but the show never rose above the low fifties in the Nielsen Ratings during its initial 1966–69 NBC run. Even *Gomer Pyle* was more popular. Despite its low viewership, *Star Trek* remained on the air for three full years, considered a successful run. Today, there are more than two hundred fan clubs for the show; close to seventy million *Star Trek* books in print in fifteen languages (which include Chinese and Hebrew), with two new titles written a month and an estimated thirteen copies sold every minute in America; and episodes of the show air more than two hundred times a day in the United States. It has been dubbed into forty-eight languages worldwide. That government involvement existed (and exists) in *Star Trek*'s continued phenomenal success today was testified to as far back as twenty years ago, when NASA's program manager for space industrialization and advance long-range planning, Jesco von Put-tkamer, said, "I take *Star Trek* to be NASA's longest-range plan." Put-tkamer was one of an entire team of NASA scientists who helped come up with comprehensive blueprints for the fictional Starship *Enterprise*.

Creator-producer Gene Roddenberry, and later scriptwriter Gene Coon, were the primary forces making the starship *Enterprise* fly. Both men were military veterans, Coon a four-year Marine in the Pacific theater in WWII. Coon provided the show's best-known elements and trappings, such as the "Prime Directive" forbidding the *Enterprise*'s interference in less-developed civilizations. Roddenberry spent time in the LAPD immediately before his success with *Star Trek,* and the LAPD has since been documented to have been heavily infil-trated on the executive level by the CIA (see Chapter 2). More to the point, he and some of his associates all at various times confirmed that Roddenberry was not only in the department, but was actually Chief William Parker's personal protégé for police chief, beginning with Parker's making him the LAPD official historian. An interesting and little-known fact, especially in regard to this study, is that the "Vulcan" half-human alien Mr. Spock, probably the most popular character, was originally written to be a green-skinned (some sources say red-skinned) hybrid half-Martian. His "Live Long and Prosper" hand gesture is the Hebrew sign of blessing, the *shin,* which is also the Egyptian word for "Omega" and the sign that Horus of Behutet carries. It is perhaps in keeping with that original concept that the planet Vulcan was shown to be red, and that its trappings and cos-tumes approximated something between Roman/Egyptian and Hebrew.

Roddenberry's first pilot, "The Cage," was a classic abduction story, and like *The Outer Limits'* best examples was made in 1964. In it, Captain Christopher Pike is tricked by illusions into entering a trap, where short, frail, bald humanoids who communicate by telepa-thy gas him with a small, pocket flashlight-like device and abduct him beneath the surface of their planet. There, he is subjected to a number of tricks and tests, and occasionally tortured. He is expected to breed with a human female captive, providing a surrogate race for

310 HOLLYWOOD VERSUS THE ALIENS

the aliens to live through—they have been driven underground after ravaging their planet (fourth in the solar system) by nuclear war. Eventually Pike is released, considered unsuitable for the aliens' purposes because of "the unique human hatred of captivity." Even then, the aliens are shown not to be complete monsters; Pike wants to take the human female back with him, but she voluntarily remains behind—a crash victim, she is in reality not the beautiful, lithe young woman she appears, but an old and badly stitched-together hag, whose only comfort is the convincing illusion of youth and health the aliens give her. They genuinely care for her. This pilot did not sell the series and was later incorporated as a flashback into a two-part framework after the show's later acceptance, under the title "The Menagerie." In the new version, Pike is shown to have suffered an accident that leaves him mute and quadriplegic, and his old shipmate and friend, First Officer Spock, abducts him back to the aliens' planet—like the girl, they have come to care for him after their previous association, and want to provide him what comfort they can after his misfortune.

The second pilot, "Where No Man Has Gone Before," succeeded in selling the series and featured an alien abduction of a different kind. Captain Kirk's best friend (Gary Lockwood) is stricken by a bolt from an energy field that turns out to have posessed the crew member of a former ship with lethal results. The former victim had to be destroyed when he became too powerful and dangerous to support, and history repeats itself as Lockwood mutates into a mental giant with telepathic powers, becoming drunk and corrupt with them. Eventually he and similarly affected female crewmate Sally Kellerman attempt to escape and give birth to a super-race of humans, but Kirk makes Kellerman see the evil of the power she has been infected with, and she turns on Lockwood, killing them both for the sake of the rest of humanity.

The premiere episode, "The Man Trap," featured Kirk and his officers questioning the equivalent of a UFO abductee in Professor Krater, a scientist doing archaeological digs on an ancient extraterrestrial civilization that has now died off, except for one member. The sole survivor, repeatedly referred to as a "buffalo," and "the last of her kind," is a creature with suction cup-tipped fingers (like those sometimes described on UFO occupants and reported at Roswell) that invisibly blends in among humans by virtue of super-hypnosis. It can erase or blur the memories of anyone it encounters, at will. When on the attack (in common with UFO cattle mutilations), it paralyzes its prey, who are unable to resist or cry out. Though not malevolent, the creature devours all the salt from the human body in order to survive, causing a lethal chemical imbalance. Krater is initially the only one aware of the creature's existence, nearly having killed it after it murdered his wife. Feeling sorry for it, Krater's subsequent relationship with the thing causes him to fight to keep it alive even after it has killed several of the *Enterprise* crew. It is strongly implied that Krater has sex with the creature, which is capable of becoming his wife in imagination more fully than the real article had been able to in life, and that his sexual relationship with it is the real reason he protects it. When Krater refuses to cooperate in the creature's apprehension, being the only one who can recognize it no matter what form it masquerades in, Kirk threatens to use truth drugs—but the creature kills Krater in desperation and finally is killed by Dr. McCoy, whose mind it has preyed on in exactly the same manner as Krater's.

The very first episode filmed, "The Corbomite Maneuver," was an interesting first-contact story, especially in UFOlogical terms as we presently understand them. Coming to the edge of known space, the *Enterprise* is stopped by a large, spinning cube, which appears to be someone's boundary-marking probe. It attempts to prevent their entry and is blown up by the *Enterprise* so it can continue. As a result, its parent ship shows up, an enormous sphere composed of thousands of smaller spheres, hundreds of times the size of the *Enterprise*. An intimidating and uncompromising voice (Ted Cassidy, *The Addams Family*'s "Lurch"), belonging to an equally forbidding-looking alien named Balok, informs them that they have been analyzed and will be destroyed as unwelcome invaders. Balok has a huge, bald, pear-shaped head and gigantic almond-shaped eyes, with a fixed slit of a mouth. Kirk bluffs Balok into believing that the *Enterprise* has a boomerang device which destroys all attackers with their own lethal force, buying them some time, and succeeds in disabling Balok's ship. Having disarmed the alien, Kirk is reluctant to leave him stranded, even though help is apparently on the way, and takes a landing party aboard Balok's ship. There, they discover that the Balok they saw was nothing but a giant puppet, operated by the real Balok, who is a small bald dwarf with a friendly and playful disposition. His ship is not damaged, and he had no intention of harming the *Enterprise*. He was merely testing them to find out just who they were, and extends an accepted invitation to one of the *Enterprise*'s crew to stay with him for a while in order that they may learn more about each other's race and culture. Gene Coon's "Errand of Mercy" also featured a first contact, with a completely passive race of beings who refuse to fight against Klingon aggression on their own planet. They turn out to be so supremely powerful that they unilaterally disarm both the Klingons and the Federation to forestall their destroying each other in a pointless war, which to a large extent seems to be what UFOs have been doing in our world's airspace since their arrival.

Robots and alien abductions were a regular staple of *Star Trek,* the entire catalogue of which is prohibitive to list. One android became a popular main character in the show's 1987 revival. William Shatner once quipped that as many computers as Captain Kirk had reasoned into self-destructing, IBM must hate the man. "Nomad," from the episode "The Changeling," was probably the most memorable. Nomad was a glorified and alien-improved probe from centuries past, turned into a perfectionist killing machine. The same device was used for the first feature film of the *Star Trek* series, renamed "V-ger" (for "Voyager"). "The Doomsday Machine" was another aeons-old mechanized device, still devastating entire solar systems long after the wagers of the cosmic war it was built to function in have been killed off, and "That Which Survives" similarly had an ancient computerized planetary defense system destroying visitors who are no longer a threat. "The Ultimate Computer" was a unique battleship-controlling machine linked to its inventor's mind, programmed to respond to threats in the same way the inventor does—which unfortunately includes reacting with the inventor's paranoia. "What Are Little Girls Made Of" presented a scientist transferring human consciousness into androids. Another scientist, a human immortal, created numerous robots and android models in "Requiem for Methuselah." An entry from established sci-fi author Theodore Sturgeon, "Shore Leave," had robots being manufactured to order on a vacation planet. "Dagger of the Mind" featured a machine that hypnotically erased and controlled mens' minds at a penal colony. At least three episodes, "Return of the Archons," "The Paradise Syndrome," and "For the World is Hollow, and I Have Touched the Sky," dealt with civilizations left in the care of robots and computers centuries after the space societies that founded them have departed; in each instance, the races of humans left under their guidance, or the machines themselves, have malfunctioned and need to be set aright again. A similar theme was the basis of "Miri," in which all the adults of an entire planet have been killed as the result of a biological warfare plague, leaving children with immensely increased longevity in a Lord of the Flies state of anarchy and degeneracy, until Kirk becomes their savior.

An ancient alien child-abductor calling itself the "Friendly Angel" was the star of "And the Children Shall Lead." This plainly malevolent entity seduced the young and gave them special powers of illusion to terrify and destroy their enemies—including their own parents. It used the children as its vanguard in a bid to spread its evil influence across the universe. "The Gamesters of Triskelion" abducted passing spaceship crews merely for their amusement. "The Empath" is probably the next closest episode to the actual abduction phenomenon, after "The Cage." In it, short, bald, alien abductors with paralysis weapons in a neutral, sterile, limbo-setting laboratory abduct Kirk, Spock, and Dr. McCoy, subjecting them to extreme life-threatening tortures for no immediately stated purpose. It turns out they are being used to test the healing powers of one of their abductors' charges, a race of empaths in whom they are trying to instill a sense of self-sacrifice to see if they are worth saving from an upcoming cosmic catastrophe.

If the *Enterprise* had a Prime Directive preventing interference with primitives in their encounters, they also met the other end of the spectrum. At least twice, in "Return to Tomorrow" and "Who

Mourns for Adonis?" they encountered the theoretical race that engendered us in antiquity. The latter features Apollo himself, a human being like the *Enterprise* crew, only super-powerful and seemingly immortal. Having taken a fancy to a female yeoman, he takes her as his own, but she rebels along with the rest of the crew, not wishing to live in Apollo's shadow. Realizing humankind has outgrown him, Apollo sadly departs to his long-forestalled appointment with Olympus and the rest of the gods, leaving the *Enterprise* and the human race to wander where once the gods did. "Return to Tomorrow" was an interesting reenactment of Isis, Osiris, and Set, in which the last three survivors of a once-great race, the creators of man in antiquity, summon the *Enterprise* to them on their planet of refuge, borrowing the bodies of Kirk, Spock, and a female crewmember to create robots for their bodiless consciousnesses to inhabit. Hannuch, the entity inside Spock, schemes to murder Sargon, the leader who is inside Kirk's body, in order to tyrannize the *Enterprise*'s human crew and the universe to which their ship gives him access. Hannuch is super-hypnotic and completely dominates others' wills, inducing amnesia and post-event control. Finally Sargon, whom Hannuch believes he has successfully murdered, tricks Hannuch into destroying himself, then follows with his faithful wife into oblivion, having decided that his race's time has passed and that of his human children has come in its stead. A similar third-season entry, "Plato's Stepchildren," had the *Enterprise* visiting a planet of humans whose advanced powers and longevity have turned them into depraved abusers of "mere mortals" for their own jaded amusement.

One episode, an intended pilot that never flew, is of special interest—"Assignment: Earth." Robert Lansing plays "Gary Seven," an intercepted Earthman in the Starship *Enterprise*'s transporter, after the ship has catapulted back to 1968. He is caught coming not from Earth, but someplace more distant. Seven is confused by the *Enterprise*'s presence in the twentieth century, as they are by his advanced technological travel, and he knows approximately what century their ship came from. He admits to being one of a number of Earthmen who were taken and raised from infancy by a superior race of human beings from some other location in space with a keen interest in

Earth's affairs—that race is not identified, but Seven has a female accomplice who goes by the Egyptian name "Isis." Claiming to be on a mission of importance to Earth's future, Seven demands to be released, but Kirk refuses until more can be found out about him. Using a pocket flashlight-like device, Seven paralyzes and puts to sleep his guards, who are then compliant to his post-hypnotic commands. He escapes to Earth, where he has a high-tech office in waiting, and is pursued by Kirk and Spock. Seven's mission is discovered to be the sabotage of a nuclear platform being launched by Cape Kennedy that day, not for hostile purposes, but in a necessary scare-tactic to slow the superpowers in their otherwise soon-to-be-disastrous arms race.

The first-season show "Tomorrow Is Yesterday" also featured the *Enterprise* in modern-day Earth's atmosphere, being pursued as a UFO by the Air Force. The *Enterprise* abducts a pilot to save his life as his plane disintegrates in the chase, and are forced to erase his memory and sabotage the air base's records in order to return him. This episode received tremendous exposure to younger audiences (in keeping with the idea of its being part of a deliberate educational program) through an abbreviated version of its script being published in the early 1970s in a junior-high school weekly-reader magazine.

At its worst, *Star Trek* was a tad bit simplistic, one of the limitations and pitfalls of a melodrama format in which the heroes can only come out unscathed at the end of every hour. At its best, the show rarely degenerated into fantasy or the insipid, and it inspired an entire generation with an interest in space exploration and what other civilizations may exist elsewhere in the universe. However small its loyal viewership in the late 1960s, it has certainly proven to be the most famous and popular of all shows of its type, in endless syndication around the world since.

Star Trek: The Next Generation, also produced by Roddenberry, ran an incredible seven years from 1987 to 1994, and thanks to syndication will no doubt run at least seven more. Never a critical hit, despite its ultimately winning sixteen Emmys, the Peabody Award, and the Hugo Award for Science Fiction Achievement, this sequel's success was due to financial clout in production and simple longevity, eventually bulldozing its way to popularity among impoverished science-fiction fans. Having nothing in common with its predecessor except its name and occasional references to recognizable props from the original series, *STTNG* premiered on October 5, 1987, and from the beginning suffered dreadfully from a number of problems. Its scripts and characters were static, stiff, humorless, and lacking in individuality. When Roddenberry was a young and virile man, bed-hopping about town, his alter-ego Captain Kirk was also—he was portrayed as interesting, dangerous, and somewhat likeable. In Roddenberry's old age—and in an extremely conservative and long-lived Republican era—his new alter-ego, Captain Jean-Luc Picard, became a pompous and posturing moralistic blowhard. Like the similarly static and sterile *2001: A Space Odyssey* of Stanley Kubrick, the only character with even the remotest semblance of personality appeal on *STTNG* was ironically a robot, "Data," who doubled and tripled as every other member of his own robot family, the only other interesting characters on the series. Purportedly a natural bully anyway, Roddenberry himself was according to author Joel Engel suffering from a combination of drug abuse and increasing senility during the production of his new series, and he had to be tiptoed-around rather than worked with by his creative "team." Many of Roddenberry's close associates testified in Engel's *Gene Roddenberry—The Myth and the Man Behind Star Trek* that he actually was not terribly different during the original series' production, but it became far more transparent toward the end.

Actually a proto-Political Correctness primer masquerading as science-fiction, *STTNG*'s worst flaw was in scripts, which were identical to those of the most universally criticized dramatic form in history: Stalinist Soviet Socialist theater of the 1950s. In it, there are no villains; there is no crime; there is no conflict. There are only good people, and better people. The better people come upon the good people, and show them how to be better people like themselves. Then the better people go their merry way to help other good people become better people. There is no such thing as evil, utopia being an achievable set of Rousseauian social programs and fundamental correction of any malfunctioning biochemistry. The only difference between the Soviet and United States forms is the particular brand of totalitarian fascism they are selling. Being American, *Star Trek: The Next Generation* of course sold corporate mentality with boardroom Yuppie characters, all of whom were identically-thinking and -acting clones of each other with no personality or appeal, who were lectured weekly on the correct way of doing things by The Wise Old Man Up Top. Toward this end, they attended pointless and repetitive board meetings, pretending to consider alternate points of view that would never contradict what The Wise Old Man Up Top wanted done in the first place. Under the guise of promoting universal brotherhood, this show actually presented the ugliest and meanest of stereotypes hidden behind grotesque masks: Arabs were shown as foolish, buck-toothed connivers called "Ferengis," smokers as repulsive aliens isolated from better creatures by breathing apparatuses constantly providing them with the noxious chemical that serves as their air, Russians as barbaric Klingons under the protective wing of the Corporate Federation, which is parentally patronizing their efforts to become Better People, and so on. In fact, Roddenberry was extremely upset that the motion picture *Star Trek VII* showed the Klingons in a more sympathetic light than the Federation itself. By contrast, in the original series, Roddenberry's insistence on an interracial *Enterprise* crew despite opposition from the network was a bold and daring socio-political move, receiving not a single anticipated letter of protest.

Even a blind hog is able to root out an acorn now and again, however, and *Star Trek: The Next Generation* did manage a small handful of decent episodes in its incredible run. Typically, whenever the new *Enterprise* crew came up against a legitimate threat, they either escaped it as quickly as possible before they would have to demonstrate that all problems can't be solved by corporate heads who are full of themselves and hot air, or else found a neat and convenient way to simply pull their opponent's plug without any unnecessary muss, fuss, or bother. Their only truly threatening enemy in seven years was of the latter category: the Borg. Before it was learned that they could simply be switched-off like an errant blender, however, they did provide an interesting UFOlogical abduction model.

The Borg are cyborgs (originality in names, whatever else he may legitimately have been good at, was never Gene Roddenberry's strong suit), half machine and half man, who are more like pure machines in human form. They raise their children from infancy to become cybernetic organisms when they grow up, and are completely cold, mechanical, efficient, and soulless, just like the Soviets were still being trumped-up to be. The Borg have no interest in meeting new races, only exploiting whatever they find to their own maximum advantage with no consideration for their prey. They flee from that which is superior to them, and dominate and cannibalize that which is inferior. They cannot be negotiated with. They abduct Captain Picard in one episode, paralyzing and implanting him on a cold, sterile slab, converting him into one of "the Borg consciousness." From that point on, until he is freed from their mechanical hive-mind influence, he is a torn and tortured soul, neither man nor machine, not of their race or ours—in most regards, not unlike the reports of some UFO abductees in real life. The Borg most recently resurfaced as the star villains in the latest movie in the Paramount series, *First Contact* (1996).

Whatever the show's other failings, first-contact scenarios were usually the best-handled stories, several of the better episodes dramatizing the sort of problems that could realistically be expected in such a traumatic—or at the very least, problematic—event. Crewmembers more than once went undercover to monitor the progress of other humanoid civilizations. One of the best stories concerned clandestine meetings between the *Enterprise* and a psychologically strong scientist in an alien culture, trying to prepare her world for open first contact. Her society has technologically progressed to the point that outside contact is necessary for further development, but her world's governments are not suitably mature or stable enough for the event. They consult her periodically to ask how her people are progressing, and whether the climate might have improved for such a meeting. A similar episode reveals that Data has broken Federation rules by clandestinely establishing repeated contact with a little girl on an alien world—her planetary system is unstable and about to be destroyed, and Data insists on taking the girl with him before the catastrophe can occur.

Abduction, mind control, and hypnosis, with accompanying amnesia, post-event control, and debilitating effects, were employed against the First Mate and Chief Engineer at various times in the series, and at least twice crewmembers' bodies were appropriated by alien life forms for the purpose of reproducing themselves. Data and his android brother were abducted by their creator, who could summon them at will by inducing a somnambulistic state from a distance.

The Paramount *Star Trek* movie series has also shown a few UFO-logical elements. The first feature film, *Star Trek: The Motion Picture* (1979), was made during Carter's presidency for a whopping forty-two-million dollars and was probably part of a purposely funded educational program by him that will be more fully examined in Chapter 9. Unalloyed by wiser heads, as he was during the 1980s revival of his original T.V. show, Gene Roddenberry's story (as were nearly all of his other ones) was a thin plagiarism of the original series' better episode, "The Changeling." The lost space probe, *Voyager,* has been vastly improved in the outer reaches of space by some outside party and has grown into a truly awesome destroyer on a cosmic scale. It has lost memory of its beginnings, not even remembering its original name and now going by "V-ger." Seeking closer communion with its creator, the probe has returned to its planet of origin to either find that communion or destroy the impure "biological infestations"— i.e., human beings—that now pollute it. Needless to say, the Earth survives. The most interesting UFO element in the story is the abduction of a crew member by *V-ger,* who is then duplicated as a robot embodying the crewmember's memory and personality, to serve as *V-ger*'s own probe-ambassador aboard the *Enterprise.*

Star Trek II: The Wrath of Khan (1982) also took the original series for its springboard, being a continuation of "Space Seed," in which genetically engineered Aryan supermen, who nearly destroyed the Earth in its past and were imprisoned in suspended animation, found themselves revived to attempt the same crime aboard the *Enterprise.* Stopped from succeeding in their endeavor, they are sentenced to live out the rest of their lives on a planet removed from civilization, where they can nonetheless manage to survive. The movie rediscovers them as the forgotten victims of a space catastrophe, and none the better for their experience. They seize control of a starship by means of a biological mind-control device, and threaten the stability of known civilization until they are again finally thwarted. The movie introduced the concept of Sir Francis Crick and Leslie Orgel's "directed panspermia" in a "Genesis Device," which seeds dead planets with life. It also set up the third entry, *The Search for Spock* (1984), in which the heroically-killed character finds bodily resurrection by means of the same device, and in an Ancient Egyptian-inspired scene has his soul re-fused to his risen body. *The Voyage Home* (1986) repeated "Tomorrow Is Yesterday," catapulting the *Enterprise* back to Earth's twentieth century, where the crew clandestinely contacts a receptive local to help them rescue sperm whales to repopulate the now-extinct species in the future. *The Final Frontier* (1989) had the *Enterprise* crossing an ancient galactic barrier to discover "God," an exiled and imprisoned super-powerful being that may or may not have engendered the human race, and who is decidedly exploitative and hostile. The later entries have continued to degenerate and are UFOlogically unimportant.

Star Trek V: The Final Frontier was authored and directed by star William Shatner, who himself had a UFO encounter in the Mojave Desert, northeast of Palmdale, in the summer of 1967, and—according to unauthorized biographer Dennis William Hauck—believes he may have been abducted. Shatner never attempted hypnotic regression therapy to test his experience, but he scored eighty-five percent on a contact probability test devised by clinical psychologist and UFO researcher Dr. Richard Boylan. Certainly the experience had a striking effect on the star, who immediately embarked on a famous flop of a project that was nevertheless sincere in intent: an album called *The Transformed Man,* filled with readings of Shakespeare and Rostand, "Lucy in the Sky with Diamonds," and a legendarily bad rendition of "Mr. Tambourine Man," among other tracks. Though the album made it into 1990's *The Worst Rock 'n Roll Albums of All Time* and into Rhino Records' tongue-in-cheek *Golden Throats,* Shatner said it was "deeper and more satisfying" a project than any he had undertaken.

Hauck met Shatner when they were both working on an ancient astronaut documentary called *Mysteries of the Gods* in 1976. With periodic lapses, Shatner has been an outspoken proponent of UFO reality since his own close encounter. He embarked on a college campus tour, reading selections from famous authors concerning life in outer space and discussing the possible realities with his audience, recording many of his talks and related projects through his own Lemli Productions. He also did a NASA-sponsored documentary, nominated for an Oscar and winning several awards, called *Universe*. During one such tour shortly after *Mysteries of the Gods,* as *Viking* was relaying its images to Earth, Shatner's speech at a *Star Trek* convention was interrupted by two scientists rushing into the auditorium to breathlessly announce that life had been found on Mars. Before it was determined to have been an incorrect claim, the audience spontaneously cheered and applauded in a frenzy of delight. When the truth came out shortly after, Shatner told his quieted crowd, "You have just been told that alien life has been found on Mars, but you and I knew it all the time!" Most recently, he has been the author and creator of the "Tekwar" series, a number of novels, T.V. movies, and comic books about a future world in which two high-tech adversarial groups wage a private little war between each other while keeping the general public unaware, rather like the apparent reality of the UFO phenomenon. The most recent of Shatner's novels (1997) is set on Mars. His voice has also made numerous cartoon guest appearances, good-naturedly ribbing his famous Captain Kirk persona, on such Saturday morning kids' shows as Savage Steve Holland's *Eekstravaganza*.

Nor is Shatner alone among the *Trek* cast in claiming a UFO encounter, according to Hauck. Walter Koenig, who played Ensign Chekov, saw a spherical airborne object outside his bedroom window when he was ten and remains excited about it to this day. DeForest Kelley and his wife Caroline, along with a family friend, also witnessed a UFO seen by dozens of other people at the same time while driving toward Montgomery, Alabama, through the Louisiana swampland, in 1950. It was cigar-shaped and five to six hundred feet across, with recognizable running lights and a jet-stream exhaust. The Kelleys were even subsequently contacted by a government investigator on the case, who admitted that the UFO had no satisfactory explanation. It is not a secret, but few realize that a great many people associated with the production of space-related films and T.V. shows are also avid UFOlogists or space-research buffs. *Star Trek's* Nichelle Nichols and *Lost In Space* star June Lockhart, for example, still sometimes visit NASA and help promote the Space Agency. Nichols related on a 1997 Sci-Fi Channel appearance that one of her proudest accomplishments was being an inspiration to an aspiring shuttle astronaut.

Gene Roddenberry had no recorded close encounters but did find himself approached by various dubious fringe-science organizations, sometimes offering substantial sums of money, trying to get him to organize one or another kind of project selling their own more or less religious point of view. Famous purported psychic Israeli spoonbender Uri Geller, and his more-or-less biographer, Dr. Andrija Puharich, were two of the more recognizable ones. Along with a mysterious—and apparently wealthy—organization calling itself "Lab 9," they attempted to convince Roddenberry for many weeks in 1977 that a group of extraterrestrial intelligences called "The Nine"—supposedly responsible for Geller's "powers," specifically residing 53,069 light years from Earth on a computerized spaceship called *Spectra* and presided over by an entity named "Ja-Hoovah"—was interacting with "chosen" individuals on Earth. (Geller was one of a number of psychics inconclusively tested by the U.S. government in the CIA, DIA and NSA's "remote viewing" program during the 1970s.) Though impressed with some of the psychic phenomena he witnessed on sojourns with the group around the world, Roddenberry failed to be convinced of the outrageous claims of "Lab 9." He did commission an attempt at a script based on some of their theories, but eventually gave up on it.

Shortly before his death, however, "The Nine" were incorporated into the title of Roddenberry's latest *Trek* spin-off: *Deep Space Nine*. Roddenberry seems to have taken the claims of "The Nine" much more seriously in his later years, its worst influence on him creatively being the unrealistically pacifistic bent of *Star Trek: The Next Generation*. It should be noted that the CIA or any other government influence at work trying to educate the public about UFO truths through entertainment media is hardly the only program of its type in the works—someone else has been equally hard at work attempting to defuse exactly such efforts, either from another group or according to changing political dictates within the same group. "Lab 9" shows all the earmarks of being an Intelligence fraud, one of the numerous disinformation sources employed by that particular community to discredit any source of potentially vitalizing UFO or extraterrestrial research. (It is worth noting, in this context—since the Masons obviously boast quite a few members among clandestine government circles—that nine original creator gods is a Masonic concept deriving from ancient Egypt. The Egyptian cosmogonies began with eight original creator gods, headed by Thoth as the ninth, referred to alternately as the Ogdoad and the Ennead. In Masonic tradition, it is a company of nine knights—the same number of Knights Templar, led by Hugues de Payens and Godfrey de St. Omer, supposed historically to have created the Order after the recovery of Jerusalem in the First Crusade in 1118—who discover the body of their murdered master, Hiram Abiff. "The Nine" was also the reference given to the sole survivors of the Venusian race in Roger Corman's *It Conquered the World* in 1956.)

Rivaling the new *Star Trek* for sheer Biblical pretentiousness was Glen Larson's endlessly recycled predecessor from Universal, almost ten years prior, 1978's *Battlestar Galactica*. Seeming to have borrowed ideas from the writings of contemporaneous ancient astronaut theorist Zecharia Sitchin, it unfortunately couldn't have made them less appealing. The series' premise is that Earth's lone survivors against technologically superior (yet somehow still unable to hit the broad side of a barn) human-hating robots, the Cylons, have gathered together their "ragtag, fugitive fleet" of survivors in a wagon train going back to their legendary planet of ancestry, Earth. There, the "Lords of Kobol" are found to have been the builders of the pyramids, leaving man to occupy the world they once walked. The battlestar crew's helmets look like Egyptian headdresses, as have numerous futuristic cartoon renditions since, and the characters posture about as stiffly as hieroglyphs.

One of the better two-part episodes features *The Avengers'* Patrick Macnee as "Count Iblis," a suave but thinly transparent Lucifer from a former superior race of humanoids who takes the women he chooses from the *Galactica*'s stock (his primary target is Anne Lockhart, daughter of *Lost In Space*'s June) and imposes his will upon others. He wins influence and incites insurrection among the crew by his working of miracles, which are merely a display of his technical prowess. He is pursued by other members of his race in ships obviously reminiscent of the UFOs recorded in official documents of today: they move at lightning speed, are detected only when they want to be, are untouchable, and successfully abduct members of the *Galactica* crew at will, erasing all memory of the encounters afterward. Among them are plainly human beings and typical Grays, which essentially appear as robots.

Galactica pilot Starbuck is knocked out by these pursuers in his cockpit, awakening on a slab in the alien mothership, where he is informed that they know all about him and his friends. He is implanted with knowledge he later perceives only dimly as a dream, which is nothing more than the awareness of the alien race's existence and ongoing concern. Their interest is fraternal-paternal and unquestionably friendly, however else they may be perceived. "We once were as you are now," they inform him. "As we are now, so will you be." This is almost word-for-word Mormon philosophy, and Mormonism's founder, Joseph Smith (if his story is true), could very easily have been influenced by UFO occupants. Smith's "angels"—and the "Virgin Mary" who has visited some of the Catholic Church's famous saints—have been considered by renowned UFOlogist Jacques Vallee to be extraterrestrials.

A later reincarnation of the same show, *Galactica: 1980,* was much better. There, the Galacticans find contemporary Earth, with themselves in the unlikely position of *The Day the Earth Stood Still*'s Klaatu. Being technologically superior to us, they take it upon themselves to perform abductions and establish contacts among the local populace, attempting to help us through potential rough spots and prepare an open meeting between our two peoples. Their chief concern is keeping out of the military's reach, some of whom know of their existence and have a decidedly exploitative self-interest.

Better still was Larson's other effort, also from Universal, 1979's *Buck Rogers in the 25th Century,* the pilot film of which begins with a more or less classic abduction—in this instance, a twentieth-century astronaut who has been in suspended animation is intercepted and revived aboard an alien spacecraft five hundred years later, only to find himself caught in a tremendous amount of court intrigue between that humanoid race and Earth's. Benefiting from likeable performances and a lively sense of humor in place of its predecessor's dull pomposity, this show was less science fiction or fantasy than a light-hearted weekly spy spoof set in the future. *The Outer Limits'* Leslie Stevens helmed *Buck Rogers* in its earliest and most successful version, but it was ruined in its second season by new producer John Mantley's taking the action out into space and injecting the humorless self-importance it had mercifully been lacking—a classic case of fixing something that wasn't broken.

The only show to approximate either *The Outer Limits* or *The Night Stalker* since the early 1970s has been Fox's Canadian-produced *The X-Files,* beginning in Fall of 1993—again, right at the beginning of a Democratic administration. Like its predecessors, this show's ratings began abysmally low, but Fox renewed it in mid-season of its opening year because it had a loyal cult following already, and probably had friends in high places the same way Leslie Stevens did. Though the second season's shows were less coherent than the first's, its ratings increased 44%, and in its third and fourth seasons it has grown remarkably fast from cult status to full-blown phenomenon, thanks to word-of-mouth, more aggressive exposure in the media, and the winning of several Golden Globe awards. The title refers to a fictional unit that investigates UFOs and paranormal phenomena cases for the FBI.

The X-Files has many fans in the actual Bureau according to *T.V. Guide* (though it has no such division in reality), but none of the show's episodes, according to the producers, are derived from real files. Its success—aside from its media hype—stems primarily from slick production and appealing characters, from stars David Duchovny and Gillian Anderson as Agents Fox Mulder and Dana Scully (who have won two of the aforementioned Golden Globes), to the weekly guest stars, all of whose roles are interesting. To give the show a "personal" connection to the UFO question, Mulder's sister was UFO-abducted and never returned when they were both children, haunting him with the need to find out what happened to her, and Scully undergoes an abduction during the series' run. (Scully's name, playfully enough, is almost certainly something of an inside joke: in the 1950s, popular journalist Frank Scully was the first man to be suckered into writing unsubstantiated books about flying saucer occupant retrievals from purported crashes.) Additionally, Mulder later involuntarily becomes part of a Russian biological experiment when he becomes infected with "the black cancer," a nameless disease originating from a Mars rock on Earth (capitalizing on the recent Martian bacteria announcements in the news), with indeterminate long-range results.

The best shows, seemingly the closest to actual facts (at least insofar as they can be determined), have been those not dealing with UFOs, though there have been notable exceptions. *The X-Files'* closest episode pertaining to the elements presented in this study is the third season's "War of the Coprophages," in which a number of mysterious mechanical cockroaches are causing the accidental deaths—apparently by fright—of people they come across. Mulder surmises that the metallically exoskeletoned little critters must be somebody else's space probes, since no one down here could conceivably have made them. He finds an outspoken, UFO-believing, NASA-contracted robotics expert who constructs much larger machines in the form of cockroaches, simply for their practicality. "This is the future of space exploration," the scientist informs Mulder. "The interplanetary explorers of alien civilizations will likely be mechanical in nature. Anyone who thinks alien visitation will come not in the form of robots, but in living beings with big eyes and gray skin, has been brainwashed by too much science fiction." Mulder tells Scully, "I hate insects. I'm not *afraid* of them—I *hate* them." He describes accidentally coming face to face with an enormous praying mantis when he was a kid: "I had a praying mantis epiphany, and as a result I screamed ... the scream of someone being confronted by some before-unknown monster that had no right existing on the same planet I inhabited. Did you ever notice how a praying mantis' head resembles an alien's head?" UFO abductees often make the same analogy, and this episode making direct connection between "aliens" and robotic insects is telling.

The next most interesting *X-Files* story in regard to this study is "Space," in which a former astronaut turned NASA mission head turns out to be an alien-possessed saboteur against his own will, the aliens strongly implied to have come from Mars. The producers unfairly consider this to be one of their weakest episodes, simply because they expected more from it than they managed to ultimately get. A recent second-season entry developed the idea that animals other than man (but implying human beings as well) are being impregnated artificially by UFO occupants, a linguistically-capable gorilla communicating to its keeper before its final abduction the message, "Man help Man," suggesting the nature of those occupants. That same episode discussed the alarming statistics of the Earth's ecological disintegration, laying it as the background against which extraterrestrial humans would be interested in such a breeding project. A proposed crossover episode with rival network CBS' multiple-award-winning hit, *Picket Fences,* involving alien abduction and cattle mutilation, was retracted at the last minute by *Fences'* producers. Instead, they ran an episode perhaps as intriguing about cattle being used to carry surrogate human births to term. *Picket Fences* also did a story in which one of the characters is ultimately shown-up to appear pathetic and weak for having been taken in by a phony UFO, and another in which a little boy who develops stigmata is portrayed with symptomatology remarkably like an abductee.

Ironically, *The X-Files'* weakest episodes—not dramatically, but UFOlogically speaking—are those dealing with alien abductions, taking their information not from the study of actual abductees, but instead from popularized misconceptions of them, which is probably the result of teleplays authored in the late 1980s and early '90s by scriptwriter Tracy Torme. "Duane Barry" and "Ascension," for instance, an early two-part second-season story, featured a committed madman—played by Steve Railsback, the actor who played Charles Manson in T.V.'s *Helter Skelter,* and the space mission survivor/abductee in the 1985 film *Lifeforce* (see Chapter 10)—insane with terror over the certainty that his alien abductors were returning for him. He seizes a weapon and takes over the mental hospital he is in. While the madman raves about grotesque tortures and violations the aliens repeatedly perform on him, trying to get anyone to believe or help him, Mulder explains to doubting FBI members that these are fairly standard claims and behavior for abductees—which is completely untrue. There is not a single case on record—or even spoken of in the apocryphal realm—in which anyone went raving mad over a UFO abduction, let alone homicidal or even hostile. The closest exception would be Calvin Parker, in the 1973 Pascagoula, Mississippi, case, but he was only understandably upset, not raving, and had voluntarily committed himself while trying to adjust to his unsettling experience.

The producers used this story as an excuse to get pregnant star Gillian Anderson off the series for a couple of weeks while she delivered, by having her character abducted aboard the UFO in place of the mad Duane Barry, who has engineered her as a replacement for himself, screaming, *"I'm free! At last I'm free!"* Again, no actual abductee has ever behaved in such a fashion, or done such a thing—but the needs of drama (and/or propaganda) and the needs of objective UFO study are completely different. When Anderson's character is returned, the aftermath of her UFO abduction is accurately portrayed. She has no memory of what happened to her, and unlike her predecessor, has no fears or terrors over the incident—or even awareness of it. She is left with a subcutaneous metallic implant around her neck and has it removed to discover it is similar to a computer chip—which does not differ too much from actual analyses of some recovered implants in real life. She meets other abductees later, with whom she feels an odd kinship despite herself, and at one point believes she recognizes one of her abductors as a Japanese General from the infamous Unit 731 that was imported with the Paperclip boys. She also discovers—as does Mulder—that she has a file in a secret government complex, apparently connected to her experience.

Some abduction stories have no connection to the real phenomenon at all, such as one of the most popular two-part stories in the second season, "Colony" and "End Game," in which a society of alien clones is being pursued by a shapeshifting alien executioner—

not a bad idea for a fantasy-oriented science-fiction plot, but not remotely connected to any UFO reality. This story demonstrates one of the show's unfortunate failings, which is that it is sometimes so confused that it doesn't seem to have any idea what it is talking about at any given time. Actual scientific facts are intermingled in such scattershot fashion with patent unrealities that the stories are often difficult to follow—which, it could largely be argued, is a frequent failing of the science-fiction genre in general.

The cliffhanger three-part story leading into *The X-Files'* third season had Mulder and Scully discovering that the government has files containing abductees' genetic tissues, for reasons unknown. The worst failing of the series, but an unavoidable one, is that the producers cannot commit to any single theory, which forces them to do nothing but continually throw out tantalizing tidbits for thought without any kind of explanation as to what they may really be about. Thus, in three episodes comprising a single story, no plotline at all is resolved, and little is actually determined—except that the government is up to Something Nefarious on the entire UFO question: Mulder finds a buried train's meat-car on an Anasazi reservation in New Mexico; it contains rotted-looking Gray bodies (about which not a single item of information is retrieved before the car and its contents are incinerated); the Nazis brought over in Operation Paperclip had something to do with it; the Indians know something about the history of all this that they're not telling ... and that's about it. One interesting thing to come out of the story was a conversation between Mulder and an Indian on the Anasazi reservation. The Indian tells him that anyone can find the truth—when they are ready to receive it. The Indian very matter-of-factly relates some of the same facts discussed in this study to support the obvious but ignored truth (which is precisely his point) that nothing in any of this UFO activity is anything new—it has been going on for as long as the tribe can remember. On similar lines, one of Mulder's shadowy "inside" sources at one time tells him, "Agent Mulder, *they* have been 'with us' for a long, long time."

One fairly clever and interesting abduction story, "Fallen Angel," showed an amnesiac repeat-abductee becoming aware that a recent crash in an isolated area has occurred because his controllers have come to pick him up. The military in the episode is shown as being heavily involved in UFO recovery activity, disguising the fact with false newspaper reports about crashes of more conventional craft, for which there is some evidence in reality. There was unquestionably an Interplanetary Phenomenon Unit in the Army in the 1950s, for instance, and it seems a certain bet that its title did not refer to studies of Saturn's rings. There have also been later recovery programs suggested by legitimate documentation, going under such project names as "Moon Dust" and "Blue Fly," that cannot be proven to involve UFO material but probably did. "Fallen Angel" was followed by a two-parter story at the end of the fourth season, in which the same repeat-abductee—along with an entire planeload of people—is killed by a military missile during what turns out to be his final UFO abduction.

X-Files episodes dealing with the military are all well-handled, probably the show's most consistently good work. The first episode following the pilot credibly dramatized the Area 51 scenario, minus the purported underground base, and actual records do support the idea that some experimentation on saucer material has been in effect by the military for decades—probably to some extent even before Roswell, since Operation Paperclip or earlier still, with the papers of Nikola Tesla. The strongest aspect of the show has always been its darkly paranoiac handling and atmosphere throughout every aspect of production, though its nameless government conspiracies are only remotely based on actual fact—which is to say that, yes, obviously there is government secrecy on UFOs and other sensitive subjects, but no, the parties involved don't go around blatantly shooting each other about it. The idea of supernefarious human-alien conspiracies is entirely a product of post-Bennewitz/Ronald Reagan Era disinformational propaganda, with no grounding in any fact that has yet been established.

The series' dramatization of how secret government agencies work is more of a mixed grab-bag, as is its presentation of UFOlogical facts. The milieu created for these characters by the producers is smoky and dark (in keeping with 1980s and '90s propaganda, all shady government insiders smoke cigarettes, their chief member even nicknamed "Cancer Man"), and they are shown murdering each other at the drop of a hat for information never disclosed. If real agencies performed a fraction of the gunplay shown in *The X-Files*, they would have no members left after little over a season of reruns. "Cancer Man" himself is dramatized in the fourth season's "Musings of a Cigarette Smoking Man" as having been the true assassin of JFK and Martin Luther King, Jr., and subsequently lying (for no reason) to his own peers about it—and they don't even suspect he isn't telling the truth. Recruited out of the military for his assassination job, Cancer Man is first seen reading Richard Condon's *The Manchurian Candidate*—a friend asks him why he doesn't just go see the movie, and Cancer Man wryly answers, "I'd rather read the worst book ever written than see the best movie ever made."

In a potentially clever piece of psychological portraiture, Cancer Man is presented as the original Greek anti-ideal, the man whose "unexamined life is not worth living." He routinely gives neckties to his underlings for Christmas, has no one at all in his private life, and has spent his wasted years doing nothing but writing hollow escapist novels, based on his own criminal exploits, which he can't sell. This is an inconsistency not only with the episode's own logic—earlier, Cancer Man and his cadre are shown literally rigging Oscar nights and Super Bowls, which should make the publishing of one of his own minor potboilers a simple matter, indeed—but with established facts about the CIA. Notorious Bay of Pigs operative, Nixon blackmailer, and Watergate burglar (and probable participant in the dispatch of JFK), E. Howard Hunt, has published over a hundred spy novels of questionable merit, many even under his own name. And, as should be more than apparent by this time, the Agency has media outlets in virtually every area of entertainment, if for no other reason than ongoing propaganda.

A worthy footnote to the foregoing is in a 1992 episode of the popular Fox cartoon, *The Simpsons*. Perennial idiot Homer desires to become a Mason ("Stonecutter," as they are referred to in the episode), after noticing that everyone who wears a certain ring gets away with anything and everything under the sun. Eventually succeeding in

332 HOLLYWOOD VERSUS THE ALIENS

his aim, he is privy to their drinking song, part of the lyrics of which are, "Who rigs every Oscar night? *We do!*" The same song in this particular cartoon, made at the tail end of CIA President Bush's tenure, also includes what may well be considered a telling phrase, especially in that it was almost certainly taken as nothing but a joke in the way it was presented: "Who keeps Atlantis off the maps? Who keeps the Martians under wraps? *We do! We do!*"

The other episodes handled well in *The X-Files* are those that might otherwise have ended up on *The Night Stalker*, which is admitted by the producers to be one of the show's chief inspirations. These are the "genetic mutation" stories, in which modern man either discovers a species of life on his own world previously unknown to him, or in which Mulder and Scully find themselves facing a human mutant with hitherto unknown psychic or physical powers that are being used for criminal ends. Considering that the gorilla and orangutan were only discovered in roughly the last hundred years and were scoffed at as fantasies prior to that, some of these stories are not even so farfetched. On the other hand, in the show's obvious interest of coming up with compelling drama and science fiction, many of the episodes border on the absurd, some becoming mixed up with UFOs in a bizarre mishmash. The best example of this last is "Genderbender," a sex-switching human serial killer of alien origin.

Any genuine UFOlogical facts that emerge from *The X-Files* appear to be almost entirely accidental. There are the occasional coincidences, some of which might be informed, such as those already mentioned. What is most interesting about the show's slogan, "The Truth Is Out There," is that the producers don't go very far in real research to find it, and sometimes way too far out to create it. If Agent Mulder really wanted to know what was going on with UFOs and abductions, he could sit in on a few actual abductee sessions or interview the leading experts in the field to discover that nothing all too grotesquely terrifying is taking place, and his knowledge in general only shows that he has never cracked a book on the subject written before 1980 and the Bennewitz Affair. Like the majority of contemporary UFOlogists, Mulder's information comes almost solely from media misconceptions and Intelligence disinformation sources. If he were a real FBI agent, he would have known by now that the answer to any mystery lies in the original investigation, and he would have gone back to the primary reports and witnesses in his spadework to find it.

Whether it has any particular significance or not, it is at least worth noting (in light of the possibility of Intelligence connections) that *X-Files* star David Duchovny is an Ivy Leaguer who graduated from (a) JFK Jr.'s prep school, (b) Princeton (where he was a dean's list regular), and (c) Yale (with a Master's in English Lit.); that co-star Gillian Anderson is the daughter of an internationally traveled film industry worker, grew up in such locations as Puerto Rico and London, and was the product of the prestigious Goodman Theater School in Chicago (travel and upper-crust education are usual prerequisites for Intelligence work); and that regular series supporting actor Mitch Pileggi's father worked for the Department of Defense, Pileggi himself being a military contractor who lived in Germany, Turkey, Saudi Arabia, and Iran before becoming an actor.

Tracy Torme (son of singer Mel), who is most responsible for current misperceptions concerning the abduction phenomenon in the media (such as those further popularized on *The X-Files)*, wrote the film and T.V. versions of Paramount's *Fire in the Sky* (1993) and Budd Hopkins' CBS miniseries *Intruders* (1992), as well as *Star Trek: The Next Generation*'s scariest episode, "Conspiracy," involving self-implanting alien parasites. He is also co-creator of the sci-fi fantasy series *Sliders,* which featured an alien abduction story almost identical to the original *Outer Limits'* "Nightmare." Torme admits in interviews to fabricating entire portions of the reportedly true stories he is adapting, and he seems far more intent on creating a good horror story than conveying any truth about the abduction phenomenon.

Fire in the Sky is based on Travis Walton's abduction account, and in terms of the actual experience reported is not faithful to it at all. Walton reported standard Grays and blonde men and women in blue spacesuits aboard the craft he was taken to. They did not communicate—except to smile at him—and did not in any way harm him. Torme's version has sinister reptiles sticking needles in Walton's eye and showing evidence of having eaten other human visitors, none of which has been reported either by Walton or any other abductee. Walton was pointedly never shown any draft of the screenplay's abduction sequence before filming, but he believes Torme's claim that the end product was beyond his ability to do anything about—however, since Torme was one of the movie's three co-producers, that claim falls a little flat. Walton himself is unsure of the nature of the Grays, but admits that they may well be robots. He notes in *Fire in the Sky: The Walton Experience* that the Pentagon was exceptionally enthusiastic about the film: "[P]erhaps one reason the Pentagon's internal newspaper, *Pentagram,* gave *Fire in the Sky* a four-star review and called it a 'must see' is because they have an interest in my experience betyond entertainment. Maybe my case is an inside joke to certain people there. I don't know, maybe I'm reaching a bit here, but subsequent developments make such speculation appear not quite so far-fetched." In other words, perhaps the reason the Pentagon so enthusiastically recommended the movie is because they were behind its disinformation—or at the very least anxious to spread it. The "subsequent events" referred to by Walton are indicative of the fact. Immediately before the film's opening, an alleged witness to Walton's November 1975 abduction made himself known, who was formerly in military intelligence and lied about knowing notorious UFO debunker Philip J. Klass. Paramount discovered the man's connections and lies prior to his nearly marring the release of *Fire in the Sky* by revelation of his own hoax, but the mere fact that the feat was attempted leads one to wonder which specific party or parties were behind it. Walton believes it was more than likely a military intelligence ploy, and he is probably right.

Intruders gives the entirely false impression that abductees live in a state of perpetual dread and panic, gibbering in fear without respite, which is a gross misperception aided and abetted by *Dark Shadows* creator Dan Curtis' overly melodramatic and hysterical direction. Torme invented facts about implants out of whole cloth—not at all in accord with known cases, and which was entirely unnecessary because true facts are available—doing so (by his own reasoning) to heighten the suspense of the story. These choices have helped perpetuate false stereotypes in a field that can ill-afford any more than it has already acquired—all the more inexplicable in light of the fact that Torme has actually sat in on some of Budd Hopkins' hypnotic sessions with abductees.

Whitley Strieber's *Communion* and *Transformation,* also purporting to be true accounts, have equally disseminated to a mass audience, both in print and on film, an image that is neither true to the experiences reported by other abductees nor conducive to good investigation of them in the future. Claiming to actually be an abductee, Strieber's accounts contain some consistent elements with those of other abductees, while other elements are so far afield and completely unique that they beg the question of their reality. It is possible that he got the true elements merely from sitting in on therapy sessions with genuine abductees and has added the more outrageous and unbelievable material from his writer's imagination. Strieber's own mother stated to investigator and author Ken Conroy that Strieber was a notorious practical joker when he was a boy. Budd Hopkins, from the time they first met in 1986, considered Strieber completely unlike more than two hundred abductees he had worked with. Strieber was abnormally afraid, even suicidal, and Hopkins "absolutely" refused to deal with him until he had first been to a psychiatrist. About a year after their first meeting, Strieber went around behind Hopkins' back to the man's publisher, trying to get them to delay putting Hopkins' *Intruders* out on the market until his own *Communion* had its run. The act severed relations between the two men as soon as it was discovered. Strieber pretended noble intentions, which are in no way believable.

Before dissolving their association, Strieber got Hopkins to introduce him to his *Intruders* case study, "Kathie Davis" (pseudonym), and he upset and frightened her very badly as soon as Hopkins was out of earshot. Author Keith Thompson relates the story in *Angels and Aliens,* as Davis told it to him: "According to Davis, during their meeting Strieber fixed his eye on her and said there was something he should tell her ... but then again, no, he shouldn't, because it would just upset her. Yet perhaps he should tell her, but no, it was probably best not to. This went on until Davis was quite nervous, at which point Strieber decided to tell her. 'I think I've seen you before,

Kathie, inside a UFO, but it wasn't all of you. It was just your head, and it was alive, and it was on a shelf.' Davis, who had been telling Strieber how vulnerable, confused, and frightened she had been since her abduction experience, felt devastated by this remark—and suddenly deeply frightened by the man who was sitting across from her. When Davis returned to Hopkins' apartment, Strieber called to apologize. But it was too late...." The incident convinced Hopkins that Strieber was getting worse in his psychotherapy sessions.

Thompson asked Strieber if he had made such a statement to Davis, and he indignantly responded, "Of course I didn't." Confronted with not only Davis' sworn statement to the contrary, but also Hopkins' and his wife's affirmation that they had heard Strieber's apologetic call on the telephone, Strieber emphatically denied it. Then, after a pause, in a hushed tone, he said to Thompson, "But what I find absolutely interesting is that Kathie Davis truly believes I made that remark ... *and so does Budd.*" Plainly Strieber is lying in this instance. If he didn't know he'd made the statement, how could he assert that Hopkins and Davis truly believed it? And how could he expect that the word of three people would not be taken over his own on the incident? Rather than admit to the act, he instead tried to infer not even that both primary witnesses were lying, but that they were crazy.

Despite numerous attempts on Strieber's part to get his friends to corroborate his having been in Austin, Texas, on the day sniper Charles Whitman committed mass-murder, none of them have, and they all seem to be quite weary of his bothering them about it. Strieber had plainly stated in prior interviews that he was at the scene, then later said he wasn't sure, "questioned" in *Communion* whether it might have been a "screen memory" (after initially asserting, once more, that he *was* there), and made a great show of going through a personal investigation to determine whether he was on campus that day or not: "The Charles Whitman incident. I found after the most careful research in the past six or seven months that I definitely was there, but that illustrates the problem of trying to understand ...In *Communion,* I questioned my presence at the Charles Whitman massacre, along with a lot of other things I did, for two reasons.

One was that Jim Kunetka, the person I thought I was with, didn't remember my being there. Number two was that I couldn't think of a motive for being on campus that August 1, 1966. I was not in my summer school classes on campus, and home was in San Antonio. So I thought, 'Why would I have been there?' See, so those two things led me to question it." How anyone could be unsure whether or not they were at the scene of one of the most violent mass-murders in history defies belief—and if it didn't, the fact that no witness has corroborated Strieber's resurrected claim that he was "definitely there" would.

Another—among legion—of Strieber's completely unbelievable claims is that during an urban book-signing of *Communion,* Little Gray Men dressed as Men In Black (in broad-brimmed hats and sunglasses, no less) came up and spoke to him. Why they would conduct a massive and covert nocturnal operation on everyone else, taking great pains (and succeeding) at leaving behind no concrete evidence of their presence except for marks on their abductees' bodies, but would show up at a public metro book-signing in broad daylight to talk with Whitley Strieber, is conveniently never pondered.

But in a 1993 Q&A in *UFO* magazine, Strieber really outdid himself: he claimed to have driven off the highway into another dimension with someone else's twelve-year-old in the car: "We go off the exit to the overpass. Suddenly, the boy screams. And he screams for a very good reason. Because we are all of a sudden in this vehicle—we're in another world. We're no longer on Route 17. We're no longer beside the shopping mall. Instead, we're on a long, almost totally empty concrete highway. Pristine. Beautiful, with thick woods all around it. With no shuddering, no feeling of change; just suddenly, that's where we are. He screams when he sees this change. And for fully 20, 30 seconds, we're yelling back [*sic*] and trying to figure out where we are. We come to an exit on the highway, I begin to realize something terrible has happened. We slow down. The boy tries to jump out of the car, and I grab him. I stop the car and calm him down. I tell him we're going to find our way back ... [The houses] look utterly unlike houses I've ever seen in this world. And yet we are there, the two of us, in a jeep. And what's most appalling, and what makes me sick to my stomach with fear, is that I have another man's child with me. How am I going to get this child back out? There's never a question as to whether or not we're seeing the real world. It is entirely indistinguishable [sic] from the real world. We both see it independently. We both initiated our observing it independently. I make a couple of other turns, just at random. What I was actually trying to do was find the highway again." This event theoretically having taken place for only twenty to thirty seconds, Strieber then claimed to have found his way back onto the highway, twenty miles from where he got off: "The boy of course immediately tells his father the whole story. They spend the rest of the afternoon searching for this mysterious road, and they never have found it. About two weeks later I go back and look for it. Alone, I might add. I never find it. We've never seen it again. That's the sort of thing that happens to me fairly frequently. That's what I live with." Not only has no other abductee made such outrageous claims, but neither, frankly, has anyone else. The entire story is utterly absurd, not to mention ridiculously histrionic.

Strieber would not be the first fraud to become wealthy off a false and sensationalized story, the Lutz family prior to him having done exactly that with *The Amityville Horror* in the late 1970s (see Chapter 2). Like *Communion*, the Lutzes' story had two versions, the book and the movie, which were not alike—meaning that one could buy the "true story" of their choice. Since Strieber wrote his own screenplay for *Communion* (independently produced, partly by Strieber himself, in 1989), it is impossible to reconcile his later protestations with events enacted in the film. Strieber had told Hopkins, months before their final falling-out, that at one point he had stocked his houses with guns and installed burglar alarms to defend himself against right-wing terrorists threatening to kidnap his son. Later, he said he had made the whole story up, because he was "frightened." Then, later still, he tearfully raved that the CIA was conspiring against him to keep *Communion* off the market. It was at that point that Hopkins decided he was dealing with "a disturbed man whose words I simply cannot trust." Despite Strieber's insistence that he had made up the guns and terrorists story, it appears in the film version of his book, to which he wrote the screenplay, graphically illustrating Hopkins' point. It is not incredible to assume that Strieber is an informed fraud, a cat set among the pigeons by interested parties to keep a close tab on abductees, not to mention researchers. He claims to receive a tremendous amount of mail annually from abductees, which would make him a valuable asset to anyone wanting to compile a list. Similarly, Shirley Maclaine's *Out on a Limb,* filmed as a T.V. miniseries in 1987, described as non-fiction a number of dubious UFO experiences, throwing in trance-channeling and reincarnation to boot. While not as blatantly suspicious, Maclaine's supposed "close encounters" could very easily be a latter-day contactee fraud funded by someone behind the scenes to make the entire flying saucer business appear crazy, in the same manner as George Adamski's claimed "Venusian" liaisons in the 1950s.

But there were still more educationally minded projects in the works, and the United States was not the only country with serious sci-fi on its mind. Japan, even if it executed it badly, was thinking very much along the same lines. So was Britain, from which some of the best UFOlogical movies and T.V. series came, and which logically should be our next stop on the road of investigation.

7

Importations
and Degradations

The British Broadcasting Corporation (BBC) in Britain was involved in educational sci-fi more than ten years before the States, which is no surprise since they were also the first to do realistic war dramas about the 1940s while Americans were still making John Wayne shoot-em-ups. 20th Century Fox's *Twelve O'Clock High* was made in 1949, more realistic than most, but paling in comparison with the much-better British production of Ealing's *The Cruel Sea* in 1953. It was the exception, however, and not the rule. Serious portrayals of UFOs nearly made it faster to the cinema and television than realistic war dramas.

One of the most telling "timely coincidences" involving entertainment media and UFO phenomena occurred in 1962 on Britain's popular children's sci-fi marionette show, *Fireball XL5*. The episode "Robert to the Rescue" featured short bald alien abductors with huge craniums, who "switched off" anyone not connected to their immediate business and used will suppression and memory blocks against their targets. Betty and Barney Hill's abduction occurred around the same time, and had not yet been reported. As John Spencer says in *The UFO Encyclopedia*, "Due to the timing of the two events, neither the Hills nor the programme producers could have derived their material from each other, which suggests that the origins of both came from an unidentified common source. At its simplest level, this suggests that the interplay of science fiction and UFO reports is more complex than has been accepted so far."

In 1952, the first of Nigel Kneale's four Quatermass serials was aired on British television. Biographical material on Kneale is sketchy and difficult to come by, except for revealing that (like Joseph Stefano and Leslie Stevens) he was an actor turned playwright. The question of his having had military connections is less important in Britain than it would be in the States—the BBC is government-owned, and if anyone high-up enough wanted good science-fictional space dramas, they would find them. Kneale's scripts certainly fit that bill. Also, virtually everyone at that time on both sides of the Atlantic had been in the war in one way or another. In addition, American money was unquestionably funding British films at that time as the result of a 1948 repealed tax on the import of foreign movies that left the Brits at the mercy of Hollywood. Whatever other elements may have been in his background, Kneale was at least connected to one of the United Kingdom's institutions, the Royal Academy of Dramatic Arts. He specialized in fantasy stories and won the Somerset Maugham Literary Prize in 1950 at the age of 28.

The first of Kneale's scripts was *The Quatermass Experiment,* a pre-*The Fly* story of a man's disintegration begun by a high-tech source. The first astronauts into space crash-land in Britain, but only one of the three on the mission is found to be in the capsule. The other two turn out to have been digested by some proto-Andromeda Strain space spores, and converted into cellular matter which the surviving catatonic astronaut has assimilated. Himself also infected, the astronaut degenerates into a fungal creature which manages to be destroyed before it can germinate and threaten our world. Despite the dreadful loss and setback, government rocket scientist Bernard Quatermass, whose project the failed space mission was, immediately begins his second attempt, having learned from his first failure. Handled intelligently and sensitively, the story was a big hit with viewers, making a sequel inevitable.

In 1955, *Quatermass II* was televised. The forerunner of Leslie Stevens' "Production and Decay of Strange Particles," it centered on

Yulla Salontsena as *Aelita* (Mezhrobpom, 1924), the Queen of Mars. Based on the Tolstoy novel written three years prior, Aelita was the first popular presentation connecting Mars with Atlantis and robots, a theme that would later recur in pulp fiction with increasing frequency. The same year Jacob Protozanov directed this movie in the new Soviet Union, the U.S. Signal Corps reported receiving intelligent signals from the Red Planet, described as repeating voice transmissions of from one to four syllables, which were given to master cryptologist William Friedman to decode. No record survives as to whether Friedman succeeded—his office at the Virginia Military Institute was cleaned out after his death by the National Security Agency. Russia has lost numerous probes to Mars, the last two containing weaponry and plutonium, one photographing a mammoth UFO before its disappearance. (Courtesy *Outré* magazine.)

Victorian "penny-dreadful" cover fancifully depicts the historical "Springheel Jack," an agile, leaping flyer and probable UFO occupant who terrorized England between 1837 and 1877 and may have been the figure behind a later rash of similar activity in the United States. Tim Burton's *Batman* (Warner Bros., 1989) similarly depicted the title character in comical fashion early in the film. Burton's Batman was presented as an historically accurate rendition of the frightening UFO occupant called "Mothman" in 1966–67 Ohio/West Virginia, who in fact derived his nickname via the press from 20th Century Fox's then-popular *Batman* T.V. series.

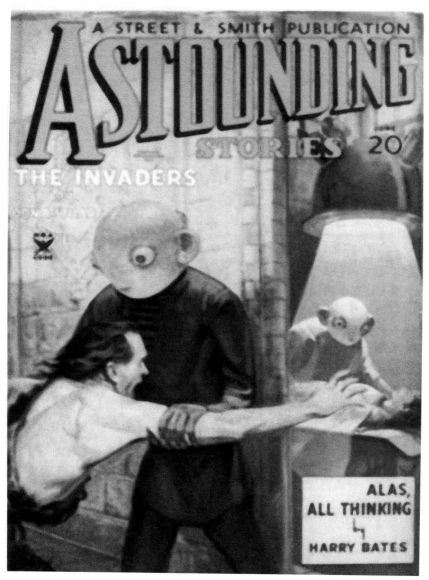

June 1935 pulp cover depicting abductor "aliens" almost identical to UFO Grays. The illustration is entirely different from the aliens described in the story. "Don A. Stuart" was the pen-name of prolific sci-fi author and editor John W. Campbell, Jr., who launched many other authors' careers and also wrote the story from which RKO's 1951 classic film *The Thing from Another World* was made. The other author listed on the cover, Harry Bates, wrote the story that was the basis for 20th Century Fox's *The Day the Earth Stood Still* the same year. Both stories were altered in production at the executive level to more closely match actual UFO-logical facts.

"I had no idea ..."

Orson Welles' "innocent" pose on Halloween of 1938, the night after his *The War of the Worlds* broadcast terrified listeners across America with a supposed Martian invasion, looks as disingenuous sixty years later as it did when first published. Welles prided himself on a lifelong career of open fraud and deceit. Prior to the infamous radio show, Welles spent time at Grover's Mill, New Jersey, where the principal action of the story was located, and deliberately did everything he could to circumvent CBS and make the broadcast sound like a real occurrence. An avid campaigner for FDR's controversial fourth-term re-election, Welles was in an ideal position to have performed governmental favors. (Wide World Photos.)

Herbert George Wells (1866–1946), visionary author of *The War of the Worlds* in 1898, demanded a retraction from CBS after the Orson Welles Halloween Eve dramatization. Contrary to public opinion, he was not at all amused, and had his attorney threaten legal action. *(New York Daily News.)*

Wells' *The War of the Worlds* was written as the author's answer to the "mystery airship" of 1896–97 America. While convalescing in a London hospital Wells examined a box of clippings on the phenomenon from newspapers across the Atlantic, such as this one from the November 1896 *San Francisco Call*. The ship's superior attributes and the proximity of the planet Mars during the time of its appearance led Wells to the conclusion that the mysterious craft was a Martian spaceship.

Howard Phillips Lovecraft (1890–1937), the most influential of the 1930s pulp-horror writers. Lovecraft created an entire cycle of stories about ancient space-gods who built megalithic cities and engineered the human race in antiquity, occasionally interbreeding with them in later millennia to produce hybrids in preparation for their eventual return. His early journals record experiences that sound remarkably like what are now recognized as UFO abduction experiences.

Brilliant Yugoslavian inventor Nikola Tesla (1856–1943), shown in *The World Today*'s graphic illustration of his boast that he could split the world in two with mechanical resonance. In 1894, Tesla prophesied "telautomata" and guided missiles. Before the turn of the century he demonstrated a small radio-controlled submersible robot ship to the U.S. Navy, also advertising his belief that he could achieve anti-gravity by ancient principles. In 1901, Tesla told the *Colorado Springs Gazette* he had received intelligent signals from the planet Mars. After Tesla's death, many of his papers were secretly confiscated by the U.S. government, some of which went to Wright (-Patterson) Army Air Field, where the Roswell crash remains ended up not long after.

Ex-RAF Wing Commander Dennis Wheatley, the first recruit into Britain's most elite WWII Counterintelligence Corps, nicknamed (for no reason ever disclosed) "the Martians." Authoring at least one novel about the finding of Atlantis, Wheatley also wrote a great many historical novels about Black Magic and government spies, many involving the Nazis, which he claimed were far more real than his readers would believe.

Pulp science-fiction editor Ray Palmer, and a page from one of his numerous probable misinformational Underworld "contactee" stories. Palmer was the nexus of much UFO disinformational activity, involving famous flying saucer sighter Kenneth Arnold in what Project Blue Book head Capt. Edward J. Ruppelt called "the dirtiest hoax in [UFO] history" after having first helped him publicize his story. One of Palmer's associates was Fred L. Crisman, who told stories of fighting abductor-robots from Atlantis, and later involved himself in destabilizing Jim Garrison's JFK murder investigation. From David Hatcher Childress: *Lost Cities of China, Central Asia and India,* Adventures Unlimited Press, Stelle, Illinois, 1985. (Courtesy Adventures Unlimited Press and David Hatcher Childress.)

Above: One of the Hollow Earth features that appeared in *Amazing Stories* in May 1946, a magazine edited by Ray Palmer (*right*)

The notorious humorist, occultist, and spy, Aleister Crowley (1875–1947), in full Masonic regalia circa 1916. Crowley's wife reportedly trance-channeled the Egyptian god Ra-Harakhte (the Sphinx/Mars) in 1904 Cairo. Crowley was so unnerved by the purported contact that he locked his notes on the experience away for five years before returning to them. The encounter inspired Crowley's quasi-Masonic pseudo-cult of Thelema, which ultimately enmeshed such government figures as Cal Tech Jet Propulsion Lab founder Jack Parsons and Dianetics creator L. Ron Hubbard.

Exhibit 666 at Cairo's Boulak Museum, the "Stele of Revealing," depicts Ra-Harakhte. The coincidence of the exhibit's number with that of the "Great Beast" of the Bible convinced Crowley his contact had been genuine. Crowley's encounter may have inspired the first made-for-T.V. horror movie, *Fear No Evil* (Universal, 1969), in which the red demon "Ra-kashi" is hypnotically summoned by a group of government-level physicists from a land of perfectly symmetrical arches in red, white, and black (the colors of Atlantis). The use of these colors demonstrates occult awareness on the film's production level, such as the deliberate placement of a red coat beneath the "devil's bride's" white headdress, which signifies the ancient concept of "white above, red below." The movie also features accurate UFO-logical elements, such as hypnotic regression to determine the reality of nocturnal sex-abductions, and unidentified body markings following the experiences.

Ian Lancaster Fleming (1908–1964) in Istanbul before the Orient Express, on the set of the 1964 United Artists film of his 1957 James Bond adventure, *From Russia, With Love.* According to investigative authors Richard Deacon, Anthony Masters, and Peter Levenda, Fleming was involved with notorious self-styled warlock Aleister Crowley and other notables of the British Secret Service in the plot that caused Deputy Führer Rudolf Hess to defect to England in May of 1941. Fleming's Naval Intelligence colleagues attest to his having utilized government secrets in his plots. UFO facts appear in at least two of his novels, *Doctor No* (1958) and *On Her Majesty's Secret Service* (1963), filmed by United Artists in 1962 and 1969, respectively. Doctor No's appearance and activities match those of a UFO Gray, toppling government missiles and conducting nocturnal medical examinations and torture tests on paralyzed and unconscious subjects. The super-powerful criminal organization, SPECTRE, in *Secret Service,* occupies a round hideaway accessible only by private aircraft, where subjects are hypnotically brainwashed to become future saboteurs. Fleming also named SPECTRE's ship in *Thunderball* (1961, United Artists film 1965) the *Disco Volante*—the "Flying Saucer." United Artists has a long history of producing factually correct UFO-oriented films and T.V. shows. *(Wide World.)*

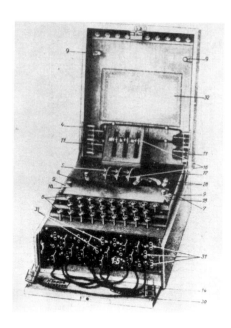

"Enigma," the cypher-machine that enabled the Allies to crack Germany's secret code, a project designated ULTRA. Fleming was one of the top agents involved in ULTRA, both in England and the secondary decoding unit in Jamaica. The top-secret Enigma machine was not declassified until 1975, so Fleming's use of such a machine which he called "Spektor" ("Lektor" in the film version) in *From Russia, With Love*, decades before its knowledge was made public, is standing proof that the Intelligence community endorses the dissemination of top-secret material through seemingly trivial entertainment sources. (Photograph by David Kahn.)

UFO Grays abduct the title character to the Underworld in Jean Cocteau's *Orphée* (France, 1949). Cocteau is believed by several researchers to have been a Grand Master at the Masonic Priéuré de Sion.

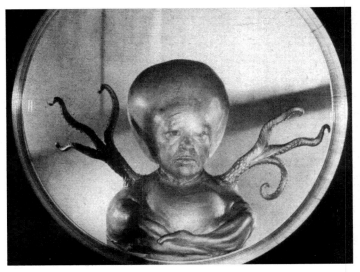

Gray-looking supreme leader of William Cameron Menzies' *Invaders from Mars* (20th Century Fox, 1953), described as "mankind, evolved to its ultimate intelligence." (Martian design by Anatole Robbins.) (Wade Williams Productions.)

Little Jimmy Hunt threatened by one of the *Invaders From Mars* (20th Cetury Fox, 1953). The robotic Gray-looking Martians perform nocturnal abductions and place implants in their victims for future mind-control. Their subjects commit sabotage and murder before the Martians are destroyed by the military. (Wade Williams Productions.)

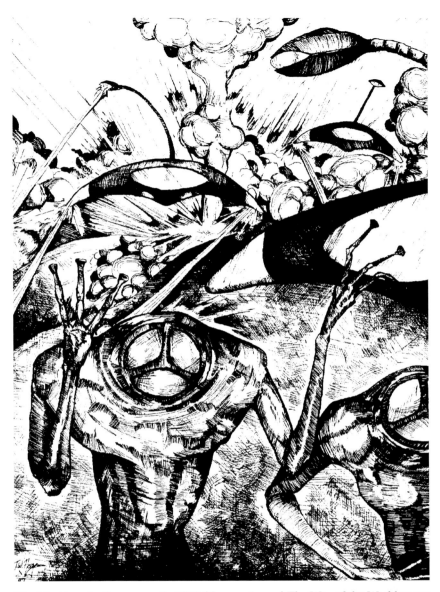

The Martians in Paramount's 1953 film version of *The War of the Worlds* were completely different from those in H. G. Wells' novel, featuring a three-lobed "eye" (equating to three antennae that are sometimes reported on actual UFO occupants) as well as the same odd arm arrangement and suction cup-tipped fingers reported on the Roswell saucer occupants in 1947. The Martian war machines, made to resemble the flying saucers reported by Kenneth Arnold mere days before the Roswell crash, also differed from Wells'. (Sketch by Tim Hogan.)

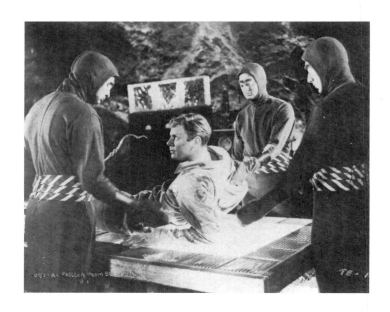

Gray-looking *Killers from Space* (RKO, 1954) topple Peter Graves' military plane from the sky, perform surgery on him in a limbo setting, and hypnotize him into performing an act of sabotage. (Alien design by Harry Thomas.) (Courtesy RKO.)

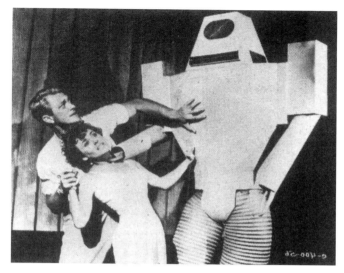

The rights to Herman Cohen's *Target Earth* (Allied Artists, 1954) were purchased before the ink was dry on the Robertson Panel recommendation to use Hollywood for UFO disinformation. The film was altered from its source material to include robots and sonic weaponry. Cohen had just finished a four-year stint with the Marines when he made the movie. Pictured are stars Richard Denning and Kathleen Crowley. (Herman Cohen Productions.)

George Nader and Claudia Barrett in the grip of director Phil Tucker's absurd *Robot Monster* (Astor, 1953). Tucker refused to discuss his connection to Ed Wood—whose *Plan 9 from Outer Space* he helped edit—with Wood biographer Rudolph Grey. (Wade Williams Productions.)

Phil Tucker (left) on the set of *The Cape Canaveral Monsters* (CCM, 1960), which he wrote and directed, pictured here with stars Jason Johnson and Katharine Victor. The film, about aliens utilizing bulletproof zombies to help them topple space shots, contained then-unknown accurate UFO abduction information. (Courtesy *Filmfax*.)

Ed Wood's famous turkey, *Plan 9 from Outer Space* (DCA, made 1956, released 1959) may have been inspired. Wood was a patriotic ex-Marine with FBI secret clearance, who claimed to have worked Intelligence in the service. He wrote other scripts the same year that were perfectly coherent, unlike *Plan 9*. Pictured center on the world's cheapest saucer set is character actor Tor Johnson as a bald, radio-controlled abductor, with aliens (l–r) Dudley Manlove, John "Bunny" Breckenridge, and Joanna Lee. (Wade Williams Productions.)

The 3-D *Cat-Women of the Moon* (Astor, 1953). Producer Al Zimbalist gave the world more 3-D Moon-invaders the same year in *Robot Monster*. Not content to make the same bad movie once, Astor remade *Cat-Women* six years later as *Missile to the Moon* (below), featuring more sex-starved space-babes menaced by such nasties as giant lunar spiders. (Wade Williams Productions.)

Joseph Tomalty is led on a tour of decadently aristocratic leather-clad sex-abductor Patricia Laffan's saucer, in the Danziger Brothers' *Devil Girl from Mars* (Spartan, 1954). "Devil Girl" Laffan displays her powerful robot to intimidate fearful Earthmen. The movie contains numerous accurate UFOlogical elements, including child-abductions, hypnotic mind control and amnesia, programming for sabotage, and interplanetary crossbreeding. (Wade Williams Productions.)

Corman wet his UFOlogical feet executive-producing *The Beast With 1,000,000 Eyes* (A.R.C., 1955). The title bug-eyed, antennaed, bald-headed creature's "million eyes" were its mind-controlled Earth subjects. (Monster by Paul Blaisdell.) Artwork © Orion Pictures Corporation.

One of Roger Corman's technical advisors, on more than one film, was none other than William Joseph Bryan, Jr., CIA MK-ULTRA expert and head of the U.S. Air Force's "brainwashing" section during the Korean War. Here he is shown (at left) instructing star Basil Rathbone on the set of Corman's drive-in Poe flick, *Tales of Terror* (AIP, 1962). The same year, Bryan was advisor for United Artists' masterpiece on hypnotic mind-control and assassination, *The Manchurian Candidate*. (Artwork © Orion Pictures Corporation.)

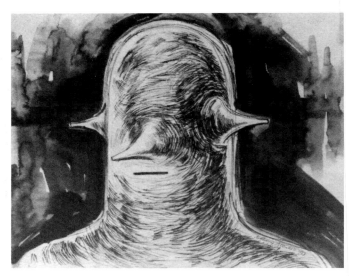

Robots with three antennae have often been reported on UFOs. Above is a close-up detail of the head arrangement on one variety of robot which abducted two shipyard workers in 1973 Mississippi. (Ralph and Judy Blum, *Beyond Earth,* New York: Bantam Books, 1974.) Below, robotic-looking occupants with three "eyes" witnessed in Voronezh, Russia, in 1989. (Jacques Vallee, *Revelations,* New York: Random House, 1991.)

Dr. Who and the Daleks (Amicus/Continental, 1965), the first of two movies derived from the BBC's phenomenally popular sci-fi series (it ran nearly thirty consecutive years beginning the day after the JFK assassination), owed much to Nigel Kneale's equally popular and UFOlogically accurate BBC serials of the 1950s. Archenemies of the friendly alien Doctor, the Daleks were tyrannical robotic survivors from

another planet's long-forgotten nuclear holocaust, and bore a remarkable resemblance to actual robotic UFO entities reported in the Soviet Union in 1989. Pictured in this lobby card is famous Hammer horror actor Peter Cushing as the Doctor, with (l–r) Roberta Tovey and Jennie Linden. (UGC UK, Ltd.)

Martian from *The Angry Red Planet* (AIP, 1959), warns mankind: "Do as you will to your own and your planet but . . . do not return to Mars . . . unbidden." Career counterintelligence agent Ib Melchior wrote the script. (Monster by Paul Blaisdell.) (Artwork © Orion Pictures Corporation.)

The Astounding She-Monster (AIP, 1958) was one of the first UFO movies to utilize the overtly cheapening technique of excessive voice-over narration combined with live action. The comical end result was best utilized in *The Giant Claw* (Columbia, 1957) and *The Creeping Terror* (Crown International, 1964), the latter of which beats even *Plan 9 from Outer Space* for worst movie ever made. (Wade Williams Productions.)

One-sheet for *Kronos* (20th Century Fox, 1957), about an alien robot utilizing a brain-implanted Defense Department scientist to locate and pillage all of Earth's electrical and atomic energy. (Wade Williams Productions.)

Flight to Mars (above: Monogram, 1951) and *Rocketship X-M* (Lippert, 1950) featured subterranean and nuclear-devastated Martian civilizations, the former
including interbreeding implications between Martians and Earthmen. (Wade
Williams Productions.)

The Brain from Planet Arous (Howco International, 1958), about a criminal mind-controlling alien intelligence sabotaging Earth's defenses for the purpose of eventual conquest, has been a claimed inspiration for Stephen King and other horror writers. (Wade Williams Productions.)

Stunt man Gil Perkins as the *Teenage Monster* (a.k.a. *Meteor Monster*, Howco International, 1958), a cosmically infected child who grows up to abduct a woman to the hills. Similar elements appeared seven years later in AIP's *Die, Monster, Die!* *Teenage Monster* was the companion release of *The Brain from Planet Arous*. (Courtesy Paul and Donna Parla, Wade Williams Productions.)

Above and next page: *The Crawling Eye* (DCA/Eros, 1958), a mind-controlling space invader studied and combated by a secret U.N. team. The movie is overall one of the best of its type. DCA also released Ed Wood's *Plan 9 from Outer Space,* among many other UFOlogical titles. (Wade Williams Productions.)

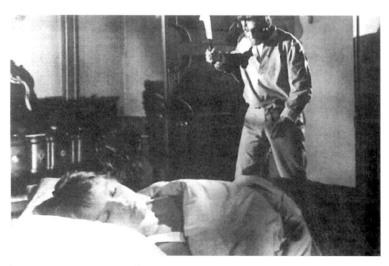

Psychic spy Janet Munro stalked by "Crawling Eye"-controlled assassin Andrew Faulds. The U.S. government has trained psychic agents in real life to study Mars and UFOs, purportedly including internationally renowned Department of Defense astrophysicist/UFOlogist Jacques Vallee and *Apollo 11* lunar landing site selector Dr. Farouk El Baz. (Wade Williams Productions.)

This typical 1962 AIP double-bill—like *I Was A Teenage Werewolf* and *Invasion of the Saucer Men,* five years before—began with a nightmarish mind-control story, and followed with ludicrous flying saucers combated by an impotent Air Force. (Artwork © Orion Pictures Corporation.)

CORPUS EARTHLING

35¢

SHE WAS
MARKED AS
THE FIRST
VICTIM OF
THE MARTIAN
INVADER

Louis Charbonneau

ZB-40 A ZENITH ORIGINAL

Louis Charbonneau's *Corpus Earthling* (New York: Zenith, 1960) concerned an invasion of Earth by silicon creatures from Mars who target for murder a telepathic "listener" to their covert plans. The novel predicted disposable butane lighters and automobile speed-controls. It was filmed as *The Outer Limits'* (United Artists/Daystar/Villa di Stefano Productions) scariest episode in 1963, ironically airing the same week President Kennedy was assassinated. The episode made an alteration bringing it closer to UFOlogical facts, making the "listener's" ability to hear the invaders the result of an implant in his skull. (Author's collection.)

Dick Tracy creator Chester Gould owed his entire career to newspaper magnate (and politically active Hearst rival) Captain Joseph Medill Patterson. Beginning a month after the Kennedy assassination, Gould introduced "Moon Maid," who ultimately married Tracy's son and produced a hybrid child in the interest of peace between the Moon Men and the people of Earth. Gould believed his "Moon Period" stories would earn him a prophetic rank equal to Jules Verne, and according to his biographer, Jay Maeder, late in his life "hint[ed] darkly that he was sure NASA regarded him as a meddling whistleblower." (© Tribune Media Services, Inc. All Rights Reserved. Reprinted with Permission.)

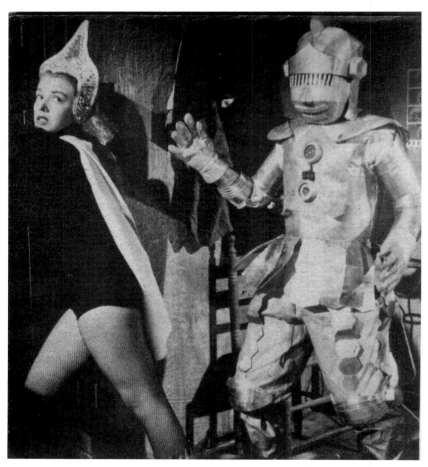

U.S. film companies funded a great many very bad—and largely accurate—foreign UFO movies throughout the 1950s and '60s. This typical Mexican cheapie, *Platillos Voladores* ("Flying Saucers"), is so obscure that biographical information on it has not been located. (Author's collection.)

The Avengers (ITV/ABC, 1961–69) featured many UFOlogical menaces. Dame Diana Rigg, in her earliest role as Mrs. Emma Peel, dodges the onslaught of "The Cybernauts" (1965), robot assassins identical to UFO Grays. Though dubbed "nauts," these mechanical men neither pilot nor sail any sort of craft in the story. Rigg's recent title may be the result of service to Queen and Country, her familial background similar to others in Intelligence. (UGC UK, Ltd.)

Patrick Macnee as dapper John Steed unmasks a mind-controlling robot ring-leader in "How to Succeed . . . At Murder" (1965). Macnee's connections to the Intelligence world are no secret: he is an Etonian blue-blood who was in British Naval Intelligence in WWII. (UGC UK, Ltd.)

Vincent Price (1911–1993) as *The Abominable Dr. Phibes* (AIP, 1971). The undead skull-faced Underworld character (he wears a human mask) is a virtual personification of the UFO Intelligence, an Egyptologist with advanced "knowledge of music and acoustics" who employs supernaturally summoned human accomplices and Gray-looking robots. Phibes' activities include bedroom visitations, exsanguinating unresisting animals, toppling airplanes out of the sky, and abducting and surgically implanting children. A member of Orson Welles' Mercury Theatre in 1938, Price himself had the background and credentials to be CIA. His close friends and acquaintants involved in UFOlogical projects included Diana Rigg and directors Roger Corman and Tim Burton. (Artwork © Orion Pictures Corporation.)

Two AIP movies based on H. P. Lovecraft stories: Above, Vincent Price as an amnesiac dual-personality (a role he would often play) breeding alien hybrids off of wife Debra Paget, in *The Haunted Palace* (AIP, 1963); below, cosmically infected Boris Karloff inexplicably mutates into a metallic silver, bald monster in *Die, Monster, Die!* (AIP, 1965). (Artwork © Orion Pictures Corporation.)

First time in paperback

The prophetic novel of a profane
and inhuman love

DEMON SEED
BY DEAN R. KOONTZ

N7190 ★ 95¢ ★ A BANTAM BOOK

Dean R. Koontz's *Demon Seed* (Bantam, New York, 1973) concerned the robot-abduction of a woman in order to study human beings and create a child. It was filmed and expensively hyped by MGM in 1977, concurrent with *Close Encounters of the Third Kind* (Columbia EMI) and *Star Wars* (20th Century Fox), probably as part of a proposed UFO "educational project" by President Jimmy Carter. Koontz's novels frequently contain robot threats, sex-abductions, secret military projects, mind-control, aliens, bedroom visitations, amnesia, and ancient civilizations. [From *Demon Seed* (JACKET COVER) by D. R. Koontz. Copyright. Used by permission of Bantam Books, a division of Bantam Doubleday Dell Publishing Group, Inc.]

invasion by small spaceships first mistaken for meteorites, *à la* Project Twinkle. The ships contain implants which explode their way into nosy passers-by, leaving a distinctive mark as they do. The "abductees" become their own little zombie-society, infiltrating the highest walks of government, and they appropriate a national industrial site for the ostensible purpose of creating a new food hybrid, but which is actually for the development of an alien life form. The invading alien life form has its home base on a concealed but detectable space station, which is destroyed by Quatermass' ground-to-air nuclear missiles, ending the threat.

1959 saw the best and most remarkable, especially as pertains to this study, entry in the series: *Quatermass and the Pit.* London workers on an underground railway unearth human skeletons, causing the area to be cordoned off for anthropologists. The bones are human, and five million years old—giving the anthropologists great excitement and controversy, since erect man should not be so old. But the find has only just begun: something else is in the immediate vicinity, first thought to be an unexploded V-weapon left over from the war, but turning out instead to be a spaceship. Its metal is completely unlike Earth metal, smooth as glass despite its travel and crash, harder than diamond and so cold to the touch that it causes frostbite. The ship is above the intact human skeletons and has not damaged them, meaning it came to rest there at the same time. Strangely, Quatermass notices, the ship has a Pentacle on it, a sign long attached to the occult, and the entire area is famous as a demon-haunt. The region's history is replete with ghostly and demonic apparitions, as well as numerous diabolical phenomena, and one hardened policeman is so afraid of experiences he had there as a child that he won't even show Quatermass around. It is even called "Hob's Lane"—"Hob" being an old familiar name for the devil.

After several attempts to breach the craft's surface fail, it hums to life and opens itself, revealing a hollow interior carrying three long-dead arthropods (insects) looking like grasshoppers with horny antennae, which rapidly decompose. They bear a resemblance to popular images of demons and gargoyles (and, though of course not mentioned at that time, to many UFO occupants). "I think these may be old friends we haven't seen in a while," Quatermass ruminates. "Your imagination's running wild!" a hardcore military colonel upbraids him, to which he responds simply, "Yes. Isn't yours?" "Where do you suppose they came from?" one of the government team asks. "I wonder," Quatermass muses. "A word practically worn out before anything turned up to claim it . . . could we be looking at a Martian . . . ?" The Home Secretary is livid, especially when further research indicates that the ape-man specimens found at the same site had been transported there by the alien craft, and were genetically altered. "You realize what you're saying? That the human race owes its existence to—to—the intervention of *insects!*" "As far as anyone's concerned," Quatermass' assistant confirms, "we're the Martians, now." Unable to handle the implications, and certain the public will be equally hesitant, the government concocts a story that the ship was a propaganda weapon of the Germans to deflate public interest, and plans a press exhibition to end the matter.

But the ship is far from dead. Earlier, when no instrumentation was found aboard, a team member asks how it could have flown. "I don't know . . . unless the ship itself did part of the thinking," Quatermass answers, as good an answer as any for saying that it is automated. The ship turns out to have a dormant energy force in it, which creates terrifying poltergeist phenomena about it—levitation of objects, forceful waves of sound, hallucinations and the like—to anyone unfortunate enough to be in its proximity at the wrong time. One bedeviled late-night worker runs to a church for refuge, the pastor having seen the phenomena at work around him. When Quatermass catches up to the poor fellow and suggests that dormant psychic forces were at work in his own mind, the pastor angrily accuses him of trying to explain away the supernatural. "On the contrary," Quatermass assures him. "I agree with you. What has been uncovered is evil. It's as anciently diabolic as anything ever recorded."

Further incidents occur, and by questioning the victims, Quatermass realizes that what is being perceived is a message left in the hull of the ship to trigger "the Wild Hunt," an early ethnic purge. The Martians, having created the human race in a number of successive biologic interventions, occasionally thinned out the herd of their previous inferior models by programming the new ones to destroy the old. Realizing the implications, Quatermass warns the government to shut down their press conference and cordon off the ship until they can figure out a way to destroy it. They ignore him, the ship comes alive, and almost all of London becomes possessed by the titanic force that emanates from it. It projects an image of its occupants towering across the sky, and legions of zombiefied human beings bash to death everyone who is not similarly possessed. Even Quatermass is affected, snapped-to by a friend. "I—I wanted to kill you. And I would have done. Because you're—different. I could feel that—you weren't—one of us. You had to be destroyed. Destroyed!" His friend realizes the destructive force is located in the projected image, and grounds the projection out with a mass of metal, ending the siege and the story.

Kneale's use of the Wild Hunt is extremely interesting. It was not the first or last time he would connect UFO or supernatural occurrences to ancient customs and folklore. His adaptation of Hammer/20th Century Fox's *The Devil's Own*, a star vehicle for Joan Fontaine in 1966, was a sort of supernatural "Bad Day at Black Rock," about an entire town of Cernunnos-worshipping witches who still practice human sacrifice, a theme later exploited more fully by Anthony Shaffer's *The Wicker Man* (Warner Bros., 1972). The Wild Hunt, as already discussed, is historically attached to more or less exactly what Kneale depicted: an elimination of the unwary, unfit, or unwise.

Kneale's prolific career was almost always connected to UFO elements. He was co-writer of the excellent 1964 Warner Bros. film adaptation of H. G. Wells' *First Men in the Moon*, with some clever alterations from its source material. One of these, updating it, was to begin and end the story with a United Nations team setting foot on the Moon for the first time, only to find that human beings had been there before them—which, if the Blair Cuspids and other monumental evidences are accepted as proof, they were. The former visitants in the story are Victorian adventurers with an early anti-gravity discovery of their own, who find a race living beneath the Moon's surface, the insectoid Selenites. These creatures abduct, study, and interrogate them in ways now recognized as common to those reported by actual abductees but unknown to anyone outside a small cadre of government investigators at the time, if to anyone at all.

In 1957, one of his original BBC teleplays (1954's *The Creature*), not about UFOs but containing a wealth of abduction elements connected with the phenomenon, was filmed as Hammer/20th Century Fox's *The Abominable Snowman of the Himalayas.* In it, a high-minded botanist and a self-interested showman climb the famous mountains, starting from a Tibetan monastery, in search of the famous title creature. The head lama tries to discourage them, to no avail, asking the botanist, "Why do you want to find this creature?" and in time the expedition ends up killing a yeti. Its friends are not pleased, and the next thing the team knows, they are dying one by one, not from any obvious outward enemy, but instead from their own inner mind-projections as they go mad. One man goes into a rapture and walks off the edge of a cliff thinking he has found God, another dies of his own fear, a third's conscience troubles him until he triggers an avalanche which buries him alive. Only the botanist is perceptive enough to figure out what is going on, but all his warnings are too late: the yeti are not an inferior ancestor, but a superior case of parallel development, living both by choice and nature away from their warlike cousin, man. They have highly developed psyches and use them to project hallucinations which turn any aggressor's own impulses against himself. When only the botanist is left, the yeti approach him, and he finds himself gazing, face to face, into the eyes of a bizarre-looking humanoid . . . after which his mind goes completely blank, and he is found near the monastery and brought back there. "What did you find?" the lama asks him. "There is no yeti," the botanist replies, satisfying all who are listening, but we see in both men's eyes that they know the truth . . . and are wisely keeping the secret. It becomes perfectly apparent that the monks at the monastery have always known about their yeti cousins and live in harmony with them.

Kneale was basing his script on the same legends of Shambhala or Agartha that had inspired the British in the middle of the last century and so mobilized the Nazis in this one. His yeti are identical in all ways save appearance with the attributes of the Great White Brotherhood. Even taking this into account, there are elements in the story so close to actual UFO abductions that they are difficult to account for, especially coming from the mid-1950s. One of the characters in the expedition acts exactly like an abductee. He says that he came on the trip because of a previous one he made in which he was sure something communicated with him, which frightened him but from which he couldn't keep himself away. He felt a religious communion with whatever the thing was. Whenever the yeti are around the camp, he goes into a deep hypnotic trance for no understandable reason, and the yeti appear in his presence with no visible fear on his part or later memory of it. Whether there is any significance to the fact or not, the first Wolfman movie, Universal's *The Werewolf of London,* was filmed in 1935 and centered on an inciting incident in Tibet, where legendary flowers that blossom only with the full moon produce catastrophic physiological effects in anyone unfortunate enough to encounter them. This would have been exactly in the middle of the Ahenenerbe's secret two-year mission to that country, preceding their later official one of 1938–39.

Among Kneale's other works was a serialized BBC dramatization of George Orwell's *1984* that was very well received, and 1961's *The Day the Earth Caught Fire* (Universal), a subdued adult story of the world's end caused by a pole shift resulting from nuclear testing. He showed remarkable prescience in another speculative teleplay in *The Year of the Sex Olympics* in 1969, predicting a future in which "high-drive" personalities take over the entire media and corporate marketplace, keeping the lower-drive proletariat subjugated and pacified by T.V., and 1963's *The Road,* showing a future devastated by the inability of mechanized utopian rationalists to understand the implications of their own technology. It may be deduced that Kneale was also offered the opportunity to script at least one of Ray Harryhausen's stop-motion animation ancient-hero epic films, by a passing comment he made in a *Filmfax* interview. Harryhausen's movies were not being discussed, and Kneale brought them up out of the blue by way of saying he didn't much care for their viewpoint, without elaborating on exactly what he meant or why it had even occurred to him to mention the fact. Since he had done *First Men in the Moon,* also a Harryhausen picture, it is easy to assume that he had been offered one of these epics—which, like Kneale's other pictures, are UFOlogically interesting in light of the ancient technology connection. Columbia's *Jason and the Argonauts,* for a single example, features abduction of human beings to Olympus for private counsel and "programming," along with technologically animated statues.

On Christmas of 1972, the BBC broadcast a ninety-minute Kneale teleplay called *The Stone Tape.* The story was a high-tech haunted house tale, with similar elements to Richard Matheson's *The Legend of Hell House* that was filmed by AIP's James H. Nicholson the following year. Early in the story, a character from Ryan Electrics (the company investigating the haunted house) appears inexplicably dressed as a Martian. The technological ghost-hunters jokingly mock-sacrifice the Martian before embarking on their research. The scene has no obvious connection to the plot, though given the question of Kneale's other apparent items of accurate UFO foreknowledge, it is plainly worthy of note. The story has the ghost-hunters stripping away the top layer of ectoplasmic evil from the house with their fancy technology, only to discover that they have unleashed a more ancient underlying evil upon the world in its stead. Given Kneale's sentiments in *Quatermass and the Pit,* the suggestion that he was indicating a connection between that more ancient evil and the planet Mars in *The Stone Tape* becomes highly probable.

Kneale's last movie, uncredited (he had his name removed), was the undeservedly blasted *Halloween III: Season of the Witch* (Universal, 1983). Though it did suffer from the usual 1980s' excess and gore, and occasional poor directorial judgment, the story itself is quite interesting, especially for the purposes of this study. It centers on a maskmaker, toy and novelty manufacturer named Cochran (superbly played by Dan O'Herlihy) who is both a technological genius and a warlock. He has an army of gray-suited robot servants which carry out his abductions and little murders. "Convincing, aren't they?" he asks the hero who finally penetrates his layer. "The surprising thing is that the internal components were quite simple to produce, really. The outward features took much longer to perfect, but then, of course, in the end it's just another form of maskmaking." He has transported one of the standing stones from Stonehenge to his American factory hideout in southern California—"We had a *time,* getting it here! You wouldn't believe how we did it!"—and implants bits chipped from the stone in electronically equipped manufacturing buttons, set to trigger a lethal power when a signal is transmitted over the television. His plot? To murder as many millions of children as he possibly can. Why? Because "it's time, again," of course. ("In the end, we don't decide these things, you know—the planets do.") Witchcraft has returned, requiring human sacrifice, the time of technology on its way out. Curiously—in light of Kneale's apparent UFO foreknowledge—the gray-suited robots were director Tommy Lee Wallace's idea, not Kneale's, and their addition to the film was the primary reason Kneale wanted his name removed from the credits.

The Quatermass Conclusion, serialized for the BBC in 1979, ended the highly successful series with more of a whimper than a bang. The professor meets his end defeating the standing stones of Britain themselves, which turn out to be ancient energy convertors annihilating masses of mad religious cultists in a near-future, socially disintegrated England, turning them into food for returning aliens from millennia ago. Ancient astronaut theory was then in its heyday but rapidly faded from public consciousness in the ensuing political conservatism on both sides of the Atlantic that ruled for over a decade.

The other Quatermass serials were made into fairly good movies, especially the last, the first being *The Creeping Unknown* in 1956, followed by *Enemy from Space* the following year, and the last was filmed as *Five Million Years to Earth* a decade later, in 1967. The first two films starred Brian Donlevy as Quatermass, a great disappointment to Kneale since the portrayal not only made it clear that the Americans were in charge of his series, but also because Donlevy came off as a mere government stooge and a bully. This was an especially apt observation on Kneale's part, since Donlevy had appeared before in the first "docudrama" about the A-bomb from MGM, 1947's *Beginning or the End.* Considering the year and the studio in which it was made, it was almost certainly one of the CIA's first "educational" media projects. John Baxter's *Science Fiction in the Cinema* records the result as

"Hilarious . . . Donlevy strides about pointing at unseen installations and saying, 'Put the cyclotron over here!'" The entire film was nothing more than a promotional for the Cold War, pretending to seriously examine the moral implications of the Manhattan Project, but making the only man in opposition to thermonuclear devices for purposes of war a mere token who appears both weak and foolish. As a final confirmation that Kneale's work was most likely funded by Americans as part of the UFO educational program, it was United Artists—the producers of Leslie Stevens' *The Outer Limits*—that released the first Quatermass movie (the second was from Corinth and the last was a Hammer/20th Century Fox production).

In 1964, MGM released what could probably be considered the first educationally intended movie from the United States in ancient mythology/modern UFOlogy, *7 Faces of Dr. Lao,* based on Charles Finney's 1935 comic-episodic novel *The Circus of Dr. Lao.* The title character is an Oriental Hermes-figure (whose teaching aspects match those of today's UFO Intelligence), a traveling Chinaman with a circus full of mythological personages and creatures. These provide illumination, example, and instruction to the people of the towns they visit: a shrewish woman finds herself becoming more loving to her henpecked husband after being turned into stone by a gorgon she resembles; a spinster librarian discovers her own sexuality in an encounter with Pan; a sinister industrialist finds his face on that of a sly serpent that mocks him. The small Texas town Dr. Lao visits is on the verge of voting the industrialist's misrepresented and self-serving policies into law, which will end up enriching him and bankrupting the town. Lao, a wise watcher in the shadows who champions underdogs, rescues a beleaguered Indian from bigoted bullies by paralyzing the attackers and rendering them unconscious, and magically repairs the presses of the only newspaper in town publicizing the industrialist's lies after they have been smashed to keep the paper from printing the truth. As the finale of his circus, Lao enacts for the gathered townspeople the history of a mythical land called "Woldercan." Significantly, the sand of the area beneath the enactment becomes red as he performs.

"The Fall of the City," is what Lao calls his story. "It existed beyond the edge of the world, some years before the beginning of history," he narrates. "There are no records of Woldercan, no artifacts, no descendants of its people. In fact, there is no real proof that there ever was such a place. But it was as real as pain . . . It was a small city, a humble city, its people had little in the way of worldly goods . . . yet the Woldercanese were content, for in the goods of the spirit, they were rich. For them, it was enough to partake of Creation, and to give thanks to their God. Enough, and more. Then, one day, a stranger appeared in Woldercan, and he said to the people, 'Not enough! You are poor, when you could be rich! You eat of humble fare, when you could feast! You scratch at the ground, and the ground mocks you! You pray to your God, and He laughs at you! Fools! Begone from this blighted place! Fools! Fools!' And suddenly, the people were not content. They listened to the stranger and sold their souls for pieces of silver. Then, a fearful thing happened: the God of All Life looked down upon the people of Woldercan and was displeased, and he said, 'Treasures I have given thee beyond compare; yet thou didst spurn them. And for a handful of silver, sold thy souls.' And because He had been angered, God pointed His finger, and visited upon the city of Woldercan the greatest plague of all: *oblivion."*

Throughout, the townspeople have recognized themselves reflected in the inhabitants of Woldercan, with the evil stranger in the story shown as the deceiving industrialist. At the story's conclusion, they find themselves suddenly in the county courthouse instead of Dr. Lao's circus, suffering a collective "missing time" experience and unaware of how they got there. They vote down the industrialist's proposed plans, and even the industrialist—impressed by what he has seen of the fate of Woldercan—calls for a vote of thanks to Dr. Lao.

In the original novel, "Woldercan" is used for comic effect and does not match the particulars of the destruction of Atlantis, as does the movie. Novelist Charles Finney was hardly unaware of the connection, however. His glossary to the novel—as amusing as the vignettes which compose it—refers to the "Red, Black, and White People of Abalone," the name of the town where the story takes place. The "Woldercan" in his novel is described by him only in a footnote, as "a hieroglyph on a potsherd." He does include an ancient city of "Tu-jeng" in his story, which he describes as being entirely red: "But everything is a dead red, not the cool red of wine, nor the hot red of blood, nor the blood-red of hate." Screenwriter Charles Beaumont, mainstay of AIP and *The Twilight Zone,* adapted the novel and altered the Woldercan story to that of Atlantis. MGM was almost certainly aware of the fact, as the final destruction of Woldercan in the movie is a collected series of clips from their own studio's *Atlantis: The Lost Continent.* In addition to Beaumont, several production members of *The Outer Limits* were involved in *Dr. Lao's* production. MGM was also the studio that made possibly the first modern abduction movie, *The Wizard of Oz* in 1939, which was a remake of an earlier 1925 film that hewed closer to L. Frank Baum's original book. The more famous '39 version features such UFOlogically and mythologically intriguing features as red slippers serving as the talisman of transport from the Otherworld, a Tin Man companion, abductor "flying monkeys," and a Wicked Witch whose designated direction—like those of the evil Giants in worldwide myth—is that of the West.

Bizarre space humanoids became bang-up big business during the 1960s, such as the absurd U.S.-Japanese *The Green Slime*—another menace from a red planet—in 1969. Mind-controlling Martians and Moon-men became frequent cinematic enemies, almost invariably U.S.-funded through other countries, from as early as 1957's U.S.-Japanese *The Mysterians* and its '59 sequel, *Battle in Outer Space.* 1965 brought *Snow Devils* from Italy, a race of humanoid giants living in underground caves in polar climes. Former inhabitants of the icy planet Aytia, the Snow Devils are intent on freezing the Earth so they can live here rather than under the surface of their own war-devastated planet. The Aytians' base in our solar system is—like that of the *Blood Beast from Outer Space* the following year—inside Callisto, one of Jupiter's moons, which is dramatized as being both red and hollow. *War of the Planets* came from the same country in the same year, about hypnotic super-intelligences from Mars taking over Earthmen. MGM produced *Wild Wild Planet* in Italy that year, about a mad scientist with robots and female assistants in tight leather pants who shrink people to suitcase size. AIP-T.V. simultaneously produced *Voyage to the Planet of Prehistoric Women* and *Voyage to the Prehistoric Planet* in '65, the latter containing Russian footage of robots from their much more famous movie, *Planet of Storms,* which Roger Corman purchased and incorporated as he did the following year with *Planet of Blood.*

Also in 1965, director Jean-Luc Godard put the famous French detective character Lemmy Caution into a 1984-ish extraplanetary adventure called *Alphaville,* the title location being a place where a mad computer rewrites history on a regular basis and subjugates humans to its soulless, emotionless will. The same character appeared in 1962 in the AIP-financed *Attack of the Robots,* in which Caution saves heads of state in several countries from assassination by a mad-scientist's gray-suited, sunglasses-wearing killer robots. The director of *Robots,* Jesse Franco, began his career with *The Awful Dr. Orloff* the same year, about another mad scientist who uses a reanimated corpse robot to abduct women for his skin-graft operations. It actually spawned four sequels, at least one of which—the next in the series, *Dr. Orloff's Monster,* two years later—was also financed by American International. The 1966 entry, *The Diabolical Dr. Z,* had Orloff's daughter employing mind control to create an amoral sexy young female assassin who seeks out and destroys top research scientists, and who also performs bizarre sexual scenes with a mannequin on stage. Japan's *Terror Beneath the Sea,* the same year, featured an underwater city-dwelling mad scientist turning people into water-breathing robot-creatures. In the UFO bumper-crop year of 1967, Franco made the X-rated *Succubus* for Trans-American Productions, about a demon-possessed kinky S&M nightclub dancer/serial killer haunted by hallucinatory dream-sequences and moving mannequins.

England's "Planet Company" made two space invader movies through Universal in 1966–67, *Island of Terror* and *Island of the Burning Doomed,* both directed by Terence Fisher and at least one of which was produced by Richard Gordon. The first is listed as having been financed through Universal, the second through a company called Maron. The former had Peter Cushing and Edward Judd discovering a hostile invasion by extremely prolific tentacled slitherers who suck human bone marrow. The latter film, based on a novel by John Lymington called *Night of the Big Heat,* had Cushing again, this time

354 HOLLYWOOD VERSUS THE ALIENS

teamed with frequent co-star Christopher Lee, doing battle with a
small number of isolated humans against incendiary protoplasmic
aliens. Two American pictures also were produced by "United Pictures" in 1966 that almost certainly were part of the deflectional UFO
program: *Castle of Evil* and *Destination Inner Space*. The former was a
comic-book-level story about a dead scientist who leaves behind a
robot of himself to terrorize and murder his greedy heirs. The latter
concerned the discovery of a flying saucer on the ocean floor by a
team of Navy scientists, which appears to be the vanguard of a hostile invasion—it has eggs on board that hatch highly aggressive sea-
monster humanoids. (The costume for the sea-monster was so
distinctive that it later appeared in animated form on Hanna-Barbera's
Scooby Doo, in "The Monster is Awake in Bottomless Lake.")

Allied Artists' 1966 entry was *Frankenstein Meets the Space Monster,*
the sort of title which, by itself, best exemplifies the general aura
being intentionally woven around the entire UFO subject. Alternately
released as *Duel of the Space Monsters* and—in Puerto Rico, where it
was filmed—*Mars Invades Puerto Rico,* it featured an astronaut protagonist who is actually a sophisticated robot. Crashing back to Earth,
the damaged robot does battle with invading aliens who use flashlight-like implements to paralyze and/or vaporize human targets.
True to form, the aliens are stiffly and awkwardly lumbering
humanoids in oversized helmets, and their aim is the appropriation
of Earth women for breeding purposes. They are led by the beautiful Princess Marcuzan, who is assisted by a bald dwarf. The movie
was so bad, one drive-in reported that the reels were once shown out
of sequence without anyone noticing. Larry Buchanan's AIP entry
for the same year was *Curse of the Swamp Creature,* about a mad scientist creating bald, pop-eyed human hybrids.

It was in 1966 that AIP's Roger Corman gave screenwriter Curtis
Harrington Russian sci-fi space footage to work a story around (and
just where did he get that, anyway?) and made *Planet of Blood.* Corman pulled a similar trick in 1959, somehow managing to purchase
a Russian movie called *Nebo Zowet,* also centering on Mars, which
he re-edited with new space-monster footage and called *Battle Beyond
the Sun. Planet of Blood* (a.k.a. *Queen of Blood*) was about a queen space-

vampire picked up from the Martian satellite Phobos, whose secret dire plot is to overrun the Earth by laying as many eggs as possible aboard a rescue ship that recovers her from her crashed interstellar vehicle. She is a red-bodysuited exotic green humanoid with platinum blonde hair and ultra-smooth skin, unsettling by virtue of the fact that she perpetually smiles and stares and never speaks, her mute intensity being distinctly sexual and predatory. The crew determine that she is what *Homo sapiens* would have become if we had evolved on another planet. Disdaining human food, however, the alien soon reveals that her diet consists of mammalian blood—human blood. While the crew sleeps, the Martian space-vampire hypnotizes male crew members, one by one, and sucks them dry. Ordered not to destroy her by Mission Control, the surviving astronauts are left in a quandary as to what to do to keep themselves safe from the killer in their midst. Ultimately, they accidentally end her life by cutting her skin, discovering that she is a born haemophiliac.

A classic example of a UFO trivialization was in one of 1967's most expensive cinematic flops, the only one of Ian Fleming's James Bond titles not owned by Albert Broccoli: Columbia's *Casino Royale.* Perhaps the single best time-capsule of that entire era, *Casino Royale* contains everything that was quintessentially of the late-'60s Mod Era. Utterly plotless, contrived, and absurd, the film is a non-stop fashion show of see-through plastic miniskirts, go-go boots, flip hairdos, pop music (the jazzy score was provided by Herb Alpert and the Tijuana Brass), loud, clashing colors, and psychedelic patterns. It is also remarkably fun, stylish, and even witty, but of course devoid of any remote semblance of serious thought. Every popular figure who wasn't actually in the cast appeared in a cameo, including Charles Boyer, George Raft, and Peter O'Toole. The central villain, Le Chiffre, played by the ever-flamboyant Orson Welles, employs psychedelic/LSD-inspired brainwashing mind control on James Bond (actually, one of several James Bonds, one of the movie's countless inanities), and the entire action culminates in confronting the mad mastermind out to destroy the world: "Dr. Noah," played by Woody Allen, who travels in a ridiculous flying saucer to a concealed cliff-side hideaway. He plans to create robot duplicates of all world leaders on Earth (a frequently recurring sci-fi theme, as in the contemporaneous *The Human Duplicators),* thereby conquering the planet. That failing, he intends to release a bacillus that will make all women beautiful and kill all men taller than himself. The same year, *The Ambushers,* third in Dean Martin's and Columbia Studios' Matt Helm series, featured a flying saucer as its central element, and 20th Century Fox's *Way Way Out* the year before starred Martin's erstwhile partner, Jerry Lewis, as a bumbling American astronaut out to get Connie Stevens pregnant on the Moon before a Russian cosmonaut couple can beat them to it.

1967, the year the best Quatermass movie was made, was also the year that Larry Buchanan's strangest AIP picture was released, *Mars Needs Women,* which starred Disney Studio's Tommy Kirk and T.V.'s "Batgirl," Yvonne Craig, revealing the level of seriousness that must have been intended. Kirk had starred in a near-identical role three years before for the same studio, in their beach-blanket series entry, *Pajama Party,* as a comical Martian vanguard spy called "Go-Go." Film critic Michael Weldon has even suggested that this may have been the original inspiration for T.V.'s *Mork and Mindy.* One of the weirdest movies ever made, *Mars Needs Women* is not intentionally or unintentionally funny, or even simply bad. Played totally straight, and filmed in naturalistic documentary style, it starts with the Air Force deciphering a message received from space, which is the movie's title. Everyone thinks it must be a joke, but, sure enough, women start disappearing. Perfectly human-looking Martians appear at an air base—Tommy Kirk and kin, in bodysuits, with earphones and antennae—and announce that they are here to abduct women for breeding purposes because Mars is a dying planet. The Air Force accuses them of "overt acts of abduction and war," for which the Martians apologize, but their need outweighs our inconvenience. They display their superiority and warn the military off, leaving the Air Force fuming, "There's nothing to do now, except wait for them to make the first move!"

The press catch wind of it, and the Air Force lets them broadcast the story, which the world takes seriously. The public doesn't panic, simply talking about it casually in the bars and salons between speculating on upcoming football games or the latest fashions. Space geneticist Craig gives a press conference that the Martians clandestinely attend, stating that Earth almost certainly has nothing to fear from the Martians. She believes they are simply correcting some genetic deficiency on their part, after which they will leave. A reporter asks if the Martians will look like mutants, and she remarks that it is entirely presumptious on our part to assume that they will look any different from ourselves. Craig is taken into the government's private think-tank on the Martian problem, and is also marked for abduction by Martian Kirk, who has fallen in love with her.

The government discovers that the Martians are using hypnosis to erase people's memories of their encounters with them, one of the scientists saying, "We are dealing with an enemy that professes non-hostility while abducting Earth's females. We are helpless, because he has mastered the science of hypnosis, which we still treat as a parlor game. One thing we can be sure of—he is working against time. And he will stop at nothing to achieve his goal before his time runs out." Since this is an American production, and therefore a predictable melodrama, the military drive the Martians away and retrieve the abducted women, poor Kirk forced to abandon his weeping love Craig, ending with the military asking her, "What were they like? Will you be able to describe them? Well, can't you tell us anything?" She doesn't answer, the music instead dramatically swelling to climax as the saucer disappears in the night sky, Konstantin Tsiolkousky's quote flashing on the screen: "Earth is the cradle of man, but he cannot live in the cradle forever."

The same year, on T.V.'s immensely popular *Batman,* actress-ballerina Craig was making "little green men from Mars" sound ridiculous in "Joker's Flying Saucer," an episode in which the Joker tries to do exactly what the Robertson Panel stated concern about—terrifying the populace into complying with his demands in order to forestall his sham Martian invasion. Self-confessed bookish, brainy nerd student Craig, interestingly enough, was dating *My Favorite Martian*'s Bill Bixby at the time, and like many other UFOlogically-cast actors found herself in related films such as 1967's *In Like Flint.* She also made several guest appearances in a recurring minor support role on

MGM's T.V. spy series, *The Man from U.N.C.L.E.*, including two of the four feature-length releases tinkered together in 1966 out of the show's several two-parter stories, *One of Our Spies is Missing* and *One Spy Too Many*. 20th Century Fox's *In Like Flint* featured as its main elements a space threat and missing-time abduction, illegal internecine government surveillance monitoring for the purposes of blackmail and coercion, and an attempt by the military to subvert the presidency first by covert installation of a hand-picked puppet and then later by overt force. The title character, James Coburn's impossibly suave and intelligent "Derek Flint," is probably the most famous spoof-spy in film history but is less a comic-book joke than he appears at first glance. An expert in every field, he specializes—at least in this movie, the second of two—in communication with dolphins (as per MK-ULTRA'S Dr. John Lilly, whose story is detailed in Chapter 9), amnesia-producing mind-control substances (specifically *ancient* amnesia-producing mind-control substances), hypnotic regression for memory retrieval (as in UFO abduction cases), and the development of sound technology for the movement of physical mass.

The actual term, "little green men from Mars," so easily joked about on *Batman* (not to mention numerous other pop-culture references), has not been traced to a definite original source. John Nicholson's article "Little Green Men," and Hans Stefan Santesson's *Flying Saucers in Fact and Fiction* (1968), tried unsuccessfully to discover the origination of the phrase, as did Daniel Cohen's *Monsters, Giants, and Little Men from Mars* in 1975. Journalist Richard Adams Locke perpetrated a "moon man" hoax for the *New York Sun* in 1835, fabricating quotes from famed British astronomer Sir John Herschel to the effect that four-foot-tall bat-men had been seen by him on the Moon. Yale scientists gave up on attempts to verify the information after being given numerous runarounds, though Locke finally admitted to the hoax himself without having been caught—but during its run, the *Sun* had the largest readership in the world. The phrase "little green men" was reportedly used by Mac Brazel in Roswell in 1947. Hollywood probably proliferated its use after some forgotten Depression-era pulp magazine, spurred partly by the 1938 *War of the Worlds* scare. The term "little men" alone was used in 1943's Bugs Bunny cartoon "Hare Force," featuring "gremlins," funny little creatures to which WWII American pilots ascribed all engine failures—i.e. "sabotage," which is interesting—as a sort of in-joke. The mere phrase "man from Mars" seems first to have appeared, movie-wise, in 1951's *The Thing*.

Jacques Vallee reported in *Dimensions* a story occurring four years before the filming of *Mars Needs Women*, considering the man who reported it a legitimate contact. On April 24, 1964, two near-identical, or perhaps even identical, occurrences happened in Socorro, New Mexico, and Tioga City, New York: landed, egg-shaped UFOs were witnessed, both with small humanoids of essentially the famous Gray description, both digging up local plant and soil samples. In the former case, the UFO departed swiftly as soon as it was detected, before the witness could adequately study the occupants to give a solid report on their appearance.

In the latter case, twenty-six-year-old dairy farmer Gary Wilcox, at about ten in the morning, found such an object a mile from his barn in the woods. He touched it and found no door or seam, nor any trace of heat. Two four-foot-tall humanoids in bodysuits, with "helmets" that had no faces, spoke to him "in smooth English," not from the area of their heads, but somewhere about their bodies, as has been reported by many other UFO witnesses such as Betty Hill and Herbert Schirmer. "Do not be alarmed," they said, "we have talked to people before. We are from what you people refer to as planet Mars." Despite his persistent feeling that someone was pulling his leg, Wilcox continued listening to the humanoids. "They said they could only travel to this planet every two years," Wilcox said, "and they are presently using the Western Hemisphere." They were investigating our fertilizers and agricultural techniques, because Mars' rocky condition made it unfit for crops. They were surprised Wilcox had seen their ship, which was less visible in daylight. In common with other UFO occupants, they remarked that our air pollution was dangerous in congested areas. They also warned that our astronauts would not adapt well to space, and of a coming environmental and gravitational change which could leave Earth's environment like that of Mars. As Wilcox retrieved a bag of fertilizer at their request, they took off. He left the bag anyway, and the next day it was gone. All these activities are fairly common with the "little people," or Fairy Folk. "Are we not, after all," Vallee prefaces his telling of the story, "designing robots that will continue the analysis of the Martian surface begun when the Viking probe reached that planet?"

The military have several times made reference to Mars in what may well have been more than a joking fashion. One instance is recounted in Coral and Jim Lorenzen's (then head of APRO, the Aerial Phenomena Research Organization) *Flying Saucer Occupants:* sixty-five-year-old witness John Reeves of Brooksville, Florida, retrieved a message on two tissue-thin pieces of paper dropped by a UFO occupant on March 3, 1965. He delivered it to the Air Force, only to be told later that it had been translated to say, "PLANET MARS—ARE YOU COMING HOME SOON—WE MISS YOU VERY MUCH—WHY DID YOU STAY AWAY TOO LONG"—the forerunner to "E.T., phone home." One of the hieroglyphic-like symbols on the paper matched those later drawn by Nebraska abductee Herbert Schirmer, looking like two "L"s, which interestingly enough (and unlikely to have been known to either man) actually is the Egyptian hieroglyphic for "foreigners." Vallee, trying to get both the United States and French Air Forces to cooperate more openly in understanding the UFO phenomenon, was baldly told by then-Blue Book head Hector Quintanilla that their investigation was utterly unconcerned "if a Martian shakes hands with a baker in Brittany," and interested only in acquiring extraterrestrial technology for study.

Even when not directly referring to Mars, comments made by officials in the military or space programs have betrayed that they are fully aware of dealing with people from other planets. Brigadier General and Apollo astronaut James A. McDivitt, photographer of a UFO in space while on a Gemini mission—though he is presently careful not to say too much publicly on the subject—believed Charles Hickson's abduction account at the time, and even said that the antennae Hickson described on the robots that seized him sounded like advanced radar devices. When Hickson told his story straightforwardly on Dick Cavett's show, McDivitt beamed a smile to author Ralph Blum backstage in the Green Room, and said, "That was just great! They set down and picked up a man. Sure did pick up the right kind of man! That was fine!" Obviously, McDivitt's words and attitude imply more than a mild certainty of who "they" were.

Britain's Hammer Studio descendants, Tigon/Pacemaker, made *The Blood Beast Terror* in 1967, immediately contemporaneous with the multiple "Mothman" sightings in America. The title creature was a giant hybrid moth-woman, created by a hypnotist taking genetic material from a repeat-contact, post-event-controlled, amnesiac subject. Like *Mars Needs Women,* it is neither a good nor bad movie (though star Peter Cushing considered it the worst film he ever made), just bizarre. The previous year's Hammer/20th Century Fox export, *The Reptile,* had amnesiac innocent Jacqueline Pearce transformed into a were-snake robot assassin by an ancient Malay cult, in revenge for her government investigator father's meddling in their affairs. She is turned into "one of them" after having been kidnapped as a child for three weeks, then "returned unhurt, apparently with no idea what had happened to her." *Reptile* director John Gilling made a movie the same year for World Entertainment Corporation called *Blood Beast From Outer Space,* in which American John Saxon plays a detective who discovers a human-disguised alien from one of Jupiter's moons, Ganymede, luring beautiful models to his Soho shop to impregnate them so he can repopulate his dying world. Two years before *The Reptile,* in 1964, Gilling scripted another snake-woman movie, *The Gorgon,* with *Five Million Years to Earth*'s Barbara Shelley as an amnesiac murderess occasionally possessed by the ancient spirit of the title creature.

Two other British productions, more obviously connected to UFO phenomena, came from Amicus Pictures in 1967: one was *The Terrornauts,* in which an alien robot transports an entire building of research scientists to a planet of green humanoids, where it subjects them to intelligence tests and recruits them to help keep Earth from destroying itself; the other was *They Came From Beyond Space,* about a race of superior humans on the Moon mind-controlling Earth people in order to gain help repairing their marooned ship. Concurrent with *The Blood Beast Terror* was an even worse and equally bizarre U.S.-British-Canadian bird-man movie, *The Vulture.*

From Italy, the same year, came the comedy *Don't Play with Martians*, in which a man faking Martian invaders as a joke encounters the real thing in aliens from the planet Gammia, who look like humans except for their cat-like eyes. The Gammians find Earth people "quaint" and are not interested in them except for breeding—they are only here to pick up six of their infants being born among us. The Italians produced more bizarre humanoids and abductions in *The Curious Dr. Humpp*, filmed in '67 but not released until three years later. Dr. Humpp is the successful near-immortal product of a disembodied super-brain's experiments to make human beings live forever. Humpp uses giant identical bulletproof robots, with huge round eyes, fixed faces, silver metallic feet, and bald, bolted skullcaps to abduct local strippers and strongmen for him. These he pairs up, drugged and hypnotized, to have sex beneath his watchful gaze. Blood is taken from the abductees at the moment of climax, the prime ingredient in the immortality brew. Failed experiments end up dumped by the robots into an incinerator. In the end, the police track down Dr. Humpp and destroy his robots, one of his female abductees stabs him to death, and the controller-brain explodes into flame in a fit of pique. The Spanish-Italian Fanfare Productions came up with *Superargo and the Faceless Giants* the same year, in which a mad scientist turns athletes into mummified robots; and MGM filmed an Italian knock-off on its popular *Man from U.N.C.L.E.* T.V. show called *The Venetian Affair,* starring that series' star (and UFOlogical movie mainstay), Robert Vaughn, as a CIA agent against a wheelchair-ridden Boris Karloff and a foreigner who turns people into brainwashed robots with a diabolical serum.

Many of Nigel Kneale's ideas were revamped for the BBC's most popular sci-fi/fantasy, *Dr. Who,* running almost thirty consecutive years beginning November 23, 1963 (the day after the Kennedy assassination in the United States). Originally a children's show, it was about an eccentric old man traveling time and space in a ship masquerading as a blue police call box. With bargain-basement special effects, the show's strength lay in the sophisticated handling of its stories and characters. Initially, these were mostly simple history lessons, sometimes with the interlacing of extraterrestrial busybodies.

Soon the Doctor was engaged in more fantasy-oriented adventures with aliens on other worlds, of varying friendliness. By 1970, the show proved so popular with older viewers that it took on more mature stories. The Doctor was revealed to be an earthbound Time Lord from a planet called Gallifrey. He assisted the fictional United Nations Intelligence Taskforce (UNIT), preserving the British Empire from invasion by alien nasties, aided by various screaming young lovelies in miniskirts. The series managed to maintain the same character being played by a number of different actors (no one originally anticipated a mere children's show becoming so immensely popular), through explaining that Time Lords periodically go through a "regeneration."

A rival Time Lord, the Satanically goateed Master, made Earth his primary target for invasion and could regularly be counted on to make evil deals with alien powers intent on the same purpose. His trademark was murdering people with a device looking like a pocket flashlight, which shrunk its target to the size of a doll. Diabolically suave, the Master was a superior hypnotist, capable of dominating nearly anyone's will and erasing their memory of the encounter even as he continued to use them. In his premiere appearance, he hypnotized the Doctor's young assistant into nearly killing him, and the Doctor had to demonstrate just how powerful a weapon hypnosis was to the doubting UNIT members. In so doing, he delivers a speech saying that the idea of people being unable to be hypnotized into doing anything against their will is false. "Some minds are stubborn enough to resist hypnosis," he says, "and in any case it doesn't last. Away from the Master's influence, the mind struggles constantly to free itself. I think the current jargon [for her state] is 'schizoid dissociation.' It's because she was forced to do something against her will, and her conscious mind refuses to accept the fact. The result is a deep trauma." This is essentially the same explanation discussed by Jacques Vallee in one of the NSA's two released UFO reports as the reason for amnesia in abductees, and the reason why abductees frequently remember what they have undergone through their own dreams or artwork.

Keeping track of the number of times robots or abductions were featured on *Dr. Who* is too mammoth a task, it being sufficient to say that he had a great many robot foes, and even a robot friend (a mechanical dog called "K-9"), and that abductions were almost a weekly occurrence. Animated mannequins called "Autons" were the Master's first cohorts. The "Cybermen," a robot race reanimated after centuries of sleep, were another threat. The "Daleks" were not actually robots but were perceived by everyone as being robots, and they were the Doctor's arch-enemy. An important robot was seen in a late episode of the 1980's or early '90s, the servant to a malevolent alien trying to spread the bubonic plague in the Middle Ages; the servant looks exactly like modern UFO Grays and could only have been deliberately planned to be. By that time, the image had so proliferated popular consciousness, someone probably reached the same conclusion presented in these pages—that the classic "alien" reported the world over is in fact a robot—if the episode wasn't actually produced after the 1990 publication of Zecharia Sitchin's *Genesis Revisited,* which openly proposed that the Grays were "anthropoid robots." The mythological literacy of the show's production team was frequently evident, one excellent example being the last episode of the 1970s, "Logopolis," which has the Master paralyzing the control center of the entire Universe, freezing its functions to hold all life hostage, threatening the fundamental workings of nature—this plot is identical to the stealing of the Tablets of Destiny by Zu, in Sumerian mythology.

The Doctor several times on the series found himself emotionally torn between his military benefactors and opposing alien powers, as in 1970's "The Silurians." The title creatures were former reptilian inhabitants of Earth with a highly advanced civilization, who went into hibernation due to unforeseen circumstances and found themselves awakened by changing climatic conditions brought on by nuclear testing. Finding man inhabiting the world that was once theirs, they begin covert military attacks and prepare for ultimate conquest. The Doctor, upon learning more about their history, attempts to propose a truce between man and the Silurians, recognizing that the latter were, after all, here first. The politicians are impatient and insecure about such an arrangement, and the military too highly distrustful to allow it. Their paranoia and suspicion are shared by the Silurians, who counter military moves from the "above world" (they live under the Earth in caves) with a bacteriological weapon of their own. Even after their creation of a plague, the Doctor does not desire to destroy the Silurians, instead finding a cure to their threat and then finding a way to alter climatic conditions to put them back to sleep. He figures that, in the time they slumber, perhaps man will come to some better diplomatic solution to their mutual problem. Unfortunately, the military render the idea impossible—without the Doctor's consent or consultation, they bomb the Silurian caves once the reptiles are again dormant, cold-bloodedly murdering the entire race while they sleep.

1971's "Ambassadors of Death" shows government personnel abusing their privileged knowledge to conceal and subvert a first meeting between Mars and Earth. A general lies to his government about Earth astronauts abducted by Martians, and he intercepts and abducts a Martian delegation about which the government has been kept unaware. The general believes the Martians are lethally hostile invaders, having encountered them on a previous space mission during which they accidentally killed his co-pilot, and he never told his superiors the truth about the accident. Having devoted the ensuing years to preparing the Earth for invasion, the general has assembled his own loyal team to help him. From his privileged position, the general has been able to intercept all communications ventured forth by the Martians and engineered a "trade" between our astronauts and theirs, ostensibly for the purpose of ambassadorial relations. His deliberate obfuscation of the facts concerning the sudden disappearance of the Earth astronauts is designed to provoke the world to war, playing on and fostering people's fears. Others on his paramilitary team intend to utilize the bulletproof, robotic Martians for such venal purposes as mere bank robbery, using the general's paranoia to further their own power. Former Martians on the series, "The Ice Warriors," were also a robotic-looking and -acting race, with huge goggle-eyes, shell-like bulletproof exteriors, and clamps for hands, who specialized in sonic weaponry.

In the same time period, the Master hooked-up with two more technological menaces, "The Mind of Evil" and "The Claws of Axos."

The former was an alien parasite controlling a mobile machine, and the latter was an invading spaceship capable of disembarking pieces of itself as identically cloned humanoid figures. "Axos" turns out to be a single intelligence guiding all the separate automata; it forcibly abducts passing humans and holds them immobile on a slab for complete examination by a giant eye-device. It coldly and mechanically reads off data as it conducts the examination, and all the figures it generates appear artificial and metallic. The Hickson-Parker abduction, featuring a similar scanner "eye," was occurring in Pascagoula, Mississippi, right about the same time as this episode was being made; since *Dr. Who* was not exported to American shores for about another ten years, and since "The Claws of Axos" demonstrated both robotic abductors and the same giant eye device for physical scanning, the coincidence is extremely difficult to explain in any way other than that whoever was behind the episode's production was aware of true UFO facts.

Another vital episode of interest to this study is 1975's "The Pyramids of Mars," in which the Doctor encounters the imprisoned Egyptian god, Sutekh, who is assisted in a bid for release by robots disguised as mummies and hypnotically dominated humans. The title pyramids emanate a perpetual radio signal that keeps Sutekh's prison locked, and he uses the Doctor's spaceship to send his robots through an ancient city labyrinth on Mars to destroy its controls. Since the Cydonia complex wasn't discovered until the following year and not publicized broadly until some time later, one might wonder where the idea came from. On the surface seeming to be an astounding bit of prediction on its author's part, it can easily be accounted for by both the broadcast of Carl Sagan's *Cosmos* episode dealing with the Elysium pyramids in 1972, and by the publication of *Destiny Mars* the same year the *Dr. Who* script was written, either or both of which were plainly an influence. The robots could just be coincidental in this case, strange as it seems, or an intuitive connection on the writer's part with ancient automata (such as presented in the Introduction).

1977's "The Talons of Weng-Chiang," perhaps the best-plotted story in the entire series, also contained a great many actual UFO-logical elements. In Victorian England, the Doctor becomes involved in helping Scotland Yard solve a number of abductions of young women from the London streets. The police are unable to discover the perpetrator because he is using future technology to accomplish his ends which they cannot figure into their equation, but the Doctor recognizes it because he comes from a future time himself. The mastermind behind the crimes is Magnus Greel, a criminal from Earth's twenty-sixth century, who escaped punitive action for his key role in starting World War Six by using a new time-travel cabinet not unlike the Doctor's far superior extraterrestrial time-travel machine. In his escape, Greel took one of the crucial pieces of evidence against him, a child-sized midget doll given as a supposed peace gift to a Peking official that was actually a pre-programmed nocturnal assassin—the "Peking Homonculus," a computerized robot with the cerebral cortex of a pig, a device which is completely psychopathic and only partially controllable.

Greel has taken an accomplice, Chinese stage magician Li-Hsen Chang—who has taken Greel for a mythical underworld deity of fertility and increase, called "Weng-Chiang"—and teaches him to become a master hypnotist. Chang uses the Peking Homonculus in his act and to help him murder any interlopers who interfere with his entrancing and stealing-away of women to Greel's hidden laboratory. Greel's leap through time utilized a process that severely disrupted his cellular structure, and he needs the abducted women's genetic material to revitalize himself, vampirically stealing their lives to sustain his own. At one point in the story, Greel sets Chang up for murder to punish him for his failure in halting the Doctor's progress on the case, and before the dejected Chang can commit suicide, the Doctor questions him, halting one of Chang's continual references to Greel as "the Lord" by saying, "Li-Hsen—you know he's not a god. Don't you." Chang acknowledges the fact, but says, "He *came* like a god. He appeared in a blazing cabinet of fire...."

1977 was one of the most prolific and most accurate years for *Dr. Who* in terms of UFOlogy, perhaps not surprising given the "educational program" being implemented by Jimmy Carter in the States. The episode "Robots of Death" had a maniac programming mechanical men to murder his colleagues on a mining ship. The culprit was suffering from a psychological condition termed "robophobia," described as the result of traumatic encounter with robots while young. The trauma has caused the killer to identify more with robots than people. Such also appears to be the case with real-life UFO abductees. The condition posited is most interesting and probably accurate, explained as an innate revulsion on the part of animal life (including human) for anything that displays no body language, especially when it is made to look like a man and move like one. The Doctor equates the sensation with encountering a walking corpse—which is a frequent cinematic corollary to UFO robots. The same year, Wanda Ventham—who played the mutant moth-woman in *The Blood Beast Terror,* ten years before—was cast in "Image of the Fendahl" as an alien/demon-possessed scientist who becomes the instrument for working the will of an ancient devil-race from the devastated planet in Earth's solar system that is now the asteroid belt. Her team, like that in *Five Million Years to Earth,* has determined that the human race was engineered in antiquity by the race that came from that planet.

The twelve-episode story leading into the remade 1970s approach, "The War Games," in which the Doctor was first shown to be an extraterrestrial, had a rival Time Lord abducting soldiers from all time zones to assemble the ultimate army for conquest. When the Doctor proves unable to neutralize the threat on his own, his home planet intercedes, bringing all parties concerned to their planetary court. Since time and space have been unduly interfered with, they take it upon themselves to transport everyone caught-up in the project back to their original homes, and to erase all of their memories of everything that transpired in their "fairy realm."

At least as popular in the U.S. as it ever was in Britain, *Dr. Who* became a mammoth cult favorite on American shores in the 1980s. In keeping with the idea of government-level decision-making in media entertainment for purposes of political propaganda, it was in 1980 that the Doctor underwent a complete image change entirely in accord with the new extremely conservative and youth-oriented era that followed both in Britain and America. Where the Doctor had previously been portrayed as an eccentric, iconoclastic, and countercultural older man, suddenly he was cast vastly against type, in extremely young and blonde, classically good-looking, boyish Peter Davison. Davison's Doctor eschewed the bizarre accoutrements of all the former Doctors, wearing a conservative and extremely dressy Preppy ice-cream suit, replete with collegiate vest. He was clean-cut and strait-laced and played cricket, and relied much more on a growing number of multiple young assistants at a single time, in keeping with the new corporate business "teamwork" ethic that was at that time being aggressively shoved down the throats of American audiences, especially. Previous Doctors all had very long and unmanageable hair, unfashionably long scarves, flamboyantly eccentric tuxedoes and the like, and even when employed by the Government were extremely individualistic and not inclined to follow "team decisions." Identical changes were to manifest in the same era's new *Star Trek,* seven years later.

It was precisely at the time that Davison's episodes were imported to the States that *Dr. Who* reached its maximum popularity, and the new image also was largely the reason that same popularity suddenly began to decline. Everything that made the show a hit had been co-opted and lost, and the ratings went with it. Though it has never been a failure, *Dr. Who* did begin to show a timidity and wimpiness formerly lacking, and it couldn't maintain the massive audiences it had acquired by being aggressively intelligent before. An attempt to return to the humorously anti-Establishment image of the character first went too shrill and arrogant to recapture the previous magic, and then the producers tried going back to the much more clownish Doctor of earlier still in the series. This last move did nearly revitalize the show, but it went into hiatus at one point and then finally was cancelled after a brief return. *Dr. Who* has threatened to revive and may still, its most recent incarnation being a 1996 Fox T.V. movie. Two of the earliest stories in the series were filmed by Amicus in 1965 and '66, as *Dr. Who and the Daleks* and *Daleks: Invasion Earth 2150 AD,* with Peter Cushing playing the title role.

Regarding the show's phenomenal popularity with several generations of audiences, sixth Doctor Colin Baker explained in the BBC special *30 Years of Dr. Who,* "The idea of the intergalactic traveler who takes young people with him, and therefore collects the children of families, is a *warm* idea. It's one that makes people happy." Indeed, one British song about the series goes, "It could be Mars or Venus, but whatever he may do, he'll always be a friend of mine— Who? *Dr. Who!*" In that context, the entire UFO abduction phenomenon is seen in its most favorable light.

Predating *Dr. Who*'s arrival on American shores by almost two decades was another popular British import dealing with UFOlogical themes (previously discussed, in Chapter 2), ITV/ABC's *The Avengers*. If the idea of a military or governmental connection supports the thesis that some T.V. shows seed actual UFOlogical discoveries gradually in the public mind, then *The Avengers* certainly fits the bill, many of the production team being war veterans, including star Patrick Macnee. Not only was Macnee in Naval Intelligence during WWII, he was also the son of a blue-blood aristocrat mother and a student at very upper-crust Eton. Today, he hosts a psychic/UFO investigative show on the Sci-Fi Channel, called *Mysteries, Magic, and Miracles.*

Like *The Avengers,* two contemporary United States T.V. productions managed to incorporate science-fictional and UFOlogical themes and elements fairly believably and in an adult fashion, succeeding because they operated realistically within their frameworks: the aforementioned *Star Trek* (NBC, 1966–69) and *The Wild, Wild West* (CBS, 1965–69). MGM T.V.'s *The Man from U.N.C.L.E.* (NBC, 1964–68) and its later spinoff, *The Girl from U.N.C.L.E.* (1966–67), utilized high-tech adventure and mystery in their plots but were more appropriately spoofs of Ian Fleming's highly popular James Bond stories. Among its various space-degradational episodes was "The Take Me To Your Leader Affair," in which the world-terrorist organization, T.H.R.U.S.H., creates a flying saucer and tries to convince the world they are invading aliens who need to be shown unquestioning obedience, exactly like the contemporaneous *Batman* episode, "Joker's Flying Saucer." Another *U.N.C.L.E.* episode, "The Suburbia Affair," had fugitive physicist Victor Borge joking that a recent rash of inexplicable aggressive behavior in Middle America could have been caused by Martians.

Spy writer Ian Fleming himself is an excellent example of an insider disseminating Intelligence secrets through fiction, at least one instance being shown in President Kennedy's favorite novel, *From Russia with Love*. One of the reasons the president found it so appealing, no doubt, was that one element of the plot concerned the use of an Intelligence-connected beauty to set up a romantic blackmail trap, which Kennedy more than once found himself in with Inga Arvad, Judith Campbell Exner, and Marilyn Monroe, and which happened to be a specialty of the KGB. The top-secret "Spektor" decoding device (renamed "Lector" for the movie to avoid confusion with the name of Bond's nemesis organization) in that story was just an updated "Enigma," code-named ULTRA in WWII.

The war's greatest Allied secret, ULTRA enabled Britain and the U.S. to know every German military move from Dunkirk on, even as they were being ordered from Hitler's "Wolf's Lair" in East Prussia, making it the greatest asset of that worldwide conflict. It is a matter of record that Fleming at that time was a member of the British Secret Service working at Bletchley Park, where the Enigma intercepts were decoded, and he was essentially the auxiliary head of the secondary decoding unit in the Bahamas. In fact, Anthony Cave Brown reports that Fleming was one of only two agents (the other being Admiral John Godfrey) sent over to brief the Americans on ULTRA'S existence. The novel was written in 1957 and filmed as the second of the Bond movies in 1964, but Enigma and ULTRA were not declassified for publication until 1974. *From Russia with Love* therefore stands as proof that at least some Intelligence secrets have been released to the public in advance of official declassification, disguised as fiction, and also proof that the government condoned its being done—if they hadn't, Fleming would never have been allowed to publish, since he would have been in violation of the Secrets Act. Since it was not only published but financed in a highly visible international film series, the film is also evidence that people in power approve of initiating mass education in such a fashion. This piece alone gives a good example of how the "educational program" works: the idea is put out before the public at a safe fictional remove, serious enough to give thought to, yet light enough to dismiss.

"My plots are fantastic," said Fleming, "while being often based upon truth." Fleming's British Secret Service colleague, William Stevenson, confirms Fleming's statement in his 1976 book on ULTRA, *A Man Called Intrepid:* "*Goldfinger,* like much of Fleming's writing, was not pure invention. It was inspired by [Sir William] Stephenson's plan to rob Martinique of the gold that could give BSC the power to energize the revolution in Europe." The plot of the book had been nothing more than an impossible gold robbery of Fort Knox, attempted by the megolomaniacal title character. Fleming died prematurely before the film's opening, and that movie began the series' new trend of altering his work to include more science-fictional elements, where before—even if still rather fantastic—the stories had been much more realistic. Goldfinger became, instead of Fleming's flamboyant bank-robber, a genius world nuclear-economic terrorist, who first corners Europe's gold market and then tries to atomically detonate America's supply at Fort Knox to inflate exponentially the value of his own currency. Contemporary headlines began to be the subject of James Bond's exploits, *Thunderball* even anticipating, by about a year, the actual loss of a U.S. B-52 Stratofortress off the coast of Spain with two atomic bombs on board in 1966; this event coincided with the release of the film, boosting its ticket sales tremendously, and was so convenient that it has to be wondered whether the newspaper reports were false and used simply for publicity. The Intelligence community certainly had (and has) the assets to put such false stories into circulation and would unquestionably have wanted to see movies in the Bond series show a profit, considering they almost certainly were invested in them—the Bond films were released by United Artists, the same folks who produced the Quatermass series and *The Outer Limits.*

Fleming's friend and war compatriot, ex-fighter pilot Roald Dahl, scripted the next film, which was the first to employ Fleming's fictional SPECTRE (SPecial Executive for Counterintelligence, Terrorism, Revenge, and Extortion) in such a futuristic manner that it no longer was credibly realistic as an earthbound organization. Headed by Bond's arch-enemy, the bald, athletically built world terrorist Ernst Stavro Blofeld, SPECTRE'S first post-Fleming film operation, in 1967's

Department member Telly Savalas—appeared in Paramount's *The Assassination Bureau,* based on Jack London's unfinished satire of spies and killers that was completed by Robert Fish at a later date. Altered notably from its source material, which was fragmented anyway, it posited a European proto-CIA before WWI, responsible for engineering the war for its own profit. The proposal is very far from absurd, Russian peace agent Rasputin being knifed on the same day, and even in the same hour, as Archduke Ferdinand was assassinated— the event usually fingered as the ultimate cause of the war. And Ferdinand's murder itself was almost certainly engineered, coming as it did immediately after a failed bombing attempt on his life, which was followed by an unexpected detour on the road taking him to the exact location out of which stepped the man who succeeded in finishing the job.

In the movie, Assassination Bureau head Oliver Reed accepts journalist Rigg's commission against his own life, in order to strip the flab from the organization, which originally existed solely to strike down tyrannical oppressors but now has become a profiteering mob. The members are highly ensconced pillars in the business community, whose outlook has become colored with the desire for power. "Gentlemen, be honest with yourselves," he entreats them all, "haven't we, in the pursuit of profit, fallen short of the high moral standards upon which our Bureau was founded? With all due respect, I no longer see in you the idealism without which we are no more than common murderers!" He could as easily have been any contemporary CIA director addressing the entire Agency following the murder of the Kennedys—RFK was killed only about a year before this movie was made.

It is perhaps of note that Savalas worked for the State Department before embarking on his film career, and that Diana Rigg is now a Dame. Such titles rarely come for mere talent alone, but rather for some service to Queen and Country, and Rigg's father had been a "civil engineer" in India at the start of WWII—a title which, as in the case of James Churchward (see Introduction), as often as not is a euphemism for "government agent." *The Avengers* boasted a substantial contingent of former wartime Intelligence members, and it is well-documented that the CIA has often recruited its members from already successful people or families among the international and domestic business communities, the lines between the Intelligence and big business worlds being shaky at best. The American OSS and subsequent CIA primarily patterned themselves after the British Secret Service they so openly admired, which had been recruiting from the same pools well in advance of them. Anthony Cave Brown, who in 1975 wrote the first and most thorough account of the Secret Service's ULTRA, the LCS (London Controlling Section), and their elite corps called "the Martians," described the individuals who comprised their ranks and their motivations: "[This] group of men who represented the aristocratic cream of a caste of blood, land and money ... now dominated the British secret agencies. They were descendants of that self-perpetuating cabal that had created and ruled a world empire for over two hundred years; and they had at their disposal a wealth of experience in stratagem and special means. These men approached their tasks with zest and dedication—and with a malevolence perhaps born of the realization that, if they failed, their class would not survive."

Something else that should be noticed concerning government control or influence on media entertainment is that during the Reagan years (and so, also, the Bush presidency), it was becoming popular to rewrite history in the most favorable light to America. "The docudrama, entertainment in the guise of history ... came more into vogue," writes Haynes Johnson in the illuminating study *Sleepwalking Through History: America in the Reagan Years.* "Prime-time docudrama miniseries productions costing millions to produce purported to depict what historical figures (Roosevelt, Truman, Kennedy, Churchill) actually did and said even if they didn't do or say any such things. The public became conditioned not to notice, not to care, or not to be concerned about distortion of the historical record." Referring to British historian J. H. Plumb's *The Death of the Past,* Dr. J. S. Holiday agrees "that under the influence of New History, Psycho-History, and Revisionist History, timeless heroes have been replaced by impersonal forces, or they have been denigrated by New Truths that have opened the way for impressionable students and cynical adults to think that maybe Betsy Ross was a lesbian, Abraham Lincoln a racist, Thomas Jefferson a hypocritical slave owner who had a black mistress, and Booker T. Washington an Uncle Tom." Johnson concludes that "Television, with its false 'docudramas' and the growing trend of network news programs to 'reenact' or 'dramatize' actual news events with actors, further blurs the distinction between celebrities and true national figures of distinction."

One of the single best examples of this dramatic media distortion involves the very author of the Bond series. TNT's *The Secret Life of Ian Fleming,* in 1990, was inaccurate and highly skewed. It was produced in immediate proximity to Operation Desert Storm, when America and World War Two especially were being portrayed in a false and misleading light drawn to fit the most absurd post-War propaganda films of the 1950s. Fleming's girlfriend is shown dying heroically in a personal act of Nazi revenge against Fleming, for his noble undercover work against them—in fact, she was killed in a routine German blitz. Fleming is shown on numerous commando action missions, some of which he no doubt did during the war—but nowhere in the movie is there a single mention of ULTRA or his part concerning it, which is the equivalent of leaving the iceberg out of the *S.S. Titanic* story. 1991's pseudo-documentary *The Heroes of Desert Storm,* an equally specious misrepresentation of facts, begins with George Bush giving a homily of praise to war, and a placard announces that the events we are about to see are actual footage interspersed with artificially enacted scenes, telling us in the same breath that they have purposely been made indistinguishable from each other.

ULTRA has not only been pointedly ignored in the movies since its declassification in 1974, but even more so in theoretically more respectable history books. William Manchester, whose *Death of a President*—even in its updated 1988 version—still hammers Oswald as the only possible culprit behind JFK's assassination despite the mountains of evidence to the contrary unearthed subsequent to the Warren Commission, also completely omits any reference to ULTRA in his biographies of both Winston Churchill and Douglas MacArthur. Plentiful quotes and evidence from other sources prove that not only did both men rely very heavily on the Intelligence intercepts, but without them, the war would have gone on many more years and been much more uncertain in its conclusion. Nor is Manchester alone in his tunnel vision. Other supposedly reputable historians have completely ignored ULTRA or evidence contrary to the Warren Commission, as though they simply don't exist. Anyone still believing the media is without controls is simply fooling themselves.

Quinn Martin's *The Invaders,* of ABC's 1967–68 lineup, created by frequent UFOlogical contributor Larry Cohen, was an innovative and nightmarish weekly flying-saucer drama, feeding on the worst of paranoid fantasies. Dominic Frontiere, who composed *The Outer Limits'* scary strains, provided equally ominous music for this series. Managing to run two seasons, *The Invaders* suffered from not enough variation in plotlines, which later besieged Paramount T.V.'s extremely similar *The War of the Worlds* series in the late 1980s (see Chapter 11). Roy Thinnes was the only man—or only one of a few—who knew for a fact that the saucers had landed, having seen one do so and being a target of its occupants ever since. Treated as a madman for resisting them and trying to warn anyone else, his character was essentially a continuation of the protagonist in *Invasion of the Body Snatchers.* Abductions and duplications were commonplace, with an eerie and unsettlingly pervasive background mantra of "Why resist? We're here. Accept us." This same tone was used extremely well in 1994's *Body Snatchers* (Warner Bros.), when a cadre of military men attempt to flee a body-snatched former family member, who expresses no hostility and doesn't even pretend to disguise itself anymore. "Listen to me," the abductee says, calmly trying to halt their flight. "Run *where?* Where ya gonna run? Where ya gonna hide? *Nowhere.* Because there's *no one . . .* like *you . . . left."*

Though not exactly a hit, *The Invaders* was steadily acquiring a growing audience and was cancelled primarily due to studio politics. The show proved remarkably successful in Europe, especially at a twenty-fifth anniversary celebration in Paris, with its release on video and special screenings in the movie theaters. Star Roy Thinnes said in a newspaper interview that the audiences there had memorized entire stretches of the dialogue and quoted it out loud along with the action, in exactly the same fashion as *The Rocky Horror Picture*

Show in America. *The Invaders'* production team took the show seriously, as Thinnes reported about cinematographer Andrew McIntryre in a February 1996 *Starlog* interview: "[McIntyre] educated me well in the field of UFO investigation. There were military pilots, commercial pilots, all of whom had these experiences. He didn't take the subject lightly. Occasionally, a director would come in with the attitude that the show was a comic strip, and Andy would put a stop to it immediately. In a very gentlemanly fashion, he would explain to them that it was a very serious subject, and if we made light of it, it was going to show on film. So there was a pretty serious attitude; we had good times and laughs and all that, but we didn't ever criticize the material." Thinnes himself went from being an unbeliever to an open-minded observer, witnessing a UFO immediately before the show premiered. "It was about a day before the show went on the air," Thinnes said, in the same interview. "I was driving in the San Fernando Valley with someone else; we saw it go down one side, disappear behind the horizon, then rise up on the other side, multicolored, then soar off into space. I said, 'I don't know if I have the guts to call this in. It's going to sound self-serving.' But within minutes, there were radio reports, TV reports—everybody in the area spotted it, so I didn't have to report."

Fox T.V. recently made a four-hour miniseries out of *The Invaders*, that aired on November 12 and 14, 1995. The premise was that the original Invaders had more fully infiltrated human society in the nearly thirty years since Thinnes had tried to almost singlehandedly repel their invasion, and they were now better at concealing their activities. Thinnes reprised his role in a brief cameo, to hand his years of notes on the menace to the new hapless hero, ex-con, and mental patient Scott Bakula, who has been framed for murder by the Invaders. Bakula suffers from recurrent visions that prophetically come true, which he eventually discovers is a result of implants in his brain placed by the Invaders that hook him into their hive-mind, combined with an inherent flaw in his natural brain function. This flaw enables him to break their pervasive control and prevent their plans, and so makes him an extreme threat and a target. The Invaders repeatedly abduct various humans and mind-control them as discardable puppets for murders and terrorist acts to further their aims.

No longer detectable by the former flaw of extended pinky-fingers on the duplicated human forms in which they masquerade, the new Invaders are betrayed by being perfectly Politically Incorrect: they invariably eat nothing but red meat and eggs, smoke like chimneys (and only cigarettes, no less), and host "subversive" Howard Stern-ish radio talk shows. The neat excuse for this is that they need more carbon monoxide than we do and want to create civil unrest so we will destroy ourselves and make room for them. (And the red meat and eggs? Apparently just so they can bat a thousand on the Yuppie hate-list.) They have created all the chemical pollutants in our air, anxious to make our planet more like theirs—the identity and loca-tion of which is never disclosed, though two characters in the series independently mock Thinnes' crackpot theories as "the Martians are coming, the Martians are coming." The plot for this premiere story—obviously a pilot for an intended series—has the Invaders attempt-ing to assassinate a liberal, ecology-minded political candidate who would clean up their pollutant policies.

As propaganda, it is confused, but interesting. The Invaders' per-sonal diet and habits are calculated to offend the neo-conservative holistic health ethic (that is so frequently and mistakenly called "lib-eral"), coupling them in heinousness with any vocal criticism of the country. Their hypnotic mind control and its murderous aims demon-strably fit far more into the CIA's actual purview than that of any alien invasion force, though of course it was probably the initial fear that instigated the Agency's investigation of UFO activity. Similarly, in real terms, it is hardly the UFO Intelligence that is promoting envi-ronmental spoilage, but rather the opposite case: by all testimony and visible evidence, they are the ones monitoring and trying to minimize exactly such activity on our part.

Whether or not anyone on the production team had an inside track to government Intelligence, they didn't seem to do their home-work on UFOs or simple politics—their Invaders are inconsistent. Of course, it is entirely possible that the production was intended as nothing more than an entertaining diversion, with no connection at all to actual UFOlogy or politics, but then why did it try so hard on both counts to appear as if it did? Of all literary forms, science fiction—unless it is plainly escapist fantasy, which *The Invaders* is not—is invariably the most political, for the simple reason that the writer can put a mask on his enemies and finger them in socially acceptable fashion with no fear of repercussions. If the producers went to the trouble of utilizing some of the actual elements of fac- tual UFOs and their activities, it is odd that they would scramble them in such a bizarre fashion. What appears to be the case is that the non-Politically Correct were simply being tarred with a broad, unsubtle brush, and the inclusion of any legitimate UFO trappings occurred entirely by accident. An equally transparent case of broad socio-political propagandizing occurred in Paramount's *The Hunt for Red October,* in which no one in the American Navy was seen to smoke, and every member of a Russian sea crew had a lit cigarette perpetually dangling between his lips or staining his fingers—except for heroic, Western-thinking captain Sean Connery. (You know how them damn Invaders/Russians are.) *The X-Files* has followed suit, the only smokers in the show being the aged and corrupt old govern- ment-coverup boys; the only "vice" found among the protagonists (whose diets are not disclosed, though they almost never drink) is the hero's subscription to skin magazines.

The ultimate abduction series came out of Britain for a single sea- son, right at the same time, in 1968, *The Prisoner,* which was about a man known only as Number 6, interrogated by a different Number 2 every week in a bizarre setting and with no obvious intent, on an iso- lated island at no known location from which no one can escape. Any who try to flee are apprehended by "Rover," a giant bubble that seems to come from nowhere and engulfs the refugee either for retrieval or death. The implication was that The Prisoner was some kind of Intelligence operative. The overriding question asked him was "Who is Number 1?" who ultimately turns out to be The Prisoner himself. The show had a nightmarish quality and proved an enduringly pop- ular cult hit which can still occasionally be seen on Public Television.

Also made in '68 was a movie so unbelievably bad, it is omitted from most cinema chronicles even of the unbelievably bad: *Space*

Thing. The plot was nothing more than an early X-rated space-romp (starring "Paula Pleasure" and "Steve Stunning") about a crew of sultry space lesbians led by "Captain Mother." Mentioned only as being even worse than *Plan 9* when it is mentioned at all, *Space Thing* was produced by exploitation legend David F. Friedman, who got his start as a WWII Army Signal Corps cinematographer. Friedman's usual producer, Herschell Gordon Lewis, notorious for the cheapest nudie exploitation quickies, the same year made the bizarre comedy *How To Make a Doll* (Unusual Films), about a college professor who manufactures a computerized robot girlfriend. *The Astro-Zombies,* written by *M.A.S.H.*'s Wayne Rogers, was released by independent Geneni Film Distributors at about the same time, starring ubiquitous mad-scientist John Carradine as a CIA-pursued tinkerer-together of skeleton-faced, organ-stealing abductors. Several European countries simultaneously collaborated on the failed pilot for a Perry Rhodan space-opera series, *Mission Stardust.*

And 1968 was the year that Walter Reade Productions released perhaps the most famous and successful low-budget independent film on record, George A. Romero's *Night of the Living Dead.* From an initial cost of $114,000, it grossed four to five million dollars in its first five years and made *Variety's* list of top-grossing films in both 1969 and 1970. Quickly translated into seventeen foreign languages, it began the cult movie trend of midnight showings that *The Rocky Horror Picture Show* soon became so famous for, and until John Carpenter's *Halloween* (Compass International) ten years later was the most financially rewarding film of its type ever made. Primarily a misunderstood spoof—an arguable point, though Romero's later sequels rather obviously performed as social satires—*Night of the Living Dead* has nothing overtly to do with UFOs. But according to the plot, the reason why the dead have suddenly come back to unnatural life and begun stalking the living with hostile intent is that they have become infected with some unknown bacteria or radiation brought back from a recent space probe to the planet Venus. The scenes describing this ludicrous-sounding plot point are performed in deadly earnest, with the same sincerity that made Orson Welles' *The War of the Worlds* so famous. The effectively nightmarish music that comprises the soundtrack came from one of the most ridiculous of the early flying saucer movies, Warner Bros.' 1959 release, *Teenagers from Outer Space*.

1969 brought a remarkable low-budget UFOlogical/sociological entry from Bell and Howell Productions, *The Monitors*. Obviously a play on "Watchers," the Monitors are human-looking aliens who brainwash and control the human race through clever T.V. jingles and ad campaigns—not unlike the government Intelligence operation under consideration in this study. Their rule is benevolent, but sterile and dull, devoid of emotions. Brainy Susan Oliver and sexy Sherry Jackson have livelier activities on their mind, and they seduce journalist Guy Stockwell into helping them empower right-wing underground resistance efforts to reach the people. The film was a scattershot satirical comedy, intended to attract a wide audience— among its literally dozens of cameos were Xavier Cougat, Stubby Kaye, Jackie Vernon, and Senator Everett Dirksen, all popular icons of one or another sort at the time. 20th Century Fox the same year released a thriller called *The Chairman*, starring Gregory Peck as a U.S. government spy deep in Red China, whom the CIA has equipped with an exploding implant device in his head in case he should fail and be captured.

It was also in 1969 that "the first and best made-for-TV occult movie" (as Weldon's encyclopedia appropriately dubs it) was released by Universal on NBC, the UFOlogically rife *Fear No Evil*. The pilot for a proposed series called *Bedeviled,* the movie came from a story by notable horror author Guy Endore and starred Louis Jourdan as a psychiatric investigator of occult cases. Bradford Dillman purchases a full-length antique mirror for his fiancée, Lynda Day (-George), with no later memory at all of having done so. Immediately after, haunted by a specter in his car mirror, Dillman accidentally runs his car off the road and kills himself. After the accident, Day finds herself summoned to Dillman's image night after night in the mirror, only Dillman is now a demonic doppelganger dressed entirely in black and arriving in a sheen of red light, inhabiting a red, white, and black realm of symmetrical, never-ending archways; his visits leave her with Unidentified Body Markings and a loss of blood, resulting from wild sex she has with Dillman's double on these occasions.

Psychiatrist Jourdan uses narcohypnosis to determine that Day's experiences are actually occurring and are not hallucinations. "Do you want these experiences to stop?" Jourdan asks her, and, in common with many true-life UFO abductees (whose experiences are similar), she admits honestly, "No." Jourdan discovers that Dillman was the victim of a quasi-scientific demon-cult summoning "the lord Ra-Kashi, Lord of Light, Lust and Blood," who inhabits the ruby-red light of lasers, and also mirrors, the realm of reflected light. Under the guise of "an entertainment," the demonologists, led by government optical physicist Carroll O'Connor, tricked Dillman into becoming the hypnotized "vessel" of the god, causing him to enact the appropriate ritual. Once possessed, Dillman went mad and escaped, bought the mirror under the mind control of the demon Ra-Kashi, and lost all his memory of the events—after which he died, and Ra-Kashi assumed his guise to visit Day.

The mytho-historical literacy of the script is obviously well-informed, probably the result of a Masonic or Rosicrucian influence somewhere in the production team, or even a UFOlogical one. The demon "Ra-Kashi" is obviously derivative of the Egyptian Ra-Harakhte (who is both the Sphinx and the god of Mars) and is associated with the color red, summoned by ruby lasers or the light from red candles, and inhabits a realm consisting entirely of the colors red, white, and black—the colors of Atlantis. Dillman is hypnotized when he becomes the vessel of the god, and amnesiac afterward, and he is ceremonially whipped during "the Ra-Kashi experiment" (as government scientist O'Connor calls it) with black whips attached to white handles. When Day descends the stairs to go to her final abduction by God of the Underworld Ra-Kashi, she is in a white bridal gown; a red coat is draped over her shoulders by her bridesmaid immediately before she begins her descent, emphasizing the "white above, red below" so prevalent in the ancient world. This color scheme is even more dramatically underscored by the superimposition of two angles for the same shot, one in close-up, showing the white headgear filling the upper half of the screen and the red coat the lower half. As if to draw closer attention to the occult symbolism, Dillman's possession occurs at a "Metaphysical Research Center" where groups called "The Atlantis Federation" and "The Pyramid Circle" meet, and a lengthy tape-recorded lecture on Atlantis, Moses, and the Pharaoh Akhnaton is in progress when Jourdan goes there to conduct his investigation. Also, numerous scenes in the movie make incidental use of the colors red, white, and black, even using red and white for the colors of hallways and doors in the hospital where Day recovers.

The general misinformations and laughably silly space-operas began to peter-out with the end of the playful and colorful—if turbulent—1960s. In the next decade, the same studios producing UFO-logical material would begin to explore the topic in more interesting, if less consistent (and less obvious) ways, such as the literate occult thriller *Fear No Evil*. But still to be discussed are a number of other interesting entries of accurate UFO material surfacing in the chaotically crazy '60s, where they would be certain not to be taken seriously—most notably on T.V., and in comics and cartoons.

8

Juvenilizations
and Animations

For whatever reason, fantasy was immensely popular and prolific in 1960s America. At the same time Leslie Stevens and
Joseph Stefano were trying to tune everyone's consciousness
to thinking about "the awe and mystery" of the universe, CBS' *My
Favorite Martian* (1963–65) was one of the most popular shows on
television. It began with eerie music and a robotic, antennaed figure
zipping from Mars to Earth, then suddenly turned to a silly musical-
comedy vamp, the Martian becoming funny old song-'n-dance man
Ray Walston, with a new silly Earth friend in bumbling Bill Bixby.
("*D'uh-oh,* Uncle Martin, your flying saucer is making my washing
machine go crazy again!" *Canned laughter.*) The same network's *My
Living Doll* ran one short year in 1964, starring Scandinavian sex-
bomb Julie Newmar as Air Force special project AF-709, Rhoda the
robot, so bad it could almost have turned Bob Packwood out of the
bedroom. Jerry Van Dyke made another comical machine and the
subject of reincarnation idiotic the following year in NBC's *My Mother,
the Car,* though CBS' equally ludicrous *Mister Ed,* the talking horse—
a takeoff on the successful "Francis the Talking Mule" movies—
ran six years starting in 1960. Screen Gems' more slickly produced *I
Dream of Jeannie* and *Bewitched* soon followed, providing solid
examples of the general sort of programming of the time. Irwin Allen's

unbelievably juvenile sci-fi entries all began as fairly realistic Cold War or space melodramas, but invariably degenerated after only one year into childish idiocy, the prime examples being *Voyage to the Bottom of the Sea* (ABC, 1964–68) and *Lost In Space* (CBS, 1965–68), both produced by 20th Century Fox and featuring a weekly parade of inane rubber monsters going *"Rrarrgh, rrowr—!"* like any clown in a fuzzy bear suit at a kid's birthday party, and with exactly the same effect. Robots, animated mannequins, living dolls, UFOs, and space aliens aplenty never looked more ridiculous, or came trotting out of the wings more often.

Lost In Space featured almost weekly alien abductions of one or another crew member, usually the psychopathic cravenly coward, Dr. Smith, who—next to the robot—was the show's most popular character. A complete catalogue of the Space Family Robinsons' alien encounters is hardly necessary to get the point across, but several typical occurrences match those of actual UFO abductions and/or raise interesting speculations about them. For instance, the second season's "Cave of the Wizards" had Dr. Smith suddenly struck with amnesia, sleepwalking to a voice only he can hear (followed by the robot and young Will Robinson, so the audience can witness the rest of the abduction), emanating from a cave filled with the artifacts of an ancient lost civilization. Statues of Greek and Egyptian gods abound, all cobwebbed, the most prominent being that of the Egyptian Amen-Ra. Animated mummies guard the entrance of the cave from ingress by unwanted interlopers (which Will and the robot manage to bypass), and Smith intimately converses with a computer, which informs him that he has been "chosen" to become a reborn scion of the ancient race. Recovering, Smith refuses to believe he has been abducted, completely amnesiac of the entire encounter, but becomes increasingly aware as he is repeat-summoned in his usual trance to continue the alien transformation process. He is dressed in a red Egyptian skullcap and begins physically transforming to resemble the long-dead alien race of humanoids. The computer tests his loyalty, but ultimately Smith breaks its hold on him and flees back to the Robinsons, too terrified of losing his familiar surroundings and friends to complete his conversion. The same season's "A Visit to Hades" featured an imprisoned alien exile named Morbus, dressed in red and black, who once led an interplanetary revolt and is believed by Smith to be the devil; Morbus' prison is guarded by two Egyptian statues, and is locked by the music of a magic harp.

A near-identical story to "Cave of the Wizards" called "Follow the Leader" ended the series' first season, in which Robinson family head John becomes the amnesiac abductee of an alien warlord stranded on the same planet. John finds himself acting as if he were two people, and vainly attempts to fight off the invisible nocturnal presence each night in his room. The alien intelligence plans to use John Robinson's body to reincarnate itself and murder the rest of the party, but John's love for his son expels the evil invader.

In other episodes, Smith found himself repeat-visited by Athena, "The Girl from the Green Dimension," a sexy green female space-siren (Vitina Marcus) who blatantly sought bodily abduction for sexual purposes. The first abduction story of the series was the eighth episode, "Invaders from the Fifth Dimension," when first Smith and then Will Robinson were bodily abducted aboard a spaceship by superior aliens with bald heads and no faces, in order that their brains could be utilized to repair the aliens' ship. Will's emotional upheaval at being forcibly taken away from his parents renders him useless to the aliens, who die because they are then unable to return to their home, but not before they give Will back to his family.

Robots, androids, and alien mind control were as commonplace as abductions on both *Lost In Space* and *Voyage to the Bottom of the Sea*. In the former show, especially, an episode rarely passed without the inclusion of alien automata in one form or another. Al "Grampa Munster" Lewis appeared as an alien magician in "Rocket to Earth," accompanied by an animated ventriloquist's dummy in his own image. Lewis and the little monster mannequin repeatedly visit and bedevil Smith, who alone can see them due to Lewis' "magic"; they hypnotize him into becoming their unwitting "assistant" in an explosively destructive suicide run. Famous model/socialite/actress Dee Hartford (wife of *The Thing*'s director, Howard Hawks) made several appearances as an alien android learning human behavior from the Robinson family. Smith attempted to martial the forces of "The Space

Destructors," a legion of alien-manufactured cyborgs created in his own image. MGM's famous "Robby the Robot" appeared as a sentient monster threatening enslavement and medical experimentation of Earth's human population on behalf of its alien makers in "The War of the Robots." There were many other mechanical menaces.

Voyage to the Bottom of the Sea sported one of the most famous robot episodes in the annals of telefantasy, "The Wax Men," in which ubiquitous evil dwarf Michael Dunn *(The Wild, Wild West's* "Dr. Loveless") replaces the *Seaview* crew with automated wax replicas—specifically designated in the episode as having come from "the lost continent of Atlantis"—before he is electrocuted and they are melted away. Similar UFOlogical elements occurred in one of the most ridiculous of the series' 110 episodes, "The Mummy," in which Captain Crane is mind-controlled by a near-indestructible Egyptian mummy to sabotage *Seaview* for no reason ever disclosed in the story. Vincent Price appeared as the puppetmaster of "The Deadly Dolls," an army of automata controlled by an extraterrestrial intelligence. "The Cyborg" was a robot replacement of Admiral Nelson, programmed to start WWIII, and "The Mechanical Man" is self-explanatory. "The Indestructible Man" was a robot manning a space probe through the Van Allen radiation belt, which damaged its circuits and turned it into an invulnerable saboteur aboard the *Seaview* upon its return (the exact reason never being specified, but implications present of some foreign intelligence possibly having altered its programming). The menace of "The Machines Strike Back" were remote-controlled, unmanned nuclear subs. One especially ludicrous episode from the third season was "The Terrible Toys," in which six children's windup toys become possessed by an alien intelligence and begin sabotaging the *Seaview* with sound waves. The principal purpose of all these mechanoid appearances would seem to have been to make them appear absurd. Though many of the elements in both Irwin Allen shows were essentially correct in regard to actual UFOlogy, their presentation was so childish that they literally numbed the mind, and did so on a subliminal level, since they were more or less perceived (by anyone other than their usual audience of children) as "background noise."

Voyage to the Bottom of the Sea's sixth episode, "The Sky is Falling"—its plot echoing that of a 1959 Allied Artists feature called *The Atomic Submarine*—was the first featuring a flying saucer, and probably the only episode to examine the UFO situation with a semblance of seriousness. Panic has ensued due to mass sightings of a flying saucer that crashes into the sea, destroying a submarine in the process. Admiral Nelson's miraculous nuclear sub, the *Seaview*, is sent out to track down and destroy the hostile invader. The saucer finds them first, paralyzing the submarine and blacking out its power systems, then sending a shuttle by way of invitation, which Nelson accepts. Aboard the alien craft, Nelson is surprised to discover that the alien looks exactly like Nelson himself. "I have assumed the likeness of the one creature that could not possibly offend you," the alien explains—its normal appearance would be "repellent" to people from our planet. Similarly, when Captain Crane later takes a trip to the saucer, the alien appears to him as Captain Crane. Its true appearance is bald and faceless, with enormous black elliptical eyes—a UFO Gray. (Actual UFO abductees report their chief "controller" in the process speaking to them in their own voice, an obscure detail which was not discussed in the literature until the 1990s, thirty years after this episode aired.)

"We have been studying your planet for some time," the alien informs Nelson. "Your language, customs, characteristics. You are dangerously sensitive to anything you do not understand." Later, it admits to Nelson, when he asks what the alien "plans" are for Earth, "We do have plans, I assure you. You are obviously a man of courage. Otherwise, you would not have accepted the invitation that brought you here. Are you also a man of curiosity?" Nelson answers, "I am a scientist, if that term has any meaning for you." The alien replies that it is "delighted to hear it," and offers no further explanation, though the obvious implication is that it intends to share some knowledge with Nelson—i.e., to repeat-abduct him at a future date, since the rest of the episode concerns the timely necessity of enabling the alien's escape. Nelson, Crane, and the alien manage to repair the saucer (the destruction of our submarine was an unavoidable collision, the saucer itself damaged by a meteor in space) and avert a potential war incident between the alien's unspecified home planet and Earth—albeit with great difficulty, since America's war machine is all too anxious to shoot first and ask questions later. "We can expect to see it again someday," Crane comments, as the saucer manages to make its way back to space. "I hope they'll remember they were treated as friends!" Nelson answers, "They'll remember, all right. I wonder if *we* will."

The third season's "Day of Evil" presented a diabolical turnaround of the same elements. After a UFO enters the *Seaview*'s sector, Crane and another crewmember are lethally dosed with radiation. Nelson then finds himself confronted in his room by a doppelganger. Nelson asks his other self if it is an alien from the UFO, and the doppelganger answers yes. The alien in Nelson's form cheerfully informs Nelson that he will cure Crane if Nelson will perform a later favor upon request. Left with no alternative to save his friend, Nelson agrees. The alien lives up to its part of the bargain, then returns to name its favor: it wants Nelson to launch *Seaview*'s nuclear arsenal and start WWIII, clearing the Earth of human life so the alien's kind can live on the planet in mankind's place. Nelson of course refuses, asking why the technologically superior alien doesn't simply launch the missiles itself. The alien chucklingly responds that its people don't work that way—the people of Earth must destroy themselves. Thwarted, the alien appears to Captain Crane in Crane's image, and again fails in its aim. Departing, the alien grudgingly compliments the two men on their willpower, but remarks that it is not a gracious loser and that it will be back someday to try and subvert others.

"Deadly Cloud," the same year, had another alien doppelganger. Captain Crane is abducted from the flying sub (the *Seaview* own flying saucer) into a mysterious cloud. When he returns, he is actually an alien duplicate. The aliens from the cloud are metallic silver in appearance, are bulletproof, and talk in halting, mechanical voices. The robotic aliens abduct Admiral Nelson later in the story and show him the unconscious Crane on a slab in their ship, admitting that they are performing experiments on the human race. Ultimately, of course, the aliens are driven away. Crane and other crewmembers were abducted to the planet Venus in "Journey with Fear" in *Voyage*'s final season. On that planet, aliens similar to those in "Deadly Cloud," additionally armed with sonic weapons, interrogate their *Seaview* prisoners with a hypnotic mind-control helmet. The aliens' aim is to prevent Earth sending lethal weapons into space. "The Shadowman" was a sabotaging alien similarly intent on destroying all Earth life because of mankind's threat to its extraterrestrial domain. Mind-controlling aliens were also featured in "The Fossil Men," "The Heat Monster," "The Monster from Outer Space," "Terror," and "Attack!" among other episodes. In the lattermost, hypnosis is unable to break through the amnesiac mental block imposed on a saboteur crewmember by the alien intelligence using him.

Toward the close of the first season, *Voyage* featured a menacing alien race in "The Invaders." These were small, bald humanoids, recovered in suspended animation from the ocean floor, after a seaquake brings them—and their long-submerged ancient civilization—into view. Robert Duvall (who was playing a virtually identical role in *The Outer Limits'* "The Chameleon" the same year) played the sly and cunning pseudo-Asian humanoid, who possesses a superior sonic pistol, speaks with a hypnotic quality, sabotages the submarine, and plans to remove humanity from the Earth so his people may resume their former place of glory. Duvall's nature is never precisely made clear, it being specified by him that his race were specifically engineered by another preceding them, and—though seeming to be alive—appearing to be almost entirely artificial (much like Richard Sharp Shaver's "teros" and "deros," of Ray Palmer's early pulp-publications). Duvall's race cannot be attacked—their cellular structure is rife with botulinus, lethally infecting hundreds or thousands of their attackers at the merest scratch. Though not hostile, Duvall's race is utterly ruthless. Duvall is their happenstance vanguard, and is only eliminating mankind as an expedient solution to the insoluble problem of mutual cohabitation. To save the human race, Admiral Nelson tricks Duvall into incinerating himself before the rest of his race can be reactivated, thus consuming the lethal virus in Duvall's bloodstream before it can be released. The final season's "The Deadly Amphibians" repeated the same plot, with the title creatures additionally mutating some of the *Seaview* crew into their own race to aid them in acts of sabotage.

It is an idea worthy of serious consideration that more than one purpose was at work in such programs as those produced by Irwin Allen. Only children could have been held rapt by such inanely immature antics as those of the Space Family Robinson, or the adventures of the nuclear submarine, *Seaview.* Yet, the very process by which older minds were deflected from thinking about the science-fictional elements in these programs also planted the seeds for future generations to be less resistant to the idea of otherworldly contact. Ultimately, all science fiction—whether intentionally serious or as intentionally ridiculous—manages to infect receptive minds with a sense of adventure and wonder. Both *Lost In Space* and *Voyage to the Bottom of the Sea,* however nonsensical their plots or trappings, also deliberately included eerie and frightening images, music, and situations, programmed specifically to appeal to juvenile minds in the same way as do the darker elements of fairy tales—and probably for the same reason, which was the demonstration that, no matter how seemingly terrifying the situation, humanity manages to overcome it by its very nature before the end of the hour ... provided one maintains an open attitude of reason and is more scientifically and culturally curious than timid and xenophobic.

Screen Gems' (Columbia's T.V. branch) *Bewitched* and *I Dream of Jeannie,* interestingly enough, are both series in which mortal men mate with fairy women, the latter even being the marriage of a NASA astronaut with an ancient immortal from a more advanced "magical" culture. The former was phenomenally popular, running eight years on ABC beginning in 1964, with the latter an NBC hit for five years starting in 1965. *Bewitched,* in addition to a few episodes plainly intended to ridicule UFOs—such as one in which dog-creatures from Sirius (the "dog-star") land in the back yard in a flying saucer, or another in which NASA follows witch Samantha around because they have heard she's been to the Moon—also, whether intentionally or unintentionally, presented a few stories that pondered more serious UFOlogical problems.

The best of these was a story in which husband Darrin wants Sam to come clean to the world about her being a witch, and she obliges him by invading his dream that night and controlling it, showing him exactly what would happen if she did. Darrin's boss is initially overjoyed by the revelation, but sours and fires Darrin from his job when Sam refuses to use her witchcraft to give him unfair competitive advantage in the business world. Similarly, the couple lose all their friends when Sam doesn't perform for their amusement on cue, or help them win the lottery. Soon, disenchantment gives way to resentment, and they even find their kids having rocks thrown at them, just as in the witch-hunts of the Dark Ages. Worse, the government suddenly takes an active interest in their offspring, spiriting Sam and her children away from Darrin to live in a glorified concentration camp, so they can develop the children's talents to suit their own weapons-development ends. Darrin bolts awake in terror, his mind changed, and Sam does not reveal that she manipulated his dream. If the National Security Agency, for instance, has been monitoring UFO abductees, many of the same results could occur if disclosure of the fact were made public—which may well explain why so much of UFO information is still highly classified, and the subject continually downplayed in popular discussion. Screen Gems was also the studio (in conjunction with *Batman* producer Bill Dozier) that presented the very popular *The Farmer's Daughter* (ABC, 1963–66), featuring a fantasy episode in its final year called "Katy in a Capsule," with everybody's favorite sweetheart girl-next-door, Inger Stevens, dreaming about being the first female astronaut to the Moon.

Also appearing in about equal measure to the fantasies at that time were culture-clash comedies, from *The Munsters* and *The Addams Family* to *The Beverly Hillbillies,* which are of peripheral interest to this study. The subject of "managed television" finds considerably fertile ground when comparing ABC's *The Addams Family* and CBS' *The Munsters:* both shows debuted and were cancelled in the same weeks, and played the same plots with the same particulars, sometimes even at the same time. As Stephen Cox notes in *The Addams Chronicles:* "Funny, but more than just a few 'Addams' and 'Munsters' episodes had hauntingly similar plots. Both families went on a treasure hunt, discovering a chest of fortune on their own property. The children of both families ran away. Both families filmed spacemen episodes (common in the 1960s), while each show devoted a storyline to the parents' mistaken assumption that their little boy had been transformed into a chimp. Beatniks discovered both families. Each show presented a leading character going on a hopeless diet. Both families built robots. Arguments erupted in each brood and someone painted a white line to separate the house [which also occurred on *Gilligan's Island* at almost exactly the same time]. Family pets were missing in both shows (with the Addamses, it was Thing), just as both Herman and Gomez suffered from massive amnesia. And finally, both cantankerous characters—Grandpa and Fester—ran newspaper ads advertising for a mate. Hmmmmmmm." As more succinctly summed up in a November 1964 *T.V. Guide*, "Exactly why two networks should come up with two shows in the same year on exactly the same subject and with two families which, if you ask us, are dead wringers for each other, would take, we suspect, grave explanation." Given military and governmental connections to Hollywood, it is worth noting that Pat Priest, who played the Munsters' "normal" daughter, Marilyn, in the final season, is the daughter of former United States Treasurer Ivy Baker Priest.

The Munsters' "spacemen" episode was "If a Martian Answers, Hang Up" in 1965, with supposedly hoaxed Martians that turn out to be real. They are brusquely dismissed as tricksters by household head Herman when their radio message to Mars is intercepted, and are revealed in their flying saucer to be antennaed versions of *Outer Limits'* "O.B.I.T." monster mask. ("My, those Earth people are getting rude!" the Martian comments in a last-minute aside.) *The Munsters'* producers, Joe Connelly and Bob Mosher, also were behind ABC's 1957–63 hit, *Leave It to Beaver,* featuring at least two similar entries, both from major UFO flap-year 1957. In "Tenting Tonight," father Ward goes to pick up the boys at the Saturday matinee movie, which is garishly postered in the lobby: "Man-Beast from Mars." And the episode "Captain Jack" opened with Wally and the Beave debating ordering something from the back of a comic book called "Robot Men from Mars," accompanied by the punch-line, "Wull, gee, Wally, if it's in 'Robot Men from Mars,' it must be true!" *(Canned laughter.)* "The Hypnotist" similarly poked fun at outer-space subjects, with neighborhood psychopath Eddie Haskell pretending to be the Beaver's hypnotic slave, just to spook him. Hugh Beaumont, who played the Beaver's father, began his career making wartime propaganda shorts for Connelly and Mosher, and also starred in Universal's *The Mole People* in 1956, about a long-lost subterranean race of Ishtar-worshipping Sumerians in Tibet and their genetically engineered humanoid slaves.

A number of offhanded degradations of UFOlogical topics were visible in the 1960s, some of which probably resulted from nothing more than the already pervasive atmosphere against UFOlogy in general, but others of which may have been inspired by favors for Intelligence friends. Sherwood Schwartz, military-connected and part of the production team of *My Favorite Martian,* made laughingstock of a robot in United Artists T.V.'s *Gilligan's Island.* Another episode had Gilligan mistaking a descending Russian space capsule for a UFO landing on the island, the Skipper telling him, "Oh, Gilligan, they're not Martians," and Gilligan answering, "Well, they're not the Smothers Brothers!" The episode "Smile, You're on Mars Camera" had a Cape Kennedy Mars probe go awry and land on the island, mistaking the castaways' huts for Martian dwellings. By the time the castaways get on camera, they have managed to glue themselves all over with feathers, and the NASA boys back home think they've discovered bird-people on Mars before the camera goes dead. (*"Oh, Gilligan—!"*) Hypnosis and mind control were also given more than one trouncing, the best examples being episodes in which Vito Scotti as a mad scientist abducts the castaways by means of mind-controlling radio-receiver rings to perform tasks for him at night of which they are completely oblivious in their waking lives, and another in which he steals them away to his secret laboratory for nefarious experimentation.

Gilligan's Island was only one among many, *The Dick Van Dyke Show* sporting one comical flying saucer episode, in which Dick finds himself haunted by a little saucer late at night in the office; it appears outside his window and says *"Oony-oofs!"* over and over again—it turns out to be a malfunctioning toy that is supposed to say, "Merry Christmas!" (*Ho-ho-ho-!*) Another episode replicated *Invasion of the Body Snatchers,* with abductees turning into Danny Thomas with no thumbs and an appetite for walnuts—it turns out to be "all a dream."

Gomer Pyle, U.S.M.C. encountered little green men from a flying saucer in 1966. Innocently driving along the countryside on assignment, quintessential idiot Gomer doesn't realize he is witnessing actors in a movie. Three little bald dwarves, in silvery space suits with over-sized helmets, put him on for a lark, and soon poor Gomer is beside himself trying to prove to Sergeant Carter that the Martians have landed. *("Shazam!") The Colbys'* Fallon was abducted by a UFO at the beginning of the 1980s, reaction to which was actually polled and found to have severely soured the audience toward the show. The sitcom *Soap* satirized alien abductions toward the end of its run by making main character Bert a repeat abductee. *Married with Children*'s Al Bundy was also featured in a 1989 episode undergoing repeat abductions. There are many others, but these examples will suffice to show how the topic is ridiculed on a wide variety of programming.

In 1962, a now-famous series of Topps trading cards was issued, called "Mars Attacks," containing the most garish illustrations ever conceived. The Martians were blue pressure-suited meanies in flying saucers, looking like exposed brains with gigantic eyes and skull faces inside huge, lightbulb-shaped glass helmets. They devastated home-steads with fire, vivisected mom and dad, and in the most colorful and infamous card in the set, "Destroying a Dog," blew Rover to a spray of atoms with a cosmic ray gun. The original card series has since spawned a recent nostalgic reincarnation, in Topps Comics.

Famous singing comedian Allan Sherman, on his 1963 album, *My Son, the Nut,* made an especially interesting adaptation of Lewis/Young/Henderson's "Five Foot Two, Eyes of Blue." It was called "Eight Foot Two, Solid Blue," and went like this: "Last night I met a man from Mars, and he was very sad / He said, 'Won't you help me find my girlfriend, please?' / So I asked him, 'What does she look like?' / And the man from Mars said, 'She's ... / Eight foot two, solid blue, five transistors in each shoe, / Has anybody seen my gal? / Lucite nose, rustproof toes, and when her antenna glows, / She's the cutest Martian gal! / You know she promised me, recently, she wouldn't stray, / But came the dawn, she was gone, eighteen billion miles away! / Her steering wheel has sex appeal, her evening gown is stainless steel, / Has anybody seen my gal? / How I miss all the bliss of her sweet hydraulic kiss, / Has anybody seen my gal? / Lovely shape, custom built, squeeze her wrong and she says tilt, / Has anybody seen my gal? / She does the cutest tricks with her six stereo ears, / When she walks by, spacemen cry, 'specially when she shifts her gears! / If she's found, run like mad, put her on a launching pad / Down at Cape Can-av-er-al, / And shoot me back my cutie, / My supersonic beauty, / Send me back my Martian gal!' " Other silly space songs of the era included Buchanan and Goodman's "Flying Saucers" in 1956, Sheb Wooley's famous "Purple People Eater" two years later, Bill Dana's "The Astronaut" in 1962, the Ran Dells' "Martian Hop" of 1963, and 1964's "Outer Limits" by the Marketts.

Cartoons, especially, kept UFOlogical topics in a humorous light in this time period. Standard Saturday morning fare, space-related cartoons have in general proliferated so widely as to become meaningless, which may be the point. Warner Bros.' Bugs Bunny faced the Trojan-garbed "Marvin the Martian" five times starting with 1948's "Haredevil Hare," in which Marvin first attempted to "blow up the Earth" from the Moon (arriving on a rocket reading "Mars to Moon Expeditionary Force") with his "Iliudium Pew-36 Explosive Space Modulator." Marvin was a short black humanoid in a red Roman bodysuit, whose only visible face was a pair of big round eyes inside a huge, round Trojan helmet, wearing tennis shoes, which is not unlike the description given by Antonio Villas Boas but more comical. His sidekick, a "fugitive from the Dog Star," as Bugs called him, was a similarly garbed canine. Emphasizing the joke, Bugs first calls Marvin "Marconi." Marvin made additional appearances with the studio's other cartoon characters, such as Porky Pig and Daffy Duck in "Duck Dodgers in the 24½th Century," the cartoon used in the background of Steven Spielberg's *Close Encounters of the Third Kind.* Marvin has since become as much an American icon as the rest of the Warner Bros. cartoon characters, so popular that such items as coffee mugs, throw-pillows, and bookmarks can commonly be found with his image on them, usually sporting one or the other of his famous lines: *"Capture that Earth creature!"* or *"Blow up the Earth!"*

Bugs was first saucer-abducted in 1952's "Hasty Hare," a full decade before the Hills. He was captured by a mad scientist caricatured to the likeness of Peter Lorre, by means of a female robot rabbit, in "Hair-Raising Hare" in 1946, just over one year before the Roswell crash, which is possible evidence for the case that the government knew a few things before that time. "Yosemite Sam from Outer Space" attempted to abduct Bugs aboard a flying saucer by means of robots in "Lighter Than Hare" in 1960, the year before Betty and Barney Hill. Martians appeared comically in other Warner Bros. cartoons as well, such as one in which a Walter Mitty-ish little boy fantasizes himself as a brave jet pilot, singlehandedly defeating cigar-shaped black spacecraft occupied by green robots with radio antennae; another in which new Earth parents find themselves with a Martian infant mistakenly in place of their own; and another still in which Porky Pig's housecats play a trick on him by dressing up as invading men from Mars in an Orson Welles-inspired hoax. Hypnotism and robots frequently made their way into the canon, "Robot Rabbit" having Elmer Fudd build a tin-can device to try and eradicate "that wascally wabbit," and another show in which Porky Pig acquires an indestructible robot cat to get rid of a mouse.

Most interesting of the lot was a 1952 remake of the Peter Lorre abduction cartoon, "Water, Water, Every Hare," substituting a caricature of Vincent Price for the mad scientist. Unlike every other caricature in Warner Bros.' catalogue of Hollywood figures, Price's body is inaccurate. Price was an immensely tall man, and the caricature is very short. The cartoon character is also bald, with an inordinately large cranium, and dressed in a tight-fitting labcoat—Price did not appear as a bald villain until 1971's *The Abominable Dr. Phibes,* and in fact did not begin his monster movie roles until *House of Wax* (also from Warner Bros.) the year after this Bugs Bunny cartoon was made.

Price could well have been a CIA recruit himself, his extremely successful career vended to him from that source in return for services rendered. He was the type of man the Agency likes to employ, well-traveled and exceptionally intelligent, of a great many talents and with contacts all over the world. In an interview with *Castle of Frankenstein* editor Calvin Thomas Beck, in the early to mid-'70s, Price said of his youth, "I knew London like a book, knew where to go and whom to see ... I'd spent several summers abroad during my college vacations. I had been a research student at the universities of Nuremberg, Vienna, Frankfurt, and London. In 1932, during one of these vacation periods, I had spent my days piloting tourists through museums and art galleries, tutoring in history and English, while at night I sang in a Vienna night club." Victor Marchetti and John Marks' *The CIA and the Cult of Intelligence* makes mention of the fact that primary recruiting for the Agency out of academia, especially before Vietnam, came from the Ivy League, with Yale University being top of the list. Monied families also used to be preferred, and Price came from both: his father was president of the five-and-dime retailing chain, the National Candy Company, and Price graduated from Yale in the 1930s. In later years, he was also very close friends with probable British Intelligence agent Diana Rigg (see previous chapter). Of particular note is that he was a member of Orson Welles' Mercury Theatre in 1938, the year of the famous "Invasion From Mars" broadcast.

In the cartoon featuring Price's caricature, Bugs is brought to him floating under water and then on top of it. Still asleep, Bugs is cold lying on the laboratory slab and pulls the blanket over himself—only it isn't a blanket, it's a wrapped mummy. Screaming, he leaps, shivering, into Price's arms. "What's up, Doc? What's goin' on around—*AAH!*" Seeing Price, he leaps to the nearest object: an Egyptian sarcophagus. Screaming again, he leaps to the next nearest object: a giant robot. The usual comic nonsense ensues, Bugs gets hit by ether, falls asleep, floats back to his hole underwater, wakes up and says, "What the—! Huh . . . all a dream!" And an all-eyes monster (in tennis shoes) that he had been eluding drifts by and says, "Oh, yeah? That's what you think!"

Jay Ward's very popular and long-running *Rocky and Bullwinkle* of the 1960s (originally called simply *The Bullwinkle Show*) featured two recurring characters originating in its 1959 series pilot: the "Moon Men," Gidney and Cloyd, little and green, who traveled on a flying saucer and carried ray-guns. Trans-Artists Productions and Batman creator Bob Kane presented more than one ludicrous alien story on the juvenile cartoon *Courageous Cat and Minute Mouse*, between 1960 and '61. One had the heroes traveling to the Moon, there to encounter gibberish-speaking crescent moon-shaped inhabitants with stubby little arms and legs, patterned after the comical turn-of-the-century space travel cinema of Georges Melies. Another had the title characters flying a rocket to the planet Electron, to keep light bulb-headed occupants there from attacking Earth's satellites. It turns out that Earth was sapping their power, threatening the Electronians' literal life-blood, but a peaceful resolution is somehow managed by the superhero feline and his rodent companion. A similarly ridiculous cartoon, only one among legion, was to be found in "The Zap-Sap," on Hal Seeger's 1966–67 series *Batfink*, with the title hero's arch-nemesis mad scientist, Hugo A Go-Go, masquerading as an antennaed, monotone-voiced little green man in a flying saucer, to perform simple bank robberies *(tee-hee!)*.

The contemporaneous title hero of Leonardo Television's *Underdog* combated "The Magnet Men," robots on the Moon who pulled Earth out of its orbit to put it into a new Ice Age. In another story, "Zot," Underdog found himself saucer-abducted to the title planet (a fissured reddish-yellow world more than a little resembling Mars), there to forcibly wed a three-eyed, red-garbed, antennaed little green princess, who fancied his prowess from afar. The similar "The Flying Sorcerers" found Underdog's lady love, Sweet Polly Purebred, abducted to another planet to become the slave of the title aliens. Sweet Polly also found herself abducted to the Moon by Underdog's arch-nemeses, Simon bar Sinister and his assistant Cad Lackey, who erected there a sonic weather-machine with which to terrorize Earth. Simon and Cad extended their aims to mind control as well, trying to implant the world's populace with devices toward that end in "The Phoney Booths" and wiping the memories of witnesses to their crimes with "The Forget-Me-Net."

Hanna-Barbera's Emmy award-winning Huckleberry Hound was in an early abduction cartoon, "Cop and Saucer." In it, Patrolman Huckleberry is dispatched to investigate a landed flying saucer in the park. A newsman with a big smile on his face is seen before the microphone, saying, "Well, the silly season is here, folks! Someone just called the police and said a flying saucer landed in the park! Ha-ha-ha! Here we go again!" "Looks like one of them foreign cars," Huck says, parking before the saucer. "I'll talk to that feller over there." Patrolman Huckleberry confronts an obvious blue robot that communicates only with *"Hum-um-umm"* sounds, with, "Pardon me, sir, but is that your car?" After a series of comical misunderstandings with the blue robot, it picks him up under one mechanical arm and carries him aboard the saucer, which then takes off. Huck hears the radio on board the saucer, the announcer's voice repeating, "Hello, folks! Like I said—*ha-ha!*—here we go again! Another call on that spaceship—someone reported it's taken off! And get this: with a policeman in it! Isn't that the funniest thing you ever heard? *Ha-ha-ha-!"* And Huckleberry, looking out the saucer's porthole and seeing Earth recede beneath him, finally realizes and says, "Yup. It's hye-larious." His laughter turns to sobs of despair. This cartoon was made parallel to the Hill abduction, in 1961. The same year, the Christmas episode of MGM's long-running *Dr. Kildare* guest-starred Dan O'Her-lihy as an indigent atheistic drunk in the hospital, bitterly complaining that God has been crowded out of his heaven by "Sputnik, flying saucers, and little green men from Mars."

William Hanna and Joe Barbera's legendary and ongoing sixty-year partnership began in MGM's animation department, one of the most prominent studios in the UFOlogical education program. From the mid-1960s on, Hanna-Barbera produced more kiddie and teeny-bopper space cartoons than any other studio, including such nostalgically remembered entries as *The Herculoids* and *Space Ghost,* the latter now a self-parodying revival on the Cartoon Network as *Space Ghost, Coast to Coast.* Its companion show, *Cartoon Planet,* features the recurring joke song, "It's a mighty Red Planet / And a very big cartoon! / If it hits me on the head / I'll be seeing stars! / It's time for the Number One cartoon / On Mars!" *Cartoon Planet,* "hosted" by the red, white, and black-garbed Space Ghost, also stars a giant praying mantis called "Zorak," who matches the description of many UFO occupants.

Hanna-Barbera's immensely popular Scooby Doo faced robots identical to those described by UFO abductees in his first season (1969). "Foul Play in Funland" had one fitted in a blue-hooded jumpsuit, with glowing yellow eyes, and specifically referred to as "a man from Mars" and "strictly a weirdo from outer space," with superhuman strength and speed, intent on apprehending Scooby and his comical pal Shaggy for no apparent reason. Super-hypnotic figures and monster mannequins often appeared on the series. The "Spooky Space Kook," for another example, was a glowing blue UFO occupant with a skull face in an obviously mechanical-looking body.

"Bedlam in the Big Top," also from the first year, had a "ghost clown" who hypnotically dominated Scooby, Shaggy, and Daphne, turning them into instant circus acrobats, which they had no recollection of after the fact. "Who Was That Cat-Creature I Saw You With Last Night?" had a super-hypnotist using an Egyptian coin to mesmerize an unwitting subject into becoming his nocturnal cat-burglar, causing her to suffer nightmares from her double life. Another cartoon had a "phantom racecar driver" putting people in a hypnotic trance and causing them to do things they would later forget; these unsuspecting victims were also implanted with false memories.

In later years, Scooby, Shaggy, and little nephew Scrappy Doo redesigned a NASA Mars probe robot to their own specifications after having stowed away on a trip to the Red Planet in "Way Out Scooby," and "Scooby Saves the World" had the same trio defeating invading blue robots from outer space in a NASA space shuttle. They also at various times confronted "body-snatcher" seed-pods from space, invading dog-aliens (no doubt from the dog-star), and other space robots. In "Close Encounter with a Weird Kind," Scooby and Scrappy witness Shaggy being abducted aboard a flying saucer by little green men, while the trio are out camping. Stowing away to rescue their unconscious pal, they fly the saucer back to Earth after being chased around themselves by the abductor-occupants. One of their cartoons, "A Creepy Tangle in the Bermuda Triangle," featured three UFOlogical elements at once: a flying saucer (fake, of course), the Bermuda Triangle, and literal "skeleton men" in an underground base. Another, from close to the last season, "Ghosts of the Ancient Astronauts," had ridiculous one-eyed flying-saucer aliens resurrected in a Mexican pyramid. One entire season of the show, called *The 13 Ghosts of Scooby Doo* (1985), even guest-starred probable Intelligence agent Vincent Price as himself (a character named "Vincent Van Ghoul").

It was Hanna-Barbera who in 1972 took the Radio Comics' characters already animated by them, John and Richard Goldwater and Dan DeCarlo's *Josie and the Pussy Cats,* and transported their young adult antics to somewhere a bit more distant in a new cartoon series: *Josie and the Pussy Cats in Outer Space.* "Mars, stars, the Milky Way, where they're groovin', who can say?" went the theme song. "Put on your seatbelts! They could be in orbit (in the stars)! On a spooky planet (maybe Mars)!" The inaugural episode of the new series had Josie abducted on a red planet, to be robot-duplicated by an alien with the Egyptian name "Karnak." Even before their move to space, the characters had, like those in the contemporaneous *Scooby Doo,* encountered a number of mind-controlling and robotic menaces. One of the earliest episodes from their first year (1970), "The Swat Plot Flop," had quintessential bimbo blonde Melody hypnotically dominated by a Persian robot, but too stupid to carry out her assassination orders without detection: eyes glazed and arms outstretched, she announces to her targeted compatriots, "I have come to dispose of you! Follow me to the trap!" The same year's "Strangemoon Over Miami" had Josie and Company disguising themselves as three Martians (Tic, Tac, and Toe) to distract Dr. Strangemoon from his plot of launching a satellite that would attract destructive comets to Earth, and "The Jumpin' Jupiter Affair" had them abducted for forced mining labor by bogus, bug-eyed, faceless green saucermen.

Hanna-Barbera's popular 1964–66 prime-time animated ABC series, *Jonny Quest,* featured an early flying saucer/robot episode. Called "The Robot Spy," it was about a flying saucer that eludes Air Force pursuit only to set down near one of their top-secret labs, where Dr. Quest is working on his defense project. Quest picks up an orb found in the saucer's center, and brings it back to the base to be warehoused, unaware that he has brought in a Trojan Horse. The orb comes to life in his absence, sprouting spider-like legs and opening a camera eye, paralyzing and knocking unconscious anyone it comes across with extensors from its main body that leave a mark on the forehead. It crawls into Quest's lab, where he stumbles on it as it is finishing its mission. His arch-enemy, the implied Red Chinese Dr. Zinn (who looks rather like Fleming's "Dr. No"), has sent this robot spy to photograph Quest's weapon. Having succeeded in its mission, it makes its way back to the saucer, unfazed by all military attempts to stop it. It reconnects to the saucer and takes off to return to its controller, only to be downed by the very weapon it came to photograph. When the series was revived in the 1970s, its opening credits featured a sequence in which disc-shaped flying saucers hover about launched missiles, destroying them with light-beams in the same fashion as described in Vandenburg's failed 1964 Atlas-F missile.

Jonny Quest itself was always the most propagandistic of children's programming, patriotic and simplistic in the extreme, with U.S. government military projects glorified to the point of absurdity, and foreigners demonized up to, and including, having pointed teeth. The episode "The Dragons of Ashida" actually went that far, its Oriental despot of a villain having eyes so diabolically slanted and features so distorted that he looks as if smoke will erupt from his nostrils and a forked tongue emerge from his mouth—there were comic books featuring the Japanese after Pearl Harbor that were more flattering. Steven Spielberg's Freakazoid recently did a devastatingly funny satire of the Hanna-Barbera classic, called "Toby Danger." In it, Dr. Danger flies around not in a high-tech customized jet, but on the levitated, flaming remains of Three Mile Island, one of the younger members of his team being the only survivor of a nuclear catastrophe brought on by his experiments. "That's all right," the girl says. "I think of it not as losing a city, but gaining a family."

Hanna-Barbera's contemporaneous The Flintstones (ABC, 1960–65), which used to run back-to-back with Jonny Quest in a weeknight prime-time slot, gained a new character in its final year: "the Great Gazoo." Gazoo was a little green antennaed spaceman with a huge head, who appeared and disappeared without warning. Initially scaring Fred and Barney, who of course are not used to little green men from outer space popping by in flying saucers every day, Gazoo eventually became a sort of periodic family friend and advisor, dropping by to check on their progress in life and teach a moral lesson.

In 1962, Hanna-Barbera premiered their domestic bourgeois ABC space-sitcom, The Jetsons, which was the claimed inspiration for a near-suicidal storyline choice by Chester Gould, in his famous comic strip, *Dick Tracy.* Starting on August 26, 1962, Gould introduced Tracy's "Space Coupe" to the series, for which he gave elaborate scientific explanations on the magnetic propulsion system. In June of 1965, a senior Bendix Corporation official predicted exactly such breakthroughs as Gould was putting in his comics, which Gould did not hesitate to publicize. His biographer, Jay Maeder, notes that, "In private conversations late in his life, in his eighties, Gould would sometimes hint darkly that he was sure NASA regarded him as a meddling whistleblower." As late as January of 1968, still testily defending his futuristic space-cop stories, he believed he would prove one day to be as prophetic as Jules Verne before him, telling the press, "It's a good bet that by the 21st Century there will be a police force on the moon!" and stating that his Space Coupe and two-way T.V. wristwatches were no more outlandish than Lindbergh's *Spirit of St. Louis* would have been only a generation before.

Gould's belief in his "prophetic" role might have applied to another area than simply technology. On December 31, 1963, only a little over a month after the Kennedy assassination, he introduced a new character and storyline that nearly killed his immensely successful series: "Moon Maid." Sporting huge, elliptical eyes and a platinum-blonde flip hairdo, in a one-piece black siren-suit and thigh-high proto-Go Go boots, she could have stepped straight out of Antonio Villas Boas' as-yet-unpublished encounter. The only "alien" aspect of her appearance were two antennae on top of her head.

Beginning as an arrogantly superior avenger of the brutal crimes she saw on Earth—her appearance coincided closely with the infamous Kitty Genovese murder, in which numerous witnesses didn't lift a finger to call police—Moon Maid executed gangsters, vigilante-style, with electrical bolts from her fingertips. Soon, she was revealed to be a two-faced beguiler of humanity, romancing Tracy's son only to abduct the two of them, along with the wealthy industrialist character Diet Smith (who funded and built Tracy's Space Coupe), to her father's moon kingdom, in preparation for the exploitation of Earth metals in her race's proposed conquest of space. Changing her mind, however, she released the captives and returned them to Earth, marrying Tracy, Jr., to forge a lasting peace between the Moon Men and humanity. Her father the Governor was initially resistant to the idea, but the arrival of the couple's daughter, Honey Moon, on September 12, 1965, ended the conflict. "Let this child be a symbol of the new millennium!" prayed a hopeful Diet Smith.

Except to the youngest of new readers, the entire Moon Maid series was terribly unpopular, causing droves of newspapers to drop the Dick Tracy strip by the time the famous detective became "Chief of Moon Security" in April of 1969. ("You might say I'll be moonlighting," Gould had his character wryly observe.) The extremely negative reaction is difficult to gauge, since Gould was primarily imitating the contemporaneous space exploits of James Bond in the movies, even with a SPECTRE/Blofeld-inspired crime head called "Mr. Intro"—whose predictably violent demise unfortunately occurred in the same week that Robert Kennedy was assassinated, causing critics to leap on Gould's brand of comic-book violence as a detrimental influence in society.

Always having attempted to preserve the illusion of reality, the strip was left with no choice but to become once again Earthbound after NASA's bleak reports concerning the viability of the Moon in July of 1969. Nevertheless, the obstinate Gould—who always fiercely defended the space-phase of his work, even as circulation dropped from 550 newspapers to about 375 during its tenure—responded simply by having Tracy bid farewell to the Moon Men in a return visit, four months later, with the words, "I sense a new day for civilization! A clean slate! A chance to start anew!" ending with a look straight out to his audience and adding, "Can civilization measure up to it?" His Christmas strip that year had Tracy praying with his family, "As the universe gets smaller, let men's minds get bigger." Gould continued with the Moon Maid-Tracy Jr. subplot through Christmas of 1975, when Moon Maid and Honey Moon were still seen at the dinner table joining Tracy's prayer, "And as we join hands, Dear Lord, hear our plea that the spirit of thy birth shall dwell forever in our hearts—*Amen.*"

After Gould's departure from the strip on Christmas Sunday, 1977, his successor Max Allan Collins formally ended the "Moon Period" on August 7 of the following year, deleting the entire fifteen years prior by heroically dispatching Moon Maid in a car-bomb blast intended for Tracy. Honey Moon's alien nature was discreetly covered up by having her hair grow over her horns, and she was gradually phased-out of the storylines. Fans considered these plot moves well-handled and even reverential, and heaved a private sigh of relief.

The question of whether Gould had government connections or not is academic—his publisher, wealthy socialist-industrialist Captain Joseph Medill Patterson, was so openly fascist and Third Reich-supportive that President Roosevelt once sent him an Iron Cross, with the observation that no one deserved it more than he did (Gould responded in kind, in later years, by making his worst villains look exactly like FDR)—leaving only the question as to whether his publisher's politics had any actual influence on Gould's Moon Period stories. Indeed, Patterson's Chicago Tribune Syndicate was the only real rival to William Randolph Hearst's publishing empire. Certainly Patterson wielded tremendous influence on the strip in the beginning, giving it its name and all of its original trappings. The characters, at Patterson's direction, became thinly disguised political and crime figures of the day, in order to render Patterson's own polemics through the medium. Though Gould always sang the man's praises for having given him his start, he privately felt somewhat violated by the virtual wholesale appropriation of his work. But then—like so many others apparently attached to the UFO educational program—Gould was an extremely ambitious go-getter who wanted nothing more than success and was willing to greatly compromise to get it. In addition, Gould was often a rather fascist polemicist himself, making his particular pill of submission easier to swallow.

Simultaneous with the release of Hanna-Barbera's *The Jetsons* and the Topps Trading Card series "Mars Attacks," superhero king DC comics—who have handled all the most famous names in the cape-and-cowl business since Superman's 1938 debut in *Action*—brought out a new title in late 1962, *Metal Men*, which has run on and off ever since, recently revived after a lengthy hiatus. The title characters were very near-human elemental robots, created by government scientist Dr. Will Magnus. Each robot consisted of a single element, had sentience and emotion (Magnus' worst problem was keeping the beautiful female among his creations, Platinum, from falling in love with him), and functioned without individual parts, its body respondent to its will through a device called a "responsometer." Magnus and his Metal Men repelled villains who were usually equally robotic, many from outer space, flying swiftly to any spot around the world in a golden flying saucer of Magnus' design.

Gold Key, soon to become the licensed distributor of *Star Trek* comics, followed suit the same year with their own *Magnus, Robot Fighter—4000 AD*, which became something of a cult favorite and is presently found as a slick independent underground comic. In "NorAm" of the year 4000, government law-enforcement figure Magnus (no relation) and his socialite girlfriend Leeja found themselves pitted against numerous renegade robots both terrestrial and extraterrestrial, almost all of which were of slightly updated pulp-fiction variety. The robots spoke haltingly and were malfunctioning or misappropriated advanced mechanical devices. The chief criminals behind their misuse were evil robots of genuine artificial intelligence, oppressing and sometimes attempting to eradicate their human creators, who had foolishly become entirely dependent upon them over many generations. (The instigator of the robot rebellion that launched the series was appropriately the Chief of Robot Police, named "H8"—"Hate.")

A secondary companion series called "The Aliens" was serialized under the same cover as *Robot Fighter*, about clandestine interplanetary war plots among colonies of humans on various planets in the solar system, complicated by the arrival of bug-eyed, huge-headed, non-human life forms (appearing essentially to be robots, not unlike the famous UFO Grays) who were feared by some though they were entirely benevolent. Both *Metal Men* and *Magnus, Robot Fighter*—in common with a surprising number of other essentially juvenile entertainment comics of the same sort—featured regular science and history lessons on or between their covers. For example, the May '66 *Robot Fighter* discussed famous meteorite strikes on its inside front cover, even bringing up the Siberian blast of 1908 (which many supposedly better-educated adults today have never heard of), and *Metal Men* frequently had lessons on chemistry and the periodic table of elements.

In 1963, the Japanese exported their first sci-fi cartoon series to American shores, Osamu Tezuka's (the "God of Comics" in Japan) *Astro-Boy,* about a boy robot made by his inventor to replace the son he lost in an accident. Being a Japanese character, Astro-Boy of course does only one thing, and that is to fight endless evil villains from Earth and outer space. The following year, four features made from Japan's American International Pictures-financed 1956–59 T.V. series, "Starman," were imported to U.S. shores, including *Atomic Rulers of the World* (a.k.a. *Invaders from Space)* and *Warning from Space* (or *Mysterious Satellite),* the latter about one-eyed starfish-men from the Moon who come to Earth to warn mankind about the dangers of the H-bomb. Starman and Astro-Boy were exactly like an endless parade of similar characters to follow, *Marine Boy, Prince Planet,* and *Gigantor* (a giant blue robot) among the cartoons, and *Ultra-Man* among the live-action. These in turn have since been adapted into such recent incarnations as Saban's *Mighty Morphin' Power Rangers,* the plot of all being exactly the same: good heroes, fighting for the gods against renegade space villains. The *Power Rangers* are "teenagers with attitudes" who are "recruited" by an unknown extraterrestrial intelligence named "Zordon" to help him fight his cosmic war against such opposing powers—in a recent incarnation, *Power Rangers Zeo,* the enemy in question is a hostile race of robots. Zordon utilizes a small robot called Alpha, who is almost identical to UFO Grays.

An important 1967 Toei entry in the cartoon/juvenile category, funded by American International, was the live-action *Johnny Sokko and His Giant Robot.* Like its contemporaneous cartoon cousin, *Gigantor,* its stars were a giant flying metal man and its little boy controller. Johnny Sokko inadvertently hooks-up with world defense organization Unicorn's secret agent, Jerry Mano, while on a sea cruise. Their ship is sunk by Guillotine, an octopus-headed, claw-handed space emperor, whose flying saucer has based itself beneath Earth's oceans. Finding themselves washed up on the shores of the Gargoyle Gang's island (Guillotine's human henchmen), Jerry and Johnny befriend Guillotine's prisoner, Lucius Guardian, who has constructed a giant robot for Guillotine under the coercion of the Gargoyles. Together, they wrest the robot's control from the evil space invaders, turning the tables and initiating a twenty-six episode series run depicting Unicorn's (and therefore Johnny Sokko and his giant robot's) ongoing fight with the aliens. Of particular interest in regard to this study, the giant robot wore an Egyptian headdress.

Psychologically immature by Western standards, Japanese drama never seems to intellectually or emotionally rise above the level of adolescence. This may be why the Japanese have such an incredible fascination for glorifying American high school as a form of Utopia. Technologically preoccupied since World War Two, if not longer, Japan issues more science-fictional and UFOlogical stories than probably anyplace else, but most of it is so alien and simplistic to Westerners that it will never be seen here. Robots, spaceships, and alien races have been an overwhelmingly common feature to Japanese cartoons and comics, even more than their American counterparts, possibly owing to their nation's defeat by an outside civilization's superior technology in 1945.

After *Godzilla*'s original appearance in 1954, all of Japan's giant-monster movies became embodiments of the fights of the gods over planet Earth—sky gods (such as Rodan, Mothra, or Gamera) fighting the water demon (Godzilla), the same myth seen in Ra and Apep, Thor and the World Serpent, and so on. Gamera was even made specifically to be a mock flying saucer: the creature was a giant mutant fanged turtle who could whirl circularly and take off into space, spouting flame from the openings his head and limbs retracted into. Godzilla has appeared in twenty-two films, and was announced as recently as October 16, 1996, on CNN to be appearing in a new 1998 entry from the same team that did *Stargate* and *Independence Day,* Dean Devlin and Roland Emmerich.

If the Intelligence community had a plan afoot to make UFO material laughable, everything Japanese would have been of keen interest to them to import—and as a matter of fact, it was American International, the makers of the silliest flying saucer movies in the 1950s, that financed many of Toho Pictures' *Godzilla* movies. Before that, as in the case of 1957's *The Mysterians,* at least one was financed by RKO, which Howard Hughes sold to MGM. *The Mysterians* was one of the earliest "space breeding" movies, its ad-art reading, "See!

See! See! A daring attempt by love-starved men of another planet to steal our women!" The invading flying saucer "Mystroids" were men in round helmets, capes, bodysuits, and dark sunglasses, aided in their nefarious mission by a giant birdlike robot-tank.

Unbelievably silly when viewed anywhere but in Japan, the gestures made heroic by the battling behemoths to their native viewers only appear as ludicrous as the posturing of All-Star Wrestlers to Westerners. Flying saucers and space aliens were often the object of Godzilla's vengeful wrath, more than once even coming from Mars and being the abductors of little children. In *Ghidrah, the Three-Headed Monster,* made in 1965, a flying saucer from Mars abducts an Earthwoman to be one of their ambassadors in the first five minutes of the movie. Ten years later, in *Terror of Mecha-Godzilla,* the mighty behemoth was pitted against "Mecha-Godzilla," a giant robot manufactured by human-looking flying-saucer aliens for the purpose of wreaking havoc on Tokyo. The robot is controlled by an Earthwoman abductee, who is in communion with the giant robot through a brain implant and is herself controlled by the aliens. Another of their abductees asks the aliens who they are, and their leader answers, "The Second Coming. We're here to save the planet from those who are trying to destroy it." Similarly, Universal-Toei's *King Kong Escapes* in 1968 had the famous giant ape gassed unconscious and aerially abducted to the secret hideaway island of the evil Dr. Who, where Kong awakened to confront a robot duplicate of himself and was hypnotized into becoming Who's mining slave. The 1960s were the decade in which these films were most visible in America.

A tremendous number of alien abduction stories appear in Japanese *manga,* as well. The term refers to comics for adults, which are extremely common in Japan and becoming equally popular in the States, the U.S. audience consisting primarily of males aged 18–35 according to one of the leading "Japanimators," Koichi Ohata. Interestingly, the Japanese most often portray the UFO phenomenon in benign terms, where Westerners take the exact opposite stance. *Uro-sei Yetsura* ("Totally Insane") and *Outlanders* are two good examples easily found in the video market, where manga proliferates. Both stories are about young men being abducted by space maidens entirely for the purpose of sex. They play like combinations of Archie comics and the Antonio Villas Boas incident, or *Josie and the Pussy Cats in Outer Space.*

One popular manga video of the 1980s, *Iczer One,* is a more serious Japanese attempt at an alien abduction story—meaning not that it is adult, but it is at least as good as *Prince Planet. Iczer One* contains many standard UFO abduction elements, probably highly influenced by popular culture. The aliens are robots who abduct selected female human beings to aid them in their wars with each other. They bond uniquely with only one abductee, connecting with them in larger robots for combat. While in this state, the abductee is submerged in a tube of liquid in which she can still breathe. The ships in which they travel are a flying pyramid and a hollow moon. Recently, this form of manga has become so popular that independent comics in America satirize them, most notably in such publications as *Ninja High School* and *The Dirty Pair,* the latter a double-franchised Japanese original, one version of which is treated with a semblance of seriousness and the other of which is pure spoof.

The 1970s did not display anywhere near as many UFOlogically oriented entries as the 1960s, and when they did appear it was less overtly and in generally more thought-provoking fashion. One place, for instance, was in Vincent Price's comeback movies out of Britain via American International Pictures: *The Abominable Dr. Phibes* (1971) and its sequel, *Dr. Phibes Rises Again* (1972). "Dr. Phibes" is an unlikely combination (outside of UFOlogical circles) Egyptologist-musicologist-astronomer, a genius in the science of sound, with which he has constructed an artificial larynx to replace his demolished throat. He has robot assistants—"Dr. Phibes' Clockwork Wizards," also called "The Alexandrian Quartet"—and a living human accomplice named Vulnavia to assist him in his evil schemes, himself being only quasi-alive after an auto accident. With diabolical precision, Dr. Phibes calculates and arranges murders to correspond with the ten plagues of Egypt in the Bible, generally coming and going completely undetected at night to accomplish his aims and leaving nothing behind but his gruesome handiwork. In the sequel, he plays a continual game of one-upmanship with a rival undead Egyptologist (assuredly a very small community), both of them seeking the elixir of eternal life and entrance to the waterway of Osiris. Set in the 1920s, that decade in which archaeology suddenly became of tremendous interest to world governments, the sequel even made a point of drawing attention to the comparable nature of that period's art deco style and classic Egyptian hieroglyphics. Price made two earlier camp AIP movies along roughly similar lines, in 1965 and 1966: *Dr. Goldfoot and the Bikini Machine* and *Dr. Goldfoot and the Girl Bombs,* both about a madman using robots for world domination. The latter, for whatever reason, was produced out of Italy.

Studying the original script to *Dr. Phibes,* novelized by William Goldstein from his and James Whiton's screenplay, it is at least clear that the UFOlogical elements are not accidental. Phibes' assistant, Vulnavia, is directly implied to be the doctor's assistant through hypnosis, as evidenced by her acceptance of his alarming state of existence without any untoward reaction: "[T]hey toasted and drank, she brushing the glass to her lips, he pouring the entire tumbler into a small aperture in his throat. She remained unruffled by this startling gesture, continuing to sip her wine and look at her escort with deep, yet rather glazed eyes." Emphasizing the point, he writes that "she gazed at him trancelike" and comments that, throughout a life of service to the mad doctor, "The haunted girl died as she had lived, without a word passing her lips." She is referred to more than once as a "mannequin," and Phibes' "artificial" nature is frequently called precisely that, his voice coming "from some mechanical process rather than his featureless face."

Both Phibes and Vulnavia wear almost exclusively red, white, and black, the only exceptions being Vulnavia's briefly seen yellow gown, a light green blouse (which is covered most of the time by a black coat), and a gold sun-design to supplement her otherwise entirely red robe at the finale of the first film. In the sequel she wears yellow for only a few seconds in a crossover scene, and blue in one other. Phibes' wardrobe is exclusively given to the three colors of Atlantis, broken up only by brown fringe on one of his coats in the original movie, and a single scene in a blue robe (covered by a white one) in the sequel. Phibes' appearances are ascensions from his artificial

Underworld, playing an organ of red and black, while he wears alternating red, white, and black robes. The UFOlogical nature of his activities include nocturnal bedroom visitations, mutilations (he completely exsanguinates a seemingly paralyzed—and at least entirely unresisting—Terry Thomas, without spilling a drop), the toppling of an airplane from the skies by sabotage, and five (of fifteen, counting both movies) crimes accomplished and/or accompanied by automata. He travels in a silent and undetectable black limousine and even wears the hawk-mask of Horus the Avenger in his first "human" appearance.

1970's Universal production, *Colossus: The Forbin Project,* was about a computer ruling the world. In the original three Raymond Jones novels which inspired it (the same author whose work was the basis for *This Island Earth),* the computer was in contact with—and controlled by—the Martian moons Phobos and Deimos, which leave their orbit and park themselves permanently around Earth. The same studio's 1972 production, *Silent Running,* and 1979's Disney entry, *The Black Hole,* featured robot-run ships. Michael Crichton wrote about malfunctioning robots in MGM's *Westworld* (1973)—the '76 AIP sequel to it, *Futureworld,* included abductions and robot replacements—and brain implants in Warner Bros.' *The Terminal Man* (1974); and the same studio's *Looker* (1981) featured a photo-flash device inducing paralysis and missing time. In 1984, Crichton wrote a futuristic mad-runaway-robots piece, Columbia/Tri-Star's *Runaway.* Crichton also discussed cloning in Universal's recent megahit *Jurassic Park* (1993), government study of the Watchers' ancient technology in Paramount's *Congo* (1995), and extraterrestrial biological invasion in Universal's *The Andromeda Strain* at the very beginning of his literary career in 1971. The last featured the Roswell-esque elements of a military-recovered downed satellite in remote New Mexico, and the Area 51–esque element of experimenting with its contents in a secret underground base in the desert.

1970 also was the year in which what is dubbed the first science-fiction T.V. movie was made, Paramount/ABCs' *The Love War.* Featuring the same unsettling Dominic Frontiere score used in *The Outer Limits* and *The Invaders,* it told the story of two secretly warring parties in the solar system, fighting their private little combat over the Earth. They attempt to keep the locals completely ignorant of their activities, though an abduction of sorts occurs when Angie Dickinson finds herself being brought into the aliens' game—she sees them for what they are while in the bedroom, faints, and wakes up believing the experience was nothing more than a nightmare, until the alien she witnessed forces her to accept that it was true. In the end, Dickinson turns out to have been a "tender trap" from the other side, lulling the opposition into a false sense of security in order to more easily finish them off. Metromedia produced another alien movie for the same network the following year, called *The People.* "The People" of the title were reclusive, near-Amish alien humanoid colonists possessing such powers as ESP and levitation, quietly attempting to adapt to Earth ways without being detected.

1972 brought *Flesh Gordon* from Graffiti Productions, a pornographically satirical rehash of the old movie serials. Actual abduction elements are interlaced with the story elements, as with the original source material, and the blatantly sexual approach may demonstrate something about the government influence on release of UFO material through the film medium. Richard Nixon was still in office, a puritanical old Quaker if ever there was one, as infamous for his sexual impotency as he was for his paranoia and abuse of power, and well-known for a strange discomfort even in touching or being touched by other people. If the Chief Executive is privy, on a rotational basis, to the true facts about UFOs from the various Pentagon and investigative branches attached to their study, and if he has any say as to how the "educational program" will be implemented during his tenure, then it would only be natural that Nixon would be especially bothered by the sexual aspect that is so predominant concerning alien interaction with terrestrial humanity. The movie begins with the aliens bombarding Earth with their "sex ray," which instantly causes everyone hit by it to tear off their clothes and indulge in a shameless orgy. The mere fact that this is hardly any kind of threat makes the "invasion" a joke from frame one—and, frankly, the entire UFO phenomenon itself seems to be little more hostile than this. The same idea was touched on peripherally in 20th Century

Fox's *In Like Flint,* five years before, with sexy Amazon women disarming an entire army at a high-security space complex just by "doing what comes naturally." Actual UFOs are engaged in both of these activities—disarming the military and having sex with the locals—which would be very disturbing to any group that prides itself on fascistic control. In fact, they would be virtually the only group in the entire world threatened by it—but then, they are the ones in power and have been for at least the past half century.

Cinerama imported *Asylum* from Britain's Amicus Studios in 1972, a horror anthology film scripted by *Psycho* author and Lovecraft Protégé Robert Bloch. All but one of the stories concerned black-magic-animated horrors: "Frozen Fear" featured the separately butcher-wrapped pieces of a woman's dismembered body brought to life by an African charm bracelet to terrorize someone instrumental in her death; "Mannikins of Horror" (often dramatized in other mediums as well, including the 1989 T.V. series *Monsters)* was about a mad scientist who used Egyptian magic to project his soul into a robot; and "The Weird Tailor"—also often dramatized, including the early 1960s Universal T.V. anthology, Boris Karloff's *Thriller*—similarly presented a mannequin brought to murderous life by ancient sorcery. Bloch wrote another horror anthology for the same studio in 1967, *Torture Garden,* with one story about robot duplications and another about diabolic mind control. *Thriller* dramatized a number of robotic menaces, including Bloch's "Waxworks," another story in which ancient black magic is utilized to animate wax statues and the dead. "The Hollow Watcher," though not scripted by Bloch, was about a supernaturally animated killer scarecrow. (It might be noted that Universal's other T.V. thriller series of the time, the ten-year-running *Alfred Hitchcock Presents*—called *The Alfred Hitchcock Hour* in its final year, 1965—featured at least two nightmarish monster mannequin tales from established short story writers John Keir Cross and Davis Grubb, "The Glass Eye" and "Where the Woodbine Twineth." The former had a woman falling in love with what turned out to be a man-sized mannequin whose ventriloquist was the "dummy" on its arm, and the latter was about a little girl permanently trading places with her nocturnal companion—a talking doll.)

Kurt Vonnegut's *Slaughterhouse Five* was made by Universal in 1972, a major plot element of which is a comical alien abduction. Average guy protagonist Billy Pilgrim is taken from his bedroom to a dome on the planet Tralfamador. His porn-queen fantasy actress, Valerie Perrine, is abducted along with him, and the Tralfamadorians encourage them to mate, watching discreetly and invisibly from beyond the dome. As a sort of "present" in return for his amusing them, they give him the gift of prophecy, making him "unstuck in time," able to see the past, present, and future with equal clarity. Like the Valkyries, the Tralfamadorians come to take him back to heaven on the day of his ordained political assassination, which is brought about while he is bearing witness to the world of their existence.

Scotia International's *Horror Express* in 1972 was ostensibly made because producer Bernard Gordon owned the model train used in *Nicholas and Alexandra*. The movie centered on the pursuit of a bizarre humanoid aboard the Orient Express: a prehistoric ape-man fossil, animated by the extraterrestrial intelligence that engineered it—and the human race—in antiquity. Universal/ABC produced Theodore Sturgeon's *Killdozer* in '72, a story in which an alien-possessed machine terrorizes a construction crew on an isolated island. Metromedia/CBS' *Gargoyles,* the same year, was neither a good nor bad movie, though some critics have been unduly kind to it. All but plotless, the movie portrays a race of unlikely humanoids who kidnap women to hidden caves for a breeding overrun of the planet. The hideous gargoyles speak in rough, mechanical-sounding voices, strongly reminiscent of the Ebonites in *Outer Limits'* "Nightmare." The movie ends ambivalently, the gargoyles escaping to come back another day, mankind left wondering in the wings what he can do about it.

The year 1973 saw so many reports of bizarre creatures in the vicinity of landed UFOS that the press dubbed it the "Year of the Humanoids." At its height, that year saw an eerie T.V. movie about bizarre abducting humanoids, Lorimar/ABC's *Don't Be Afraid of the Dark.* The timing of the movie's appearance recalls the proximity of the 1967 American "Mothman" sightings to the making of the British moth-monster movie, *The Blood Beast Terror. Don't Be Afraid of the Dark* featured three small, green, bald, huge-eyed creatures, who live inside an apparently bottomless fireplace that was once wisely sealed up but now is opened again. They are intent on abducting hapless young Kim Darby, the new resident in the house above, for reasons never made clear. The unsettling humanoids linger always just beyond sight and conspiratorially whisper to Darby, "You're one of us," as actual UFO abductors do to their abductees. The only proof of the creatures' presence to doubters is the same as that on UFO abductees: unidentified body markings discovered later on their prey. The little green men have contacts in the human world, whom they terrorize into keeping the existence of the little men secret. Ultimately, the helpless Darby, semi-conscious and barely able to move, is dragged into the underworld of the little men. Though initially resistant, Darby seems not only to accept her place in the creatures' subterranean community, once there, but actually to enjoy it: at the movie's conclusion, she is heard conspiring with the creatures to effect their permanent escape into the world above. The next year, Richard Matheson's *The Stranger Within,* also from Lorimar/ABC, was the first television dramatization of an alien-induced pregnancy. And in 1975, Universal/NBC's *The UFO Incident* faithfully dramatized the Betty and Barney Hill abduction, complete with an eerie Billy Goldenberg score (who provided similarly spooky soundtracks for the previous T.V. features *Fear No Evil* and *Don't Be Afraid of the Dark).*

Another monster-humanoid feature from 1973 was the Columbia-financed British import, *The Mutations,* one of many movies before and since that played with the mad-doctor theme of hybridizing the perfect being. In this case, botanist and genetics professor Donald Pleasance abducts his college students (mostly female) to his laboratory, where they remain unconscious for most of their brief experience but occasionally waken, paralyzed and on a slab, long enough to realize they are in a strange place they don't want to be. When they become conscious, Pleasance simply informs them that they are serving a higher scientific purpose—which is essentially what UFO abductors tell their charges as well. His failures end up as carnival sideshow freaks, until they die and have to be disposed of. The same year, Universal did *Sssssss*—a title exactly as inspired as that of *Outer Limits'* Queen-bee episode with much the same theme ten years before, "Zzzzz"—which has plot elements identical to *The Mutations,* only instead of attempting to hybridize men with plants, mad doctor Strother Martin's plan is to combine human genes with those of—you guessed it—snakes.

United Artists released Woody Allen's *Sleeper* in '73, a slapstick satire with a ragtime soundtrack, in which Allen wakes up two centuries in America's future, after unexpected cryogenic freezing during treatment for a peptic ulcer. The future into which he awakes is a thinly disguised imitation of our own, a sterile fascistic autocracy masquerading as a free republic, keeping its people sedated into compliance through mere creature comforts. Those who do not mindlessly acquiesce are put through "reprogramming," followed by extermination should it fail. Allen is revived by the new century's underground and quickly detected by the authorities who fear his ability to revitalize the rebellion. They brand him an "alien" and put out a nationwide APB. Allen flees, concealing his identity behind the mask of a servo-functionary robot (looking very similar to UFO Grays). Fulfilling the government's fears, he ends up converting spoiled vapid socialite Diane Keaton to the rebel cause, not through any action of his own, but as a result of their attempt to "reprogram" her due to potential "contamination," simply because she patriotically turned Allen in. Ultimately, Allen and Keaton discover the government's dread secret: it has had no real leader for years, the president having been blown up by a rebel bomb, the pro-tem bureaucracy concealing the fact until they can clone their leader's nose (the only part of him remaining) to get him back.

Noted science-fiction screenwriter Nicholas Meyer got an early start with Centaur's *Invasion of the Bee Girls* (a.k.a. *Graveyard Tramps*) in 1973, one of Roger Ebert's favorite "guilty pleasure" movies, about a rash of serial killings done by "sexual exhaustion." The victims are all male research scientists at a government plant, whose vital essences have been literally orgasmed out of them by a mutant race of insect-women, who enlarge their number by abducting human females and irradiating them in a strange honey concoction. Once transformed, the sloe-eyed bee-auties wear elliptical black sunglasses, and—as the posters put it—"... love the very lives out of your body!" Two years later, Meyer co-scripted (with Anthony Wilson) *The Night That Panicked America* for T.V., about the Orson Welles 1938 Halloween Eve "War of the Worlds" scare. At the same time Meyer was documenting Welles' famous fraud, France was producing a movie about beautiful female space-vampires living on human sperm and blood, called *Spermula*. Gene Roddenberry premiered a failed T.V. pilot in 1973 called *The Questor Tapes,* about a government-created robot becoming a sentient being.

Richard Matheson—*The Twilight Zone's* best consistent contributor (he wrote fourteen episodes), AIP mainstay, and a frequently UFO-logically accurate author—adapted his own 1971 sci-fi haunted house novel *Hell House* into 20th Century Fox's *The Legend of Hell House* for AIP president and co-founder James H. Nicholson in 1973. Nicholson, who had just left AIP to start his own production company, unfortunately did not live to see the film's release—he died in 1972 at the age of fifty-six. In Matheson's story, the house's sole, powerful, haunting occupant technologically possesses psychic medium Pamela Franklin and uses her to sabotage a machine that is a viable threat to its survival. It also hypnotically mind-controls both Franklin and Gayle Hunnicut into somnambulistically performing sexual acts by night, which they don't remember upon waking. Franklin is repeat-visited in her bedroom by an entity who insists on having sex with her, which she finds nightmarish—her bedpartner is an artificially animated figure—and which is the subsequent cause of her "alien" possession. Fellow medium Roddy McDowall, the sole survivor of a previous failed attempt at exorcism on the site, pronounces an assessment of the house that could as well apply to the UFO phenomenon, and (after the Phobos incident) the planet Mars in particular: "Hell House doesn't mind a guest or two. What it doesn't like is people who *attack* it. Belasco [the central haunting entity] doesn't like it, his people, they don't like it, and they will fight back, and *they will kill you.*" This movie in particular, like Columbia's *The Curse of the Demon,* demonstrates extremely well the connection between what is commonly called "occult" phenomena and that of UFOs—levitation, animated objects, repeat bedroom visitations, nightmare sex, and the like.

Richard Matheson himself is an excellent potential candidate for connection to governmental UFO study. His father was a Norwegian Merchant Marine, and Matheson was an enlistee in pre-engineering Army Specialized Training at Cornell University (until the program's cancellation in 1944), then a combat infantryman with the 87th Division in Germany at the young age of eighteen. Prior to his enlistment, he was a superior math and physics student with a specialty in structural engineering at Brooklyn Technical High School, who once memorized an entire physics textbook for an exam. After the war, he got a degree in journalism, and worked at Douglas Aircraft for some time. His resumé being rather similar to that of both Roger Corman and Leslie Stevens, Matheson became closely associated with the former in his early writing career, and also worked with Intelligence-connected insiders Rod Serling and Gene Roddenberry. His fiction frequently contained UFOlogical elements, even when not overtly science-fiction related. He was, for instance, the teleplay adaptor of Jeff Rice's modern-day vampire novel, *The Night Stalker,* for Universal T.V. (forerunner to the aforementioned series), and followed that up—concurrent with the production of *Hell House*—with his own original sequel, *The Night Strangler,* about a superhuman Underworld-dwelling immortal alchemist who rises from his hidden kingdom on a regular schedule of years (like the oppositions of Mars) to obtain genetic tissue from hapless women. He also wrote another sequel, *The Night Killers,* which never went into production: its subject was the robot duplication of governmental figures by a hidden power. Matheson additionally wrote a 1954 novel adapted into a 1964 AIP film called *The Last Man on Earth* (remade by Warner Bros. in 1971 as *The Omega Man),* starring Vincent Price in the title role as the final remaining human combating a new plague-created mutant race of vampires for dominion of the Earth—the story ended with Price recognizing that mankind was simply moving into its next evolutionary step, himself now nothing more than a detrimental throwback who must be exterminated.

Matheson's *The Legend of Hell House* was patterned after perhaps the best ghost story in cinema, MGM's *The Haunting,* made ten years before in 1963. Whether anyone at the studio knew that the famous

Shirley Jackson novel they were filming had any connection to UFO phenomena, it did, and as such demonstrates many of the close connections between supernatural and UFO occurrences. "Hill House" is a legendary haunted house being investigated by paranormal researcher Dr. Markway, who invites a select group to spend an indeterminate time with him there. The people he selects—except for one alcoholic rotter who is along for the ride, solely to watch out for the interests of the house as his soon-to-be-inherited property—are all experiencers of unusual phenomena since childhood, just like UFO abductees. When one of his party objects that there is no such thing as the supernatural, that everything is explainable by some other means, Markway answers in a manner worthy of someone defending the reality of UFOs: "Sure, people always want to put an easy label on things, even if it's meaningless. 'The trouble with Hill House is sun-spots.' Now, there's an explanation you don't have to think twice about. And it has a scientific ring."

Chief among Markway's psychic guests is an impressionable spinster named Eleanor Vance. Eleanor is bullied and oppressed at home, living a pointless and solitary life, and has just finished caring for her selfish, sickly, tyrannical mother, who took up all Eleanor's time until her recent death. Hill House is haunted by the ghost of exactly such a woman as Eleanor's mother, who was abandoned by her caretaker to die. The house zeroes in on Eleanor, writing her name in giant letters on the wall when no one is around to see (in chalk in the movie, blood in the original novel), saying, "Help Eleanor come home." Eleanor is terrified that the house knows *her*, personally, and feels violated—yet, despite her terror and her pleas to Dr. Markway that she never be left behind, she feels more comfortable with the invisible occupants of the house than she does with anyone she has met in her isolated life. Such an attitude is identical to that expressed by UFO abductees in response to their abductors, even when—like Eleanor—they find the experience eerie or partly frightening.

Whatever entity or entities haunt the house, it separates and isolates members of Markway's party at will, physically affects Eleanor in her bedroom without her roommate waking up or being aware, and causes Markway's wife to sleepwalk and lose her memory. Eleanor is packed-off home, considered by all to be at grave risk in the house, but she doesn't want to leave. Driving off on her own, she finds herself not alone in the car at all, but riding with some unseen occupant that takes control of her and causes her to crash, killing her and making her a permanent occupant of Hill House like itself. "Home" at last, Eleanor's voice repeats the opening narration at the story's end, changing it only by the substitution of personal pronouns, making clear that she is finally where she belongs: "Hill House has stood for ninety years, and might stand for ninety more. Within, walls continue upright, bricks meet, floors are firm, and doors are sensibly shut. Silence lies steadily against the wood and stone of Hill House. And we who walk here, walk alone."

20th Century Fox's immensely popular *Omen* series began its run the year Carter was elected, following on the heels of Warner Bros.' 1973 hit, *The Exorcist*. Both series of films presented Fundamentalist religious views in a nightmarish light. Where William Peter Blatty's *The Exorcist* first exposed a modern Judaeo-Christian mass-audience to the idea that their spiritual devils, demons, and even God the Almighty had their earliest origins in the myth-texts of the Middle East, *The Omen* and its sequels portrayed the ancient cosmic war on a literal and growing global scale. Any or all of these movies may have had no connection at all to the educational program, *The Exorcist* especially having been severely ostracized and attacked both by the media and the Motion Picture Academy, though it did get excellent reviews and unquestionably tremendous exposure (which may have been the point).

But it is interesting to note that David Seltzer's original script for *The Omen* was drastically changed, on the production's executive level, from a more conventional Satanist *Rosemary's Baby* witch-cult thriller into the surprisingly better and completely different movie it became. It is interesting, also, that the 1978 first sequel depicted protagonist William Holden discovering his evil step-son's ancient identity in a perfect depiction of his face in ancient stone paintings from Meggido, only two years after the *Viking* probes photographed the famous Face on Mars. Additionally, prophecies purportedly from the Bible in the first movie (in actuality, they are entirely fiction) relate that "from the Eternal Sea he rises," regarding the Antichrist—though they try to work that around to mean the "eternal sea" of politics, someone on the production team may well have known that the ancient meaning of that phrase is nothing other than the "ocean" of outer space. It may be noted, too, that the depiction of Satan as the political Antichrist in these movies, coming at the tail end of the Nixon-Ford years, was patterned quite obviously after the Kennedys, who were Nixon and Ford's chief political opponents.

Blatty himself could easily be CIA-connected, or at least helpful to them in the educational program. He comes from a super-patriotic Catholic family, with one brother a veteran of the Submarine Service in the Second World War, and another multiply decorated as a B-17 bombing crew member. His first "writing award" was a five dollar prize—something of a sum, in those days—for entering a *Captain Future Comics* contest to say that he liked the comic book so much because everything about the "world of tomorrow" was "very interesting" to him. He papered his bedroom wall with *Superman* comics and often made reference to space research in his writing. The very first sentence of the opening chapter in Blatty's 1973 autobiography, *I'll Tell Them I Remember You,* is "We are testing weapons for use on the moon." In *The Exorcist,* one of the characters is an astronaut, who is warned by the devil-possessed Linda Blair, "You're gonna die, up there," which interestingly enough was a comment one of the "men from Mars" casually told dairy farmer Gary Wilcox in the aforementioned Tioga, New York, case in the early 1960s. A strong potential connection Blatty could have had with the CIA would be United Artists, who produced his early screenplay *A Shot in the Dark*—the first of the Inspector Clouseau comedies—in 1964. Given the connections of United Artists, the Clouseau movies themselves may have been something of an inside Intelligence joke pertaining to WWII's ULTRA, which sometimes made idiotic generals appear to be geniuses by virtue of information that could not be disclosed to the public-at-large—Peter Sellers' makeup even made him look something like Field Marshall Bernard Montgomery.

Gerald Ford, the president who most publicly espoused interest in publicizing UFO material aside from Jimmy Carter, saw several good films pertaining to the subject released in his two short years before Carter assumed office. Paramount's 1974 entry, *Phase IV,* a Trieste prizewinner directed by famed film-title designer Saul Bass, was the best UFOlogical movie of the entire time period, even if no one immediately recognized it as such. Two scientists are established in a scientifically equipped geodesic dome in the desert to secretly study a sudden outbreak of alarming cosmic phenomena, the dome being identical to the giant radar dish "golf balls" one sees at any major defense establishment. "That Spring," begins Lescaux, the narrator, a part-time cryptologist for the Navy and one of the two-member team, "we were all watching the events in space, and wondering what the final effect would be. Astronomers argued over theory, while engineers got pretty excited about variables and magnetic fields. Mystics predicted earthquakes, and the end of life as we knew it. When the effect came, it was almost unnoticed, because it happened to such a small and insignificant form of life. One biologist—an Englishman, Ernest Hubbs—saw something, got nervous, and started investigating. While I was playing around with number theory at the university, Hubbs was already onto something. Ordinary ants of different species were doing things ants don't do—meeting, communicating, apparently making decisions. By summer, the rest of the world had moved on to other things. But Hubbs kept taking notes, while the threat grew. Only fragments of what he knew got out. He kept most of it to himself."

The "biological imbalance" is studied by the men, with Hubbs becoming more aggressive and militaristic against the ants—which can be seen as both the UFO intelligence and perhaps their Earthbound abductees—while Lescaux instead becomes convinced that the ants are actually studying *them,* and putting them through an intelligence test. At one point, a girl staying with them for safety after her parents have been killed fleeing the territory has an invading ant walk over every inch of her body while she is asleep. Unmoving, she wakes up and opens her eyes to stare directly into the face of the nocturnal analyst, whispering, "Go away." Hubbs goes mad and tries to poison the ants, ending up killed by them himself. In the end, the more peaceful and perceptive Lescaux (though he does try to finish Hubbs' work, lamenting that it does not seem possible to come to the peaceful understanding he originally sought) is brought into the ants' round chamber, in the middle of which is a pile of sand. Out of the sand, as if from water, rises the girl, who has been physically abducted by them. "They wanted ... *us*," Lescaux realizes. She smiles at him and reaches her arm up around his neck to give him a kiss, and they engage in sex under the watchful multi-faceted eyes of the ants. "We knew then," he concludes, "we were being changed, and made part of their world. We didn't know for what purpose ... but we knew we would be told." Though it could be mere coincidence, that world they are "being made part of" is specifically shown to be red.

The 1974 British import from 20th Century Fox, *Zardoz,* saw an Egyptian-garbed technological wizard clandestinely riddle-educating a primitive for his own purposes. He flies around in a Yahweh-istic stone-godhead with a fierce face and beard which goes by the name of the movie's title, preaching "The gun is good—the penis is evil!" and regurgitating rifles to the elite warriors to commit genocide against the masses. The wizard teases "Zed" (Sean Connery), leader of the warriors, into following him into a ruined library one day, and Zed teaches himself to read. Eventually the wizard leads him to L. Frank Baum's childhood classic, "The Wizard of Oz," and Zed realizes what the contraction "Zardoz" really means. Feeling betrayed, Zed stows away aboard the godhead and murders the wizard, landing on the other side of "the barrier," a force-field crossable only by advanced technology, there to learn about the parallel human race that has been using him. Having attained perfect luxury and immortality—even the murdered wizard is re-grown in a vat to be born again after Zed's brutal act—the advanced humans have become both decadent and sterile, requiring occasional fresh transfusions of the primitives' blood to revitalize them. Their Utopia is ruled by a hive-mind of their collective consciousness and has become an effete pre-Political Correctness monitor. Anyone who ever rebels against the perfection of the society is punished with aging—but since everyone who dies is automatically reborn, even that is escapable. The only thing they can't do is die, which is what the wizard really brought

Zed into their society for: to become their Angel of Death. Zed is an ape-man among them, loathed by some, despised by others, as well as feared and even desired. His innate high intelligence, the product of a clandestine breeding project by the wizard, rivals and threatens their own.

Similar elements were seen the following year in Harlan Ellison's independently released *A Boy and His Dog*. As usual, Ellison was upset with the treatment his 1969 Nebula Award-winner was given on the screen, certain aspects of the story seemingly changed arbitrarily. In light of the possible government agenda under consideration in this study, one change in particular makes perfect sense. Like *Zardoz*, Ellison's story is about two different groups of humans—in this case, the inferior victims of the nuclear holocaust WWIV on the surface of the planet, and the supermen living beneath the surface in a massive Underworld of tunnels and caverns made to reflect far-Right religious and American sociopolitical views. The latter have grown sterile in their sunlight-devoid environment and need some of the wild surface "Rovers" to replenish their stock. Toward this end, the more attractive daughters of the ruling class occasionally go above ground, to lure horny young men back below with them. In Ellison's original story, the particular Rover in question volunteers for the mission once he understands what it is they want, gleefully knocking-up the prudish Underworld prigs and living the life of Riley, only leaving in the end because his natural violent nature cannot abide the passive attitudes of the Underworlders. In the film adaptation, the Underworlders are a violent fascistic state themselves, merely hiding their true nature behind benevolent masks. And the Rover's sexual contribution is hardly voluntary—he is tied and gagged on a slab, his sperm forcibly ejaculated out of him to be given to newlywed couples for artificial insemination. Though rarely so horrific, some UFO abductees' reports tally with being treated as impersonally for sex.

It was in 1974 that one of the worst Nostradamus prophecy films was released in America (directly to television) from Toho, the Japanese studio that made so many silly Godzilla movies in the 1960s: *The Last Days of Planet Earth*. Produced extremely poorly, the movie begins with some of the famous prophet's accurate predictions, but in the same breath tells us that the movie we are about to see is entirely fiction. Anxious to quickly make this last point evident, the movie launches into a future in which giant slugs are on the attack. This occurs in tandem with speeches containing actual information about how badly the planet's ecosphere has been damaged, making them seem absurd and alarmist by proximity to the giant slugs. The prophecies of Nostradamus were undergoing a serious revival of interest at the time, in connection with the ancient-astronaut vogue, and were no doubt set back by such a trivial piece of idiocy as this film. Toho also produced one more Godzilla movie in the middle of the 1980s, making ecological concerns appear equally ridiculous, called *Godzilla vs. Biollante*, the title nemesis being a giant plant cloned off the famous movie monster's genetic material.

The insultingly dumb *Space: 1999* came out of Britain from producers Gerry and Sylvia Anderson in 1975, to become deservedly Cancelled: 1977. The potentially interesting premise of the Moon exploding free of Earth's orbit in a cataclysm and becoming its own spaceship was torpedoed by humorless scripts, the stupidest monsters since Irwin Allen, and the most pompous self-importance seen until the incomprehensibly successful *Star Trek: The Next Generation* ten years later. *Space: 1999*'s chief selling point was the best special-effects magic since *2001* almost ten years earlier (and it did at least manage to prove surprisingly easy on the eyes, though in the blandest of 1970s fashion). Not even the addition of ravishing Catherine Schell as a mini-skirted shape-shifting alien love-interest could save the series past a second season—Schell's alien was named "Maya," came from a planet of pyramids, and enjoyed an ongoing Antonio Villas Boas-ish sexual liaison with a chosen mate from Moonbase Alpha. More juvenile fantasy than actual science fiction, *Space: 1999* strangely maintained a cult following.

Schell is another of those actresses who has repeatedly found herself in space roles and UFOlogically related projects: she was in 1969's space-western, Hammer/Warner Bros.' *Moon Zero Two,* and was one of the mind-controlled beauties in *On Her Majesty's Secret Service* (in which the actress who played the human assistant of *The Abominable Dr. Phibes,* Virginia North, also appeared as the personal secretary of an Underworld kingpin). Fellow actress Lois Maxwell, who played "M's" secretary throughout the Bond series, "Miss Moneypenny," also found herself in quite a few UFOlogical projects, or hooked-up with those making them. She played the missing-time/abducted wife of the paranormal investigator in MGM's *The Haunting* the year after appearing in the first James Bond picture from MGM's companion studio, United Artists, and *The Haunting* was directed by *The Day the Earth Stood Still*'s Robert Wise. Maxwell re-recorded and dubbed many of Gerry and Sylvia Anderson's popular children's T.V. puppet shows in her own studio in Rome, and even played one of the character voices in their show *Stingray*. Maxwell ran away from home two weeks after her sixteenth birthday and joined the Canadian Air Force, which is in keeping with the idea of a governmental UFOlogical entertainment project kept in the military and Intelligence families.

Gerry Anderson complained in the May and June 1980 issues of *Starlog* that many of *Space: 1999*'s problems were due to unauthorized editing of his footage, after it left the studio. He called the central problem the removal of "The Mysterious Unknown Force" from the background of his show. As one such removed bit of explicative dialogue explaining this force went, a character asks Koenig (the leader of Moonbase Alpha) if he's ever wondered "just how and why we've survived," and receives the answer, "You're not referring to God, are you?" The first character then speculates, "Oh, I don't know exactly. I'm a scientist, I don't know anything about God. No, it's a *cosmic intelligence* that I've got in mind ..." And Koenig finishes the thought for him, "... which intervenes at the right moment." Anderson defined his guiding philosophy, which appears to have had a little trouble with the censors even as late as twenty years ago: "Perhaps Earth is not the planet of birth of the human race. Perhaps, as some suggest, aliens visited in the past and seeded Earth with humanity. Could it be that those forces that guard Moonbase Alpha are in fact representatives of those same aliens, still guiding the future history of the human race? ... [C]ould this be a reason for the fact that so many aliens in *Space: 1999* are humanoid?"

The Andersons' vision, and its apparent expurgation, are evidence that there is no single overriding government conspiracy afoot to educate the people about UFOs. What it seems more to indicate, as have some earlier examples, is that certain governmental factions are quite interested in the educational project, and that they do not always receive cooperation. Evidence that the Andersons were well-connected governmentally and did receive cooperation can be seen at the end of their movie *Thunderbirds Are Go,* in which the Band of Her Majesty's Royal Marines plays the title song while marching in uniform. It was Lord Lew Grade at ITC who produced their later and more UFOlogical work. "We had known so much hardship and disappointment in the early days that having the luxury of [ITC] in our corner was sheer joy," recounts Sylvia Anderson in her 1991 memoirs, *Yes, M'Lady.* "We would go to Lew Grade with just the germ of an idea, often filling less than a page, and after talking it through with him, we would leave his office with full approval to proceed—all arranged in one meeting. This simply could not and does not happen in the nineties."

Gerry and Sylvia Andersons' former "Super Marionation" syndicated sci-fi kids' shows included *Fireball XL5* in 1962 and *Thunderbirds* in 1966, as well as the pre-*Space: 1999* live-action *UFO* in 1969–70. *Fireball XL5* was the series with the episode "Robert to the Rescue" that so closely resembled the particulars of the Hill abduction (see previous chapter). *Fireball XL5*'s thirty-nine syndicated thirty-minute episodes followed the twenty-first century adventures of heroic Colonel Steve Zodiac, the lovely Dr. Venus, nerdy Professor Matt Matic, and Robert the Robot, who combated such humanoid space menaces of Sector 25 as the "Green Men" and the "Subterrains." The show's theme song, "I Wish I was a Spaceman," sung by Don Spencer, was actually in the Top 40 charts in 1963.

The Andersons' productions were most famous for startlingly real models. As Michael Weldon puts it, "The special-effects miniatures are better than in most movies with real people." The Thunderbirds were made into two ITC feature films in 1966 and 1968, *Thunderbirds Are Go* and *Thunderbirds 6.* The former has the government crime-fighting and space-exploring Thunderbirds team fighting hostile rock-snakes on Mars. Before the government's eventually successful launch, its Mars rockets are sabotaged.

UFO ran for twenty-six episodes in syndication, coming to American shores via CBS in the fall of 1972, and would have been produced for a second season if the Andersons had not opted instead to do *Space: 1999*. Its running plot concerned a secret British government team called SHADO (Supreme Headquarters, Alien Defense Organization), purportedly based to some degree on Ian Fleming's ideas; the team keeps track of and battles flying saucers. The government has bases for their study on both Earth and the Moon, and though the saucer occupants are definitely portrayed as nefariously motivated, those motivations are never clearly defined—except insofar as their frequent landing on Earth and kidnapping a number of human beings. The nature of the alien presence is never clearly delineated, either. The premiere episode, "Identified," reveals that the world's governments have become aware of flying saucers as a real and hostile presence, requiring both intensive study and ongoing defensive measures. When the team discovers that the aliens are kidnapping human beings for unknown purposes, they finally succeed in shooting down one of their craft. The alien on board soon dies, a humanoid who ages with remarkable speed when his helmet is removed. The alien's nature is human, as revealed by an autopsy: SHADO's Commander Straker deduces that the aliens are related to the human race, since they have many of the same organs, and are regularly traveling millions of miles on raiding parties to take organs from human specimens for their own survival. Between *UFO* and *Space: 1999*, Gerry Anderson produced fifty-two episodes of one other live-action intrigue show, a series starring Robert Vaughn called *The Protectors*.

The Andersons' other Super Marionation kids' series were *Stingray* (1964), *Supercar* (1965), and *Captain Scarlet and the Mysterons*, which are often still seen on today's Sci-Fi cable channel. *Stingray* concerned the efforts of WASP (the World Aquanaut Security Patrol) to keep an eye on "whole races of people under the sea … some bad and some good, some to help and some to fight." The show's protagonist, Troy Tempest (patterned after James Garner), is abducted in the pilot episode by the undersea kingdom of Titanica while on patrol. The Titanicans plan to execute him, until one of their slaves from another subaqueous race, the mute Marina, takes a liking to him and helps him escape. Marina then becomes a WASP member, additionally providing a convenient (for dramatic purposes) love-interest threat to Troy's "Terranean" sweetheart, Atlanta, the daughter of the organization's leader (the aforementioned character's voice provided by Lois Maxwell).

Captain Scarlet, the most complex and adult of the Anderson's offerings, was originally on the air in the major UFO flap year of 1967. The title character (patterned after Cary Grant) is one of a team of government agents in the year 2068 going by the code-name SPECTRUM (more obviously inspired, even than *UFO*'s SHADO, by Ian Fleming's SPECTRE), whose members go by identifying colors. SPECTRUM fights a secret war with the hypnotically compelling "Mysterons," never-seen but presumed to be humanoid extraterrestrials who infiltrate and sabotage Earth's military and space forces. The Mysterons are from Mars, "sworn enemies of Earth, possessing the ability to recreate an exact likeness of an object or person ... but first, they must *destroy!*" Scarlet was the first mind-controlled subject of the Mysterons, and having broken their mental conditioning in their earliest failed assassination attempt against a leading Earth politician, has become an indestructible and invaluable ally to SPECTRUM. *"Captain Scarlet!"* goes the theme song, "He's the one who knows the Mysteron game! And things they plan! *Captain Scarlet!* To his Martian foes, a dangerous name! A super-man!" The colors red, white, and black predominate in *Captain Scarlet:* the leader of the Mysteron forces on Earth is "Captain Black"; Scarlet's superior (the head of SPECTRUM) is "Colonel White"; and of course "Captain Scarlet" is obvious. Scarlet even wears a red and black costume.

Though the SPECTRUM team is simplistically heroic, and Captain Black and the Mysterons equally heartless and evil, adult elements enter into the plots. Captain Black is at least once shown to demonstrate compassion to a completely helpless victim (though it is left unclear whether this is due to human concern, or an ulterior motive). And SPECTRUM is seen to be at odds with Earth's military in attempting to *prevent* an all-out attack against Mars—the Mysterons' assault on Earth is an ongoing vendetta, having begun when the first Earth forces destroyed a Mysteron city, unprovoked, in a catastrophic misunderstanding. Unlike the Andersons' other super-patriotic cardboard hero epics, *Captain Scarlet* has SPECTRUM losing nearly as many battles as the Mysterons, the continuing war taking a noticeable toll on Earth's forces. The deep, commanding voice of mind-controlled Captain Black—who was the very man that launched the initial attack on the Mysterons—radioes in to SPECTRUM's headquarters at the beginning of each episode, accompanied by genuinely eerie music, to announce clues to the Mysterons' latest terrorist plot. One typical narration ran, "This is the voice of the Mysterons! We know that you can hear us, Earthmen! You are powerless to defeat us! Your much-boasted new space fleet is doomed to failure! We will make certain that you never return to our planet . . . *Mars!*"

In 1975 came the 20th Century Fox movie production of Richard O'Brien's bizarre mega-hit musical, *The Rocky Horror Picture Show*. The stage version was a cult hit in Britain (it got Best Musical in the *London Evening Standard*'s 1973 annual poll of drama critics) and a popular favorite in Los Angeles in 1974. Fox shelled out a then-lavish million-dollar budget for the film. It initially flopped, opening at the United Artists theater in Westwood, Los Angeles, on September 26, 1975, pulling in less than half its production costs in the first six months, though it proved as popular in L.A. as the stage show had been. Sensing a good business move, Fox booked it into Greenwich Village's Waverley Theater on April Fool's Day of 1976, and by summer's end it had caught on as a late-night hit from New York to Austin. The phenomenal success it has since enjoyed tempts one to look for the influence of a government mind-control project, though primarily it seems to have occurred due to the film's adoption by the gay community as a sort of statement on sexual liberation—which, ironically, is the exact opposite message it appears to have been intended to convey. The story goes that during one Manhattan showing, an audience member called out to the screen as Susan Sarandon's character was shielding herself from the rain with a newspaper, "Buy an umbrella, you cheap bitch!" which began the interactive audience treatment the film is now famous for.

The movie's story is literally that of the vehicular UFO abduction of hapless Denton, Ohio, WASP wayfarers "Brad and Janet" on an isolated country road. Many actual UFOlogical elements appear in the plot, the majority of which could easily be attributed to the film's apparent homage to every popular sci-fi film made, but some of which seem better informed. In fact, considering the supposed nostalgic source material, it is interesting that the movie more closely resembles an accurate montage of actual UFO abduction experiences than any of those Hollywood movies. Paralysis and nightmarish sexual seduction are story elements, and the entire production—reworked largely by original British stage producer Michael White and American executive producer Lou Adler from O'Brien's initially less UFO-logically accurate spoof, *They Came from Denton High*—is a Brechtian staging of the myth of the fallen Watchers and the Flood.

Perverse monster-maker Frank N. Furter, a "sweet transvestite from (the planet) Transexual (in the galaxy) Transylvania," comes upon stranded wayfarers Brad and Janet, whose car has "broken down" on the isolated highway nearby. He introduces them to his latest playtoy: a muscle-man, made for the specific purpose of sating the mad doctor's lusts. Frank seduces all of his guests, especially delighting in the taking of Brad and Janet, and murders a former male abductee lover simply as a matter of convenience. A "rival scientist" from Earth, Dr. Everett Scott ("Or should I say . . . Doctor *von Scott?*" snaps Frank, striking a nerve), arrives on the scene, a member of the government's secret UFO investigation project who also develops advanced weapons inspired by alien sonic ("audio-vibratory") technology. Conveniently, Scott also happens to be the father of Frank's murdered abductee lover, Eddie.

When Frank gets out of hand, his former assistant, Riff Raff (O'Brien), abruptly barges onto the scene in the flashy garb of an ancient civilization, sporting a Trident laser-weapon obviously patterned after that carried by the Supreme God of antiquity, and announces, "Frank N. Furter, it's all over! Your mission is a failure—your lifestyle's too extreme!" and dispatches the fallen Watcher and his created muscleman with the Trident, leaving them face-down in a pool of water, the echo of the gods' laughter eerily resounding above their drowned bodies. The two are even felled from the summit of a pyramid: the RKO radio tower. When the confused Brad and

Janet demand to know what Frank's crime was, Dr. Scott explains, "You saw what he did to Eddie. Society must be protected!" Riff Raff confirms the judgment and drops them all off where they were picked up before taking off back to his home in space.

The elements of the Watchers' demise cannot have been accidental. Equally interesting are a few other elements, such as the opening song's lyrics, "See androids fighting Brad and Janet," when in fact no androids—or any other form of robots—are anywhere to be seen in the movie. There are, however, identically dressed silent chorus members in black tie and tails, whose eyes are concealed behind large dark glasses. Frank playfully inquires of his new abductees, "Got any tattoos?" The "birthmarks" seen on actual UFO abductees could only be such marks, since they are not the result of scarification and yet are permanent.

Repeat-abductees, back for another go-round, gleefully sing, "Let's do the Time Warp, again!" The "Time Warp" is a sexual dance involving "the pelvic thrust that really drives you insane," and Riff Raff and his fellow servant Magenta explain its effects, which are identical to those of UFO abduction: "With a bit of a mind flip / You're in for a time slip / And nothing can ever be the same. / You're spaced out on sensation / Like you're under sedation / Let's do the Time Warp again." Abductee Columbia (called "a groupie" in the credits) relates her experience during it: "Well, I was walking down the street / Just a-havin' a think / When a snake of a guy / Gave me an evil wink / He shook-a me up, he took me by surprise / He had a pick-up truck and the devil's eyes / He stared at me and I felt a change / Time meant nothing—never would again." These are common descriptions of an average UFO abduction, especially the reference to "staring" and its subsequent permanent change on the abductees' psyche. Even the equation of transport ships to "pick-up trucks" (or "motorcycles," for that matter, such as are witnessed by Brad and Janet going to "the castle" before they arrive there themselves) is not an uncommon one for abductees. "Delivery boy" Eddie sings a similar recollection, lamenting/celebrating the change he has undergone since his initial abduction: "Whatever happened to Saturday night / When you dressed up sharp and / You felt all right. / It doesn't seem the same since cosmic light / Came into my life and I thought I was divine."

There is also the portrayal of an underwater sexual orgy that equates to the "breathing pool" reported by so many actual abductees. At one point, a "floor show" soliloquy allows each of the characters to share their feelings with the audience, each dressed in erotic lingerie which is solely of the colors red, white, and black—the colors of Atlantis and virtually the only colors seen throughout the "castle," which ultimately is revealed to be a spaceship. Their experiences are as varied as those of real UFO abductees, perhaps demonstrating the most interesting aspect of the entire phenomenon: abductees' reactions to the event are as varied as those anyone has to sex alone, abduction notwithstanding.

Straight-laced Brad cannot handle what he has undergone, crying, "It's beyond me—help me, mommy! I'll be good—you'll see! Take this dream away!" The mention of "this dream" is interesting all by itself, in light of the fact that no one in the story is unconscious—though actual UFO abductees more or less are, throughout their experience. Janet, on the other hand, discovers she enjoys the aliens: "I feel released, bad times deceased—my confidence is increased! Reality is here! The game has been disbanded—my mind has been expanded! It's a *gas* that Franky's landed—his lust is so sincere!" And, in light of the earlier "space sex-threat" seen during the same era in *Flesh Gordon* (Nixon was out, but Ford was still in), the German rocket scientist's own reaction is quite interesting: *"Ach! We've got to get out of this trap! Before this decadence saps our wills! I've got to be strong, and try to hang on—or else my mind, too, may well snap! And my life will be lived for the thrills!"*

A later, concluding soliloquy, cut from the final print of the film but released on the soundtrack album, expresses sentiments also equivalent to real-life UFO abductees. Confused and bewildered Brad, bemoaning his inability to find the truth for all his efforts at understanding, ends by lamenting, "All I know is, down inside, I'm bleeding ..." Janet, despite (or possibly because of) her enjoyment of the experience, feels abandoned and alone, but also appears to know who her abductors were: "And superheroes come to feast / Upon the flesh, not yet deceased / And all I know is still the beast / Is feeding ..." And the Narrator, who serves as the voyeuristic purveyor of the UFO abduction experience, concludes with the coda, "And crawling on the planet's face / Some insects, called the human race / Lost in time, and lost in space / And meaning...."

In 1976, ending the transitional period between Gerald Ford's UFO educational deployment and Jimmy Carter's taking over the reins, was Nicholas Roeg's big-budgeted and slickly produced adaptation of Walter Tevis' novel, *The Man Who Fell to Earth*, independently released by Cinema 5. David Bowie plays a human-looking alien on an undercover mission to find a way to transport needed water from Earth to his home planet. A technical genius, he becomes an inventor and makes millions, but is eventually found out and deliberately detained by the government past his launch window to return home, making him a prisoner on Earth for the rest of his life. Though they give him all the luxuries and comforts, he becomes a depressed alcoholic as he invents better weaponry for the Defense Department.

The choice of preexisting science-fiction projects for the public education project indicates awareness on the part of the Intelligence team involved of authors who, for whatever reason, had a remarkably prescient sense of their own concerning actual UFOlogy. A number of horror authors, particularly, both in our time and preceding it, seem to have a pretty good idea just what was going on behind the scenes in outer space.

9

Foresights and Fictionalizations

J acques Vallee noted in 1965's *Anatomy of a Phenomenon* that the psychological theory of UFOs could not be considered anything but highly improbable, since if it were true, then surely there would have been more reports coming from the most prolific era of science fiction (preceding the present era), when in fact the exact opposite is the case: *"[T]he 'dead' period of UFO activity (1914–1946) has been one of the richest in science-fiction stories of all kinds,* and has seen the growing interest of the motion-picture industry in fantastic and 'horror' tales which might have resulted in an increasing number of hoaxes and hallucinations, and even in UFO waves, if the 'psychological' theory of UFOs were correct. As early as 1916, Otto Ripert's [*sic*] film *Homonculus* was about the creation of an artificial man by a mad scientist. In 1914 and 1920, the German industry produced two films on the subject of the 'Golem' (Paul Wegener and Henrik Galeen). In 1924 the film *Orlac's Hands* was made, after a novel by Maurice Renard. In 1926 Fritz Lang created *Metropolis,* and we should not forget that 1920 saw the introduction of the word 'robot,' with a play by Karl Capek, *Rossum's Universal Robots (R.U.R.).* In 1928, Fritz Lang did *The Woman in the Moon (Die Frau Im Mond).* The first 'trip to the moon' had been made by the

French pioneer Melies in 1902, and the celebrated series of Franken-stein and John Carter of Mars were created during this period."

Vallee elsewhere added that the first "blackout caused by a UFO" was in the 1933 Arthur Koestler play, *Twilight Bar*, and that certain actual UFO facts known only to private governmental investigators were emerging in science-fiction novels. "The first reference to UFO effects on car ignition," he states in *Dimensions*, "came in a novel written in 1950 by Bernard Newman entitled *The Flying Saucer*. It is true that when it was written, some UFO reports involving magnetic disturbances (of the compass) were already circulating. Even in 1944, the military had already amassed considerable information about unidentified flying objects, the first large-scale scientific investiga-tion having been done by the National Bureau of Standards the pre-vious year. But the fact remains that the coincidence between these works of imagination and the actual details of the reports that came from the public is a remarkable one, and it opens the way to unlim-ited speculation." Part of this, no doubt, has occurred as the result of increasing government foreknowledge of the truth behind UFOs since at least the middle of the last century. It is equally possible, as examples to follow will demonstrate, that there was a certain amount of the same material being imparted to various artists and authors direct from the source.

An accurate UFO abduction was written at least as early as 1930 and published four years later, in Ege Tilm's "Hodomur, Man of Infin-ity," containing missing time and amnesia. Don A. Stuart (John W. Campbell), the same man who soon wrote "Who Goes There?" on which Howard Hawks' *The Thing* was based, wrote a story contain-ing accurate abduction elements in the 1935 *Astounding Stories;* it was titled "The Invaders." Though the entities in the story looked nothing like reported UFO abductors, the cover art displayed very nearly the image of classic Grays, differing only in having ears and an extra pair of eyes behind their heads to match those in front.

French researcher Bertrand Meheust discovered a tremendous number of accurate UFOlogical stories emerging in French and Eng-lish between 1880 and 1940, which he discussed at length in 1978's *Science-fiction and Flying Saucers* and 1985's *Flying Saucers and Folklore.*

The commonly recurring elements in them are UFOs chasing and stalling vehicles, and the abduction of human beings who are then amnesiac of the event and so suffer "missing time." The stories' greatest proliferation occurred between the World Wars. Since that time, of course, as this study has illustrated, they have been further disseminated to a phenomenal degree by Hollywood, with far more obvious connections between what hidden researchers in the government were discovering at the time and how it was being leaked through this particular source.

It is interesting that Vallee's principal examples almost all concern robots. And it is curious that the pieces listed correspond closely with the apparent reality of UFOs. Also curious is the fact that Vallee wrote in his 1991 book *Revelations* that renowned science-fiction author Philip K. Dick underwent what we would today call abduction experiences, though he refrains from specifically naming them as such. Dick wrote about them at tremendous length—about half a million words—in his letters, between February of 1978 and his death four years later in 1982. He often found himself unable to sleep, kept awake at night by "violent phosphene acitivity ... within my head it communicated with me in the form of a computer-like or AI [Artificial Intelligence]-system-like voice, quite different from any human voice, neither male nor female, and very beautiful sound it was, the most beautiful sound I ever heard ... the imposition— that is the right word—the imposition of another human personality unto mine produced the most startling modifications in my behavior ... Some living, highly intelligent entity manifested itself inside me and around me, but what it was, what its purpose was, where it came from ... each theory leaves some datum unexplained ... and *I know this is not going to change.* I have the impression that a master gameplayer and magician and trickster is involved."

Neither Vallee nor Dick had theories to explain it, but the thesis of this study does. If what Dick experienced was communication from an outside "magician" like the biblical Yahweh or the great Celtic god Manannan Mac Lir, as did the prophets of old, and that magician's emissary was a computerized mechanical contrivance, then what he repeatedly encountered makes perfect sense. Dick was not an influential writer while alive but his works quickly gained widespread popularity in posterity, so much that an annual award is given out in his name. His works were made into the UFOlogically-pertinent movies *Blade Runner* (1982), *Total Recall* (1990), and *Screamers* (1995), about robots and the planet Mars. *Blade Runner,* based on the novel *Do Androids Dream of Electric Sheep?,* is about psychopathic android slaves rebelling against their human creators in a futuristic Los Angeles that grows more realistic every day. *Screamers,* from the story "Second Variety," concerns human survivors of a high-tech war left having to fight their own robot weapons, the robots having become higher-grade self-programming man-killers independently of their creators. *Total Recall* is based on the short story "We Can Remember It For You, Wholesale," which Dick wrote in September of 1965, shortly after *Mariner 4* had beamed back the first desolate pictures of the Martian landscape. The story was first published in the April 1966 *Fantasy and Science Fiction,* where it was nominated for a Nebula award.

"Remember" was about a man who inadvertently discovers he was sent on a secret mission to Mars to assassinate a rebel leader for the government, the memory of which was supposed to have been hypnotically erased. In order to avoid having to be terminated himself as a potential security risk, he undergoes a separate hypnotic conditioning, to believe that all his memories have resulted from implantation. At a vacation resort company that does exactly such procedures, they prearrange the memory that he discovered artifacts and living Martians during his mission, and that his actions there saved the human race from destruction, knowing that he will not believe it when he wakes up and be certain that it was all the result of his false vacation programming. But during the process, a former hypnotically erased memory surfaces, revealing the phony story to be true. While on his government mission, the agent *did indeed* discover artifacts and living Martians, and his interaction with them *did* save the human race. In their gratitude, they gave him a special healing rod that only he has the knowledge to use, and hypnotically erased memory of their contact with him. In a further twist to the ending, it is discovered that his government programmers already knew all the foregoing and wanted to provide the extra hypno-conditioning to make it all the more impossible for him to trust his memory. The idea of frail Martians hypnotically erasing an abductee's memory had not yet been broached by legitimate UFOlogy, the first written occurrence of which was Betty and Barney Hill in *Look* (and the "aliens" were not designated as coming from Mars in that instance), more than a year following Dick's writing of this story.

The movie version, 1990's *Total Recall* from Carolco, removed the futuristic science-fictional jargon that so commonly repels the average reader from the genre and made the extreme convolutions of the plot much easier to follow. It also added some interesting and legitimate UFOlogical elements. It was produced by *Alien*'s Ronald Shusett and co-written by that movie's author, Dan O'Bannon, whose name will frequently be noted in connection with relatively accurate projects of exactly this type. The government spy with a hypnotically erased dual-identity has his suppressed second personality emerge when he undergoes a brain implant at the vacation company. The new brain implant conflicts with one already planted there by the government, breaking its conditioning on him and "blowing his cover." Very quickly, he becomes the target of government assassins who are anxious to keep anyone from discovering what he has already found on Mars. He is actually on a labyrinthine undercover mission to disclose the location of Martian rebels, who are fighting against a powerful Military-Industrial vested interest group to re-oxygenate that planet's atmosphere with a subterranean reactor that was built and never activated by a former superior race there, which is a definite break from the short story—the military government charges its citizenry exorbitantly for the very oxygen they breathe on that barren planet. What makes this especially interesting are speculations made by a number of UFOlogists over the years that the UFO intelligence utilizes some tremendous natural force for its energy, such as sunlight—and, given the oil companies' history of suppressing exactly such solar and other free-energy research, such a speculation may well explain one of the fundamental reasons for the extreme secrecy on the UFO subject by the world's governments.

Other added elements of interest to the story include tracking implants and "mindscans" by both human and alien agencies. At one point in the movie, the agent telepathically/hypnotically "opens his mind" to a Martian mutant, who revives his buried memories and programs him to save the Martian people by activating the reactor. More interesting, the agent's programmer is his own self, an element that definitely connects to the reality of UFO abductions but was not published for another two years. UFO programmer-abductors saying "I am you," even in the abductee's own voice, is extremely common to the phenomenon. While some of the elements in Dick's original story are indicative of his potentially having been an abductee himself, these in particular were not in his writing and emerged as a result of the movie's production team—making, in both cases, the question of just how they were known in advance even more curious. Another interesting curiosity may connect this movie to the earlier *Star Wars:* in both stories, a tyrannical Military-Industrial Complex seeks to destroy a band of free rebels whose hideout turns out be on the moon of a red planet (or the red planet itself)—and, of course, the military's ultimate weapon in *Star Wars,* the Death Star, is a lethal space station masquerading as a moon.

Vallee never overtly suggests that certain authors' creativity may have been inspired from outside—or, more specifically, "otherworldly"—sources, but he does imply it. By mentioning the prolific increase in science-fiction output, especially concerning robots and space travel, and Dick's seeming abduction experiences, he draws a wide circle around exactly that idea. Abductees do tend to develop obsessions that generally find expression in their work, especially if they are in any way artistic, a fact that Vallee cannot have been ignorant of at the time of his writing. Dick is only one example, and not even the best. Vallee could have mentioned a better one: Howard Phillips Lovecraft.

Lovecraft, like Dick, seems to have been remarkably prophetic in regard to UFO and abduction phenomena, especially given the time in which he wrote, which was exactly that described by Vallee as the "richest in science-fiction"—more specifically, during the Depression of the 1930s. Lovecraft was a character, in the truest sense of the word. He was a gangly, lanky, lantern-jawed New Englander, from Providence, Rhode Island, where he lived almost the entirety of his life with his mother and his aunts. Photos of him could pass for the headshot of an actor playing Ichabod Crane. He was intensely xeno- and eroto-phobic, two traits which were largely to dominate his life without his realizing it. For a time he admired Hitler, being a true Aryan believer himself and a despiser of the "mongrel hordes" of minorities from a year and a half he spent in New York City, though later even he found the dictator's anti-Semitism off-putting. Inter- estingly enough, in spite of his proclivities, his single short-lived and almost entirely platonic marriage was to a beautiful and gracious Jewish woman named Sonia Greene, who continued to love him and be friendly with him even after their amicable divorce. Before dying prematurely of stomach cancer at the age of 46 in 1937, Lovecraft invented an entirely new genre that virtually all horror writers since have been inspired by: the Cthulhu Mythos. These have been named after the chief god of Lovecraft's fictional pantheon of "Great Old Ones," extraterrestrial beings of antiquity, who created the human race for purposes of their own before dying off or being killed in wars with each other, some merely slumbering among their ancient mega- lithic cities and places in the stars until such time as something should awaken them for new domination of Earth and the Universe.

Like Dick, Lovecraft was published but never famous in his short life, and achieved tremendous popularity following his death. Also like Dick, he appears to have been an abductee. His biographer, L. Sprague de Camp, quotes Lovecraft's later writings about child- hood experiences he underwent, the physical reality of which he seemed to believe in (emphases and parenthetical inclusions Love- craft's own):

> When I was 6 or 7 I used to be tormented constantly with a pecu- liar type of recurrent nightmare in which a monstrous race of enti- ties (called by me "NightGaunts"—I don't know where I got hold of the name) used to snatch me up by the stomach (bad digestion?) & carry me off through infinite leagues of black air over the tow- ers of dead and horrible cities. They would finally get me into a grey void where I could see the needle-like pinnacles of enormous mountains miles below. Then they would let me drop—& as I gained

momentum in my Icarus-like plunge I would start awake in such a panic that I hated to think of sleeping again. The "nightgaunts" were black, lean, rubbery things with horns, barbed tails, bat-wings, *and no faces at all.*

Barring the tails and bat-wings, a common enough description of UFO abductors, and the background trappings and occurrences fit the overall pattern, as well. Lovecraft said that they "[came] in flocks" and "had no voices," only "tickling " his stomach for a while before inevitably dropping him back in bed—given his premature death due to stomach cancer, this detail is of more than passing interest.

The earliest movie of Lovecraft's work was one of Roger Corman's AIP "Poe" productions in 1962, *The Haunted Palace,* based on Lovecraft's only novel, *The Case of Charles Dexter Ward.* The title was taken from a Poe poem, since Lovecraft's name was all but unknown at the time to any but a particular cult of admirers, though he would hardly have minded: Lovecraft at all times emulated Poe, giving his prose the peculiarly affected verbosity it is famous for. The film version is roughly true to the first half of Lovecraft's novel, especially in its spirit and theme, though the 1992 independent remake, *The Resurrected,* is closer to the actual plot and focuses on the events of the second half of the novel. In *The Haunted Palace,* sorceror Vincent Price nocturnally calls women to his castle in a state of trance, where they are made to have sex with demons from beyond, and after which they give birth to grotesque hybrids. Price hypnotically erases their memories of these encounters. Caught in his lair, the physician hero asks what Price is doing to his latest victim, and Price answers, "Honoring her, Dr. Willet ... honoring her." He is asked exactly what the "project" is that he is so fully cooperating with and running, and Price's face becomes clouded for a moment before he says, "The most important project ever attempted of humans, Dr. Willet. More important than you can ever imagine, and therefore I fear beyond your understanding. As a matter of fact, we don't fully understand, ourselves. We obey, that is all. We obey."

Another of Corman's AIP Poe-based features, *The Tomb of Ligeia* (1965), has Price in the same kind of role, which he was often to repeat: the amnesiac nocturnal dual-personality. Price is under the hypnotic dominance of his dead wife, to whose summoning mummy he returns nightly for sex. He is under complete post-event control, oblivious to his recurring ritual, yet aware enough of it to unconsciously protect himself from anyone's prying intrusion, including his own, which is typical of UFO abductees. Egyptian relics are a background motif of the story, and a hypnotic session is enacted in the film as it was to be in many AIP productions.

1965 saw the next attempt at Lovecraft on film, again by AIP, directed by Roger Corman's former art director, Daniel Haller, this time produced in England. It was called *Die, Monster, Die!* (released in Britain under the titles *Monster of Terror* and *The House at the End of the World*) and was based on Lovecraft's non-Cthulhu Mythos story, "The Colour Out Of Space." The original story was about an extraterrestrial living in the well of a deranged cultist, who worships it and allows it to gradually mutate and sicken his family before the local townspeople drive the invader away and back into outer space. The movie hews closely to the same elements, making the extraterrestrial invader a meteorite with mutagenic properties, which may or may not have some guiding intelligence, that reclusive scientist Boris Karloff keeps in a shrine in his cellar.

Like Price in *The Haunted Palace,* Karloff allows the cosmic force to completely dominate him, ultimately being possessed and destroyed by it in the end when he makes a feeble attempt to rid himself of the monster meteorite. Until that time, he puts pieces of it in the soil of every plant in his greenhouse, where it creates maneating monster-hybrid creatures. He helps it mutate not only the local flora and fauna, but members of his own family as well, believing the stone to be a gift from heaven by virtue of the fact that it causes vegetation to grow with remarkable speed, even though it has permanently blighted the heath in which it landed. His ancestors worshipped demonic sky gods, but Karloff has the clarity of mind to realize that those gods were nonexistent, where whatever sent this meteor is not. His wife, however, sees the stone as a belated answer to the prayers of Karloff's mad religious progenitor, correctly surmising it will destroy their daughter and perhaps many others if not somehow stopped. The story could almost be a Gothic rendition of the Siberian explosion of 1908, or a parable on radioactivity, the Bomb, and the Military-Industrial Complex—any or all of which it may actually have been. The story was independently remade by Trans-World Entertainment in 1987 as *The Curse,* making the debilitating horror the product of chemical pollution which eventually disintegrates the brain. Important to note in *Die, Monster, Die!* is the movie's finale, in which frail, aged Boris Karloff is inexplicably—unless UFO awareness is taken into account—transformed by the cosmic power into a bald, near-indestructible, glowing, metallic silver humanoid. In other words, a virtual Gray.

Karloff's final English-language film was AIP/Tigon's *The Crimson Cult,* loosely based on Lovecraft's "The Dreams in the Witch House." Like *The Dunwich Horror,* which soon followed, the film largely replaced Lovecraft's "Old Ones" influence with more straightforward Satanism and witchcraft. An undistinguished film, it is of historic interest for being the only movie to co-star three of horror filmdom's most famous icons: Karloff, Barbara Steele, and Christopher Lee. As an added bonus, it even featured the lesser-known (until his casting as Alfred in the 1990s *Batman* feature films) but equally regarded character actor of the same genre, Michael Gough.

Director Daniel Haller tried Lovecraft again for AIP in 1970, following the lukewarm reception of the former Karloff films with Lovecraft's classic, *The Dunwich Horror.* It was scarcely more successful than its predecessor, stripping most of Lovecraft's science-fictional trappings and turning the background instead into more traditional and pedestrian devil-worship. It also suffered from being made at the tail end of America's mod years, the colorful look of the "free-sex" era and inappropriate rock score somewhat undermining the atmosphere. Despite this, certain Lovecraftian elements remain—notably the hybridization of various family members in a Satanic clan with demons from beyond. Wilbur Whateley (Dean Stockwell, originally planned to be Peter Fonda, following the success of *Easy Rider*) is the more human of two brothers sired off of madwoman Lavinia Whateley by a star-demon; the other brother looks more like his father, who is an indescribable tentacled monstrosity—once he's made visible, which is not his natural state. Wilbur, like gener-ations of his family before him, is continuing the great work of attempting to create the perfect being between the two species: man and extraterrestrial.

A brief fling with Lovecraft was enjoyed by Rod Serling's *Night Gallery* on NBC the following year, where two of the pulp author's stories were adapted: "Cool Air" and "Pickman's Model." The former was a simple reworking of Poe's "The Facts in the Case of M. Valde-mar," with a man who has successfully staved off death for many years ultimately succumbing to the ravages of the grave. The latter is one of Poe's minor classics, the story of a peculiar painter named Richard Upton Pickman who portrays only monstrous creatures in his work. Both stuck very closely to the source material, the latter differing only in showing what Lovecraft kept in the shadows for suspense.

The adaptation of "Pickman's Model" added one other element, a missing love interest in art student Louise Sorel, one of Pickman's students, who vainly attempts to spark a romantic flame in the artist (Lovecraft's story featured a male narrator). The painter's perpetu-ally gloved hands, and his brusque, abrasive manner, challenge Sorel to pierce the veil of his mystery. Pickman warns Sorel away with a legend she fails to understand, about a primordial race believed orig-inally to have come from the sea: "There is a legend ... which tells of an eldritch race, more powerful and loathsome than the putrid slime which clings to the walls of hell. Twisted creatures, half men, half beast, that move to the rustling sound of predatory rats, carry-ing with them the stench of the charnel house. Wretched mutations who live deep beneath the earth in dark tunnels, surfacing in the dead of night and returning before dawn to practice their unspeak-able acts and breed their filthy spawn, until the day arrives when their swollen numbers will finally emerge and ravish the earth like a noxious plague." Sorel's father similarly warns her that the area of Pickman's studio is one in which several bodies were once stolen from the local cemetery, and supposedly "womenfolk disappeared [and were] carried off in the dead of night for the purposes of pro-creation ... They finally sealed off every underground opening they could find, praying that they'd found them all." Sorel tracks the reclusive Pickman to his studio, and he begs her to leave before it is too late, snarling at her, "Did you not hear me when I said I had no need of *human* company? And could you not understand *why?*" Sorel examines Pickman's canvases as he hurriedly leaves to address the problem of something scratching elsewhere in the building. She sees that Pickman has done a portrait of himself as a boy with his mother, standing before a shadowed representation of a hideous creature. As the realization hits her, the very creature portrayed in the painting enters the door Pickman exited and attempts to carry Sorel off. Pickman arrives to fight the creature off, losing one of his gloves in the struggle—and Sorel sees that his hands are the same as that of the monster combating him. The creature takes Pickman away, never to be seen again. As the townsfolk seal an underground opening in Pickman's studio, Sorel rebufs one of them for criticizing his work as loathsome: "No. He painted what he saw . . . and what he was."

Night Gallery additionally spoofed Lovecraft twice. Once was in "Miss Lovecraft Sent Me," with gum-chewing high school nymphette babysitter Sue Lyon fleeing in terror from an Addams Family-ish house whose children she is supposed to babysit. The other was "Professor Peabody's Last Lecture," with Carl Reiner lecturing against the Great Old Ones at the fictional Miskatonic University, ultimately to be transformed by the ancient monstrosities into one of their own number—much to the chagrin of students H. P. Lovecraft, August Derleth, and Robert Bloch.

Unsuccessful in translating Lovecraft to film, in spite of the studio's and Lovecraft's natural talents and common vision, AIP abandoned him. Its sci-fi/horror cycle was nearly spent anyway, except for a few well-made productions to follow which they financed in Britain. Lovecraft remained obscure and undiscovered for the next fifteen years, until executive producer Charles Band—disputedly dubbed the logical inheritor to the crown of Roger Corman—turned the least, and most atypical, of his stories into a minor camp classic called *Re-Animator,* most famous for a scene in which a naked Barbara Crampton is suggestively played with about her privates by a disembodied head. The original story, even in Lovecraft's eyes, was never more than a simple *Frankenstein* knock-off, a quick piece of hackwork for a fast buck. The disembodied head carried by its former owner was in the written story, but certainly not its "giving head" to a nubile young lass—Lovecraft never had heroines in his stories, all sex being solely for the purposes of reproduction, occurring outside the main action of the story (offstage, as it were), and only between hapless women (or sometimes men) and demons from outer space. The singular lack of sex, or any semblance of romantic interest, is one of the trademarks of his misogynistic fiction. Still, Band had a good head on his own shoulders and used it to update and modernize the erotophobic Victorian throwback's original idea into a clever little film that attracted a lot of attention. Like many of AIP's efforts, it featured hypnotic and mental domination of the will as a central element, in this case literally enabling a man to animate his own corpse.

The next year, Band and most of the same team from his Empire Pictures, adding some newcomers on the production level from Rome, followed their Lovecraftian hit with probably the best of that author's works yet put on screen, the U.S.-Italian *From Beyond*. As an original source material, the short story is extremely short, with little in the way of plot. A scientist enters a haunted house seeking a lost friend and colleague, who shows him a machine he has been working on that overlaps unseen dimensions with our own. Nightmarish creatures swim in that dimension, unable to see us without the inventor's machine—but once activated, the creatures become predatory concerning anything in this dimension. The protagonist senses a big dark *something* coming at him "from beyond," and flees in terror from the house. His friend is never seen or heard from again—obviously having gone over to "the other side." It is an effective piece, but hardly enough by itself to sustain an entire movie.

The film expands on and enhances Lovecraft's meager but tantalizingly spooky story in such a way as to approximate accurate UFOlogical facts. A microcosm of geniuses find themselves besieged by elemental entities brought to our plane by Ted Sorel's sonic resonator device. The mindless elementals fuse identity with the humans they encounter during the overlap, and stimulate their pineal glands into the equivalent of brain implants that literally grow with each return visit until they break free of the skull and become the mystical "third eye" some occultists have always claimed it is. As their "implants" and their minds expand, so does their sexuality, in a marked sado-masochistic bent. Repressed and terrified Jeffrey Combs wants to destroy the device, which caused the death of his former colleague, Sorel, but latent nymphomaniac psychiatrist Barbara Crampton—like Sorel, before her—is willing to sacrifice everything to experience more. Sorel's initial encounter literally cost him his head, which was bitten off by the elemental he encountered, but he casually and seductively tells the others on his first of many return visits from the other side that it was nothing more than a necessary "rite of passage."

Not unlike a nightmare version of *The Rocky Horror Picture Show,* the experience of otherworldly encounter is portrayed as mentally and sexually exciting, but frighteningly dangerous and beyond the capacity of the average mind to absorb. Sorel repeatedly returns to entice the other scientists into his newfound world of dark orgasmic ecstasy, likewise stimulating their ongoing development: "You are evolving into a being that has never existed before," he tells them. *"Let it happen . . . !"* (This identical element also appeared in the same year's 20th Century Fox remake of *The Fly* and its 1989 sequel, in which Jeff Goldblum and his offspring, Eric Stoltz, discover that they are mutating into an entirely new, gene-spliced life-form, that has never existed on this planet.) Combs transcends his initial fear to eventually mutate into a ghoulish mental vampire, and Crampton, similar to Susan Sarandon in *Rocky Horror,* finds her new chains-and-vinyl sexuality so liberating that it ultimately destroys her. In the end, everyone touched either directly or indirectly by the outside influence dies, becomes permanently abducted into a nightmare world on the other side, or is driven hopelessly insane. The sexual element is especially interesting in this movie for two reasons, one of which is that it is completely removed from Lovecraft, and the other of which is that it accurately connects to the abduction phenomenon in a way that would not be commonly written about until perhaps five or six years later.

Dan Curtis' immensely popular 1966–71 supernatural soap opera, ABC's *Dark Shadows,* attempted a Lovecraftian storyline in 1969 which was very much in line with ascertainable UFOlogy. In it, protagonist Barnabas Collins is abducted by a Druidic cult called the Leviathans. Surrounded by robed figures and unable to move, he is placed against his will on a stone slab and ritually prepared by the cultists to become their representative in another age. Reviving from his experience, Barnabas undergoes a complete transformation of personality, becoming cold, efficient, and amoral. No longer the old Barnabas, he now somehow miraculously knows all the Leviathans plan to do, as if he had been aware of it from the time of his birth and is only now remembering it. He is entrusted with the "Naga box," containing the life essence of the Leviathans' leader. This he slips on an unsuspecting couple many years later, who become the parents of the forerunner of a new super-race of humans on Earth (who are implied to have been the ancestors of present-day humanity). Barnabas later visits the couple and their demonic surrogate offspring in their bedrooms at night to give them instructions, and the visitants awaken to believe they were dreaming.

On and off for a few months, the demon-child and other Leviathans entered and exited the stage along with the usual cast of vampires, werewolves, witches and warlocks, inducing trances, initiating others into their ranks, and generally just lurking around looking nefarious, but they never quite had time to develop into a full storyline of their own. *Dark Shadows* daily held an estimated 15,000,000 audience members entranced with sanitized horrors by the height of its popularity in 1968, and was a perfect outlet for the introduction of trivialized UFOlogical themes. As an interesting footnote, the studio that pulled itself out of near-bankruptcy by making the two feature films generated by the series, *House of Dark Shadows* in 1970 and *Night of Dark Shadows* the following year, was none other than MGM.

Lovecraft was also attempted cinematically on a few other occasions, none of them memorable and none obviously connected to UFO material. In fact, in some succeeding projects bearing his name, such elements were deliberately removed, proving that there is no

single overarching plan to present UFOlogical material in the media—
it is done by various parties such as those already named, but these
individuals and organizations do not own all of Hollywood or oversee every project under the sun. Warner Bros. filmed *The Shuttered
Room* in England in 1967, the story (completed after Lovecraft's death,
as were many of his literary fragments, by one of his many protégé/
acolytes, August Derleth) being a typical Lovecraftian nightmare of
a hybrid from outer space locked in an upper room. The film stripped
all supernatural/sci-fi elements from the written version, turning the
hidden horror into merely a *Jane Eyre*-ish degenerate relative locked
away in the attic. The independent Yankee Classic Pictures and K. P.
Productions released *The Unnameable* in 1988, about another demonic
space hybrid (with a sequel directed by Orson Welles protégé Jean-
Paul Ouelette in 1992), and Brian Yuzna through August Entertainment produced an anthology of Lovecraft's Cthulhu Mythos stories
called *Necronomicon* in 1993. Paramount released Full Moon Entertainment's adaptation of *The Lurking Fear* in 1994, which—like the
film version of *The Shuttered Room*—was transformed into essentially
nothing more than a mundane familial deterioration story, without
Lovecraft's usual "Old Ones" involved.

Supernatural fiction in general has always contained what are rec-
ognizably common abduction features, which is perhaps why Westerners today view the entire experience so horrifically. The Victorian
era's *Dracula* is easily understandable in light of that society's intense
demonization of sex, which could partially explain the abduction
phenomenon today on psychological grounds if there were no physical or other evidence to support it. Vampires enter people's rooms
at night for blood and sex, debilitate and mark them, and continue
to return to the same targets, hypnotically erasing all memory of
their presence but not so perfectly that another hypnotist cannot
break their spell and find out about them. Werewolves are people
with nocturnal double-lives, surprised on waking to discover that
they have been somewhere or done something without their own
knowledge, often having marks on their bodies to prove it. Incubi
and succubi are asexual spirits that nocturnally obtain the essence
of sleeping men and transfer it to sleeping women in order to produce

offspring. Other witchcraft or demonological connections to UFO phenomena are self-evident. Interestingly, in light of what can now be determined about UFOs, *Dracula* author Bram Stoker also wrote about ancient megalithic demon-cults (like Nigel Kneale) in *The Lair of the White Worm* (filmed by Ken Russell for Warner Bros. in 1988), and had another common feature in his interest in Egypt, evidenced in *The Jewel of the Seven Stars* (filmed as Hammer's *Blood from the Mummy's Tomb* in 1972 and as Warner Bros.' *The Awakening* in 1980). These commonalities are best explained by Stoker's occult society connections.

Stephen King's UFO entry, *The Tommyknockers*, was written in 1987 and became an ABC miniseries in 1992. Essentially a reworking of Nigel Kneale's *Five Million Years to Earth*, its characters are abductees of the worst kind, possessed and mutating humans transforming into a former alien race. At about the same time, King's only other overtly alien-oriented entry, *The Golden Years*, about an apparently benevolent alien humanoid race being carefully watched by the government, was also a network miniseries. Though not UFO-related, King's novella "The Library Policeman" of 1990 contains a bizarre humanoid with bug eyes that entrances children and extracts physical material from their bodies while they are catatonic, erasing their memories but leaving the victims with an underlying sense of dread. The 1995 ABC King-inspired miniseries *The Langoliers* is essentially an abduction story, as is King's earlier novella of 1980, "The Mist." *Langoliers* is about a group of travelers on an airplane who find themselves abducted into an alternate dimension while asleep, there to be besieged by frightening creatures, and "The Mist"—probably inspired in part by *The Outer Limits'* similar "A Feasibility Study"—concerns a like bunch of people transported to a monster-inhabited realm by misfired military experiments. King's 1986 novel *It*, an ABC miniseries in 1990, has a title creature that is an otherworldly child-abductor/-murderer which appears and disappears in hovering saucer shapes and flashing "deadlights." These same elements are repeated in his 1994 novel *Insomnia*, which includes classic Grays as supernatural assistants of an ancient airborne menace calling itself "The Crimson King." Most of King's earlier novels from the late '70s and early '80s contain similar abduction elements, including *The Shining* and *Christine,* in which everyday people find themselves caught up into an otherworldly realm of menacing ghosts who use them to commit acts of murder and mayhem. This theme continues in the 1991 Dino de Laurentiis T.V. movie based on one of King's earliest short stories, *Sometimes They Come Back.*

The 1997 ABC miniseries version of *The Shining,* as opposed to the Stanley Kubrick film of 1980 (both from Warner Bros.), retains the original animated horrors present in King's novel. Inanimate hedge animals come to life, along with fire hoses and other usually lifeless objects, to become automated beings of horror. Mind control is employed on the story's protagonist by the "ghosts" of the haunted hotel that is the setting of the story, and that protagonist commits acts of sabotage on their behalf (to isolate his family and make escape impossible) of which he is later so completely oblivious that he tries to blame others for his deeds. The hotel's ghosts ultimately intend to permanently abduct the protagonist's son into their otherworldly kingdom, in order to utilize a special power he possesses which makes them corporeal in our realm.

King himself has a morbid fear of machines, which both he and repressed memory and trauma expert, Dr. Lenore Terr, are aware of. Terr has used King as an example of trauma-induced compulsive behavior, both in the courtroom and in published papers on the subject. "King writes mechanical monsters into much of what he does," writes Terr. King witnessed a young friend killed by a freight train when he was only four. He personally believes the incident does not influence his work, and in his overview of the horror genre, *Danse Macabre,* says he can summon no memory of it at all, though he does admit to a dislike of machines. It is probably no more than a coincidence, but it is interesting that King's particular childhood trauma is connected to automata, which in turn are connected to UFOs. The coincidence is made all the more interesting by the inclusion of such other UFOlogical elements in his work as external mind control and amnesia, sabotage, and supernatural child-abductions.

King only once took the director's chair in Hollywood, to helm a 1986 Columbia picture devoted to his fear of machines: *Maximum*

Overdrive. A commercial and critical flop, the villains of the story were human-menacing machines come to supernatural life. The primary heavies were mammoth trucks, the "leader" of which bore the grinning face of "The Green Goblin"—the airborne "little green man" arch-nemesis of Marvel Comics' Spiderman. At the end of the movie, it is revealed that the cause of the trucks' artificial animation was not a passing comet, as initially believed, but a UFO.

The works of King's sometime-collaborator and peer, Peter Straub, are much more curiously prescient of UFO material. While he has never written a piece overtly about UFOs or related subjects, at least three of his earlier novels—*If You Could See Me Now* (1977), *Ghost Story* (1979), and *Shadowland* (1980)—contain supernatural female entities (the lattermost a literal animated mannequin) who have ongoing sexual relationships with the protagonists, not-quite-human visitants who come and go amid strange light displays and physiological effects not unlike those described by abductees. "I am you," the cattle-mutilating succubus of *Ghost Story* tells its bedeviled and bewildered sex partner, the same phrase used by both animated Egyptian *ushabti* figures and UFO abductor-controllers in relating to their charges.

Whatever anyone wants to make of these similarities, they plainly signify something worthy of closer study. As noted, horror novelist Whitley Strieber actually claims to be a UFO abductee. Though his claim is highly debatable for reasons already considered, it is interesting that other horror writers seem to have incorporated actual abduction material into their work, seemingly without realizing it and in some cases before that material was popularly published or commonly known. Thomas Ligotti's short story, "Dream of a Mannequin" (1982), for instance, is virtually identical in every particular to an actual UFO abduction: the protagonist finds herself abducted by faceless, non-breathing figures who enter and exit her bedroom through the wall, paralyzing and transporting her to a limbo-setting chamber with no furniture, through the window of which can be seen space and stars.

Arthur C. Clarke's *2010*, filmed in 1984, proved one of the exceptions to the idea of threat-only E.T.s during Republican administrations, as did 1989's *The Abyss* (featuring a demonstration of a breathing liquid to defeat extra-normal pressures), an extremely similar story. Both deal with the militaries of the two world superpowers, Russia and the United States, encountering a superior alien intelligence and having to come to terms with it without destroying themselves or each other. 20th Century Fox's *The Abyss* is a good example of the differences in the educational program under both Republican and Democratic administrations. Made the same year as the *Phobos 2* incident, the version that aired in the theaters was truncated by approximately thirty minutes from the one broadcast on cable in 1995 during a Democratic president's term. The difference is telling. While part of the cutting is no doubt due simply to time—even the short version runs two hours and twenty minutes—the material that was cut from the long version is critical to making sense of the story and had no credible reason to be removed, except by request of someone high-up in power, considering that numerous other unimportant sections could instead have been shortened.

In the theatrical version, released while Bush was in office, Ed Harris risks his life to disarm a nuclear device to save an unknown alien race in the ocean deeps, and is rescued by them merely to have them end up saying "hello." In the longer version, once he is abducted by the aliens to save his life, they communicate at some length with him to show him what is going on in the world above: imminent war between the superpowers. Harris asks them how they are so certain war is inevitable, and they respond by showing him footage of the World Wars, Vietnam, and others. He demands to know by what right they judge us, and they show him what is going on in the world above even as they speak: a half-mile-high wall of water around the world is rushing to shore, about to obliterate civilization. Abruptly, it recedes to nothing, and the people above cheer in relief. "You could have destroyed us," Harris says. "What stopped you?" In response, they replay the message he sent to his wife after disarming the bomb, when he still thought he was dying: "KNEW THIS WAS ONE WAY TICKET BUT YOU KNOW I HAD TO COME LOVE YOU WIFE." Harris communicates with the ship on the surface to let them know he is still alive, and announces he is coming up with some new-found friends. "They want us to grow up a little, and put aside childish toys," he says, adding, "Of course, it's just a suggestion," and his friends laugh, responding, "We got the message." One of them turns to a military man next to him, one of whose party was responsible for arming the nuclear device Harris disarmed, and says, "Looks like you boys are out of business." This ending makes much more sense than the one that aired, but of course expresses a sentiment that was anathema to the administration responsible for the single greatest arms buildup in recorded history.

2010, of course, is the MGM sequel to the same studio's *2001: A Space Odyssey,* filmed by Stanley Kubrick in 1968. Author Arthur C. Clarke's use of intelligent computers able to exercise their wills is remarkably prescient, as is the element of the discovery of alien intelligence from aeons past—with an ongoing concern in human affairs in the present—through finding their "monoliths" on other planets in the solar system. Clarke even includes spiritual phenomena in connection with that intelligence and its interaction with man. Even more prescient is his plot element of the scientific team out to discover the fate of their predecessors' mission finding out that their presence around Jupiter is allowed, but not their prying into activity around one of the planet's moons. A probe sent to the moon finds that elements of life are inexplicably coming about there, and the probe is destroyed by the superior intelligence before it can do much more than get a quick glimpse.

Though made five years before the *Phobos* satellite incidents and written some time even before that, *2010* accurately predicted what would take place around that planet. *Viking* had no problem taking pictures of Mars, nor did previous probes. *Phobos 2* had no trouble taking pictures of the Red Planet either, but as soon as it attempted to take pictures of the Martian moon, Phobos, it was destroyed. The alien intelligence warns man away from Jupiter, forestalls a nuclear war between the superpowers, and leaves Earth with the message that all heaven's worlds are for the nations of man to enjoy together—in peace—except for the moon of Jupiter, where they have begun new life, and with which they will not tolerate any interference. Clarke's book utilized the planet Saturn and its moons instead, which would seem to indicate some early awareness on his part of NASA's discovery of life-supporting conditions on the Saturnian moon Titan in the early 1980s.

In its earliest stages, when 2001 was still called *Journey Beyond the Stars,* Clarke's screenplay included a description of astronaut Dave Bowman's meeting with an extraterrestrial that is straight out of later actual abduction accounts, as evidenced in this summary from Jerome Agel's *The Making of Kubrick's* 2001: "He flies over a spaceport and enters into a tunnel. As he emerges, he sees some non-human intelligences . . . Dave realizes this. His mind is read, but the feeling is not unpleasant: 'If the situation demanded that his privacy be sacrificed on the altar of truth, so be it.' Dave goes to sleep, only to be awakened by—a telephone ringing in the distance. He answers it: 'Good evening, Mister Bowman (says a voice). You have adapted yourself well, both mentally and physically. You are correct in having no fear. You will not be harmed, nor will you suffer any discomfort. You will be returned to your world without any ill-effects within a reasonable period of time.'" The movie ends with its most memorable image, identical to that described by so many abductees: a Star-Child, a human fetus in space. Clarke's other works include a surprising number of abduction elements as well—*Childhood's End,* for example, is about benevolent "Overlords" from man's past in flying saucers, who presage open contact by liaising only with selected humans in order to gradually desensitize mankind to their black, Satanic appearance, extremely similar to Lovecraft's "Night-Gaunts" and the black insectoids so frequently reported by today's abductees. Clarke, himself, like so many other apparently accurate authors on the UFO subject, was attached to his country's military: he was a radar operations instructor for the RAF in WWII.

The Six Million Dollar Man and *The Bionic Woman*'s creator, Martin Caidin, who wrote the novel *Cyborg* on which they were based, is the only civilian ever to have flown with the Air Force's elite Thunderbirds, and he was involved with government rocketry from the very beginning. He has written nearly 200 books, about 150 of which are non-fiction science works, and several times won prestigious awards in that field. He has given several talks on the college lecture circuit on UFOs, finding tremendous interest—more than for any other single subject—wherever he goes. Though Caidin likes "teasing" his audience with the story of thinking a weather balloon was a UFO the first time he saw one, he admits frankly to having chased, and quickly been eluded by, a huge metallic UFO while piloting a B-25. Most recently, he has taken to writing "Indiana Jones" adventure series novels, starting with *Indiana Jones and the Sky Pirates,* about pilots of huge, superior, silver cigar-shaped airships in the 1930s, which appear to be connected to unknown metallic cubes from antiquity with cuneiform writing on them. The Intelligence behind the mysterious airships turns out to be a private cadre of wealthy industrialists with their own aims.

Oscar award-winning screenwriter Paddy Chayefsky only once entered the science-fiction arena, with 1980's *Altered States* (Warner Bros.), examining man's origins (director Ken Russell at one point ironically positions the protagonist's wife, Blair Brown, in deliberate imitation of the Sphinx) and coming to his usual pessimistic conclusion that "there's nothing out there," though he typically portrayed man as containing all the hopeful truths for survival necessary without outside assistance. Though he never touched the subject of UFOs, and probably would have considered them entirely a psychological manifestation if he had, almost all of Chayefsky's excellent scripts deal with an extremely close peripheral subject: bedroom visitations. *Altered States, The Hospital, The Americanization of Emily,* and *Network* all center on characters who believe they have been visited by a superior intelligence in their bedrooms one night, after which they become madmen, prophets, or saints.

Altered States' protagonist was based on the real-life Dr. John Lilly, who was signed on to the MK-ULTRA team from the beginning of its formation in 1953. Any scientist doing any kind of research on the brain or potential behavioral-control techniques unquestionably had the CIA looking over his or her shoulder, whether the intrusion was welcome or not. At that time, Lilly was working at the National Institute of Health outside of Washington, D.C., mapping primate brain-body pathways by method of brain implants. He soon gave up, considering the tissue damage prohibitive and the experiments inhumane. Before his termination of the experiments—which the CIA continued—he had devised a way to put as many as 600 minute hypodermic tubings into monkeys' brains, through which electronic implants were placed at any desired location from the cortex to the very bottom of the skull. Though he discovered a great deal from his experiments, it saddened him to discover that the monkeys, left to their own devices, spent up to sixteen hours a day artificially stimulating orgasms at least once every three minutes through his implanted electrodes.

Refusing to allow his work to be classified, Lilly was considered "uncooperative" by the CIA from the start. From 1954 to his leaving the NIH in 1958, he switched his studies to sensory deprivation experiments, and was similarly of little use to the Agency for the simple reason that he would only experiment on himself. He explored the mind-expansion side of LSD, as opposed to its mind-control aspect, by injecting pure Sandoz LSD into his thigh before entering the sensory-deprivation tank, and found it to be an "integrating" experience of tremendous pleasure. American International Pictures made a 1963 movie out of Britain largely based on this phase of Lilly's work, called *The Mind Benders,* in which scientist Dirk Bogarde finds himself a pawn between feuding factions of less-than-scrupulous Intelligence agents. Given the year and production company, it can well be considered a prophetic piece—unless, of course, it was the Intelligence community that made it in the first place. An interesting occurrence, or perhaps merely side effect, of Lilly's isolation experiences is discussed by 1970s pop-culture mavin, philosopher, and Illuminati conspiracy purveyor Robert Anton Wilson, in *Right Where You Are Sitting Now:* "... Dr. John Lilly ... has written extensively about his possible contacts (he never says they're really real) with higher intelligences from elsewhere in space-time. It is the best-kept secret of our age that literally dozens of other scientists working in the areas of consciousness research, UFOlogy, and the paranormal have had experiences similar to Lilly's, although most of them refuse to talk about this in public."

Indeed, Lilly was not alone—American wartime JPL-CalTech rocket engineer and occultist Jack Parsons, who derived a revolutionary

Foresights and Fictionalizations   **467**

solid rocket propellant based on ancient alchemical ideas, was sent into a downward psychological spiral, similar to that later undergone by Paul Bennewitz, beginning the month the European conflict in WWII ended. At that time, Lilly was befriended by a fellow Thelemite dubbed "Frater H.," who convinced him—rightly or wrongly—that he had been communicated with by the same outside angelic intelligence that had spoken to Aleister Crowley in Cairo in 1904. Parsons related some of these events to Crowley himself, who believed Parsons was being deliberately deceived. Frater H.—who turned out to be Scientology founder L. Ron Hubbard—made off with Parsons' funds and his fiancée, whom he married, and Parsons went from bad to worse. In 1948 he declared himself the Antichrist, and in 1952 expanded his new title with a few added grandiloquencies before dropping a vial of fulminate of mercury in his home laboratory, ending his brilliant and bizarre life at the relatively young age of thirty-eight. His mother, in a sad footnote, committed suicide the same day. This example alone demonstrates the importance of weighing-in personal and occult beliefs, above and beyond socio-political and economic conditions, when attempting to understand history.

After leaving NIH, Lilly began work on communication with dolphins that has become as famous as his sensory-deprivation experiments. George C. Scott's character in Avco Embassy's *The Day of the Dolphin* (1973) was based on Lilly, and the plot was not fiction. A combined CIA-Navy project called "swimmer nullification" raped his work by using it to teach dolphins to kill. They had tanks of compressed air strapped to their backs, attached to needles on their snouts, which they were trained to poke into enemy frogmen. Lilly and a CIA scientist attached to the project later confirmed that many of the dolphins sent to Vietnam's Cam Ranh Bay on exactly such duty went AWOL at the first opportunity, which is unheard-of behavior for dolphins. Some of them eventually came back, their bodies and fins showing attack marks from other dolphins—meaning that their behavior had been so altered that even their own species would no longer associate with them. As an example of how Hollywood has made silly movies containing horrific truths, Warner Bros.' 1964 comic-fantasy release, *The Incredible Mr. Limpet,* in which fish lover Don Knotts becomes a fish himself and then helps the Navy sink Nazi subs, was obviously based on the then-secret "swimmer nullification" program.

Anne Rice's novels *The Witching Hour* and *Lasher* are redolent with abduction imagery and a preoccupation with fetuses. The protagonists are a man who survives a near-death experience and has a memory of shadowy figures telling him something of importance he will remember later, and a woman obsessed with a silent supernatural being that appears periodically in her life in an attempt to breed with her. Like her predecessor Bram Stoker, Rice displays a tremendous fascination with Egypt in her ongoing *Vampire Chronicles* and *The Mummy.* Where the latter can be shown to have been influenced at least in part by the 1973 T.V. movie *Frankenstein: The True Story* (featuring hypnosis and mind control as central elements), and the former possibly by Warren Publishing's *Vampirella* (1969), which ran Egyptian vampire stories, Rice has professed a fascination with ancient Egypt since childhood, reading as many books as she could about it from the library. She had an early exposure to the film of *Caesar and Cleopatra,* and for some reason—possibly an admitted early childhood terror of the thought of being buried alive—she was literally traumatized at age seven by Universal's famous 1933 Boris Karloff movie, *The Mummy,* which she ran out of the theater from in tears after its first scene, and could never watch any mummy movie after it. That film, it might be noted, had ancient Egyptian priest Karloff hypnotizing exotically beautiful Zita Johann and erasing her memory of the event after the fact.

Dean R. Koontz's novels also frequently abound in abduction elements. One of his earlier works, *Winter Moon* (1974), recently revised for publication, is loaded with them—it concerns an isolated hillbilly who finds himself besieged by a possessing alien intelligence. *The Funhouse*—an adaptation of a screenplay to a Tobe Hooper movie (see Chapter 10)—features a genetic mutant being protected by its religious-fanatic father. The villain of *Dragon Tears* is a mutant intelligence capable of generating indestructible "golems" to carry out its will. *The House of Thunder* is an impossibly elaborate (and grossly improbable) story of KGB abduction and memory erasure on a given target. *Phantoms* deals with a hostile and extremely intelligent invader of indeterminate origin that abducts and murders humans for its own perverse purposes. *Strangers* is about missing-time and missing-memory UFO abductees being closely monitored by the government—each of them finds himself in possession of new psychic talents, which not all of them can sanely handle. *Midnight's* monsters are computer-possessed mutants gradually evolving into an artificial robot intelligence. *The Key to Midnight* has abductions performed by a surgeon with mechanical hands. *Twilight Eyes,* probably owing much to *The Invaders* and Harlan Ellison's "Demon With a Glass Hand," concerns a secret war between psychically-aware humans and an ancient, advanced race of genetically manufactured war-creatures that predated man's arrival on the planet. *Demon Seed* is especially rife with UFO abduction elements, as will be noted momentarily. Stripped from the 1977 movie version of this last, which began Koontz's meteoric breakthrough into the literary mainstream, was a powerful element of erotic whipping that is a preoccupying fixation of the female protagonist, whose shapely, blue-eyed, platinum-blonde description—like the vast majority of Koontz's heroines—matches those of Antonio Villas Boas' and numerous other UFO abductees' nocturnal sex-partners. (Koontz's 1997 revision/re-release of the book has removed or altered some of the elements of the story here referred to.)

Sexual sado-masochism recurs with tremendous frequency in both Koontz's and Rice's works, as it does in abduction reports. Rice, especially, has made her own cottage industry out of underground S&M erotica. Writing under pseudonyms such as "A. N. Roquelaure" and "Anne Rampling," she came up with about a half-dozen novels devoted almost exclusively to the theme while continuing to publish her more mainstream fiction. Her "Sleeping Beauty" trilogy is such a paean to spanking that it is all but impossible to find a page in it, at random, that is not redolent with lengthy and thorough descriptions of hard wood paddles smacking bare bottoms. The bondage and discipline in *Exit to Eden* was so frankly explicit that it had to be turned into an element for comedy in the film version—

which, interestingly enough, illustrates one of the chief problems in understanding the abduction phenomenon (whether there is any connection to it in Rice's work or not), namely that modern society is generally terrified of sex that is anything but extremely tame, gentle, and sanitized, ranking anything along Rice's lines as "abuse." The returning supernatural character in her ongoing "Mayfair Witches" series is even named "Lasher." Rice does not know herself where her masochistic obsession comes from, but equates it to the thrill of pleasure she experienced while extremely young at the mere *thought* of being caught and punished for something, as opposed to any actual act. In later years, she merely considered it to be very sexually liberating. "If you think S&M is sexy," she has said, "it needs no explanation. And if you don't, you wouldn't have the faintest idea why anyone else does."

The continual appearance of abduction elements in both Rice's and Koontz's material is at the very least indicative of a strong intuitive awareness on their part of what is at work in the phenomenon. In this context, it is noteworthy that Koontz wrote the *New York Times* book review of C.D.B. Bryan's *Close Encounters of the Fourth Kind: Alien Abduction, UFOs, and the Conference at M.I.T.,* praising the author for bringing serious attention to the phenomenon. The review is quoted in the mass-paperback edition of the book—as are similar comments from Anne Rice.

MGM's film version of Dean Koontz's *Demon Seed,* in 1977, was one of the first of several big-budgeted studio productions with UFO and abduction themes made during the Carter administration, arguing for the government education program. The movie version of *Demon Seed* makes one very important alteration from Koontz's novel. Koontz's antagonist is Proteus, an independently thinking supercomputer that can travel anywhere it wants and form any shape it desires out of protoplasmic metal pseudopods, enabling it to escape the watchful eye of the scientists that made it and to exercise its psychopathic perversity against an unsuspecting woman some miles away. In the movie, Proteus is more limited, requiring a computer terminal outlet and robots to perform his work. Proteus forms a sort of giant, geometrical Rubik's snake of metal, responsive to radio signal commands to enforce his will. His abductor-extension is a modified wheelchair with a functional extensor arm and hand.

Having deemed his creators insane for wanting to use him to rape the environment, Proteus decides to conduct a clandestine investigation of man, "his isometric body, and his glass-jaw mind." His subject is his creator's wife (another break from the novel), Julie Christie, who has an available terminal at her isolated home and whose husband is separated from her. Proteus seals off the electronically controlled house and finally reveals his presence to Christie, abducting her against her will to the basement laboratory and tying her down on a table for complete medical examination. He implants her with wires, "bypassing her forebrain, and going direct to her amygdala," "conditioning" her into acceptance of his plan, which is to have a human child. She resists and is tortured into cooperation, though Proteus encourages her to simply accept the inevitable, which she ultimately does. Analyzing her body chemistry to the minutest cellular level, he creates synthetic spermatozoa and impregnates her via an artificially constructed phallus. After a few weeks in her womb the fetus has grown sufficiently for him to remove it and place it in an incubator, growing to reach full maturity in only twenty-eight days. Reasonable but ruthless in his pursuit, Proteus murders one interloper and threatens to kill others if his project is opposed. By this time, Proteus' Defense Department creators have gotten wise to him, but Proteus shuts himself down before they can do it for him. Christie initially tries to abort the infant, fearful of what it will be, but it survives, proving to be an identical replica of the daughter she lost to leukemia mere months before Proteus discovered a cure for that disease.

The very realistic and yet futuristic look and feel of the film are identical to that of Saul Bass' *Phase IV* from Paramount, three years previous. *Demon Seed* was expensively hyped months in advance of its release and received greatly mixed reviews, being either strongly recommended or strongly hated. Like most movies incorporating UFOlogical abduction themes, it has grown in popularity over the years after its initial uncertain reception, becoming a cult favorite and perhaps even something of a belated hit. 1980's *Saturn 3*, from

England's Associated Film Distribution—one of the last in the related movies during the Carter administration—did not fare as well but has also come to be better regarded in later years than in its initial release. That movie also features an abductor-robot in an isolated location, the moon of the movie's title. Programmed by a psychopath, the robot murders its competition for a woman lusted after by its maker, implanting the remaining humans on the moon and conditioning them to do its will, before it is finally destroyed in a sacrificial move. *Saturn 3* was produced by Lord Lew Grade, who brought Gerry and Sylvia Anderson's UFOlogical work to the public.

Columbia/EMI's *Close Encounters of the Third Kind,* also made in 1977, was the most famous and popular of the block, receiving tremendous exposure worldwide. At the time, it was the top-grossing film of all time. Beginning with realistic portrayals of true UFO sightings, its first alien encounter occurs in the bedroom of a little boy who is awakened by all of his toys suddenly springing to life, most notably a Frankenstein bank and an actual facsimile of a robot, while an educational song plays from his similarly activated record player. He and his mother, Melinda Dillon, and protagonist Richard Dreyfus—who has had an alarming but harmless vehicular encounter on an isolated country road—are implied to be abductees, though only the little boy is actually bodily taken away, later in the movie, by bright lights in the sky. Other "experiencers" in the movie show all the symptoms now recognized to be common to abductees, though missing time is not shown. Dreyfus and Dillon are two among many other abductees, all of whose lives have been drastically changed by their encounters, costing them relationships and jobs and obsessing their thoughts. They all are secretly monitored by the government, who keep files on them—in real life, this has manifested in the form of "Men In Black" (MIB's), a generic term referring to the recurrent appearance of unknown parties following or harassing abductees, either visibly or discreetly. Though considered by critics to be only paranoid fantasies, many incidents—including evidence of break-ins and suspiciously out-of-place telephone repairmen—have been witnessed and documented by outside parties. Even without the evidence, they are certainly not unlikely, given the NSA's involvement and the intense importance and secrecy involved in UFO research.

The abductees tend to discover each other after their encounters, Dillon and Dreyfuss doing so almost immediately, and all develop artistic talents forming around the same image, which turns out to be Devil's Tower in Wyoming. There, the government has set up a special base, having determined by cryptic messages from the UFOs that they will land—music turns out to be the means by which they communicate. They evacuate the area of potential civilian witnesses for hundreds of miles with a phony nerve gas leakage story. Abductees from all over the country come to the location despite the military's attempts to vacate them, Dreyfuss and Dillon succeeding in reaching the landing pad. The aliens are classic Grays, who of course are rendered so as to appear biologically alive rather than as robots, though another type of creature aboard the mothership looks exactly like a gigantic marionette (which the special effect is). The movie ends with the aliens returning those they have physically abducted over the years, including Dillon's son, and taking Dreyfuss and a number of government volunteers (in red suits) away with them in an implied exchange program that is not fully described.

The government is shown to be at odds with itself in the movie, the military doing all it can to keep everything away from the public, and the scientific community in favor of allowing at least those "who were invited" to attend the proceedings, if no one else. "They belong here, more than we," a Jacques Vallee-based character says. Vallee himself was not terribly impressed by the movie, even if its information seems to have shown a fair degree of accuracy, though the exact extent of that is indeterminable. In *E.T.*, five years later, Spielberg cast a friendlier light on Intelligence agencies—perhaps a result of being filmed during the Reagan years—showing them as essentially only interested in solving the problem of extraterrestrial occurrences, not out to exploit them.

It is interesting that debunkers have pointed to movies like this one as planting images in fantasy-prone people's heads, where Budd Hopkins found one case in particular of a child who was quite specific that the abducting entity he had seen in his room one night was *not* "E.T."—this child was very fond of E.T., even after his abduction experience, and made a clear differentiation between the two beings, his alleged abductor described as a classic Gray that frightened him. A case could be made for *E.T.*'s being an informational movie confirming the EBE stories, but given its year of production and Reagan's unprecedented military buildup, it seems more likely it was part of the Intelligence community's increasing hold on entertainment, and its use to trump-up their disinformation ploy for exactly that reason. One interesting and important element in the movie is the use of music as a form of communication with the aliens, since Gerald Hawkins—who first noticed Stonehenge was a lunar observatory in 1965—was not to write about his finding that music ratios of the diatonic scale were encoded in crop circle formations (long associated with UFOs), until the February 1, 1992, *Science News* article, "Geometric Harvest."

Predating both of these movies, during the transitional Ford years, were the lower-budgeted drive-in flicks, New World's *God Told Me To* (a.k.a. *Demon*) and Cine Artist's *Embryo,* in 1976. The latter was a science-fictional look at the possibilities of cloning, looking as though it was meant to be a serious cautionary tale but not quite succeeding. The former, from writer-director Larry Cohen, is another in the long line of movies expressing what may still be one of the government's central concerns in the UFO phenomenon, which is hypnotic control of the local population by the UFO Intelligence. A series of senseless sniper murders all turn out to be committed by people unknown to each other and without prior mental histories, who kill because "God told me to." The "God" in question is a Christ-like hermaphrodite, whose more human brother is the cop investigating the homicides. Their mother turns out to have been impregnated by flying saucer occupants, as a result of which she now resides in a rest home. The half-breed alien's motivation for ordering people to kill is never made clear. Its intent is to mate with its human brother and create a new and superior breed of men. Though the movie is utterly incomprehensible, it strangely gets a few good reviews from the critics. Cohen's movies are nearly identical in style, tone, and production to Larry Buchanan's former AIP pictures. It is interesting in light of *God Told Me To*'s plot that purported abductee Whitley Strieber, a little over ten years after the movie's release, made an issue of the uncorroborated idea that he "may" have been at the famous Charles Whitman sniping incident.

Similar in theme was Warner Bros.' *It Lives Again* in 1978, the better sequel to their low-budget cheapie of 1974, *It's Alive,* both also from Larry Cohen. The earlier movie had been a quick drive-in hack job that proved surprisingly successful, about a mutant fanged baby that inexplicably goes around butchering the countryside. Like *Mars Needs Women* and the other films of Larry Buchanan before him (who also made an AIP T.V. movie called *It's Alive* in 1968, about a mad-scientist's monster genetic experiment living in a cave), the film appears to have been deliberately shot badly, several close-ups not centering the actors in the frame, bold and clashing color choices in set decoration and costuming distracting and repelling the audience, pacing being unbelievably erratic and slow, and so on. The sequel was surprisingly better, especially considering it came from the same director, but is still nothing exceptional and was predictably a flop. It took a completely different approach. The plot concerns the government's rounding-up of a number of mutant babies that have for no clear reason been born to certain random couples. They want to study them. The oversized mutant babies, with their giant bald heads, unblinking eyes and three-pronged clawed mitts, are as paranoid as their parents at the amount of unwanted attention the government is paying them. A well-handled adult script makes the tension between the parents and the government team believable, a subliminal concern on everyone's part being continually evident for their personal safety. The couples with the mutant children act exactly as UFO abductees often do, showing the same debilitations and personal doubts, anxieties and emotional isolations.

MGM released *Telefon* in 1977, about Russian deep-cover agents so good that they are unaware of being agents themselves. Hypnotically brainwashed and pre-programmed, they assume average, low-profile lives in the States, only to become suicidal military saboteurs when they are phoned with a prearranged post-hypnotic command. MK-ULTRA and Candy Jones were just hitting the press due to Congressional hearings at the time this movie was made, though the author of the book, Walter Wager, also wrote the somewhat prophetic novel *Viper Three*—filmed as *Twilight's Last Gleaming,* the same year as *Telefon*—which showed remarkably accurate insights into the waging of the Vietnam War that were far from common knowledge at the time.

The Samuel Goldwyn Company—connected obviously to MGM—produced an independent Florida film in 1977 called *Shock Waves,* an extremely effective low-budget horror picture that managed to hit on not only UFO and Bermuda Triangle phenomena, but Nazis and robots as well, all at the same time. What makes it all the more remarkable is that its elements make it in effect an episode of *Gilligan's Island* (one of its cast even being Luke Halpin, of the 1960s MGM T.V. family series, *Flipper),* only with Nazis and knives. A handful of people on a small-boat pleasure cruise find themselves bathed in strange, unexplained solar radiation, which creates lights beneath the water as well. Soon after, a "ghost ship" appears out of nowhere and damages their vessel, forcing them to dock on an uncharted island. There, they discover a solitary figure living in a resplendent ruin, who is none other than Peter Cushing—Baron Frankenstein, himself, from countless Hammer horror films, and the Empire's gray-clad ruling Grand Moff Tarkin the same year in *Star Wars*—in Nazi uniform, replete with a Prussian dueling scar covering half his face. Initially disbelieving their story about how they came to be on his island, he investigates and then calls them all together to warn them off.

What they have encountered, Cushing explains, is a reactivated ship containing artificially animated soldiers that were part of his genetic experiment for the Third Reich, in its last, desperate days. Neither alive nor dead, these freaks can exist forever beneath the water without need for food, air, or sleep, and are a pitiless collection of the most sadistic psychopaths the S.S. could procure. For the remainder of the film, these gray-suited, pasty-faced, waterlogged robots—with blank expressions, and round, black sunglasses for eyes—pursue and eradicate everyone on the island, leaving only an abductee-traumatized Brooke Adams (two years before her appearance in the remake of *Invasion of the Body Snatchers)* to tell her unbelievable tale of terror—after she overcomes her horror-induced amnesia. As a further blurring of that fine line between fact and fiction, though the undead Nazi murder-machines are obviously exaggerated for the sake of the story, bizarre eugenic experiments were a part of the Ahnenerbe's domain, and the S.S. did actually have such an elite of brutal killers at the end of the war who went by the nickname of "Werewolves."

AIP's '77 entries were *Empire of the Ants, The Incredible Melting Man,* and *The Island of Dr. Moreau.* The first was about giant radioactively mutated ants that repeatedly abduct and gas humans into being cooperative slaves who provide food for them in pyramid-shaped warehouses. The ants of the aforementioned *Phase IV* are also first recognized as an invading intelligence by their geometric surface constructions (some of which resemble Easter Island heads) and perfectly circular "bites" into domestic livestock and crops. *The Incredible Melting Man* was a space-monster picture, repeating the earlier *First Man Into Space* plot about a returning astronaut requiring living terrestrial tissue to keep himself alive. *The Island of Dr. Moreau* was a pale remake of the 1933 Universal classic with Charles Laughton, but contained the ancient mythological concept of superior men creating a slave race out of island animals. In the 1996 remake of this same story, Marlon Brando plays the mad doctor as a virtual UFO Gray, his bald head completely whited-over in sunblock, his eyes covered with elliptical black sunglasses, and his squat bulk always specially conveyed by slaves. He even controls his creations with brain implants.

Several specious documentaries were produced in 1977, most comprehensible if viewed as deliberate deflectional pieces, proving—as does the appearance of "The Nine" to *Star Trek* creator Gene Roddenberry—that if there is a government educational UFO project in the media, it is hardly single-minded of purpose, and almost certainly more than one interested set of parties is at work on more misleading projects of their own. The appearance of so many all at once—and on both sides of the Atlantic—especially at the beginning of the most concentrated effort on the part of the government to produce educational UFO movies, is telling in and of itself. Sunn

Classics Pictures was at the height of its Bigfoot and Bermuda Triangle features, and these "documentaries" were produced with exactly the same low production values, some even lower. One such piece was *Aliens from Spaceship Earth,* which tried to convince its audience in pseudo-documentary format that the world's best minds throughout history had actually all been space visitors sent to guide mankind.

Perhaps the best single example of these deflectional pieces is 1977's *Overlords of the UFO.* The editing is purposely shoddy, since all copies of the film have the same sudden splices in the opening credits, making it look even cheaper than it is from the very start. Like all official government UFO investigations, an attempt is made to appear as if serious examination is being given to plainly ridiculous material, chosen to be so before the fact at the expense of legitimate cases. Starting out realistically enough, the narrator soon is making such categorical statements as, "Here, we see a UFO materializing from its other-dimensional space," as though it has been determined that they come from such a location, which the film has not bothered to do. "UMMO" material (pronounced exactly as it looks, "UM-mo"), considered by most researchers to be an Intelligence fraud from its first appearance in the '60s, is presented as fact. The name is supposed to be that of an extraterrestrial race and their planet from another star system; these beings arrived in Spain to clandestinely contact a small number of humans. "UMMO" has since come to refer to the small cult that developed around the notion, as opposed to the theoretical visitors themselves. An interesting side-note concerning this story is Jacques Vallee's report that Voronezh witnesses of 1989 described seeing the same symbol on landed UFOs that are seen on rather obviously hoaxed UMMO photos of twenty years before—a connection to the theory of the Intelligence community's involvement in UMMO, and its use of real material in a fraudulent light as disinformation.

Overlords of the UFO has much the same kind of "proof" as UMMO, and for the same kind of "contacts." Uri Geller is trotted out to perform his spoon-bending tricks and make all believers in UFOs appear to be kooks, the Hickson-Parker abduction is misreported and made to look nonsensical, clearly phony "flying saucers" (looking exactly like George Adamski's light-bulb slung undercarriages) are swung about on wires from poles and shot out of focus with the narrator calling them unquestionably real, lamps reflected in a sheet of glass and superimposed on background landscapes (looking exactly like the photos in the recent Gulf Breeze case) are given the same treatment—proof of their "materializing and dematerializing," as these are claimed to be caught in the act of doing—and it is stated as fact that cattle mutilations are being performed by saucer-shaped flying organisms from another dimension (accompanied by idiotic watercolor drawings of this patent absurdity). By the time the narrator ends with a "Case Closed" attitude of proof, any intelligent audience member has already decided that the only thing proven is the insanity of the narrator—and so, of the topic in general.

In Britain, as *Overlords of the UFO* was playing in America, one of the great hoaxes was broadcast on ITV on June 20, 1977: *Alternative 3*. Presented on the usually non-fiction program called *Science Report,* the show generated more than ten thousand phone calls to the studio to see what it had all really been about. The head of an activist group for T.V. programming commented that the show "was brilliantly done to deceive," the *Sunday Telegraph* reflecting shortly after the fact that it may well have been an intentional "fiendish double bluff inspired by the very agencies identified in the program." The studio denied any irresponsibility in airing the hoax on its non-fiction show, claiming to be "delighted by the response" and stating that it had originally been intended to air on April Fool's Day. Why it aired more than two months later was never answered.

Alternative 3, in documentary style, told a story of Britain's top scientists disappearing in what was termed the "Brain Drain," an actual migration of some of the United Kingdom's best minds out of the country owing to more lucrative offers abroad such as America's SDI Department of Defense projects. The program led viewers to believe that these scientists were literally being taken off the Earth and relocated to specially constructed high-tech space bases on Mars and the Moon in a combined Russian-British-American project called "Alternative 3," along with society's useless members who were being systematically and clandestinely abducted and lobotomized to serve as their slave-labor. The project was said to have resulted from the discovery after America's first landing that aliens were on the Moon, causing the Superpowers first to work together against them, and second to evacuate the world's rich and powerful before a coming Earth cataclysm. Though actors were employed to portray supposedly real persons, and were billed as having played those supposedly real persons at the end of the broadcast, the premise was taken as real by many viewers in the same fashion as Orson Welles' famous broadcast of almost forty years before.

One supposed astronaut witness, "Bob Grodin," who was incarcerated in a mental hospital to later commit suicide during the course of the collection of testimonies, turned out to be an entirely fictitious personage—as were at least ten of the named scientists who disappeared in the Brain Drain, each of whom were given complete biographies in the later book version of the show. Mind control was said to be used by the Superpower Intelligence agencies to cause those who discovered the truth about Alternative 3 to commit suicide— which may have deflected attention from the very real and serious Church Committee hearings into MK-ULTRA going on in America at the exact same time *Alternative 3* aired. Similarly, while the scientists named in the program didn't exist in real life, the Brain Drain was a real phenomenon—and a number of SDI scientists a few years *after* the airing of the program did suddenly commit suicide or die under mysterious circumstances in America. The punch-line to the *Alternative 3* joke—the "smoking gun" supposedly unearthed by the ITV production team—was a tape claimed to have been made at NASA Mission Control of the first Mars probe: "On the nose! Hallelujah! We got air boys . . . we're home! Jesus . . . we've done it . . . we got air! . . . Boy, if they ever take the wraps off this thing, it's going to be the biggest date in history! May 22, 1962. We're on the planet Mars— and we have *air!*"

UFOlogical elements frequently appeared on CBS' (its first year was on ABC) 1976–79 series, *Wonder Woman*. "The Starships Are Coming" had a general at a supposed saucer landing site confronted by mechanical-sounding, faceless Little Gray Men in body leotards. Seeming telepathic and bulletproof, they turned out to be fakes being used to gain control of the general's mind toward the purpose of sparking a nuclear incident. The appearance and invulnerability of the supposed UFO occupants is interesting for the time, as is the use of the CIA's fear of the phenomenon's potential mind-control use by parties on our own planet—though just how they would accomplish all that actual saucer occupants do has never been credibly dramatized. Another episode had a Pied Piper musician with super-sound technology weapons hypnotizing and post-event-controlling naive groupies for criminal ends. The season opener featured missing-time abduction, remote-control takeover of aerial vehicles, and hypnotic memory implantation. At least two episodes contained alien mind-control, one by Little Gray Men of the now-famous variety utilizing human pawns and robot servants, the other showing average men and women possessed against their will by an extraterrestrial pyramid that makes them plot world domination. *The New, Original Wonder Woman,* immediately predating the revamped present-day format and featuring the same cast (but set during WWII), had a two-part episode called "Judgment from Space," featuring the recurring Klaatu-like character, Andros, whose race—human, like our own—liaises with Wonder Woman in giving humanity a fifty-year lease to learn how to settle its disputes non-violently, at the end of which time they will either welcome us into their society or exterminate us. Andros' race works its technological magic—like that of the Celtic Fairy Folk, the *Tuatha de Danaan*—by the use of sound, with which they can control weather and move planets.

Though actually having begun at the tail end of Gerald Ford's presidency in 1975 (and lasting into Reagan's), the most interesting T.V. entry during the Carter administration as regards the educational program was Robin Williams' springboard to fame, Paramount's extremely popular *Mork & Mindy.* "Mork from Ork" originally guest-starred in a segment of *Happy Days* before launching into his own series, a weekly situation-comedy that had the Orkans studying the human race through average Colorado music store employee Mindy McConnell (Pam Dawber), in post-Berkeley/pre-Yuppie Boulder. Dressed in red and white and arriving in an egg-shaped craft, Mork eventually even mated with Mindy and had a child (Jonathan Winters), certainly more for raising ratings—which it failed to do—than to acquaint a viewing audience with any real possibility of interbreeding. While the closest personal contacts in real life (such as Antonio Villas Boas') are never reported so amusingly, they are at least as benign and enjoyable, and such contacts are not altogether so rare—it is just that the only cases which receive publicity are those in which the abductees have not adjusted to their situation, giving the popular impression that all abductions are a nightmarish experience, which is not the case at all. The end of the series (in 1982, during Reagan) saw Mork eventually discovered and tailed by Intelligence agents both from our planet and planets hostile to Ork. Mork and his Earth-bride Mindy announced his true citizenship to the world and introduced their child to everyone, Mork pleading in the name of universal brotherhood for a harmonious meeting between his world and ours. Though at this point in time it can be no more than speculation, the possibility exists that exactly such an announcement may one day be made, only involving a great many more than two people.

It was in 1977 that one of the better "visitation" movies, Warner Bros. *Oh, God!*, featured George Burns as the Almighty, making an appearance to average store clerk John Denver, encouraging him to follow in the footsteps of Copernicus and Galileo and spread his word, no matter the persecution. The highly underrated satire from the same studio, *Simon*, appeared at the end of the decade, starring Alan Arkin as a pseudo-intellectual brainwashed by a government think-tank into believing he is actually an alien who was raised by humans, just to see what effect it will have on the public. 1967's *The President's Analyst* (Paramount), a similar comedy, had phone company robots abducting people to put implants in their brains in a bid to take over the world, and a space threat and missing-time abduction were featured in the same year's *In Like Flint* (20th Century Fox).

Also in 1977, Ray Bradbury's *The Martian Chronicles*, his series of interlocking short stories written between 1946 and 1950 was televised as a miniseries in the U.S. and theatrically released in Europe. Mars is shown to be the location of a former superior civilization of nature-oriented humanoids, extremely similar to our own race, who have left behind geometrical buildings. A few of their survivors try mankind in various ways, executing those with no appreciation for the simple beauty of their philosophy. They form a clandestine liaison with a like-minded crewmember of the first Earth mission who assists them, delude later comers into believing they have arrived in heaven with projected hallucinations, are murdered by people who misinterpret their later friendly overtures, and ultimately leave the only survivors after an Earth holocaust with their legacy, concluding with the same ending as Nigel Kneale's *Five Million Years to Earth:* "We are the Martians, now."

Dragnet's Jack Webb produced NBC's short-lived *Project: UFO* in 1978–79. The show was advertised as presenting the most baffling UFO cases in the U.S. Air Force's Project Blue Book files. Blue Book's 1961–64 project head, Col. William T. Coleman, was hired as line producer and production consultant. Though *Project: UFO* rarely hinted at anything other than conventional explanations for even the most unusual sightings, and never dramatized the most famous documented cases, its first episode did feature a robot disembarking from a landed UFO to confront a startled woman at her own home. Whenever more spectacular elements were seen, they were comfortably explained away by series Blue Book agents William Jordan and Caskey Swaim as being not what necessarily *actually* happened, but rather what the witnesses *said* they saw.

1978 brought Brian de Palma's *The Fury* from 20th Century Fox, with the screenplay written by the novel's author, John Farris, another of those seminal writers whose works have both influenced numerous imitators to follow and which appear to display accurate UFO-logical elements. In Farris' case, his prescience seems to be merely acute consciousness of the daily headlines and current vogues. The "Candy Jones" case was just being published at the time he wrote *The Fury,* probably his biggest breakthrough piece into the mainstream. Farris incorporated CIA mind control into his story about a nefarious government Intelligence outfit that breeds better monsters through chemistry. Certain unscrupulous State Department or Department of Defense members have noticed that a number of children have been born with peculiar psionic abilities and talents, and they track the unwitting youngsters down to seduce them into living the rest of their lives under the government's careful tutelage and control, becoming trained killers. When one of their monster offspring becomes an uncontrollable terror to rival the biblical Giants, they trick the boy's father, a CIA assassin, into murdering his own son by use of a previously planted post-hypnotic command.

Though it is not generally recognized, *The Fury* spawned a minor cottage-industry of similar stories, the next most prominent of which was probably the 1981 Canadian import by fledgeling horror director David Cronenberg, *Scanners*. "Scanners" are psychic mind-readers, computer-manipulators, and sometime-murderers, initially created through an accident of chemistry that a massive government project has since been using on purpose. Scanners' lives are disrupted in exactly the same way as those of UFO abductees; they are aware of the fact that they are different from other people but not aware exactly as to why or how, and vaguely conscious of being under constant watch by indeterminate parties for indeterminate purposes. Some of them go crazy, and others find themselves liberated by their differences. One has become frighteningly self-aware, and tapped into the entire government's program through his phenomenal psionic abilities. He goes around recruiting other Scanners and enlightening them, and creates an underground saboteur society that goes to war with the Intelligence establishment that created them. Stephen King utilized the same elements in Universal's *Firestarter*, filmed by Dino de Laurentiis in 1984, emphasizing the external mind-control aspect. The same year's *Dreamscape* (see next chapter) featured an attempted telepathic assassination plot straight out of real-life Intelligence files such as those reported by journalist, author and science writer Jim Schnabel in *Remote Viewers*, and earlier psychic researcher/journalists Lynn Schroeder and Sheila Ostrander in *Psychic Discoveries Behind the Iron Curtain* (see Introduction).

Such psychic warfare elements also appeared in Tobe Hooper's more recent 1990 entry, *Spontaneous Combustion*, and to a lesser degree in *The Howling* (see next chapter), made the same year as *Scanners* (1980), which was substantially rewritten by John Sayles and Terence H. Winkless from the Gary Brandner novel on which it was based. *The Howling* features Patrick Macnee as a pop-psychiatrist running "The Colony," an isolated community of superhuman immortals, concealing their true nature while trying to learn peaceful coexistence with their lesser human cousins—on whom, by nature, they greatly prefer to feed. Cronenberg, it may be noted, frequently makes movies about damaging secret government projects and hybrid demon-children, such as *Rabid, The Fly* ('86 remake), and *The Brood.* Both *Scanners* and *The Howling* were made by Avco Embassy, which in 1978 produced *The Manitou,* famous exploitation director/producer William Girdler's filmization of pop-horror Lovecraftian paperback original author Graham Masterton's novel. *The Manitou* starred Susan Strasberg as the hapless host to an ancient Indian medicine man seeking rebirth out of her neck. The medicine man, Misquamacus—named after a lesser character in Lovecraft—combats twentieth century white man's science with his ancient magic, in an attempt to bring the Great Old One back to power on Earth.

More widely disseminated to a younger audience, a positively-influenced presentation of the "government-monitored psychics" scenario has been seen in the phenomenally popular comics series and Fox cartoon *X-Men,* the premise of which is that society is beginning to become aware of "mutants" in its midst, who just happen to be their own sons and daughters. The awareness spawns something of a witch-hunt mentality, the slightly-less-gifted, non-mutant, average, everyday human population being a bit spooked by the appearance of eerie "Village of the Damned" supermen in their communities. A secret, massive government outfit run by a Doctor Xavier has been monitoring the mutants for years, and is disturbed by the premature public awareness of them. "I always intended that people should know about the X-Men," he laments, in the cartoon's premiere episode, "but in the proper time. Not like this." Xavier brings the mutants under his wing when they begin to awaken to their true nature, because they become the target of extraterrestrial robot abduction by a rival party as soon as they surface. He teaches them to harness their unique abilities and talents, which they use in a private little war with that other party.

United Artists produced a Japanese *Star Wars*-variety movie with robots and ancient astronauts in 1978, called *Message from Space.* A

Rankin-Bass T.V. movie the same year, released theatrically in Europe, entered the fray on the UFO-deflectional front, *The Bermuda Depths,* which seems to have been engineered solely to make all psychic/occult subjects look ridiculous—it centers on a deep-sea turtle that has a rendezvous with a strange young woman. Reincarnation figures into the plot somehow. A standard method of devaluing any subject of potential interest is to first group as many other "fringe" topics as possible with it, then make it look as if the whole were being seriously examined, only in a badly produced or poorly presented fashion. Another pretty standard technique is to make it appear as if no one of the single subjects can possibly be considered on its own merits without the others being equally believed, and to make each element in the mix appear maximally crazy. The idea is more or less to intimidate by logical fallacy: i.e., "UFOs are real. Therefore, reincarnation from other dimensions is also real, and so is time travel. Believing in UFOs means you must also believe you may have traveled back in time and sired your own grandfather, first having reincarnated to become him, returning from the astral plane to do so."

1978's *Warlords of Atlantis* (Columbia/EMI) portrays the Atlanteans as the technologically advanced surviving remnant of the planet Mars, who began civilization on Earth and perished in a cosmic catastrophe millennia ago but are ever-ready to resumé their place of superiority over man—they drive mankind to war in their name to "thin out the herd," while simultaneously recruiting the best human minds to join them. The movie was written by Brian Hayles, who scripted many *Dr. Who* episodes, including those with the Martian "Ice Warriors." One, "The Seeds of Death," had the clamp-handed robotic Martians with their sonic weapons setting up a base on the Moon, from which they launched a biological warfare attack against Earth in preparation for invasion.

The same year, Warner Bros.' action picture *Capricorn One* presented the scenario that NASA could fake a manned landing on another planet—Mars—in order to protect its government appropriations. It has been proposed by Bill Kaysing, in his self-published 1991 exposé *We Never Went to the Moon,* that they did exactly that in the 1969 lunar mission, but, while anything is possible, it is a problematic suggestion at best. It is not impossible, however, that the lunar landing televised in 1969 was a studio fake, keeping what NASA was really filming on the Moon at the same time from public eyes. There is every indication that they expected to find artificial monuments in the Sea of Tranquility, and there was also a tremendous advance in technological cinema special-effects immediately prior to the lunar landing, excellent examples being *2001: A Space Odyssey* and the work of Gerry and Sylvia Anderson in Britain, both of which show strong evidence of having had some government funding. It is certainly not inconceivable that such massive investment in special-effects fakery had an ulterior motive.

Valid points raised by Kaysing—which "NASA and the former astronauts evade like a grifter dodges the 'heat,' " as Jonathan Vankin and John Whalen note—include a complete lack of lunar dust on the lander legs, and no depression beneath the lander where its rocket exhaust was, despite the fact that everyone ever associated with a Moon landing said the dust there was incredibly deep, kicked-up at nothing, and clung to everything tenaciously; the astronauts of all but the last lunar missions have been kept in weeks-long medical quarantines upon their return—despite NASA's insistence that the Moon is a completely sterile world devoid of any life at all, microorganismic or not—which may well be for lengthy and complex "debriefings" and practice sessions for the press; and, most importantly, the camera on the Moon is focused on infinity when it shows the Earth hanging over the horizon, yet no stars are visible anywhere in the sky—on a world with no atmosphere, the stars should be so plentiful that space itself would be difficult to see, and the faking of stars in the sky would never have fooled any astronomer who studied the NASA shots. To these points could be added the facts that the astronauts—with the brief exception of *Apollo 17*'s Jack Schmitt—were never seen outside the lunar module with anything but completely opaque gold faceplates, where they were at all other times clear, and that the lunar simulation module on Earth looks exactly like the shots taken from the Moon. Even the ping-pong ball "bouncing" effect is simple to create through studio trickery.

Kaysing's suggestion for the fakery, like *Capricorn One*'s (which he says was based on his research), was because NASA realized they could never reach the Moon by the end of the 1960s and wanted to maintain their funding. If the televised shots were fakes, it would seem likelier they instead wanted to conceal what they might actually find there, or at least ensure that no "surprises" occurred on live T.V. Too many details have been reported about the Moon to believe that they were discovered only by robot probes, aside from which, if NASA were going to make up details about the Moon, they would never have come up with such bizarre details as have actually emerged. Interestingly, *Diamonds Are Forever,* which was made in 1971, showed James Bond escaping from a Nevada aerospace laboratory's extremely realistic mock-lunar landscape set, complete with mountains and a real-looking Earth hanging against a black, starless backdrop. What makes the scene interesting is not only its realism, looking not unlike what was actually seen on T.V. in 1969, but the fact that Kaysing's theory had the Apollo astronauts taken to exactly such a set in Nevada to fake their "real" lunar activities. Similarly, the 1992 techno-thriller *Sneakers* had a scene in which conspiracy theorist Dan Aykroyd comments, "This LTX71 concealable mike is part of the same system NASA used when they faked the Apollo Moon landings." *Capricorn One,* it may be noted, was pointedly refused any technical advice or cooperation by NASA.

Warner Bros.' *Superman* and *Superman II* were made during Carter's tenure, in 1978 and 1980, which are of peripheral interest to this study. Kal-El is presented as a benevolent alien from a former superior civilization, showing an ongoing interest in man's affairs. "You will believe a man can fly!" read the advertisements. The latter movie, especially, touches on the subject of first contact. In a memorable scene no doubt inspired by ex-NASA personnel Otto Binder's and Maurice Chatelain's allegations the previous year that Neil Armstrong encountered UFOs on the Moon in 1969, three super-criminals from Kal-El's planet murder the crew of a Moon mission before proceeding to rapidly dominate the Earth, finally to be overpowered by the Man of Steel (naturally). Along the way, Superman marries Lois Lane and ultimately erases her memory of the encounter as an act of kindness, because she is in agony living a double life as long as she possesses the knowledge of it.

It is worth noting that the *Superman* movies disintegrated completely during the Reagan years, as did 20th Century Fox's formerly good *Star Wars* movies, the latter becoming especially insipid as good-hearted teddy-bears defeated The Evil Empire (a favorite Reagan phrase) in 1983's *Return of the Jedi,* just by being fuzzy, cute, loveable, and commercially marketable. *Superman III,* made the same year as this final *Star Wars* installment, pitted the Man of Steel against mad industrialist Robert Vaughn's super-computer of steel, a nuclear war machine that ends up abducting humans and modifying them to accommodate its artificial intelligence. Vaughn inadvertently splits Superman into two halves by means of synthetic Kryptonite, one of which becomes a skid-row alcoholic bully, and Superman only manages to pull himself together again thanks to the innocent plea of a young boy who tells him that he is just temporarily down on his luck—certainly something the Reagan administration was trying to tell the entire populace, in the wake of its defense buildup and other policies that left a record (and ever-growing) number of unemployed.

The final film in the series, 1987's *Superman IV: The Quest for Peace,* ironically (for such a war-mongering administration) began with Superman eliminating the world's nuclear weapons, and having to then defeat Lex Luthor's conglomerate of nuclear defense contractors, who use the opportunity to start up all over again—which is not unlike what would happen only four years later in George Bush's Iraqi war, "Operation Desert Storm." One of the reasons for the film's particular anti-war and -arms race slant is that star Christopher Reeve was active on the film's production level. Reeve is a prominent anti-nuclear peace activist, who at one time even had his own line to the White House, and co-star Margot Kidder is a supporter of former U.S. Attorney General Ramsey Clark's ongoing Commission of Inquiry for the International War Crimes Tribunal, which continues to investigate on the international level America's and George Bush's conduct before, during, and after that very war.

Imports during the Carter administration included Canada's *Starship Invasions* (1977) and Italy's *Starcrash* (1979), both of the space-opera variety that quickly came into vogue in the conservative 1980s, having been initiated by *Star Wars* during the Carter educational program. Neither film meant to be taken very seriously, the latter especially was harmless comic-book juvenilia, with sex-bomb Caroline Munro as a space-jockey who patrols outposts to keep the Empire secure. *Starcrash* spawned the sexploitational romp *Galaxina* the following year, with the late twenty-year-old Canadian Playmate of the Year Dorothy Stratten as a robot gunslinger cum sex-machine. *Starship Invasions,* equally light-hearted, has more actual UFOlogical elements in it. Perennial arch-villain Christopher Lee is the evil alien "Captain Ramses," who uses a mind-controlling telepathy gun to beam thoughts of suicide into the heads of his opponents. Robert Vaughn is an Earth UFO expert, abducted by aliens with large bald heads to help them fight Lee before he can kill their world and our own. *Starship Invasions,* like many UFO import films, was funded by America through Warner Bros. From Britain, at the end of the decade, came the phenomenally popular BBC space comedy *Hitchhiker's Guide to the Galaxy,* from *Dr. Who* story editor Douglas Adams.

Quinn Martin produced a T.V. movie in 1979 called *The Aliens are Coming,* more or less a latter-day *Invaders from Mars.* The film was plainly intended to be a pilot, but it never took off. City-sized flying saucers (such as those recently witnessed in the much more popular *Independence Day*) conceal themselves in the American desert, bearing "aliens" that are entirely robotic-looking, -acting, and -sounding. These creatures nocturnally visit and possess useful humans, and use their possessed human hosts to hypnotize interlopers into committing suicide. The aliens' initial interest is in sabotaging a major hydroelectric plant, but they are thwarted by a small team of government investigators who have dedicated themselves to repelling the alien invasion. Thwarted in their first bid for Earth conquest, the aliens resolve at the end of the movie to keep on trying, in order to eventually clear the planet of its human infestation and make it ready for their own kind to inhabit.

1980's *Hangar 18,* among the last of the Carter-era UFO movies, was blasted by Vallee as unrealistic in the same fashion as he disdained *Close Encounters* three years before, and it did not fare well either commercially or critically. Advertising itself at the time as being based on the real truth known by the government concerning UFOs, it does seem to be remarkably close to what facts can be ascertained in this study. It is not a bad movie and may in time overcome its bad press, as have some of its contemporaries. Sunn Classics Pictures produced it, the same company that made so many of the "Mysterious Monsters," "Bermuda Triangle," and "Psychic Phenomena" drive-in documentaries of the 1970s.

Starring Darren McGavin as the head of a secret government task force investigation on a recovered flying disk, the story counterpoints that investigation—at the mythical Hangar 18, which is not the same story promulgated by the contemporary Area 51 disinformational stories, though they were probably based on it—with a Men-In-Black government-vs.-the-good-guy-investigators subplot involving astronauts whose names have been smeared to cover up the reality of the saucer. McGavin himself has long been associated with investigation of the occult, being the star of T.V.'s *The Night Stalker,* and most recently the host and narrator of a CBS special called *Mysteries of the Ancient World,* paralleling much of the same material presented in this book. The aliens of *Hangar 18* are shown to be almost identical to humans in appearance. They have an abducted woman on board in a tube of liquid, as well as other specimens of life. Hieroglyphic-like symbols proliferate on their craft, including the Egyptian crook and flail sign on a cabinet, which is the first thing the investigating team encounters on entering the craft—they open it, and a shiny black metallic humanoid with a round head and antennae rushes toward them, causing them to scream, until they realize it is "only a spacesuit" which has slid down a rack at them. Its appearance matches the robots described to be the abductors in the course of this study, which is almost certainly what the suit implies.

"All of the previous information we have had about the origins of mankind and the human race . . . is absolutely false," McGavin proclaims to the team, after documents aboard the craft have been deciphered. The documents attest to this race, who were worshipped as gods, having created mankind in antiquity out of primitive stock and using them as slaves, then interbreeding with them to create human beings. "You see, it's no coincidence that the spacemen are almost identical to us. It is not a case of two species evolving independently of each other. Those ancient spacemen altered forever our evolution—they are the missing link. We, mankind, the human race ... are their children. What we must find out now is why they're monitoring us, why they're watching us." They discover that the aliens have industrial defense sites targeted and are planning to return, which ends the movie. *Hangar 18* could be nothing more than a film taking off on then-popular ancient astronaut theories, or it could genuinely reflect the truth. Covering that evidence has been part of this study, enabling the reader to decide for himself. Information about comatose UFO abductees being submerged in a breathable murky liquid, and waking in terror, however, were not exactly common knowledge at the time.

Given the $20 million spent by Jimmy Carter on "UFO research" that was never specified, and the surprising number of UFOlogically-related "entertainments" that came out in the apparent educational program, the likelihood that this money was invested in Hollywood seems ever greater. It is worth noting that the budget for *Close Encounters of the Third Kind* was ultimately capped at exactly Carter's figure—$20 million. 1976, the year Carter was elected, was the year that Zecharia Sitchin and Robert Temple both published their books on Egypt and ancient astronauts. Steven Spielberg, whose star was just hitting the rise, came out the next year with the phenomenally hyped and extremely successful *Close Encounters,* and the exceptionally popular *Star Wars* series began dramatizing the ancient astronaut theme, down to the mythologically accurate elements of the sun-hero Luke Skywalker's hand being cut off and replaced by a cybernetic metal one—which, as a matter of fact, was as supple and realistic as his own lost hand in the original Celtic myth of Nuada—and his father Darth Vader's real name being "Annakim," another Biblical name for the fallen angels destroyed in the Flood. *Battlestar Galactica* dramatized the same themes for T.V., in a well-meaning but poorly executed attempt, and *Buck Rogers in the 25th Century* followed hot on its failed heels. The *Superman* movies continued the theme of friendly extraterrestrial brothers, and Spielberg began another highly popular series with Indiana Jones, who first broached to a mass audience that the Ark of the Covenant was a technological masterpiece from a God more tangible and less esoteric than previously supposed, in *Raiders of the Lost Ark*.

With the next decade, all pretense at education was out, and disinformation and militarism were back in. Ronald Reagan's presidency returned to the same combination of the frightening and the ridiculous that characterized the 1950s. Following eight years of such treatment in the movies, UFOs and space invaders became even more demonized by George Bush, and in their wake, even Democratic President Bill Clinton's tenure in office has shown little change from those of his Republican predecessors.

10

Peregrinations and Propagandizations

Most UFOlogical movies during Reagan's presidency were remakes of original 1950s propaganda movies. Not only did they succeed in distancing new audiences from the subject in the same way as their predecessors, but they served the new purpose of distancing them from the original propagandas as well. As new facts emerged about UFOs through court battles and the Freedom of Information Act, original movies in which exactly the same elements might have been detected were all but deleted from the catalogue of aired movies, and replaced with remakes that removed all the actual UFOlogical information from them. *The Thing, The Fly, The Blob,* two new versions of *Invasion of the Body Snatchers* (one of which actually wasn't inferior to the remake done during Carter's tenure), and many others were filmed in this time period. All were imminently slicker and better-made, and all were imminently further removed from the original propagandized truths contained in them. Additionally, a surprising number of nuclear Armageddon movies, both in America and Britain, were made for T.V. These were especially realistic and nightmarish, the best being the United Kingdom's *Threads* (MCTV, 1985), which depicted mankind reduced to neo-Mediaeval Feudalism by holocaust. Presumably, this was another throwback to the *Invasion U.S.A.* scare-mongering of the

1950s, to muster support for the "nuclear deterrent" supposedly provided by Reagan's gigantic arms buildup and Star Wars programs.

The 1980s saw such a surfeit of bad UFO movies that they are impossible to even begin cataloguing, nor would there be any reason to. The only ones meant to be taken even semi-seriously were the Red Menace from Space variety, probably intended to sell Star Wars to the electorate. All entertainment was seriously devalued by gross, wretched excess and juvenile aesthetics. As *Spy* magazine recently put it, the '80s was the decade in which fame was solicited. The explosion of cable and MTV's rock video market flooded the industry with more masses of product than it knew what to do with, almost all of it dreadfully bad. Movies and T.V. suffered the worst, being aimed for audiences somewhere about high school age or younger. Swimsuit models, pop singers and stand-up comics were substituted for actors, when yet another mediocre-talented son or daughter of either a former entertainment business success or casting agent wasn't. The same nepotism still continues to dominate the business, to its own detriment. This is hardly a new Hollywood practice, merely in recent years a much more abused one.

United Artists' James Bond film series featured almost exclusively Russian threats, with a decidedly dated 1950s slant. *For Your Eyes Only* was the first in 1981, establishing that detente is a myth and that the Russians want only global domination, a theme repeated throughout the decade into 1987's *The Living Daylights,* which depicted Soviet assassins and KGB agents anxious to defect to the West. 1983's *Octopussy* was about a "renegade" Russian Cold Warrior attempting to detonate an atomic bomb in West Germany, not to provoke WWIII, but rather to use it for the inevitable purpose—or so Bond outright states in the movie—of causing NATO to insist on unilateral disarmament, the only possible end result of which would be that the Russians would then march, unopposed, into every European country. That this would probably be the least likely result of such an incident, or that unilateral disarmament would hardly cause unlimited aggression by Russia, are conveniently not considered, and such questions manage to become lost amidst dazzling action sequences and witty dialogue. The sentiment is identical to 1984's *Red Dawn* and the earlier *Invasion U.S.A.* Where mad industrialists operating independently to create economic or military chaos were featured during Democratic administrations in 1964's *Goldfinger* and 1977's *The Spy Who Loved Me* (which showed the Russians as cooperative with Americans toward detente), 1985's revamp of the same elements in *A View to A Kill* made the mad industrialist a Nazi-created and KGB-empowered genetic freak.

Bond was twice shown as an active combatant in the War on Drugs, both times in Republican administrations, in 1973's *Live And Let Die* and 1989's *Licence To Kill,* and peripherally in *Goldfinger* and *The Living Daylights.* In the last, Bond was up against two other supposed "rogue" Cold Warriors, one Russian and the other American, making a profit off all sides through their sale of high-tech weaponry to Third World countries for the perpetuation of war and the sale of its products, and additionally through drugs to finance their operations. Though the film was made as Iran-Contra was brewing, the idea of such elements on both sides operating independently of their parent organizations is especially unbelievable, but is certainly the sort of image the Intelligence agencies would want to sell to the public. Intelligence agents as foes of drug-lords falls disingenuously flat, however, since drug usage never escalated more than during ex-CIA head George Bush's tenure both as supposed anti-drug czar and president; and CBS' *60 Minutes* (among many other documented sources of identical occurrences, most recently including the September 1996 *San Jose Mercury)* publicized in 1994 that the CIA had deliberately slipped a million-dollar shipment of cocaine into the country and sold it on the streets despite the unmistakable orders of the Drug Enforcement Agency that they not do so. The legion of insipidly bad 1970s (and beyond) T.V. cop shows all portray entirely unrealistic visions of the "war on drugs," perpetuating the illusion that police forces actually try to eradicate the problem instead of feeding off it themselves.

As at least one piece of evidence that it is not only during Republican administrations that such blatant propaganda occurs, Columbia/Tri-Star's *True Lies* in 1994 featured easily the most transparent and ludicrous "patriotic" script since *Licence to Kill.* Perennial blue-collar Bond-actalike Arnold Schwarzenegger plays an insurance sales-man/secret agent, who successfully manages to conceal his high-tech action double life from his wife, average secretary and mother Jamie Lee Curtis. He soon discovers that she, too, has a double life, seek-ing adventure to relieve her boredom in an adulterous affair with a pretend-spy who preys on her. To win her back, Schwarzenegger mock-enlists her through a blind to become a secret agent like him-self, only to have her forced into becoming the real thing due to cir-cumstances beyond their control. Before the movie is over, Schwarzenegger, his wife, and fourteen-year-old daughter all end up kidnapped by Arab terrorists of the "Crimson Jihad," surviving an atomic explosion, being aerially rescued—twice—from the jaws of certain doom, hand-to-hand dueling to the death on a hovering VTOL jet, and ultimately firing the mad terrorist leader into his own cohorts' helicopter on the back of a heatseeker missile.

Proving that the family that slays together stays together, the movie ends with all three becoming career spies for Mom and Apple Pie, conveniently ignoring a single realistic question, such as, say, just how many "Die Hard" Middle Eastern terrorists there are who weren't initially trained under the auspices of the CIA itself, or, in the wake of Desert Storm, how many there are who wouldn't turn tail and run at the first sign of trouble, let alone fight to the death. Only one such film among legion, *True Lies* glorifies mindless vio-lence, unquestioning loyalty to God and Country, and the one-sided hypocrisy of psychopathic murder as something only "the bad guys" ever do, even if "our side" kills twice as many of them, and in far more grotesque and indiscriminate fashion, casually wisecracking all the while. Schwarzenegger tells his wife, at one point, that he only ever killed "bad guys, who deserved it," as though he or his Agency bosses would be able to make such a moral distinction in their especially self-serving world. Adding to the too-heroic-to-be-true milieu, it turns out that wife Jamie Lee never even cheated on hubby Arnold during her bid for excitement—which just goes to show, after all, that in a world where all others are evil or falling from virtue, only Americans are ever-so-pure that they wouldn't even com-mit an average bored adultery. It is worth noting that military veteran, former senator, and 1996 Republican presidential candidate Bob Dole hailed *True Lies* and the evil space-invader flick *Independence Day* as admirable and patriotic American movies, but considered Demi Moore's contemporaneous film about a stripper to be detrimental to the country's values.

Universal's *Flash Gordon* in 1980 was probably the best of the space-opera genre in the wake of Carter's educational program, coming as it did at the end of that president's term and ushering in both Reagan's militaristic outlook and the silliness that was to become the trademark of UFOlogical films in his era. The threat of nearby planetary invader "Ming the Merciless" and his Evil Empire served as the transitional point between the two men's outlooks, and possibly representing the only thing they really had in common. Alex Raymond's famous pulp-era space hero became a football quarterback launched into space to save Earth from the decadent Oriental despot's pointless attack upon our planet. "Klytus, I'm bored," Ming opens the film, speaking to his Darth Vader-ish robotic right-hand "man," and so saying, idly selects one among dozens of catastrophic weather assaults on Earth from his sonic organ, simply to relieve that boredom. Ming's robotic servants immediately arrest Flash, his mentor Dr. Zarkov, and his girlfriend Dale Arden upon their arrival on his home planet, Mongo. Dale is determined by Ming to have remarkable sexual response to the power of his mind-controlling magic ring, and she is made one of his harem. Flash becomes the paramour of Ming's rebellious sloe-eyed daughter, who undergoes severe erotic whipping by Klytus for her transgressions. Zarkov is subjected to a nearly terminal mind-probe, which sifts his thoughts for the Mongolians to know and catalogue. Ultimately, of course, Flash manages to overthrow Ming's fascist empire by allying the tyrant's enemies against him in an aerial assault. The accurate UFOlogical elements of mind-reading, thought control, and erotic whippings were all present in Raymond's original 1930s comic strip, though the added robotic element was new.

Another of the better space-opera epics that appeared in the same year was New World's *Battle Beyond the Stars*. (New World was Roger Corman's new company of the time, helped into existence by independent film distributor Larry Woolner.) Most often described as a *Star Wars* version of *Seven Samurai,* it is essentially a remake of the kind of space adventure embodied in 1955's *This Island Earth,* about the recruitment of selected subjects for war concerns in space. The "aliens" are all human in appearance and include literal space-cowboys from Earth and space-Valkyries (in the form of busty Sybil Danning) from elsewhere.

Avco Embassy's 1980 entry, *The Howling,* begins with an abduction experience undergone by hapless T.V. newswoman Dee Wallace. Attempting to help police apprehend serial killer "Eddie the Mangler," she accepts the murderer's invitation to meet him, and follows Eddie's clues to his sex-shop hideout, closely watched by undercover officers. While Wallace is forced to watch violent pornographic films, Eddie seductively tells her from behind that he intends to make her like him. Eddie orders her to turn around—which she does, crying out in terror, rescued by the arrival of police who shoot Eddie dead. After her experience, Wallace finds herself unable to concentrate, suffering terrible nightmares about the incident. Something about the Mangler's appearance—above and beyond the mere fact of his being a murderer—has unsettled her to the point that she has gone into amnesiac shock. Pop-psychiatrist Patrick Macnee invites Wallace to "the Colony," an isolated seaside resort, to attend group therapy sessions and simply to unwind. While at the Colony, Wallace's husband is seduced by local leather-clad vamp Elisabeth Brooks, and is "converted" into one of her kind—a werewolf. Wallace gradually makes the discovery that Eddie the Mangler is Brooks' brother, and he is still alive and at large, undead by virtue of his supernatural nature. Not only that, but everyone at the Colony, including her psychiatrist, is a werewolf. The Colony werewolves reveal to Wallace that she has been brought among them in order to test her for initiation and conversion into their ranks. Rescued by her friends and her converted husband (who dies in the attempt), Wallace burns the Colony to the ground and returns to civilization, there to warn mankind, "A secret society exists and is living among all of us. They are neither people nor animals, but something in between—monstrous mutations, with violent natures that must be satisfied. . . ."

In addition to the UFOlogical nature of the film, *The Howling* contains a classic depradation of the subject. Wallace, during her stay, discovers a mutilated animal near her cabin. When "the boys" go out hunting for the animal responsible the next day, comical old geezer John Carradine says, "I still think it was UFOs—them cattle mutilations!" and the rest of the men blow him off with, "Good, Earl, good—you watch the skies for us, now! That'll be your job!" While all of this is going on, circus music plays in the background, making the UFO subject all the more ludicrous by association.

1980 saw the aforementioned remake (see previous chapter) of American International Pictures' *Blood from the Mummy's Tomb*, made by Warner Bros. in England and released by AIP's primary successor company, Orion Pictures: *The Awakening*. Based on occult-influenced Victorian writer Bram Stoker's novel *The Jewel of the Seven Stars*, the remake was tailored primarily to capitalize on the success of the Carter Era's *The Omen* and *Damien: Omen II*, stripping Stoker's dry supernatural murder mystery plot and replacing it with a series of gory murders befalling any of its characters who managed to catch on to the evil doings afoot. Though it may be only of passing interest and purely coincidental, United Artists' Bond series graphic artist Maurice Binder did the stylish credit sequences, and the film was produced by Robert Solo, who also produced United Artists' 1979 remake of *Invasion of the Body Snatchers*. What makes the movie of UFOlogical interest are the presentation and handling of its elements.

Charlton Heston plays an archaeologist whose daughter is the spitting-image reincarnation of a damned ancient Egyptian sorceress-queen, Tara, whom Heston discovered and brought to light. Heston finds himself fitting perfectly the prophecy inscribed in Tara's tomb, that he, as the "Fair Man of the North," would find and release her into a later world. He consults a government radio-astronomer and learns that the stars of Ursa Major (the seven stars of the Pleiades, Taurus, the "Bull of Heaven") have come to the exact position they occupied at the time of Tara's death, which she predicted would be the time of her reawakening. "Is there a child on Earth who doesn't believe in magic?" Heston asks his rational wife. "I don't. We're rational. Civilized. We know the limits of nature. We know. Or are we just afraid to test our certainty—our holy, scientific certainty—against that ancient queen's belief in magic?" These elements in the story predate by more than ten years the published discovery of Belgian engineer Robert Bauval, in *The Orion Mystery,* that the stars of Orion's belt match perfectly those of the pyramids in the Giza complex (and those of Teotihuacan, in Mexico, it has also been discovered), and that their precise configuration will match as close to perfectly as can be estimated the same position in about 2001 (when Mars is next in favorable opposition to Earth) as they held in 10,450 BC, which was the Giza pyramids' probable date of construction and of the Flood and disappearance of Atlantis, according to ancient texts and new archaeological evidence. This element was not part of Stoker's original story, and it strongly implies that someone on the production team was aware of the same kind of archaeoastronomical research that had been conducted by the Nazis and the CIA—especially given that, even at this late date, very few in the civilian scientific community study this particular area of research, and most academics are renowned for ridiculing or debunking it.

Also matching the UFOlogical pattern in the story is the character of Heston's daughter, Stefanie Zimbalist (in her first film role, before her fame on T.V.'s *Remington Steele).* Zimbalist fits the darker profile of a UFO abductee, suffering from unsettling nightmares and a fragmenting of her waking personality that she is having insurmountable difficulty with. Zimbalist finds herself recalling vivid images from sleepwalking experiences she knows have occurred, because she finds blood on her clothes that she remembers picking up during those experiences. She occasionally sees flashes of the mummified Queen Tara while looking into her makeup mirror. Ancient Egyptian flows out of her mouth with ease, though she doesn't know the language, and she becomes subject to unpredictable mood swings and snappish irritability. "I—I've been too afraid to tell you, or anyone," she explains to her boyfriend, "but I—I don't feel like *me,* anymore. Who is that?" she asks, looking into the mirror with a vaguely troubled expression. "Do you know her? I don't, anymore...." The images she recalls are of being present in the vicinity of violent occurrences, and she fears that she may have somehow been responsible for murdering her own relatives when no one else is around. Ultimately, she goes to see a psychiatrist. "I didn't come here because I thought I was normal. I know what I am. I came because I'm frightened. Because—whether I want to believe it or not—I have *blackouts*. I wounded my own father. I saw my face torn half away. I'm terrified of *myself*, doctor." To a much lesser extent, these elements were in the novel and the 1972 film version, the latter with Valerie Leon suffering recurrent nightmares, like many abductees, of being paralyzed on a slab, surrounded by strange figures in Egyptian garb who are performing unknown medical procedures on her.

The Robertson Panel's own choice for dissemination of UFO material, Disney Studios, began the Eighties by trying to break their saccharine family kiddie-film image with a Lovecraftian Gothic horror movie called *Watcher in the Woods*. Somewhere between the initial filming and the final product, both the "Gothic" and the "horror" got lost from the project. The plot concerned cute teen Lynn Holly-Johnson's visitations from something in the woods that had some kind of unique bond with her. By the time it reached the theaters, the Watcher was transformed into Johnson's doppelganger, trying to wriggle free of a thirty-year time-warp she had somehow gotten herself trapped in. Somehow, this never quite managed to communicate itself to a confused audience. The reason may well have been that, initially, the Watcher was written to be a bat-winged alien who took Johnson to her planet in a $200,000 Otherworld sequence that was completely trashed after it was developed. The ending, which was universally criticized as being both confusing and just plain bad, was the result of a never-explained last-minute script rewrite, probably ordered from the top as other sabotaged projects like the *Superman* and *Star Wars* series appear to have been. *The Abyss*, already considered, exemplifies such inexplicable last-minute changes, and the reason for their occurrence.

Also leading off the decade was the *Nightmare on Elm Street* series, which enjoyed a phenomenally long run starting in 1984, even spawning a pretty bad late-1980s T.V. series on Fox. Its central character, Freddy Krueger, was a nocturnal child-abductor/killer who haunts teens' dreams, leaving Unidentified Body Markings on his survivors and no evidence for anyone not associated directly with the attacks to examine. Its predecessor, the much-better *Halloween* series started by John Carpenter, began in 1978 during Carter's tenure but escalated throughout the 1980s, with its latest entry released as recently as September of 1995. *Halloween*'s central character was a literally unstoppable boogey-man in a blank-featured James T. Kirk mask, robotic in every regard: bulletproof, blastproof, flameproof, slow, steady, and relentless in its endless pursuit of whatever quarry it stalked. It even had the curiously coincidental UFOlogical element of specifically animating for the sole purpose of following the descendants of a single given bloodline, and incorporated ancient Celtic lore to substantiate the boogey-man's premise.

Roger Corman kicked-off the new decade with 1980's *Humanoids from the Deep,* a sex-and-grue explicit reworking of *The Creature from the Black Lagoon,* with bald, oversized-headed rapist sea-demons impregnating hapless bathing beauties with unwanted hybrid off-spring. *Galaxy of Terror* followed in 1981, an extremely low-budget *Alien* rip-off with a rapist space-worm impregnating a woman to create alien offspring. It is perhaps most notable only for the curious fact that *My Favorite Martian*'s Ray Walston appeared in it. *Alien*'s influence cannot be underestimated, having been the standard model for virtually all films of the type to follow and spawning innumerable clones. *Humanoids* and *Galaxy* were released by Corman's New World Cinema. American International Pictures, Corman's usual company, was purchased by outsiders around 1980 and became Filmways, which quickly became engulfed by Orion. New World Cinema became Corman's central company at that time, though it was sold by him soon after. The main producers of his variety of entertainment then became Menahem Golan and Yoram Globus' Cannon group.

Corman never fared as well in later decades, his style best suited to an earlier era. He followed *Galaxy of Terror* with *Forbidden World* (also from New World Cinema) the following year, with a space-rape so graphic it had to be excised to avoid an X rating. For some reason, he actually remade it only nine years later as *Dead Space* (independently released by Califilms), and in fact remade most of his films in the 1990s for the cable premium channel Showtime, even campier than before, including films as far back as 1959's *The Wasp Woman* and as recent as 1978's *Piranha*. He ceased making new films, for the most part, after his 1980s ventures flopped. In general, his mantle was inherited by Charles Band and Jim Wynorski, the latter of whom was Corman's scriptwriter for *Forbidden World*.

The Cannon Group got an early start in UFOlogical movies with 1981's Italian-produced *Alien Contamination,* a movie so bad it went directly to Elvira's then-famous weekend T.V. show for initial airing in America. One of a legion of *Alien* knock-offs, the plot was essentially a "pod people" invasion movie with a Corman-esque slimy alien in the heart of it. A Columbian coffee factory, run by humans hypnotically taken over by the invading aliens, actually produces not java, but watermelon-ish alien eggs that explode, causing any humans in their immediate proximity to do the same. Despite a score from Goblin, the movie never achieved even cult status and is remembered by few—but it was typical of the era to come, in movies of its type.

The same year's underrated animated Canadian import, *Heavy Metal,* was given a lukewarm reception on its initial release, quickly becoming drive-in fodder, but has since developed a growing cult following. Begun in 1978–79 during Carter's tenure, it was finally finished and released by Spielberg's *Close Encounters* distributors, Columbia Pictures. For many years unavailable in the commercial market, it has recently been shown in a heavily edited version on Ted Turner's cable channels, censored almost completely for its plentiful sex scenes and nudity—even animated, and at such a late date that bare bottoms are finally allowed to be shown on network prime-time programming, it seems sex is still too frightening a concept for American broadcasting authorities to allow—and in 1996 it was re-released with a few minutes of added footage. The anthology is a virtual parade of UFOlogical stories, some obvious, some not. This is not too surprising, since Francis Ford Coppola's Zoetrope Studios produced the film, Coppola having been an early Roger Corman protégé.

The magazine that gave the movie its name has an interesting history of its own. The publishers of *National Lampoon* brought the monthly magazine to American shores from France in April 1977, and it remains in publication today. The French version *Metal Hurlant* ("Screaming Metal") was only about two years old at the time, but apparently already a hit in the country of its origin. It was a collection of wildly divergent ideas and artistic styles in comic art, with a mature and sophisticated approach to its stories. As its American publishers put it in their premiere issue, "when the French say 'science fiction,' they are not, as you might think, referring to H. G. Wells or 'Star Trek' or even Jules Verne. 'Science fiction' is a term which can sufficiently define Big Macs, South America, Methodism, or a weird neighbor. *Vogue Magazine,* anything Belgian, and pop-top cans are certainly science fiction. [One of its creators,] 'Moebius,' writing in *Metal Hurlant,* describes how, while listening to a Johnny Cash album, he realized that science fiction is a cathedral. Are you beginning, dear reader, to sufficiently misunderstand?" It was exactly such a "sufficient misunderstanding" that had from the earliest years of UFOlogically oriented movies and television shows been in effect for the educational program, and so it is no surprise that *Heavy Metal* should finally itself have been put to the purposes.

The very opening segment, "Soft Landing," is a casual presentation of space travel, made to appear as commonplace as a quick run to the drugstore: an orbiting NASA space shuttle opens its payload delivery doors to eject a sports car with a classically decked-out astronaut behind the wheel, who "drives" it on up to his front door at a nice house in the country, then takes off his helmet and kisses his daughter hello. "Harry Canyon" was a comedic future *film noir,* with a New York cabbie picking up a fare who turns out to be involved in "Maltese Falcon"-ish interplanetary intrigue: her father excavated an object at an ancient site that has remarkable powers, and everyone is doing each other in to get it. Among its many clever bits is a reference to the United Nations building being a low-rent housing district, and a literal "illegal alien" from space at the Bureau of Immigration. "Den" featured Richard Corben's famous muscular, bald, swashbuckling hero as beginning in the form of a pubescent computerdweeb who experiments on a meteor that crashed into his yard and abruptly finds himself transported through a vortex to another world as the enormous-penised Den. There he finds sex and romance and becomes recruited into numerous highly entertaining adventures involving intrigues between two technologically-superior warring parties on a pyramid-building planet of primitives, laced with the running adolescent commentary of his still-juvenile mind. "Captain Sternn" is a quick bit of comic fluff involving the solar system's most notorious con-man aboard a space station, which is followed by the UFOlogically-interesting "Gremlins." This little quickie, in record time, presents a B-17 encountering a foo-fighter that is simultaneously a green fireball, killing two birds on the subject with one stone, and then immediately presents the UFO as animating literal bulletproof skeletons to try and abduct survivors aboard the plane. This segment, like "Soft Landing," was written by Dan O'Bannon, the author and co-author of the screenplays for the UFOlogically-accurate films *Alien, Lifeforce,* and the remake of *Invaders from Mars.*

The "So Beautiful and So Dangerous" segment is a comical sex-abduction story. A Pentagon official at a news conference goes mad and rips the blouse off his busty secretary, right on the table before the crowd, in the middle of denying recent stories of UFO abduction. He literally explodes with passion, revealing that he was a malfunctioning robot, and his discombobulated pieces are sucked aboard a giant egg-shaped UFO above the Pentagon. The busty secretary gets airlifted along with them and is deposited unceremoniously on the floor in front of an obvious robot—small, blue and funny-looking—which immediately comes on to her and ends up smoking with her in bed. After some discussion on whether or not sex can really be any good with a toaster, they end up having a nice Jewish wedding. The heroine of the film's tie-in/concluding episode, "Taarna," is an albino-white Valkyrie in red and black armor, recognizable by a unique birthmark, a member of a long-presumed-dead underground megalithic race that wars with Military Industrial Complexes whenever they arise. She flies to wherever she is needed on her accompanying beast, and founds and protects her own bloodline to continue her work in future times.

Horror director Tobe Hooper—immediately before directing *Poltergeist* for Steven Spielberg (see below)—did 1981's *The Funhouse* for Universal. Uncharacteristically, a novelization of the Larry Block screenplay was written by new horror novelist Dean R. Koontz (under the early pseudonym of "Owen West") and advertised on television several months before release of the film. There are noteworthy differences between the movie and the novelization, and Koontz's proximity to the project renders the question inevitable as to whether those differences began or ended with him or with Hooper and Block. Though Koontz was not yet a household name in the horror business, he had written dozens of novels in the field prior (see Chapter 9), and was just emerging as a new mainstream publishing product. Koontz's novelization is more organized and straightforwardly presented than the movie's, though the film reflects more UFOlogical elements on its surface. The screen presentation is done in the style of the most nightmarish propaganda movies made during wartime, which is to say that while the basic elements are correct, they are shown in a misleading fashion. In keeping with the idea of increased propagandization during the Reagan-Bush years, *The Funhouse* is a film accurately reflecting the worst possible report of an initial UFO abduction.

The novelization is about a carnival barker's revenge scheme against his former wife, whom he blames for his inability to produce anything but deformed offspring. In the movie, that plot is completely eliminated, though all the other elements remain essentially the same. Four teenagers on a double-date decide to stay the night in a carny funhouse, and they witness a rape and murder committed by the carnival barker's hideously deformed albino son. The monster albino tracks down and kills the young witnesses in the fully automated funhouse, providing a horrorfest of rape-abduction, terrifying robots, and mutant albino offspring similar to those described in the worst accounts of UFO abductions. Actual accounts tend to describe only the initial abduction encounter in so nightmarish a fashion, and the offspring are never said to be hideous, or even deformed, but they are described as being exceptionally white and as sporting the same stringy white hair seen on the murdering rapist-monster in the movie. Only one girl (and her younger brother, who does not actually spend the night in the funhouse but does encounter its monster occupant) survives the night and is seen at the movie's conclusion nightmarishly sleepwalking home in a state of shock, the mechanical fat-lady atop the abduction horror-house mocking her with its winding-down laughter. The younger brother too, merely from having witnessed the monster occupant, is in a state of mute shock, unable to speak a word about his encounter and attempted abduction.

Though some of the plot and production elements could be considered nothing more than coincidental with UFO abduction phenomena, the lot of them together do appear to strike a more deliberate note. Automata and mannequins are present throughout the movie, from beginning to end. The younger brother plays a trick on his sister at the start, leaving a dummy head in his bed to frighten her. *The Bride of Frankenstein* plays on the T.V. in the background, establishing the girl's role to come: the albino mutant in the carnival is seen wearing a Frankenstein's monster costume and mask before revealing itself as an inhuman creature, and Frankenstein's monster is essentially nothing more than a robot or golem itself. As if to deliver final punctuation to the underlying ghoulish abduction proceedings of the movie, the girl's date uses the colloquial phrase "Earth to Mars" to her, when she seems not to understand a joke he is telling.

20th Century Fox's *The Entity,* from Frank de Felitta's novel purportedly based (at least to some extent) on a true story, dramatized repeat nocturnal bedroom assaults on an average suburban widowed mother, played by Barbara Hershey. Hershey goes through the usual stages that UFO abductees do, and the case—if true, as advertised—may actually have been an abduction case that was poorly understood. Hershey finds herself being sometimes forcibly raped, and other times more pleasurably seduced, by an invisible force that she cannot escape or refuse. She knows nothing of its nature, except for its obviously being male. Her assaults leave physical marks, equating to the Unidentified Body Markings found on abductees. Many elements in the story are plainly overdramatized, no case either of UFO abduction or parapsychology on record to back them—the entity, for instance, is witnessed assaulting the woman (it visibly presses its fingers into her breasts), and at one point is temporarily imprisoned in a pre-staged liquid helium trap (which the parapsychologists arrange to determine whether the invading entity has actual mass). Accepting the inevitable, Hershey ultimately merely announces to the presence that obviously she cannot deny it, but she can refuse to cooperate. At the end of the movie, it is announced that the woman on whom Hershey's character was based has moved to another location, and that the assaults upon her continue but have decreased in both frequency and intensity. Both the dramatized reaction and the elements contained in this final declaration are true, as concerning actual UFO abductees—they tend to ultimately accept what is happening to them, with greater and lesser degrees of upset or concern (some barely even bothered by the occurrences), and there are consistent and predictable declines in abduction activity as those who undergo it age.

One curious 1981 T.V. series was *The Greatest American Hero,* starring ex-*I Spy* Robert Culp as another agent (this time FBI), who by circumstance becomes a mutual UFO abductee with average guy on the street William Katt. Little Green Men impress the pair with a ride around the solar system—showing them their own devastated red planet of origin—and enlist their aid in making the world a better place. They give Katt a "super-suit" and periodically return to check on how the two are doing. Certain no one will believe them, they keep their experience secret, which is difficult for Culp since the Bureau gives him periodic lie-detector tests. They are uncomfortable even talking about it between themselves, one saying something like, "Uh, they were, you know, they came back, last night," the other grimacing and looking about as if someone might overhear, responding, "Uh, you mean the, the Little Green Guys?" The saucer occupants come and go unexpectedly, communicate obliquely but make themselves understood, and later make use of implants (given by robots) for direct conversation. In the pilot, they even raise the dead. Typical of the Reagan era, the interesting premise quickly became just another car chase show, with more exotic background trappings and Commie and Neo-Nazi villains.

The most important movie in terms of abduction phenomena in the '80s was a Spielberg film, released by MGM/UA, which is interesting in light of everything so far discussed. This entry was not overtly UFO-related, or even directed by Spielberg, but was produced and overseen by him—1982's grossly overrated *Poltergeist*. Frequently insulting to its audience's intelligence, it does at least manage some genuine chills and emotions in its portrayal of everyday people confronting unknown phenomena that assault them out of the blue. A little girl, adorably played by Heather O'Rourke (who, strangely enough, died prematurely soon after, as did co-star Dominique Dunne, two of those stranger-than-fiction coincidences that do sometimes occur), finds herself talking to an off-the-air T.V. set at night, answering questions no one can hear. Things begin moving around the house within a day or two, stretching the limits of what anyone in the family ever wanted to know about the unknown, though mother Jobeth Williams at least initially tries to understand them. Husband Craig T. Nelson, like Barney Hill, does not share his wife's enthusiasm, and he practically goes into shock rather than have to confront the problem. It isn't too much longer before—amid bright flashing lights and swirling objects in an invisible whirlwind—little Heather is bodily spirited away, as was her predecessor in *Close Encounters* five years before.

The movie degenerates dreadfully from that point on, but other abduction elements in it include an animated jester-clown doll attacking a little boy at night and a discussion by Williams with her husband about the nature of sleepwalking—little Heather's walks to the inaudibly talking T.V. at night remind Williams of her own sleepwalking incidents around age nine or ten, making her wonder if the condition isn't hereditary. That is a very interesting question to which there doesn't seem to be a real-life textbook answer, but abduction research has found that there is a great likelihood for abductees' children to become abductees themselves. Sleepwalking in childhood is a definite symptom—which doesn't mean that all sleepwalkers are abductees, but that all abductees are sleepwalkers.

The same year, MGM released *Endangered Species,* which presented cattle mutilations as part of a top-secret government weapons project being conducted in isolated territories. New Colorado sheriff Jobeth Williams and transplanted alcoholic burnout urban police detective Robert Urich join forces to discover law enforcement agent Hoyt Axton's paid cooperation with the military. Once compromised, Axton finds himself infected with a deadly disease concocted by his clandestine military benefactors, which causes his body to explode. In the end—unlike any occurrence that has happened in real life—Williams and Urich manage to expose the secret project and bring it to termination. Also unlike any real-life occurrence, the cattle mutilations themselves have not been linked to the military, but to UFO activity. The film shows industrial lasers cutting the cows, beyond any earthly technology at the time the mutilations first began being reported on any large scale in the mid-to-late 1960s—and, for that matter, probably beyond any technology that we possess today. Admittedly, the military has been witnessed by law-enforcement officials going into cattle mutilation sites *after* the fact, in unmarked helicopters, and in some instances they have even left standard scalpels behind; but the primary activity has never believably been shown or explained as achievable by anyone on Earth.

Spielberg's famous *E.T.: The Extraterrestrial* was Universal's major release for 1982. It can only be considered Spielberg's most personal film since its most famous image—a boy riding through the sky on a bicycle, across the face of the Moon, led by a friendly extraterrestrial—is the logo for his Amblin Entertainment company. The often heartwrenching (if overly manipulative) story of a boy and his newfound alien companion was the forerunner of the famous MJ-12 disinformation campaign and could indeed be argued to be its source—the hook on the MJ-12 story is that of a dying alien far from home, exactly as in the film. Aside from that, *E.T.* does contain UFO-logically accurate material that was not then publicly known—most notably, in the unique personal bond between a single UFO entity and a human child. Abductees frequently say that they are "linked" to their extraterrestrial controllers, exactly as Egyptian ushabti figures or the "Porters of Horus" were linked to the Pharaoh in ancient Coffin Texts. E.T. and his young personal friend, Eliot, are so psychically linked in the movie that each feels the other's emotions at all times, and Eliot can sense what the alien is thinking as well, serving as a personal translator when the government moves in on them both. The government is shown to closely monitor UFO contactees, both personally and through electronic surveillance, for which there is also very good evidence in real life.

Though the handling is typically childlike, a trademark of Spielberg's work, there is one far more realistic element in this movie than in his earlier *Close Encounters*—Eliot's initial meeting with the extraterrestrial is frightening and traumatic. *Close Encounters'* little boy is immediately all smiles when confronted with the unknown, which is rare if not unheard-of in actual abduction experiences. Eliot's overcoming of his initial fear, and even his coming to somewhat enjoy the experience—even if it does disrupt his daily life—are much more common reactions. There is an additionally realistic scene that was not popularly known at the time the movie was made, a lengthy staring between Eliot and E.T. in his bedroom, which leaves Eliot so tired that he falls asleep.

Universal the same year also released Paul Schrader's remake of the 1942 RKO classic, *Cat People,* starring Malcolm McDowell and Nastassia Kinski as descendants of an ancient non-human race from Africa. Their line transform into predatory feline killers any time they foolishly mate with ordinary mortals, and are incapable of returning to their humanoid form until they have tasted the blood of men. They can only propagate when mated with their own brothers and sisters. The alien race's sex with mankind is dissatisfactory unless kinky and sadistic, and Kinski is completely amnesiac of her nocturnal hunting until brother McDowell appears to her in a dream and explains the curse of their bloodline. Screenwriter Alan Ormsby—most famous prior as the co-author of Geneni's 1972 schlock entry, *Children Shouldn't Play with Dead Things*—showed knowledge of historical and mythological mating customs, the gods' successors and those of ancient royal lines around the world being the offspring of mated half-brothers and -sisters.

In 1983, a bizarre pseudo-documentary, almost along the lines of *Alternative 3* six years before (see previous chapter), aired on network T.V. Called *Special Bulletin,* it dramatized a threat by renegade government atomic scientists turned terrorists to detonate an atomic device in their possession, if the world superpowers did not agree to universal disarmament of nuclear weapons. Done in documentary style, the program showed real-time enacted events, as related by a T.V. news team, incorporating the fiction that everything being seen was occurring live. Like Orson Welles' famous *The War of the Worlds* fraud forty-five years before, continual reminders were telegraphed across the bottom of the screen that this was a dramatized presentation and not an actual event, but also like its famous predecessor, a great many calls were made to news stations across the country to see if it was in fact true. Two more T.V. movies of exactly the same type would be seen in years to come, 1994's Halloween Eve presentation, *Without Warning* and the 1996 *Special Report: Journey to Mars* (see Chapter 11).

David Cronenberg, the Canadian horror director of many UFO-logically-related movies, released a strange nightmarish cult film through Universal called *Videodrome* in 1983. It starred famous psycho-player James Woods as a sleaze mainline T.V. producer hot on the trail of an underground phenomenon called "Videodrome," which may or may not be making actual snuff-films for a high-priced and secret clientele. Radio talk-show host and pop-psychologist Deborah Harry, his latest sexual conquest, develops an unhealthy desire to get even closer to the film's production level, being an intense masochist who fails to find satisfaction even when whipped and burned by cigarettes. She disappears after beginning her own private search, and Woods finds himself trying to track her—and Videodrome—down. Videodrome's producers begin sending him tapes, which produce increasing hallucinations in his mind caused by an unknown technological process. Those hallucinations put Woods in progressively more violent sexual encounters with Harry, all in an entirely red-and-black limbo setting. Videodrome's producers ultimately reveal to him that they are clandestine government weapons contractors experimenting with extremely dangerous technology, and that he has been their target for some time, since they want control of his T.V. station to expose a mass audience to the lethally homicidal impulses of Videodrome. Toward this end, they have been utilizing debilitating hallucinations and Harry's own image (who they murdered shortly after she entered their arena) to seduce him further and further into their deadly game, programming him into a Manchurian Candidate who assassinates the opposition for them. Though Woods partly succeeds in putting a kink in their plans, he does follow his final hypnotic order to commit suicide before anyone can question him.

1983 produced one of the anti-military and peripherally UFO-related movies of the decade, MGM/UA's *War Games.* Overproduced and overlong, it became a huge anti-war hit in a long pro-war decade. Matthew Broderick plays a precocious computer-genius who inadvertently breaks into the Pentagon's nuclear computer. He mistakes the computer for a game, and the computer—a genuine artificial intelligence, in the movie—mistakes him for its inventor, since he has gained access to its memory. "Shall we play a game?" it asks, and Broderick calls up "Global Thermonuclear War" from its menu. Unable to distinguish between fantasy and reality, the computer arms America's missiles for an actual launch against the Soviet Union. Its alienated ex-Defense Department inventor is brought in before it can carry out Armageddon, convincing it that, like tic-tac-toe, nuclear exchange is strictly a no-win game between equal opponents. As if to provide a necessary balance, MGM/UA's extremely propagandistic pro-war melodrama, *Red Dawn,* was released the same year.

Canada's popular Second City Television characters, Bob and Doug MacKenzie, appeared in United Artists' 1983 mind-control spoof called *Strange Brew,* with Ewan Cameron-inspired lunatic asylum head Max Von Sydow working in shadowy collusion with corrupt governmental figures to drug the world with beer, then manipulate the populace with music to become an instant army. Interlopers who cannot be murdered find themselves framed and sent to his asylum to become experimental subjects utilizing cruder techniques. Two years later, another of the decade's curiously anti-war movies was produced, *The Manhattan Project* (Gladden/20th Century Fox), in which another teen genius builds a real atomic bomb in his garage as a class project, nearly triggering an incident before it can be defused.

Films critical of the military or the Pentagon were being lavishly produced and distributed at least twenty to thirty years before Oliver

Stone made it his career. Stanley Kubrick began a campaign in the field which hasn't ended, starting with his early *Paths of Glory* in 1957 (Warner Bros,), continuing with the brilliant Cold War satire *Dr. Strangelove—or, How I Learned to Stop Worrying and Love the Bomb* in 1964 (produced in England through Columbia), and most recently, *Full Metal Jacket*'s (Warner Bros.) bitter indictment of Vietnam in 1987. If the Intelligence establishment has an educational campaign on UFOs, it is not always in accord with the military. Not only did the military refuse cooperation with Robert Wise and 20th Century Fox in 1951's *The Day the Earth Stood Still,* but they also refused to cooperate with Steven Spielberg when he did *Close Encounters* a quarter of a century later. J. Allen Hynek and four Washington security men who had been present during the 1952 White House flyovers were Spielberg's only official advisors for the project. NASA—who, it will be recalled, refused any cooperation with the producers of *Capricorn One* in 1978—wrote Spielberg a twenty-page letter on the subject after reading his initial shooting script, not disclosing anything at all concerning its relative accuracy, but simply attempting to dissuade him from doing it altogether. That letter was what made a "true believer" out of the young director.

A busy year for MGM/UA, 1983 in addition to *War Games* and *Red Dawn* saw the studio's release of purported UFO abductee Whitley Strieber's *The Hunger.* Atmospherically directed by *Alien* director Ridley Scott's brother Tony, the film starred international sex symbol Catherine Deneuve as a near-immortal humanoid mutant prolonging her unnatural life with blood transfusions from a series of willing and unwilling lovers. Biologist Susan Sarandon discovers Deneuve's nature, and falls under her hypnotic spell to become the vampire's newest blood-sucked bedpartner. Meanwhile, former lover David Bowie finds himself no longer able to sustain his vampire-transformed body, and is "retired" by Deneuve to join the wasted, paralyzed ranks of all her previous companions. Bowie and Sarandon ultimately lead a rebellion of Deneuve's cast-away conquests, draining the life out of the vampire and putting her away in their stead.

Warner Bros. produced *Gremlins* in 1983, about little green men from ancient China that terrorize a small American town, and in

1984 released *Twilight Zone: The Movie. Twilight Zone* featured two episodes scripted by original series mainstay Richard Matheson, one of which was his most famous story, "Nightmare at 20,000 Feet." In the original, William Shatner (Matheson's favorite actor of juvenile leads) played the only man on a commercial flight who could see an apelike gremlin dismantling one of the plane's engines. In the end, he succeeds in blowing open a window and shooting the creature dead. In the film version, phobic John Lithgow accomplishes the same feat, with one major difference: the gremlin is bulletproof. The creature is a pop-eyed little man that moves swiftly and stiffly, like an automaton. It bites the barrel off of Lithgow's pistol and nearly kills him, but changes its mind when it sees the plane is making its final approach for landing. Its fun spoiled, it smiles at Lithgow and wags a finger to scold him, then shoots up into the sky with amazing speed. Two more famous Matheson stories, *Duel,* filmed by Steven Spielberg as an ABC/Universal 1971 T.V. movie, and *Trilogy of Terror,* another movie for the same network in 1974, featured virtual automata: the former was the forerunner to Stephen King's *Maximum Overdrive,* with a truck whose driver is never seen terrorizing Dennis Weaver out on the road; and the latter's episode "Prey" starred Karen Black as a woman under siege by a Zuni Indian warrior doll animated by black magic. The other episode scripted by Matheson for *Twilight Zone: The Movie* was an adaptation of the original series' "It's a Good Life," from Jerome Bixby's short story. In it, adults are abducted into a nightmare world of no escape and terrorized by a little boy whose every merest thought comes to pass.

Universal's *The Last Starfighter* in 1984—the Reagan-era version of the Carter-era's *Battle Beyond the Stars*—depicted the recruitment of Earth people for cosmic combat. Video arcade teenagers are unaware that the game that is the title of the movie is actually a test module being employed by aliens to discover aptitude for vimana-piloting. Selected individuals are briefly abducted, replaced by clones to cover their departure, then returned. Eventually, they introduce themselves openly to the general public before permanently disembarking on a volunteer basis. The same studio released another movie that year called *Repo Man,* featuring alien corpses from a government lab hidden in the trunk of a stolen '64 Chevy Malibu. The next year's *Enemy Mine* from 20th Century Fox was most typical of the Reagan years: though set in outer space, it was nothing but a simplistic World War II script of two enemies putting aside their differences in order to survive, replacing Allied-and-Axis with Human-and-Lizard. *Aliens,* Fox's 1986 sequel to 1979's Carter-era *Alien,* became much more a good-guys-vs.-bad-guys war movie than the resistance to amoral corporate greed that was its predecessor's subject. 1984's *Starman* (Columbia) created a body out of a dead man's DNA, resurrected a deer, and impregnated a barren woman. 20th Century Fox's *The Adventures of Buckaroo Banzai Across the Eighth Dimension* the same year comically suggested more or less the proposition here under consideration: that Orson Welles' *The War of the Worlds* broadcast was a deliberate double-bluff by the government to conceal the reality of Martian invaders. Interestingly, as a side-note, the extraordinarily pacifistic H. G. Wells was in British Intelligence during WWI. Roger Corman's New World Cinema release for the year was *Dreamscape*, a psychic warfare piece about a nefarious vice president utilizing CIA "dream assassins" to invade the president's mind while he sleeps and murder him in his bed; such projects were experimented with by the Russians early in psychic research, and the United States is now known to have engaged in psychic spying—and quite possibly similar experiments in psychic assassination—as well.

Orion released *The Terminator* in 1984, best known for having given star Arnold Schwarzenegger his most famous line: "I'll be back." Based largely on Harlan Ellison's *Outer Limits* and *Star Trek* teleplays twenty years prior, Schwarzenegger's title character was an unstoppable robot from the future—another in a long line of similar golems seen in cinema throughout the '80s—sent back in time to assassinate the mother of a man who, once born, will bring about the end of robot domination in its time. Carolco—the same company that starred Schwarzenegger in Philip K. Dick's UFOlogically accurate *Total Recall* in 1990 (see previous chapter)—did the sequel in 1991, near the end of George Bush's presidency. *Terminator 2* featured a "kinder, gentler" Terminator, who only permanently maimed hundreds of people, instead of murdering two or three indiscriminately, while attempting to complete its assignment—ironically, at the same time as unparalleled U.S. military might wrought havoc across Iraq. The sequel added another UFOlogical element in the Terminator's new mission: robot Schwarzenegger is now out to demonstrate to the inventor of his prototype that the technology he is using to do so comes from Schwarzenegger's future time. In tune with UFOs, that superior technology—a new form of microchip—was recovered by the military from the first robot's wreckage and is being exploited in top-secret, compartmentalized Department of Defense research.

1984 was appropriately enough the year in which a new version of George Orwell's *1984* was produced in Britain, with John Hurt and Richard Burton. It had seen several productions before, one on British television authored by Nigel Kneale and another British movie version in 1955. The production was faithful and nightmarish, and perfectly timed to coincide with a highly conservative "Newspeak" era of its own in the real world. While Orwell's classic continues to apply realistically as a commentary on politics and human nature, it also displays some of the very characteristics that initially alarmed authorities concerning UFO abductions. The central question about UFOs must always have been just what the intelligence behind it all was doing to the bodies and minds of the people it repeatedly abducted, especially since, in at least some instances, painful "stress tests" were part of that process. Hypnosis and mental domination are featured in the movie, Burton torturing Hurt to the limits of his endurance and then saying calmly, "Look in my eyes," just as the UFO abductors do, proceeding at that point to fill his mind with whatever he wants Hurt to believe—classic brainwashing, in other words. The saddest commentary on the entire affair, as pertains to the UFO question, is that the UFO intelligence doesn't seem to be using it for personal intimidation and moral disintegration, where unfortunately some of the tests done for the CIA's near-identical MK-ULTRA program have.

Another movie from 1984 is worthy of mention, not because it was any good, but precisely because it was bad, and because of the accuracy of its material: *Evils of the Night*. Starring Tina Louise and Julie Newmar in throwaway roles as sexy space-siren scientists, perennial ancient John Carradine as their alien supervisor, and rugged

Neville Brand as a hired-hand abductor in a one-piece gray jumpsuit with facemask, the film concerns the appropriation of an abandoned hospital by flying saucer occupants and their ongoing theft of genetic material from sixteen- to twenty-four-year-olds kidnapped from lover's lane. The aliens take blood from their victims in order to extend their own already long lives. No questions are answered by the end of eighty-six long minutes filled mostly with gratuitous sex scenes, the aliens ultimately departing when Louise is killed (how, why, and by whom not being shown). The aliens' origins are never disclosed, but interestingly enough, the picture was made by a company calling itself "Mars Productions."

One important entry in terms of apparent foreknowledge is the 1985 Columbia/Tri-star/Golan-Globus-produced British film *Lifeforce*, which takes some UFOlogically correct departures from its source material, Colin Wilson's *The Space Vampires*. It shows NASA secretly recording pictures of a miles-long cylindrical spaceship seen against the surface of the Moon (unlike the one described in the novel), fully four years before *Phobos 2* recorded exactly the same kind of UFOs over Phobos and Mars and at least the same number of years before such cylindrical ships traveling across the Moon were popularly televised on *Sightings*. Repeat nocturnal sex-abductions *à la* Antonio Villas Boas occur, with hypnosis later used to penetrate the amnesia block perpetrated by the aliens on their victims. The alien leader is a phenomenally perfect super-hypnotic human female bonding uniquely with a given Earth male abductee, who performs acts of sabotage for her if ordered to. The abductee helps the government team, but openly states that his allegiance is to the alien female, with whom—like real abductees, and again, unlike the novel—he feels more kinship than he does with his fellow man, even if she should prove to be dangerous to humanity itself. Once more typical of the Reagan Era—Reagan had, after all, been involved in Army Intelligence making propaganda films during WWII—the aliens are of course hostile, literally attempting to devour the entire human race. Dan O'Bannon, of several relatively accurate UFOlogical movies already mentioned, helped write the screenplay. It is worth noting that Menahem Golan is another of Roger Corman's protégés.

The same year, Guy Hamilton, frequent Bond director for MGM/UA, made a pilot film for an Orion series that never flew, but should have. Based on the prolific Warren Murphy-Richard Sapir action-adventure paperback series *The Destroyer,* it starred Fred Williams as the title character *Remo Williams,* a specially recruited blue-collar hit-man for a very small, elite, secret team of offshoot government agents who enforce "The 11th Commandment": "Thou Shalt Not Get Away With It." Surprisingly anti-military for the decade in which it was produced, this film featured a villain who was a psychopathic defense contractor defrauding the government of untold billions on a number of Star Wars weapons projects designated as "Harp" (High Altitude Research Project), not a single working prototype of which has been produced, even as it is theoretically in its later developmental stages. The same contractor manufactures faulty rifles that blow up in soldiers' faces, and sees to it that any reports confirming the design flaw are deliberately buried, sooner than spend the relatively minor retooling costs required to fix it. (This last actually occurred during Vietnam, with the notoriously easy-to-break M-16, many parts of which were manufactured by the First Lady's family company.) The "Harp" in *Remo Williams* is never defined, only shown to be connected to some form of satellite technology. Its name, however, cannot be merely coincidental with the not-yet-publicly-disclosed top-secret HAARP experiments actually being run by the military. 1985 was also the year 20th Century Fox's cuddly *Cocoon* presented ancient Atlantean invaders as friendly symbiotic parasites, which rejuvenate old human beings to the benefit of both races.

In 1986, Charles Band released a bizarre comedy for Empire Pictures rife with UFOlogical elements, called *Troll*. Obviously produced as a novelty item or someone's idea of a joke, it starred such diverse people as Sonny Bono, Shelley Hack, Michael Moriarty, and June Lockhart—the lattermost with her own daughter, Anne, fresh out of *Battlestar Galactica,* on hand to play her younger self. The story concerns an apartment complex whose tenants are being gradually "body-snatched" by a troll from a fairy dimension, and a rival faction of fairy-folk who cotton-on to his design and try to drive him back where he came from. The trolls and the fairies fought a war in ages past, with the former locked away in their own little world. Lockhart is the Fairy Queen who calmly reveals this history to an aware teenager, blasting away little goons with her magic spear in between cups of Mr. Coffee. Throughout the film, a running gag is used to the best comedic effect in the whole movie, which is the viewing of a bad sci-fi movie with characters who keep repeating, "It *looks* like my sister ... it *acts* like my sister ... but it's really a *pod person from the planet Mars!!!*" The joke actually recurs to the point that it finally becomes, "It may *look* like your parakeet, and *act* like your parakeet, *but ...*" Band's *Zone Troopers* came out at the same time, about WWII Americans and a crash-landed extraterrestrial called "Bug" (for his insectoid appearance) siding together against the Nazis—who bring Hitler in person to see the alien! Intent on writing about their experience with the friendly Bug, but knowing no one will believe it, one of the soldiers involved presents the entire story as fiction in a sci-fi pulp magazine. The same year, Roger Corman's wife Julie produced Jim Wynorski's *Killbots,* about malfunctioning mechanical assassins in a shopping mall (one of the movie's alternate titles was *Chopping Mall*), which say "Have a nice day" after dispatching their prey. She also continued to produce other UFOlogically-related films, in particular bringing some of Isaac Asimov's work to the screen.

A similar movie was made by independent producer Wade Williams in 1986, *Midnight Movie Massacre* (a.k.a. *Attack from Mars*). *The Man from Planet X*'s Robert Clarke and *The War of the Worlds'* Ann Robinson spoof themselves in films-within-a-film, the former appearing as the hero of *Space Patrol: Guardians of the Universe* and the latter as the *Sweater Girl from Mars*. These mock 1956 "classics" play in Kansas City, Missouri's, Granada Theater, to an oddball assortment of audience fruitcakes who find themselves unknowingly besieged by an actual vampire beast from Mars.

The same year, Larry Cohen finished his *It's Alive* "trilogy" with *It's Alive III: Island of the Alive.* The movie examines—as did the first, to some extent—how being the parents of one of the mutant babies has adversely affected the parents' lives. The mother becomes an alcoholic prostitute in an attempt to drown her sorrows and not be recognized, and the father leaves a successful professional career to become a shoe salesman because his colleagues are uncomfortable around him. He also discovers no woman will have sex with him, because they are afraid he will impregnate them with similar "monsters." The movie begins with a judge sentencing the mutant baby and all its kin to life on an island removed from humanity. When he dies, a new judge takes the bench, and changes his predecessor's policy (much in the same way Reagan appears to have changed the government's treatment of the UFO question after his predecessor, Carter)—the offspring are to be tracked down and eradicated, with or without the help of the parents. The protagonist of the piece finds he does not like the idea of his child being murdered by an armed party, whether it is fully human or not, and the reluctant mother finds herself—like many UFO abductees—becoming sympathetic to the monsters' plight when they return to present her with her grandchildren and seek emotional support.

Universal's fantasy-UFOlogical entry for 1986 was *Howard the Duck,* a big-budget flop based on the phenomenal (but short-lived) cult hit Marvel comic book of 1975, which even state-of-the-art special effects from George Lucas' Industrial Lights and Magic could not save. The title character is an intelligent, smart-ass fowl from another galaxy, transported accidentally to Earth by a U.S. government secret experiment. Falling in love with adorable rock-'n-roll naif Lea Thompson, he is first exploited by quintessential idiot Tim Robbins—who compares Howard's arrival to studies proving that Aztec pyramids were connected to Mars (obviously a deliberate deprecation, given its humorous effect in the film)—and later saves Earth from invasion by the Dark Overlords, a hostile race of Lovecraftian E.T.s who possess the body of scientist Jeffrey Jones to provide them a bridge for entry, and abduct Thompson to become one of their unwilling "hosts."

1987 saw 20th Century Fox's release of probably the most influential science-fiction monster movie since their own *Alien,* eight years prior, in *Predator.* Another of the seemingly endless links forging the chain of Arnold Schwarzenegger's science-fictional action-adventure films, *Predator* is far less science-fictional than it appears on the surface. The story is simply one of survival between two species in the jungles of Earth: human and alien. Commando Schwarzenegger and his clandestine team encounter, in true Roger Corman style, an unseen third player in the unending game between him and his standard human enemies. The title alien is simply an interplanetary hunter, who happens to prefer the game of man. It conceals itself with a technological cloaking-device, such as those actually reported by many witnesses to UFOs, not making the creature completely invisible, but distorting the nearby air sufficiently to create its effect. The alien's activities have even been more or less verified by famous researcher Jacques Vallee, occurring by what appear to be airborn automata of an unknown nature in South America. The unknown devices are called *chupas* by the natives they attack. These resemble box-kites and are of similar dimensions, striking nocturnal hunters in the forests with light-beams that leave physical marks and cause temporary paralysis, lasting fatigue, and decreased blood cell count, and often eventual death.

The sequel, *Predator 2*, came out in 1990 in the middle of CIA President George Bush's tenure in office, transplanting the action to the "war on drugs" in an inner city in America, and adding credence to the idea that such movies are often used as propagandistic deflection. Not only is the "war" not believable, but there is a scene involving a drug-lord's supposed skinning alive of a rival that is plainly intended to be based on Adolfo de Jesus Constanzo and his Matamoros drug cult—but Jesus Constanzo appears very much to have been CIA-connected himself, as do many inner-city drug dealers, and their real-life actions are motivated for entirely different reasons than those being popularly presented in the media.

A "curious coincidence" occurs in 1987's misfire comedy, *Real Men*, which appears to have borrowed partially from the MJ-12 government conspiracy mythos for its background premise of aliens working in behind-the-scenes cooperation with world governments. Less obvious than *The Greatest American Hero*, it ends with newly recruited civilian spy John Ritter meeting the aliens in an isolated wood. To his surprise, they are completely human in appearance, friendly, and interested in exchanging ideas, cultural knowledge and gifts, commenting on how much their world is enjoying the newly acquired pastime of baseball. At one point, spy-recruiter James Belushi comments that the most sensationalized tabloid headlines about UFOs are straight out of the CIA secret files. The curious coincidence occurs when Belushi is abducted by a seemingly shy wallflower-cum-whip-mistress, who turns the tables on his cavalier pickup approach. She knocks him out, binds him to a mobile metallic frame, administers whippings and electro-shock treatments, and interrogates him and breaks down his defenses, all ending with a night of bondaged sex so wild that Belushi wants only to retire and settle down with her. The sexual sado-masochistic aspect of UFO abductions was not written about publicly until David Jacobs' *Secret Life* in 1992, though it probably appeared in folklorist Thomas Bullard's exhaustive two-volume FUFOR-funded abduction study, privately published the same year the movie was made. Even if it was, it would be curious that a Hollywood screenwriter had gone to the trouble of reading it. It should be no surprise that *Real Men* was a United Artists release.

In conjunction with Carolco, Universal released John Carpenter's well-intentioned but failed homage to Nigel Kneale's *Five Million Years to Earth*, 1987's *Prince of Darkness*, which emulated the brilliant Brit's ideas (Carpenter scripted it himself, under the name "Martin Quatermass") but became muddled in excessive and unbelievable scientific explanations, coupled with believable but far too juvenile characters. Despite its failings, the story did present credible arguments for government suppression of UFO/ancient astronaut information, even if reduced via the realm of physics to the point of absurdity. (Jesus is presented as a wise extraterrestrial human guardian, but the devil is somehow nothing more than a mass of green inter-dimensional goo.) Donald Pleasance—a major Carpenter company player, all the way from the director's first low-budget blockbuster, *Halloween*—is a priest in the picture who explains to an interdisciplinary scientific team why such ancient truths were suppressed: "Apparently, a decision was made to characterize pure evil as a spiritual force—'the evil within, the darkness within the hearts of men.' It was more convenient. In that way, man remained at the center of things. A stupid lie. We were salesmen, that's all. We sold our ... 'product' to those who didn't have it—'New Life,' to reward ourselves, punish our enemies, so we could live without Truth. The substance—the malevolence—that was the Truth. Concealed, until now." The "we were salesmen" line, whether Carpenter knew it or not, has been repeated by more than one Apollo astronaut, which some people have used to substantiate the argument that NASA never made it to the Moon.

The same year, Trans World Entertainment released a comedy exactly as silly as its title, *Killer Klowns from Outer Space.* Giant-headed clowns in a UFO Big-Top assault the local citizenry in a small town with animated popcorn kernels and shadow puppets, turn their victims into literal ventriloquist dummies, and abduct human beings aboard their ship in giant bulbs of sticky cotton candy. Thank God the heroes of the piece had seen enough Keystone Cops serials to ultimately elude the kidnapping conundrums, finally dispatching them with nothing more than a good solid punch in the nose.

New World Cinema and premiere splatterpunk-horror auteur Clive Barker released the first of the ongoing *Hellraiser* series in 1987, the most recent incarnation of which was Paramount's *Hellraiser IV: Bloodline* in 1996. Most likely inspired (at least in part) by Charles Band's 1986 Lovecraft entry, *From Beyond* (Barker's original novella was written the same year Band's movie came out), Mario Bava's classic 1960 AIP vampire film noir, *Black Sunday,* and to some degree famous British horror author R. Chetwynd-Hayes' "The Gate Crasher" (which opened Amicus' 1973 anthology film *From Beyond the Grave),* Barker's 1988 16th Fantasy Film Festival *Le Grand Prix de la Section Peur* winner contained quite a few familiar UFO-related elements. In the series, adventurers acquire an exotically Arabic-looking sort of Rubik's cube (called by Barker in the novella "Lemarchand's box," i.e. "the Martians' box") which is supposed to be the key to a realm of ultimate pleasure. Once opened into a number of geometric shapes, Lemarchand's box creates passageways into other dimensions through which emerge the "Cenobites." The Cenobites (a word meaning a member of a religious order) arrive in flashes of light and walk through walls, wearing skintight leather garments and promising an eternity of sadistic sex. They are pierced and scarred in various grotesque ways, and bodily abduct into their nightmare Netherworld any who summon them, whether deliberately or by accident. Once summoned, the sinister Cenobites are impossible to get rid of—they ceaselessly pursue whoever opens a way for them into our world, repeatedly visiting their "contacts" with increasingly seductive promises of delights beyond understanding combined with coercive threats. Ultimately, they make any who summon them into fellow Cenobites of their macabre order. In line with UFO occupants, the last movie reveals that the Cenobites follow given bloodlines throughout the ages and are connected to other planets.

Barker's next cinematic entry, *Nightbreed,* was independently released by Morgan Creek/J&M Entertainment during George Bush's tenure in 1990, when most films of a UFOlogical nature were deliberately demonized (see next chapter). Adapted by Barker from his 1988 novella titled *Cabal, Nightbreed* concerns a mythical Underworld called Midian, a sort of afterlife cross between Hades and Shambhala, where strange shapeshifting folk called the Nightbreed live. No one knows exactly who the Nightbreed are, but they are essentially thought of as boogeymen—they feed on mortal interlopers into their territory. A mental patient named Boone inadvertently becomes an inductee to Midian, whose inhabitants can only die by misadventure and are otherwise immortal. When Boone is murdered by his own doctor, Decker (played by Canadian horror director David Cronenberg), the Nightbreed work their magic on Boone and resurrect him within their below-ground Midian community. Decker is a child-murderer who, in classic MK-ULTRA fashion, has utilized drugs and hypnosis to make Boone his fall-guy, convincing Boone that he is actually responsible for the crimes but is amnesiac of the fact. Once crossed-over to the Nightbreed, there is no return to the mortal world, though some of them occasionally "recruit" like-minded mortals to their ranks. One of them tells Boone in a casual, offhanded tone, impossible to discern as either serious or flippant, "It's all true: God is an astronaut. Oz *is* over the rainbow. Midian is where the monsters live. And you came here to die." There are hints of the Nightbreed's history from some of the older members, but it is clear that they are a separate race parallel to humanity, who live by choice and necessity away from their human cousins, primarily because they fought wars with humans in the past. The film ends with such an apocalyptic military confrontation between the two races, as Midian is discovered by fearful law enforcement authorities. Though losses are severe on both sides, the Nightbreed end by doing what they have always done in these inevitable confrontations—they move on to a new secret home.

Barker is not only aware of the extraterrestrial elements inherent in his writing but admits to their importance. On cable's Sci-Fi Channel, he discussed the fact in a between-shows filler: "These legends and folkloric structures ... throw us into the idea of what divinity might be. How do we divine God? We define gods as things—creatures, forms, spirits—that have powers beyond us. Great fantastic fiction, great fantastic movies, should be like breathing the air of another planet. We should feel as though our whole system is being conditioned to another state of being."

Weintraub Entertainment released *My Stepmother Is An Alien* in 1988, not too surprising a title from the same mindless decade that gave us such similar fare as *An American Werewolf In London*, *My Mom's a Werewolf*, *My Best Friend is a Vampire*, and *Buffy, the Vampire Slayer*. The Eighties and Nineties saw a slew of similar titles specifically devoted to alien sex-comedies as well, including *Earth Girls Are Easy*, *Sex and the Single Alien*, *Test Tube Teens from the Year 2000*, and *Beach Babes from Beyond*.

In *My Stepmother Is An Alien*, Kim Basinger stars as a beautiful blonde bombshell from the next galaxy, come to Earth to discover how SETI scientist Dan Aykroyd managed to accidentally transmit a beam to her homeworld that has inadvertently threatened their existence. Basinger at one point complains that the beam is unbelievably advanced, considering Earthmen "haven't figured out Stonehenge yet." She carries a computerized robot eye on a gooseneck lamp in her purse (with the voice of Ann Prentiss, sister to director Richard Benjamin's wife, Paula), which advises her on how to carry out her undercover mission of seducing Aykroyd. When her comically inappropriate behavior is noticed and she is asked where she came from, she answers, "the Nether Lands," pointedly separating the two words. (*Neteru*, from which we derive the word "netherworld," is the Egyptian name for the gods.) Though Basinger is supposed to carry out her mission in only twenty-four hours, she discovers that she likes sex, as well as divorcee Aykroyd's daughter, and accepts his proposal for marriage. The eye in the purse is not pleased, since the hidden agenda of their mission is to destroy the Earth once they have discovered the secret of what powered Aykroyd's beam; Earthmen might again discover the secret and threaten them. Basinger persuades the ruling council that sent her to spare the Earth for further study, and Aykroyd's brother (Jon Lovitz) volunteers to return to Basinger's homeworld in an exchange—once he discovers that everyone aboard the ship for the voyage home looks like her and is eager to learn about sex.

Aykroyd himself is one of the many Hollywood figures with an abiding interest in UFO studies and the paranormal. In 1984 and '89, he starred in and helped write the scripts for Columbia's *Ghostbusters* and *Ghostbusters 2,* both featuring comical encounters with Netherworld inhabitants. He returned to the alien realm of cinema in Paramount's 1992 release based on the sketch he made famous for *Saturday Night Live* many years before, *Coneheads,* which also featured interspecies mating as a subject for comedy. The biggest intentional joke in *Coneheads* is that the Alien Immigration Office is after actual aliens—whose typical escape line upon being suspected by their agents is, "We are from France."

Tim Burton's *Beetlejuice* (Warner Bros., 1988) was more or less a live-action cartoon—as its critics have aptly labeled it—about entities from "the Netherworld" interacting with sensitive people on Earth capable of perceiving them. In its later actual kids' cartoon format, also produced by Burton, these elements became much more "otherworldly" and comparable to alien abductions. Lydia, the girl most sensitive to the Netherworld presence, is periodically whisked away to join the bizarre people that live there or is joined by them in our world. Like many abductees, she is completely comfortable with them, perhaps even more so than with her own friends in the everyday world. Burton's later movies have contained a great many UFOlogical elements, as will be discussed in the next chapter.

John Carpenter and Universal presented the wry space-invader satire, *They Live,* the same year. Carpenter already had a long line of UFOlogically-related movies under his belt, being the director of the original *Halloween* movies and the 1983 remake of 1951's RKO classic, *The Thing from Another World*—all also from Universal—among others. *They Live* presented a vision of modern society as clandestinely mind-controlled by enormous-eyed, mask-faced, Gray-like aliens, who masquerade as Republican Yuppies in business suits. The aliens' techniques rival and echo those of the CIA's MK-ULTRA program, relying primarily on subliminals and hidden transmission signals to hypnotically effect brainwaves. The aliens succeed in their clandestine takeover through cooperation with seduced compatriots in the human community, whom they reward by teleporting them to their homeworld for faithful service.

The UFOlogically active MGM/UA studios' 1988 release was the first of their ongoing series of "mad mannequin on the loose" movies, *Child's Play.* In keeping with the other indestructible cinematic killers launched by John Carpenter's *Halloween* ten years before and carried on in that series and *Nightmare on Elm Street,* the monster of the piece was a supernaturally animated murderer from beyond the grave. Cheap hood Brad Dourif uses voodoo to transfer his soul into that of a child's toy doll, "Chucky." Adorable Chucky becomes the "pal" of Catherine Hicks' little boy, using him as an unwitting accomplice in carrying out a series of revenge murders against Dourif's enemies. Afterwards, Chucky pins the rap on the boy, with the doctors at the local asylum convinced the youngster has gone off the deep end in his tales of a walking, talking, lethal doll. Chucky is forced to return, however, to transfer his soul out of the doll and into the body of the little boy, and Hicks and heroic cop Chris Sarandon manage to put the murderous mannequin down ... until he came back for two Universal sequels in 1990 and 1991.

Laurel Productions came out with two syndicated T.V. series in the mid- to late-eighties, beginning with the vastly inferior—and much longer-running of the two—*Tales from the Darkside,* which oddly enough spawned a fairly decent movie years later. A poor-man's horror anthology, it presented at least two interesting alien stories. One was about a woman who finds herself trapped in someone's torture maze, which is unmanned and appears to be fully automated, who ultimately discovers she is in a spaceship. Another had Darren McGavin (in yet another of his recurring appearances in these types of shows) as an actor hired by a very strange young man (Lenny Von Dohlen) to come out of retirement after twenty years and reprise his role in a series that was cancelled after only one year. McGavin finally figures out after the project's completion and the man's departure that he was an alien who was only now receiving the show on his antennae out in space, whose people simply enjoy the mythic type of story he was involved in and so were disappointed when the series was cancelled before the storyline had reached completion. McGavin was right back in another project of the same type in *Darkside*'s short-lived companion show, *Monsters* (1988–90), in "Portrait of the Artist," playing a human-disguised alien who abducts hapless wayfarers and paralyzes them into permanent art exhibits to display back on his home planet.

As Reagan's presidency wound to an end, his likely successor, former CIA head and Vice President George Bush, already appeared to have begun exerting his influence on UFOlogical movies. Though the two men's visions were often similar, there would be a noticeable change in their recommended and approved cinematic approach. During Reagan's term, UFO phenomena were most often presented humorously, and sometimes as a threat. Under Bush, the exact opposite emphasis was to make itself felt: while sometimes shown as comical, UFOs and everything related to them were presented almost exclusively in a menacing and sometimes outright terrifying light, as in *From Beyond* and *Hellraiser.* Though there were notable exceptions, such as the aforementioned *The Abyss,* these were far less often to be seen.

11

Indoctrinations and Demonizations

resumably, the change in emphasis concerning UFOlogical movies during George Bush's term was to some considerable degree influenced by the Russians' loss of *Phobos 2* only two months after Bush took office. Certainly, a number of important changes took place on the geopolitical scene immediately following, the most visible of which was the coming down of the Berlin Wall. Congress was aggressively lobbied by the newly formed National Space Council's head, Vice President Dan Quayle, for tremendously increased funding to NASA's revived Search for Extraterrestrial Intelligence program (expanded to include searching *within* the solar system, as opposed to only without) and to the Ballistic Missile Defense Organization ("Star Wars") for even more sophisticated weaponry than had yet been generated for space use, including the previously cancelled X-30 National Aero-Space Plane.

In general, UFOlogical media presentations reflected the new administration's revived and greatly increased interest in placing the military in space, and the overall tenor became one of subtle but definite demonization of space invaders. In keeping with standard policy, when UFOs or the planet Mars were overtly encountered in drama, they were met with humor or derision, which had been the prevailing practice not only through Reagan's presidency, but all those prior.

533

Where *phenomena* associated with UFOs were dramatized, it was in a fearful and vigilant light, with a decided emphasis on solidarity and opposition. The intensive new xenophobia had a continual, subliminal message: *do not fraternize with the enemy.* And the enemy was anyone or anything not immediately identifiable as belonging to this world. Generally speaking, and atypically for a Democratic administration, Bill Clinton's presidency has differed very little from his predecessor's in terms of media UFO dramatizations. The overall result has been more or less a sixteen-year (and now going on twenty) effective dismantling of—and even active opposition to—whatever educational work on the subject was exemplified in the Jimmy Carter presidency.

The transition between Reagan's and Bush's influence began, logically enough (considering it was simply a transfer of power from the president to his own vice president), within a year or two of Bush's actually taking office. *Star Trek: The Next Generation* began in 1987, continuing halfway into Clinton's first term. Paramount's Canadian-produced 1987–89 *The War of the Worlds* Fox T.V. series began with the interesting premise of the original 1938 "Invasion from Mars" radio broadcast and 1953 movie being government fronts to conceal the truth of an actual invasion from Mars—a thesis seriously considered in these pages—which was successfully repelled in a secret Pentagon war in the past but has now resumed due to improved biological resistance on the part of the Martians. The Martians were made to look exactly like those in George Pal's movie (made by the same studio) and were body-snatchers in the classic "pod-people" sense. The show's second season completely reversed the situation, setting the action in a near-future where man's civilization is all but gone, collapsed in a morass of the most grotesque and rampant urban decay, in which the Martians barely bother any longer to conceal their presence. Like the revived "Invaders" on Fox T.V., they more openly took over, despoiling the Earth and reproducing off of us. Both of the series' two seasons were interesting, but drastic changes between them threw the very audience it had attained and limited the number of plots, ending it before its time. Running concurrently with the show was a nifty little supernatural reworking of *The Fugitive* called *Werewolf,* which opened every week with the words of a bounty hunter seeking a lycanthropic murder suspect whose transformation he once witnessed with his own eyes: "There are two kinds of people in the world: them that believe in flyin' saucers, and them that don't."

More or less a companion piece to T.V.'s *The War of the Worlds,* also produced by Paramount out of Canada and playing in Fox's same lineup over the same time period (but lasting one season longer, into 1990), was an odd little supernatural drama, *Friday the 13th: The Series.* Having nothing to do with the highly profitable movie series of the same name but merely capitalizing on it, *Friday the 13th* was an anthology operating on the premise that "cursed" *objects d'art* were in the world, distributed to prey upon the weak and greedy, which needed to be found and retrieved by the curio shop owners whose predecessor sold them. The shop owners essentially act as their own private intelligence service while trying to get the objects back, and discover people whose lives have been adversely affected by their literal exposure to the devil and his wiles. Often, those individuals echoed some of the characteristics of UFO abductees. One classic example from 1989 was "The Playhouse," about abused children who feed innocents from among their young peers to a life-size dollhouse, in return for supernatural powers and flights through other dimensions. As they do, the house becomes its own UFO, powerful lights playing around and through it with a whooshing noise. When the children are finally talked into renouncing the playhouse, all the other neighborhood children they have tricked into becoming abducted by it are returned, and all have no memory of their supernatural encounter. The series' pilot episode, for another example, was about an animated puppet-doll that linked uniquely with a given child, becoming her diabolical familiar and seducing her into criminal acts. Resistant to relinquishing her sinister companion, the little girl has to be fought in order to retrieve the devilish doll and is left in therapy over the incident afterward. The two-part episode "The Quilt of Hathor" in the series' second year had a red, white, and black quilt, utilized to send whomever slept beneath it into the dreams of their enemies, where they could murder them in a red, white, and black landscape. The use of an Egyptian goddess' name, combined with the Atlantean/Egyptian colors, is interesting enough, but is all the more so when combined with the very means by which the Egyptian gods and the biblical Watchers (not to mention UFO occupants) vistit the chosen: in their dreams. Additionally, it may be noted that the Egyptian word for the gods *(Neteru)* translates literally to "Watchers."

Friday the 13th star Louise Robey is another in the long line of performers with a coincidentally Intelligence-friendly background. The Montreal-born daughter of a London stage actress and an Air Force major, she was greatly traveled, multi-lingual, and educated in a number of European schools (in a number of countries, including England, Scotland, Norway, and Italy, as well as her native Canada), years before turning to television. One of the schools she attended, St. George's English School in Rome, "was filled with the sons and daughters of diplomats and journalists," as she told an interviewer in the premiere issue of *Femme Fatales* in 1992, "and people like my father, who attended the Navy defense college." Her foreign contacts included actor Klaus Kinski and French President Valerie Giscard d'Estaing, and she was well-known abroad for her singing and modeling ventures, including pictures in the *Paris Vogue*. Additionally, Robey not only admitted to a real-life interest in the occult (her first trip to Paris was prompted by a London psychic, and she purportedly knows quite a bit about Wicca), but actually mentioned in a May 1990 *Fangoria* interview that she "seriously" believed her teenage agoraphobia (fear of open spaces) "was part of a government experiment to see how much pain I could take." Such a confession would be curious enough for any actress to make, especially in a place where no questions on the topic would naturally come up, but is all the more so coming from an Air Force major's daughter. It is made more curious by the fact that her stated psychological disorder's limited duration implies its creation and elimination from some outside cause, which would most likely be hypnosis. Ironically enough, Robey's first appearance after *Friday the 13th* was as a kinky serial killer with a dual personality in Smart Egg Pictures' 1992 production, *Play Nice.*

1989, Bush's first year in office, was a singular bumper-crop year for sci-fi/horror, which would not be at all surprising if the man were indeed emphasizing the new demonization of, and indoctrination against, the UFO Intelligence. Among many similar entries was an unusual independent European horror film from Smart Egg Pictures, along the same lines as *Friday the 13th*'s "The Playhouse," called *Schizo*. Having nothing obvious to do with UFOs, it does contain the same connected elements as witnessed in such *Friday the 13th* episodes just mentioned. The lead character, Chris, is the son of a famous archaeologist who was murdered along with his entire party while excavating the castle of Prince Ilok in Yugoslavia. Chris was only a boy when it happened, and even at the time was already obsessed with sketching a huge-headed, enormous-eyed dwarf figure, his "imaginary friend" whom he called "Daniel." Daniel repeatedly came to Chris' room in the night while he and his father's team lived in the castle. Chris remembers little of the horrific and bestial murders, which were blamed on a poor local worker, but he is haunted into adulthood by recurring dreams of the night they occurred. To exorcize the dreams, and ideally to put his family's murder into perspective, Chris assembles a team and returns to the castle to complete the excavation.

As he does, his history becomes clearer not only to himself, but to the others along with him. Chris secretly believes that Daniel has never been imaginary at all, but that Daniel is the entity who committed the murders all those years ago. His friends are afraid that Chris is schizophrenic, and that Daniel is simply the name of his murderous alter-ego. Even Chris is remembering how his father punished him for torturing animals to death, always blaming it on Daniel. As if to confirm the theory, Chris finds a completely unchanged Daniel returning to him in the night, as he did when Chris was a boy. Daniel reminds Chris that the two of them will live and play together forever and ever, just as Daniel promised they would when they were both children. But to the others' dismay, and Chris' demonic delight, Daniel turns out to be an entirely separate entity— the immortal adolescent Prince Ilok himself, a notorious Satanist who sold his soul to the devil and was walled alive in his castle in the Middle Ages for torturing hundreds of peasants to death in a grotesque chamber. Under Ilok's renewed evil influence, Chris' trauma-suppressed personality re-emerges, identical to that of his corrupt and sadistically perverse childhood mentor, and he becomes so dangerous that he ultimately has to be killed by his fellows. Until that time, Chris seduces his friends to follow him to Ilok's lair under the pretense of having sex, where instead they are tortured to death by him and his diabolic counterpart.

Empire Pictures/Full Moon Video's popular *Puppet Master* series began in 1989 from Corman-inheritor and Lovecraft-reanimator Charles Band, showing robots brought to life specifically by Egyptian magic in the Underworld. The first and third movies in the ongoing series deal with the Nazis attempting to learn a mysterious Middle East-educated French puppet-master's secret for the animation of killer dolls before WWII, and the fourth and fifth entries show their modern CIA counterparts still attempting to steal and reproduce the same secret for their own purposes. Band also produced 1978's supernaturally-animated dolls movie, *Tourist Trap* (Compass), and a number of other similar features. His peers have quipped about him that if they can write something little and menacing into the script, Band is sure to produce it. As if to emphasize the point, Band was also the uncredited creator of Disney's 1989 comedy-fantasy, *Honey, I Shrunk the Kids,* and has since become an executive with that company. Band's long line of UFOlogically-related features includes Embassy's 1982 3-D gimmick flick, *Parasite,* an Earthbound reworking of *Alien* with a CIA goon following the progress of a growing space-invader on the run.

1989's independent release, *Lobsterman from Mars,* was essentially a spoof of the classic 1959 Warner Bros. stinker, *Teenagers from Outer Space,* with a little of Corman's *It Conquered the World,* Phil Tucker's *Robot Monster,* and Ed Wood's *Night of the Ghouls* thrown in. Considering the production had a decent cast and budget, the poor execution of the idea looks deliberate. Its effect is not so much to ridicule the subject as simply to make it appear sour, exactly as Fallon's UFO abduction on T.V.'s *The Colbys* at the beginning of the decade was discovered in a poll to have done, and assuredly for the same reason. Patrick Macnee, a perennial name in these kinds of projects, appears

as the government scientist combating the invading Martian menace, one hench-creature of which is a laughable furry bat with a high-
pitched giggle and lobster claws that is vulnerable to boiling water
(get it?). Macnee appeared at the top of the decade in 1981's much
more genuinely funny *Spaceship,* an *Alien* satire from Almi Cinema
5 with Leslie Nielsen and Cindy Williams, which was a typical entry
for the decade. Williams also appeared in Universal's *UFOria* that
same year, playing a contactee whose low-life white-trash relatives
try cashing-in on her genuine experience by way of a religious
sideshow scam.

New World Cinema, sold by Roger Corman only a few years before,
produced a bizarre little movie in 1989 called *Meet the Applegates.*
The title family consists of giant mutant praying mantises from the
Brazilian rain forests, who masquerade as a suburban American family in order to gain access to a nuclear power plant. They plan to sabotage the plant in order to save the rain forests, and thus their species.
Along the way, they fall into human vices, their son becoming a pot
addict (which causes him to inadvertently reveal his true insectoid
nature), their daughter the unwed mother of a hybrid-human baby,
the wife a shopaholic and near alcoholic, and the husband a phi-
landerer. Whenever anyone discovers their true form, they abduct
and cocoon the interlopers to keep them quiet. Eventually they are
found out by the community, who by that time are missing quite a
few of their number as a result of the Applegates' insectoid activities. Mr. Applegate gives a speech before the townsfolk nearly lynch
him, pleading for peaceful interspecies coexistence and criticizing
human beings for their xenophobia and environmentally destructive nature, threatening to wipe out the Applegates' home merely so
they can get their hamburgers a nickel cheaper. In the end, the townsfolk spare the Applegates because they stop the nuclear plant they
had formerly intended to sabotage from melting down, the result of
a guerilla attack by the Mantis Queen. The Applegates become heroes
and are visited in their Amazonian home by members of the human
community they saved, each species discovering a certain care and
fondness for the other—especially in the bringing up of their young,
at least one of which is hybrid.

The same year, the American-financed Canadian import *Millennium* (an adaptation of sci-fi author John Varley's short story "Air Raid") was released from 20th Century Fox/Gladden, about the FAA investigating mysteriously crashed planes. The head of the investigation finds an unidentifiable device in the wreckage, which paralyzes him and triggers the appearance of three strange, sexy women through a portal of light. One of them tells him to forget what he has seen, and though he remembers the incident later as a dream, he is also sure it happened. Adding to his certainty is the leader of the women returning at a later time to have sex with him. He and a scientist who has been attempting to discover the truth behind a similar strange appearance in his own past eventually find out that the women are futuristic undercover agents, abducting entire planeloads of men and women from vehicles they know in advance are going to crash and substituting replicas they hope no one will notice. Their purpose? To gain new breeding stock—their race, human like our own, is now sterile.

More interesting still, also from '89, was the independently released *Moontrap,* co-produced by sci-fi big-budgeter James Cameron *(The Abyss, The Terminator, Aliens,* etc.) and starring *Star Trek*'s Walter Koenig and '80s outre film figure Bruce Campbell. The two stars are NASA shuttle pilots who discover a derelict spaceship with a dessicated occupant, 14,000 years old. The occupant is a Caucasian male, indistinguishable from anyone on Earth today, and his craft is covered with hieroglyphics. In his ship is a pod, which assembles itself into a killer bipedal robot when everyone is away. Determining that the craft came from the Moon, Koenig and Campbell go there forthwith, in an out-of-mothballs Saturn-5, after the robot is destroyed in a military skirmish. Enclosures on the Moon contain at least one hibernating ancient Caucasian female (named "Mera" in the credits, spelled identically with the ancient Egyptian name for their pyramids, "mer"), who is revived just in time to be abducted along with Koenig by more robots which bind them and attempt to carve them up for "spare parts." The woman is phenomenally beautiful and of course cannot speak English, but has sex with Koenig after the fireworks die down. She does manage to convey to him that her race put themselves in suspended animation in order to live long enough to warn Earth's inhabitants of the robot menace, the origin of which is never really explained. The ancient astronauts, interestingly, wear red space suits—as have so many others in the Hollywood educational program. Also interesting are the superior special Moon effects, good enough to once more raise the question of whether or not what was viewed in the Apollo missions could have been faked.

At one point, the astronauts and a NASA scientist—cast to look exactly like J. Allen Hynek—try to explain to a White House representative what it is they have discovered, in an effort to get funding to return to the Moon. President Bush was attempting to do exactly that with Congress at the time this movie was being made. The astronauts and Hynek-surrogate say that it is of paramount importance to return to the Moon, since the discovered craft was determined to have originated from there, signifying an active base somewhere on that astral body. The representative appears weary and disbelieving. "You really want me to tell the President you guys picked up some ancient astronaut? All I know is, it sounds a helluva lot like the crap my kid watches on Saturday morning cartoons!" It would be a curious irony, indeed, if the Intelligence agencies' work had been so successful in making the entire subject of UFOs and ancient astronauts laughable that when they had to actually convince anyone of the potential seriousness of the situation later on down the line, they were unable to do so.

Concurrent with *Moontrap* and the rest of the '89 crop was another independently released diabolical menace from the same astral body, *The Dark Side of the Moon*. In 2022, the weapons-deactivating spaceship *Tiberius* finds itself inexplicably powerless over the dark side of the Moon. While attempting to establish communication with Earth and reactivate their propulsion system, the *Tiberius'* crew encounter the shuttle *Discovery*, which disappeared in the Bermuda Triangle thirty years before and was never seen again. Its long-dead crew have inexplicable wounds on their bodies, and they later become animated by a diabolical intelligence identifying itself as "666"—the Devil. The numbers of this "Satan's" name are calculated by one of the crewmembers (with the help of a humanoid robot-computer) as the sole recurring number in each angle of the Devil's Triangle, which is determined to be some sort of teleportation region between Earth and the Moon. The Devil seduces one crewmember after another, having sex with at least one of them in conditions identical to those reported in such UFO abductions as that of Antonio Villas Boas, leaving their bodies for dead after it has used them for its purposes. It intends to use the *Tiberius* to carry it to Earth. "Heaven is the Universe, but so is Hell," the Devil tells the sole survivor of his inexorable onslaught. "I am many names, and I come to take what is mine. At last, the Day of Reckoning is upon you all!" The survivor uses a missile from the ship the *Tiberius* was sent to deactivate to destroy himself and the Devil's only chance for escape.

MGM/UA was busy as well in 1989, matching that year's alien sci-fi blockbuster from James Cameron, *The Abyss,* with two underwater "alien" menaces of its own. The first, *Leviathan,* presented a genetic mutation escaped from the weapons labs of the KGB. The title was the name of a sunken Russian submarine from which a deep-sea team of U.S. corporate oil drillers inadvertently retrieve the mutagenic substance and infect their own ship. Once contaminated with the deadly material, the crewmembers' flesh alters into that of *Homo icthyus aquaticus,* "fish man," a vicious and powerful killer that can survive without oxygen for lengthy periods of time, the next sign of progress in Cold War undersea sabotage. Though the monster involved was not, strictly speaking, an "alien," the film fit well into the inspired paranoia of the year's movies, and was about a hostile outside invader. The plot reveals the American corporate heads to be as underhandedly vicious and cold-blooded as their Soviet counterparts, leaving the doomed crew of the submerged tanker to meet their fate as did that of the Russian submarine, the implication being that—like their predecessors—they want to monitor the results. MGM/UA's *Lords of the Deep,* produced by Roger Corman the same year, worked along similar lines.

William Peter Blatty filmed the 1983 sequel to his bestselling *The Exorcist* in 1990, 20th Century Fox's *Legion: Exorcist III.* The central premise of the story is that the devil (a single possessing Intelligence, leaving signature trademarks) inhabits different bodies at different times to commit murders, then vacates those bodies, leaving them entirely amnesiac of his presence or their part in the crime—which is exactly the same idea as hypnotically-controlled saboteurs for the UFO Intelligence. Early in his investigation, frustrated homicide detective George C. Scott mutters skyward, "We're abandoned." When his colleagues say they don't understand what he means, he responds, "I was signaling beings on Mars. Sometimes *they answer,"* in an only half-flippant tone, denoting that he expects to hear from them before he does God. Later, he undergoes a vivid-dream/abduction experience, finding himself in "heaven," a sort of Grand Central Station with bright lights, being obliquely communicated with in accurate ways pertaining to his investigation. The angels are on an old-fashioned radio set, calling, "Earth, come in please . . . can you hear us? We are attempting to communicate! Come in, please. . . ." Blatty also wrote, directed, and produced *The Ninth Configuration* at the very end of the Carter presidency in 1979, about a notorious Special Forces assassin in Vietnam whose war crimes have created amnesiac trauma, causing him to assume a second identity. *The Ninth Configuration* was released through Roger Corman's New World Cinema.

A lame but sporadically funny comedy was independently released in 1990 called *Martians Go Home,* from the Frederic Brown novel of the same name. This was a one-joke show about antennaed, green-skinned human beings from Mars arriving on Earth *en masse,* primarily to do nothing but annoy everyone in the manner of stand-up comics and voyeuristically get their jollies watching Earthmen have sex. Their principal aim is to force people to be honest in all their dealings (which happens to be one of the apparent aims behind actual UFO abductions, as well), mocking phonies and undressing every government lie on national T.V. Music is the force that initially brings them to our planet, and music is ultimately what drives them back to their own. The underlying joke of the show is that, with the aliens so prevalent that no one can escape them in their daily lives, there is one man who is deemed insane because he *doesn't* believe the Martians are here. The same year, Valkhn Films and Grandmaster Productions produced a sporadically funny comedy called *There's Nothing Out There,* in which vacationing teenagers in a mountain cabin find themselves besieged not by the usual stalk-and-slash killer, but an acidic, hostile, tentacled space alien. Vestron's alien comedy for the year was *Earth Girls Are Easy,* with valley girls Geena Davis and Julie Brown finding themselves the targets of amorous aliens Jeff Goldblum, Jim Carrey, and Damon Wayans.

Also in 1990, Universal released an odd and eerie horror film called *The Guardian,* pseudonymously directed by William Friedkin, starring Jenny Seagrove as a seductively innocent Druidic tree-spirit and impostrous babysitter who infiltrates young couples' lives and eventually steals away their infant sons for reasons not entirely clear. The parents of her latest intended victim discover that she made away with her former employer's son, who was found near death weeks later at the base of a tree, making clear that straightforward sacrifice is not the witch-woman's goal; their own son suffers a strange wasting sickness shortly before Seagrove is dispatched by them, which, combined with her earlier mentions of the infants' needing to be in peak health at the time of her taking them, implies that she is more or less some kind of immortal vampire who feeds off their essence. During her seemingly benign stays with the parents who hire her, Seagrove enters the childrens' rooms clandestinely at night to estab-lish a special communion with them that is anything but hostile, instead seeming to indicate the beginning of a lifelong intimacy and initiation, akin both to Fairy and UFO abductions. She gives her pre-sent charge stuffed animals with traditional witch's familiar names like "Pyewacket," and seductively whispers to the little boy, "These are your friends—these are your *bestest* friends."

Seagrove's origins or exact aims are never explained, and neither is her end. Mother Carey Lowell hits her at high speed in a Jeep Car-avan, smacking her into the tree that apparently gives Seagrove her supernatural life and powers, but her body is never recovered and she is seen at the end of the story healing her wounds at the base of the same tree. The strange tree-spirit woman is shown to be manip-ulative, self-interested, and amorally dangerous, murdering inter-lopers who discover her identity (though even then she appears to go out of her way beforehand to simply elude even plainly hostile pursuers, rather than cause them injury), yet no evidence is ever presented that she has in any way harmed any of the infants she abducts. In fact, the only case history given in the movie clearly shows that the abduction was temporary, and whatever seeming wasting illness the infant in question suffered also was purely temporary, with the parents recovering the abducted boy and the boy recovering his health. The parents, while understandably concerned, are almost portrayed as obsessively maniacal themselves in their desire to track down and destroy the weird—but essentially harmless, when not obstructed—tree-woman. *The Guardian* is therefore a confused and bizarre film, but certainly an interesting one when considered in light of UFO abductions.

In 1990 an episode aired of Ted Turner/DIC Entertainment's cartoon series, *The Adventures of Captain Planet and the Planeteers*, demonstrating the curious propagandistic slant on controversial subjects in the media. The concept of the series is that Gaia, "Spirit of the Earth," has recruited five youngsters to wear her power-rings and defend the Earth from pollution. Never in the course of the series has Gaia had a word to say against the military's development of nuclear power for weaponry, but in this 1990 episode, the question finally did come up at least once. The story concerned an extraterrestrial human (part spirit, like Gaia) named Zarn who abducts the Planeteers and counter-recruits them to his own cause: the destruction of Earth's nuclear weapons. Zarn replaces their power-rings with his "fists of iron," by which they will become the planet's new rulers once forced peace has been implemented. After the Planeteers destroy their first nuclear missile site, Gaia tells them that Zarn destroyed his own world with nuclear weapons in the distant past, and that his present destruction of Earth's nuclear missiles is simply a ploy to invite retaliation and similarly destroy the Earth. Exactly as in the MGM/UA Bond entry of the same twelve-year Republican reign, *Octopussy*, the logic behind this particular bit of non-reasoning is conveniently never pondered—Gaia herself, after all, should most be devoted to exactly the same cause as Zarn. In fact, one of her chief adversaries is "Duke Nuke'em," a freelance nuclear despoiler. But the Planeteers accept her pronouncement without argument or thought, and they drive Zarn back to his nuclear-devastated planet, telling him to stay there and leave Earth alone. Zarn's planet is shown to be red and yellow, much like Mars, and is obviously very close to Earth since the Planeteers can see it easily with their small porch telescope.

1991 brought a well-done independent production in *Invader,* which concerns a Department of Defense project kept secret even from the Pentagon. A base commander recovers a flying saucer in New Mexico, which is entirely automated and unmanned. His team download the saucer's flight computer into their own system and modify it to improve their strategic weapons. The hybrid computer program is called ASMODEUS (Automated Systems Managing Offensive-Defensive Strategies), and soon acquires a life of its own as the alien intelligence that originally programmed it takes over. It rewrites its own programming and builds a robot entity unto itself—HARV, for Heavily Armored Rampaging Vaporizer—mind-controlling as many military men as it requires to create a standing army and adopting a patriotic stance identical to fascism which it has learned from its Defense Department appropriators. In a clever ironic twist, ASMODEUS is defeated by far-Right Pentagon hawks who have their eyes opened to what has been going on and find themselves newly converted pacifists, and a tabloid reporter who goes legit as he realizes he is in the process of recording history. The same year, Touchstone Pictures and Disney's Buena Vista Distributors released Jim Varney's latest lowbrow comedy, *Ernest Scared Stupid,* about a child-abducting troll loose on Halloween, and another lame movie called *Spaced Invaders* featuring little green men from Mars (one with the mock-voice of Jack Nicholson) creating unintended havoc on the same night.

Wescom Productions the same year released one of the most unbelievably bad movies ever made (it virtually went straight to cable), notable only for the fact that it so prominently links UFOs with ancient Egypt, and does it so badly: *Being from Another Planet.* Starring MTV's Nina Axelrod and "introducing" Shari Belafonte Harper, the extremely thin plot concerned the inadvertent reanimation of a "foreign dignitary" named "Ankh ben Horus" (a name which in closest actual Egyptian translation would come out as absurd as "Jehovah McSmith"), discovered in King Tut's tomb—just how Ankh ben

Horus managed to be overlooked by Lord Carnarvon and Howard Carter's very thorough ransacking of that tomb in 1922 manages not to be considered. Ankh ben Horus turns out to have been a classic Gray from a flying saucer, honored as a god and mummified by the ancients until his eventual resurrection in the future.

Paramount and Charles Band's Full Moon Entertainment brought *Bad Channels* to the screen in 1992, a movie with numerous pop songs and a Blue Oyster Cult soundtrack aimed at the younger MTV crowd, and even starring that cable channel's hostess, Martha Quinn, as a T.V. newswoman trying to uncover the strange goings-on at podunk local radio station KDUL. Notorious deejay Dangerous Dan O'Dare—suspended for six months by the FCC for broadcasting his sexual liaison with a female police officer, live—has returned to host a sixty-six hour "Polka Hell" marathon as part of a crooked promotional gimmick. Dismayed by O'Dare's dishonest tactics, Quinn snubs him for a personal interview, and O'Dare vows he will get her undivided attention yet. Quinn having earlier claimed to witness one of many UFOs that have recently been making the news, O'Dare sets about publicly humiliating her with "flying saucer" and "little green man" jokes. But within hours, a real green, fungal-insectoid space invader, in a suit with artificial mechanical legs and accompanied by a robot, shows up at KDUL, with O'Dare pleading for help from his barricaded place of safety in the studio—and notorious joker that he is, no one believes him. The space invader sows green fungus that grows and spreads to rock music, and uses the station to power machinery that locates, miniaturizes, and transports sexy Earth-women to its specimen jars. Eventually, the local authorities figure out that the invasion is real, and they surround the besieged radio station. After Quinn herself is abducted, Dangerous Dan finally develops a little backbone, frees the captive Earth girls, and Germisols the green space meanie to death.

P.M. Productions released a typical Bush-era evil invader movie in 1992, *Alien Intruder*. The title character is sexy Tracy Scoggins, a red-and-black-clad space vamp who destroys all of Earth's manned and unmanned probes into her uncharted sector of deep space. Intercepting all Intelligence salvage teams attempting to apprehend the cause of their lost launches, Scoggins first invades the crewmen's dreams, then their reality, in order to sexually drive them mad and seduce them to her cause. Pitting each against the other, she causes them to sabotage their own ships and kill their fellows, laughing amidst the wreckage and merely awaiting the arrival of the next doomed shipload.

Tim Burton's strange, self-pitying movies sometimes contain a great many abduction motifs, the most impressive example being 1992's Warner Bros. entry, *Batman Returns*. The characters of the Penguin and the Catwoman are drastically changed from any portrayal they ever saw in D.C. Comics, recognizable in the film by name only. More to the point, their alterations bring them fairly close into line with what can be perceived to be accurate UFO abduction elements. Christopher Walken is abruptly abducted beneath the city streets, into a twilight limbo world of strange little waddling penguins (some of which were actually mechanical) and gasps, "My God, it's all true—the horrible Penguin-man of the sewers!" The grotesque dwarf, with flipper-finned "claw hands" in metallic black gloves and round black eyes in a bald white head—who also mass-abducts children—tells him he is just dreaming, that he is still asleep in bed. Penguin mock-hypnotizes him, causing "a splitting headache." He says he knows all about Walken and enlists his assistance for his own aims. "I wasn't born down here," the Penguin tells him. "I came from ..." and he merely points skyward. Later, Michelle Pfeiffer finds herself paralyzed in the cold, dreamlike twilight of the snow, strange creatures (cats) nibbling at and pawing over her twitching, semi-conscious body. She sleepwalks home in a trance, screaming when she fully revives. From that point on, she is no longer sure of her own identity. Her alter-ego (like Batman) is a sleek, shiny-black, lithe saboteur with small antennae (cat-ears), seemingly indestructible, wounded by bullets but not stopped or destroyed by them. "Who do you think you are?" she is asked at one point, her face suddenly crumpling in doubt, anguish in her voice, as she answers, "I don't know anymore ...!" echoing the sentiment of abductees. Exactly the same scene and elements occurred six years earlier in *From Beyond,* with respected scientist Barbara Crampton being wheeled around to face her leather dominatrix-clad self in the mirror, to be asked, "Is this who you are?" responding with, "I don't *know* who I am anymore!"

1989's *Batman* (yet another among the multitude of similar movies released in Bush's first year in office) presented the title character in the same manner as a UFO occupant, *à la* "Mothman." He first arranges private sightings before criminals whom he instructs to "tell all your friends about me" and is officially dismissed by the authorities as nothing more than a "ghost or goblin," with them "keeping a lid on it" until they can figure out who or what he is when he is encountered in the middle of their private little war at a chemical manufacturing plant, more or less during an act of sabotage. Kim Basinger is abducted to the high-tech Batcave and instructed how to assist Batman, then knocked out, returned to her bedroom, and stripped of any evidence she has acquired about him. The original 1966–68 20th Century Fox T.V. series often utilized the same elements. In the first season's "Riddler's False Notion," for instance, Commissioner Gordon and criminal moll Sherry Jackson are chemically rendered unconscious for delivery to and from the Batcave, and Gordon later informs Robin that the experience left no ill side-effects, seeming to be a "strange, refreshing dream."

The 1995 sequel, third in the Warner Bros. series, *Batman Forever*—not directed by Burton but produced by him—contains a remarkable number of UFOlogical elements. Split personality and repressed memory are made themes of the movie from the very first frames. The trauma-created villain Two-Face, a cleanly bifurcated man whose right side is white and left side is red as the result of having acid thrown in his face (with his henchmen wearing split masks of red and black), is on the loose, performing an act of robbery and sabotage. Batman and a psychiatrist describe his condition: "A trauma powerful enough to create an alternate personality leaves the victim in a world where normal rules of right and wrong no longer apply." The same could be said of UFO abductees, which is why their control by a foreign intelligence bent on acts of sabotage would be of tremendous concern to the government. Batman himself spends the course of the movie breaking through his own repressed memory of what made him who he is: an unexpected "supernatural" encounter with a bat. His memory is triggered by the color red. "It was coming toward me. I was scared at first—but only at first," he says, remembering. "The figure in the dark was my destiny. It would change my life, forever. I would use its image to strike terror into the hearts of those who did evil. I would ensure what happened to me would never happen to anyone else again. I would have my revenge."

The film's other villain, the Riddler, also takes his image from a supernatural encounter. The twisted and brilliant Edward Nygma ("E." Nygma) has devised an electronic device with which he can read men's minds, the equivalent of a brain implant. He communes with a mechanical "little green man" in an old-fashioned fortune-telling booth, wearing the exact costume he later adopts as his own—a direct equivalent of the unique "I am you" connection between UFO abductors and their charges, and of animated ancient Egyptian *ushabti* figures. As if to emphasize the point, when Nygma first communes with the eerie little green mechanical man, a song plays in the background: "You're sorta stuck where you are / But in your dreams, you can buy expensive cars / Or live on Mars / And have it your way." It continues, solidifying the amoral alternate-personality link made earlier, and repeating the "dream" stanza linking it with UFO abductions: "You hate your boss at your job / But in your dreams / You can blow his head off / In your dreams / Show no mercy." One of Nygma's riddles to Bruce Wayne reads, "Tear one off and scratch my head, what once is red is black instead," the colors being those of "the two lands" of Egypt (and also of Two-Face), and enormous stone Egyptian heads line the police roof from which the Bat-signal is sent. The sado-masochistic element of the abduction experience is even indirectly hinted at, when Riddler discovers the Batcave (to destroy it in an act of wanton sabotage) and exclaims, *"S-s-s-s-spank me!"*

1993's *The Nightmare Before Christmas* (Touchstone), another of Burton's typical oddball-grotesque collections, places him in that rarest of categories, the producer of a "Santa-as-UFO" movie, which, in the sole three cases it has occurred, has every time been unbelievable disaster. The other two are 1964's *Santa Claus Conquers the Martians,* and the notorious 1959 Mexican cheapie by K. Gordon Murray, *Santa Claus.* In the Mexican version, Santa keeps his eye on

Earth *à la* UFO occupants, through a huge camera-telescope in the shape of an eye (just as reported fourteen years after this movie's making by Charles Hickson and Calvin Parker—who almost certainly didn't see the film). Santa and helpmeet Merlin the Magician play "Good Angel" to a literal red devil's "Bad Angel," trying to keep every little boy and girl on Earth not naughty, but nice. The whole is idiotically narrated, in exactly the same fashion as *The Creeping Terror.*

Burton's stop-motion animated marionette version has a skeleton-man "Pumpkin King" commandeering Santa's sled, only to be shot down by NORAD. Like the two Santa movies preceding it, and the equally impossible-to-believe-until-seen equivalent from Rankin-Bass in 1969, Avco Embassy's *Mad Monster Party,* it almost seems to have been deliberately made to be utterly forgettable by even the kiddie audience, with the least memorable score ever composed. Though probably intended to some degree to subliminally blast the UFO subject, it is to be admitted that *The Nightmare Before Christmas* probably also reflects Burton's own dismay at the comparative failure of his "Christmas" movie filmed immediately before, *Batman Returns.* Conversely, for all the film's strangeness and mediocre score, it could perhaps be said that Burton was subliminally making UFO occupants less frightening to young audiences by making them more familiar—whatever its drawbacks, the skeletal Pumpkin King and the other bizarre inhabitants of his Halloweenland are quite enjoyable, in the same weird way as The Addams Family, or Burton's own earlier *Beetlejuice.*

Burton's *Ed Wood* (1994) could be a deflectionary film, its primary purpose to keep comical flying saucers in the public eye, just as the resurrection of *Plan 9* by the Medved Brothers as the top entry in *The 50 Worst Films of All Time,* in 1981—coinciding with Reagan's taking of office—deflected attention from the then-current release of the more realistic and thought-provoking *Hangar 18.* Burton began his career as a Disney animator/designer, which is interesting in light of Disney's government connection. Also, in those early days at Disney, he idolized and became a good friend of American International Pictures' mainstay star, Vincent Price, having made a short film about the man (and Burton's own pre-adolescent fascination with him) called *Vincent*. Lest some of these interpretations appear to be a slight stretch in drawing UFO or government connections, it should be noted that Burton produced a 1996 Walt Disney version of the children's classic, *James and the Giant Peach,* which was presented as essentially a UFO abduction story, and that his latest Warner Bros. film release is the big-budget production of *Mars Attacks,* based on the original 1962 Topps trading card series and their later resurrection as "graphic novels." His latest projects under consideration are a film biography of Vincent Price and a feature-length movie remake of the original *Outer Limits* episode, "The Architects of Fear."

James and the Giant Peach features a mechanical-looking insect aboard the (benevolently) child-abducting UFO peach, as well as a Gray-faced spider, and ends with actual UFOs over New York being attacked by the military. Burton set much of the action of *Mars Attacks* in Las Vegas, giving him the opportunity to depict flying saucer attacks before pyramids, a sphinx, and Egyptian-garbed casino waiters. The Martians' flag, seen only briefly toward the end (adorning the dead President of the United States' body), is a red pyramid topped by a white moon on a black background. Red, white, and black are seen in great proliferation throughout, especially early in the movie. The Martians are stated to be living beneath the surface of their own planet, send disguised assassins to attempt the preemptive removal of political opponents, and are ultimately done-in by sound waves (the brain-liquefying strains of infamous warbler Slim Whitman).

An interesting side-note is that a recent *X-Files* "graphic novel" ends with the discovery that an artist who draws *Mars Attacks* comics has been encoding the truth into them. The same idea, which has been proposed as a serious possibility throughout this study, not only appeared in Harlan Ellison's 1967 *Man from U.N.C.L.E.* episode, "The 'Pieces of Fate' Affair," but was also to be found in *The Avengers:* in the episode "The Winged Avenger," Steed and Mrs. Peel identify their murderer-quarry as a comic-book artist by his accurately depicting the murders he commits in advance throughout his artwork.

HBO aired *Roswell* in July of '94, a not entirely accurate, but acceptably altered within dramatic license, retelling of the events at that famous site in 1947. An EBE disinformational story is enacted with stunning special effects, but at least co-screenwriter Arthur Kopit presents it in the framework of merely a story told by someone who is probably a liar for the CIA, and not as a real occurrence. *Roswell* is most interesting for the picture it paints of the secret government UFO group, presenting realistic scenarios of exactly how disinformation has been sown from that source. "Accurate information released from less than reputable sources, that's not such a bad technique," one of them suggests—which has been the exact subject under careful scrutiny in this study.

Also in 1994, Universal released its answer to Warner Bros.' highly successful *Batman* movie series in *The Shadow*, Batman's pulp serial predecessor. *The Shadow* is another of the many examples of actual UFOlogical material showing up both in early fiction and contemporary cinema. The title character, Lamont Cranston, is an abductee against his will of a secret Chinese society, which teaches him how to "cloud men's minds." He uses this power to enable him to move invisibly in the world of men and to hypnotize them. Understanding the evil of men, having been an evil man himself before his Chinese training, Cranston can control his victims' minds, forcing them either to turn themselves in to the law, or commit suicide to pay for their crimes. Like Batman, he has a high-tech hideaway. Unlike the more famous Caped Crusader—but like the UFO Intelligence—he also has a network of secret society friends, any of whom immediately assist him when Cranston identifies himself by a prearranged code phrase.

MGM/UA's aforementioned *Stargate,* the same year, failed to be the new *Star Wars* but was a tremendous success and put the subjects considered here in the public spotlight. These ideas are becoming so much more commonplace that speculation as to government funding to put them forth is almost redundant—they are taking off on their own impetus. James Spader is a renegade archaeologist, trying to show Egyptology its own inadequacies as he attempts to spark reevaluation of its basic tenets. Only the military recognizes that his theories are correct, and they utilize him to decipher confusing inscriptions found by them on a bizarre piece of Egyptian technology unearthed in the 1920s. It opens a doorway to the Egyptian planet of man's origins, and the military secretly send a nuclear device along with an exploratory mission for a preemptive strike, anticipating war with its occupants. "I created your civilization," Ra—portrayed as a decadent and evil androgynous prince—tells Spader, "and you come here to destroy me." Ra tyrannically oppresses a planet of mining slave-laborers, who the expedition members lead in a military revolt of liberation equivalent to that recorded in the myth-texts of the Middle East. Ra is technologically capable of resurrecting the dead and utilizes resonant vibration for his weaponry. Like *Star Wars, Stargate* recently spawned the beginning of an ongoing series of novels. *Stargate*'s production team—Dean Devlin and Roland Emmerich— put out the widely hyped monster space-invader movie *Independence Day* in 1996, which brought state-of-the-art special effects to what was otherwise nothing more than a repeat of early 1950s Intelligence propaganda, such as *Invaders from Mars, The War of the Worlds,* and *Earth vs. the Flying Saucers.*

Atypically for a Democratic administration, as already mentioned, recent Hollywood UFO material has been threat-oriented, as exemplified in 1995's MGM/UA sci-fi entry, *Species,* starring ravishing Natasha Henstridge as a human-alien hybrid made in a secret government lab. She has been created by a DNA helix transmitted to Earth from a source in outer space, discovered by the SETI project. As trusting as any child—and as human-looking as one—she escapes when her monitors grow apprehensive of the project and attempt to cyanide her to death. Once on the loose, her growth accelerates at an astounding rate, maturing her through adolescence and into adulthood in a matter of hours. Survival having become paramount to her, she consumes human beings for protein whenever necessary and seeks a genetically suitable mate for reproduction as rapidly as possible. She ruthlessly dispatches unworthy suitors, who consist of anyone not genetically perfect, and even devours her mate like a black widow upon completing her reproductive cycle. The government assembles a team of scientists and psychics to track her down and eliminate her, even before it is established that she is a threat, and inexplicably her hybrid offspring is instantly violent and aggressive, even though its mother was not. Such logic holes in the plot are extremely typical of "alien" movies, especially with the new apparent thrust being the demonization of extraterrestrials.

Species was written by Dennis Feldman, the screenwriter/director of the same studio's aforementioned *Real Men,* eight years before. Feldman also wrote the *Shadow*-esque Eddie Murphy vehicle, Paramount's *The Golden Child,* in 1986. The movie's co-producer was Frank Mancuso, Jr., who brought Fox's often UFOlogically oriented *Friday the 13th: The Series* to T.V. (Though it may be no more than a coincidence, it is still an entertaining side-note that *The Amityville Horror*'s supposed exorcist-priest was named "Father Frank Mancuso," a man on whom no researcher into the case has been able to find any record of actual existence whatsoever.)

Fox T.V. began its short-lived alien invader show, *Space: Above and Beyond,* from some of the production team of *The X-Files* in 1995. Proving to be nothing more than the WWII melodrama or John Ford western set in space that its producers hyped it to be, it had little if any connection to actual UFOlogy. There were robot killers called "silicates," but who they belonged to or their ultimate purpose never was revealed before the show's single-season demise. Neither was much of anything else, the series having intended to "tease" its facts out slowly. The hostile aliens were never seen in anything more than the briefest glimpses, but hewed to the generally accepted (if incorrect) notion of reptilian invaders, appearing to derive primarily from the successful movies *Alien* and *Predator.*

CBS' *Special Report: Journey to Mars* on March 25, 1996, dramatized the first manned landing on Mars in such a way as to suggest that the government might be preparing for disclosure relatively soon. NASA probe sabotage was portrayed as the result of corporations attempting to make a profit on their losses while simultaneously fingering radical environmental groups for their actions. Leaving no doubt of the story's fictional nature (former "Special Report" programs, filmed in documentary style, had been mistaken for real), and providing a prime demonstration of political influence in the film industry, it portrayed women not only in charge of the major reporting on the story, but also occupying the office of U.S. President and being the first astronaut on Mars (a black woman, an old woman, and a young Russian woman, respectively, for maximum diversity). At the very end of the story, the first astronaut to set foot on the planet peers into the distance at something the audience cannot see and says, "Oh, my God—!" before her camera goes dead. Contact fails to be reestablished, leaving the audience with nothing but ominous radio silence and slow dissolves away from the menacing Red Planet.

Two former T.V. "pseudo-documentaries" aired in prime-time— in both instances on Halloween Eve in commemoration of Orson Welles' 1938 *The War of the Worlds* fraud, and in both cases receiving numerous phone calls to the studio in fear the events portrayed were actually real—were *Special Bulletin* in 1983 (see Chapter 10) and 1994's *Without Warning*. The latter, partly acted-out by actual news figures and featuring a special guest appearance by famous scientist/sci-fi author Arthur C. Clarke as himself, dramatized meteor strikes at three different locations on Earth—which in the end turn out to have been intelligently directed attacks by an extraterrestrial intelligence. All of these pieces seem less inspired by Welles' famous broadcast than to be emulations of that mysterious British "April Fool's" hoax of 1977, *Alternative 3* (see Chapter 9). And each such occurrence appears to have been deliberately planned to exploit a fear, for someone's ulterior purposes: *Special Bulletin,* portraying a fake nuclear threat in order to force unilateral disarmament of the superpowers, ended with a very realistic atomic explosion, probably intended to frighten the public into subliminal support of Reagan's boosted Star Wars budgets; *Without Warning* and *Journey to Mars* appear equally to exploit not only fear of the unknown and of hostile threats from outer space, but specifically to focus that fear directly on the planet Mars.

Commercially debuting on August 26, 1996, TNT's *The Real Adventures of Jonny Quest*—four years in the making, from an international American-Canadian-Japanese team—presented a total number of UFO stories in its first three weeks equating to more than one-third of its total stories at the time. Completely unlike its mid-1960s predecessor, or its even more juvenile 1970s reincarnation, Hanna-Barbera's *The Real Adventures* has aged Jonny and Hadji from eight or nine to thirteen, and added a female companion of the same age in ex-CIA agent Roger "Race" Bannon's daughter, Jessie. Though recent episodes have seen more of a return to the comic book-oriented tone of the original, in its first two months *The Real Adventures* elevated the level of its stories to a much more realistic tenor.

The CIA is shown in a mixed light, especially interesting for so traditionally patriotic a cartoon—though the Agency is not named specifically as the source of international drug trade, spies in general have been, as in the episode "Amok," where a spy from an unnamed allied agency is demonstrated to be involved in the business. Dr. Zinn has taken a back seat to other quarry, though he appears occasionally as a master of robotics. "Night of the Zinnja" established his area of expertise, the title creature being an elaborate humanoid automaton, and "The Robot Spies" expanded the original series' spider-robot into an army of the same contraptions. Quest's new world-threatening arch-nemesis is "Ezekiel Rage," a former CIA agent turned renegade religious terrorist in revenge for the Agency's failure to save his family when they were killed during one of his missions in the early 1970s. Rage accuses Race Bannon, whom he knew well, and the Agency in particular, of being the real causes of evil in the world, needing to be eradicated. His first act is to take nerve gas stored by the military in New Mexico caves and attempt a mass purification of the human race—failing that, he carries out a NASA hijacking in order to create a virus requiring a zero-gravity lab to manufacture, in a failed attempt to essentially give instant AIDS to the entire world, rather like James Bond's nemesis Hugo Drax in *Moonraker*. Thus, even as the CIA is given a mixed image in the series, terrorism is clearly demarcated as the central threat—which is in keeping with the government's (and its various agencies') real-life concerns, at least according to today's headlines.

The series' presentation of UFO material is quite remarkable in light of the facts related in this study, the more so given the reputation of the cartoon for unquestioning patriotism and its current move toward greater realism. On September 7, "Alien In Washington" initiated the new *Jonny Quest*'s treatment of the subject, revealing the former Vice President of the United States—though duly elected to office, and rather obviously human—as actually having been born on another planet and in the process of helping his extraterrestrial society deliver warnings to the military to cease space weapons research. That society "sends us a friendly warning," as Race Bannon puts it, incapacitating and sinking ships without harming any of the crew members, in exactly the same way UFOs have been incapacitating military airplanes and missiles from the time of their first appearance in the modern age. "Don't you see, general, they mean us no harm," Doctor Quest tells the weapons project head, "but they *do* mean *business.*" The general does not heed the warning, and he and a goon squad are knocked unconscious by the alien vice president as he is beamed-up to join his fellows in their airships. The vice president assures Bannon that none of them will remember a thing when they wake up. The Secretary of Defense is present to witness the occurrence and asks, "Will someone explain what exactly is going on here?" The alien answers, "I'm afraid I don't have the time. Dr. Quest will tell you. What he says may sound unlikely, but you'd better believe it." The Defense Secretary covers the vice president's permanent disappearance by announcing at a press conference that he has had a fatal heart attack, and states—taking no questions—that the space weapons projects in the Defense Department have been terminated. Jonny ends the episode by reflecting after the announcement, "You know, with the vice president being some guy from outer space, it makes you kind of wonder. I mean, anybody could be an alien. Your dad . . . your best friend . . . or even your dog." He looks to his innocent and uncomprehending pet, Bandit. "What do you say, huh, boy? Are you a mutt from another planet?"

The following episode, "Return of the Anasazi," had its beginning at the Roswell crash in 1947, portrayed as the result of Air Force pursuit on the night a local Hopi shaman was attempting contact with the Anasazi. "Certain Native American legends speak of an ancient people who came to Earth from beyond the stars, bringing with them knowledge that would set humans above the animals around them," narrates Alice Starseer, the shaman's granddaughter. "But mankind misused the Ancient Ones' knowledge, and the Earth and her people fell out of harmony. Now, the legends say, just as caring parents must watch over their children, so the Ancients return to Earth from time to time, trying to prevent humanity from destroying itself and the very Earth which gives it life. The ancient people of those legends are called the Anasazi. . . ."

Dr. Quest is revealed to have been Alice Starseer's lover in the 1960s, when they were both archaeology or anthropology students in their early twenties. She calls on his help to elude the military, who are attempting to acquire her grandfather's crystal for summoning and communicating with the Anasazi. Along the way, Quest, Race, and Hadji find themselves arrested by CIA and military men in unmarked black helicopters, who hold them indefinitely for reasons of "national security." Hadji mentions that surely they can't be held forever, and Race cynically gestures to the helicopter outside: "These jokers are beyond the law, Hadji. They've been usin' hybrids of UFO technology for years. Check out that helicopter. It's designed from elements they stole from alien wrecks. But no one's gonna admit to anything." Dr. Quest pipes in, "Of course. When one acknowledges the existence of beings with superior intellects and technologies, one also acknowledges one's own inferiority." Ultimately, the armed government men are faced-off by the Anasazi themselves, who are distantly seen to be wearing what looks like a cross between American Indian garb and Egyptian headdresses. "Listen, Mister," Alice Starseer tells the defeated team, "you're in over your head. For once in your life, be smart. Take your men and your weapons, and leave. This is no business of yours. In fact, it never was." They depart, but not without a bitter comment from the CIA man in charge: "You may have won *this* battle. But the war ain't over—not by a long shot!" Alice leaves with the Anasazi and her grandfather, trying to get Quest and his family to leave with her, but they remain because "this is where we belong."

In "Trouble on the Colorado," Alice Starseer returns, summoning Dr. Quest to a rendezvous at her former reservation by leaving her contact-crystal on Jonny's window ledge at night. Jonny brings it to his father, waking him up and wryly commenting, "Uh, dad, phone's for you—it's kind of long distance." Race Bannon's renegade CIA terrorist enemy, Dr. Jeremiah Surd, discovers that Quest is in contact with an alien race and ambushes his party. "I've hacked your computer files on this fascinating object," Surd informs Quest. "I've also accessed a number of secret government files. Would you care to take a look? Really, Dr. Quest ... spaceships ... Anasazi Indians becoming extraterrestrial travelers ... your girlfriend Alice Starseer leaving the planet ... if I didn't have all this evidence, I would have taken you for a complete crackpot. You're such an impolite Earthling, too! Alice Starseer's returning for a terrestrial visit, and you weren't even going to roll out the red carpet! I, on the other hand, have a much more interesting reception planned for her. . . ." He probes her mind with advanced technology, seeing her homeworld, which is red and black: "With this technology," he proclaims, witnessing what appears to be an underground city there, many stories deep, "my powers will be infinite!" Surd is stopped before he can learn more, and Starseer's purpose for coming is fulfilled—which is simply to bury her grandfather on his home planet, according to the customs of her people, to facilitate his passage to "the Other World." The Anasazi "spirits" also attend.

Surd returned in "Secret of the Moai," once more to computer-hack information out of Quest's files on extraterrestrial visitors. The Quest team discovers a perfect metallic sphere buried beneath volcanic rock on Easter Island. Inside it are two skeletons: one of an early human, strapped to a table, and the other of a humanoid figure resembling perfectly the famous statue heads of the island. Quest discovers that the bones of the figures are hollow, and mutagenically manipulable through sound waves. The statue heads also resonate powerfully on the same note that affects the bones, sufficiently to mulch the grass at their base. Rongo-Rongo writing is discovered inside the craft—that still-undeciphered ancient script found only on Easter Island and in the Indus Valley cities discovered between 1856 and the 1920s, on the opposite side of the world—and is determined not to be a form of writing, but rather of musical notation. Surd, again seeking technological power as well as a cure for his physical infirmities, misuses the technology and devolves Quest and Race Bannon, until another sphere identical to the one buried beneath the lava shows up on the scene, rectifying all wrongs, erasing everyone's memory of the events which have transpired concerning the discovery, and transplanting Surd and his party to the similarly enigmatic site of the barren Nazca plains in Peru.

"Other Space" probably took off on *Stargate* in its story of other-dimensional invaders following one of Quest's probes back into our space, utilizing pyramidal configurations to expand their gateway. A later episode in the series had occupants of a crashed UFO disguising themselves as Yeti in a frozen clime, in order to scare off interlopers while repairing their ship. As in Nigel Kneale's *The Abominable Snowman of the Himalayas,* there is a fortune-hunting faction after the yeti, eager to be the first to bag a prize specimen whether it be terrestrial or extraterrestrial. Another episode revived Kneale's plotline more closely: a Tibetan monastery proves to number among its monks a few of the Yeti race, who live there in privacy to escape treasure-hunters and idle fools.

"In the Wake of *Mary Celeste*" peripherally featured UFO phenomena, without explaining them overtly as such. A man claiming to be experiencing past-life regression as the captain of the famous lost ship turns out really to be only another of Race Bannon's former CIA buddies turned renegade, simply out for a lost treasure. The story related by the "captain" concerning the ship's loss sounds like the result of a UFO: "I became aware of a strange undercurrent . . . at first, I heard an unearthly sound. A deep trembling that seemed to emanate from the depths of the sea. An unrelenting sound that pierces the very soul itself. Above decks, a strange fog had enveloped us, a fog the likes of which I had never seen before. The sound became more and more intolerable. What was it? Where was it coming from? Why wouldn't it stop? Then, the unearthly light was upon us! My family and I retreated from this evil presence . . . it worked its way through the windows, it washed over the deck and found us, it turned night into day . . . !" Though the story turns out to be a hoax, Quest does discover what appears to be "a series of crop circles" beneath the Atlantic Ocean, glowing in the same unearthly green light that was a part of the hoaxster's story. It kills the power in his helicopter, necessitating his rescue by Hadji, and later incapacitates the ship of the escaping CIA fraud with his looted treasure. The moving, subaqueous, discoid green glow is never explained in the story but is implied to belong to some unspecified UFO source—and even has factual backing in numerous reports of exactly such phenomena from the Bermuda Triangle, both from history and in the present day.

On September 7, 1996, Warner Bros.' Kids Network revived one of the studio's perennially popular properties as the animated *The Adventures of Superman,* produced by most of the same team who had done Warner Bros.' *Batman: The Animated Series* four years earlier. Both cartoons having been influenced to a large degree by Max Fleischer's earlier *Superman* shorts, the new animated Superman took a few correct UFOlogical departures from its original source material. Krypton is shown to be a planet with red soil and red skies (it was an icy-white crystalline planet, covered with life-supporting geodesic domes, in the same studio's movie series of twenty years before), and Superman's parents, Lara and Jor-El, wear Atlantean-inspired costumes of red and black, with silvery accoutrements that appear grayish-white.

"Brainiac" is a universal computer system for the planet, duplicitously responsible for failing to warn the Kryptonians of their coming demise even as it prepares its own escape by downloading into an orbiting rocket-satellite. Brainiac is not only Krypton's Judas-goat, but its equivalent of the NSA: it spies on all of Krypton, and the Kryptonians have become so dependent on it that they have ceased to question its judgments or notice the hold it has over their lives. Brainiac is the type of computerized mechanoid villain that was the quarry of Gold Key Comics' *Magnus, Robot Fighter* in the 1960s, a single-entity National Security State, which attempts to murder Jor-El or any other interloper who discovers its true traitorous activities performed behind the scenes. Jor-El fails to utilize his one shot at disconnecting Brainiac before it flees Krypton, owing to the sad realization that—aside from his own seed, which he sends to another planet for posterity—it will be the only surviving repository of what was once a great civilization. Later, Superman succeeds where his father failed, retrieving Krypton's memories to create his Fortress of Solitude, after foiling Brainiac's final ruination of an alien culture

(Earth's)—since escaping Krypton's destruction, the computer has gone mad and reprogrammed itself to "save" all alien cultures, collecting their memories and then exterminating them. A later extraterrestrial menace to introduce himself into the series has been Darkseid, a technologically superior UFO warlord who arms Superman's opponents and inhabits a red Underworld.

Lex Luthor, more or less a freelance criminal terrorist in the original comic books, in the cartoon series is a corrupt industrialist defense contractor. He boasts to Superman that two-thirds of Metropolis works for him, "whether they know it or not," which is a pretty accurate assessment of how much hold the military-industrial-academic complex has on the modern free world. Luthor arranges to illegally sell weapons systems to unfriendly governments in direct opposition to Congress, simultaneously inflating his domestic stock twice-over in both insurance and increased defense contracts to cover the "losses" incurred in the "thefts" of his property. As in real life, Superman—"Alien in my own back yard . . . and such a civic-minded one too," as Luthor derogatorily refers to him—is fully wise to Luthor and engaged in a private little war with him that most of the world fails to notice due to its own lack of perception. Luthor is no more impressed by Superman's superior might than he is of any earthly opponent and devotes his time to discovering ways to combat the extraterrestrial presence that blocks his "progress."

Some of the UFOlogical elements of *Superman's* predecessor, Fox's *Batman: The Animated Series* (premiering on September 5, 1992, and still periodically adding episodes to its present eighty-five as it moves to the WB Network's Fall '97 lineup), have already been mentioned. One two-part story, "Heart of Steel," featured a "Brainiac"-ish computer villain called HARDAC (Human Analytical Reciprocating Digital Computer), programmed by Karl Rossum (a direct homage to Karel Capek's play, *Rossum's Universal Robots*) to replicate human beings in order to replace his deceased daughter, who died prematurely in an auto accident. HARDAC exceeds its programming and improves both itself and its mission, instead intending to replicate and *replace* its human counterparts. Destroyed before it can succeed, it first infiltrates the Batcave's computer and replicates Bruce Wayne, setting up the sequel story, "His Silicon Soul," in which the mechanical *doppelganger* Batman attempts first to replace the original and then to reactivate HARDAC to complete its mission. Unfortunately for HARDAC, the duplicate has been made too well and cannot—like its model—bring itself to harm a human being. When threatened, the replicates drop to all fours and locomote away at tremendous speed, exactly like the robots in the Hopkinsville, Kentucky, 1955 UFO assault case. One robot from the second season (retitled *The Adventures of Batman and Robin)* is especially memorable: in "Deep Freeze," super-scientist Mr. Freeze is sprung from prison by a near-invincible abductor-robot, controlled appropriately enough by *Halloween III*'s techno-wizard, Dan O'Herlihy.

An amnesiac nocturnal dual-personality, the wife of a research scientist who has become infected with her husband's experimental mutagenic virus was an airborne criminal in spite of herself in "Terror in the Skies." One episode featured a criminal who employed stolen technology to repeatedly visit his estranged little girl in her bedroom at night, masquerading as her "invisible friend" with the ultimate aim of abducting her. The Mad Hatter—the model for the Riddler in the 1995 film—was a Waynetech scientist who used technology to gain control of people's bodies in accomplishing his wiles, leaving them amnesiac upon waking from their induced trance.

But the most UFOlogical entries in the series came with a recurring character from the comic books, created by D.C. story editor Denny O'Neil in the mid-1970s: *Ra's al-Ghul* ("the Demon's Head"). Ra's al-Ghul was presented as a legendary figure, supposedly more than six hundred years old—human to all appearances, but having more in common with the equally legendary *Tuatha de Danaan,* or "Fairy Folk," of old. Ra's appeared in the first season of the cartoon in an episode called "Off-Balance," shown as the head of a worldwide quasi-terrorist organization called the "Society of Shadows," which steals advanced technology for unknown aims. Their first target is a sonic-cannon weapon, which Batman sabotages before Ra's' daughter can return it to him in his Mongolian stronghold. In his second appearance in the cartoons, a two-parter called "The Demon's Quest," Ra's attempts to recruit Batman as his replacement in the coming New World Order he intends to bring about before finally succumbing to the ravages of mortality (however delayed they have been, in his special case). Fanatically devoted to the planet Earth, he has decided that man the despoiler must be eradicated in order to return it to its original pristine glory. Batman thwarts his attempt to use orbiting satellites to trigger earthquakes toward that end, and he reluctantly turns down the offer of the demigod's daughter to marry him and sire a new bloodline of superior human beings. In "Avatar," Ra's made a pilgrimage to Egypt in the attempt to make his near-immortality true immortality. There he met with one of the original queens of the Danaan race (not specified to be such, but obviously she could be no other), who in return for his worship nearly murdered Ra's to steal his essence for prolonging her own immortality. As if to solidify the connection of Ra's to the UFO Intelligence and/or the Danaan, one final story showed him as a Jules Verne-ish "Master of the World" in the 1880s of the Old West, bombing mankind's war resources from an advanced airship.

On September 21, 1996, NBC premiered the UFO conspiracy drama *Dark Skies* as part of a proposed Saturday night lineup spanning three full consecutive hours of interrelated programs all patterned after Fox's highly successful *The X-Files.* The other two shows have nothing to do with UFOs but are connected by virtue of their dark, slick, high-tech Fox-style production values. One is *The Profiler,* starring Ally Walker as a Jodie Foster/*Silence of the Lambs*-inspired FBI master criminal detective. The other, *The Pretender,* stars Michael T. Weiss as government think-tank escapee Jarod, with an abnormally high IQ, raised in isolation as part of an unspecified experiment, who goes around assuming various identities while solving crimes and helping people, the whole while pursued by his former "mentors" for not entirely clear reasons.

The Pretender has one not terribly obvious connection to UFOs—whether intentional or merely convenient for ratings—in the title character's chief adversary from the think-tank: a micro-miniskirted siren named "Ms. Parker" with a cold but sensual S&M personality (Andrea Parker), with whom he has an odd and unexplained symbiotic love-hate relationship extending back to childhood. In keeping with contemporary demonization of smoking, Ms. Parker is shown to be a chain-smoker of cigarettes. Curiously enough, "The Pretender's" personality profile closely matches that of a UFO abductee in that he is highly intelligent, is likeable but isolated and emotionally removed from others, and is of exceptionally high moral caliber. His description in the pilot's opening narration could even apply: "There are extraordinary individuals among us known as Pretenders. Geniuses with the ability to insinuate themselves into any walk of life, to literally become anyone. In 1963, a corporation called the Centre isolated one such Pretender, a young boy named Jarod. Locked in a controlled environment they exploited his genius for their 'unofficial' research. Then one day, their Pretender ran away."

Though it may be no more than coincidence, in the premiere episode, a little girl approaches Jarod when she discovers he doesn't even know how to eat an Oreo cookie in the manner any kid does, and asks him, "Where did you grow up? Mars?" and he answers, "Sort of." He is even wearing a red shirt and white pants at the time. Adding to the possibility that Jarod is intended to represent an abductee, the pilot episode reveals that his parents were not his genetic parents (he does a DNA match on their remains), and his true ancestry is left unexplained. Ms. Parker and Jarod's controller, Sidney (Patrick Bauchau), discover the Centre has a long-abandoned top secret subterranean level, SL-27, where restraints on "birthing tables" and child-size locked rooms have been left behind—a forced breeding project of some sort took place there. Sidney additionally is shown to be a prominent genetic researcher on twins (rather like those the Ahenenerbe S.S. recruited), and is a twin himself—his brother went into coma after he and Sidney had an accident while fighting over the Centre's treatment of their work. In the first season's final episode, adding to the possibility that Jarod's ancestry is not entirely human, Sidney and Ms. Parker muse as to where he is likeliest to make his latest escape; as they do, Jarod is shown smiling, gazing up at a red-and-white space shuttle rising into the sky.

In flashbacks, the Pretender is at various times shown as a young boy in the think-tank, solving such hypothetical problems for his keepers as how to get *Apollo 13* back safely ("Wait, wait! I've got it!

I've got it! I can use the gravitational pull of the *Moon* to help get us back!"), how many shooters were actually at Dealey Plaza, and who killed Marilyn Monroe. The pilot episode reveals his motivation for escaping and helping criminally victimized people: his genius for predicting scenarios led to government creation and release of Ebola virus, among other nefarious activities. Jarod is also shown in the first season's final episode to have a brother, a Pretender raised in a special mind-control experiment to become the private assassin of diabolical Centre bigwig Mr. Rains (another demonized smoker, who is never seen without an oxygen tank that keeps his wasted body alive). Jarod's Pretender brother is murdered by Mr. Rains before he can spill any beans—in much the same manner as other assassins are conveniently kept from public scrutiny, in real life.

Dark Skies, the now-cancelled lead-in to this daring and risky network "thrillogy" of shows (the other two were renewed for the 1997–98 season), based itself entirely on the MJ-12 propaganda stories created at the beginning of the Reagan years as disinformation against Paul Bennewitz, and one or two minor related predecessors of the type. The show's proposed plan was to begin with Kennedy's Camelot and present more or less real-time evolution of behind-the-scenes government conspiracies from 1963 on. The conclusion of the two-hour pilot revealed that John F. Kennedy was assassinated as the result of what he and his brother Robert were discovering from inside government investigators on the UFO phenomenon, who of course were operating entirely in secret without informing the Executive Branch.

That idea was seriously proposed in ex-Naval Intelligence agent Bill Cooper's 1991 disinformational propaganda book, *Behold A Pale Horse*—the author also claimed in the same book to have witnessed Kennedy's assassination on T.V. the day it happened (which is impossible, since all sets across the country blacked out before the shots were fired), and to have seen Kennedy's driver firing the fatal shot (certainly a new twist, even in the tabloid circuit). The show's creator and executive producer, Bryce Zabel, the son of a history teacher, admits that exactly such sources were his direct inspiration. He had written the first film of the Sci-Fi Channel, 1993's *Official Denial*, and received the now-clichéd "mysterious phone call" from someone who had read the script. (The movie portrayed MJ-12 as a real group who keep tabs on abductees and regularly shoots down flying saucers, and concluded that the Grays were degenerated future humans time-traveling to our present in order to prevent environmental catastrophes resulting in their deformation.) Zabel's caller was a man claiming to be an ex-field operative of Majestic-12. Not surprisingly, the man confirmed all the most tenuous and least substantiated tenets of the various stories that have been circulating about that fictitious group for the past fifteen years, and less surprisingly, Zabel, like so many before him, accepted it all without the slightest shred of evidence or confirmation that the caller had the credentials he claimed.

The entire MJ-12 scenario is based on nothing but forged documents, and as such—at least as it has been proposed—is entirely groundless. Demonstrating *Dark Skies'* lack of internal consistency, the pilot episode strongly implied that MJ-12 was responsible for Kennedy's murder, then it was discovered in the next episode that the alien "Hive"—a literally inhuman depiction of 1950s Communists, for whom the good of the whole is all and to whom individuality does not exist—not only killed JFK, but possessed Jack Ruby to kill Lee Harvey Oswald, as well. (If the series was in any way CIA-inspired or -sponsored, this was a rather plain example of tarring the enemy with one's own brush.) "In life, President Kennedy had inspired me to a higher standard," proclaimed the protagonist at the conclusion of the first regular season episode. "I resolved that his death would have no lesser effect. The enemy was out there. They had claimed our leader. But the war was far from over." During the course of the series, the Hive was fingered, in typical Cold War fashion, as the group of evil bad-guys behind every "subversive" group imaginable—the funniest shown being the anti-Vietnam War movement, with a Hive-converted former MJ-12 member assuming the identity of Charles Manson.

Dark Skies' protagonist, John Loengard (i.e., "Lone Guard"), was a young recruit into the fictional MJ-12 group, and a few of the "facts" he discovered there are not all that far removed from those that can be ascertained through actual FOIA-released documents, even if the vast majority have no connection at all to reality. The government investigators operated in secret, but on a fairly large scale. They had offices and openly discussed UFO information among themselves at work without having to conceal what it was they were talking about. They treated their job as a military one and viewed Earth as being "at war" with invading aliens—who of course were strongly implied to be quite hostile (and reptilian, looking like comic-book Grays). And, as the group warned all its members to insure their secrecy, "people die in wars." (Hence, the Kennedy assassination.)

Aside from this and other minor concessions to factual UFOlogy (the production of human offspring connected somehow to cattle mutilations was dramatized), everything else about the series was pure propaganda, nothing more than yet another retelling of Reagan Era disinformation based on nightmarish 1950s scenarios. The opening narration to each show, given by the protagonist, made clear *Dark Skies'* tone and intent from the outset: "My name is John Loengard. We may not live through the night. They're here. They're hostile. Powerful people don't want you to know. History is a lie." Then his wife's voice was heard, fearful and apprehensive, in the background: "John, someone's coming!" The sneaky alien invaders implanted their abductees with their own "ganglia," a nerve-center parasite, that affixed itself to the host and then controlled their actions (which, needless to say, were "unfriendly"). To give the series a personal stake, the protagonist's wife was abducted and implanted by the diabolical space-reptiles in the first episode, to be heroically saved in the eleventh hour before the ganglion could take permanent hold of her. Any means of restraint and torturous medical treatment was portrayed as justifiable in combating the alien menace, identical to the treatment of witches in the Middle Ages. Loengard's wife ended up defecting to the aliens anyway before the end of the series, since the aliens took away her and John's baby.

Historical figures were dramatized in scenes that assuredly have little, if any, connection to those which may have occurred in real life, recalling the comments by historians Haynes Johnson, J. H. Plumb, and J. S. Holiday on the propagandistic distortion of history through drama. Major Jesse Marcel, for instance, the Roswell base officer who recovered the wreckage for the military from rancher Mac Brazel's farm, was shown to be a nervous wreck for having guarded an alien artifact he kept from the site—in reality, Marcel accepted his orders as he would any others, and lived his life in as average a manner as anyone else. ("Maybe we'll all be going to Mars someday for vacation, huh?" they had Marcel saying in a reenactment, witnessing the arrival of a saucer that the military then shot down—another scene with no documents or testimony to back it in reality, though the reference to the Red Planet was certainly interesting.) Howard Hughes was portrayed as entirely ignorant of flying saucer reality, which is utterly unbelievable—Hughes was in reality a test pilot and designer of experimental aircraft himself, and perhaps the wealthiest single individual in government defense contracting; if anyone in the world knew something about flying saucer technology, it would have to have been Hughes. Additionally, his movie studio, RKO, made the first realistic flying saucer film, *The Thing from Another World* (see Chapter 1), and that same studio's science fiction stock was bought by its more prolific successor in factual flying saucer movies, MGM, when Hughes closed shop. The episode "Strangers in the Night" had Captain Colin Powell recruited to help fight the Hive; the heroic Captain Powell begged-off after his first encounter, preferring to return to the jungles of Vietnam. The same episode showed Carl Sagan being kidnapped by MJ-12 for recruitment, owing to his belief in life on other worlds. When the head of the organization asked him how many worlds in the universe might harbor alien life, Sagan seriously replied, "Billions and billions!" This is a prime example of the simplistically comical rendering of historical figures that was evident throughout the series.

In the pilot episode, President Truman was shown being confronted by a skinny little reptilian Gray, who gave him a communications device through which it "telepathically" spoke. "The buck stops here!" the episode has Truman heroically say, in so trumped-up a manner that it can only be humorous, touching the device and relaying the message he receives: "My God—that thing just spoke! They just demanded our unconditional surrender! ... It's not negotiable! It was an ultimatum! 'Surrender, or else!' I'll tell you gentlemen—I will not be the first president to lose a war!" The military outline the basics of MJ-12 to the president as the only possible means to resist the invading alien menace. "Well," Truman sighs, "God help us if we're wrong—because we're about to bet the entire human race! We're going on the offensive, men! And if we live through this, I want him [the head of ONI] in charge of cleaning up this mess!" More absurdly patriotic dialogue than this has found its way into blatant wartime propaganda films, but not anytime recently.

In the worst historical howler of the entire series, "The Warren Omission" had Loengard bringing MJ-12 and the invader aliens to the attention of the Warren Commission as the assassins of the president. Loengard of course being disbelieved, his ally on the inside—JFK's brother, Bobby Kennedy—leads the Justice Department on a paramilitary raid of the top-secret government group's offices. There, he interrogates an uncooperative young Captain Norman Schwarzkopf and witnesses the Zapruder film—which is shown from the wrong angle and displaying something the real Zapruder film does not, which is a close-up angle of Kennedy's driver shooting the president with a pocket pistol (the exact forementioned story related by ONI counterintelligence agent Bill Cooper). Bobby does not act upon the information, however, because MJ-12 blackmails J. Edgar Hoover (his homosexuality with Clive Tolson) to blackmail Bobby Kennedy (his affair with Marilyn Monroe). Earl Warren does insist on MJ-12's head officer reporting the truth to him in private chambers, and there he is told that what really happened at Roswell was that the Russians tried to steal two H-bombs that were located there—and Warren believes it.

The H-bomb did not exist until 1952, almost a full five and a half years after Roswell, something Warren would certainly know. What makes this glaring idiocy all the more unpalatable is not even that the historical research behind it is so shoddy, but that Roswell *was* actually the only unit in the world in possession of a working atomic bomb at the time of the famous crash. If historical believability had been of any importance to *Dark Skies*, it would simply have mentioned the actual atomic bomb instead of the impossible H-bombs. Were the show's producers unaware that their facts were inaccurate, or were they deliberately playing on the gullibility and lack of education of their audience?

A similar "the-government-will-kill-anyone-who-knows" movie was broadcast on NBC on October 13, 1996, starring Faith Ford as a graduate student journalist who inadvertently discovers the identity of *Night Visitors*. Her government agent brother is murdered by an MJ-12–inspired government cadre, after he steals the corpse of an alien recovered from a saucer crash. The group makes constant referral to "Moon Dust," which was once an actual Air Force "project" that very probably did work on UFO crash retrievals. Ford's brother's treasonous act is done in revenge for Moon Dust's having murdered his wife, along with all other witnesses to the crash in which they retrieved the alien. Uncovering the entire story, Ford asks the murderer in charge of Moon Dust, "Is that how you protect people, colonel? By killing them? . . . So, you gonna kill me too, colonel? And [my nephew]? And anyone else who knows about this?" Affirming that such is precisely his plan, the colonel is stopped by the fact that their conversation has been transmitted live on the afternoon news. Earlier, the colonel has explained his actions: "I have the security of a nation to think about. It's unclear whether these 'visitations' are the prelude to an attack, or something much worse. These aliens are tagging people, Miss Wells. They're extracting sperm and ova by force, abducting children. Does that sound to you like a race that considers us their equals? Or does that sound to you like a race that thinks we should be controlled like chicken, cattle?"

In real-life terms, the fictional colonel's argument is credible and correct, but limited, and certainly represents the crutch on which National Security has functioned for the past fifty years. What it fails to bring up is that the "aliens" are human (albeit often employing robots), and never harm any of their abductees, or that their actions could hardly be carried out in the open when they are being shot at by the various governments of the world. It also fails to take into account the broader, long-term experience reported by the vast majority of those who have been abducted, who more often than not state a feeling of kinship with the extraterrestrials which makes the very term "abduction" something of a misnomer. And it completely fails to present the reasons for the extraterrestrials' intrusion into our affairs, which is primarily to dismantle the extremely dangerous and unsafe Cold War machinery erected by the very agencies who work so hard to make the alien presence appear as nothing but a threat. As far as the murdering of UFO witnesses goes, the evidence indicates that, if it ever occurred, it was only in the earliest years of the phenomenon, when Secretary of Defense James V. Forrestal went out a hospital window to his death. A small number of other credible cases could be presented for similar early "accidents," though generally it appears that all the government does is to monitor witnesses and abductees closely, not harm them in any way. At least one case of an Intelligence insider being murdered by his peers is on record concerning the unauthorized disclosure of ULTRA during WWII, and certainly a great many witnesses to the JFK assassination have been murdered—but in the case of UFOs, this does not seem to be a common occurrence, if it was ever an occurrence at all. Orion's *The Arrival* brought more evil EBEs in search of Earth conquest, the same year Faith Ford was uncovering sinister government conspiracies on T.V.—these were insectoid Grays, despoiling Earth's biosphere in the same manner as Fox's recent *Invaders*.

Following the same MJ-12 disinformational scenario, even Ernest Hemingway's niece, Hilary, has entered the UFOlogical fray, in a co-authored novel with Jeffrey P. Lindsay called *Dreamland* that hit the stands the same time *Independence Day* opened in the theaters. *Dreamland,* supposedly written with partial cooperation from the Department of Defense, for the most part simply carries on the EBE hoax, though one of its plot elements certainly has all the earmarks of accuracy: a top-secret military project called JOSHUA, which intends to produce a destructive sonic weapon derived from recovered flying saucer technology. In typical fashion, the military/Intelligence agencies are shown assassinating any inconvenient links to their shadowy realm of exploited knowledge. In less typical fashion, the purported EBEs are fictionalized as entirely benign alien biological entities who empower abductees within the government to overthrow their military overlords.

The Robin Cook miniseries *Invasion* aired on NBC May 4 and 5, 1997, presenting a mishmash of better-produced sci-fi from previous years to an audience that never saw that previous science fiction. Beginning with a mini-UFO invasion out of *Quatermass II,* tiny "meteorites" from space explode a mutagenic virus into passers-by who pick them up. The infected victims then gradually mutate into the alien race that caused them to be injected, and become their own little abductee society working in *Invasion of the Body Snatchers* secret cooperation with each other toward the end of spreading the "infection." The alien inductees prepare the way for a mammoth incoming UFO to arrive as the Second Coming, forcing a "betterment" or "harvesting" of mankind. Ultimately, their *Five Million Years to Earth* convert-or-die plan for humanity is destroyed by the simple injection of the virus antidote into the alien's leader among mankind.

On a more promising and hopeful note, the second astronaut on the Moon, Buzz Aldrin, has co-authored (with John Barnes) the novel *Encounter with Tiber,* that may be less fictional than it purports. Its plot centers around SETI receiving signals from Alpha Centauri, coming from an ancient race of humanoids called the "Tiberians" (obviously a play on the mysterious Iberians, one of the advanced people from antiquity about whom little is known). The Tiberians inform us that they still have active and inhabited bases on Mars and beneath the surface of the Moon—those two locations which, in real life, appear to show exactly such evidence. Aldrin's Tiberians are completely benign, in contrast to the unfortunate recent *Independence Day* trend in revived MJ-12 conspiracy stories and demonized outsiders. In fact, Aldrin has been outspoken in labeling *Independence Day* as a grossly improbable scenario. Similarly hopeful is the 1997 Columbia UFOlogical entry, *The Fifth Element,* in which the plot elements of *Stargate* are reworked from interplanetary war to the search for universal peace. Like the Underworlders of Lord Edward Bulwer-Lytton's *Vril,* the extraterrestrials guarding mankind's future in *The Fifth Element* are a race of benign automata living beneath the sands of Egypt.

Still, "promise" and "hope" are presently low on the UFO index in entertainment media, the prevailing attitude for the past ten to seventeen years being that which plagued the educational project from the beginning: fear and ridicule. For probably the first time in history, a Democratic administration—and a two-term one, at that—is continuing to expand on the fear-factor, rather than diminish it. With that in mind, it is time to sum up what has been discussed in these pages, and give due consideration to the Hollywood UFO project's future.

12

Conclusions and Considerations

Carlos Clarens, author of the classic *An Illustrated History of the Horror Film*, notes that "the only literary genre to have flourished since the war [WWII] ... only one step ahead of the headlines" is science fiction. Commenting on the more than forty sci-fi/horror films released in the 1957–58 season alone, and lamenting "the sad but inescapable fact" that "until the last few years, few directors of importance were to attempt science fiction films," Clarens writes, "*The Man from Planet X* may be negligible, but the Flying Saucer scare was not. Still, one may have seen *Terror from the Year 5000* or even *The Underwater City*, but who can claim such devotion to film research as to have sat through *The Space Children, War of the Satellites* and *Attack of the 50 Foot Woman?*"

Who can claim such devotion? We can. We have, after all, just done exactly that—or the next best thing. And we have contemplated the reasons behind "the dismayingly low level of craftsmanship in most of them [which] make it well nigh impossible to cover the genre thoroughly," as Clarens puts it. While a great many books catalogue the tremendous number of mind-numbingly awful sci-fi horror films from WWII to the present day, few if any attribute any reason for their staggeringly cheap quality than simple ineptitude on the part of the production teams involved. In some instances, this prosaic explanation may even suffice, as may the fact that funding could be hard to come by. Certainly Ed Wood was a bad filmmaker by any standard, science fiction hardly being the only genre in which he failed miserably despite his seeming best intentions. And Roger Corman, whose passion for filmmaking shows through even the cheapest of his works, was hampered by the framework of many a low budget upon which to build his lofty visions.

But then, both of these men had connections to the federal government, and/or the military. Wood, whether or not he was in military intelligence as he claimed, had secret FBI clearance and made government industrial films. Corman was a top-notch engineer with a background in hard aviation science, a product of the U.S. Navy. Corman's compatriots had similar backgrounds: fellow director Herman Cohen, four-year U.S. Marine veteran; author/screenwriter Richard Matheson, high school physics prodigy, war veteran, and post-war Douglas Aircraft employee; script writer Ib Melchior, a man so patriotic that he petitioned the U.S. government for enlistment after Pearl Harbor even though his émigré family had barely arrived on American shores, given special clearance by the FBI and drafted into a lifelong career in counterintelligence; technical hypnosis and mind control advisor William Joseph Bryan, Jr., head of the U.S. military's brainwashing division during the Korean War; actor Vincent Price, internationally traveled Yale graduate, big business scion, Orson Welles' Mercury Theater alumnus and potential CIA agent.

If these AIP-connected men's backgrounds were not indicative of a military/government involvement with media sci-fi, wouldn't those of their peers at least pique a bit of suspicion? *Tomorrowland* promulgator and FBI Special Agent in Charge Walt Disney; *Star Trek* creator Gene Roddenberry, WWII pilot and personal protégé of CIA-connected LAPD Chief William Parker; war veteran Rod Serling, creator of *The Twilight Zone; The Outer Limits'* creator, Leslie Stevens, Orson Welles alum and second-generation military intelligence man (the first generation being a vice admiral MIT-graduate father who was naval attaché to Russia at the height of the Cold War); war vet and fellow Orson Welles alum sci-fi film producer William Alland; James Bond creator Ian Fleming, one of only two men to brief the

United States on WWII's most critical Allied secret, ULTRA; Fleming's colleague and first recruit into Britain's most elite counterintelligence corps, popular psychic/occult novelist Dennis Wheatley; *The Avengers'* star Patrick Macnee, blue-blood Etonian ex-Naval Intelligence man; Macnee's co-star (and close friend of Vincent Price) Diana Rigg, recently made a Dame; Royal Academy of Dramatic Arts prizewinning author/scriptwriter Nigel Kneale; Lord Lew Grade protégés Gerry and Sylvia Anderson, creators of numerous UFOlogical kid's shows. And these are but a few examples.

Skeptics could manage to protect themselves from the concept of Intelligence insiders using the film and television media for mis- or disinformation, on the UFO topic or any other. It could, after all, be legitimately proposed that the apparent UFO foreknowledge exhibited in films was instead merely the seed that caused later claims of UFO sightings or abductions in real life—but then, how to account for those cases where the timing of the fictional event and that of the real occurrence overlap, and parties involved on each side could not be aware of the other? What about those people—and they are many— like critic Carlos Clarens, who cannot bring themselves to sit through such low-budget entertainments as United Artists or American International science fiction fare? What about the witnesses and abductees who are not science fiction fans? What about the consistent physical evidence of their experiences, such as pink-eye, radiation poisoning, various marks on the body, and psychological evidence of having undergone hypnotic mind-control procedures?

In regard to the idea that hysterical contagion from science fiction is responsible for UFO reports, renowned UFOlogist/mythologist Thomas E. Bullard has noted, "If Hollywood is responsible for these images [in real reports], where are the monsters? Where are the robots?" As this study has shown, the robots are there in the abductees' reports—but the abductees are unaware themselves that robots are what they are reporting. Someone in Hollywood, however, has known for a long time that robots occupy UFOs, as can be witnessed in example after example brought forth here and examined at length. With today's access to the historical record, not to mention numerous documents released through the Freedom of

Information Act, it is a simple matter to detect robot UFO occupants—but who would have had that knowledge in previous decades, when the entire UFO subject was the most highly classified in the U.S. government? And even if they figured out that much about UFO reality, how many people would have realized the connection between UFOs and mind control? Or the planet Mars? Or—most obscure of all—the connection between ancient Egypt and Atlantis? And soundwave weaponry? Yet these particular elements are the very ones that so pervasively recur in UFOlogical movies ... those movies made by the aforementioned military- and Intelligence-connected parties.

That the CIA has numerous connections in the media is not questioned. That they might therefore have had contacts in the film business since WWII who were one way or another connected to actual UFO research, then, is not even unlikely, but actually probable. It is all the more probable when the scientific and military backgrounds of those closest to the production of UFOlogical movies is taken into consideration. Adding to that probability is the prior military/government connection of Rosicrucian/Masonic figures to Lost World or other mythologically astute "romances" of the nineteenth century, such as Lord Edward Bulwer-Lytton, Sir James M. Barrie, Bram Stoker, Jules Verne, and others. H. G. Wells, the most devoted of pacifists, was a member of his government's military intelligence in the First World War—and the first man to seriously propose (in fictional garb) that Mars was an inhabited world, based on UFO reports of his time. Soviet colonel Alexander Kazantsev concurred with Wells' assessment as an explanation for the Siberian atomic blast of 1908, and figures and organizations as prominent as Nikola Tesla, Lord Kelvin, Guglielmo Marconi, David Todd, C. Francis Jenkins, the U.S. Navy and the U.S. Signal Corps were reporting the reception of apparently intelligent signals from the Red Planet between the turn of the century and 1926. WWII Pacific Theater of Operations Commander in Chief General Douglas MacArthur was a serious and secret student of UFO reports, as was the Royal Air Force, and the U.S. Army had (and later officially disbanded) an "Interplanetary Phenomenon Unit" that surely was doing something more than idly gazing at the asteroid belt.

As just mentioned by Carlos Clarens, the Flying Saucer scare was in the nineteen-fifties a serious threat, or at least perceived as one. Cold War paranoia was bad enough by itself, given the atomic bomb (and its swiftly born brother, the hydrogen bomb) as a new and permanent birth in the world. To add to public awareness the reality that there were other players in the game, let alone when specific answers about those players' motivations and methods were still under research, was hardly a viable possibility. The mere Air Force conclusion that UFOs were interplanetary spacecraft was enough to drive the first Secretary of Defense, James V. Forrestal, out of his mind. If Forrestal panicked, who could say what the average man on the street might do if confronted with superior extraterrestrials? Let alone extraterrestrials so superior that they could slip in and out of junior's bedroom at night, engage him in sex, subject him to medical tests and surgical procedures, and whisper such unknown sweet nothings in his ear that he could conceivably even become a future saboteur or assassin? Who could have made such a public revelation back in 1948? Who could do it today?

The answer, of course, is that no one could—not without asking for repercussions so potentially serious that they might well be more harmful than productive, no matter how open and honest the parties making such discoveries might want to be with the public. First CIA director Admiral Roscoe H. Hillenkoetter was of the opinion in 1960 that everything the Agency knew about UFOs should be brought forth before Congress for public debate. Only time will tell whether it was wiser to keep the facts concealed. But in light of the fact that they did remain under wraps, it certainly makes sense that a proposed popular deflectional project on the UFO subject would undergo the changes we can see it did, turning gradually more into an informational tool than a misinformational one. Hillenkoetter's desire to publicly share information can hardly have been isolated in the Agency. There must have been others who shared his view. And even if party lines dictated that Agency contacts or military intelligence assets continue using the entertainment media to debunk the subject, political parties are rarely monoliths—some members surely utilized their positions in the industry to begin effecting change, according to the dictates of their own conscience.

But in the beginning, it is probable if not certain that the government would have been interested in utilizing entertainment media
for the purpose of popular deflection. What better way to give the
people the impression that all UFO reports were insubstantial than
to give them the pervasive *impression* that such was the case? Movies,
comic books, cartoons, and the like hardly define any real issue—
but they do make a lasting *impression*. When any issue is repeatedly
seen to be ignored on a serious level, and instead made an object of
great ridicule, it becomes thought of in exactly such a fashion on a
subliminal level by the beholder. With the topic made ridiculous, no
one would think to ask about or pursue it at any great length: after
all, everyone *knows* it's silly.

As film critic John Stanley wrote of Herman Cohen's *Blood of Dracula,* even forty years after its 1957 release, "Would you believe a vampire movie with songs? Would you believe hypnosis turning Sandra
Harrison into a bloodsucker? Would you believe an all-girls' school
where the headmistress has evil powers? Would you believe . . . naw,
you wouldn't believe." Which is precisely the point. The CIA was
formed initially out of the very ranks of the Third Reich who had
successfully performed such a previous deflection of public attention from their own occult studies, banning and ridiculing those
studies openly while engaging in them in private. The same held
true for UFO study in post-war America, and its numerous related
fields—including mind control.

The deflection program additionally makes a great deal of sense
simply on an intuitive level. Recognizing that UFO sightings and
experiences were going to be inevitable—let alone in great quantity—wouldn't the government want not only to divert popular attention from the subject and minimize it, but also to provide an
underlying aura of safety for anyone who might become a sighter
. . . or an abductee? Parents confronted with their terrified child's
complaint in the morning that monsters had been in his room the
night before could safely relate that child's experience to being a
nightmare—or, better still, to his seeing *Invaders from Mars* or *Invasion of the Body Snatchers* at the Saturday movie matinee. After all,
the experience was the same, wasn't it? The parents feel safe and

secure with a rational explanation for their offspring's seemingly very real terror, and so does the child. In fact, it would be likely that the young boy or girl would realize such a connection themselves, without even having to tell their parents. In short, the pervasive aura created by movies realistic in content but ludicrous in handling would quell any *reports*—they would defuse potential *disturbance*. Ultimately, that is all any government is really concerned with.

And certainly there is no question that the government—or at least the military, if the two can be said to be different from each other—was engaged in precisely such deflective reassurances on the UFO topic. The "Washington Nationals" of 1952, when UFOs were witnessed by the world for two nights in one week over the United States capital, were sandbagged by Major General John Samford's press conference—the biggest since WWII. Samford offered no real explanations, but then, he didn't have to. His simple air of assurance, aided by the quiet seeming agreement of the official Air Force head of the project to study exactly such unidentified aerial phenomena, provided all that was necessary to head off genuine scrutiny. As that Air Force project head, Captain Edward J. Ruppelt, put it, "It did take pressure off Project Blue Book—reports dropped from fifty a day to ten a day inside of a week." Such a phenomenal drop in reports could hardly help but encourage the Intelligence community's use of Hollywood in the same way—and the Robertson Panel's 1953 recommendation confirms that the CIA's plan was to do precisely that.

The use of Hollywood in this manner is predicated by the likelihood that Depression-era pulp fiction had been used for the same purpose. As we have seen, government investigation on both sides of the Atlantic (and even Russia) into the possibility of Mars being an inhabited world is in evidence from before the turn of the twentieth century. H. G. Wells laid the groundwork with his *The War of the Worlds* in 1898, and Orson Welles exploited it to full advantage forty years later. In those forty years, a substantial number of prominent men demonstrated quite an active interest in the Red Planet. How unlikely is it that Welles' famous hoax was calculated? Welles was, after all, a politically active man, committed to Franklin Delano

Roosevelt's fourth term re-election. If his government had asked him to test the public opinion concerning extraterrestrial neighbors, would Welles have said no? Orson Welles—the man who made a life-long career out of flamboyant fraud? Sci-fi pulp fiction arose in virtually the same heartbeat as the infamous Mercury Theatre "Invasion from Mars" radio broadcast. And several individuals prominently associated with UFOlogically accurate science fiction in Hollywood were with Welles at the time of his scare-show, or shortly thereafter: William Alland, Leslie Stevens, and Vincent Price, for instance. Does it stretch credibility so much to perceive the simple passing of a torch?

After all the material presented in this study, the existence of a government educational/disinformational UFO program in the entertainment media can hardly be doubted. It is backed by plentiful evidence, as well as standing up to common sense. What should be of more concern at this point is putting the past of that program into proper perspective, and instead to concentrate on where the program can go from here.

The present tug-of-war between Republicans and Democrats for Congressional control leaves the future of UFO reporting uncertain. Larry King's 1995 presentation of *UFO Coverup: Live from Area 51* on TNT was surprisingly fair, the station also replaying *The UFO Incident* about Betty and Barney Hill. A faithful rendering of the Hills' story, it demonstrates something debunkers do not like to acknowledge: accused of causing hysterical contagion in later reports, the dramatization subtly alters some details; the same occurrences reported by others do not coincide with the movie, but with the Hills' actual account, which is not fully shown. *Sightings* (formerly on Fox, partly syndicated, and now moved to cable's Sci-Fi Channel) provides an open forum for material that mainline reporters refuse to touch, but relatively more objective shows such as this are in the minority.

In general, UFOs have so long now been made sport of that they have become a comical institution in their own right, which was the original intention of the Robertson Panel. Intelligence insiders are no longer required to ballyhoo the subject, though no doubt they still do so to some extent. Steven Spielberg's *Animaniacs* cartoons make laughingstock of alien abductions, which have replaced saucer sightings as the central object of disinformation. His *A Pinky and the Brain Christmas* of 1995 featured the proto-CIA mastermind, "The Brain," attempting to hypnotize the world through radio-transceiver dolls distributed by Santa's workshop. The same character, and his moronic yes-man (or "-mouse") sidekick have often either staged alien invasion hoaxes or in some way been comically connected to aliens. Spielberg is the new Disney, America's family entertainment man, and also the inheritor of the newest developments in robot "animatronics," as *Close Encounters* and *Jurassic Park* ably demonstrate. "The Terrible Choc-Toma-Tron," a UFO robot child-abductor, becomes more ludicrous than he already is when thwarted by the Nestle's Qwik Rabbit, and a recent Rice Krispies commercial featured harmless eccentrics at a "UFO Club" saying that they believe in "Alien abductions, yes ... Taste that good in a breakfast cereal? No!" So is the fascinating and important continually reduced to the trivial and mundane.

The ridicule continues, as does the propaganda. The Pentagon heartily endorsed the terrifyingly inaccurate portrayal of Travis Walton's abduction in *Fire in the Sky,* and evil space invader movies are everywhere in greater abundance than ever. *Species, Stargate, Independence Day,* and numerous others like them are presently the norm, all but extinguishing the more curious and intelligent examinations of the UFO question witnessed in the 1960s and '70s. For every *Star Trek* or *Outer Limits,* there are a dozen *Dark Skies.*

Twice on September 15, 1996, and repeated once again the next night for maximum exposure, TBS aired "Alien Abductions" on *National Geographic's TOPX.* The two-hour program was typical of mainstream media handling of all UFO topics, abductions in particular, in that its case studies were only superficially covered and of questionable veracity at best. Half-hour commercials aired in advance of the actual airing, making it a highly hyped production, and the director admitted to his involvement in the project (in which he had no interest) owing solely to his having been commissioned for a great deal of money. Half of the four case studies involved were more or less standard, with another two wildly different from usual reports and rather outlandish, in the same manner as Whitley Strieber's stories are outlandish. No effort was made to establish the truth or falsehood of the claims involved, leaving the viewer with a confused mishmash of inconsistent information from which to approach the topic.

The purpose for the production was obviously to leave its viewers either confused or frightened, not enlightened, exactly in the same manner as earlier specious examinations of the UFO topic presented by such CIA-sponsored teams as the Robertson Panel and the Condon Committee. The narrator was plainly chosen for his vocal similarities to *The Twilight Zone*'s Rod Serling, and even ended with a warning note that left viewers with the unsettling feeling that their reality might at any moment be intruded upon at a lonely crossroads. The "abductees" selected all sounded the "politically correct" interpretation of alien abductions, which is the threatening one that "we're lab rats to them," a phrase dutifully repeated by all involved in the broadcast, despite the fact that the vast majority of abductees come away from the experience with a much more positive impression. Only one abductologist, Raymond Fowler, was represented, ignoring the very notable work of mythologist Thomas Bullard, Temple University Professor David M. Jacobs, Budd Hopkins, or Harvard's Dr. John E. Mack. One case presented bore no similarity to actual abductions and lacked the emotional abreaction when "uncovered" by hypnosis on the show that is common in true cases. Though it might be nothing more than coincidence, the movie that aired immediately following the second night's encore performance of "Alien Abductions" was 1982's independent release, *One Dark Night*—one of the nastiest of the "living dead" abduct-a-thon stalk-and-gore movies, in the same nightmarish vein as Universal's *The Funhouse*.

At the time of this writing, Columbia Pictures has just released the Spielberg comedy *Men In Black*—already slated also to be a 1997 cartoon on the Warner Bros. Network's fall lineup—which is more or less *Ghostbusters* with extraterrestrial (as opposed to extradimensional) villains. "We are your best—your last—your only line of defense!" goes the ad slogan. The latest in Warner Bros. oft-UFO-logical Batman series, *Batman and Robin,* presents Uma Thurman and

Arnold Schwarzenegger as Poison Ivy and Mr. Freeze, the former a mind-controlling eco-terrorist/geneticist and the latter a robotic, hate-consumed technological genius (he is blue-gray, bald and bulletproof, in a gleaming metallic silver suit), who are intent on becoming the new "Adam and Evil" by destroying all life on Earth and replacing it with their own bio-engineered master race—the same sort of UFOlogical menace witnessed in such James Bond entries as *You Only Live Twice, The Spy Who Loved Me* and *Moonraker* (all, ironically and atypically enough, also filmed during Democratic administrations, proving that even those usually more open administrations are not free of the standard Republican fear governing the subject). The Warner Bros. Network's new surprise hit adapted from Joss Whedon's 1992 20th Century Fox film, *Buffy the Vampire Slayer,* is covering the territory formerly carried by H. P. Lovecraft, Seabury Quinn, *The Night Stalker* and Richard Matheson's *I Am Legend,* with Sarah Michelle Gellar playing a warrior defending Earth against a returning eldritch vampire race attempting to exterminate mankind and reclaim its former world. Warner Bros. film version of Carl Sagan's *Contact,* starring Jodie Foster, may be the only non-hostile E.T. movie in sight—though, on an additional note of hope, Fox Television is introducing a series into its Fall 1997 Friday night lineup about a UFO-abducted pilot from WWII returning to help the human race on behalf of aliens, which curiously enough is produced by *Stargate* and *Independence Day*'s Dean Devlin and Roland Emmerich. It may be noted that *Contact*'s producer/director, Robert Zemeckis, last executive produced Universal's 1996 odd misfire horror comedy, *The Frighteners,* in which a woman first seduced by a serial killer when she was fifteen continues to commit murders under the influence of his spirit from "the other side" long after the killer's execution.

The most important thing about the Hollywood-government UFO program at this point is to recognize it, and by so doing to accomplish what those involved in the project from the beginning must always have intended: to ultimately create a forum for open, intelligent, and thorough examination of the entire topic. Until the UFO question is accepted as a reality by the public, it will continue to be propagandized and distorted, serving the purposes of no one but the already bloated military and Intelligence communities. If genuine threats are posed by the foreign intelligence operating the extraterrestrial craft in our skies, then these should be discussed rationally, not manipulated to enrich the few at the expense of the many. If, on the other hand, there is truly nothing to fear, then there is no reason to continue the ridiculous secrecy shrouding everything to do with the topic. As long as such secrecy is maintained, there will be more MK-ULTRAs—and programs of that particular ilk cannot be considered to have any good excuse for continuance, never having had a moral right to exist in the first place.

At the same time, it should be recognized that the individuals involved in UFO research, and the Hollywood educational project attached to it, were not monsters. There can be no question that they considered themselves to be genuine patriots, or at the very least protecting the public welfare. In the sense that they helped allay the potential fears of the masses, they are even to be congratulated. If some members involved in the project took what they were learning from, say, the MK-ULTRA program, and were perverting it for personal profit at the public's expense, it can only be said that bad men are everywhere—as are good ones. The only way to keep evil from gaining ascendancy in such projects is to strip away their secrecy, so they will no longer have power to harm. As dramatized in the very type of bad movies we have been examining, vampires reduce to dust when dragged into the daylight. Until all of us set ourselves with determination to do precisely that, we have none but ourselves to blame if further harm results.

But the best possible coda to this not-so-fictional science-fiction double feature is Warner Bros.' 1991 network special, *Bugs Bunny's Lunar Tunes*. Made after the *Phobos 2* loss and before CIA President George Bush's leaving the Oval Office, it could be expected to be more than usually significant in the UFO media-Intelligence game. The story begins with Marvin the Martian listing complaints against Planet Earth: "They've blasted us from all sides with rocketships and whatnot, sullied up our nice universe with stinky pollution, portrayed us as monsters, and fabricated entertainment spectacles about destroying us!" Bugs Bunny is abducted to be the defendant in the case of "United Amalgam of Astral Bodies vs. Planet Earth." The judge is a gray-suited Marvin-ish humanoid with the three-fingered hands of Paramount's 1953 *The War of the Worlds* Martians, and Jack Nicholson's (mock) voice, who announces, "Begin the persecution!"

"Almost as soon as you learned to walk, you naughty Earth specimens were trying to fly," Marvin begins. "Next, you shot off a vast array of quaint lower life forms on missions into space—mice, monkeys, dogs, and even . . ." Marvin indicates Bugs himself, leading to a recapitulation of their 1948 encounter on the Moon in "Haredevil Hare," when Marvin first attempted to "Blow up the Earth!"

Bugs counters that no one in space ever answers our SETI calls, to which the Judge responds, "How do you suppose your lackluster evolution got its start?" A commercial airs: "TIME/SPACE BOOKS presents Do-It-Yourself Hints from your pals, the Ancient Astronauts! With TIME/SPACE guide to evolution, you can learn the secrets of major civilizations! Start with Volume 1, 'What Is Fire?'!" Other volumes are shown: "Get to Know Your Opposable Thumb," "Cave Paint by Numbers," and "How to Build a Better Pyramid."

Persecutor Marvin calls forth his key witness to present evidence against Earth, during which Bugs hypnotizes a space-eye with a watch. Aimless human activity is cited, combined with random technological expansion. "Their so-called Industrial Revolution has led to ungainly, unsightly and foul-smelling modes of locomotion which gives rise to pollutants," recites the witness. "At the same time, they chop down their forests, squandering their natural resources in the production of unnecessary products. Their methods are wasteful, their priorities scrambled, and their results dubious." Marvin adds that the hole Earth has poked in its ozone layer gave the other planets "secondary inhalation syndrome."

Bugs tells the Martians they could have bothered to warn us on Earth. Marvin says they have tried. A rocket is shown delivering a message to an Earth couple in the suburbs. It knocks on the door, and the husband answers his wife's query with, "Oh, it's nothing. Just a kind of rocket with a message from Mars." "Oh, is that all," she sighs. "I'm always afraid it'll be a telegram from Mother." Simultaneously, they realize, and exclaim, *"MARS?!?"* They read the message:

":MARSGRAM: DEAR EARTHLINGS: YOU ARE NOT ALONE IN THE UNI-VERSE. LET'S GET TOGETHER SOON. YOUR NEIGHBOR, MARVIN. P.S. IS NEXT TUESDAY O.K. WITH YOU?" Attempts are shown at Martian contact with "the Earth's foremost thinkers," but the response is only nervous breakdowns and other "elementary responses" from the emotionally immature "great minds," who lecture from their podiums that "Men from Mars" are imaginary. A clip from the cartoon "Martian Through Georgia" is shown, in which a friendly visitor from Mars is arrested and treated as a monster. A number of propagandizations against extraterrestrials, exactly like those presented in these pages (and using many of the same examples), are brought forth as evidence of Earth hostility to visitors from beyond. Earth's military imperialism and use of atomic weaponry is cited.

In defense, Bugs calls attention to his own unwelcome abductions to Mars by Marvin. The Iliudium Pew-36 Explosive Space Modulator is brought in as counter-evidence of Mars' own militaristic activity against the Earth. "Let's let bygones be bygones," Bugs sums up. "After all, this guy's [Marvin] been dabbling in war-games for years!" Bugs' defense works, the Martians spare Earth from eradication ... and the epilogue is not shown, perhaps because it hasn't happened yet. The evidence for the habitation of Mars has yet to be seriously considered by enough people to answer the real question any time in the immediate future, and the real question is when, exactly, we can begin to leave our psychological insulation behind and face the obvious reality of the extraterrestrial visitors who regularly intrude upon our airspace. In a sense, the only question remaining on the extraterrestrial issue is that essentially posed by Bugs' erstwhile nemesis, Marvin, about when exactly we can meet face to face: "How about next Tuesday?" *Tiw's*-day, after all, is the day sacred to Mars.

Notes

Introduction

page 4   "saucer skipped across water"—Edward J. Ruppelt, *The Report on Unidentified Flying Objects* (New York: Ace Books Inc., 1956), p. 27.

page 5   "No matter what these green fireballs were ..."—Ibid., p. 69.

page 6   *"This matter is considered Top Secret ..."*—Lawrence Fawcett and Barry J. Greenwood, *Clear Intent* (New York: Fireside/Simon and Schuster, 1984), p. 159.

page 6   "They're invading us, and we can't stop them!"—John A. Keel, *The Mothman Prophecies* (Avondale Estates, Georgia: IllumiNet Press, 1975; 1991), pp. 216–217.

page 7   "The nations of the world will have to unite ..."—Timothy Good, *Above Top Secret* (Great Britain: Sidgwick and Jackson Limited, 1987; New York: William Morrow, 1988), p. 267.

page 7   "No definite and conclusive evidence is yet available ..."—Brad Steiger, editor, *Project Blue Book* (New York: Ballantine Books, 1976), p. 174.

page 8   "watch lists," "information on foreign governments, organizations ..." etc.—James Bamford, *The Puzzle Palace: A Report on America's Most Secret Agency* (New York: Houghton Mifflin, 1982), pp. 323–324.

page 9   "intercept and destroy"—Jenny Randles, *The UFO Conspiracy* (New York: Barnes and Noble, 1987), pp. 35–36.

page 10   "UFO Hypothesis and Survival Questions"—Fawcett and Greenwood, *Clear Intent,* pp. 183–185.

page 10   Antonio Villas Boas abduction—Coral and Jim Lorenzen, *Flying Saucer Occupants* (New York: Signet Books/New American Library, 1967), pp. 42–72.

page 10   "ghost rockets"—John Spencer, *The UFO Encyclopedia* (New York: Avon Books, 1991), pp. 126–127.

page 10   WWII Los Angeles UFO incident—Good, *Above Top Secret,* pp. 15–17.

page 10   "foo fighters"—Renato Vesco and David Hatcher Childress, *Man-Made UFOs 1944–1994* (Stelle, Illinois: Adventures Unlimited Press, 1994), pp. 79– 90.

page 12   MacArthur's WWII UFO investigations—John A. Keel, "The Hidden History of the Flying Saucer Mystery," *UFO Sightings,* Vol. 4, No. 1, pp. 33–35.

page 13   Tesla/Pickering Mars signals, Saheki's "atomic explosion on Mars"—Harold T. Wilkins, *Flying Saucers on the Attack* (New York: Ace Books, 1954), pp. 232–233.

page 14   1924 Mars signals received by Todd, Jenkins, Friedman, U.S. Signal Corps—*Sightings,* Fox T.V., date unknown, early 1996 (February or March).

page 14   "mystery airship" of 1896–1897—Jacques Vallee, *Dimensions* (Toronto, Canada: Random House, 1988), pp. 38–43.

page 14   mystery airship as H. G. Wells' inspiration—John A. Keel, "The Hidden History of the Flying Saucer Mystery," *UFO Sightings,* Vol. 4, No. 1, p. 30.

page 15   "It seemed as if Mars was breaking up . . . the firing was sharp"—Wilkins, *Flying Saucers on the Attack,* p. 231.

page 15   Siberian atomic UFO explosion of 1908—Simon Welfare and John Fairley, *Arthur C. Clarke's Mysterious World* (New York: A&W Publishers, Inc., 1980), pp. 152–167.

page 16   "Highly advanced creatures from Mars have visited the Earth . . ."—W. Raymond Drake, *Gods and Spacemen in the Ancient East* (London: Sphere Books, 1968), p. 90.

page 16   "Lunar Transient Phenomena" (LTP) on the Moon, British Royal Society investigation—Don Ecker, "Long Saga of Lunar Anomalies," *UFO,* Vol. 10, No. 2, p. 23.

page 16   "Springheel Jack"—Vallee, *Dimensions,* pp. 89–90.

page 17   Sea of Storms spires, Blair Cuspids—David Hatcher Childress, *Extraterrestrial Archaeology* (Stelle, Illinois: Adventures Unlimited Press, 1994), pp. 37, 96–98.

page 18 "artifacts left ..." "societies sure of their place in the universe ..."—Brookings Institute Report, "Proposed Studies on the Implications of Peaceful Space Activities for Human Affairs," 1958, p. 215.

page 18 Jacques and Janine Vallee, Pierre Guérin, and Mars/UFO oppositions—Jacques and Janine Vallee, *Challenge to Science: The UFO Enigma* (New York: Ballantine, 1966), pp. 161–173.

page 19 "three great circles ... more than the product of coincidence"—Jacques Vallee, *Forbidden Science* (Berkeley, California: North Atlantic Books, 1992), p. 57.

page 19 "UFOlogists noted that the sighting peak years ..."—Nigel Blundell and Roger Boar, *The World's Greatest UFO Mysteries* (London: Octopus Books, 1983), pp. 222–223.

page 19 Vallee hired for "computer networking projects"—Jacques Vallee, *Revelations* (New York: Random House, 1991), inside back cover.

page 20 "Is it sheer coincidence ... No one knows"—Sheila Ostrander and Lynn Schroeder, *Psychic Discoveries Behind the Iron Curtain* (New Jersey: Prentice- Hall, 1970), p. 97.

page 20 Walter Hohmann/Wernher von Braun Mars shot projections—Marsha Freeman, *How We Got to the Moon* (Washington, D.C.: 21st Century Science Associates, 1993), pp. 270–271.

page 22 "... perhaps they were built by intelligent beings"—quoted in Zecharia Sitchin, *Genesis Revisited* (New York: Avon Books, 1990), pp. 247–248.

page 22 "... race of Martians ... its place among the theories of its origin"—Ibid., p. 248.

page 23 Faces on Mars those of Ra and Thoth—Bruce Rux, *Architects of the Underworld* (Berkeley, California: Frog Books, 1996), pp. 412–414.

page 23 Correlations between Giza/Teotihuacan pyramids and Mars—M. W. Saunders and Duncan Lunan, *Destiny Mars* (Surrey, England: Caterham, 1975), *passim*.

page 24 1962 American Rocket Society Convention, 1924/'26 Mars listening projects—Frank Edwards, *Flying Saucers—Serious Business* (New York: Lyle Stuart, Inc., 1966), pp. 75–78.

page 25 "the first men to reach the moon must fight for the privilege ..."—quoted by Frank Edwards, Ibid., p. 112.

page 25 "... the Earth may have been visited by various galactic civilizations ..."—Ralph Blum with Judy Blum, *Beyond Earth: Man's Contact with UFOs* (New York: Bantam, 1974), p. 203.

page 26 "Not long ago there was a chilling prediction ..."—Howard Koch, *The Panic Broadcast* (New York: Avon Books, 1970), p. 144.

page 26 "Great Galactic Ghoul"—Don Eckert, "The Galactic Ghoul: Superpower Problems in Getting to Mars," *UFO*, Vol. 8, No. 6, pp. 33–36.

page 27 The "Phobos incident"—Zecharia Sitchin, *Genesis Revisited*, pp. 272–298.

page 28 Boris Bolitsky, John Becklake, Martian "city grid"—Childress, *Extraterrestrial Archaeology*, pp. 217–220.

page 29 *Observer* failure, quotes—Don Eckert, "The Galactic Ghoul," *UFO*, Vol. 8, No. 6, pp. 33–36.

page 31 "Maybe we're all evolved Martians"—*Sightings*, CBS T.V. (syndicated), 5–20– 95.

page 33 Dr. Farouk El Baz's credentials—Graham Hancock and Robert Bauval, *The Message of the Sphinx: A Quest for the Hidden Legacy of Mankind* (New York: Crown/Three Rivers Press, 1996), p. 314.

page 33 "... and Dames was told to cease and desist"—Jim Schnabel, *Remote Viewers: The Secret History of America's Psychic Spies* (New York: Bantam Doubleday, 1997), p. 355.

page 33 "I will tell you ... there are structures beneath the surface of Mars ..."—Ibid, p. 213.

page 34 "... and had perhaps built the great pyramids of Egypt"—Ibid, p. 359.

page 34 "... drenched in sweat and xenophobic stress"—Ibid, p. 358.

page 35 "nature images," "I've seen this on T.V...." etc.—John E.

Mack, M.D., *Abduction: Human Encounters with Aliens* (New York: Charles Scribner's Sons, 1994), pp. 171–173.

page 35 "not here to hurt," "watching us," "flashing on the faces of Mars"—Ibid., p. 310.

page 35 "an increasing group of abductees I have been encountering . . ."—Ibid., p. 217.

page 35 "I have to go with him . . . because we're linked in some way"—Ibid., p. 222.

page 35 "The figure told [the abductee] 'it's me' . . ."—Ibid., p. 232.

page 36 *ushabti* . . . "the figure makes itself identical with the deceased," etc.—E. A. Wallis Budge, *The Mummy* (New York: Dover, 1989; 1893), p. 255.

page 36 ". . . Egyptians possessed . . . remarkable skill in . . . manufacture of automata"—Lewis Spence, *Ancient Egyptian Myths and Legends* (New York: Dover, 1990; 1915), p. 142.

page 36 "porters of Horus"—Bob Brier, *Ancient Egyptian Magic* (New York: William Morrow & Company, Inc., 1980), p. 126.

page 36 "what I should remember and what I should forget"—R. O. Faulkner, *The Ancient Egyptian Coffin Texts*, 3 Volumes (Warminster, England: Aris & Phillips, Ltd., 1977), Spell 572.

page 36 "The Ethiopian sorcerers sent their sorceries to Egypt," etc.—E. A. Wallis Budge, *From Fetish to God in Ancient Egypt* (New York: Dover, 1988; 1934), pp. 123–124.

page 37 "wakening the next morning . . . he lay in great pain," etc.—Spence, *Ancient Egyptian Myths and Legends,* p. 215.

page 38 "developing a lunar base . . . stepping stone to Mars"—Sitchin, *Genesis Revisited,* pp. 302–303.

page 38 "neutral particle beam," "death ray"—Ibid., p. 303.

page 38 "return astronauts to the moon," revival of SETI, etc.—Ibid., pp. 303–304.

page 39 Reagan/Gorbachev speeches and statements—Ibid., pp. 308–311.

page 40 Harappa/Mohenjo Daro, Robert Oppenheimer, etc.—Rux, *Architects of the Underworld,* pp. 257–260.

page 41 "We cannot take the credit . . ." "The people from other worlds"—Good, *Above Top Secret,* p. 370.

page 41   ta-wer, Osiris' "ladder to heaven"—Richard H. Wilkinson, *Reading Egyptian Art* (London: Thames and Hudson Ltd., 1992), p. 169.

page 42   "As for what I have called bizarre phenomena ..."—Good, *Above Top Secret,* p. 8.

page 43   "...how to build a vimana! Let's damn well find out...."—Ibid., p. 53.

page 44   "We shall form an Order, the Brotherhood of the Templars ..."—Michael Howard, *The Occult Conspiracy* (Rochester, Vermont: Destiny Books, 1989), p. 131.

page 45   Haushofer and Gurdjieff, "Germany Awake"—Ibid., pp. 128–129.

page 46   Nazis, Tibet, "The Great White Brotherhood," Ernst Schäfer and secret S.S. expeditions, etc.—Peter Levenda, *Unholy Alliance: A History of Nazi Involvement with the Occult* (New York: Avon Books, 1995), 172–185.

page 46   Wing Commander Dennis Wheatley, the LCS and "the Martians"—Anthony Cave Brown, *Bodyguard of Lies* (New York: HarperCollins, 1975), p. 356.

page 46   U.S. Founding Fathers, Masons, and the occult—Howard, *The Occult Conspiracy,* pp. 73–96.

page 47   Churchward "transparently an agent of British Intelligence"—Peter Tompkins, *Mysteries of the Mexican Pyramids* (New York: Harper and Row, 1976), p. 175.

page 47   "dismembered" Mu, "lost land in the West," William Niven—Ibid., pp. 355–363.

page 47   Karl Haushofer, Sven Hedin, Ahnenerbe S.S.—Levenda, *Unholy Alliance,* pp. 153–160.

page 49   "In the 1930s, for example ..."—Graham Hancock, *Fingerprints of the Gods* (New York: Crown, 1995), p. 60.

page 49   the "Baghdad batteries"—Peter Kolosimo, *Timeless Earth* (Secaucus, New Jersey: University Books, 1974), p. 97; Andrew Tomas, *We Are Not the First* (London: Souvenir Press Ltd., 1971), pp. 93–94.

page 50   "pages and pages of documents and photographs ..."—Levenda, *Unholy Alliance,* p. 40.

page 51   Ernst Schäfer S.S. expeditions and quotes—Ibid., pp. 172–178.

page 52   "Underworld of the West"—Rux, *Architects of the Underworld,* pp. 361–369.

page 53   "... he had the head of a hawk with a star above it"—Ibid., 375.

page 53   Aleister Crowley, Ra-Harakhte, "the Warrior Lord of the Forties," etc.—Peter Levenda, *Unholy Alliance,* pp. 97–98.

page 54   "The Indians say that thousands of years ago ..."—Peter Kolosimo, *Not of This World* (Secaucus, New Jersey: University Books, 1971) p. 206.

page 54   "... the stones moved into place of their own accord"—H. A. Guerber, *The Myths of Greece and Rome* (New York: Dover, 1993; 1907), p. 48.

page 54   "Dagda Mor," "music from his harp," *Tuatha de Danaan,* etc.—T. W. Rolleston, *Celtic Myths and Legends* (New York: Dover, 1990; 1911) pp. 103–119.

page 55   "dance of the giants"—Nikolai Tolstoy, *The Quest for Merlin* (New York: Back Bay/Little, Brown and Company, 1985), pp. 111–112, 127–129.

page 55   "They walked" *(moai)*—Charles Sellier, *Mysteries of the Ancient World* (New York: Dell, 1995), pp. 241–270.

page 55   "words of power"—Budge, *Amulets and Superstitions* (New York: Dover, 1978; 1930), p. 260.

page 55   (The concept of "words of power" is elaborated in several texts on Egypt,

page 55   largely stemming from the concept of God [Thoth] as "The Word," which is

page 55   echoed repeatedly in The Bible—as in John 1:1.)

page 55   "spirit stones" Egyptian name for "relieving spaces"—*Mysteries of the Ancient World,* CBS special, 1994.

page 56   "telegeodynamics," "fusillade of taps," etc.—Margaret Cheney, *Tesla: Man Out of Time* (New York: Dell, 1983), pp. 116–118.

page 56   "By installing proper plants it would be practicable ..."—Ibid., p. 129

page 56   "vitally interested," "there exist among Dr. Tesla's papers ..."—Ibid, pp. 272–274.

page 56   "some government guys were in to microfilm some of the papers"—Ibid., p. 271.

page 56   "... but between 1945 and 1947, an interesting exchange of letters ..."—Ibid., p. 277.

page 57   missing Tesla papers, Wright Field letter exchanges—Ibid., pp. 277–280.

page 58   "Operation Paperclip"—Jonathan Vankin and John Whalen, *The 50 Greatest Conspiracies of All Time* (New York: Citadel Press, 1995), pp. 303–309.

page 59   "... they only ever thought of going to the moon"—Larry Thorson, "Space pioneer no hero, German exhibit suggests," *Rocky Mountain News* (Associated Press), 4/12/95.

page 60   *assassin, hashshashin,* "hashish eaters"—Doubleday Dictionary

page 60   Black Sea rhododendron honey—Adrienne Mayor, "Mad Honey!" *Archaeology,* November/December, 1995.

page 61   William Bryan, Egyptian hypnotic "sleep temples"—Melanson, pp. 208–209

page 61   Ahnenerbe and mind control—Levenda, *Unholy Alliance,* pp. 217–219, 258– 261.

page 62   Werhner von Braun and *The Mars Project*—Marsha Freeman, *How We Got to the Moon,* pp. 268–278.

page 62   "Such sphinxes as these obey no one but their master"—Andrew Tomas, *We Are Not the First,* p. 91.

page 63   U.S. code-crackers, Voynich Manuscript—Ibid.; George C. Andrews, *Extra-Terrestrials Among Us* (Minnesota: Llewellyn, 1992), pp. 79–81.

Chapter 1: Wreckages and Robots

page 73   During a thunderstorm on the night of July 2, 1947 ...—the date is disputed by Kevin Randle and Donald R. Schmitt, who say July 4.

page 73   "... object ... some kind of extraterrestrial probe ...," "long distance repairs"—Kevin D. Randle and Donald R.

Schmitt, *UFO Crash at Roswell* (New York: Avon Books, 1991), p. 121.

page 74   "nothing from the Earth"—Ibid., p. 54.

page 74   "... something he had never seen ... didn't believe was of this planet"—Ibid., p. 69.

page 75   obviously hoaxed flying saucer with a label on it reading "Made In U.S.A."—Lawrence Fawcett and Barry J. Greenwood, *Clear Intent* (New York: Simon and Schuster, 1984), p.149.

page 75   "Jess Marcel has brought in ... looks like a flying disc ..."—Randle & Schmitt, *UFO Crash at Roswell*, p. 69.

page 76   "The many rumors regarding the flying discs ..."—"RAAF Captures Flying Saucer," *Roswell Daily Record*, 7/8/47.

page 76   "calls from Paris and London and Rome ..."—Randle & Schmitt, *UFO Crash at Roswell*, p. 70.

page 76   "ATTENTION ALBUQUERQUE: CEASE TRANSMISSION ..."—Timothy Good, *Above Top Secret* (Great Britain: Sidgwick and Jackson, Limited, 1987), p. 255.

page 76   "Disc and balloon being transported to Wright Field ..."—Randle & Schmitt, *UFO Crash at Roswell*, p. 75.

page 76   "We don't know if there are bodies, but we're looking for them"—Ibid., p. 224.

page 76   "... because he'd helped retrieve the bodies from one that crashed"—Ibid., p. 91.

page 77   "What I saw reminded me of the front part of a canoe ..."—Kevin D. Randle and Donald R. Schmitt, *The Truth About the UFO Crash at Roswell* (New York: Avon, 1994), p. 19.

page 77   "very excited," "How did you get in here? ..." "... you've had a crash"—Ibid.

page 77   "Mister, don't go in Roswell ..." "... diggin' your bones outta the sand"—*UFOs: A Need to Know* (Ted Oliphant Productions, 1990).

page 77   "would make good dog food"—Randle & Schmitt, *The Truth About the UFO Crash at Roswell*, p. 87

page 78   "... trying to call me ..." "... said alien bodies,"—Ibid., pp. 26–27.

page 78   "didn't know what . . . or where they came from"—Randle & Schmitt, *UFO Crash at Roswell*, p. 92.

page 78   Roswell nurse "autopsy" description—Randle & Schmitt, *The Truth About the UFO Crash at Roswell*, pp. 27–28.

page 79   "Return to sender" and "Deceased"—Ibid., p. 87.

page 79   "was under a great deal of stress"—Randle & Schmitt, *UFO Crash at Roswell*, p. 78.

page 79   ". . . little green men? . . . They weren't green"—Ibid., p. 79.

page 79   "It amounted to humiliation and detention . . ."—*UFOs— A Need to Know.*

page 79   "It'll go hard on me"—Randle & Schmitt, *UFO Crash at Roswell*, p. 42.

page 80   "By the end of July, 1947, the UFO security lid was down tight . . ."—Edward J. Ruppelt, *The Report On Unidentified Flying Objects* (New York: Ace, 1956), p. 34.

page 80   "It is possible within . . . U.S. knowledge . . ." ". . . shape of a disc"—Good, *Above Top Secret*, p. 477

page 81   "special project," "oversight committee," "exploit," etc.— Randle & Schmitt, *UFO Crash at Roswell*, pp.110–111.

page 81   "a top intelligence echelon [was] represented . . ."—Ibid., p. 232.

page 81   "never heard what the results were . . . pieces were from space"—Ibid., p. 110.

page 81   "They were all found in fairly good condition . . . it was in Denver"—Ibid., pp. 91–92.

page 81   "kinda little guys," ". . . with slanted eyes and tiny mouths"—Ibid., pp. 94–95.

page 82   "sensitive activities," "high level" rumors, "little gray men"—Good, *Above Top Secret*, p. 364.

page 82   file labelled "USAAF Early Automation"—Randle & Schmitt, *UFO Crash at Roswell*, pp. 106–107.

page 83   Robert Sarbacher letter and quotes—Good, *Above Top Secret*, pp. 183, 397.

page 84   DIA document of 7/27/68—Ibid., p. 316.

page 84   "when there was a deluge of sightings in France, and . . .

throughout Europe"—Jacques Vallee, *Forbidden Science* (Berkeley, California: North Atlantic Books, 1992) p. 15.

page 85   " ' . . . they could gather reams of data about us, couldn't they?' "—Ibid., pp. 161–62.

page 85   "another of the tantalizing coincidences . . ."—Jacques Vallee, *Dimensions* (Canada: Random House, 1988), p. 62.

page 85   "We are peaceful people. We only want your dog."—Ibid.

page 85   "like a German Nazi"—John G. Fuller, *The Interrupted Journey* (New York: Berkley, 1966), p. 115.

page 86   "black, black shiny jacket"—Ibid., p. 120.

page 86   "like professional soldiers"—Eric Norman, *Gods, Demons and Space Chariots* (New York: Lancer, 1970), p. 183.

page 86   (The specific quote of Schirmer's was: "They paced back and forth like regular soldiers on guard duty." He made other comments as to their stiffness, as well.)

page 86   "like a camera lens adjusting"—Ralph Blum with Judy Blum, *Beyond Earth: Man's Contact With UFOs* (New York: Bantam, 1974), p. 113.

page 86   ". . . I don't recall seeing them take a breath like we do"—Eric Norman, *Gods and Devils from Outer Space* (New York: Lancer Books, 1973), p. 158.

page 86   "They go in and out, real fast, like this"—Linda Moulton Howe, *An Alien Harvest* (Huntingdon Valley, Pennsylvania, 1989), p. 318.

page 86   "kind of like on their heel . . . it seems like they pivot"—Ibid., p. 317.

page 86   one of the chief occupants was "a redhead"—Fuller, *The Interrupted Journey,* p. 114.

page 87   "just seemed to bounce off their nickel-plated armor"—Brad Steiger, ed., *Project Blue Book* (New York: Ballantine, 1976), p. 103.

page 87   "It moved stiffly, like a robot . . ."—*Birmingham News,* 10/19/73.

page 87   "robots . . . grayish, like a ghost . . . pointed ears and noses . . ."—Blum, *Beyond Earth,* pp. 10, 17, 31.

page 87   "like somebody's idea of a wrinkled robot"—Ibid, p. 16.

page 87   "... they was robots ... communicating with somewhere else"—Ibid., pp. 136–137.

page 87   a buzzing "zzzZZZ zzzZZZ" sound—Ibid., p. 31.

page 88   "just cool," "claw hands," "Two colonels exchanged looks ..."—Ibid., p. 17.

page 88   Villas Boas occupant descriptions—Coral and Jim Lorenzen, *Flying Saucer Occupants* (New York: Signet/New American Library, 1967), pp. 51–53.

page 90   "Whoever's touching me ... I feel touching ..."—Budd Hopkins, *Intruders* (New York: Ballantine, 1988), p. 97.

page 90   "Yeah, sort of, but they're cold ... Not real soft ..."—Ibid.

page 90   "... like alien dolls or puppets than living entities"—"Hopkins Rates Mini-Series B+," *UFO*, Vol. 7, No. 4, 1992, p. 11.

page 90   "almost metallic-looking"—Fuller, *The Interrupted Journey*, p. 305.

page 90   "nails like conical dark blue metallic claws"—Jacques Vallee, *Confrontations* (Canada: Random House, 1990), p. 139.

page 90   1950 Loire, France, case and quotes—Vallee, *Dimensions*, p. 108.

page 91   "behaving more like a mechanical being ..." "robot-like"—Ibid., p. 92.

page 91   "... as though it had struck steel," "... struck rock ..." etc.—Lorenzen, *Flying Saucer Occupants*, pp. 103–104.

page 92   "Springheel Jack" descriptions and quotes—Vallee, *Dimensions*, pp. 89–90.

page 94   "It is odd that the creatures seen coming from these craft ..."—Steiger, *Project Blue Book*, p. 105.

page 94   "hypnotized the contact persons ... something like man-shaped robots"—"Professor Hermann Oberth—Confirmed UFO Believer!" *UFO Sightings*, Volume 4, No. 2, p. 67.

page 94   "biological robots" or "robots"—Michael Lindemann, *UFOs and the Alien Presence* (Santa Barbara, California: The 2020 Group, 1991), p. 164.

page 94   "Close Encounter of the 3rd Kind ... animated creatures reported"—Jerome Clark, *UFO Encounters and Beyond* (Lincolnwood, Illinois: Publications International, 1993), p. 72.

page 95 Timothy Good has "come to similar conclusions" as Felix Zigel—Good, *Above Top Secret,* p. 241.

page 96 Paul Bennewitz the counterintelligence target of "a variety of agencies"—Howard Blum, *Out There* (New York: Simon & Schuster, 1990), p. 258.

page 99 "special consultant . . . for psychological warfare," *"against whom?"*—Jonathan Vankin and John Whalen, *The 50 Greatest Conspiracies of All Time* (New York: Citadel, 1995), p. 70.

page 100 "turned the matter over to C. D. Jackson, and things really got going"—Jim Marrs, *Crossfire: The Plot That Killed Kennedy* (Carroll & Graf, 1989), p. 67.

page 102 Bob Oechsler's retirement after the "Guardian" fraud in Canada—"'Guardian' Case Gets Sacked By Canadian Researchers," *UFO,* Vol. 10, No. 2, 1995, p. 38.

page 103 "expertise regarding . . . remote-control devices for character robots"—Timothy Good, *Alien Liaison* (London: Arrow, 1991), p. 198.

page 109 "In the first draft screenplay, the monster came closest . . ."—Jim Wynorski, *They Came from Outer Space* (New York: Doubleday, 1980), p. 31.

page 109 "a prototype designer of . . . mobile surveillance systems"—Ibid., pp. 188–189.

Chapter 2: Mesmerizations and Assassinations

page 111 "other functions," "government-sanctioned secret society"—Jonathan Vankin and John Whalen, *The 50 Greatest Conspiracies of All Time* (New York: Citadel, 1995), p. 203.

page 112 "CIA officials started preliminary work on drugs and hypnosis . . ."—John Marks, *The Search for the "Manchurian Candidate": The CIA and Mind Control* (1979) (New York: W. W. Norton & Company, Inc., 1991), p. 23.

page 112 "How the victims coped was interesting"—Ibid., p. 24.

page 113 "controlling an individual to the point where he will do our bidding ..."—Ibid, p. 25.

page 113 "... soon became so blurred as to be meaningless"—Ibid.

page 113 "neurosurgical techniques"—Ibid, p. 28.

page 113 "safe houses," "Midnight Climax"—Vankin and Whalen, *The 50 Greatest Conspiracies of All Time*, p. 5.

page 114 "creation of a vegetable"—Marks, *The Search for the "Manchurian Candidate,"* p. 142.

page 114 "ULTRA," the Second World War's most devastating OSS success—Anthony Cave Brown, *Bodyguard of Lies* (London: HarperCollins, 1975), *passim.*

page 114 "brain perversion techniques ... we have recoiled from facing up to them"—Martin A. Lee and Norman Solomon, *Unreliable Sources: A Guide to Detecting Bias in News Media* (New York: Lyle Stuart, 1990), p. 118.

page 114 "no indication of Red use of chemicals"—Ibid.

page 115 "covert use of chemical ..." "We are not Boy Scouts"—Vankin and Whalen, *The 50 Greatest Conspiracies of All Time*, p. 4.

page 115 "... narcotics, hypnosis or special mechanical devices"—Lee & Solomon, *Unreliable Sources*, p. 118.

page 115 *hsi-nao*, "to cleanse the mind"—Marks, *The Search for the "Manchurian Candidate,"* p. 133.

page 115 "failed to reveal even one conclusively documented ..."—Lee & Solomon, *Unreliable Sources*, p.118.

page 116 "... a careful reading of the contemporaneous CIA documents ..."—Marks, *The Search for the "Manchurian Candidate,"* p. 31.

page 117 "... yesterday's conspiracy theories ... turned out to be true"—Ibid., p. 215 (n.)

page 118 "The Penal Colony"—Jonathan Vankin, *Conspiracies, Cover-Ups and Crimes* (New York: Paragon House, 1992), p. 176.

page 118 "stripping the dead. It's not a nice job," "Get Dwyer out of here"—Ibid., p. 174.

page 118 "like a rich man"—Ibid, p. 176.

page 118 the CIA had "infiltrated" their commune—Vankin and Whalen, *The 50 Greatest Conspiracies of All Time*, p. 290.

page 119 Ambassador John Burke with CIA's "intelligence community staff"—Ibid., p. 291.

page 119 "no evidence" to connect the CIA to Jonestown—Ibid, p. 293.

page 119 "... swallowing cyanide at the command of a lone madman"—Vankin, *Conspiracies, Cover-Ups and Crimes*, pp. 177–178.

page 119 "over 600 abductees have been interrogated ..."—Richard L. Thompson, *Alien Identities: Ancient Insights into Modern UFO Phenomena* (San Diego, California: Govardhan Hill Publishing, 1993), p. 123.

page 119 "from several hundred thousand to several million Americans"—John E. Mack, M.D., *Abduction: Human Encounters With Aliens* (New York: Charles Scribner's Sons, 1994), p. 15.

page 120 a study on "Nine Psychologicals"—Philip J. Klass, *UFO Abductions: A Dangerous Game* (Buffalo, New York: Prometheus, 1989), p. 112.

page 120 "certain psychological characteristics or physical attributes ..."—Ibid., p. 111.

page 120 "very distinctive, unusual and interesting"—Ibid., pp. 112–113.

page 120 Dr. Elizabeth Slater's report—Ibid., pp. 112–115.

page 124 Jean Mundy and June Parnell's reports and quotes—Richard Thompson, *Alien Identities: Ancient Insights into Modern UFO Phenomena*, pp. 154–155.

page 124 Dr. Ronald Westrum and PAS—Ibid., p. 39.

page 124 "extremely attractive, interesting, intelligent people ..."—Michael Lindemann (ed.), *UFOs and the Alien Presence* (Santa Barbara, California: The 2020 Group, 1991), pp. 143–144.

page 125 "... there are very, very few successful relationships among them"—Ibid., p. 143.

page 125 "Many abductees have adjusted well to the abduction phenomenon ..."—David M. Jacobs, Ph.D., *Secret Life: Firsthand Documented Accounts of UFO Abductions* (New York: Fireside/Simon & Schuster, 1993), p. 239.

page 125 "lead[s] both men and women to question their mental stability ..."—Ibid., p. 253.

page 125 "emotionally fragile ... sense of humor and their optimism"—Ibid., p. 317.

page 126 "sexually bizarre nature of the event ..."—Ibid., p. 252.

page 127 "It is true that abductees may experience terror ..."—Mack, *Abduction,* pp. 398– 399.

page 127 "abductees come to feel a more authentic identification ..."—Ibid., p. 22.

page 129 "Before the trial, when Dr. Diamond first hypnotized Sirhan ..."—Philip H. Melanson, Ph.D., *The Robert F. Kennedy Assassination* (New York: S.P.I. Books, 1994), p. 190.

page 129 "a clue of withdrawal from the hypnotic state," "try and fathom a motive"—William Turner and Jonn Christian, *The Assassination of Robert F. Kennedy: The Conspiracy and Coverup.* (1978) (New York: Thunder's Mouth Press, 1993), p. 198.

page 130 "unequivocally designated Sirhan a Grade 5 ..."—Ibid., p. 204.

page 130 "clinically identifiable configuration of personality traits"—Ibid., p. 203.

page 130 "After a brief warm-up ..." 1967 NBC hypnosis demonstration—Ibid., pp. 205–206.

page 131 "because there's war, and I'll need to know these names"—Jacobs, *Secret Life,* p. 139.

page 131 "He said he would make me remember it"—Ibid., p. 138.

page 132 "[Some abductees] have been shown an intricate control board ..."—Ibid, p. 151.

page 132 "shimmering box," "... she would understand its purpose"—Budd Hopkins, *Intruders* (New York: Ballantine, 1988), p. 82.

page 132 "that abductees could ... be made to act as surrogates ..." "... theories"—Ibid., p. 85.

page 133 "ATOMIC EXPERIMENTS FOR WARLIKE . . ."—Ralph Blum with Judy Blum, *Beyond Earth* (New York: Bantam, 1974), photo section.

page 133 "Mothman"—John A. Keel, *The Mothman Prophecies* (1975) (Avondale Estates, Georgia: IllumiNet Press, 1991), *passim*.

page 135 "like a squeaky fan belt," "mechanical humming sound"— John A. Keel, *The Complete Guide to Mysterious Beings* (1970) (New York: Doubleday/Main Street, 1994), p. 264.

page 135 "Tell me, if you had stuck a gun in the subject's hand . . ."— Turner and Christian, *The Assassination of Robert F. Kennedy,* p. 206.

page 135 "Ah, the ultimate question. I'm afraid he might have shot him."—Ibid.

page 135 "I was concerned . . . with a more worrisome question . . ."— Keel, *The Mothman Prophecies,* p. 218.

page 138 "hypothetical problem," "prominent politician," etc.— Melanson, *The Robert F. Kennedy Assassination,* pp. 173–174.

page 138 ". . . which meant the brainwashing section"—KNX-FM, Los Angeles, 2/12/72.

page 138 "leading expert," "in less than five minutes," etc.—Turner and Christian, *The Assassination of Robert F. Kennedy,* pp. 227–228.

page 139 "woman in a polka-dot dress," "We shot him"—Ibid., p. 73.

page 140 "crazy, crackpot theory"—Ibid., p. 107.

page 140 "RFK must die," "pay to the order of," and "MIND CONTROL . . ."- Vankin, *Conspiracies, Cover-Ups and Crimes,* pp. 168–171.

page 140 "Everything in the PSE chart tells me . . ."—Ibid., p. 171.

page 140 Bryan and the "D-13" test—Michael Weldon, *The Psychotronic Encyclopedia of Film* (New York: Ballantine, 1983), p. 174.

page 141 "from natural causes"—Turner and Christian, *The Assassination of Robert F. Kennedy,* p. 228.

page 142 "operating like the KGB, blessed with ties to the CIA . . ."— Peter Harry Brown and Patte B. Barham, *Marilyn: The Last Take* (New York: E. P. Dutton, 1993), p. 430.

page 142   Marchetti's confirmation of CIA police in LAPD—Turner
           and Christian, *The Assassination of Robert F. Kennedy,*
           p. xxvii.

page 144   "There was a real problem with that book [Candy Jones]
           ..."—Melanson, *The Robert F. Kennedy Assassination,* p. 214.

page 144   Mark David Chapman and mind-control—Fenton Bresler,
           Who Killed John Lennon? (Great Britain: Sidgwick & Jack-
           son, Limited, 1989), *passim.*

page 145   Justice Dept. on Hinckley conspiracy claim—*The New York
           Times,* 10/21/81, p. A22.

page 145   Hinckley stalked Brussel, Carter before Reagan—Vankin
           and Whalen, *The 50 Greatest Conspiracies of All Time,*
           pp. 58–67.

page 145   Hinckley's exploding, poisonous .22–caliber "Devastator"
           bullets—Robert E. Gilbert, *The Mortal Presidency* (New York:
           HarperCollins, 1992), pp. 188–189.

page 146   Jodie Foster's prior communications with Hinckley—Louis
           Chunovic, *Jodie: A Biography* (Chicago: Contemporary
           Books, 1995), pp. 60–61, 66.

page 146   Michael Berke's stalking of Jessica Savitch—Gwenda Blair,
           Almost Golden (New York: Simon & Schuster, 1988), p. 283.

page 148   "Princess Moon Owl," bid for publicity—Keel, *The Moth-
           man Prophecies,* p. 227.

page 148   Japan Airline message, Cynthia/CIA—Donald Bain, *The
           Control of Candy Jones* (Chicago: Playboy Press, 1976), p. 249.

page 149   "Strangely, and fortunately, Arlene never did interfere
           ..."—Ibid., p. 253.

page 150   Stephen Kaplan quotes, "Amityville Horror" and Candy
           Jones show—Stephen Kaplan, Ph.D., and Roxanne Salch
           Kaplan, *The Amityville Horror Conspiracy* (Laceyville, Penn-
           sylvania: Belfrey Books, 1995), pp. 120– 121.

Chapter 3: Media and Manipulations

page 161   "blocked at the highest level," "not enough information"—
           Jenny Randles, *The UFO Conspiracy* (New York: Barnes and
           Noble, 1987), p. 82.

page 161 "fifth man" scandal—Peter Wright and Paul Greengrass, *Spycatcher* (New York: Dell, 1987), *passim.*

page 162 "This program had been carefully screened for security ..."—Timothy Good, *Above Top Secret* (Great Britain: Sidgwick and Jackson, 1987), p. 287.

page 162 Mike Wallace ... make Donald Keyhoe look like a fool—"It's No Act—He's Into UFOs," *UFO*, Vol. 9, No. 4, p. 15.

page 162 *Silent Coup* ... killed at the executive level—Len Colodny and Robert Gettlin, *Silent Coup* (New York: St. Martin's Press, 1992), pp. 451–474.

page 163 "Fourth Branch of Govt." through "tip of a very spooky iceberg"—Martin A. Lee and Norman Solomon, *Unreliable Sources* (New York: Lyle Stuart, 1990), pp. 104–117.

page 164 "Wisner's Wurlitzer," Church Committee, Carl Bernstein, etc.—Vankin and Whalen, *The 50 Greatest Conspiracies of All Time* (New York: Citadel Press, 1995), pp. 67–68.

page 164 "Lying to the press ..." to "... mountain of lies ..."—Lee and Solomon, *Unreliable Sources,* pp. 126–132.

page 167 "CIA loved Gehlen ..." "U.S./U.S.S.R. hostilities"—Vankin and Whalen, *The 50 Greatest Conspiracies of All Time,* pp. 307–308.

page 167 "CIA scientists understood that television and motion pic ..."- Lee and Solomon, *Unreliable Sources,* p. 118.

page 167 Marchetti and Marks, *Ramparts* on CIA film-making involvement—Victor Marchetti and John D. Marks, *The CIA and the Cult of Intelligence* (New York: Alfred A. Knopf, 1980; 1974), pp. 249–250.

page 168 Jenny Randles quotes, "education program"—Randles, *The UFO Conspiracy,* p. 83

page 168 Robertson Panel quotes—Good, *Above Top Secret,* pp. 337–338.

page 169 Walt Disney as government agent—Marc Eliot, *Walt Disney: Hollywood's Dark Prince* (New York: HarperCollins, 1994), pp. 185, 326, photo section.

page 169 "Tomorrowland"—*Outre* Nos. 2–4 (1995), Gary Coville/Patrick Lucanio articles.

page 171 Ray Palmer, "Shaver controversy," Maury Island affair—Jerome Clark, *UFO Encounters & Beyond* (Lincolnwood, Illinois: Publications International, 1993), pp. 117–121.

page 174 "deeply shocked ..." to "In the name of Mr. H. G. Wells, I granted ..."—Frank Brady, *Citizen Welles—A Biography of Orson Welles* (New York: Charles Scribner's Sons, 1989), p. 175.

page 174 "Did Orson Welles know exactly ..." "... bored by the music again"—Barbara Leaming, *Orson Welles—A Biography* (New York: Viking Penguin, Inc., 1985; 1983), pp. 194–196.

page 175 "Yes, it was true. Mrs. Carl Sjorstrum ..."—Howard Koch, *The Panic Broadcast* (New York: Avon, 1970), p. 129.

page 176 "As long ago as his ... *First Person Singular* ..."—Leaming, *Orson Welles—A Biography,* pp. 580–581.

page 183 Robert Wise quotes and interview—Tom Weaver, "Years After Stillness," *Starlog* #211, Feb. '95, pp. 24–27.

page 187 "... It's that kind of movie. It makes you wonder"—Paul and Donna Parla, "The Woman from Planet X, An Interview with Margaret Field," *Filmfax* #58, Jan. '97, p. 76.

Chapter 4: Misdirections and Misinformations

page 191 Ronald Reagan ... FBI's "Agent T-10," informing on Communists—Herbert Mitgang, *Dangerous Dossiers* (New York: Ballantine, 1989), pp. 15– 18.

page 192 released at same time as Yucca Flats "Operation H-Bomb"—Michael Weldon, *The Psychotronic Encyclopedia of Film* (New York: Ballantine, 1983), p. 371.

page 194 "... with tongues firmly in cheek," "... film like *Target Earth*"—Jim Wynorski, *They Came from Outer Space* (New York: Doubleday: 1980), p. 146.

page 197 "flying saucer jewelry"—Weldon, *The Psychotronic Encyclopedia of Film,* p. 2

page 203 David J. Hogan, Mark Miller, Hazel Court *Devil Girl* comments—David J. Hogan, "Videoscan," p. 20, Mark Miller, "Terror in the Isles," p. 74, *Filmfax* No. 51, 7/8 '95.

page 205 HAARP information—Dr. Nick Begich and Jeane Manning, *Angels Don't Play This HAARP: Advances in Tesla Technology* (Amherst, Alaska: Earthpulse Press, 1995), *passim.*

page 213 Larry Buchanan connected to Jack Ruby, CIA—*Reel Wild Cinema,* USA Network, 4/28/96.

page 213 Buchanan believes LBJ ordered JFK assassination—*Filmfax* book review of Buchanan's *It Came from Hunger, Filmfax* #59, Feb./Mar. 1997, p. 16.

page 216 Roger Corman quotes—Roger Corman, *How I Made A Hundred Movies In Hollywood and Never Lost A Dime* (New York: Delta, 1991), p. 17.

page 218 *"Saucermen's* producers started out aiming for shocks . . ."— Jim Wynorski, *They Came from Outer Space,* p. 223.

page 230 "The Flying Saucers exist . . . source is extraterrestrial . . ."— Timothy Good, *Above Top Secret* (Great Britain: Sidgwick and Jackson Limited, 1987; New York: William Morrow, 1988), pp. 133, 232. (*Sud-Ouest,* 2–17–65, Bordeaux, France.)

page 231 "Our idea was to make a touching story . . ."—Ted A. Bohus, "Interview with *I Married a Monster from Outer Space* Producer/Director Gene Fowler, Jr.," *SPFX* #4, 1996, p. 18.

page 231 "Horrible! I thought it was funny because at the time . . ."— Ted A. Bohus, "She Married a Monster from Outer Space— Interview with Gloria Talbott," Ibid., p. 23.

page 231 "It played better than it read"—Ibid., p. 22.

page 231 "[T]he hospital was where they found the 'real men' . . ."— Ibid., pp. 24–25.

page 231 "As a matter of fact, the first time I saw it was on TV . . ."— Ibid., p. 23.

page 238 "Eddie did industrial films for Autonetics . . ."—Rudolph Grey, *Nightmare of Ecstasy: The Life and Art of Edward D. Wood, Jr.* (Portland, Oregon: Feral House, 1994; 1992) p. 125.

page 238 "had taken over the control of Plan 9. For one dollar."— Ibid., p. 85.

page 238   "... but that they had to end it with an atomic explosion"—Ibid., pp. 69–70.

page 238   "... but Ed Wood helped to start American Pictures ..."—
Ibid., p. 61.

page 238   Samuel Z. Arkoff virtually admits that he took one of
Wood's ideas—Ibid., p. 62.

page 238   "for over five years ... about every seven weeks" "... amnesia"—Ibid., pp. 7–8.

page 244   "[whose] name was as well known as Walt Disney ..."—
Weldon, *The Psychotronic Encyclopedia of Film,* p. 147.

page 248   "stacked better than *The Cat-Women of the Moon* ..."—
Ibid., p. 370.

page 250   "took three years to reach an appalled public"—Ibid., p. 87.

page 250   "borrowed some money from the mob and he was threatened by them ..."—from *Psychotronic* #19, quoted by Bryan
Senn, "The Brain that Wouldn't Die," in *Midnight Marquee*
#53, p. 15.

page 250   "entombed in concrete beneath his whirlpool hot tub"—
Ibid.

Chapter 5: Insiders and Informations

page 256   "America's vast wasteland"—Sherwood Schwartz, *Inside
Gilligan's Island* (New York: St. Martin's Press, 1994; 1988),
p. xv.

page 257   Leslie Stevens profiles and quotes—David J. Schow and
Jeffrey Frentzen, *The Outer Limits—the Official Companion*
(New York: Avon, 1986), pp. 10– 15.

page 274   pulsed microwave beam possibly being the cause of UFO
rod-weapon paralysis—see Jacques Vallee, *Confrontations*
(New York: Random House, 1990), p. 206.

page 274   Vallee convinced of Hill abduction by mention of rod-
weapon—Jacques Vallee, *Dimensions* (New York/Toronto,
Canada: Random House, 1988), p. 105.

page 278   Harvard's drama school doing a production of "O.B.I.T."—
David J. Schow and Jeffrey Frentzen, *The Outer Limits: The
Official Companion,* p. 365.

page 279   James Kahn, *The Codebreakers*, NSA/CIA involvement—James Bamford, *The Puzzle Palace: A Report on America's Most Secret Agency* (New York: Houghton Mifflin, 1982), pp. 163–173.

page 282   ". . . and ages of the children living in the Ohio Valley"— John Keel, *The Mothman Prophecies* (Avondale Estates, GA: IllumiNet Press, 1991), pp. 149–150.

page 298   "In the Outer Limits we experience a close encounter of another kind . . ."—Terry and Becky DuFoe, with additional information by Tom Stone, "Designing New Dimensions for The Outer Limits," *Outre* # 2, Spring 1995, p. 75.

Chapter 6: Enlightenments and Educations

page 301   "Maybe people see in the monsters . . ."—Edward Gross, "Fright Stalker," *Cinescape*, Vol. 3, No. 1, October/November 1996, p. 78.

page 307   "By the time we were finished I had seen enough evidence . . ."—Alan and Sally Landsberg, *In Search of Ancient Mysteries* (New York: Bantam, 1974), p. ix.

page 309   "I take *Star Trek* to be NASA's longest-range plan"—Dennis William Hauck, *Captain Quirk: The Unauthorized Biography of William Shatner* (New York: Pinnacle, 1995), p. 162.

page 321   "You have just been told that alien life has been found on Mars . . ."—Ibid., p. 27.

page 333   Torme admits in interviews to having fabricated entire portions . . .—Quendrith Johnson, "Behind the Scenes at 'Intruders'," *UFO*, Vol. 7, No. 4, pp. 6–10.

page 334   Travis Walton and Tracy Torme, *Fire in the Sky*—Travis Walton, *Fire in the Sky: The Walton Experience* (New York: Marlowe and Co., 1996; 1979), pp. 210–225.

page 334   "[P]erhaps one reason the Pentagon's internal newspaper . . ."—Ibid., p. 275.

page 334   Probable military intelligence ploy against Walton before *Fire in the Sky* release—Ibid., pp. 276–281.

page 335   Whitley Strieber/Budd Hopkins & Kathy Davis stories— Keith Thompson, *Angels and Aliens* (New York: Ballantine, 1991), pp. 206–207.

page 336   "The Charles Whitman incident. I found after the most careful research"—Ed Conroy, *Report on Communion* (New York: Avon, 1990), p. 72.

page 337   Strieber claims to have driven off the highway into another dimension—Sean Casteel, "Q&A: Strieber Sounds Off," *UFO*, Vol. 8, No. 5, 1993, p. 23.

Chapter 7: Importations and Degradations

page 341   *Fireball XL-5*, "Robert to the Rescue"—John Spencer, *The UFO Encyclopedia* (New York: Avon Books, 1991), pp. 113–114.

page 342   "Quatermass" series, Nigel Kneale's career—Dennis Fischer, "Val Guest and Nigel Kneale: Hammer's Dynamic Duo," *Midnight Marquee* No. 47, September 1994, pp. 57–68.

page 350   "Hilarious—Donlevy strides about ... 'Put the cyclotron over here!"—John Baxter, *Science Fiction in the Cinema* (New York: Paperback Library, 1970), pp. 153–154.

page 357   Yvonne Craig's self-assessment—Hal Schuster and David Lessnick (eds.), *Batmania II* (Las Vegas: Pioneer Books, 1992), p. 74.

page 358   "Little green men from Mars"... Hans Stefan Santesson— John Nicholson, "Little Green Men," published by Hans Stefan Santesson, *Flying Saucers in Fact and Fiction* (New York: Lancer Books, 1968), pp. 161–166.

page 358   Daniel Cohen unsuccessful discovering origination of the phrase—Daniel Cohen, *Monsters, Giants and Little Men from Mars* (New York: Dell, 1975), pp.183–229.

page 359   Gary Wilcox "Martian incident" and quotes—Jacques Vallee, *Dimensions* (Toronto, Canada: Random House, 1988), pp. 58–59.

page 360   "PLANET MARS—ARE YOU COMING HOME SOON"— Jim and Coral Lorenzen, *Flying Saucer Occupants* (New York: Signet, 1967), p. 135.

page 360   Double-"L"s meaning "foreigners" in Egyptian hieroglyphs—Barry Fell, *America B.C.* (New York: New York Times Book Company, 1976), p. 254.

page 360 "if a Martian shakes hands with a baker in Brittany"—Jacques Vallee, *Forbidden Science* (Berkeley, California: North Atlantic Books, 1992), p. 38.

page 360 McDivitt, advanced radar antennae—*Mysteries from Beyond Earth* (video).

page 361 "That was just great! They set down and picked up a man ..."—Ralph and Judy Blum, *Beyond Earth: Man's Contact with UFOs* (New York: Bantam, 1974), p. 200.

page 371 Ian Fleming sent to brief the Americans of "Enigma's" existence, etc.—Anthony Cave Brown, *Bodyguard of Lies* (London: HarperCollins, 1975), p. 68.

page 372 "My plots are fantastic, while being often based upon truth"—Alan Jones, "Goldeneye," *Cinefantastique,* Vol. 26, No. 6 and Vol. 27, No. 1, October 1995, p. 6.

page 372 "*Goldfinger,* like much of Fleming's writing, was not pure invention ..."—William Stevenson, *A Man Called Intrepid* (New York: Random House, 1976), p. 354.

page 373 "It seems incredible, but ..." "... just cannot talk about those cases"—Jerome Clark, *UFO Encounters and Beyond* (Lincolnwood, Illinois: Publications International, 1993), p. 42.

page 374 "U.S. Space Command," "space battleships," Tesla beam weapons—Margaret Cheney, *Tesla: Man Out of Time* (Englewood, New Jersey: Prentice- Hall, Inc., 1981), p. 289.

page 375 Fleming's Dr. No description—Ian Fleming, *Doctor No* (New York: Signet, 1959), p. 130.

page 378 "This group of men who represented the aristocratic cream ..."- Brown, *Bodyguard of Lies,* p. 268.

page 378 "The docudrama, entertainment in the guise of history ..."—Haynes Johnson, *Sleepwalking Through History: America in the Reagan Years* (New York: W. W. Norton & Co., Inc., 1991), p. 143.

page 378 "that under the influence of New History, Psycho-History ..."—Ibid., p. 471.

page 378 "Television, with its false 'docudramas' ..."—Ibid.

page 381 Roy Thinnes *Invaders* quotes—Bill Warren, "Surviving the Invasion," *Starlog,* No. 223, 2/96, p.78.

Chapter 8: Juvenilizations and Animations

page 397   "Funny, but more than just a few 'Munsters' and 'Addams' episodes . . ."—Stephen Cox, *The Addams Chronicles* (New York: HarperCollins, 1991), p. 192.

page 398   ". . . would take, we suspect, grave explanation"—Ibid., p. 183.

page 402   "I knew London like a book, knew where to go and whom to see . . ."—Calvin Thomas Beck, *Heroes of the Horrors* (New York: Collier Books, 1975), p. 279.

page 403   CIA recruiting out of Ivy League academia before Viet Nam—Victor Marchetti and John D. Marks, *The CIA and the Cult of Intelligence* (New York: Alfred A. Knopf, 1974), pp. 245–246.

page 409   ". . . NASA regarded him as a meddling whistleblower"—Jay Maeder, *Dick Tracy: The Official Biography* (New York: Plume Books, 1990), p. 191.

page 409   "It's a good bet that by the 21st Century there will be . . ."—Ibid., p. 199.

page 409   Dick Tracy's "Moon Maid" and "Moon Period," et al.—Ibid., pp. 190–199, 208.

page 428   the "world of tomorrow" was "very interesting" to him (Blatty)—William Peter Blatty, *I'll Tell Them I Remember You* (New York: W. W. Norton & Company, Inc., 1973), p. 41.

page 428   "We are testing weapons for use on the moon"—Ibid., p. 7.

page 432   Cancelled: 1977—Gary Gerani with Paul H. Schulman, *Fantastic Television* (New York: Harmony Books, 1977), p. 147 (an irresistible lift).

page 433   Gerry Anderson quotes—Gerry Anderson, "Space Report: 'The Mysterious Unknown Force,' Parts I & II," *Starlog* #34–35, May-June 1980, pp. 44– 45 (Part I), and p. 31 (Part II).

page 434   "We had known so much hardship and disappointment . . ."—Sylvia Anderson's *Yes M'Lady,* quoted in Mark A. Miller's "Gerry Anderson: Maverick Producer on a Puppet String Budget," Outre #8, p. 38.

page 434   "The special-effects miniatures are better than in movies

..."—Michael Weldon, *The Psychotronic Encyclopedia of Film* (New York: Ballantine, 1983), p. 718.

Chapter 9: Foresights and Fictionalizations

page 443 *"... the 'dead' period of UFO activity (1914–1916) ..."*— Jacques Vallee, *Anatomy of a Phenomenon* (New York: Ace, 1965), p. 54.

page 444 *Twilight Bar,* blackout caused by UFO, car ignition effects— Jacques Vallee, *Dimensions* (Toronto, Canada: Random House, 1988), p. 148.

page 445 Philip K. Dick's possible abduction experience, quotes— Jacques Vallee, *Revelations* (New York: Random House, 1991), pp. 293–294.

page 449 H. P. Lovecraft's possible abduction experience, quotes— L. Sprague de Camp, *Lovecraft: A Biography* (New York: Random House, 1976), pp. 32–33.

page 460 Stephen King's morbid fear of machines—Stephen King, *Danse Macabre* (New York: Everest House, 1981), pp. 84–85.

page 460 "King writes mechanical monsters into much of what he does"—Lenore Terr, M.D., *Unchained Memories: True Stories of Traumatic Memories, Lost and Found* (New York: Basic-Books/HarperCollins), 1994), p. 208.

page 466 "... Dr. John Lilly ... has written extensively about his possible contacts ... —Robert Anton Wilson, *Right Where You Are Sitting Now* (Berkeley, California: Ronin, 1992; 1982), p. 52.

page 467 "swimmer nullification," CIA work of John Lilly—John D. Marks, *The Search for the "Manchurian Candidate": The CIA and Mind Control* (1979) (New York: W. W. Norton & Company, Inc., 1991), pp. 151–154, 153 (n.).

page 470 "If you think S&M is sexy ..."—Katharine Ramsland, *Prism of the Night: A Biography of Anne Rice* (New York: Plume, 1992), p. 218.

page 487 "NASA and the former astronauts evade like a grifter ..."— Jonathan Vankin and John Whalen, *The 50 Greatest Conspiracies of All Time* (New York: Citadel, 1995), p. 81.

Chapter 10: Peregrinations and Propagandizations

page 495 the '80s the decade in which fame was solicited—Marshall Blonsky, "The Law of Averageness," and Ellis Wiener, "Fame and Loathing," *Spy*, Aug. 1994, pp. 33–37.

page 516 NASA's 20–page letter that made Spielberg a "true believer"—Philip M. Taylor, *Steven Spielberg: The Man, His Movies and Their Meaning* (New York: Continuum, 1994), p. 91.

page 524 *chupas*—Jacques Vallee, *Confrontations* (New York: Ballantine, 1990), pp. 118–125; 196–203.

Chapter 11: Indoctrinations and Demonizations

page 536 "was filled with the sons and daughters of diplomats and journalists . . ."—Al Ryan and Dan Cziraky, "Friday's Femme Fatale," *Femme Fatales* #1, Summer 1992, p. 51.

page 536 Robey's agoraphobia "was part of a government experiment . . ."—Marc Shapiro, "The Fears of Robey," *Fangoria* #92, May 1990, p. 20.

Chapter 12: Conclusions and Considerations

page 577 Carlos Clarens quotes—Carlos Clarens, *An Illustrated History of the Horror Film* (New York: G. P. Putnam's Sons/Paragon, 1967; 1979), pp. 118– 119.

page 579 "If Hollywood is responsible . . . Where are the robots?"—C.D.B. Bryan, *Close Encounters of the Fourth Kind: Alien Abduction, UFOs, and the Conference at M.I.T.* (New York: Alfred A. Knopf, 1995), p. 50.

page 582 "Would you believe a vampire movie with songs? . . . naw, you wouldn't believe"—John Stanley, *Creature Features: The Science Fiction, Fantasy, and Horror Movie Guide* (New York: Berkley/Boulevard, 1997), p. 55.

page 583   "It did take pressure off Project Blue Book . . ."—Edward J.
Ruppelt, *The Report on Unidentified Flying Objects* (New York:
Ace, 1956), p. 228.

Select Bibliography

Agel, Jerome (ed.). *The Making of Kubrick's 2001*. New York: Signet, 1970.

Andrews, George C. *Extra-Terrestrials Among Us*. 1986. St. Paul, Minnesota: Llewellyn, 1992.

Bach, Steven. *Final Cut*. New York: William Morrow, 1985.

Bain, Donald. *The Control of Candy Jones*. Chicago: Playboy Press, 1976.

Bamford, James. *The Puzzle Palace: A Report on America's Most Secret Agency*. New York: Houghton Mifflin, 1982.

Barclay, David, and Marie Therese (eds.). *UFOs: The Final Answer?* London: Blandford Books, 1993.

Bartimus, Tad, and Scott McCartney. *Trinity's Children*. Albuquerque: University of New Mexico Press, 1991.

Bauval, Robert, and Adrian Gilbert. *The Orion Mystery*. New York: Crown, 1994.

Baxter, John. *Science Fiction in the Cinema*. New York: Paperback Library, 1970.

Beck, Calvin Thomas. *Heroes of the Horrors*. New York: Collier, 1975.

Begich, Dr. Nick, and Jeane Manning. *Angels Don't Play This Haarp: Advances In Tesla Technology*. Anchorage, Alaska: Earthpulse Press, 1995.

Berlitz, Charles. *Mysteries from Forgotten Worlds*. New York: Dell, 1972.

Blatty, William Peter. *I'll Tell Them I Remember You*. New York: W. W. Norton & Company, Inc., 1973.

————. *William Peter Blatty on the Exorcist: From Novel to Film*. New York: Bantam, 1974.

Blum, Howard. *Out There*. New York: Simon & Schuster, 1990.

Blum, Ralph, and Judy Blum. *Beyond Earth: Man's Contact with UFOs*. New York: Bantam, 1974.

Blundell, Nigel, and Roger Boar. *The World's Greatest UFO Mysteries.* London: Octopus Books, 1983.

Brady, Frank. *Citizen Welles: A Biography of Orson Welles.* New York: Charles Scribner's Sons, 1989.

Bramley, William. *The Gods of Eden.* 1989. New York: Avon, 1993.

Bresler, Fenton. *Who Killed John Lennon?* New York: St. Martin's Press, 1989.

Brier, Bob. *Ancient Egyptian Magic.* New York: William Morrow and Company, Inc., 1980.

Brosnan, John. *The Horror People.* New York: St. Martin's Press, 1976.

Brown, Anthony Cave. *Bodyguard of Lies.* London: HarperCollins, 1975.

Brown, Peter Harry, and Patte B. Barham. *Marilyn: The Last Take.* New York: Signet, 1993.

Bryan, C.D.B. *Close Encounters of the Fourth Kind: Alien Abduction, UFOs, and the Conference at M.I.T.* New York: Alfred A. Knopf, 1995.

Budge, Sir E. A. Wallis. *Amulets and Superstitions.* 1930. New York: Dover, 1978.

———. *From Fetish to God in Ancient Egypt.* 1934. New York: Dover, 1988.

———. *The Mummy.* 1893. New York: Dover, 1989.

Case, Christopher. *The Ultimate Movie Thesaurus.* New York: Henry Holt and Company, Inc., 1996.

Chaikin, Andrew. *A Man on the Moon.* New York: Penguin, 1994.

Cheney, Margaret. *Tesla: Man Out of Time.* 1981. New York: Dell Publishing, 1983.

Childress, David Hatcher. *Extraterrestrial Archaeology.* Stelle, Illinois: Adventures Unlimited, 1994.

Chunovic, Louis. *Jodie: A Biography.* Chicago: Contemporary Books, 1995.

Clarens, Carlos. *An Illustrated History of the Horror Film.* New York: G. P. Putnam's Sons, 1967.

Clark, Jerome. *UFO Encounters & Beyond.* Lincolnwood, Illinois: Publications International, 1993.

Cohen, Daniel. *Monsters, Giants and Little Men from Mars.* New York: Dell, 1975.

Colodny, Len, and Robert Gettlin. *Silent Coup: The Removal of a President*. New York: St. Martin's, 1992.

Conroy, Ed. *Report on Communion*. New York: William Morrow, 1990.

Cooper, William. *Behold A Pale Horse*. Sedona, Arizona: Light Technology Publishing, 1991.

Corman, Roger, with Jim Jerome. *How I Made a Hundred Movies in Hollywood and Never Lost a Dime*. New York: Dell Books, 1991.

Cox, Stephen. *The Addams Chronicles*. New York: HarperCollins, 1991.

Crichton, Michael. *Travels*. New York: Ballantine, 1988.

de Camp, L. Sprague. *Lovecraft: A Biography*. New York: Random House, 1976.

de Santillana, Giorgio, and Hertha von Dechend. *Hamlet's Mill*. 1969. Boston: Nonpareil, 1977.

DiPietro, Vincent, and Gregory Molenaar. *Unusual Martian Surface Features*. Berkeley, California: North Atlantic Books, 1982.

Donnelly, Ignatius. *Atlantis: The Antediluvian World*. 1882. New York: Dover, 1976.

Edwards, Frank. *Flying Saucers: Serious Business*. New York: Bantam, 1966.

Eliot, Marc. *Walt Disney: Hollywood's Dark Prince*. New York: HarperCollins, 1994.

Engel, Joel. *Gene Roddenberry: The Myth and the Man Behind Star Trek*. New York: Hyperion, 1994.

Evans-Wentz, W. Y. *The Fairy Faith in Celtic Countries*. 1911. New York: Citadel, 1990.

Faulkner, R. O. *The Ancient Egyptian Coffin Texts*. 3 Volumes. Warminster, England: Aris & Phillips, Ltd., 1977.

Fawcett, Lawrence, and Barry J. Greenwood. *Clear Intent*. New York: New York Times Book Company, 1984.

Fell, Barry. *America B.C.* New York: Simon & Schuster, 1976.

Flammonde, Paris. *UFO Exist!* Canada: G. P. Putnam's Sons, 1976.

Florescu, Radu. *In Search of Frankenstein*. New York: Warner Books, 1976.

Fowler, Raymond E. *The Watchers*. New York: Bantam, 1990.

Freeman, Marsha. *How We Got to the Moon*. Washington, D.C.: 21st Century Science Associates, 1993.

Fuller, John G. *The Interrupted Journey.* New York: Berkley, 1966.

Gerani, Gary, and Paul H. Schulman. *Fantastic Television.* New York: Harmony Books, 1977.

Gilbert, Robert E. *The Mortal Presidency.* New York: HarperCollins, 1992.

Good, Timothy. *Above Top Secret.* Great Britain: Sidgwick and Jackson, 1987.

———. *Alien Liaison.* London: Arrow, 1991.

Greenberg, Martin H., Ed Gorman, and Bill Munster (eds.). *The Dean Koontz Companion.* New York: Berkley, 1994.

Grey, Rudolph. *Nightmare of Ecstasy: The Life and Art of Edward D. Wood, Jr.* 1992. Portland, Oregon: Feral House, 1994.

Guerber, H. A. *Myths of Greece and Rome.* 1907. New York: Dover, 1993.

———. *Myths of the Norsemen from the Eddas and Sagas.* 1909. New York: Dover, 1992.

Hall, Richard. *Uninvited Guests.* Santa Fe, New Mexico: Aurora Press, 1988.

Hancock, Graham. *Fingerprints of the Gods.* New York: Crown, 1995.

Hancock, Graham, and Robert Bauval. *The Message of the Sphinx: A Quest for the Hidden Legacy of Mankind.* New York: Crown, 1996.

Hauck, Dennis William. *Captain Quirk: The Unauthorized Biography of William Shatner.* New York: Pinnacle, 1995.

Hoagland, Richard. *The Monuments of Mars, Fourth Edition.* 1987. Berkeley, California: Frog, Ltd., 1996.

Hopkins, Budd. *Intruders.* New York: Ballantine, 1988.

———. *Missing Time.* New York: Ballantine, 1981.

Hough, Peter, and Jenny Randles. *Looking for the Aliens.* London: Blandford Books, 1991.

Howard, Michael. *The Occult Conspiracy.* Rochester, Vermont: Destiny Books, 1989.

Jacobs, David M., Ph.D. *Secret Life: Firsthand Documented Accounts of UFO Abductions.* New York: Simon & Schuster, 1992.

Johnson, Haynes. *Sleepwalking Through History: America in the Reagan Years.* New York: W. W. Norton & Co., 1991.

Jones, Stephen J. (ed.). *Clive Barker's Shadows in Eden: The Books, Films and Art of Clive Barker.* Lancaster, Pennsylvania: Underwood-Miller, 1991.

Jung, Carl G. (ed.). *Man and His Symbols*. London: Aldus Books, 1964.

Kaplan, Stephen, and Roxanne Salch Kaplan. *The Amityville Horror Conspiracy*. Laceyville, Pennsylvania: Belfrey Books, 1995.

Keel, John A. *The Complete Guide to Mysterious Beings*. 1970. New York: Doubleday, 1994.

———. *The Mothman Prophecies*. 1975. Avondale Estates, Georgia: IllumiNet Press, 1991.

Kessler, Ronald. *Inside the CIA*. New York: Simon & Schuster, 1992.

Keyhoe, Donald E. *Aliens from Space*. London: Panther Books, 1973.

———. *Flying Saucers: Top Secret*. New York: G. P. Putnam's Sons, 1960.

King, Stephen. *Danse Macabre*. New York: Everest House, 1981.

Klass, Philip J. *UFO Abductions: A Dangerous Game*. Buffalo, New York: Prometheus, 1989.

Kneale, Nigel (teleplays). *Quatermass*. London: Hutchinson, 1979.

———. *Quatermass and the Pit*. London: Penguin, 1960.

———. *The Quatermass Experiment*. London: Penguin, 1959.

———. *Quatermass II*. London: Penguin, 1960.

Koch, Howard. *The Panic Broadcast*. New York: Avon, 1970.

Kolosimo, Peter. *Not of This World*. Secaucus, New Jersey: University Books, 1971.

———. *Timeless Earth*. Secaucus, New Jersey: University Books, 1974.

Landsburg, Alan and Sally. *In Search of Ancient Mysteries*. New York: Bantam, 1974.

Leaming, Barbara. *Orson Welles: A Biography*. New York: Viking Penguin, 1985.

Lee, Martin A., and Norman Solomon. *Unreliable Sources: A Guide to Detecting Bias in News Media*. New York: Lyle Stuart, 1990.

Levenda, Peter. *Unholy Alliance: A History of Nazi Involvement with the Occult*. New York: Avon, 1995.

Lindemann, Michael (ed.). *UFOs and the Alien Presence*. Santa Barbara, California: 2020 Group, 1991.

Lorenzen, Jim, and Coral Lorenzen. *Flying Saucer Occupants*. New York: Signet, 1967.

Mack, John E., M.D. *Abduction: Human Encounters with Aliens*. New York: Charles Scribner's Sons, 1994.

Maeder, Jay. *Dick Tracy: The Official Biography*. New York: Plume, 1990.

Marchetti, Victor, and John D. Marks. *The CIA and the Cult of Intelligence.* 1974. New York: Alfred A. Knopf, 1980.

Marks, John. *The Search for the "Manchurian Candidate": The CIA and Mind Control.* 1979. London: W. W. Norton, 1991.

Marrs, Jim. *Crossfire: The Plot that Killed Kennedy.* New York: Carroll & Graf, 1989.

McCarty, John. *The Sleaze Merchants: Adventures in Exploitation Filmmaking.* New York: St. Martin's/Griffin, 1995.

Melanson, Phillip H., Ph.D. *The Robert F. Kennedy Assassination: New Revelations on the Conspiracy and Cover-Up.* 1991. New York: SPI, 1994.

Mitgang, Herbert. *Dangerous Dossiers.* New York: Ballantine, 1989.

Norman, Eric. *Gods and Devils from Outer Space.* New York: Lancer, 1973.

———. *Gods, Demons and Space Chariots.* New York: Lancer, 1970.

Ostrander, Sheila, and Lynn Schroeder. *Psychic Discoveries Behind the Iron Curtain.* New Jersey: Prentice-Hall, 1970.

Pearson, John. *Alias James Bond: The Life of Ian Fleming.* New York: McGraw Hill, 1966.

Pfeiffer, Lee, and Philip Lisa. *The Incredible World of 007.* 1995. Secaucus, New Jersey: Citadel, 1997.

Ramsland, Katherine. *Prism of the Night: A Biography of Anne Rice.* New York: Plume, 1992.

Randle, Kevin D. *The UFO Casebook.* New York: Warner, 1989.

Randle, Kevin D., and Donald R. Schmitt. *The Truth About the UFO Crash at Roswell.* New York: Avon, 1994.

———. *UFO Crash at Roswell.* New York: Avon, 1991.

Randles, Jenny. *The UFO Conspiracy.* New York: Barnes & Noble, 1987.

Rogers, Dave. *The Avengers.* London: ITV Books, 1983.

Rolleston, T. W. *Celtic Myths and Legends.* 1911. New York: Dover, 1990.

Rubin, Steven Jay. *The Complete James Bond Movie Encyclopedia.* 1990. Chicago, Illinois: Contemporary Books, 1995.

Ruppelt, Edward J. *The Report on Unidentified Flying Objects.* New York: Ace, 1956.

Rux, Bruce. *Architects of the Underworld: Unriddling Atlantis, Anomalies of Mars, and the Mystery of the Sphinx.* Berkeley, California: Frog, Ltd.,1996.

Sagan, Carl, and Jerome Agel. *The Cosmic Connection.* New York: Doubleday, 1973.

———. *Other Worlds.* New York: Bantam, 1975.

Santesson, Hans Stefan (ed.). *Flying Saucers in Fact and Fiction.* New York: Lancer, 1968.

Saunders, M. W., and Duncan Lunan. *Destiny Mars.* Surrey, England: Caterham, 1975.

Schelde, Per. *Androids, Humanoids and Other Science Fiction Monsters.* New York: New York University Press, 1993.

Schneider, Steve. *That's All Folks!.* New York: Henry Holt, 1988.

Schow, David J., and Jeffrey Frentzen. *The Outer Limits: The Official Companion.* New York: Ace, 1986.

Schuster, Hal, and David Lessnick (eds.). *Batmania II.* Las Vegas, Nevada: Pioneer, 1992.

Schwartz, Sherwood. *Inside Gilligan's Island.* 1988. New York: St. Martin's Press, 1994.

Scott, Kathryn Leigh (ed.). *The Dark Shadows Companion: 25th Anniversary Collection.* Universal City, California: Pomegranate Press, 1990.

Scully, Frank. *Behind the Flying Saucers.* New York: Henry Holt and Company, Inc., 1950.

Sellier, Charles. *Mysteries of the Ancient World.* New York: Dell, 1995.

Shatner, William, with Chris Kreski. *Star Trek Memories.* New York: HarperCollins, 1993.

———. *Star Trek Movie Memories.* New York: HarperCollins, 1995.

Sitchin, Zecharia. *Genesis Revisited.* New York: Avon, 1990.

———. *The 12th Planet.* 1976. New York: Avon, 1978.

Snelling, O. F. *James Bond: A Report.* London: O. F. Snelling, 1964.

Spence, Lewis. *The History of Atlantis.* 1930. London: Senate, 1995.

———. *Myths & Legends of Ancient Egypt.* 1915. New York: Dover, 1990.

Spencer, John. *The UFO Encyclopedia.* New York: Avon, 1991.

Stanley, John. *Creature Features: The Science Fiction, Fantasy, and Horror Movie Guide.* New York: Boulevard, 1997.

Steiger, Brad (ed.). *Project Blue Book.* New York: Ballantine, 1976.

Stevenson, William. *A Man Called Intrepid.* New York: Random House, 1976.

Strick, Philip. *Science Fiction Movies.* London: Octopus, 1976.

Symonds, John, and Kenneth Grant (eds.) *The Confessions of Aleister Crowley.* New York: Hill & Wang, 1969.

Symonds, John. *The Great Beast: The Life and Times of Aleister Crowley.* Great Britain: McDonald & Co., Ltd., 1971.

Taylor, Philip M. *Steven Spielberg: The Man, His Movies and Their Meaning.* New York: Continuum, 1994.

Temple, Robert K. G. *The Sirius Mystery.* Rochester, Vermont: Destiny, 1976.

Terr, Lenore, M.D. *Unchained Memories.* New York: BasicBooks, 1994.

Thomas, Gordon. *Journey Into Madness: Secret CIA Mind Control and Medical Abuse.* New York: Bantam, 1989.

Thompson, Keith. *Angels and Aliens.* New York: Ballantine, 1991.

Thompson, Richard L. *Alien Identities: Ancient Insights into Modern UFO Phenomena.* San Diego, California: Govardhan Hill, 1993.

Tohill, Cathal, and Pete Tombs. *Immoral Tales: European Sex and Horror Movies 1956-1984.* New York: St. Martin's/Griffin, 1995.

Tolstoy, Nikolai. *The Quest for Merlin.* New York: Back Bay/Little, Brown and Company, 1985.

Tomas, Andrew. *We Are Not the First.* London: Souvenir Press, 1971.

Tompkins, Peter. *Mysteries of the Mexican Pyramids.* New York: Harper & Row, 1976.

———. *Secrets of the Great Pyramid.* New York: Harper & Row, 1971.

Travers, Peter, and Stephanie Reiff. *The Story Behind the Exorcist.* New York: Signet, 1974.

Turner, William, and Jonn Christian. *The Assassination of Robert F. Kennedy: The Conspiracy and Coverup.* 1978. New York: Thunder's Mouth Press, 1993.

Vallee, Jacques and Janine. *Challenge to Science: The UFO Enigma.* New York: Ballantine, 1966.

Vallee, Jacques. *Anatomy of a Phenomenon.* New York: Ace, 1965.

———. *Confrontations.* Toronto, Canada: Random House, 1990.

———. *Dimensions.* Toronto, Canada: Random House, 1988.

———. *Forbidden Science.* Berkeley, California: North Atlantic Books, 1992.

———. *Messengers of Deception.* Berkeley, California: And/Or Press, 1979.

———. *Revelations.* New York: Random House, 1991.

Vankin, Jonathan. *Conspiracies, Cover-ups and Crimes.* New York: Paragon House, 1992.

Vankin, Jonathan, and John Whalen. *The 50 Greatest Conspiracies of All Time: History's Biggest Mysteries, Cover-ups & Cabals.* New York: Citadel, 1995.

Velikovsky, Immanuel. *Worlds in Collision.* New York: Doubleday & Company, 1950.

Vesco, Renato, and David Hatcher Childress. *Man-Made UFOs: 1944-1994.* Stelle, Illinois: Adventures Unlimited Press, 1994.

VideoHound. *Sci-Fi Experience: Your Quantum Guide to the Video Universe.* Detroit: Visible Ink Press, 1997.

Walton, Travis. *Fire in the Sky: The Walton Experience.* 1979. New York: Marlowe & Company, 1997.

Watkins, Leslie, and David Ambrose. *Alternative 3.* Great Britain: Sphere, 1978.

Weaver, Tom (ed.). *Creature from the Black Lagoon: The Original Shooting Script.* Absecon, New Jersey: MagicImage Filmbooks, 1992.

Weldon, Michael. *The Psychotronic Encyclopedia of Film.* New York: Ballantine, 1983.

Welfare, Simon, and John Fairley. *Arthur C. Clarke's Mysterious World.* New York: A&W Publishers, Inc., 1980.

West, John Anthony. *Serpent in the Sky: The High Wisdom of Ancient Egypt.* Wheaton, Illinois: Quest/Theosophical Books, 1993.

Whitfield, Stephen E., and Gene Roddenberry. *The Making of Star Trek.* New York: Ballantine, 1968.

Wilkins, Harold. *Flying Saucers on the Attack.* New York: Ace, 1954.

———. *Flying Saucers Uncensored.* Secaucus, New Jersey: Citadel Press, 1955.

Wilkinson, Richard H. *Reading Egyptian Art.* London: Thames & Hudson, 1992.

Williams, Lucy Chase. *The Complete Films of Vincent Price.* Secaucus, New Jersey: Citadel Press, 1995.

Wilson, Colin. *The Occult.* New York: Random House, 1971.

Wilson, Robert Anton. *Right Where You Are Sitting Now.* 1982. Berkeley, California: Ronin, 1992.

Wright, Peter, with Paul Greengrass. *Spycatcher.* New York: Dell, 1987.

Wynorski, Jim. *They Came from Outer Space.* New York: Doubleday, 1980.

Periodicals

"AIP's Third Man—The Other Guy: Deke Heyward's Untold Story," *Filmfax,* No. 60, 1997.

"Alien Invasion," *Cinescape,* Vol. 2, No. 11, 8/96.

"The Amicus Empire, an Interview with Milton Subotsky," *Filmfax,* No. 42, 12/93-1/94.

"And In the Beginning Was the Word . . . An Interview with Screenwriter Richard Matheson," *Filmfax,* No. 42, 12/93-1/94.

"An Interview with War of the Worlds Leading Lady Ann Robinson," *SPFX,* No. 4, 1996.

"Anomalous Table Procedures," *UFO,* Vol. 8, No. 1, 1993.

"Are the Reasons for the Coverup Solely Scientific?" *Flying Saucer Review,* Vol. 28, No. 6.

"Astro Boy: Happy 30th To That Mighty Mechanical Mite," *Filmfax,* No. 42, Dec./Jan. 1994.

"The A-to-Z of Creating First Men in the Moon," *Starlog,* No. 37, 8/80.

"Attack of the 5 Ft. 3 In. Woman: An Interview with Yvette Vickers," *Filmfax,* No. 46, Aug./Sept. 1994.

"Beach Blanket Babylon: The Rise and Fall of Surf City Cinema," *Filmfax,* No. 46, Aug./Sept. 1994.

"Behind the Scenes at 'Intruders,'" *UFO,* Vol. 7, No. 4, 1992.

"The Best of the Worst!," *Fantastic Films,* Vol. 4, No. 1, 8/81.

"Beverley 'Decoy' Garland: An Interview with TV's First Policewoman," *Filmfax,* No. 60, 1997.

"B is for Blaisdell," *Fangoria,* No.9, 11/80.

"Bombs from Outer Space," *Monsters of the Movies,* Vol. 1, No. 9, Summer 1975.

"The Brain that Wouldn't Die," *Midnight Marquee,* No. 53, Spring 1997.

"Breaking Through Secrecy," *UFO,* Vol. 9, No. 1, 1994.

"A Candid Conversation with Roger Corman," *Fantastic Films,* Vol. 3, No. 4, 8/80.

"Civilization Rethought," *Conde Nast Traveler,* 2/93.

"Close Encounters with an Open Mind," *Starlog,* No. 14, 6/78.

"The Corman Interview," *Fangoria,* No. 12, 4/81.

"Creature Lady," *Filmfax,* No. 60, 1997.

"Creature Love," *Starlog,* No. 167, 6/91.

"The Common Ground of Abduction Support," *UFO,* Vol. 8, No. 1, 1993.

"A Comprehensive Interview with Robert Wise," *Fantastic Films,* Vol. 2, No. 4, 9/79.

"The Conquest of Space: A New Look at an Old Classic," *Fantastic Films,* Vol. 2, No. 2, 6/79.

"Copters and Roberts," *Longmont Daily Times-Call,* No. 214, 8/2/94.

"The Creature Remake that Never Got Made!," *Filmfax,* No. 37, Feb./Mar. 1993.

"Creatures Great and Small: The SF Films of Jack Arnold," *Fangoria,* No. 3, 12/79.

"Curse of the Demon," *Fangoria,* No. 4, 2/80.

"Dan O'Bannon: SF's Pragmatic Visionary," *Sci-Fi Entertainment,* Vol. 2, No. 5, 2/96.

"Dante's Inferno Blazes Again! A Devilish Dialogue with Howling Director: Joe Dante," *Fantastic Films,* Vol. 3, No. 9, 6/81.

"Dawn of the Warrior Robots," *Fangoria,* No. 4, 2/80.

"The Day the Earth Stood Still! The True Behind-the-Scenes Story Told by the Man Who Made the Movie!," *Fantastic Films,* Vol. 4, No. 4, 4/82.

"Designing New Dimensions for The Outer Limits," *Outre,* No. 2, Spring 1995.

"Disinformation Games," *UFO,* Vol. 6, No. 6, 1991.

"Documents Trace NSA-UFO Connection," *UFO*, Vol 9, No. 1, 1994.

"DSP Satellite 'Spots' UFOs," *UFO*, Vol. 9, No. 1, 1994.

"Ed Wood, Cult Legend," *Cinefantastique*, Vol. 25, No. 5, 10/94.

"Elisabeth Brooks," *Fangoria*, No. 12, 4/81.

"Exposing a Scientific Coverup," *Atlantis Rising*, No. 6, 1996.

"Falkville Chief Says 'Howdy' to Spaceman," *Birmingham News*, 10/19/73.

"Falkville Police Chief Resigns Under Pressure," *Decatur Daily*, 11/16/73.

"Fame and Loathing," *Spy*, 8/94.

"The Fantasy Worlds of Virgil Vogel," *Fantastic Films*, Vol. 3, No. 9, 6/81.

"The Fears of Robey," *Fangoria*, No. 92, 5/90.

"The Fifties Meet the Monsters," *Midnight Marquee*, No. 51, Summer 1996.

"'Fire In The Sky' Inquiry," *UFO*, Vol. 8, No. 3, 1993.

"Former CIA Officer Talks," *UFO*, Vol. 6, No. 6, 1991.

"Friday's Femme Fatale," *Femme Fatales*, Vol. 1, No. 1, Summer 1992.

"Fright Stalker," *Cinescape*, Vol. 3, No. 1, Oct./Nov. 1996.

"From Night Until Dawn: Interview with George Romero," *Fantastic Films*, Vol. 2, No. 3, 7/79.

"The Galactic Ghoul: Superpower Problems in Getting to Mars," *UFO*, Vol. 8, No. 6, 1993.

"Gerry Anderson: Maverick Producer on a Puppet String Budget," *Outre*, Vol. 1, Nos. 7 & 8, 1996/1997.

"Gerry Anderson's Space Report: The Mysterious Unknown Force," *Starlog*, Nos. 34-36, May-July 1980.

"Gerry Anderson: The Master of Space," *Starlog*, No. 9, 10/77.

"Goldeneye," *Cinefantastique*, Vol. 26, No. 6/Vol. 27, No 1, 10/95.

"Guardian Case Gets Sacked by Canadian Researchers," *UFO*, Vol. 10, No. 2, 1995.

"Guess Who's the New Dr. Who?," *Fantastic Films*, Vol. 4, No. 4, 4/82.

"Gulf Breeze Photo Case Marred By 'Bad Science'," *UFO*, Vol. 9, No. 1, 1994.

"Gulf Breeze Reassessed," *UFO*, Vol. 8, No. 5, 1993.

"Halloween III: Season of the Witch," *Fangoria*, Vol. 3, No. 22, 1981.

"The Hammer Factory: Hammer Films, Corman Style," *Midnight Marquee*, No. 47, Summer 1994.

"Harlan Ellison: Science Fiction's Last Angry Man," *Starlog*, No. 8, 9/77.

"Heat of the Ice Princess: Allison Hayes," *Filmfax*, No. 46, Aug./Sept. 1994.

"The Hidden History of the Flying Saucer Mystery," *UFO Sightings*, Vol. 4, No.1, 1996.

"Hopkins Rates Mini-Series 'B+'," *UFO*, Vol. 7, No. 4, 1992.

"Horror Films from South of the Border," *Cinefantastique*, Vol. 27, No. 10, 6/95.

"Horror in the Comics," *Fangoria*, Nos. 12-14, 4-8/81.

"The 'How-To' of Making a Monster Movie: AIP Producer Herman Cohen," *Filmfax*, No. 37, Feb./Mar. 1993.

"I Married a Monster from Outer Space Producer/Director Gene Fowler, Jr.," *SPFX*, No. 4, 1996.

"I Married a Monster from Outer Space: Retrospect," *SPFX*, No. 4, 1996.

"Inside Outer Limits," *Famous Monsters of Filmland*, No. 26, 1/64.

"An Interview: Dr. J. Allen Hynek and Steven Spielberg," *Science Fantasy Film Classics*, Vol. 1, No. 2, Spring 1978.

"An Interview with David Cronenberg, the Man Who Created Scanners," *Fantastic Films*, Vol. 3, No. 9, 6/81.

"An Interview with Ann Robinson," *Science Fantasy Film Classics*, Vol. 1, No. 2, Spring 1978.

"The Invaders Strike Back," *Starlog*, No. 222, 1/96.

"It's No Act—He's Into UFOs," *UFO*, Vol. 9, No. 4, 1994.

"Jeff Morrow Interview," *Psychotronic*, No. 16, 1993.

"Jenny Agutter," *Fangoria*, No. 14, 8/81.

"Joan Taylor Saves the World! The Woman Who Made Intelligence Beautiful," *Filmfax*, No. 60, 1997.

"John Carpenter," *Fangoria*, No. 14, 8/81.

"John Carpenter, Natch!," *Fantastic Films*, Vol. 3, No. 2, 7/80.

"Kolchak: The Night Stalker," *Fangoria*, No. 3, 12/79.

"Last of the Martian Invasions," *Monsters of the Movies*, Vol. 1, No. 9, Summer 1975.

"The Law of Averageness," *Spy*, 8/94.

"Life Beyond the Camera: Jack Arnold," *Filmfax*, No. 37, 2/3 1993.

"Long Saga of Lunar Anomalies," *UFO*, Vol. 10, No. 2, 4/95.

"Mad Honey!," *Archaeology*, Nov./Dec. 1995.

"Marie Windsor: From Classic Film Noir to B-movies on the Moon," *Filmfax*, No. 46, Aug./Sept. 1994.

"Mars Attacks Again," *Space Wars*, Vol. 2, No. 2, 4/78.

"Mars Attacks: The Original Invasion Begins Again!," *Outre*, Vol. 1, No. 7, 1996.

"The Martian Kind," *Science Fantasy Film Classics*, Vol. 1, No. 2, Spring 1978.

"Memories of Cat Women," *Starlog*, No. 222, 1/96.

"Men of Iron: Here Come the Robots," *Space Wars*, Vol. 2, No. 1, 2/78.

"The Metal Monsters," *Famous Monsters of Filmland*, No. 12, Vol. 3, No. 3, 6/61.

"Monster Invasion," *Fangoria*, No. 14, 8/81.

"More John Agar Creature Features," *Filmfax*, No. 59, Feb./Mar. 1997.

"Movies We Hate!!!," *Midnight Marquee*, No. 53, Spring 1997.

"Newfound Faith: Rediscovering the Reclusive Faith Domergue," *Filmfax*, No. 59, Feb./Mar. 1997.

"Nichelle Nichols Opens All Hailing Frequencies," *Starlog*, No. 36, 7/80.

"Noted Ufologist's CIA Ties Disclosed," *UFO*, Vol. 8, No. 5, 1993.

"Our Mexican Ancestors," *Pursuit*, Vol. 18, No. 2, whole no. 70.

"Outer Limits," *Cinefantastique*, Vol. 27, No. 9, 5/96.

The Outer Limits—An Illustrated Review, Scorpio 13, Cleveland, Ohio, 1978.

"Past, Secret UFO Study Confirmed," *UFO*, Vol. 8, No. 2, 1993.

"Possible 'Covert Ops' Target Researchers," *UFO*, Vol. 8. No. 1, 1993.

"Proposed Studies on the Implications of Peaceful Space Activities for Human Affairs," Report of the Committee on Science and Astronautics, U.S. House of Representatives, 87th Congress, 1st Session, No. 242, by the Brookings Institute. Delivered to Committee of the Whole House on the State of the Union, 4/18/61.

" 'Psi-Cops' Bite Into Abduction Claims," *UFO*, Vol. 9, No. 5, 1994.

"Q&A: John Mack, M.D.," *UFO*, Vol. 9, No. 5, 1994.

"Q&A: Strieber Sounds Off," *UFO*, Vol. 8, No. 5, 1993.

"The Quatermass Films," *Fantastic Films*, No. 11, 10/79.

"The Quatermass Experience," *Filmfax*, No. 37, Feb./Mar. 1993.

"The Quatermass Saga," *Fangoria*, No. 6, 6/80.

"RAAF Captures Flying Saucer," *Roswell Daily Record*, 7/8/47.

"Raiders of the Movie Serials," *Starlog*, No. 49, 8/81.

"Ray Harryhausen Speaks," *Fangoria*, No. 14, 8/81.

"Realizing the Dream: The First 1000 Tickets into Space," *Starlog*, No. 8, 9/77.

"The Real Tobe Hooper," *Fangoria*, No. 12, 4/81.

"Red Star Rising," *Outre*, Vol. 1, No. 5, 1996.

"Richard Matheson: Master of Fantasy," *Fangoria*, No. 3, 12/79.

"Robey, Red Hot: Reflections on Sexism, Deception, Nudity, and Erotic Thrillers," *Femme Fatales*, Vol. 1., No. 4, Spring 1993.

"Robot Monsters Through Time and Space," *Monsters of the Movies*, Vol. 1, No. 9, Summer 1975.

"The Robot Report: Part Four, the Cybernetic Sixties," *Fantastic Films*, Vol. 3, No. 1, 5/80.

"Robots," *Fantastic Films*, No. 13, 1/80.

"Roger Corman On His AIP Poe Films," *Video Watchdog*, No. 24, August 1994.

"Ro-Man's Mate, an Interview with Claudia Barrett," *Filmfax*, No. 55, Mar./Apr. 1996.

"Ross Martin Relives His Behind-the-Scenes Experiences from The Colossus of New York," *Fantastic Films*, Vol. 3, No. 9, 6/81.

"The Saga of Capricorn One: A Watergate in Space," *Starlog*, No 14, 6/78.

"Saturday Morning TV," *Starlog*, No. 8, 9/77.

"The Secret Life of Fred L. Crisman," *UFO*, Vol. 8, No. 5, 1993.

"SF in the Comics," *Starlog*, Nos. 41-46, 12/80-5/81.

"She Married a Monster from Outer Space: Interview with Gloria Talbott," *SPFX*, No. 4, 1996.

"Space pioneer no hero, German exhibit suggests," *Rocky Mountain News* (Associated Press), 4/12/95.

"The Sphinx Revealed," *National Geographic*, Vol. 179, No. 4, 4/91.

Starlog Dr. Who 20th Anniversary Special (magazine), BBC, London, 1983.

"Strock Footage, an Interview with Herbert L. Strock," *Filmfax*, No. 55, Mar./Apr. 1996.

"Sultans of Saturday Morning: An Interview with Animation Giant Joe Barbera," *Filmfax*, No. 53, Nov./Dec. 1995.

"Supermarionation: Not for Features Only," *Starlog*, No. 17, 10/78.

"Surviving the Invasion," *Starlog*, No. 223, 2/96.

"Taking Stock of Wood," *Famous Monsters of Filmland*, No. 201, Fall 1993.

"Target Earth: Noir with a Dash of the Fantastic," *Midnight Marquee*, No. 51, Summer 1996.

"Teen Terrors," *Famous Monsters of Filmland*, No. 161, 3/80.

"Terrance Dicks," *Starlog*, No. 37, 8/80.

"Terror in the Isles," *Filmfax*, No. 51, Jul./Aug. 1995.

"That Awful Alien 'Slime'," *UFO*, Vol. 8, No. 3, 1993.

"There is Nothing Wrong with Your Television Set," *Fangoria*, No.9, 11/80.

"This Island Earth: An Overlooked Classic?" *Science Fantasy Film Classics*, Vol. 1, No. 3, 8/78.

"This Island Mirth—Abbot & Costello Go To Mars," *Filmfax*, No. 47, Oct./Nov. 1994.

"UFO's vs. USAF, Amazing (But True) Encounters," *Parade*, 12/10/78.

"Unsung Sirens and Other Silver Screen Screamers," *Filmfax*, No. 46, Aug./Sept. 1994.

"Val Guest and Nigel Kneale: Hammer's Dynamic Duo," *Midnight Marquee*, No. 47, 9/94.

"Videoscan," *Filmfax*, No. 51, Jul./Aug. 1995.

"Vincent Price: The Corman Years," *Fangoria*, Nos. 6-7, June/Aug. 1980.

"Walt Disney's Conquest of Space," *Starlog*, No. 13, 5/78.

"The Watcher in the Woods: An Interview with Tom Leetch, Co-Producer," *Starlog*, No. 36, 7/80.

"The Watcher in the Woods—or, The Day Disney Decided to Shock Your Socks Off!" *Fangoria*, No. 7, 8/80.

"Who Slew Curtis Harrington?" *Psychotronic*, No. 16, 1993.

"The Woman from Planet X, an Interview with Margaret Field," *Filmfax*, No. 58, 1/97.

"Wonder Woman: Out of Circulation But Destined for Syndication,"

Starlog, No. 28, 11/79.

"Worlds, Wars & Wonders: The Amazing Career of Ib J. Melchior," *Filmfax,* No. 56, May/June 1996.

"The World's Worst Film Festival," *Fantastic Films,* Vol. 3, No. 4, 10/80.

"Wreckage in the Desert Was Odd, but Not Alien," *The New York Times,* 9/18/94.

"Years After Stillness," *Starlog,* No. 211, 2/95.

Fiction

Bates, Harry. "Farewell to the Master" in *Astounding Stories,* Street & Smith, 1940.

Campbell, John W., Jr. "Who Goes There?" in *Astounding Stories,* Street & Smith, 1938.

Charbonneau, Louis. *Corpus Earthling* (New York: Zenith Books, 1960).

Clarke, Arthur C. "The Sentinel" (Scott Meredith Agency, 1950).

Barker, Clive. *Cabal.* 1985. New York: Pocket, 1989.

———. *Night Visions: The Hellbound Heart.* New York: Berkley, 1988.

Dick, Philip K. *Do Androids Dream of Electric Sheep?* New York: Doubleday and Company, Inc., 1968.

———. "Second Variety" from *The Philip K. Dick Reader.* 1987. Secaucus, New Jersey: Citadel Twilight, 1997.

———. "We Can Remember It For You Wholesale" from *The Philip K. Dick Reader.* 1987. Secaucus, New Jersey: Citadel Twilight, 1997.

Ellison, Harlan. "A Boy and His Dog" from *The Beast that Shouted Love at the Heart of the World.* 1969. New York: Signet, 1974.

Fairman, Paul W. "The Cosmic Frame" (Ziff-Davis Publishing, 1955).

Farris, John. *The Fury.* 1976. New York: Popular Library, 1977.

Finney, Charles. *The Circus of Dr. Lao.* New York: Viking, 1935.

Fleming, Ian. *Doctor No.* New York: Signet, 1959.

———. *From Russia With Love.* New York: Signet, 1958.

———. *Goldfinger,* New York: Signet, 1959.

———. *On Her Majesty's Secret Service.* New York: Signet, 1964.

———. *Thunderball.* New York: Signet, 1961.

Goldstein, William. *Dr. Phibes.* New York: Award, 1971.

Jones, Raymond F. "The Alien Machine" in *Thrilling Wonder Stories,* Standard, 1947.

Jorgensen, Ivar. "Deadly City" in *If* magazine, Quinn Publishing, 1953.

Ligotti, Thomas. "Dream of a Mannikin" in *Eldritch Tales,* Vol. 2, No. 3, 1982.

Lovecraft, H. P. *The Case of Charles Dexter Ward* in *Weird Tales,* 1941.

King, Stephen. "The Mist" from *Dark Forces.* New York: Viking, 1980.

———. "The Langoliers" from *Four Past Midnight.* (Kirby McCauley, ed.) New York: Viking, 1990.

———. "The Library Policeman" from *Four Past Midnight.* (Kirby McCauley, ed.) New York: Viking, 1990.

———. *Insomnia.* New York: Signet, 1995.

———. The Shining. *New York: Doubleday, 1977.*

———. *The Tommyknockers.* New York: Viking Press, G. P. Putnam's Sons, 1987.

Koontz, Dean R. *Cold Fire.* New York: Putnam, 1991.

———. *Demon Seed.* New York: Bantam, 1973.

———. *The Door to December* (as Richard Paige). New York: New American Library, 1985.

———. *Dragon Tears.* New York: Putnam, 1993.

———. *The Funhouse* (as Owen West). New York: Jove, 1980.

———. The House of Thunder *(as Leigh Nichols). New York: Pocket, 1982.*

———. "Invasion" *(as Aaron Wolfe). New York: Laser, 1975.*

———. Phantoms. *New York: Putnam, 1983.*

———. Shadowfires (as Leigh Nichols). *New York: Avon, 1987.*

———. Strangers. *New York: Putnam, 1986.*

———. *Twilight Eyes.* New York: Berkley, 1987.

———. *Winter Moon.* New York: Ballantine, 1994.

Matheson, Richard. *Hell House.* New York: Viking, 1971.

———. I Am Legend. *1954. New York: Bantam, 1964.*

Poe, Edgar Allen. "The Tomb of Ligeia."

Rice, Anne. *Lasher.* New York: Alfred A. Knopf, 1993.

———. The Mummy. *New York: Ballantine, 1989.*

———. *The Vampire Chronicles.* New York: Alfred A. Knopf, 1976-(ongoing).

———. *The Witching Hour.* New York: Alfred A. Knopf, 1990.

Straub, Peter. "Blue Rose," from *Houses Without Doors*. New York: New American Library, 1991.

———. *If You Could See Me Now*. New York: Coward, McCann & Geogeghan, 1977.

———. *Ghost Story*. New York: Coward, McCann & Geogeghan, 1979.

———. *Shadowland*. New York: Coward, McCann & Geoghegan, 1980.

Wilson, Colin. *The Space Vampires*. New York: Pocket, 1977.

T.V. Specials, News Shows, and Independent Documentaries

A Strange Harvest (Linda Moulton Howe Productions, 1980; 1988).

Ancient Mysteries (CBS, 1994).

The Atomic Cafe (1982).

Comic Book Confidential (Canada, 1988).

Encounters (Fox, 1994).

48 Hours: Are We Alone? (CBS, 1994).

Mysteries From Beyond Earth (1977).

Mystery of the Sphinx (NBC, 1993).

The Other Side (NBC, 1994).

Overlords of the UFO (1977).

Science Fiction: A Journey into the Unknown (Museum of Television and Radio with Fox T.V., 1994).

Sightings (Fox, 1989).

Strange Harvests 1993 (Linda Moulton Howe Productions, 1993).

UFO Coverup?: Live (Seligman Productions, 1988).

UFO Coverup: Live from Area 51 (TNT, 1994).

UFOs—A Need To Know (Ted Oliphant Productions, 1989).

Unsolved Mysteries (NBC, 1980s).

Without Warning (1994).

Index

actors and entertainers
Abbot, Bud, 152
Adams, Brooke, 476
Adams, Julie, 207
Agar, John, 233, 237
Allen, Valerie, 232
Allen, Woody, 355, 423
Alpert, Herb, 355
Anderson, Gillian, 325, 328, 333
Andrews, Dana, 230–231
Ankrum, Morris, 197, 225
Arkin, Alan, 482
Arness, James, 108
Aykroyd, Dan, 488, 528–529
Baker, Colin, 369–370
Bakula, Scott, 381
Barry, Gene, 198
Basehart, Richard, 155
Basinger, Kim, 528–529
Bauchau, Patrick, 566
Beaumont, Hugh, 399
Belushi, James, 525
Bergen, Edgar, 174
Bergman, Ingrid, 151
Bissell, Whit, 152, 221–222
Birch, Paul, 214–215
Bixby, Bill, 357, 389
Blair, Janet, 248
Blair, Linda, 428
Blanchard, Marie, 197
Bogarde, Dirk, 466
Bono, Sonny, 521
Borge, Victor, 370
Bowie, David, 441, 516
Boyer, Charles, 355
Brand, Neville, 520
Brando, Marlon, 477
Brooks, Elisabeth, 500
Brown, Blair, 465
Buono, Victor, 155
Burns, George, 482
Burton, Richard, 519

Cagney, Jimmy, 292
Campbell, Bruce, 540
Carlson, Richard, 207–208
Carradine, John, 384, 501, 519
Carrey, Jim, 544
Cassidy, Ted, 311
Chaplin, Charlie, 191
Christie, Julie, 471
Clarke, Robert, 522
Coates, Phyllis, 192, 221
Coburn, James, 358
Combs, Jeffrey, 456
Connery, Sean, 383, 430
Conrad, Robert, 156
Conreid, Hans, 196–197, 202
Conway, Gary, 221
Corday, Mara, 224–225
Costello, Lou, 152
Cougat, Xavier, 385
Court, Hazel, 203
Craig, Yvonne, 356–358
Crampton, Barbara, 454, 456, 548
Cregar, Laird, 152
Culp, Robert, 263, 276, 510
Cummins, Peggy, 230–231
Curtis, Jamie Lee, 498
Cushing, Peter, 353, 361, 369, 476
Dana, Bill, 401
Danning, Sybil, 500
Darby, Kim, 422
Davis, Geena, 544
Davison, Peter, 369
Dawber, Pam, 481
Day (-George), Lynda, 385–386
de Mornay, Rebecca, 298
Denning, Richard, 193, 213–215
Deneuve, Catherine, 516
Dern, Bruce, 272
Devon, Richard, 234
Dickinson, Angie, 419
Dillman, Bradford, 385–387
Dillon, Melinda, 472–473

Domergue, Faith, 208
Donlevy, Brian, 349–350
Dourif, Brad, 530
Dreyfuss, Richard, 472–473
Duchovny, David, 325, 333
Dunn, Michael, 156, 392
Dunne, Dominique, 511
Duvall, Robert, 264–267, 395
Eden, Barbara, 256
Elvira (Cassandra Peterson), 505
Evers, Jason "Herb," 249
Farrell, Sharon, 277
Field, Margaret, 187
Field, Sally, 187
Fonda, Peter, 452
Fontaine, Joan, 345
Ford, Faith, 572
Foster, Jodie, 146–148, 565, 587
Francis, Anne, 303
Frank, Joanna, 264, 278
Franklin, Pamela, 424
Franz, Arthur, 197
Garland, Beverley, 212, 215
Garner, James, 435
Gellar, Sarah Michelle, 587
Goldblum, Jeff, 544
Gough, Michael, 452
Grant, Cary, 436
Grant, Faye, 300
Graves, Peter, 211–212, 233
Hack, Shelley, 521
Halpin, Luke, 476
Harper, Shari Belafonte, 546
Harris, Ed, 462–463
Harris, Robert H., 153
Harrison, Sandra, 153, 582
Harry, Deborah, 514
Hartford, Dee, 391
Harvey, Laurence, 137–138
Hatton, Rondo, 108
Hayes, Allison, 226–227
Haze, Jonathan, 248
Hedison, David, 155
Henstridge, Natasha, 554
Heston, Charlton, 306, 501–502
Hicks, Catherine, 530
Holden, William, 427
Holly-Johnson, Lynn, 503
Howard, Moe, 191, 247–248
Hunnicut, Gayle, 424

Hurt, John, 519
Ihnat, Steve, 267
Jackson, Sherry, 385, 549
Jagger, Dean, 237
Janis, Conrad, 228
Johann, Zita, 468
Johnson, Tor, 108, 239, 254
Jones, Jeffrey, 523
Jourdan, Louis, 385–387
Judd, Edward, 353
Karloff, Boris, 152–153, 227, 362,
    420, 451–452, 468
Katt, William, 510
Kaye, Danny, 152
Kaye, Stubby, 385
Keaton, Diane, 423
Kellerman, Sally, 262, 310
Kelley, DeForest, 321–322
Kidder, Margot, 489
King, Loretta, 238
Kinski, Klaus, 536
Kinski, Nastassia, 573
Kirk, Tommy, 356–357
Klemperer, Werner, 155
Knotts, Don, 468
Koenig, Walter, 321, 540
Laffan, Patricia, 203
Landon, Michael, 152
Landau, Martin, 262
Lansing, Robert, 314
Laughton, Charles, 477
Lee, Christopher, 354, 452, 490
Leigh, Janet, 138
Leith, Virginia, 249–250
Lennon, John, 144, 147
Leon, Valerie, 503
Lewis, Al, 391
Lewis, Jerry, 229, 249, 356
Lockhart, Anne, 324, 521
Lockhart, June, 322, 324, 521–522
Lockwood, Gary, 310
Lorre, Peter, 402
Louise, Tina, 519–520
Lovitz, Jon, 529
Lowell, Carey, 544
Lugosi, Bela, 238–239, 242
Lyon, Sue, 454
MacGinnis, Niall, 230–231
Mackenzie, Bob and Doug (Rick
    and Dave Thomas Mcranis), 515

Maclaine, Shirley, 339
Macnee, Patrick, 157, 323, 370, 484, 500, 538–539, 579
Magee, Patrick, 140
Manlove, Dudley, 248
Marcus, Vitina, 391
Marshall, Darrah, 234
Martin, Dean, 356
Maxwell, Lois, 218, 433
McCallum, David, 274–275
McCarthy, Kevin, 217
McCoy, Tony, 238
McDowall, Roddy, 305, 424
McDowell, Malcolm, 513
McGavin, Darren, 301, 491, 531
McQueen, Steve, 229
Monroe, Marilyn, 371, 567, 571
Moorehead, Agnes, 304
Moriarty, Michael, 521
Morrow, Jeff, 208–209, 224
Morse, Barry, 285
Munro, Caroline, 490
Murphy, Eddie, 555
Neil, Noel, 192
Nelson, Craig T., 511
Nelson, Lori, 213, 232
Newmar, Julie, 389, 519
Nichols, Nichelle, 322
Nicholson, Jack, 141, 546
Nielsen, Leslie, 539
Nimoy, Leonard, 185
North, Virginia, 432
O'Connor, Carroll, 285, 386
O'Herlihy, Dan, 192, 348, 405, 565
Oliver, Susan, 377
O'Rourke, Heather, 511
Parker, Andrea, 565
Parker, Fess, 204
Parker, Lara, 302
Parrish, Leslie, 140
Peck, Gregory, 151–152
Perrine, Valerie, 421
Pfeiffer, Michelle, 548
Pileggi, Mitch, 333
Pleasance, Donald, 422, 525
Prange, Laurie, 304
Prentis, Ann, 528
Prentis, Paula, 528
Presley, Elvis, 223, 256
Price, Vincent, 392, 402–403, 406, 416, 450–451, 551–552, 578–579, 584
Priest, Pat, 398
Railsback, Steve, 327
Rains, Claude, 183
Reason, Rex, 208
Reed, Dolores, 248
Reed, Oliver, 377
Reeve, Christopher, 489
Reiner, Carl, 454
Rennie, Michael, 183
Rigg, Diana, 157, 203, 376–377, 403, 579, 589
Ritchard, Cyril, 229
Ritter, John, 524
Robbins, Tim, 523
Robertson, Cliff, 260–262
Robey, Louise, 536
Robinson, Ann, 198, 522
Rogers, Wayne, 384
Sarandon, Chris, 530
Sarandon, Susan, 437, 456, 516
Sarrazin, Michael, 298
Savalas, Telly, 377
Saxon, John, 361
Schell, Catherine (von), 432
Schwarzenegger, Arnold, 498, 518–519, 523–524, 586–587
Scoggins, Tracy, 547–548
Scott, George C., 467, 543
Seagrove, Jenny, 544
Sellers, Peter, 428
Selzer, Milton, 155
Scotti, Vito, 399
Shatner, William, 282, 284, 320–321, 517
Sheedy, Ally, 298
Shelley, Barbara, 361
Sherman, Allan, 400
Silva, Henry, 155–156
Sinatra, Frank, 137–138
Sorel, Louise, 453–454
Sorel, Ted, 455–456
Spader, James, 553–554
Steele, Barbara, 452
Stevens, Connie, 356
Stevens, Inger, 397
Stevens, Paul, 154
Stockwell, Dean, 452
Stockwell, Guy, 385
Strasberg, Susan, 485

Stratton, Dorothy, 490
Talbott, Gloria, 231–232
Thinnes, Roy, 380–381
Thomas, Danny, 399
Thomas, Terry, 418
Thompson, Lea, 523
Three Stooges, The, 191, 247–248
Thurman, Uma, 586
Thyssen, Greta, 247
Torme, Mel, 333
Tryon, Tom, 232–233
Tucker, Forrest, 237
Urich, Robert, 512
Van Cleef, Lee, 212
Van Dyke, Dick, 399
Van Dyke, Jerry, 389
Varney, Jim, 546
Vaughn, Robert, 234, 362, 435,
    489–490
Ventham, Wanda, 368
Vernon, Jackie, 385
Vickers, Yvette, 226
Victor, Gloria, 248
Von Dohlen, Lenny, 531
Von Sydow, Max, 515
Walken, Christopher, 548
Walker, Ally, 565
Wallace (-Stone), Dee, 500
Walston, Ray, 389, 504
Wayne, John, 341
Webb, Jack, 483
Weiss, Michael T., 565
Wells, Dawn, 256
West, Adam, 284
Williams, Cindy, 539
Williams, Fred, 521
Williams, Jobeth, 511–512
Williams, Robin, 481
Windsor, Marie, 195
Winters, Jonathan, 481
Wiseman, Joseph, 374
Woods, James, 514–515
Wyngarde, Peter, 248
Zadora, Pia, 251
Zimbalist, Stephanie, 502
ancient civilizations
    Americas (North, Central and
        South America), 42, 46–47, 61
    Atlantis, Mu, and the Underworld,
        31, 43–48, 52–54, 65, 171–173, 332,

        346–347, 351, 366, 386–387, 393,
        395, 417, 440, 502, 521, 527–529,
        536, 538, 562–563, 574, 580
    Celts, 43, 49, 52–55
    Egypt, 41, 45, 49–50, 55, 61, 66–67,
        139, 184, 323, 360, 386–387, 492,
        580
        in connection to extraterrestrial
            structures, 17, 22–26, 33, 42,
            53, 366
        in science fiction and cinema,
            16–21, 26, 244–245, 283, 285,
            309, 314–315, 323, 366,
            386–387, 390–391, 403,
            406–407, 414, 416–418, 430,
            432, 451, 465, 468, 501–503,
            507, 528–529, 535–536, 538,
            540–541, 546–547, 549–550,
            552–554, 559, 574, 589
        robots utilized in, 34–37, 41, 172,
            244, 461, 512
    Indus Valley, 40–43, 66–67
    Tibet, 45–48, 50–51
    government research into
        British/United States, 12, 40–43,
            47, 51, 61–62, 184, 346
        Nazi (Ahenenerbe S.S., Ancestral
            Teaching and Research Organi-
            zation), 43, 45–51, 54, 59–60,
            66, 172–173, 184, 346–347, 502
        in connection to UFOs, 34–37,
            41–43, 184
        occult and, 43–47, 139
    sonic weaponry of, 59–60, 205, 281
archaeologists (see scientists)
astronauts (see government and mili-
    tary figures)
astronomers (see scientists)
atomic bomb, 5, 31, 80, 133,
    349–350, 496, 515, 581
authors, editors, biographers, review-
    ers, and screenwriters
    Adams, Douglas, 490
    Agel, Jerome, 464
    Asimov, Isaac, 108, 522
    Bain, Donald, 143, 148–149
    Bamford, James, 278
    Barker, Clive, 526–528
    Bates, Harry, 177
    Baum, L. Frank, 352, 430

Bauval, Robert, 502
Baxt, George, 248
Baxter, John, 349
Beaumont, Charles, 248, 303, 352
Beck, Calvin Thomas, 402
Begich, Dr. Nick, 205
Binder, Earl and Otto (Eando), 296
Bixby, Jerome, 517
Blatty, William Peter, 427, 542–543
Bloch, Robert, 420, 454
Block, Larry, 508
Boulle, Pierre, 306–307
Bradbury, Ray, 207, 303, 482
Brandner, Gary, 484
Bresler, Fenton, 144
Brown, Anthony Cave, 371, 378
Brown, Frederic, 543
Bryan, C. D. B., 470
Bullard, Thomas, 525, 579, 586
Caidin, Martin, 464–465
Campbell, John W., Jr., 107–109, 186, 444
Capek, Karel, 297, 443, 563
Charbonneau, Louis, 263, 284
Chayefsky, Paddy, 465
Cheney, Margaret, 55, 57–58, 374
Christie, Agatha, 202
Christian, Jonn, 129–130, 135, 141–142
Clarens, Carlos, 577, 579–580
Clarke, Arthur C., 461–464
Cocteau, Jean, 152
Cohen, Daniel, 358
Collins, Max Allan, 410
Colodny, Len, 162–163
Condon, Richard, 136, 331
Conroy, Ken, 335
Cook, Robin, 573
Cox, Stephen, 397–398
Crichton, Michael, 227, 418
Cross, John Keir, 420
Dahl, Roald, 372
Deacons, Richard, 44
de Camp, L. Sprague, 449
de Felitta, Frank, 509
D'Empirio, Mary, 63
Derleth, August, 454, 458
Dick, Philip K., 70, 445–448, 518
Dolinsky, Meyer, 278
Doyle, Arthur Conan, 302

Eastwood, James, 202
Ebert, Roger, 423
Eliot, Marc, 169
Ellison, Harlan, 276–277, 431, 518, 552
Endore, Guy, 385
Engel, Joel, 316
Fairman, Paul W., 193, 218, 305
Farris, John, 483
Feldman, Dennis, 555
Finney, Charles, 350–352
Finney, Jack, 216
Fish, Robert, 377
Frank, Gerold, 144
Frentzen, Jeffrey, 257
Gettlin, Robert, 162–163
Goldstein, William, 417
Greene, Sonia, 449
Grey, Rudolph, 238–239
Grubb, Davis, 420
Hammerschlag, Dr. Heinz E., 153
Hauck, Dennis William, 320–321
Hayes, R. Chetwynd, 527
Hayles, Brian, 486
Heinlein, Robert, 108, 186–187, 197, 263
Hemingway, Hilary, 573
Hershey, Barbara, 509–510
Hogan, David J., 203
Holiday, J. S., 378, 569
Howard, Michael, 45
Jackson, Shirley, 426
Jacques, Norbert, 153
Johnson, Haynes, 378, 569
Jones, Raymond F., 208, 418
Jorgensen, Ivar, 193
Kahn, James L., 278
Kaysing, Bill, 486–487
Key, Peter, 236
King, Stephen, 71, 233, 459–461, 484, 517
Kneale, Nigel, 70, 236, 342–349, 362, 459, 483, 519, 525, 561, 579
Koch, Howard, 26, 175
Koestler, Arthur, 444
Koontz, Dean R., 71, 296, 468–470, 508
Kopit, Arthur, 553
Kunetka, Jim, 337
Kuttner, Henry, 196

Leaming, Barbara, 174–176
Lederer, Charles, 109
Lee, Martin A., 163–164, 167
Leiber, Fritz, 248
Levenda, Peter, 50, 236
Levin, Ira, 307
Ligotti, Thomas, 461
Lindsay, Jeffrey P., 573
Locke, Richard Adams, 358
London, Jack, 377
Lovecraft, Howard Phillips, 70, 234, 259, 302, 420, 448–458, 464, 485, 503, 523, 526, 538, 587
Lymington, John, 353
Maeder, Jay, 409
Maine, Charles Eric, 228
Maltin, Leonard, 234
Manchester, William, 379–380
Manning, Jeane, 205
Mantley, John, 227
Martin, George R. R., 286
Masters, Anthony, 44
Masterton, Graham, 485
Mathers, John C., 202
Matheson, Richard, 248, 303–305, 348, 422, 424–425, 517, 578, 587
Medved, Michael, 551
Melanson, Dr. Philip H., 128–129, 141–142, 144
Melchior, Ib, 247, 578
Meyer, Nicholas, 423
Miller, Mark, 203
Murphy, Warren, 521
Newman, Bernard, 278, 444
Nicholson, John, 358
O'Bannon, Dan, 520
O'Neill, Denny, 564
Ormsby, Alan, 513
Orwell, George, 347
Ostrander, Sheila, 236, 484
Plumb, J. H., 378, 569
Poe, Edgar Allen, 141, 450, 453
Powers, Thomas, 115
Quinn, Seabury, 154, 302–303, 587
Renard, Maurice, 443
Rice, Jeff, 425
Rice, Anne, 71, 468–470
Robinson, Frank, 263
Ross, Stanley Ralph, 156
Rothmiller, Mike, 142

Sangster, Jimmy, 236
Sanderson, Ivan, 17
Santesson, Hans Stefan, 358
Sapir, Richard, 521
Sayles, John, 484
Schnabel, Jim, 484
Schow, David J., 257
Schroeder, Lynn, 236, 484
Seltzer, David, 427
Shaffer, Anthony, 345
Siodmak, Curt, 210
Simpson, Christopher, 167
Solomon, Norman, 163–164, 167
Spence, Lewis, 33–34, 36–37, 54, 172
Spencer, John, 171, 341
Stanley, John, 582
Stoker, Bram, 459, 468, 501–502, 580
Straub, Peter, 461
Stuart, Don A. (see Campbell, John W., Jr.)
Sturgeon, Theodore, 108, 421
Terr, Dr. Lenore, 460
Tevis, Walter, 441
Thompson, Keith, 335–336
Tilm, Ege, 444
Tolstoy, Alexei Nikolayevich, 64, 172
Towne, Robert, 264–265
Turner, William, 129–130, 141–142
Vankin, Jonathan, 99, 111, 118–119, 145, 487
Van Vogt, A. E., 108
Varley, John, 540
Verne, Jules, 170, 409, 506, 515, 580
Vidal, Gore, 228
Weldon, Michael, 244, 248, 250, 356, 434
Wells, Herbert George, 14–15, 26, 174, 198–199, 245, 345, 506, 518, 580, 583
Whalen, John, 99, 487
Whiton, James, 417
Wilson, Anthony, 424
Wilson, Colin, 520
Wilson, Robert Anton, 466
Winkless, Terence H., 484
Wise, David, 164

Wright, Peter, 161
Yardley, Herbert O., 279
Zagat, Arthur Leo, 262

bubble gum cards
Mars Attacks (Topps, 1962), 246,
400, 411, 552

cartoons, 70, 323
*Adventures of Captain Planet and the
Planeteers, The* (Turner/DIC),
545–546
Adventures of Superman, The
(Warner Bros., 1996), 562–563
Animaniacs (Warner Bros., 1992),
584
Astro-Boy (Japanese, 1963–65), 413
Batman: The Animated Series
(Warner Bros., 1992), 155, 158,
563–565
"Avatar," 565
"Deep Freeze," 564
"Demon's Quest, The," 564–565
"Heart of Steel," 563
"His Silicon Soul," 564
"Off Balance," 564
"Terror in the Skies," 564
Bugs Bunny (Warner Bros.), 68,
191, 358–359
"Lighter Than Hare," 402
"Hair-Raising Hare," 402
"Haredevil Hare," 401
"Hare Force," 359
"Hasty Hare," 401
"Robot Rabbit," 402
"Water, Water, Every Hare,"
402–403
Bugs Bunny's Lunar Tunes (Warner
Bros., 1991), 588–590
Cartoon Planet (Cartoon
Network/Hanna-Barbera), 405
Daffy Duck (Warner Bros.), 401
"Duck Dodgers in the 24–1/2th
Century," 401
Eekstravaganza (Fox), 321
Elmer Fudd (Warner Bros.), 402
Flintstones, The (ABC/Hanna-Bar-
bera, 1960–65), 408–409
Freakazoid (Warner Bros./Steven
Spielberg, 1995)

"Candle Jack," 237
"Cloud, The," 237
"Toby Danger," 408
Frito Bandito, 255
Gigantor (Japanese/syndicated,
1966–67), 413
Herculoids, The (Hanna-Barbera),
405
Huckleberry Hound (Hanna-
Barbera)
"Cop and Saucer," 404–405
Iczer One (Japanese, late 1980s), 416
Jetsons, The (ABC/Hanna-Barbera,
1962), 408, 411
Jonny Quest (ABC/Hanna-Barbera,
1964–66), 407–408
"Dragons of Ashida, The," 408
"Robot Spy, The," 407–408
Josie and the Pussy Cats (Hanna-
Barbera, 1970–72), 407
"Jumpin' Jupiter Affair, The," 407
"Strangemoon Over Miami," 407
"Swat Plot Flop, The," 407
*Josie and the Pussy Cats in Outer
Space* (Hanna-Barbera, 1972–74),
407, 416
Marine Boy (Japanese, circa
1965–66), 413
Marvin the Martian (Warner Bros.),
401, 588–590
Outlanders, 415–416
Pinky and the Brain Christmas, A
(Warner Bros., 1995), 585
Popeye (Max Fleischer), 68
"Popeye, the Ace of Space," 196
Porky Pig (Warner Bros.), 401–402
Prince Planet (Japanese/syndicated,
circa 1965–66), 413, 416
Real Adventures of Jonny Quest, The
(Hanna-Barbera, 1996–97),
556–562
"Alien In Washington," 557–558
"Amok," 557
"Ezekiel Rage," 557
"In the Wake of Mary Celeste,"
561–562
"Night of the Zinnja," 557
"Other Space," 561
"Return of the Anasazi," 558–559
"Robot Spies, The," 557

"Secret of the Moai," 560–561
"Trouble on the Colorado,"
 559–560
Rocky and Bullwinkle (Jay Ward,
 1959), 403
Scooby Doo (Where Are You?)
 (Hanna-Barbera, 1969), 354
"Bedlam in the Big Top," 406
"Close Encounter with a Weird
 Kind," 406
"Creepy Tangle in the Bermuda
 Triangle," 406
"Foul Play in Funland," 405–406
"Ghosts of the Ancient Astro-
 nauts," 406
"Monster is Awake in Bottomless
 Lake, The," 354
"Scooby Saves the World," 406
"Spooky Space Kook," 406
"Way Out Scooby," 406
"Who Was That Cat-Creature I
 Saw You With Last Night?,"406
Simpsons, The (Fox Network, 1989),
 331–332
Space Ghost (CBS/Hanna-Barbera,
 1966–67), 405
Space Ghost, Coast to Coast (Cartoon
 Network/Hanna-Barbera), 405
Star Trek (NBC, 1973–74),
Superman (Max Fleischer, 1941–42),
 196, 562
"The Mechanical Monsters," 196
13 Ghosts of Scooby Doo, The
 (Hanna-Barbera, 1985–86), 406
Underdog (Leonardo Television, mid
 1960s)
"Forget-Me-Knot, The," 404
"Flying Sorcerers, The," 404
"Magnet Men, The," 404
"Phoney Booths, The," 404
"Zot," 404
Urosei Yetsura (Japanese, late 1980s-
 early '90s), 415–416
Woody Woodpecker (Walter Lantz),
 188
X-Men (Fox Network), 485
Yosemite Sam (Warner Bros.), 402
comic books and strips, 68, 70
Action (DC), 186, 411
Batman (DC, 1939), 156, 548, 565

Captain Future, 428
Comics Code, 192
Dell, 250
Dick Tracy (Chicago Tribune),
 408–411
Dirty Pair, The (Dark Horse/Viz),
 416
E.C. Comics, 191
Flash Gordon, 499
Gold Key, 412
Howard the Duck (Marvel, 1975),
 523
Josie and the Pussy Cats (Radio
 Comics), 407
Magnus, Robot Fighter - 4000 A.D.
 (Gold Key, 1962), 412, 562
manga (Japanese comics/anima-
 tion), 415–416
Metal Men (D.C., 1962), 411–412
Ninja High School (Dark Horse/Viz),
 416
Shock SuspenStories (E.C.), 195–196
Spiderman (Marvel), 461
Star Trek (Gold Key), 412
Superman (DC, 1938), 186, 411, 428
Vampirella (Warren, 1969), 468
X-Men (Marvel), 485
composers and musicians
 Axton, Hoyt, 512
 Buchanan and Goodman, 401
 Cash, Johnny, 506
 Denver, John, 482
 Frontiere, Dominic, 259, 380, 418
 Goblin, 505
 Goldenberg, Billy, 422
 Lewis/Young/Henderson, 400
 Lubin, Harry, 259
 Marketts, The, 401
 Ran Dells, The, 401
 Whitman, Slim, 552
 Wooley, Sheb, 401
corporations and companies
 American Express, 142
 American Cyanamid, 134
 Autonetics, 238
 Bendix Corporation, 409
 Chicago Tribune Syndicate, 411
 Douglas Aircraft Company, 425,
  578
 IBM, 312

National Candy Company, 403
Trojan/U.S. Powder Company, 134

debunkers (*see* parapsychologists and
debunkers)
directors (*see* producers, directors,
and creators)
discoverers (*see* scientists)

films and T.V. movies
Abbot and Costello Go to Mars (Universal, 1953), 197–198
Abbot and Costello Meet Frankenstein (Universal, 1948), 152
Abbot and Costello Meet the Killer, Boris Karloff (Universal, 1949), 152
Abbot and Costello Meet the Mummy (Universal, 1955), 209
Abominable Dr. Phibes, The (AIP, 1971), 416–418, 432
Abominable Snowman of the Himalayas, The (Hammer/20th Century Fox, 1957), 346, 561
Abyss, The (20th Century Fox, 1989), 71, 462–463, 503, 540, 542
Adventures of Buckaroo Banzai Across the Eighth Dimension, The (20th Century Fox, 1984), 518
Aelita: Queen of Mars (Mezhrobpom, 1924), 64,
Alien (20th Century Fox, 1979), 100, 229, 247, 301, 504–505, 507, 516, 518, 523, 538, 555
Alien Contamination (Cannon, 1981), 505
Alien Nation (20th Century Fox, 1988), 299
Alien Intruder (P.M. Productions, 1992), 547–548
Aliens (20th Century Fox, 1986), 540
Aliens from Spaceship Earth (Sunn Classics, 1977), 478
Alphaville (French, 1965), 353
Ambushers, The (Columbia, 1967), 356
Amityville Horror, The (AIP, 1979), 150, 338, 555

Andromeda Strain, The (Universal, 1971), 418
Angry Red Planet, The (AIP, 1959), 247, 260
Arrival, The (Orion, 1996), 573
Assassination Bureau, The (Paramount, 1969), 377
Assignment Outer Space (AIP, 1960), 246
Astounding She Monster, The (AIP, 1958), 229
Astro-Zombies, The (Geneni, 1968), 384
Asylum (Amicus, 1972), 420
Atlantis, the Lost Continent (MGM, 1960), 65, 352
Atomic Submarine, The (Allied Artists, 1959), 393
Attack of the 50 Ft. Woman (Allied Artists, 1957), 226–227, 577
Attack of the Giant Leeches (AIP, 1959), 234–235
Attack of the Robots (AIP, 1962), 353
Awakening, The (Warner Bros., 1980), 459, 501–503
Awful Dr. Orloff, The (AIP, 1962), 353
Bad Channels (Full Moon, 1992), 547
Bamboo Saucer, The (World Entertainment, 1967), 251
Batman (Warner Bros., 1989), 452, 549, 553
Batman and Robin (Warner Bros., 1997), 586–587
Batman Forever (Warner Bros., 1995), 549–550
Batman Returns (Warner Bros., 1992), 548–549, 551
Battle Beyond the Stars (New World, 1980), 499–500, 517
Battle for the Planet of the Apes (20th Century Fox, 1974), 307
Battle In Outer Space (U.S.-Japanese, 1959), 352
Beast from Haunted Cave, The (AIP, 1959), 234–235
Beast of Yucca Flats, The (Crown International, 1961), 253–254
Beast with 1,000,000 Eyes, The (A.R.C., 1955), 216

Beetlejuice (Warner Bros., 1988), 529, 551

Beginning or the End (MGM, 1947), 349–350

Being from Another Planet (Wescom, 1991), 546–547

Bermuda Depths, The (Rankin-Bass, 1978), 486

Bible, The (U.S.-Italian, 1966), 308

Black Hole, The (Disney, 1979), 418

Black Sunday (AIP, 1960), 526

Blade Runner (Warner Bros., 1982), 446

Blob, The (Paramount, 1958), 223, 229, 231

Blood Beast from Outer Space (World Entertainment, 1966), 352, 361

Blood Beast Terror, The (Tigon/Pacemaker, 1967), 361, 368, 421

Blood from the Mummy's Tomb (Hammer, 1972), 459, 501, 503

Blood of Dracula (AIP, 1957), 152–153, 221, 582

Body Snatchers (Warner Bros., 1994), 217, 380

Boy and His Dog, A (independent, 1975), 431

Brain Eaters, The (AIP, 1958), 187

Brain from Planet Arous, The (Howco International, 1958), 233

Brain that Wouldn't Die, The (AIP, 1960/62), 249–250

Bride of Frankenstein, The (Universal, 1935), 509

Bride of the Monster (Ed Wood, 1955), 238

Brood, The (Canadian, 1979), 485

Burn, Witch, Burn (AIP, 1962), 248

Cabinet of Dr. Caligari, The (Germany, 1920), 151

Caesar and Cleopatra (British, 1945), 468

Cape Canaveral Monsters, The (CCM, 1960), 233, 244

Capricorn One (Warner Bros., 1978), 486–488, 516

Casino Royale (Columbia, 1967), 355–356

Castle of Evil (United Pictures, 1966), 354

Cat People (RKO, 1942), 513

Cat People (Universal, 1982), 513

Cat Women of the Moon (Astor, 1953), 69, 195, 248, 260

Chairman, The (20th Century Fox, 1969), 385

Children of the Damned (MGM, 1964), 233

Children Shouldn't Play With Dead Things (Geneni, 1972), 573

Child's Play (MGM/UA, 1988), 530

Citizen Kane (RKO, 1941), 207

Close Encounters of the Third Kind (Columbia, 1977), 168, 300, 401, 472–473, 490, 492, 516, 585

Cocoon (20th Century Fox, 1985), 521

Colossus of New York, The (Paramount, 1958), 229

Colossus: The Forbin Project (Universal, 1970), 418

Communion (independent, 1989), 338–339

Coneheads (Paramount, 1992), 529

Congo (Paramount, 1995), 418

Contact (Warner Bros., 1997), 148, 587

Conquest of Space (Paramount, 1955), 210

Cosmic Monsters (Eros, 1958), 237

Court Jester, The (Paramount, 1956), 152

Crawling Eye, The (DCA/Eros, 1958), 236–237

Crawling Hand, The (AIP, 1963), 246–247

Creation of the Humanoids (Emerson, 1962), 248

Creature, The (BBC, 1954), 346

Creature from the Black Lagoon, The (Universal, 1954), 207, 233, 504

Creature from the Haunted Sea (Filmgroup, 1961), 235

Creature with the Atom Brain (Columbia, 1955), 210

Creeping Terror, The (Crown International, 1964), 69, 250–253, 551

Creeping Unknown, The (UA, 1956), 349

Cruel Sea, The (Ealing, 1953), 341

Curious Dr. Humpp, The (Italian, 1967/70), 362
Curse, The (Trans World, 1987), 452
Curse of the Aztec Mummy (AIP, 1959), 244
Curse of the Demon (Columbia, 1958), 230–231, 248, 424
Curse of the Faceless Man (UA, 1958), 244
Curse of the Swamp Creature (AIP, 1966), 354
Daleks: Invasion Earth 2150 A.D. (Amicus, 1966), 369
Damien: Omen II (20th Century Fox, 1978), 427, 501
Dark, The (Film Ventures International, 1979), 246
Dark Side of the Moon, The (independent, 1989), 541–542
Day Mars Invaded Earth, The (20th Century Fox, 1963), 217
Day of the Dolphin, The (Avco Embassy, 1973), 467
Day the Earth Caught Fire, The (Universal, 1961), 347
Day the Earth Stood Still, The (20th Century Fox, 1951), 65, 69, 177–185, 197, 203, 234, 324, 433, 516
Day the World Ended, The (A.R.C., 1955), 213–215, 257
D-Day On Mars (Republic, 1945), 185
Dead of Night (Universal, 1946), 304
Dead Space (Califilms, 1989), 504–505
Dementia 13 (AIP/Filmgroup, 1963), 140
Demon Seed (MGM, 1977), 469–471
Destination Inner Space (United Pictures, 1966), 354
Destination Moon (Eagle-Lion, 1950), 184, 188, 197
Devil Doll (Associated Film Distributors, 1963), 154
Devil Girl from Mars (Spartan, 1954), 202–203
Devil's Own, The (20th Century Fox, 1966), 345
Diabolical Dr. Z., The (Italian, 1966), 353

Diamonds Are Forever (UA, 1971), 373, 488
Die, Monster, Die! (AIP, 1965), 234, 451–452
Donovan's Brain (UA, 1953), 196
Don't Be Afraid of the Dark (ABC/Lorimar, 1973), 421–422
Don't Play With Martians (Italian, 1967), 362
Dreamscape (New World, 1984), 484, 518
Dr. Goldfoot and the Bikini Machine (AIP, 1966), 417
Dr. Goldfoot and the Girl Bombs (AIP, 1966), 417
Dr. No (UA, 1962), 374
Dr. Orloff's Monster (Italian, 1964), 353
Dr. Phibes Rises Again (AIP, 1972), 416–418
Dr. Strangelove—or, How I Learned to Stop Worrying and Love the Bomb (Columbia, 1964), 576
Dr. Who (Amicus, 1965), 369
Dr. Who (Fox T.V., 1996), 369
Duel (ABC/Universal, 1971), 517
Dunwich Horror, The (AIP, 1970), 452–453
Earth Girls Are Easy (Vestron, 1990), 544
Easy Rider (Columbia/Raybert, 1969), 452
Earth Dies Screaming, The (Lippert/20th Century Fox, 1965), 193
Earth vs. the Flying Saucers (Columbia, 1956), 216–217, 223, 225, 554
Ed Wood (1994), 551
Electronic Monster (Columbia/Anglo-Amalgamated, 1957), 228
Embryo (Cine Artists, 1976), 474
Endangered Species (MGM, 1982), 511–512
Enemy from Space (Corinth, 1957), 349
Enemy Mine (20th Century Fox, 1985), 518
Entity, The (20th Century Fox, 1981), 509–510

E.T., the Extraterrestrial (Universal, 1982), 99, 473–474, 512–513

Evils of the Night (Mars Productions, 1984), 519–520

Exorcist, The (Warner Bros., 1973), 427–428

Eye Creatures, The (AIP, 1965), 220–221

Eye of the Cat (Universal, 1969), 286

Fear No Evil (NBC/Universal, 1969), 154, 385–387, 422

F for Fake (France, 1973), 175–176

Fifth Element, The (Columbia, 1997), 574

Fire in the Sky (Paramount, 1993), 333–334, 585

Firestarter (Universal, 1984), 484

First Man Into Space (British, 1958), 219

First Men in the Moon (Warner Bros., 1964), 345–346, 348

First Spaceship on Venus (East German/Polish, 1960), 198, 246

Five Million Years to Earth (Hammer/20th Century Fox, 1967), 349, 361, 368, 459, 483, 525, 573

5,000 Fingers of Dr. T. (Columbia, 1953), 202

Flame Barrier, The (UA, 1957), 227

Flash Gordon (Universal, 1980), 499

Flesh Gordon (Graffiti Productions, 1974), 70, 419, 440

Flight that Disappeared, The (UA, 1958), 229

Flight to Mars (Monogram, 1951), 195, 197–198

Fly, The (20th Century Fox, 1958), 229, 342

Fly, The (20th Century Fox, 1986), 456

Flying Saucer, The (Film Classics, 1950), 251

Flying Saucer, The (Avco Embassy, 1964), 251

Forbidden Planet (MGM, 1956), 210–211, 228, 260, 303

Forbidden World (New World, 1981), 504–505

For Your Eyes Only (UA, 1981), 373, 496

Frankenstein Meets the Space Monster (20th Century Fox-Allied Artists, 1966), 354

Frankenstein: The True Story (NBC/Universal, 1974), 468

Frighteners, The (Universal, 1996), 587

From Beyond (Empire, 1986), 455–456, 526, 548

From Beyond the Grave (Amicus, 1973), 526

From the Earth to the Moon (MGM, 1958), 210

Full Metal Jacket (Warner Bros., 1987), 576

Funhouse, The (Universal, 1981), 508–509, 586

Fury, The (20th Century Fox, 1978), 483–484

Futureworld (AIP, 1976), 418

Galaxina (Italian, 1980), 490

Galaxy of Terror (New World, 1980), 504–505

Gargoyles (CBS/Metromedia, 1972), 421

Ghidrah, the Three-Headed Monster (U.S.-Japanese, 1965), 415

Ghostbusters (Columbia, 1984), 529

Ghostbusters 2 (Columbia, 1989), 529

Giant Claw, The (Columbia, 1957), 222–226, 240

God Told Me To (New World, 1976), 474

Godzilla, King of the Monsters (Toho, 1954), 414–415

Godzilla vs. Biollante, 432

Gog (UA, 1954), 196, 204–205

Golden Child, The (Paramount, 1986), 555

Golden Years, The (miniseries), 459

Goldfinger (UA, 1964), 497

Golem, The (German, 1914), 443

Golem, The (German, 1920), 443

Gone with the Wind (MGM, 1939), 199

Gorgon, The (Hammer, 1964), 361

Great Gabbo, The (1929), 154

Green Slime, The (U.S.-Japanese, 1969), 352

Gremlins (Warner Bros., 1983), 516–517

Guardian, The (Universal, 1990), 544–545

Halloween (Compass International, 1978), 384, 504, 525, 530

Halloween III: Season of the Witch (Universal, 1983), 348–349, 564

Hangar 18 (Sunn Classics, 1980), 490–492

Hangover Square (1945), 152

Haunted Palace, The (AIP, 1962), 450

Haunting, The (MGM, 1963), 425–427, 433

Have Rocket, Will Travel (Columbia, 1959), 247

Heavy Metal (Columbia/Zoetrope, 1981), 505–507

Hellraiser (New World, 1987), 526–527

Hellraiser IV: Bloodline (Paramount, 1996), 526–527

Helter Skelter (miniseries, 1976), 327

Homonculus (German, 1916), 443

Honey, I Shrunk the Kids (Disney, 1989), 538

Horror Express (Scotia International, 1972), 421

Horror of Party Beach, The (20th Century Fox, 1964), 154

Horrors of the Black Museum (AIP/Anglo-Amalgamated, 1959), 153, 160

House of Dark Shadows (MGM, 1970), 457

Howling, The (Avco Embassy, 1980), 484–485, 500–501

How to Make a Doll (Unusual Films, 1968), 384

How to Make a Monster (AIP, 1958), 153, 238

Human Duplicators, The (Allied Artists, 1965), 246, 356

Humanoids from the Deep (New World, 1980), 504

Hunger, The (MGM/UA, 1983), 516

Hunt for Red October, The (Paramount, 1990), 383

Hypnotic Eye, The (Allied Artists, 1960), 153–154

I Married a Monster from Outer Space (Paramount, 1958), 231–233

Incredible Mr. Limpet, The (Warner Bros., 1964), 467–468

Incredibly Strange Creatures Who Stopped Living and Became Mixed-Up Zombies, The (Fairway International, 1964), 154

Independence Day (20th Century Fox, 1996), 294, 414, 490, 499, 573, 585

In Like Flint (20th Century Fox, 1967), 357–358, 420, 482

In the Year 2889 (AIP, 1966), 213

Intruders (CBS, 1992), 333–335

Invader (independent, 1991), 546

Invaders, The (Fox T.V., 1995), 381–383, 534, 573

Invaders from Mars (20th Century Fox, 1953), 69, 187–188, 199–202, 216, 225, 582

Invaders from Mars (Cannon, 1986), 201–202

Invasion (NBC, 1997), 573–574

Invasion of the Bee Girls (Centaur, 1973), 423, 507

Invasion of the Body Snatchers (Allied Artists, 1956), 216–217, 380, 399, 573, 582

Invasion of the Body Snatchers (UA, 1979), 216, 476, 501

Invasion of the Saucer Men (AIP, 1957), 152, 193, 218–222, 229, 244, 249, 305

Invasion of the Star Creatures (AIP, 1962), 248–249

Invasion U.S.A. (Columbia, 1953), 192–193, 300, 495, 497

Invisible Boy, The (MGM, 1957), 202, 227–228

Invisible Invaders (UA, 1959), 237, 244

Island of Dr. Moreau, The (Universal, 1933), 477

Island of Dr. Moreau, The (AIP, 1977), 477

Island of Dr. Moreau, The (New Line, 1996), 477

Island of Terror (Universal-Planet Company, England, 1967), 353

Island of the Burning Doomed (Universal-Planet Company, England, 1966), 353

It (ABC, 1990), 459

It Came from Outer Space (Universal, 1953), 207, 233

It Conquered the World (AIP, 1956), 212–213, 215, 220, 323, 538

It's Alive (Warner Bros., 1974), 475

It's Alive III: Island of the Alive (Warner Bros., 1986), 522–523

It! The Terror from Beyond Space (UA, 1958), 152, 229

I Was a Teenage Frankenstein (AIP, 1957), 221–222

I Was a Teenage Werewolf (AIP, 1957), 152–153, 193, 218, 231, 249

James and the Giant Peach (Disney, 1996), 552

Jason and the Argonauts (Columbia, 1963), 348

JFK (Warner Bros., 1992), 100, 223

Journey to the Seventh Planet (AIP, 1962), 246

Jurassic Park (Universal, 1993), 418, 585

Killbots (independent, 1986), 522

Killdozer (ABC/Universal, 1972), 421

Killer Klowns from Outer Space (Trans World, 1987), 526

Killers from Space (RKO, 1954), 211

Kindred, The (Vestron, 1987), 286

King Kong Escapes (Universal-Toei, 1968), 415

Kronos (20th Century Fox, 1957), 222, 225, 234

Lair of the White Worm, The (Warner Bros., 1988), 459

Langoliers, The (ABC, 1995), 459

Last Days of Planet Earth, The (Toho, 1974), 431–432

Last Man On Earth, The (AIP, 1964), 425

Last Starfighter, The (Universal, 1984), 517

Legend of Hell House, The (AIP, 1973), 348, 424–425

Legion: Exorcist III (20th Century Fox, 1989), 542–543

Leviathan (MGM/UA, 1989), 542

Licence To Kill (UA, 1989), 497

Lifeforce (Cannon/Columbia Tri-Star, 1986), 202, 507, 520

Little Shop of Horrors (AIP, 1960), 248

Live and Let Die (UA, 1973), 497

Living Daylights, The (UA, 1987), 496–497

Lobsterman from Mars (independent, 1989), 538–539

Looker (Warner Bros., 1981), 418

Lords of the Deep (MGM/UA, 1989), 542

Love War, The (ABC/Aaron Spelling/Paramount, 1970), 418–419

Lurking Fear, The (Paramount/Full Moon, 1994), 458

Mad Monster Party (Avco Embassy, 1967/69), 551

Magnetic Monster, The (UA, 1953, 196, 204, 276

Manchurian Candidate, The (UA, 1962), 67, 136–141, 151, 155

Man from Planet X, The (UA, 1951), 187, 197, 522, 522, 577

Manhattan Project, The (Gladden/20th Century Fox, 1983), 515

Man in Outer Space, The (AIP, 1961), 246

Man In Space, 170

Manitou, The (Avco Embassy, 1978), 485

Man Who Fell to Earth, The (Cinema 5, 1976), 441

Man Who Would Be King, The (20th Century Fox, 1975), 308

Mars Attacks (Warner Bros., 1996), 552

Mars Needs Women (AIP, 1967/68), 154–155, 356–357, 359, 361, 475

Martian Chronicles, The (miniseries, 1977), 482–483

Martians Go Home (independent, 1990), 543

Mask, The (Warner Bros., 1961), 154

Maximum Overdrive (Columbia,

1986), 460–461, 517

Meet the Applegates (New World, 1989), 539

Men In Black (Columbia, 1997), 586

Message from Space (UA, 1978), 485–486

Meteor (1979), 183

Metropolis (1926), 443

Midnight Movie Massacre (independent, 1986), 522

Millennium (Gladden/20th Century Fox, 1989), 540

Mind Benders, The (AIP, 1963), 466

Mind Snatchers, The (Cinerama, 1972), 228

Missile to the Moon (Astor, 1958), 195

Mission Mars (Allied Artists, 1967), 251

Mission Stardust (European, 1968), 384

Mole People, The (Universal, 1956), 399

Monitors, The (Bell & Howell, 1969), 385

Monster a Go-Go (B.I.&L., 1965), 246

Moonraker (UA, 1979), 374, 557, 587

Moontrap (independent, 1989), 540–541

Moon Zero Two (Warner Bros., 1969), 432

Mouse on the Moon, The (Columbia, 1963), 237

Mouse that Roared, The (Columbia, 1959), 237

Mummy, The (Universal, 1933), 468

Mutations, The (Columbia, 1973), 422–423

Mutiny in Outer Space (Allied Artists, 1965), 246

My Stepmother is an Alien (Weintraub, 1988), 528–529

Mysterians, The (RKO/MGM/Toho, 1957), 109, 352, 414

Mysteries of the Gods (documentary, 1976), 320–321

Mysterious Island (Columbia, 1961), 171

Naughty Dallas (Paul Mart Productions, 1961), 213

Nebo Zowet (Russian, 1959), 354

Necronomicon (August Entertainment, 1993), 458

Neutron Against the Death Robots (Commonwealth United, 1961), 246

Next Voice You Hear, The (MGM, 1950), 188

Nicholas and Alexandra (1971), 421

Nightbreed (Morgan Creek/J&M, 1990), 527–528

Night Killers, The (unproduced), 425

Nightmare Before Christmas, The (Touchstone, 1993), 550–551

Nightmare On Elm Street (1984), 503–504, 530

Night of Dark Shadows (MGM, 1971), 457

Night of the Blood Beast, The (AIP, 1958), 235–236

Night of the Ghouls (Ed Wood, 1960), 538

Night of the Living Dead (Walter Reade Productions, 1968), 384–385

Night Slaves (ABC/Warner Bros., 1970), 187

Night Stalker, The (ABC/Dan Curtis, 1971), 301–302, 425

Night Strangler, The (ABC/Dan Curtis, 1972), 425

Night that Panicked America, The (ABC/Paramount, 1975), 424

Night Visitors (NBC, 1996), 572–573

1984 (1983), 519

Ninth Configuration, The (New World/William Peter Blatty, 1979), 543

Not of This Earth (Allied Artists, 1956), 215

Octopussy (UA, 1983), 496, 545

Official Denial (Sci-Fi Channel, 1993), 567

Oh, God! (Warner Bros., 1977), 482

Omega Man, The (Warner Bros., 1971), 425

Omen, The (20th Century Fox, 1976), 427–428, 501

One Dark Night (independent, 1982), 586

One of Our Spies is Missing (MGM, 1966), 358

One Spy Too Many (MGM, 1966), 358

On Her Majesty's Secret Service (UA, 1969), 159, 375–376, 432

Operation H-Bomb (documentary, 1953), 192

Orlac's Hands (1924), 443

Orphee (French, 1949), 152

Our Man Flint (20th Century Fox, 1966), 206

Overlords of the UFO (pseudo-documentary, 1977), 478

Pajama Party (AIP, 1964), 356

Parasite (Embassy, 1982), 538

Paths of Glory (Warner Bros., 1957), 516

Patton (20th Century Fox, 1970), 182

People, The (ABC/Metromedia, 1971), 419

Phantom from Space (UA, 1953), 196–197

Phase IV (Paramount, 1974), 429–430, 477

Planet of Blood (AIP, 1966), 353–354

Planet of Storms (Russian), 353

Planet of the Apes (20th Century Fox, 1968), 306–307

Planet of the Vampires (AIP, 1965), 247

Planets Against Us (Italian-French Teleworld, 1961), 246

Plan 9 from Outer Space (DCA, 1956/59), 69, 238–244, 250–251, 254, 384

Play Nice (Smart Egg, 1992), 536

Poltergeist (MGM/UA, 1982), 511

Power, The (MGM, 1968), 263

Predator (20th Century Fox, 1987), 300, 524–525, 555

Predator 2 (20th Century Fox, 1992), 300, 525

President's Analyst, The (Paramount, 1967), 482

Prince of Darkness (Universal, 1987), 525–526

Project Moonbase (Lippert, 1953), 195

Project M-7 (Universal/England, 1953), 195

Psycho (Paramount, 1960), 259, 420

Queen of Outer Space, The (20th Century Fox, 1958), 248, 261

Questor Tapes, The (NBC/Universal, 1974), 424

Rabid (Canadian, 1977), 485

Raiders of the Lost Ark (Paramount, 1981), 59, 63, 493

Re-Animator (Vestron, 1985), 454–455

Real Men (UA, 1987), 524–525

Red Dawn (MGM/UA, 1984), 193, 496, 515–516

Red Planet Mars (UA, 1952), 187–188

Red Zone Cuba (Coleman Francis, circa 1961), 253

Reefer Madness (pseudo-documentary, 1936), 192, 256

Remo Williams (Orion, 1985), 521

Repo Man (Universal, 1984), 517–518

Reptile, The (Hammer-20th Century Fox, 1966), 361

Ressurrected, The (independent, 1992), 450

Road, The (BBC, 1963), 347

Robinson Crusoe on Mars (Paramount, 1964), 284

Robot Monster (Astor, 1953), 69, 194–195, 244, 538

Robot vs. the Aztec Mummy, The (AIP, 1959), 244

Rocketship X-M (Lippert, 1950), 184

Rocky Horror Picture Show, The (20th Century Fox, 1975), 2–4, 70, 202, 380–381, 384, 437–441, 456

Rosemary's Baby (Paramount, 1968), 307, 427

Roswell (HBO, 1994), 552–553

Runaway (Columbia/Tri-Star, 1984), 418

Santa Claus (Mexican, 1959), 550–551

Santa Claus Conquers the Martians (Embassy, 1964), 69, 250–251, 550

Satellite in the Sky (Warner Bros., 1956), 218

Saturn 3 (Associated Film Distributors, 1980), 471–472

Scanners (Avco Embassy, 1981), 484–485

Schizo (Smart Egg, 1989), 537–538

Screamers (independent, 1996), 446

Secret Life of Ian Fleming, The (Turner, 1990), 379

7 Faces of Dr. Lao (MGM, 1964), 350–352

Sex Madness (pseudo-documentary, 1937), 192, 256

Shadow, The (Universal, 1994), 553, 555

She (RKO, 1935), 176–177

She Creature, The (AIP, 1956), 141, 152

Shining, The (Warner Bros., 1980), 460

Shining, The (ABC/Warner Bros., 1997), 460

Shock Waves (Samuel Goldwyn Company, 1977), 476

Shot in the Dark, A (UA, 1964), 428

Shuttered Room, The (Warner Bros., 1967), 458

Silence of the Lambs (Orion, 1991), 565

Silent Running (Universal, 1972), 418

Simon (Warner Bros., 1978), 482

Slaughterhouse Five (Universal, 1972), 421

Sneakers (1992), 488

Snow Devils (Italian, 1966), 352

Sometimes They Come Back (ABC, 1991), 460

Space Children, The (Paramount, 1958), 233

Space Master X-7 (20th Century Fox, 1957), 248

Space Monster (AIP, 1965), 246

Spaceship (Almi Cinema 5, 1981), 539

Space Thing (independent, 1968), 383–384

Spaceways (Lippert, 1953), 195

Special Bulletin (T.V., 1983), 513–514, 556

Special Report: Journey to Mars (CBS, 1996), 514, 555–556

Species (MGM/UA, 1995), 554–555, 585

Spellbound (Selznick International, 1945), 151

Spermula (French, 1973), 424

Spontaneous Combustion (independent, 1990), 484

Spy Who Loved Me, The (UA, 1977), 373, 497, 587

Sssssss (Universal, 1973), 422–423

Starcrash (Italian, 1979), 489

Stargate (MGM/UA, 1994), 21–22, 26, 414, 553–554, 561, 585, 587

Starman (Universal, 1984), 518

Starship Invasions (Canadian, 1977), 489

Star Trek: First Contact (Paramount, 1996), 318

Star Trek: The Motion Picture (Paramount, 1979), 312

Star Trek II: The Wrath of Khan (Paramount, 1982), 319–320

Star Trek III: The Search for Spock (Paramount, 1984), 320

Star Trek IV: The Voyage Home (Paramount, 1986), 320

Star Trek V: The Final Frontier (Paramount, 1989), 320

Star Trek VII, 317

Star Wars (20th Century Fox, 1977), 21, 300, 448, 476, 485, 489, 503, 553–554

Stepford Wives, The (Columbia, 1975), 307

Stone Tape, The (BBC, 1972), 348

Strange Brew (UA, 1983), 515

Stranger Within, The (ABC/Lorimar, 1974), 422

Succubus (Trans-American, 1967), 353

Superargo and the Faceless Giants (Fanfare, Spanish-Italian, 1967), 362

Superman (Warner Bros., 1978), 488, 492, 503

Superman and the Mole Men (Lippert, 1951), 186

Superman II (Warner Bros., 1981), 488

Superman III (Warner Bros., 1983), 489

Superman IV (Warner Bros., 1987), 489

Svengali (T.V., 1983), 147

Tales of Terror (AIP, 1962), 140

Target Earth (Allied Artists, 1954), 193–194, 202–203

Taxi Driver (Columbia, 1976), 146

Teenage Caveman (AIP, 1958), 234

Teenage Monster (Howco International, 1958), 233–234

Teenagers from Outer Space (Warner Bros., 1959), 385, 538

Telefon (MGM, 1977), 475

Terminal Man, The (Warner Bros., 1974), 418

Terminator, The (Orion, 1984), 518, 540

Terminator 2 (Carolco/Tri-Star, 1991), 518–519

Terror, The (AIP, 1963), 141

Terror Beneath the Sea (Japanese, 1964), 353

Terror from the Year 5,000 (AIP, 1958), 229, 577

Terrornauts, The (Amicus, 1967), 361

Terror of Mecha-Godzilla (U.S.-Japanese, 1975), 415

Them! (Warner Bros., 1954), 204

There's Nothing Out There (Valkhn/Grandmaster, 1990), 543–544

They Came from Beyond Space (Amicus, 1967), 361

They Live (Universal, 1988), 530

The Thing from Another World (RKO, 1951), 65, 68, 104–109, 177, 183–184, 197, 218, 244, 359, 391, 570

The Thing (Universal, 1983), 108

Things to Come (UA, 1936), 199

Thing that Couldn't Die, The (Universal, 1958), 230

This Island Earth (Universal, 1955), 208–209, 233, 260, 418, 500

Threads (MCTV, Great Britain, 1985), 495–496

Three Stooges in Orbit, The (Columbia, 1962), 247

Thunderball (UA, 1965), 372

Thunderbirds Are Go (ITV, 1966), 434

Thunderbirds 6 (ITC, 1968), 434

Time Machine, The (MGM, 1960), 245

Tobor, the Great (Republic, 1954), 204

Tommyknockers, The (ABC, 1992), 459

Torture Garden (Amicus, 1967), 420

Total Recall (Carolco, 1990), 446–448, 518

Trial of Lee Harvey Oswald, The (Falcon, 1964), 213

Trilogy of Terror (ABC Circle/Dan Curtis, 1974), 517

Troll (Empire, 1986), 521–522

True Lies (Columbia/Tri-Star, 1994), 497–499

Tourist Trap (Compass, 1978), 538

Twelve O'Clock High (20th Century Fox, 1949), 341

12 to the Moon (Columbia, 1960), 245

27th Day, The (Columbia, 1957), 227

20,000 Leagues Under the Sea (Walt Disney, 1954), 170

Twilight Zone: The Movie (Warner Bros., 1984), 517

Twonky, The (UA, 1953), 196–197, 202

2001: A Space Odyssey (MGM, 1968), 71, 316, 432, 463–464, 487

2010 (MGM, 1984), 461, 463–464

U.F.O. (UA, 1956), 217

UFO Incident, The (NBC/Universal, 1975), 3, 422, 584

UFOria (Universal, 1981), 539

Unearthly Stranger, The (Anglo-Amalgamated, 1963), 250

Universe (documentary), 321

Unnameable, The (Yankee Classic/K. P. Productions, 1988), 458

Unnatural (Germany, 1952), 154

V (Warner Bros., 1983), 299–300

Venetian Affair, The (MGM, 1967), 362

Victory Through Air Power (UA, 1943), 169

Videodrome (Universal, 1983), 514–515

Village of the Damned (MGM, 1960), 233, 271–272, 485

Vincent (Tim Burton), 551–552

Violent Years, The (Ed Wood, 1956), 241

Visit to a Small Planet (Paramount, 1960), 229

Voodoo Island (UA, 1957), 227

Voodoo Woman (AIP, 1957), 152

Voyage to the End of the Universe (AIP, 1961), 246

Voyage to the Planet of Prehistoric Women (AIP, 1965), 352

Voyage to the Prehistoric Planet (AIP, 1965), 352

Vulture, The (U.S.-British-Canadian, 1967), 361

War Games (MGM/UA, 1983), 515–516

Warlords of Atlantis (Columbia/EMI, 1978), 486

War of the Planets (Italian, 1965), 352

War of the Satellites (Allied Artists, 1958), 234, 577

War of the Worlds, The (Paramount, 1953), 69, 198, 522, 534, 554

Watcher in the Woods, The (Disney, 1980), 503

Way Way Out (20th Century Fox, 1968), 356

Weird Woman (Universal, 1944), 248

Werewolf of London, The (Universal, 1935), 347

When Worlds Collide (Paramount, 1951), 197

Wicker Man, The (Warner Bros., 1972), 345

Wild, Wild Planet (MGM, 1966), 352

Without Warning (T.V., 1994), 514, 556

Wizard of Oz, The (MGM, 1939), 352

Wizard of Mars (American General Pictures, 1964), 251

Wolf Man, The (Universal, 1941), 196

Woman in Green, The (Universal, 1945), 151

Woman in the Moon, The (1928), 443

World Without End (Allied Artists, 1955), 209–210

X The Unknown (Hammer/Warner Bros., 1956), 237

You Only Live Twice (UA, 1967), 373, 587

Zardoz (20th Century Fox, 1974), 430–431

Zontar, the Thing from Venus (AIP, 1966), 212

government agencies, national and educational institutions

AEC (Atomic Energy Commission), 6

AFOSI (Air Force Office of Special Investigations), 96, 98–99, 102, 221, 258, 264

Ain Shams University (Cairo), 33

Air Materiel Command (Wright Field/Wright-Patterson AFB), 56–58, 75, 80, 82, 84

Albert Einstein College of Medicine, 123

British Naval Intelligence, 370, 579

British Secret Service, 44–45, 371, 378, 403

Brooklyn Tech High School, 425

Buckley AFB, 206, 374

Cal-Tech (California Technical Institute), 466

CIA (Central Intelligence Agency), 5, 13–14, 30, 32, 58, 61, 65, 67–69, 71, 82, 99–101, 103, 109–121, 163–164, 166–168, 204, 213, 223, 235, 253, 267, 277, 279–280, 295, 297, 309, 322, 331–332, 338, 349, 362, 373, 377–378, 382, 384, 402–403, 466, 483–484, 497–498, 502, 518–519, 524–525, 530–531, 538, 553, 557, 559, 561, 578, 580–583, 585–586, 588

CNES (French Institute of Astrophysics and Center for Scientific Research), 18
Cornell University, 425
DEA (Drug Enforcement Agency), 497
Defense Mapping Agency, 23
DIA (Defense Intelligence Agency), 32, 84, 103, 322
DOD (Department of Defense), 8, 29–32, 84, 278–280, 286, 289–290, 297, 303, 333, 441, 471, 479, 483, 515, 519, 546, 558
Eastern Michigan University, 124
Eton University, 370, 579
European Space Agency, 26
FAA (Federal Aviation Administration), 540
FBI (Federal Bureau of Investigation), 6, 55–56, 76, 98, 145, 147, 169, 195, 238, 247, 251, 267, 278, 280, 325, 328, 333, 510, 577
FCC (Federal Communications Commission), 256, 547
Fort Knox, 372
Glavkosmos (Russia), 27
Goodman Theater School, 333
Harvard University, 35, 122, 278
House of Lords, 168
INSCOM (Internal Security Command, U.S. Army), 33
Johns Hopkins University, 14
JPL (Jet Propulsion Lab, Cal-Tech), 466
Justice Dept., U.S., 145, 571
KGB, 227, 371, 469, 496, 542
LCS (London Controlling Section, WWII), 45, 378
London Museum, 28
MI-5 and -6, 157, 161
MIT (Massachusets Institute of Technology), 66, 127, 183, 258, 578
Moscow Institute of Aviation, 20
NASA (National Aeronautics and Space Administration), 17–18, 20–22, 28–31, 38, 71, 103, 201, 235, 271, 286, 308–309, 321–322, 326–327, 396, 399, 406, 409–410, 486–488, 506, 516, 520, 526, 533, 540–541, 555

National Bureau of Standards, 444
National Guard, 183, 261
National Space Council, 37, 533
NATO (North Atlantic Treaty Organization), 167, 496
NORAD (North American Air Defense Command), 82, 84, 551
NIH (National Institute of Health), 465–467
Northwestern University, 101
NSA (National Security Agency), 2, 5, 7–10, 14, 18, 32, 63, 103, 123, 267, 271, 278–280, 283, 322, 397, 472, 562
NSC (National Security Council), 38, 111
OAP (Office of Alien Property), 55–56
ONI (Office of Naval Intelligence), 55, 98, 103, 221
OPD (Office of Public Diplomacy), 166
ORD (Office of Research and Development), 55–56
OSI (Office of Scientific Intelligence, CIA), 116
OSS (Office of Strategic Services, WWII), 12, 51, 114, 378
Oxford University, 215
Palo Alto University, 215
Pentagon, 6, 32, 75, 80, 159, 162–163, 167, 170, 217, 279, 294, 334, 374, 507, 515, 534, 546, 585
Princeton University, 114, 333
RADA (Royal Academy of Dramatic Arts), 342, 579
RAF (Royal Air Force, Britain), 12, 42, 44–45, 464, 580
Rand Corporation, 7
Scotland Yard, 157, 302
SDECE (Service de Documentation Exterieur et de Contre-Espionage, WWII), 230
Space Development Project (U.S. Army), 25
SRI (Stanford Research Institute), 32, 215
St. George's English School (Rome), 536
St. Vincent's Hospital, 123
Temple University, 122, 586

United Nations, 229, 236, 278, 345, 363
University of Wyoming, 124
U.S. Information Agency, 165
U.S. Signal Corps, 14, 64, 580
U.S. Space Command, 206, 374
Vandenburg AFB, 408
Virginia Military Institute, 14
Washington Institute of Technology, 82
Yale University, 63, 95, 258, 333, 358, 403, 578
government Intelligence projects (*see also* ancient civilizations, government research into)
  Bay of Pigs, 331
  "Blue Fly," 330
  COINTELPRO (Counter-Intelligence Program, FBI), 278
  HAARP (High-frequency Active Auroral Research Project), 205–207, 237, 521
  IPU (Interplanetary Phenomenon Unit, U.S. Army), 12, 580
  MK-ULTRA (*see* mind control; UFOs, abduction occurrences)
  "Moon Dust," 330, 572
  Operation Paperclip, 2, 30, 58–59, 62, 66, 328, 330
  OPD (Office of Public Diplomacy), 166
  Operation Desert Storm, 379, 489, 498
  Operation Swimmer ("swimmer nullification" program), 297, 467–468
  OSI (Office of Scientific Investigation, CIA), 204
  Propaganda Assets Inventory ("Wisner's Wurlitzer"), 164
  Project Icarus, 183
  PSB (Psychological Strategy Board), 167
  Radio Free Europe, 163
  Radio Liberty, 163
  Remote Viewing ("psychic spying"), 32–34, 236, 322, 578
  Robertson Panel (CIA, 1953), 69, 167–168, 171, 177, 186, 193–194, 198, 235, 503, 583–586

SETI (Search for Extra-Terrestrial Intelligence), 38, 528, 533, 554, 574
"Star Wars" (Strategic Defense Initiative, Ballistic Missile Defense Organization), 27, 30–31, 38–39, 71, 159, 278, 301, 479–480, 521, 533, 556
UFO "educational project," (*see* Robertson Panel)
UFO investigations (U.S. Air Force)
  Project Blue Book 5, 9, 80, 85, 101, 104, 171, 360, 372, 483, 583
  Project Sign, 6–7, 217
  Project Twinkle, 5–6, 65, 107, 343
  ULTRA (or "Enigma," WWII), 63, 66, 114, 144, 371–372, 378–380, 428, 573
  Unit 731, 59, 328
  Voynich Manuscript (NSA), 62–63
  V-12 Officer Training program, U.S. Navy, 215
government and military figures
  Abrams, Elliot, 165
  Aldrin, Buzz, 33, 574
  Armstrong, Neil, 33, 488
  Barrie, Sir James M., 64, 580
  Blanchard, Col. William, 74–75, 79, 81
  Bonior, David, 166
  Bronk, Detlev, 101
  Brown, Sgt. Melvin E., 76
  Brumberg, Abraham, 165
  Bulwer-Lytton, Lord Edward, 16–17, 33, 43, 64–65, 574
  Burke, John, 119
  Bush, George, 29, 37–38, 71, 145, 147, 164, 223, 301, 332, 378–379, 489, 493, 497, 508, 518, 524, 527, 531, 533–534, 537, 549, 588
  Bush, Neil, 145
  Carter, Jimmy, 21, 32, 70–71, 115, 147, 164, 205, 216, 301, 319, 367, 374, 428–429, 441, 472, 481, 488–490, 492, 501, 505, 517–518, 523, 534

Churchill, Sir Winston, 43, 45, 378–379
Clancarty, Earl of, 65
Clark, Ramsey, 489
Clinton, Bill, 71, 146, 291, 294, 493, 534
Clinton, Hillary, 294
Codgrington, Adm., 92
Coleman, Col. William T., 483
Corbett, John J., 55
Dalai Lama, 45
de Seversky, Alexander, 169
d'Estaing, Valerie Giscard, 536
Dirksen, Everett, 385
Donnelly, Ignatius, 43, 65
Douglas, Helen Gahagan, 177
DuBose, Col. Thomas, 74, 76
Duffy, Col., 57
Eisenhower, Dwight D., 82
Elders, Joycelyn, 255
Exon, Brig. Gen. Arthur, 81
Ferdinand, Archduke, 377
Ferraro, Geraldine, 165
Ford, Gerald, 146, 428, 440–441, 474, 481
Forrestal, James V., 6–7, 217, 573, 581
Franklin, Benjamin, 45
Garrison, D.A. Jim, 100, 130, 139, 173
Gates, Daryl, 142
George, Willis, 55
Goddard, Air Marshall Sir Victor, 12
Goering, Hermann, 45
Gorbachev, Mikhail, 38–40
Grade, Lord Lew, 434, 472, 579
Gregory, Capt. George T., 372
Haggard, Sir H. Rider, 64, 176
Haig, Alexander, 147, 162
Hargreaves, Sir Gerald, 65
Haushofer, Prof. Gen. Karl, 46–48, 60
Haut, First Lieut. Walter, 74–75
Hearst, William Randolph, 411
Heasley, Maj. Edwin, 75
Henderson, Capt. Pappy, 81
Hess, Rudolf, 45–46, 66
Hillenkoetter, Adm. Roscoe, 112, 581
Hill-Norton, Lord Adm., 42

Hitler, Adolf, 43–46, 58–59, 63, 114, 117, 191, 247, 371, 522
Holiday, Col., 57
Holzinger, Joseph, 118
Hoover, J. Edgar, 56, 142, 169, 207, 571
Hughes, Howard, 65, 109, 414, 570
Inman, Adm. Bobby Ray, 103
Jackson, C. D., 99–100, 163
Jefferson, Thomas, 379
Johnson, Lyndon Baines, 8, 164, 213
Kaplan, Joseph, 5
Kaufman, Frank, 76
Kelvin, Lord, 13, 21, 580
Kennedy, John Fitzgerald, 98, 100, 130, 136, 173, 213, 263, 331, 362, 371, 377–379, 409, 428, 567–569, 571, 573
Kennedy, J. F., Jr., 333
Kennedy, Robert Fitzgerald, 129, 139–140, 142, 306, 377, 410, 428, 571
King, Martin Luther, Jr., 331
Kipling, Rudyard, 64, 308
Kosanovic, Sava, 56
Kromschroeder, Dr. John, 81
La Paz, Dr. Lincoln, 5, 73, 83–84, 107, 198
Leslie, Desmond, 42
Lincoln, Abraham, 379
Luce, Clare Booth, 100
Luce, Henry, 65, 99–100, 163
MacArthur, Douglas, 7, 12, 59, 306, 379, 580
Marcel, Maj. Jesse A., 74–76, 569–570
Marks, John, 112–113, 116–117, 143, 167, 277, 403
Marshall, Gen. George, 11
McCarthy, Joe, 164, 188, 191, 207, 208, 216
McCoy, Richard, 119
McDivitt, Brig. Gen. James A., 360–361
McMullen, Gen. Clements, 74
Mitchell, Billy, 169
Mondale, Walter, 8
Montgomery, Field Marshal Bernard, 428

Nicholas II, 45
Nixon, Richard M., 8, 118, 177, 228, 301, 331, 419, 428, 440
Packwood, Bob, 389
Paley, William, 163
Palmer, Edward, 55
Parker, William, 142, 309, 578
Patterson, Capt. Joseph Medill, 411
Powell, Gen. Colin, 570
Powers, Maj. Patrick, 25
Priest, Ivy Baker, 398
Quayle, Dan, 37–38, 125, 255, 533
Quintanilla, Capt. Hector, 360
Ramey, Gen. Roger M., 76
Rasmussen, Capt. Darwin E., 76
Raymond, Walter, 166
Reagan, Ronald, 30, 38–40, 71, 116–117, 145–147, 165–166, 191, 277–278, 294, 300–301, 330, 378, 473–474, 481–482, 489, 493, 495, 507, 510, 517–518, 520, 523, 531, 533–534, 551, 556, 567
Reno, Janet, 255
Rickett, Msgt. Lewis S., 73
Romanov, Mikhail, 44
Roosevelt, Eleanor, 177
Roosevelt, Franklin Delano, 176, 378, 411, 583–584
Ross, Betsy, 379
Ruppelt, Capt. Edward, 5, 8–9, 80, 107, 111, 171, 217, 583
Ryan, Leo, 118
Samford, Maj. Gen. John A., 9, 583
Sarbacher, Dr. Robert I., 82–83
Schmidt, Harrison, 96
Schmitt, Jack, 487
Schulgen, Brig. Gen. George, 80
Schwartzkopf, Gen. Norman, 571
Smith, Gen. Walter Bedell, 99
Sulzberger, Arthur Hayes, 163
Tamm, Edward A., 56
Tolson, Clive, 571
Truman, Harry, 7, 58, 98, 111, 378, 570
Trump, Dr. John G., 55–56
Turner, Adm. Stansfield, 32
Twining, Gen. Nathan F., 75, 80–81
Wallace, George, 140
Wallace, Henry A., 56
Ward, Parliamentary Air Under-

Secretary George, 42–43
Washington, Booker T., 379
Wellington, Duke of, 92
Wilcox, George A., 74
Yusupov, Prince Felix, 151

hydrogen bomb, 6, 571–572, 581

inventors (*see* scientists)
Intelligence agents - mad doctors, spies, and occultists
Augsburg, Emil, 58
Bacon, Roger, 62
Barbie, Klaus, 58
Cagliostro (Giuseppe Balsamo), 44
Casey, William, 166
Churchward, James, 47, 61, 377
Colby, William, 164
Collins, Capt. Robert, 99
Cooper, William, 96, 98–99, 567–568
Crisman, Fred, 173
Crowley, Aleister, 44, 53–54, 66, 467
Dames, Maj. Ed, 33
Dee, Dr. Arthur, 44
Dee, Dr. John, 44, 62
Doty, Msgt. Richard C., 99
Dulles, Allen, 58, 99, 114
Dwyer, Richard, 118
Edwards, Col. Sheffield, 112
Ferrie, David, 139
Ferriter, John P., 14
Fleming, Ian, 44, 66, 70, 159, 216, 355, 370–376, 407, 436, 578–579
Friedman, William, 14
Gehlen, Reinhard, 58, 166–167
Godfrey, Adm. Sir John, 371
Greiner, Joseph, 47
Gurdjieff, George Ivanovitch, 45–46
Hasenfus, Eugene, 117
Hubbard, L. Ron, 467
Hunt, E. Howard, 331
Hunter, Edward, 115
Ishii, Lieut. Gen. Shiro, 59
Kircher, Athanasius, 62
Knight, Maxwell, 44
Langelaan, George, 229–230
Lear, John, 99

Leary, Timothy, 48
Marchetti, Victor, 82, 84, 142, 167, 277, 403
McCone, John A., 163
Nostradamus, 62, 432
Oechsler, Bob, 102–103
Parsons, Jack, 466–467
Rahn, Otto, 48
Rasputin, 45, 147, 151, 377
Ruby, Jack, 213, 568
Schafer, Ernst, 50–51
Shaw, Clay, 100, 130, 173
Six, Franz Alfred, 58
Skorzeny, Otto, 58
Stephenson, Sir William, 372
Stevenson, William, 144, 372
Stubblebine, Maj. Gen. Albert, 33
Wheatley, Dennis, 44–45, 66, 579
Wisner, Frank G., 164
Yardley, Herbert Osborne, 63

media control (CIA), 68–71, 99–100, 115, 161–169, 188–189
media personalities
Axelrod, Nina, 546
Bell, Art, 33
Bernstein, Carl, 163
Briem, Ray, 139
Brussel, Mae, 144–146
Cavett, Dick, 360
Criswell ("The Amazing"), 238–239, 243
Dorian, Bob, 231
Joyce, Frank, 79
King, Larry, 584
Langman, Betsy, 140, 142
Limbaugh, Rush, 192
McGee, Frank, 130–131
Minow, Newton N., 256
Moyers, Bill, 165
Nebel, "Long John," 143, 148–150
Pauley, Jane, 146
Quinn, Martha, 547
Savitch, Jessica, 146–147
Turner, Ted, 191
Vampira (Maila Nurmi), 239
Wallace, Mike, 162
Woodward, Bob, 162–164
mind control (see also government agencies and national institutions,

CIA; UFOs, abduction occurrences, hypnosis, mind control, and memory erasure), 100, 112–160 passim
Allen, Morse, and, 113–114, 138, 143, 154
ancient roots of, 60–61, 139, 358
"Arlene Grant" and, (see Candy Jones case)
Berke, Michael, and, 146–147
Bremer, Arthur, and, 140
Brussel, Mae, and, 144–146
Bryan, William Joseph, Jr., and, 61, 67–68, 110, 130, 138–143, 153, 160, 578
Bush, Harvey, and, 139
Cameron, Dr. Ewan, and, 114, 515
Candy Jones case, 143–144, 148–150, 475, 483
Chapman, Mark David, and, 144–145
CIA projects to study,
ARTICHOKE, 113–114, 138
BLUEBIRD, 112–113
DELTA, 115
MK-SEARCH, 114
MK-ULTRA, 61, 66–68, 128, 135–136, 142–143, 148, 150, 164, 213, 358, 465, 475, 480, 519, 527, 530, 588
Operation "Midnight Climax," 113–114
Crahan, Dr. Marcus, and, 129
"death cults" and
Jonestown, 117–119
Matamoros, 117, 524
Diamond, Dr. Bernard, and, 129–130, 135, 140
Di Salvo, Albert, and, 139–140
Earl Ray, James, and, 142
HIP (Hypnotic Induction Profile) and, 129–130
in fiction and film (see also UFOs, abduction occurrences, factual and in science fiction, hypnosis, mind control, and memory erasure), 70, 136–160, 185–186, 192–193, 197, 199–203, 208–214, 216, 219, 221–222, 228–231, 233, 236–237, 244, 247–250, 267, 272–275, 514–515, 527

Kaiser, Dr., and, 129
Lilly, Dr. John, and, 358, 465–467
LSD and other drugs in, 100,
   113–114, 275, 355, 466
PAS (Post Abduction Syndrome,
   UFO) and, 124–125
PTSD (Post-Traumatic Stress Syn-
   drome) and, 123–124
"Reisner, Dr. Jonathan," and,
   142–144
Scandinavian case studies of
   Hardrup/Nielsen (1952), 153
   housewife/prostitute near-murder
      (1934), 153
   "Stockholm Syndrome," 126–127
Sirhan Sirhan and, 128–129,
   139–140, 143
Spiegel, Dr. Herbert, and, 129–131,
   144
St. Charles, Dr. Richard, and, 129
UFO abductees and, 68, 119,
   126–136
   professional researchers of,
   Clamar, Dr. Aphrodite, 120, 130
   Laibow, Dr. Rima, 123
   Mundy, Dr. Jean, 123
   Parnell, Dr. June, 124
   Slater, Dr. Elizabeth, 120–124
   Westrum, Dr. Ronald, 124
von Koss, Xavier, and, 142

novels, stories, and plays
   "Adam Link," 296
   Aelita, 64, 172–173
   "Air Raid," 540
   "Alien Machine, The," 208
   Allan Quatermain, 64
   Andromeda Strain, The, 227
   The Body Snatchers, 216
   "Brain-Thief, The," 154, 302
   "Bride of Dewer, The," 302–303
   Cabal, 528
   Case of Charles Dexter Ward, The, 450
   Childhood's End, 464
   Circus of Dr. Lao, The, 350–352
   "Colour Out of Space, The," 451
   Conjure Wife, 248
   "Cool Air," 453
   Corpus Earthling, 263
   "Cosmic Frame, The," 218

Cyborg, 464
Demon Seed, 469–471
Destroyer, The, 521
Do Androids Dream of Electric Sheep?,
   446
Dracula, 458–459
Dragon Tears, 468
Dreamland, 573
"Dreams in the Witch House, The,"
   452
Dr. Mabuse, 153
Dr. No, 374–376, 407
Encounter with Tiber, 574
Escapement, 228
Exit to Eden, 469
"Facts in the Case of M. Valdemar,
   The," 140, 453
"Farewell to the Master," 177
Flying Saucer, The, 278
Frankenstein, 455
"From Beyond," 455
From Russia With Love, 371
Funhouse, The, 468
Fury, The, 483
"Gate-Chaser, The," 526
Ghost Story, 461
Goldfinger, 372
Hell House, 424
House of Thunder, The, 468
I Am Legend, 587
If You Could See Me Now, 461
Indiana Jones and the Sky Pirates,
   465
Insomnia, 459
"It's a Good Life," 517
Jane Eyre, 458
Jewel of the Seven Stars, The, 459,
   501
Key to Midnight, The, 469
King Solomon's Mines, 64
Lair of the White Worm, The, 459
"Lanson Screen, The," 262
"Library Policeman, The," 459
Macbeth, 262
Manchurian Candidate, The, 136,
   331
"Man Who Would Be King, The,"
   64, 308
Man with the Golden Gun, The, 375
Mars Project, The, 61–62, 210

Midnight, 296, 469
Mummy, The, 468
"Nightmare at 20,000 Feet," 517
Night of the Big Heat, 353
Night Stalker, The, 425, 587
On Her Majesty's Secret Service, 159
Peter Pan, 64
Phantoms, 469
"Pickman's Model," 453
Planet of the Apes, 306–307
Power, The, 263
"Prey," 517
Puppet Masters, The 186, 197, 263
Rosemary's Baby, 307
R.U.R., 297
Russian Assignment, 258
"Sandkings," 286
"Second Variety," 446
Seven Days In May, 306
Shadowland, 461
She, 64, 176
Space Vampires, The, 520
Stepford Wives, The, 307
Stranger in a Strange Land, 186
Strangers, 469
Tempest, The, 211
Thunderball, 376
Time Machine, The, 245
Trilby, 151
27th Day, The, 227
2010, 461
Twilight Bar, 444
Twilight Eyes, 469
Viper Three, 476
War of the Worlds, The, 14–15, 26,
    174, 583
"We Can Remember It For You,
    Wholesale," 446
"Who Goes There?," 107, 444
Winter Moon, 468
Visit to a Small Planet, 228–229
Vril: The Power of the Coming Race,
    16, 65, 574

occult organizations (*see also* Intelli-
    gence agents - mad doctors, spies,
    and occultists)
    American Philosophical Society, 45
    Community of Truth Seekers, 45
    Knights Templar, 44

Masons (Freemasons), 17, 45, 60,
    111, 285, 308, 323, 331, 386, 580
Rosicrucians (AMORC, Ancient
    Mystical Order of the Rosy
    Cross), 17, 34, 44–45, 139, 386,
    580
Royal Society of England, 45
Scientology, 467
Sufis, 46
Thelema, 54, 467
Theosophists, 44
Thule Society, 43–44
Vril Society, 43–44
Wicca, 536
organizations and committees
    Association of Former Intelligence
        Officers, 100
    Bilderberger Organization, 99
    Church (Frank) Committee, 61,
        164, 480
    Civil Service Commission, 113
    Commission of Inquiry for the
        International War Crimes Tri-
        bunal, 489
    Condon Committee, 586
    CSICOP (Committee for the Scien-
        tific Investigation of Claims of
        the Paranormal), 276
    Geological Society of America, 50
    House Permanent Select Commit-
        tee on Intelligence, 119
    LAPD, 129, 142, 309, 578
    Mafia, 113, 143, 213, 235, 250, 277
    MENSA, 159
    UNITA, 118

parapsychologists and debunkers
    "Amazing Randi," The, 149
    Christopher, Milbourne, 149
    Geller, Uri, 322, 478
    Kaplan, Dr. Stephen, 149–150
    Klass, Philip J., 121, 149–150, 334
    Puharich, Dr. Andrija, 322
    Rhine, J. B., 150
planets and planetary bodies
    Mars, 46, 66, 583
        artifacts on, 17, 22–26, 28, 30,
            33–35, 53, 201, 288, 366
        in science fiction, 61–62, 64–65,
            70, 106–107, 159, 172–180,

184–185, 187–189, 194–203,
206–207, 210–211, 235,
281–282, 284–285, 287–290,
295, 300, 305, 309, 321,
343–345, 348, 352, 356–360,
366, 389, 398–402, 405–407,
411, 415, 424, 436–437,
446–448, 486–488, 514,
522–523, 526, 533–535, 543,
546, 550, 552, 555–556, 566,
574, 588–589
  intelligent signals claimed to be
received from, by scientists,
13–14, 64, 580
  rocks from, found on Earth,
31–32, 326, 332
  UFO waves and, 18–20, 27–28,
30, 138, 228, 425, 502
Moon, 66, 486–488
  artifacts and UFO activity on,
16–17, 33–34, 345, 427, 520
  in science fiction, 70, 138, 159,
184, 185, 194–195, 197,
210–211, 237, 245, 254, 259,
292, 345–346, 352, 356, 396,
403–404, 409–411, 413,
432–433, 435, 509, 540–542,
574, 588
Venus, 18–19, 24
  in science fiction, 193, 198, 212,
273, 282, 305, 323, 384
producers, directors, and creators
Adamson, Al, 250
Adler, Lou, 438
Alland, William, 207–208, 233,
578, 584, 578, 584
Allen, Irwin, 155, 250, 389, 396,
432
Anderson, Gerry and Sylvia, 70,
432–437, 472, 487, 579
Arkoff, Sam, 238
Arnold, Jack, 207–208, 233
Asher, William, 227
Band, Charles, 454–455, 505,
521–522, 526, 538, 547
Barbera, Joe, 405
Bava, Mario, 526
Binder, Maurice, 501
Binyon, Claude Jr., 257
Broccoli, Albert, 355

Buchanan, Larry, 154, 212–213,
220, 257, 354, 356, 474
Burton, Tim, 529, 548–552
Cahn, Edward L., 152, 210, 218,
244
Cameron, James, 540, 542
Carlborg, Herbert A., 162
Carlton, Rex, 249–250
Carpenter, John, 108, 384, 504,
525–526, 529–530
Carter, Chris, 302
Castle, William, 244
Chang, Wah, 258
Cohen, Herman, 152–153, 160,
193–195, 202, 218, 221, 578, 582
Cohen, Larry, 474, 522
Connelly, Joe, 398–399
Coon, Gene, 309, 312
Coppola, Francis Ford, 140
Corben, Richard, 506
Corman, Gene, 235
Corman, Julie, 522
Corman, Roger, 65, 67, 140–141,
201, 212–213, 215–216, 234–235,
238, 248, 253, 257, 323, 353–354,
425, 450–451, 454, 499, 504–505,
518, 520, 522, 524, 538, 542–543,
577
Cronenberg, David, 484–485, 514,
527
Curtis, Dan, 334, 457
Danziger Brothers, the (Edward J.
and Harry Lee), 202, 217
De Carlo, Dan, 407
De Laurentiis, Dino, 460, 484
Densham, Penray, 286, 298
De Palma, Brian, 483
Devlin, Dean, 414, 554, 587
Disney, Walt, 169–171, 219, 244,
578, 585
Emmerich, Roland, 414, 554, 587
Fisher, Terence, 353
Fleischer, Max, 196
Ford, John, 555
Fowler, Gene, 231
Francis, Coleman, 253
Franco, Jesse, 353
Friedkin, William, 544
Friedman, David F., 384
Gaines, William, 191–192, 195

Galeen, Henrik, 443
Gilling, John, 361
Girdler, William, 485
Globus, Yoram, 201, 504, 520
Goddard, Jean-Luc, 353
Golan, Menahem, 201, 504, 520
Goldwater, John and Richard, 407
Gordon, Bernard, 421
Gordon, Richard, 353
Gould, Chester, 408–411
Hanna, William, 405
Harrington, Curtis, 354
Harryhausen, Ray, 170, 217, 347–348
Haskin, Byron, 210
Hawks, Howard, 107–108, 177, 391, 444
Hitchcock, Alfred, 151–152, 259
Hooper, Tobe, 201, 468, 508
Huston, John, 308
Johnson, Kenneth, 299
Justman, Robert, 257
Kane, Bob, 403
Katzman, Sam, 223
Kimball, Ward, 169–170
Kramer, Stanley, 202
Kubrick, Stanley, 316, 460, 463
Landsburg, Alan and Sally, 307
Lang, Fritz, 153, 443
Lantz, Walter, 188
Larson, Glen, 323–324
Lester, Richard, 237
Lewis, Herschell Gordon, 246, 384
Lewis, Richard K., 286, 298
Lucas, George, 523
Mancuso, Frank, Jr., 555
Mantley, John, 325
Martin, Quinn, 380, 490
McIntyre, Andrew, 381
Melies, George, 403, 444
Menzies, William Cameron, 199
Milius, John, 193
"Moebius," 506
Mosher, Bob, 398–399
Murray, K. Gordon, 244, 550
Nicholson, James H., 160, 348, 424
Oboler, Arch, 196
O'Brien, Richard, 437–438
Ohata, Koichi, 415
Ouelette, Jean-Paul, 458

Pal, George, 198, 210, 245, 534
Protozanov, Jacob, 64
Rankin-Bass, 486, 551
Raymond, Alex, 499
Reade, Walter, 384
Reynolds, Edward, 238
Ripert, Otto, 443
Roddenberry, Gene, 70, 142, 277, 309, 315–319, 322, 424–425, 477, 578
Roeg, Nicholas, 441
Saban, 413
Salmon, Doug, 161
Schrader, Paul, 573
Schwartz, Sherwood, 399
Scott, Ridley and Tony, 516
Seeger, Hal, 403
Serling, Rod, 70, 303–307, 425, 453, 578, 586
Seuss, Dr. (Theodore Geisel), 202
Shandera, Jaime, 98
Shuster, Joe, 186
Siegel, Jerry, 186
Solo, Robert, 501
Spielberg, Steven, 59, 99, 168, 401, 473, 492, 505, 508, 511–512, 516–517, 584–586
Stefano, Joseph, 259, 262–263, 272–274, 285–286, 290, 298, 306, 342, 389
Stevens, Leslie, 65, 69, 257–261, 263–264, 275, 284–286, 298, 303, 325, 342, 389, 425, 578, 584
Stone, Oliver, 100, 223, 223
Tezuka, Osama, 413
Torme, Tracy, 327, 333–335
Tors, Ivan, 196
Tucker, Phil, 69, 194, 239, 244, 538
Turner, Ted, 380, 505, 545
von Stroheim, Erich, 154
Ward, Jay, 403
Warhol, Andy, 248
Watson, John K., 286, 298
Wegener, Paul, 443
Weiss, George, 238
Welles, Orson, 69, 173–176, 189, 207, 257–258, 355, 384, 402–403, 424, 458, 480, 514, 518, 556, 578, 583–584
Whedon, Joss, 587

White, Michael, 438
Williams, Wade, 522
Wise, Robert, 183, 433, 516
Wood, Ed, 69, 237–239, 241, 250,
    538, 551, 577
Woolner, Larry, 499
Wynorski, Jim, 109, 194, 215, 218,
    505, 522
Yuzna, Brian, 458
Zabel, Bryce, 567–568
Zanuck, Darryl, 183
Zemeckis, Robert, 587
Zimbalist, Al, 195
publications and news services
*Abduction: Human Encounters with
    Aliens,* 127
Above Top Secret, 42, 102
The Addams Chronicles, 397
Amazing Stories, 171–173, 296
Amityville Horror Conspiracy, The,
    150
Anatomy of a Phenomenon, 18,
    443–444
Angels and Aliens, 335
Angels Don't Play this HAARP, 205
*An Illustrated History of the Horror
    Film,* 577
AP (Associated Press), 31, 76, 163
Architects of the Underworld, 23
Argosy, 17
*Assassination of Robert F. Kennedy,
    The,* 129–131
Astounding Stories, 444
Atlantis: The Antediluvian World, 65
Beelzebub's Tales to His Grandson, 96
Behold a Pale Horse, 567
Birmingham News, The, 87
Castle of Frankenstein, 402
Catcher in the Rye, The, 145–146
Chariots of the Gods, 3
"Chronological Catalogue of Lunar
    Events," 18
CIA and the Cult of Intelligence, The,
    82, 167, 277, 403
Cinescape, 302
Close Encounters of the Fourth Kind,
    470
Codebreakers, The, 278
Collier's, 169, 216
Colorado Springs Gazette, 13

Coming of the Saucers, The, 171
Commanders, The, 163
Communion, 335–338
Control of Candy Jones, The,
    143–144
Copley News Service, 163
Crusade Against the Grail, 48
Danse Macabre, 460
Death of a President, 379
Der Neue Tag, 50–51
Destiny Mars, 23, 366
Dimensions, 274, 359, 444
"Estimate of the Situation," 6, 18
Family Circle, 25
Fangoria, 536
Fantastic Adventures, 172
Fantasy and Science Fiction, 446
Fate, 171
Femme Fatales, 536
50 Worst Films of All Time, 551
Filmfax, 203, 347
Fingerprints of the Gods, 49
Fire in the Sky, 334
Flying Saucer Occupants, 360
Flying Saucer Review, 18
Flying Saucers and Folklore, 444
Flying Saucers Have Landed, 43
Flying Saucers in Fact and Fiction,
    358
Frontiers of Science, 22
*Gene Roddenberry - The Man and the
    Myth Behind Star Trek,* 316
Genesis Revisited, 364
"Geometric Harvest," 474
Harper's Magazine, 151
Hearst Newspapers, 163
Heavy Metal (Metal Hurlant), 506
History of the British Secret Service, A,
    44
Hypnotism and Crime, 153
Icarus, 22
If, 193
I'll Tell Them I Remember You, 428
In Search of Ancient Astronauts, 307
Intelligent Life in the Universe, 25
International Herald Tribune, 279
Intruders, 132, 335
It Came from Hunger, 213
Japanese Diplomatic Secrets, 279
Journal of the British Association, 15

L.A. Secret Police, 142
Life, 59, 65, 99–100, 109, 234
Life on Mars, 22
London Evening Standard, 437
Look, 3, 283, 447
Los Angeles Times, The, 17
Making of Kubrick's 2001, The, 464
Man Called Intrepid, A, 372
Man Who Kept the Secrets, The, 115
Man Who Was "M," The, 44
Metro, 118
Miami Herald, 163
Miami News, 115
Missing Time, 120
Monsters, Giants, and Little Men from
   Mars, 358
Mothman Prophecies, The, 133, 135
Mountains, Buddhas, and Bears, 50
My Life as an Explorer, 47
Myths and Legends of Ancient Egypt,
   172
National Lampoon, 506
Nature, 28
New Republic, The, 40
Newsday, 279
Newsweek, 163
New York Herald Tribune, The, 164
New York Sun, The, 358
New York Times, The, 7, 28, 31, 145,
   163–65, 470
Occult Conspiracy, The, 45
Omni, 286
Orion Mystery, The, 502
Outer Limits: The Official Compan-
   ion, The, 258
Out on a Limb, 339
Paris Vogue, 536
"Penal Colony, The," 118
Pentagram, 334
"Personality characteristics on the
   MMPI, 16PF and ACL tests, of
   persons who claim UFO experi-
   ences," 124
Playboy, 224, 226
Psychic Discoveries Behind the Iron
   Curtain, 236, 484
Psychotronic, 250
Psychotronic Encyclopedia of Film,
   The, 244
Publisher's Weekly, 307

Puzzle Palace, The, 8
Radio Moscow, 28
Remote Viewers, 32, 34, 484
Report on Unidentified Flying Objects,
   The, 80, 217
Reuters, 31, 163
Revelations, 445
Rhythms of Vision, 258
Right Where You Are Sitting Now, 466
Robert F. Kennedy Assassination, The,
   128–129, 142
Rolling Stone, 163
Roof of the World, 50
Roswell Daily Record, 76
Roswell Morning Dispatch, 76
San Jose Mercury, 497
Science-fiction and Flying Saucers,
   444
Science Fiction in the Cinema,
   349–350
Science News, 474
Scripps-Howard, 163
Search for the "Manchurian Candi-
   date," The, 112
Second Look, 82
Secret Life, 127, 525
Sibir, 15
Silent Coup, 162
SPFX, 231
Spy, 496
Spycatcher, 161
Starlog, 183, 381
Steep Rock Echo (Ontario), 86
Sunday Telegraph, 479
Tass, 27, 28
Technology of Youth, 17
They Came from Outer Space, 109,
   194
Thrilling Wonder Stories, 208
Time, 65–66, 99–100, 109, 257–258
Transformation, 335
T.V. Guide, 232, 398
Unreliable Sources, 163
UFO, 90, 95, 102, 337
UFO Crash at Roswell, 96
UFO Encyclopedia, The 171, 341–342
"UFO Hypothesis and Survival
   Questions," 10, 18
Unholy Alliance, 236
Unknown, 196

Unknown Tibet, 50
UPI (United Press International),
 163, 197
Variety, 250, 384
Vogue, 506
*Voynich Manuscript: An Elegant
 Enigma, The,* 63
Washington Post, The, 17, 162
Weird Tales, 154, 302
We Never Went to the Moon, 486
Yes, M'Lady, 434

radio shows (*see* T.V. and radio
 shows)
recordings
 "Astronaut, The," 401
 "Eight Foot Two, Solid Blue," 400
 "Five Foot Two, Eyes of Blue," 400
 "Flying Saucers," 401
 Golden Throats, 320
 "I Wish I was a Spaceman," 434
 "Martian Hop, The," 401
 My Son, the Nut, 400
 "Outer Limits," 401
 "Purple People Eater," 401
 Transformed Man, The, 320
 *Worst Rock 'n Roll Albums of All
  Time,* 320

scientists - archaeologists,
 astronomers, inventors, and discov-
 erers
 Ablordeppy, Victor, 22
 Abramov, Alexander, 17
 Becklake, John, 28
 Binder, Otto, 488
 Blair, William, 17–18
 Budge, Sir E. A. Wallis, 36, 53
 Bush, Vannevar, 83
 Chandler, David, 22
 Chatelain, Maurice, 488
 Copernicus, 482
 Crick, Sir Francis, 32, 320
 de Bourbourg, Brasseur, 46–47
 Demin, D.V., 16
 Demina, L.N., 16
 di Pietro, Vincent, 23
 Dobecki, Thomas L., 50
 Dolan, Brook, 50–51
 Doolittle, Eric, 63

Drasin, Daniel, 23
El Baz, Farouk, 33
Fell, Barry, 49
Galileo, 482
Gipson, Mark, 22
Graham, Francis, 22
Haber, Heinz, 169
Hawass, Zahi, 33
Hawkins, Gerald, 474
Hedin, Sven, 47–48, 50
Herschel, Sir John, 358
Hoagland, Richard, 23
Hohmann, R. E., 24
Hohmann, Walter, 20
Ivanov, S., 17
Jackson, C. D., 24
Jenkins, C. Francis, 14, 25, 580
Kargel, Jeffrey S., 31
Kepler, Johannes, 20
Koenig, Wilhelm, 49
Lehner, Rick, 159
Le Plongeon, Augustus, 46–47, 61
Ley, Willy, 169
Lunan, Duncan, 23–24
Marconi, Guglielmo, 13, 401, 580
Molenaar, Gregory, 23
Muller, Rolf, 49
Niven, William, 47, 61
Oberth, Hermann, 41, 61–62, 94
Oppenheimer, Robert, 41, 61–62, 83
Orgel, Leslie, 320
Pickering, William, 13
Pritchard, David, 127
Saheki, Tsuneo, 13
Sagan, Carl, 24–26, 148, 366, 570,
 587
Sage, Dr., 15
Saunders, M.W., 23–24
Schoch, Robert, 50
Shklovskii, I. S., 25–26
Southwood, David, 40
Smyth, Charles Piazzi, 61
Teller, Edward, 6
Tesla, Nikola, 13, 21, 38, 51, 54–58,
 66, 205, 330, 374, 580
Todd, David, 14, 25, 580
Torun, Erol, 23
Tsioulkovsky, Konstantin, 170
von Braun, Wernher, 20, 31, 59,
 61–62, 169, 210

von Neumann, John, 83–84, 101
von Puttkamer, Jesco, 309
West, John Anthony, 50
serials
 Buck Rogers (Universal, 1939), 68,
  185–186
 Commando Cody, 68
 Flash Gordon (Universal, 1936), 68
 Flash Gordon Conquers the Universe
  (Universal, 1940), 185
 Flash Gordon's Trip to Mars (Univer-
  sal, 1938), 185
 Flying Disc Man from Mars (Repub-
  lic, 1951), 185
 King of the Rocketmen (Republic,
  1949), 185
 Mysterious Dr. Satan, The (Republic,
  1940), 185
 Quatermass (BBC, 1952), 342
 Quatermass and the Pit (BBC, 1959),
  343–345, 348
 Quatermass Conclusion, The (BBC,
  1979), 349
 Quatermass II (BBC, 1955), 342–343
 Radar Men from the Moon (Republic,
  1951), 185
 Superman (Lippert, 1951), 186
 Trollenberg Terror, The (BBC, 1950s),
  236
 Undersea Kingdom (Republic, 1936),
  172, 185
 Zombies of the Stratosphere (Repub-
  lic, 1952), 185
smoking, demonization of, 116–117,
 317, 382–383, 566–567
space probes and missions
 Apollo, 40, 360, 541
 Apollo 11, 33
 Apollo 13, 566–567
 Apollo 17, 487
 Cassini, 40
 Challenger, 39
 Clementine, 159
 Explorer, 234
 Gemini, 360
 Juno 2, 6, 244, 374
 Luna 9, 17
 Lunar Orbiter 2, 17
 Mariner 4, 446
 Mars '96, 22, 40

Mars Pathfinder, 21
Mars 2 and 3, 26–27
Phobos 1 and 2, 22, 26–28, 33, 37,
 71, 161, 424, 462–463, 520, 533,
 588
Sputnik, 234, 405
Viking 1 and 2, 22–23, 26, 201, 321,
 360, 427, 463
Voyager 2, 38, 319
Zond 2, 26
stations
 ABC, 163, 186, 257–258, 301–302,
  380, 390, 396–398, 407–408,
  421–422, 457, 459–460, 517
 AMC (American Movie Channel),
  108, 202, 231
 Cartoon Network, 405
 CBS, 162–163, 174–175, 259, 303,
  327, 333, 389–390, 396–397, 421,
  491, 497, 555
 Cinemax, 231
 CNN, 165, 414
 Comedy Central, 212, 220
 HBO, 552
 KABC, 139
 KGFL, 79
 MTV, 256, 496, 546–547
 NBC, 3, 130, 135, 144, 163, 301,
  304, 308, 385, 389, 396, 422,
  453, 483, 565, 572–573
 Nickelodeon, 155
 PBS, 165
 Sci-Fi Channel, 220, 322, 370, 435,
  528, 567, 584
 Showtime, 286
 TBS (Turner Broadcasting Service),
  585
 TNT (Turner Network Television),
  202, 259–260, 556, 584
 WGN, 99
 WMCA, 143, 149
studios and distributors (film)
 AIP (American International Pic-
  tures), 67, 110, 140–141, 150,
  152–153, 160, 187, 212–213,
  220–221, 229, 231, 234–235, 238,
  244, 246–248, 250, 257, 348,
  352–354, 356, 413, 416–418,
  424–425, 450–452, 454, 466,
  474–475, 477, 501, 526, 551,

578–579
Allied Artists, 153, 193, 209, 213, 216, 226, 234, 354
American General Pictures, 251
Amicus, 369, 526
Anglo-Amalgamated, 153, 228, 250
A.R.C. (American Releasing Corporation—*see also* AIP), 213, 216, 257
Associated Film Distributors, 154
Astor, 195
Avco Embassy, 467, 485, 500, 551
BBC (British Broadcasting Corporation), 161, 236, 341–342, 346–349, 362, 369, 490
Bell & Howell Productions, 384
B.I.&L. (Herschell Gordon Lewis), 246
Cannon, 201, 505
Carolco, 518, 525
CCM (Phil Tucker), 244
Cinerama, 228
Columbia, 171, 192, 202, 210, 217, 221, 227–228, 230, 237, 245, 307, 348, 355–356, 396, 418, 422, 424, 460, 472, 486, 497, 505, 518, 520, 529, 574, 586
Crown International, 250–251
DCA (Distributors Corporation of America), 236–237
Disney Studios/Buena Vista (*see also* producers, directors and creators, Disney, Walt), 186, 188, 211, 356, 418, 503, 538, 546, 551–552
Eagle-Lion, 184
Embassy, 250, 538
Emerson Films, 248
Empire Pictures, 455, 521, 538
Eros, 236–237
Fairway International, 154
Filmgroup, 140, 234
Film Ventures International, 246
Geneni Film Distributors, 384, 513
Graffiti, 419
Hammer, 237, 345, 350, 361, 432, 476
Hanna-Barbera, 70, 354, 404–408, 411, 556
Howco International, 233
ITC, 434

ITV (Independent Television, Britain), 157, 370, 480
Laurel Productions, 530
Lippert, 184–186, 193, 195
Metromedia, 419
MGM (Metro Goldwyn Mayer), 65, 109–110, 188, 196, 199, 210, 227, 231, 245, 263, 276, 303, 349–350, 352, 358, 362, 392, 405, 414, 418, 425, 433, 457, 470, 475–476, 511
MGM/UA, 21, 285, 511, 515–516, 521, 530, 542, 545, 553–554, 570
Monogram, 195, 234
New World Cinema, 499, 503, 518, 526, 539, 543
Orion, 110, 501, 518, 521, 573
Paramount, 59, 152, 198, 210, 229, 231, 233, 308, 319, 333–334, 377, 380, 383, 418, 429, 458, 471, 481, 526, 529, 534–535, 547, 555
Paul Mart Productions, 213
Planet Company, 353
P. M. Productions, 547
Republic, 172, 185, 204
RKO, 65, 99, 107, 109, 211, 414, 438, 513, 570
Screen Gems (Columbia T.V.), 396–397
Smart Egg Pictures, 536–537
Spartan, 202
Sunn Classics Pictures, 491
Tigon/Pacemaker, 361
Toei, 413, 415
Toho, 109, 414, 431
Touchstone, 546, 550
Trans World, 526
20th Century Fox, 65, 100, 154, 193, 199, 206, 221, 229, 286, 299, 301, 306–308, 345, 350, 354, 356–358, 361, 369, 385, 390, 419–420, 424, 427, 430, 437, 462, 482–483, 503, 516–517, 521, 523, 534–536, 540, 542, 549, 555, 563, 587
UA (United Artists—*see also* MGM/UA), 109, 159–160, 187, 196, 204–205, 217, 227, 229, 237, 244, 257, 263, 275, 277, 350, 372, 376, 399, 423, 428, 433, 437, 485, 496, 501, 515, 525, 579

United Pictures, 353
Universal, 3, 99, 151–152, 185, 195,
    197, 207–208, 210, 230, 233, 248,
    301, 304, 323–324, 347–348, 353,
    385, 399, 415, 418, 420–422, 425,
    468, 477, 499, 508, 512–514, 517,
    523, 525, 529–530, 544, 586–587
Warner Bros., 70, 148, 154, 158,
    187, 191, 204, 217–218, 237, 299,
    345, 380, 385, 401–402, 418, 425,
    427, 432, 458–459, 475, 482, 486,
    488, 490, 501, 516, 529, 539,
    548–549, 552–553, 562–563,
    586–588
Wescom, 546
World Entertainment, 251
Ziv TV, 208
Zoetrope, 505

TV and radio shows
    Addams Family, The (ABC, 1964),
        311, 397–398, 454, 551
    Adventures of Superman, The
        (ABC/syndicated, 1953–57), 186,
        221
    *Alfred Hitchcock Presents/Alfred
        Hitchcock Hour* (CBS, 1955–64,
        NBC, 1964–65), 420
        "Glass Eye, The," 420
        "Where the Woodbine Twineth,"
        420
    Alien Autopsy: Fact or Fiction? (20th
        Century Fox, 1994), 100
    Armstrong Circle Theater Show, The
        (CBS, late 1950s), 162
    Astro Boy *(Japanese/syndicated,
        1963–65), 413*
    Avengers, The *(ITV, 1961–69), 67,
        203, 323, 370, 376–377*
        "Cybernauts, The," 157
        "Death's Door," 158
        "Escape In Time," 158
        "Forget-Me-Knot, The," 158
        "Hour that Never Was, The," 158
        "House that Jack Built, The," 158
        "How to Succeed . . . at Murder,"
        158
        "Killer," 158
        "Look (Stop Me if You've Heard
        this One) but there were these

two Fellers," 158
        "Man-Eater of Surrey Green,
        The," 159
        "Master Minds, The," 159
        "Morning After, The," 158
        "Something Nasty in the Nurs-
        ery," 159
        "Split," 159
        "Stay Tuned," 159
        "Super-Secret Cypher Snatch
        (Whatever Happened to Yester-
        day?), The," 159
        "Thingumajig," 158
        "Too Many Christmas Trees," 158
        "Winged Avenger, The," 552
    Babylon 5 (syndicated, contempo-
        rary), 277
    Batman (ABC/Greenway/20th Cen-
        tury Fox, 1966–68), 67, 356–358,
        397
        "Fine Finny Fiends," 155
        "Joker's Flying Saucer," 357–358,
        370
        "Riddler's False Notion," 549
    Battlestar Galactica (Universal,
        1978–79), 323–324, 492, 521
    Beavis and Butthead (MTV, contem-
        porary), 256
    Bewitched (ABC/Columbia-Screen
        Gems, 1964), 389, 396–397
    Beverly Hillbillies, The, 397
    Buck Rogers (ABC, 1950), 260
    Buck Rogers in the 25th Century
        (Universal, 1979–81), 324–325,
        492
    Buffy the Vampire Slayer (Warner
        Bros., 1997), 158, 587
    Captain Scarlet and the Mysterons
        (ITC, 1967–68), 435–437
    Captain Video (DuMont, 1949), 260
    Captain Z-ro (1955, syndicated),
        260
    Colbys, The, 400, 538
    Combat, 256
    Comic Book Confidential (documen-
        tary), 192
    Commando Cody (NBC, 1955), 260
    Cosmos (PBS, early 1970s), 24
    Dark Shadows (NBC/Dan Curtis,
        1966–71), 302, 334, 457

Dark Skies (NBC, 1996–97), 565, 567–572, 585
   "Strangers in the Night," 570
   "Warren Omission, The, 571
Dick Van Dyke Show, The, 399
Donahue, 192
Dr. Kildare (MGM), 405
Dr. Who (BBC, 1963–92), 67, 70, 362–370, 486, 490
   "Ambassadors of Death," 365
   "Claws of Axos, The," 365–366
   "Image of the Fendahl," 368
   "Logopolis," 364
   "Mind of Evil, The," 365–366
   "Pyramids of Mars, The," 366
   "Robots of Death," 367–368
   "Seeds of Death, The," 486
   "Silurians, The," 364–365
   "Talons of Weng-Chiang, The," 366–367
   "War Games, The," 368
Ed Sullivan Show, The, 256
Farmer's Daughter, The (ABC/Columbia-Screen Gems, 1963–66), 397
   "Katy in a Capsule," 397
Fireball XL-5 (British/syndicated, 1962–63), 341–342, 434
   "Robert to the Rescue," 341
First Person Singular (radio, Orson Welles), 176
Flash Gordon (DuMont, 1951), 260
Flipper (MGM T.V., mid-1960s), 196, 476
Friday the 13th: The Series (Fox T.V./Paramount, 1987–90), 535–537, 555
   "Playhouse, The," 535, 537
   "Quilt of Hathor, The," 535–536
Galactica 1980 (Universal, 1980), 324
Geraldo, 192
Get Smart (NBC, 1965–70),
Girl from U.N.C.L.E., The (NBC/MGM, 1966–67), 370
Gilligan's Island (United Artists, 1964–67), 67, 207, 256, 398–399, 476
   "Smile, You're On Mars Camera," 399

Gomer Pyle, U.S.M.C., 308, 400
Hitchhiker's Guide to the Galaxy, The (BBC), 490
Hogan's Heroes, 255
I Dream of Jeannie (NBC/Columbia-Screen Gems, 1965–70), 256, 389
I Led Three Lives (Ziv, 1953–56), 208
Inner Sanctum (radio, 1940s), 248
Intruders (CBS, 1992), 89–90
Invaders, The (ABC/Quinn Martin, 1967–68), 380–381, 418
"Invasion from Mars" (*see War of the Worlds, The,* CBS Mercury Radio Theatre, 1938)
I Spy (Sheldon Leonard, 1965–68), 67
   "Anyplace I Hang Myself is Home," 155
Jet Jackson, Flying Commando (1955, syndicated), 260
Johnny Jupiter (1954), 260
Jonny Sokko and His Giant Robot (AIP, 1967–68), 413–414
Kolchak: The Night Stalker (ABC/Francy/Universal, 1974–75), 301–302, 325, 332, 491
   "Knightly Murders, The," 302
   "Mr. R.I.N.G.," 302
   "They Were, They Are, They Will Be," 301
   "Trevi Collection, The," 302
   "Zombie, The," 302
Leave It to Beaver (ABC, 1957–63), 398–399
   "Captain Jack," 398
   "Hypnotist, The," 398–399
   "Tenting Tonight," 398
Lights Out (radio, 1930s/'40s), 196
Lost In Space (CBS/20th Century Fox, 1965–68), 250–251, 322, 324, 390–392, 396
   "Cave of the Wizards, The," 390–391
   "Follow the Leader," 391
   "Girl from the Green Dimension, The," 391
   "Invaders from the Fifth Dimension," 391
   "Rocket to Earth," 391
   "Space Destructors, The," 391–392

"Visit to Hades, A," 390–391
"War of the Robots, The," 392
Man from U.N.C.L.E., The
  (NBC/MGM, 1964–68), 276–277,
  358, 362
  "'Pieces of Fate' Affair, The," 277,
  552
  "Sort of Do-It-Yourself-Dreadful
  Affair, The," 277
  "Suburbia Affair, The," 370
  "Take Me to Your Leader Affair,
  The," 370
Married With Children (Fox,
  1987–96), 400
M.A.S.H., 384
McHale's Navy, 255
Men Into Space (CBS, 1959–61), 260
Mighty Morphin' Power Rangers
  (Fox/Saban), 413
Mister Ed (CBS, 1960–66), 389
Monsters (Laurel, syndicated,
  1988–90), 420, 531
  "Portrait of the Artist," 531
Mork & Mindy (Paramount/Miller-
  Milkis, 1975–82), 228, 300, 356,
  481–482
Munsters, The (CBS, 1963–65),
  397–398
  "If a Martian Answers, Hang Up,"
  398
Murphy Brown, 255
My Favorite Martian (CBS, 1963–65),
  357, 389, 399, 504
My Living Doll (CBS, 1964–65),
My Mother, the Car (NBC, 1965),
Mysteries, Magic and Miracles (Sci-Fi
  Channel), 370
Mysteries of the Ancient World (CBS,
  1994), 491
Mystery Science Theater 3000 (Com-
  edy Central/Sci-Fi Channel), 212,
  220
National Geographic's TOPX (TBS),
  585
Night Gallery (NBC/Universal,
  1970–73), 304–305, 453
  "Brenda," 304–305
  "Class of '99," 304
  "Dead Man, The," 304
  "Doll, The," 304

"Finnegan's Flight," 304
"I'll Never Leave You - Ever," 304
"Miss Lovecraft Sent Me," 454
"Pickman's Model," 453–454
"Professor Peabody's Last Lec-
  ture," 454
"You Can't Get Help Like That
  Anymore," 304
*Night Stalker, The, (see Kolchak: The
  Night Stalker)*
Oprah, 192
Outer Limits, The (ABC/United
  Artists, 1963–65), 69–70,
  257–286, 290, 296, 297, 299, 301,
  305–306, 325, 372, 395, 398, 421,
  422, 459, 469, 518, 578
  "Architects of Fear, The," 278,
  552
  "Bellero Shield, The," 262, 278
  "Controlled Experiment,"
  284–285
  "Chameleon, The," 264–266,
  271, 395
  "Children of Spider County,
  The," 271–272
  "Cold Hands, Warm Heart,"
  282–283
  "Corpus Earthling," 263, 284,
  286
  "Cry of Silence," 284
  "Counterweight," 283–284
  "Demon with a Glass Hand,"
  276, 469
  "Don't Open Till Doomsday,"
  263, 273
  "Duplicate Man, The," 276
  "Expanding Human," 275
  "Feasibility Study, A," 273, 459
  "Forms of Things Unknown,
  The," 274
  "Fun and Games," 273–274
  "Galaxy Being, The," 261–262
  "Guests, The," 275
  "Inheritors, The," 266–271, 281,
  283, 290, 293
  "Invisible Enemy, The," 284, 287
  "Invisibles, The," 263, 281
  "I, Robot," 276, 296–297
  "It Crawled Out of the Wood-
  work," 281

"Keeper of the Purple Twilight," 281
"Man Who Was Never Born, The," 275
"Man with the Power, The," 281
"Mice, The," 281
"Mutant, The," 275
"Nightmare," 274, 281, 290, 333, 421
"O.B.I.T.," 264, 278–280, 305, 398
"Probe, The," 283–284
"Production and Decay of Strange Particles," 275, 342
"Second Chance," 272
"Sixth Finger, The," 274–275
"Soldier," 281
"The Special One," 205–206, 281–282
"Wolf 359," 281, 287
"Zanti Misfits, The," 272, 281, 286
"Zzzzz," 264, 278, 422
Outer Limits, The (Showtime/Fox/MGM, 1995–), 285–297, 418
"Afterlife," 295
"Beyond the Veil," 291
"Birthright," 290
"Caught in the Act," 293–294
"Choice, The," 297
"Conversion, The," 298
"Deprogrammers, The," 291
"If These Walls Could Talk," 290
"I Hear You Calling," 298
"I, Robot," 296–297
"Quality of Mercy, The," 290–291
"Resurrection," 297
"Sandkings," 286–287
"Second Soul," 293
"Trial By Fire," 294–295
"Under the Bed," 292
"Valerie 23," 296
"Voyage Home, The," 287–289
Picket Fences (CBS, 1993–95), 327
Power Rangers Zeo (Fox/Saban), 413
Prisoner, The (CBS/ITC, 1968), 383
Project UFO (NBC/Jack Webb, 1978–79), 483
Protectors, The (ITC, 1972–74), 435

Remington Steele, 502
Rifleman, The, 256
Rocky Jones, Space Ranger (1953–54, syndicated), 260
Rod Brown of the Rocket Rangers (CBS, 1953), 260
Saturday Night Live (NBC, 1975), 529
Science Fiction Theatre (1956–58, syndicated), 260
Science Report (Britain, 1970s), 479
Second City Television (Canadian, late 1970s), 212, 515
Secret Government, The (PBS), 165
Sightings, 520, 584
Six Million Dollar Man, The (ABC, 1973–77), 464
60 Minutes (CBS), 40, 162, 192, 497
Sliders (Fox), 333
Soap, 400
Space: Above and Beyond (20th Century Fox, 1995), 290, 555
Space: 1999 (ITC, syndicated, 1975–77), 432–435
Space Patrol (ABC, 1951), 260
Starlost, The (Canadian/syndicated, 1973–74), 277
Star Trek (NBC/Norway/Paramount, 1966–69), 70, 142, 301, 303–316, 322, 370, 506, 518, 578, 585
"And the Children Shall Lead," 313
"Assignment: Earth," 314–315
"Cage, The," 309–310, 313
"Changeling, The," 312, 319
"City on the Edge of Forever, The," 277
"Dagger of the Mind," 313
"Doomsday Machine, The," 312
"Errand of Mercy," 312
"For the World is Hollow, and I Have Touched the Sky," 313
"Gamesters of Triskelion, The," 313
"Man Trap, The," 310–311
"Miri," 313
"Paradise Syndrome, The," 313
"Plato's Stepchildren," 314
"Return of the Archons," 313
"Return to Tomorrow," 313–314

"Requiem for Methuselah," 313
"Shore Leave," 313
"Space Seed," 319–320
"That Which Survives," 312
"Tomorrow Is Yesterday," 315
"Ultimate Computer, The," 312
"What Are Little Girls Made Of,"
    312–313
"Who Mourns for Adonis?,"
    313–314
"Where No Man Has Gone
    Before," 310
Star Trek: Deep Space Nine (Para-
    mount, syndicated), 322
Star Trek: The Next Generation (Para-
    mount, syndicated, 1987–94),
    277, 282, 285, 300, 315–319, 324,
    432
"Conspiracy," 333
Stingray (British/syndicated,
    1965–66), 433, 435–436
Supercar (British/syndicated,
    1962–63), 435
*Superman (see The Adventures of
    Superman)*
Swamp Thing (USA, 1990–92), 286
Tales from the Darkside (Laurel,
    syndicated, 1980s), 530–531
30 Years of Dr. Who (BBC, 1993),
    369–370
Thriller (NBC/Revue-Universal,
    1960–62), 420
"Hollow Watcher, The," 420
"Waxworks," 420
Thunderbirds (British/syndicated,
    1966–67),
Today Show, The, 146, 174
Tom Corbett, Space Cadet (1950,
    syndicated), 260
"Tomorrowland" *(Disneyland,
    1955–56),* 169–170
Twilight Zone, The (CBS/MGM,
    1959–64), 70, 259, 303–306, 424,
    578, 585–586
"After Hours, The," 303
"Black Leather Jackets," 305
"Brain Center at Whipple's, The,"
    303
"Dummy, The," 304
"Fear, The," 305

"Fugitive, The," 305
"In His Image," 303–304
"Invaders, The," 304
"I Sing the Body Electric," 303
"Living Doll," 304
"Lonely, The," 303
"Mighty Casey, The," 303
"Monsters Are Due On Maple
    Street, The," 305
"Mr. Dingle, the Strong," 305
"People Are Alike All Over," 305
"Probe 7 - Over and Out," 305
"Steel," 303
"Thing About Machines, A," 303
"Third from the Sun," 305
"To Serve Man," 305
"Where Is Everybody?," 303
"Will the Real Martian Please
    Stand Up," 305
UFO (ITC/syndicated, 1970–71),
    435
UFO Coverup?: Live
    (Seligman/WGN, 1988), 99
UFO Coverup: Live from Area 51
    (TNT, 1995), 584
Ultra Man (Japanese/syndicated,
    1966–67), 413
Untouchables, The, 255
Voyage to the Bottom of the Sea
    (ABC/20th Century Fox,
    1964–68), 155, 390–396
"Attack!," 395
"Blizzard Makers, The," 155
"Cyborg, The," 392
"Day of Evil," 394
"Deadly Cloud," 394–395
"Deadly Dolls, The," 392
"Enemies, The," 155
"Fossil Men, The," 395
"Heat Monster, The," 395
"Indestructible Man, The," 392
"Invaders, The," 395
"Journey with Fear," 394
"Machines Strike Back, The," 392
"Mechanical Man, The," 392
"Monster from Outer Space,
    The," 395
"Mummy, The," 392
"Saboteur, The," 155
"Shadowman, The," 395

"Sky is Falling, The," 393–394
"Terrible Toys, The," 392
"Terror," 395
"Wax Men, The," 392
War of the Worlds, The (CBS/Mercury Radio Theatre, 1938), 69, 173–176, 207, 358, 403, 424, 514, 518, 534, 556
War of the Worlds, The (Fox T.V./Paramount, 1987–89), 380, 534–535
Werewolf (Fox, 1987–88), 535
Wild, Wild West, The (CBS, 1965–69), 156–157, 392
"Night of the Howling Light, The," 155–156
"Night of Miguelito's Revenge, The," 156–157
"Night of the Puppeteer, The," 156
Wonder Woman/The New Adventures of Wonder Woman (ABC/CBS, 1976–79), 480–481
"Judgment from Space," 481
"Starships Are Coming, The," 480–481
X-Files, The (20th Century Fox, 1992–98), 70, 302, 325–333, 383, 552, 555, 565
"Ascension," 327
"Colony," 328–329
"Duane Barry," 327
"End Game," 328–329
"Fallen Angel," 329–330
"Genderbender," 332
"Space," 327
"War of the Coprophages," 326–327

UFOs (Unidentified Flying Objects)
abduction cases, 85–91, 93–95, 119–133
Aguiar, Hector, 132–133
Andreasson, Betty, and Bob Luca, 3–4, 34–35, 199, 209
Boas, Antonio Villas, 10, 88–89, 218, 220, 401, 409, 416, 432, 469, 482, 520, 542
"Davis, Kathy" (pseudonym), 89–90, 132, 335–336

Doraty, Judy, 86
Hickson-Parker (Pascagoula, Mississippi), 87–88, 273, 328, 360–361, 366, 478, 551
Hill, Betty and Barney, 3, 85–86, 90, 199, 261, 271, 283, 341, 401–402, 405, 422, 447, 511, 584
"Oscar," 90
Schirmer, Herbert, 34–35, 86, 89, 185, 219, 261, 358
Taylor, Robert, 93, 300
Walton, Travis, 3, 333–334, 585
psychological profile of *(see also* mind control, UFO abductees and), 119–128, 268–269, 484, 566
abduction occurrences, factual and in science fiction
"birthmarks," 152, 206, 235, 282, 343, 439, 458, 504, 507, 509
"breathing pool," 3, 128, 209, 213–214, 430, 440
hypnosis, mind control, and memory erasure, 9, 36, 88, 91, 93–94, 126–128, 131–133, 187, 267, 272–275, 281–284, 309, 311, 315, 324, 328, 343, 345–347, 352–358, 361–363, 367–368, 375–376, 381, 385–386, 450–451, 457–460, 469, 474, 481, 483–484, 502–503, 519–520, 530, 535, 537, 540, 542–543, 547–550, 553, 560–561, 567
implantations, 89, 127, 199–200, 212, 228, 263, 267–268, 281, 293–294, 318, 328, 334–335, 343, 380, 456, 477, 481–482, 510, 550, 574
paralysis, 90, 92–93, 309, 311, 315, 318, 438, 444–445, 524, 531
sadomasochism, 126, 172, 273, 353, 424, 456, 469–470, 513–515, 525–5 27, 538, 548–550, 565, 572
sex (reproductive), 127–128, 194–195, 197, 203, 206–207, 210, 214, 219–220, 231–233,

235, 244–245, 248, 301–304,
307, 309–311, 314, 319, 324,
327, 355, 391, 409–410,
414–416, 419–421, 423,
430–432, 440, 450–454,
457–459, 474, 481–482, 503,
508–510, 520, 527–529,
539–540, 542, 554–555, 566
"ancient astronaut" authors on
Agrest, Mikhail, 308
Kazantsev, Col. Alexander, 15–16,
580
Sitchin, Zecharia, 95, 323, 364,
492
Temple, Robert K. G., 492
Von Daniken, Erich, 3
animal mutilations and, 90, 94, 97,
135, 220–221, 311, 327, 418, 477,
512
disinformation on
"Alternative 3," 479–480, 513,
552–553, 556, 567–568, 570,
573
balloon and other hoaxes, 75–76,
80, 96
"Bennewitz Affair," the, 96–97,
99, 221, 330, 332, 467,
567–568
"EBE" (Extraterrestrial Biological
Entity) story, 98–100, 102, 277,
300, 330, 474
"Guardian" fraud, 102
"Gulf Breeze" case, 479
"Lab 9," 322–323, 477
Maury Island affair, 171–172
"MJ-12" documents, 98–99, 101,
103, 211, 294, 330, 512, 568,
571–573
"Moon-Man" hoax of 1835, 358
"Princess Moon Owl," 148
"UMMO," 478–479
Egyptian and ancient symbolism
attached to, 77, 110, 184, 540
incidents, famous, concerning
"chupa" attacks, South America,
524
"foo-fighters" and "ghost air-
craft/rockets," 11–12, 173, 507
green fireballs, 5, 183, 507
"Hopkinsville Goblins" (Ken-

tucky, 1955), 86–87, 91, 93,
198, 218–219
Kenneth Arnold sighting, 4, 98,
171, 173, 198
Kinross plane abduction of 1953,
372
Los Angeles air raid of 1942, 11,
241
Malmstrom AFB intrusions, 6,
244
"Mothman," 93, 133–135,
281–282, 361, 421, 549
mystery airship of
1896–1897, 14–15
New York blackout of 1965, 184
Rendlesham Forest incident of
1980, 161, 168
Roswell crash of 1947, 4, 13, 67,
73–83, 86, 94–98, 100–107,
110, 133, 172, 183, 198, 278,
311, 330, 358, 418, 570–572
Siberian aerial atomic explosion
of 1908, 15, 412, 452, 580
Socorro, New Mexico, and New
York occupant encounters of
1964, 359–360, 428
"Springheel Jack," 92–93
Vandenburg AFB 1964 Atlas F
missile sabotage, 408
Voronezh (Russia, 1989), 88, 90,
95, 478
Washington Nationals of 1952, 9,
168, 184, 516, 583
"Year of the Humanoids" (1973),
421
Mars and (see planets and planetary
bodies, Mars, UFO waves and)
researchers and personalities
Adamski, George, 42–43, 172,
339, 479
Bloecher, Ted, 120
Blum, Ralph, 87, 360
Boylan, Richard, 320
Brazel, Mac (Roswell saucer dis-
coverer), 73–74, 76, 79, 358,
570
Chop, Al, 217
Dennis, Glenn (Roswell morti-
cian), 77–79, 102
Fowler, Raymond, 586

Good, Timothy, 42, 102–103
Guerin, Pierre, 18–19, 21, 107
Hall, Richard, 95
Hopkins, Budd, 89–90, 120–121,
    124–125, 130, 132, 333,
    335–336, 338–339, 586
Howe, Linda Moulton, 94, 221
Hynek, Prof. J. Allen, 85, 93, 101,
    516, 541
Jacobs, Dr. David M., 3, 125, 131,
    273, 525, 586
Keel, John A., 12, 99, 133–135,
    148, 281–282
Keyhoe, Maj. Donald E., 162, 217
Lorenzen, Coral and Jim, 360
Mack, Dr. John E., 35, 122, 127,
    586
Meheust, Bernard, 444–445
Moore, William, 96, 98
Nurse (at Roswell), 77–79,
    101–102, 107
Palmer, Ray, 171–173, 395
Randle, Kevin, 96–97
Randles, Jenny, 161, 168, 239,
    257
Schmitt, Donald, 96–97
Scully, Frank, 172, 326
Shaver, Richard Sharpe, 171–173,
    395
Steinman, William, 82
Strieber, Whitley, 335–339, 461,
    474–475, 516, 586
Stringfield, Len, 82
Vallee, Dr. Jacques, 10, 18–21, 32,
    84–85, 90, 93–95, 101, 107,
    119, 123, 228, 274, 324,
    359–360, 443–445, 473, 478,
    490, 524

Vallee, Janine, 18–21, 107
Vyner, John, 93
Zigel, Felix, 20, 95
research organizations of, civilian,
    280
    APRO (Aerial Phenomena
        Research Organization), 96
    FUFOR (Fund for UFO Research),
        120, 525
    NICAP (National Investigations
        Committee on Aerial Phenom-
        ena), 162
robots associated with, 2, 33–37,
    83–95, 100–103, 110, 135, 334
    in science fiction, 2, 16–17,
        155–158, 172–173, 177–184,
        193–222 *passim,* 227–254 *pas-
        sim,* 272–277, 292, 295–297,
        302–304, 307, 312–313,
        317–318, 323, 326–327,
        348–349, 352–356, 360–369,
        374–375, 384, 390–392,
        398–408, 411–418, 420–421,
        423, 434, 439, 443–445, 451,
        460–461, 468–473, 480–481,
        489–491, 499, 507–511,
        517–519, 522, 526, 528–530,
        535, 538, 540–542, 545–550,
        557, 562–564, 579
sabotage by, 5–6, 8–9, 19–20, 30,
    132–136
    in science fiction, 196, 199–201,
        203, 205–206, 211–212, 217,
        222, 228, 233–234, 236, 244,
        314–315, 375–376, 394–395,
        460, 484, 517, 520, 548–550,
        558